New Views of Mormon History

New Views of Mormon History

A Collection of Essays in Honor of
Leonard J. Arrington

Edited by
Davis Bitton and
Maureen Ursenbach Beecher

University of Utah Press
Salt Lake City

1987

Library of Congress Cataloging-in-Publication Data

New views of Mormon history : a collection of essays in honor of
   Leonard J. Arrington / edited by Davis Bitton and Maureen Ursenbach
   Beecher.
      p. cm.
   Bibliography: p.
   Includes index.
   ISBN 0–87480–304–7 : $19.95
   1. Church of Jesus Christ of Latter-day Saints — History.
2. Mormon Church — History. 3. Arrington, Leonard J. I. Arrington,
Leonard J. II. Bitton, Davis, 1930–. III. Beecher, Maureen
Ursenbach.
BX8611.N44 1987
289.3'32'09 — dc19
CIP   87–18787

Contents

Introduction

DAVIS BITTON

Leonard James Arrington is the single most important Mormon historian of his generation. We shall explain why that is so, but first it is appropriate to become acquainted with the man.

The Noah Arrington family was a Mormon family, originally from Tennessee, that early in the century had looked for a place to put down roots. The Magic Valley area of Idaho was being opened up to farming, thanks to irrigation made possible by a new dam, and the Arringtons settled there.

If it was not frontier in the nineteenth-century sense, it was also decidedly not city living. Twin Falls, the metropolis of Magic Valley, was a small town, and the Arrington farm was located far enough away that they did not think of themselves as anything but farmers. They worked hard. Babies were delivered by a midwife, Leonard arriving as the third child of Noah and Edna Grace Corn Arrington on 2 July 1917. The family lived in a two-room, frame house. Electricity and indoor plumbing were luxuries they did without for several years.

Young Leonard showed every indication of wishing to become a farmer himself. He took part in all the chores and arduous farm labor along with his parents and siblings. During his high school years, when he joined the Future Farmers of America, he had an impressive poultry project. The historian of later years could look back in amusement at the "chicken farmer," but it was in fact serious business, with careful attention to breeds, feeding, culling, and marketing.

The Arringtons took their Mormon religion seriously. Noah Arrington was bishop of the ward (congregation). The children participated in the various programs of the church and, like others, delivered talks and prayers. There is a pecking order within Mormondom, and the farming areas of southeastern Idaho are not at its top. Nevertheless, wherever located, a bishop is the leader of his flock, and the values and teachings of this religious background would become ingrained in Leonard, never to disappear.

One of the turning points of Leonard Arrington's life was the decision, when he was a senior in high school, to go on to college. This was not a foregone conclusion. He was already well on his way to understanding much about farming, thanks to his practical and FFA experience. He could easily have concluded that pursuit of higher education would simply put him several years behind in building up his own economic base. The year of his high school graduation, 1935, was in the midst of the Great Depression, and funds for sending off a son to college would not be easy to come by. Nevertheless, a scholarship offer from the University of Idaho combined with Leonard's strong desire and willing support from parents, and in the fall of 1935 off he went. Moscow, Idaho, might have seemed like outer space to eastern sophisticates, but to a farm lad it was a bastion of higher learning that had much to offer.

This eighteen year old was bright. He was ambitious. He had already demonstrated leadership ability both in his church and in his high school FFA activities (he even became a national officer of FFA). Now he was ready to expand his horizons, but at first he stayed close to his home base and majored in agricultural economics. It seemed then like a short step from simple agriculture but eventually would lead to other short steps—from agricultural economics to economics, from economics to economic history, from economic history to history.

Although Leonard studied hard and held part-time jobs to help in his support, he did find time for social life. He made friends and participated in the Mormon fraternity Lambda Delta Sigma. He also enjoyed intercollegiate debate. The young man obviously had "people skills" and verbal aptitude. He was no recluse.

His intellectual horizons were expanding. He remembers reading a lot of books, novels such as Samuel Butler's *The Way of All Flesh*, nonfiction such as Will Durant's *Story of Philosophy*, and even some of the writings of George Santayana. One might wonder how fully he understood what he was reading or how much stuck, but clearly he was stretching and growing beyond the subject matter of his college classes.

Religious development during college years, or the lack thereof, is often crucial. Quite commonly those with minimal religious background become confirmed in a secular approach to living, many with rigid, conservative religious upbringing abandoning what now seem like outgrown beliefs. Fortunately, as Leonard sees it, he came in contact with a Mormon institute teacher ("institutes of religion" as centers for religious, social, and intellectual support for Mormon students had just recently come into existence) in the person of George S. Tanner. Tall, unaffected, jovial, his own Arizona rural background often showing through, Tanner was just the man for students like Leonard. Tanner had studied at the University of Chicago and was interested in the wider world of religious scholarship, but he was also full of common sense. In any case, with such support reinforcing his own individual determination Leonard remained a believing and practicing Latter-day Saint.

By the time of his graduation he had become interested in pursuing a graduate degree and, hearing of a program in economics that interested him, applied to and was accepted by the University of North Carolina. He had hardly been out of Idaho when, at age twenty-two, he headed for the South.

At Raleigh came an important addition to his life that was probably not in the plans: Grace Fort. A charming young Baptist who worked as a hairdresser, Grace proved irresistible. An original blind date was followed by a series of joint activities and increasing affection.

Also not in the plans was World War II. Leonard, like others of his age, volunteered for military service. After basic training he was assigned to a prisoner-of-war processing unit and sent to North Africa. This was followed by the Italian campaigns during 1943 and 1944. He learned Italian from prisoners of war and attended several Italian operas. Even though only a PFC, he was appointed *controllore* of the Central Institute of Statistics in Rome, a significant position in the military government. The Idaho farm boy had come a long way. He also wrote letters to Grace almost every day, and she reciprocated.

Returning to Raleigh after the war in 1946, Leonard finished the courses required for his Ph.D. degree. Since technically the degree was in economics, it has to be seen as crucial to his later course that, with the permission of Professor Milton Heath (and also encouraged significantly by letters from Mormon apostle John A. Widtsoe) he chose to write a dissertation on the economic history of the Mormons. On such decisions careers hinge.

Still working on the dissertation and needing an income, Leonard accepted a position at Utah State Agricultural College (now Utah State University) in Logan. He taught classes in economics, sat in on history classes from S. George Ellsworth, and besides finishing the dissertation began publishing articles on aspects of Mormon economic history. Grace Fort Arrington, whose interest in the Mormons had originally been aroused by reading Vardis Fisher's *The Children of God*, liked her Mormon neighbors. When she heard anti-Mormon statements from some members of her Protestant congregation, she decided to join the Mormons. Children came along in due order—James, Carl, and Susan. For many years Logan was the family home.

When the dissertation, extensively revised, was published in 1958 under the title *Great Basin Kingdom* by Harvard University Press, it quickly established Leonard as a leader among those bringing professionalism to the study of the Mormon past. He continued to publish articles, many of them, during the late 1950s and through the 1960s. In 1963 Leonard was invited by Walter Prescott Webb to give two televised lectures on the Mormons in a series by eminent American historians such as Samuel Eliot Morrison and Allan Nevins.

In 1965 Leonard became founding president of a new organization, the Mormon History Association, which he had done more than anyone else to bring into being. About the same time he was one of the advisory editors of the new journal *Dialogue: A Journal of Mormon Thought*. He also participated in organizations such as the Western History Association (he was founding editor of its journal for two years), the Agricultural History Society, and the Pacific Coast Branch of the American History Association. Energy and productivity had become two of his most striking traits.

The family continued active in their Mormon ward. In fact, Leonard served as a member of a stake presidency in Logan, which of course gave him many experiences in seeing the LDS Church as it affected individual lives. He met general authorities when they came to participate in stake conferences.

If the Church of Jesus Christ of Latter-day Saints had use for a historian who had the respect of his professional colleagues, who was active in the church, and who had a track record of being able to get things done, Leonard would seem to be the man. The Church Historian's Office in Salt Lake City, however, had traditionally been under an apostle, Joseph Fielding Smith having occupied the position for a half century. The librarians and archivists were for the most part not professionally trained and had been instructed to "guard" the documents, which they construed as requiring them to examine the notes of researchers and refuse access when it appeared the intention was unfriendly. Some of the staff, however, were very helpful as well as competent. Leonard had had firsthand experience with this state of affairs, having often done research in Salt Lake City.

Miraculously, so it seemed, changes began to occur. Recognizing the need for improved procedures, Joseph Fielding Smith hired some able younger people and encouraged some of his staff to attend meetings of national archival associations. Steps were begun that would lead to improved procedures of accessioning and storing the precious sources. When Joseph Fielding Smith became president of the church, Apostle Howard Hunter, the new Church Historian, continued efforts to upgrade and professionalize the whole operation.

Then, in 1972, as part of an extensive reorganization, Leonard J. Arrington was called to be the Church Historian. This was his title, though he did not have exactly the same functions as had been exercised by his predecessors. They had been essentially administrators; this task continued to be given to a general authority, a managing director. The Historical Department of the Church, as it was now known, was made up of the following divisions: Library, Archives, Arts and Sites, and History Division. It was the History Division that was under Leonard Arrington, who served as its head between 1972 and 1982. (His title was changed from Church Historian to Director of the History Division in 1977.) This was a full-time calling. The Arrington family (actually the children had pretty well left the nest by now, only daughter Susan still living at home) moved from Logan to Salt Lake City.

Leonard's accomplishments during his ten years with the History Division are too extensive to detail here. He coauthored (with Davis Bitton) *The Mormon Experience: A History of the Latter-day Saints* (1979), did much of the work on his later prizewinning biography

Brigham Young: American Moses (1985), and supervised a staff of a dozen or so historians in projects that eventuated in speeches, task papers, an admirable oral history program, and an incredible number of books and articles. The Arrington group had no monopoly on Mormon history, of course, but it would be hard to deny that in many respects they were at the cutting edge.

Another reorganization began in 1980 and was completed by 1982. For reasons that can be guessed at but perhaps not fully known, Leonard and his remaining staff were transferred to Brigham Young University, where they continue as the Joseph Fielding Smith Institute for Church History. Even earlier Leonard had had a connection with BYU. He had held the first Charles Redd chair in Western history there, teaching about two or three classes per year, and had been Director of the Redd Center. Earlier he passed on the directorship of the Redd Center and now, having reached the mandatory retirement age, has done the same with the Smith Institute. Not one to vegetate, he continues active and interested, teaches some classes, and writes and publishes.

To bring his personal life somewhat up to date, it should be noted that his beloved Grace died in 1982. He has since married Harriet Ann Horne, who has historical interests herself, and provides endearing support and gracious companionship.

II

In general we prefer to let Leonard Arrington's scholarly work speak for itself. The bibliography included in this volume is sufficient representation of his prodigious output. However, some observations may be appropriate.

To begin with the quantitative, it is worth noting that the Arrington publications are not just numerous overall; they are also remarkably spread out over his adult career. Once he got started, he kept at it. Soon he got into his own rhythm, and not a year would pass without at least some publication. Usually there were several titles—book reviews, articles, perhaps a book, addresses at scholarly (and some nonscholarly) meetings. This historian was not one to spin his wheels. Projects were begun, methodically pursued step by step, and sooner or later, depending on the length or complexity of the topic, brought to a conclusion by submitting a final draft to a publisher. As year followed year, the Arrington bibliography grew.

Then note the variety. There is economic history, of course, but Leonard did not stay permanently fixed to that one kind of history. Intellectual history through the study of novels. Local history in articles on Idaho. Institutional history of defense installations and banks. And biography. And of course general interpretive history. In each of these areas, and possibly others, Leonard has made a mark.

Although like every other scholar or writer who has put in his share of time as an individual taking notes from the primary sources or working at drafts at his typewriter, he has been anything but a loner. While still at Utah State University he enlisted the aid of students and budding historians in a series of articles on defense establishments in Utah. He continued this teamwork approach to projects, nicely described in his article entitled "The Historian as Entrepreneur," after his appointment as Church Historian. Many of the articles for which he is listed as coauthor came out of consultation and cooperation with younger scholars. Often he would provide the original impetus, even the extensive notes and outlines, which his collaborator would then use to produce a draft. Leonard would go over the draft then and make whatever changes or improvements seemed necessary.

When the organization that had initiated the project insisted it appear under Leonard Arrington's authorship, he complied, while acknowledging extensive assistance, sometimes under the revealing phrase "assistance tantamount to co-authorship." A certain number of publications that came out during his tenure with the Historical Department of the Church—but by no means all—were of this nature.

When undertaking a project he quite typically thinks in terms of breaking it down and enlisting the help he will require. Those who have participated, by now a dozen or more, do not seem to complain. He gives them experience. He is open in acknowledging what they have done. If he is employing them, as for example when he used some advance royalties from Knopf to pay research assistants to provide notes from the Brigham Young manuscripts, he is fair and professional. What he did, in a way, was to apply in historical research and writing attitudes of teamwork and collaboration already considered standard procedure in the physical sciences. There had been an earlier operation of this kind in history—that of Hubert Howe Bancroft, whose mammoth projects on the American West were the product of his own organizing skills combined with the legwork and diversified talents of several younger assistants. Leonard was never inclined to running too tight of a ship; he was not dictatorial and did not insist on controlling everyone's total time. But there was a spirit of cooperation, of sharing, of mutual awareness of the variety of projects underway. It was a truly remarkable pattern of engaging in the historian's craft. And if publications are the measure, the bibliography of the publications of Leonard's team at the History Division—published in *Dialogue: A Journal of Mormon Thought* in 1983—should amply demonstrate that the approach bore fruit.

It was not only his own little group, those collaborating with him on projects, or, after 1972, those employed as the staff of the History Division of the Historical Department of the Church, that Leonard helped. Other historians working in the general area of Mormon history usually sought and obtained his assistance, which could range from specific suggestions, sharing sources already in his files, endorsing projects and assisting in obtaining the use of archival materials, or simply encouragement.

It may not be too much to say that for several years everyone working in Mormon history benefited from the avuncular, beneficent presence of Leonard Arrington. And by no means was the encouragement restricted to Mormons. Responsible researchers of all kinds were similarly encouraged. Jan Shipps has written: "His efforts to establish an atmosphere of openness early on when he occupied the position of Church Historian made me know that my 'Gentile' status did not and would not keep me from making an effort to write about the Mormon past. There was an ambience that made non-LDS (RLDS as well as 'Gentile') historians feel welcome and able to participate fully in the Mormon history enterprise. Leonard set the tone."

While he can be the scholar's scholar, Leonard Arrington has considered part of his role, especially since 1972, to be that of communicating interest and enthusiasm about history to ordinary people. He has given countless talks to study groups, churches, and service clubs. With a good sense of the occasion and the audience, he does not try to impress with his erudition. Some of his publications, too, have been intended for a general audience. These include, in addition to articles in magazines, his coauthored *Saints Without Haloes* and *Sunbonnet Sisters*. If such popular fare had been the total of his production, he could be seen quite simply as a kind of journalist or purveyor of information researched by others. The fact is, however, that even if all such general or popular products are screened from his bibliography, the solid, scholarly works that remain are still significant and impressively numerous.

No one excels in everything, and it is probably accurate to note that Leonard has done better in some areas than in others. Originally an economic historian, he has done much of his work in that area. Some have argued that his magnum opus will always be *Great Basin Kingdom*. Some say that biographies, with the possible exception of *Brigham Young: American Moses*, are not what he does best, tending to be competent, thorough, valuable, but not brilliant, not inspired. His writing style is straightforward, workmanlike, rather than colorful or fast paced. Intellectual history and the new social history he either leaves to others or, when something seems important to his project, enlists the help of someone more at home in those areas. With Jon Haupt, then a graduate student in history at UCLA, he cooperated in a fascinating and valuable study of Mormons as portrayed in nineteenth-century fiction. So, while recognizing his own limitations, Leonard has shown an interest in pushing at the edges and benefiting from alternate perspectives.

Most of what he does he does very well. He does not need to apologize for his style; it does the job and has been sufficiently effective to win for him many laudatory reviews. The kind of history he turns out, the best of it, simply cannot be ignored by anyone working seriously in the area of its concern.

We wish to call attention to two homely virtues that, perhaps because they are character traits rather than skills, do not receive very much specific attention in the training of historians. The first is a capacity for hard work. During graduate study the necessity of diligence is so inescapable, so necessary for survival, that it needs no further encouragement. But how many historians of Leonard Arrington's age can look back on a scholarly productivity comparable to his? Some, but not many. It simply does not happen without dedication, discipline, just sticking to the task week after week, month after month, year after year. Leonard is a model in this respect. Without fanfare he simply assumes that he will be working on several projects and that all of them will, one by one, come to completion. At a time when many people would have been quite content to rest on their laurels, Leonard both enjoys his achievements and continues working on other projects. During his graduate school period he learned about "the Puritan ethic" and "the bourgeois virtues"; one suspects that the Idaho farm boy did not need those labels to be a hardworking achiever at whatever he did.

Then there is his joviality, his friendliness. These are not usually high in the catalogue of scholarly virtues; the life of the scholar is often assumed to be solitary. The assumption undoubtedly goes back at least to the ancient Greeks, who had much to say about the contemplative life. Of course there is a core of truth to the assumption: one must ultimately face the blank page and with pen (or typewriter or computer keyboard) put down word after word. But people skills should not be ignored. In Leonard's case they have enabled him to function as a teacher that students remember, as a member of historical associations who is liked and honored with office, as a communicator about history not only to other professionals but, as noted above, to people of all kinds. And he has lived his professional life in an atmosphere that is electric with activity and projects and friendly participants.

What is the life of the mind without joy? Is it worth it if the experience becomes a chore, a tedious necessity, a gloomy trap? Richard Hofstadter once wrote of the fun and excitement of scholarship at its best. Compared to many occupations that are essentially repetitious and mechanical, the work of a historian has to be almost one of celebration. It is an activity of exploration and discovery, it is interesting, it makes a difference. At least this is history as we have experienced it in the presence of a generous, estimable, and cheerful senior colleague, Leonard James Arrington—who, whatever anyone may or may not do with official labels, will for all who understand always be considered for his generation Mormonism's church historian.

In 1986 Leonard Arrington was named a Fellow of the Society of American Historians, a select group founded by Allan Nevins, whose membership is maintained at 200 and is "limited to those authors who have written at least one book of genuine distinction." Clearly, Leonard's competence and signal contributions are recognized by his scholarly peers.

Obviously, not everyone who holds Leonard Arrington in esteem is represented in the present book. Knowing the impossibility of including everyone, we originally invited participation by most of those we knew of who had had some kind of close relationship with Leonard and who were themselves working in the field of Mormon history. No doubt we overlooked some people. Others whose names are not included here failed to meet our deadline or submitted something outside the parameters of this book. We understand the human condition enough to empathize with those who did not manage to complete a contribution, and we ask forgiveness of those who might have wished to be included. We, too, are human.

The group of participants represented in the following pages is not insignificant. They tend to be in the early or middle range of their scholarly careers. It is not going too far to say that represented within this volume are many of the solid contingent at the heart of professional research into Mormon history. Richard Bushman spoke for all of us when he said of Leonard Arrington and this project, "No volume would be wholly worthy of the man, but I think we can say we have done our best."

New Views of Mormon History

PART ONE

Early Mormonism, Aspects of History and Theology

Mormonism's formative period, roughly that bounded by Joseph Smith's birth in 1805 and his death in 1844, has long been studied from whatever points of view presented themselves to each succeeding generation. In this first section four scholars well published in the subject look yet again at those first years, each from his own position and discipline.

Secular historians have noted the record-keeping penchant of the Mormons; Mormons themselves usually offer only weak explanations, citing the Doctrine and Covenants injunction that there be "a record kept among you." In the first essay of this section, "The Book of Mormon in Early Mormon History," Richard Bushman, professor of history at the University of Delaware and recent president of the Mormon History Association, traces the persistence and importance of record-keeping to Book of Mormon peoples, seeing Joseph Smith and the nineteenth-century Mormons as intellectual successors of that ancient tradition of the creation and preservation of records.

Dean C. Jessee, an associate in the Joseph Fielding Smith Institute for Church History at Brigham Young University, is unsurpassed for his meticulous editing of the papers that document the beginnings of the Mormon faith. His *Personal Writings of Joseph Smith* and his forthcoming work on Parley P. Pratt demonstrate the insights to be gained from scrupulous fidelity to the written artifacts of the movement. In a more narrative vein, he here collects the writings of Mormon leaders, Joseph Smith primarily, in an essay titled, " 'Walls, Grates and Screeking Iron Doors': The Prison Experience of Mormon Leaders in Missouri, 1838–1839."

More theological in approach, the essays by Thomas G. Alexander and David J. Whittaker see Mormonism in its "line upon line, precept upon precept" development. Alexander, professor of history and director of Brigham Young University's Charles Redd Center for Western Studies, is author of the recent *Mormonism in Transition*. In " 'A New and Everlasting Covenant': An Approach to the Theology of Joseph Smith," he looks at covenant theology in its prerestoration Christian manifestations, and then compares early Mormon concepts of covenant-making.

David Whittaker, archivist for Brigham Young University, is an acknowledged expert in Mormon imprints of the nineteenth century. In his essay, "The 'Articles of Faith' in Early Mormon Literature and Thought," he traces through tracts and treatises of early church leaders the development of what became thirteen official statements of belief.

The Book of Mormon in Early Mormon History *

Richard L. Bushman

Was Joseph Smith a magician? That question has always lingered over the early history of Mormonism, but in recent years interest in the issue of magic has been renewed. The flurry of excitement over the short-lived Hofmann letters, with their evidence of a magical outlook in the 1820s, turned the attention of Mormon historians as never before to the broader scholarship on folk magic. There we have found a growing literature on an underground world of magical practices among Christians throughout the western world. Keith Thomas's massive work *Religion and the Decline of Magic* demonstrated beyond question the prevalence of magical beliefs in early modern England, and scholars working in the American field have found ample evidence of such beliefs persisting into the nineteenth century. Alerted by the Hofmann letters and these studies of American religion, historians of Mormonism who reviewed the record with magic in mind discovered here and there many signs of magic among early Mormons. Even with the Hofmann letters out of the picture, magic is now entrenched in the story of Mormonism's founding. The excitement of the new discoveries, sustained by the general scholarly interest in magic, has even tempted some to toy with the idea that Joseph Smith was essentially and above all a magician and that magical beliefs lay at the very heart of nineteenth-century Mormonism.

---

* This essay in an earlier form was presented as a presidential address to the Mormon History Association on 3 May 1986 in Salt Lake City, Utah. John W. Welch and John L. Sorenson offered useful criticisms of the essay while it was in preparation.

In the midst of the interest aroused by the new discoveries, we must not lose sight of other, more familiar materials that bear on the question of Joseph Smith's development and the mission of the early church. More particularly, we should not forget the Book of Mormon. In that volume, we have over five hundred pages of source material, incontestably produced before 1830, that also relate to Smith's character and culture. Furthermore, most of the evidence about magic comes from the minds of others and bears the mark of their preconceptions; the Book of Mormon came from Joseph Smith's own lips, giving it a special claim on our attention. There seems to be little question that Smith did follow practices that we would call magic, but before we sum him up in that one idea, we should weigh the few hundred words on that theme against the tens of thousands of words in the Book of Mormon. What do they imply for the Prophet's character? If believers object that the Book of Mormon does not contain Smith's own words, they would surely agree that something to which he gave so much effort affected his thinking and provides insight into his mental world. By the same token, nonbelievers must agree that writing the Book of Mormon puts Smith beyond the ranks of ordinary folk magicians.

My purpose then is to reflect on the relationship of the Book of Mormon to the young Joseph Smith and to early Mormonism. Unfortunately, the relationship is far from clear, one reason perhaps for the neglect of the book's meaning in the early life of the Prophet. One connection is beyond dispute: the mission to the Lamanites in 1830 and 1831 obviously emerged directly from the Book of Mormon conception of the gathering of Israel in the last days. But beyond that, the interplay of the book, the Prophet, and the early church is not easily described. Book of Mormon themes that we think should have resonated in Smith's life or in the early church came to nothing. One would think that the passages on the Gadianton secret society would have aroused Smith and his followers to active involvement in anti-Masonry, but the early Mormons apparently paid no heed, even when the Anti-Masonic Party was at the peak of its influence. Or why was not Alma the Younger's conversion made the model for early Mormon conversions? Alma's experience of conviction of sin and reliance on Christ for redemption from the pains of hell followed the standard evangelical pattern closely enough for any nineteenth-century American to recognize the similarities. Yet Mormons never sought conversions of that sort. Mormons tried to instill belief in the Prophet and in the Book of Mormon, faith in Christ, and repentance when they preached for conversion, quite a different thing from the ubiquitous revival preaching of the day which resembled more Alma's way than Joseph Smith's. Grant Underwood has found that Mormons quoted the Book of Mormon far less than the Bible, even in sermons among themselves. Apart from the mission to the Lamanites, the Book of Mormon seems to stand apart from Joseph Smith and the early church, complicating the task of determining what it reveals about the character of the young Prophet.[1]

Rather than search for specific doctrines or ideas linking the Book of Mormon to Smith and early Mormonism, we are better advised, I believe, to consider the Book of Mormon in its broadest outlines and to look for connections at a slightly higher level of abstraction. It is important to recognize that the Book of Mormon was more than a patchwork collection of theological assertions, or a miscellany of statements about the Indians, like, for example, Ethan Smith's *View of the Hebrews*. We may miss the point if we treat the Book of Mormon as if it were that kind of hodgepodge. Sometimes we employ a proof text method in our analyses, taking passages out of context to prove a point. We seek to associate a few words or an episode with Smith or his time, the Masons here, republican ideology there, then a touch of Arminianism or of evangelical conversion preaching. While that kind of analysis may have its uses, it has had disappointing results, and the danger is that we will lose sight of the larger world which the book evokes. The genius of the Book of Mormon, like that of many works of art, is that it brings an entire society and culture into existence, with a religion, an economy, a technology, a government, a geography, a sociology, all combined into a complete world. For purposes of analysis, we must, of course, call forth one thread, one theme, one idea at a time, but we must also bear in mind the existence of this larger world and relate individual passages to greater structures if we are to find their broadest meaning. Perhaps by stepping back and considering this larger world of the Book of Mormon, we will perceive connections with early Mormonism that otherwise remain invisible.[2]

In this spirit, I turn to a particular aspect of Book of Mormon culture: its preoccupation with records. I wish to draw out this single theme and relate it as far as possible to the larger structures of Book of Mormon culture, in the hope that a connection with Smith and the early church will come into view. The fundamental question for this inquiry is: why is there a Book of Mormon? A record was made, hidden, discovered, translated, published. Why did that happen? The question of why a Book of Mormon can be asked from many perspectives, but I wish to pose the question from the perspective of the book itself. Within the story's larger frame, why all the record-keeping? Why the immense effort lasting over centuries? Why the care to convey the records from one generation to the next? Why did Mormon, in the midst of his many troubles, work through the voluminous records to write a history? And going from the record-keepers themselves to their theology, what kind of a God makes so much of records? Why open a dispensation of the gospel with the translation of an ancient book? Since Mormon himself answered the question on the first page, we may conclude nothing further need be said. But the title page of the Book of Mormon is only the beginning, or perhaps more accurately it is the culmination and end. By recreating the Book of Mormon world as it relates to records, we may catch a glimpse of how Smith fits into the picture.[3]

The narrative draws readers into the business of records in the very first sentence. Nephi introduces himself as a record-maker — "therefore I make a record of my proceedings in my days" — and goes on to testify of the record's truth before telling a single event. We learn in the first chapter that Nephi's father, Lehi, also keeps a record and get a complicated explanation of how Nephi will abridge his father's record as well as keep his own. Besides launching us into the story of the family's visions and adventures, Nephi self-consciously informs us about the mechanics of getting it all down and of managing the various records being made.[4]

Once the family has abandoned its home for the wilderness, the first major incident has to do with records. The return for Laban's plates lets the reader know immediately that records loom large in this culture. Lehi asks his sons to accomplish a seemingly impossible task — to get the brass plates from a powerful, armed, truculent official who has no desire to give them up. The father knows he places his sons' lives at risk, yet insists. They not only jeopardize their lives but offer all the family's gold, silver, and precious things for the plates. In the end, Nephi, against all his instincts, kills for the record. He explains the murder of Laban by saying that "I knew that the Lord had delivered Laban into my hands for this cause—that I might obtain the records according to his commandments." The reasoning is that "it is better that one man should perish than that a nation should dwindle . . . in unbelief." We learn at once that in the Book of Mormon world religious culture depends on and grows out of records.[5]

It should come as no surprise that at the end, Mormon, the redactor for whom the book is named, introduces himself as a record-keeper just as Nephi had. Mormon's introductory line is "now I, Mormon, make a record of the things which I have both seen and heard," and he tells at once how Ammaron his predecessor informed him of the plates' location in Shim and charged him to continue the record. In the course of battling the Lamanites as Nephite civilization came to an end, Mormon moved the plates from one safe location to another, and in the midst of all his troubles managed to write a history from the beginning. The records pass to Moroni, who opened his account with the familiar tag, "Behold I, Moroni, do finish the record of my father."[6]

In between Nephi and Moroni we never lose sight of the records. Their descent is meticulously accounted for. In the first portion of the history, before King Benjamin, the kings, the descendants of Nephi, passed down one set of records; the other set went through descendants of Nephi's brother Jacob.[7] We lack of course the kingly record, but the Jacobean record tells us step by step of the passage from one record-keeper to another. For a time in Omni, the transmission of the records was nearly all that was written about.[8] Throughout the Book of Mormon there is a recurrent clanking of plates as they pass from one record-keeper to another. To my mind, it is noteworthy that there is nothing like this explicit description of records and record-keeping either in the Bible or in books current in nineteenth-century America.[9]

Looking back, we explain this interest in records teleologically, that is, by the final result. The Book of Mormon had a foreordained mission to fulfill in our time, before the end of the world. The record had to be kept, we say to ourselves, to accomplish the purposes outlined by Mormon on the title page. But that is only half the story. Records were intricately interwoven into the structures of Nephite society. Records had an ongoing function, apart from their ultimate purpose, making the process significant in the record-keeper's own times and not in the future alone.

We catch a glimpse of this function in an exchange between two groups of Nephites as related in the Book of Mosiah. Around 120 B.C. the Nephites occupied two regions, one around the city of Zarahemla and another in the land of Nephi. At the prompting of his people, King Mosiah in Zarahemla commissioned sixteen men led by Ammon to find the other group, which Ammon succeeded in doing. It was at the point of contact that records came into play. Once King Limhi recognized Ammon as an emissary of the Zarahemla Nephites, he sent a proclamation among his people calling them to a meeting at the temple. Before them all and before Ammon's band, Limhi read from two histories. One was the history of his own people since their arrival in the land of Nephi, and the other was the history of the people in Zarahemla to the point where his people departed. Then Limhi turned to Ammon and asked him to tell the history of the Zarahemla people since the separation, which Ammon did, including King Benjamin's famous address. That ceremony concluded, Limhi dismissed the people, but the telling of histories was not yet at an end. Limhi also brought to Ammon the written records of the people to be read. The reunion of the two long-separated peoples apparently required a recitation of their histories, involving not only the two leaders Limhi and Ammon, but the entire people.[10]

Eventually Limhi's people reunited with Mosiah's people in Zarahemla, and once again the exchange of histories took place. The way Mormon put it is that "Mosiah received them with joy; and he also received their records," as if the joining of two peoples entailed the joining of their records. Mosiah, like Limhi previously, also called all of the people together. The people from Nephi sat in one body and those from Zarahemla in another, and Mosiah read and had read the record of Limhi's people from the time they left Zarahemla until their return. Another record was read as well. Part of Limhi's people, under the leadership of Alma, had earlier splintered off and made their way back to Zarahemla about the same time. Though pursued and harried by enemies, Alma's small band had kept its record, which Mosiah read aloud before all the people. Once again the reunion of the three groups entailed the recitation of their various histories in a large public ceremony.[11]

In Mormon's account of the people's reaction, we are also given a glimpse of what the ceremony meant. The recitations went beyond mere ritualistic formality. Hearing them, the people "were struck with wonder and amazement." A great variety of emotions played over them. They "were filled with exceedingly great joy" at the deliverance of their brethren. On the other hand, "they were filled with sorrow, and even shed many tears of sorrow" at the thought of the people killed by the Lamanites. The "goodness of God" exemplified in the stories caused them to give thanks, while the "sinful and polluted state" of the Lamanites filled the people "with pain and anguish." Far from a boring lesson in history, the rehearsal of the stories thrilled and excited the listeners. The recorded histories entered into the imaginations of the people and stirred and instructed them.[12]

The two kings, Limhi and Mosiah, apparently desired their peoples to know the stories of other groups, and formal procedures had been worked out for conveying this knowledge. At the same time, the people themselves wanted the knowledge and delighted in the poignant emotions the histories evoked. This was the pattern again when it came to translating the Jaredite record on the twenty-four gold plates. King Limhi early on had asked Ammon about translation, and Ammon had told the king about Mosiah's gift of seership. But when Limhi and Mosiah were united, Mosiah's people were the ones to urge immediate translation. The record says Mosiah had to work on the plates "because of the great anxiety of his people; for they were desirous beyond measure to know concerning those people who had been destroyed." When Mosiah finished the translation, the "account did cause the people of Mosiah to mourn exceedingly, yea, they were filled with sorrow; nevertheless it gave them much knowledge, in the which they did rejoice."[13] Histories nourished and instructed people within the world of the Book of Mormon. They were the bread and meat of their conceptual lives.

This process of passing histories from one people to another went beyond the immediate value to the people who heard the stories. Within the Book of Mormon world, records were tied to a broad conception of human society and of world history. Records did not come into being as an isolated phenomenon but as a necessary component of an elaborate historical pattern. To begin with, it must be recalled that the Nephites, far more than the Israelites, conceived of "global" societies. The Bible refers to scores of "ites," the various tribal peoples and nations who lived in the lands bordering Canaan. But the Israelites' geographical images did not stretch much beyond the Middle East and the Mediterranean. Only obscurely did the prophets call up faint pictures of America or the Orient. Not so with the Nephites. Consistent with their own migration, they had a much more extended image of the earth and its nations. The Nephites conceived of human society as consisting of many peoples scattered across the earth. Significantly, they believed that many of these nations kept records. There were many nations, and many records. And the records were the means by which the nations defined their roles in world history.

The Nephite conception of multiple nations began with Israel. In his effort to explain the meaning of their lives to his little band washed ashore in a strange land, Nephi enlarged upon Isaiah's idea of Israel scattered to the isles of the sea. Their own condition, Nephi insisted to his people, was not aberrant but typical. "For it appears that the house of Israel, sooner or later, will be scattered upon all the face of the earth, and also among all nations." Already "the more part of all the tribes have been led away; and they are scattered to and fro upon the isles of the sea." And the rest were soon to follow.[14] The Nephites were but one fragment among many of the original Israel, and as a dispersed fragment were prototypical. In time all of Israel would be spread about the earth.

Each of these fragments, Nephi told his people, kept its record of God's revelations to it. God spoke to the Jews just as he did to the Nephites and, as the scripture said, "I shall also speak unto the other tribes of the house of Israel, which I have led away, and they shall write it." Each fragment of scattered Israel had its written record, and that was not all. Nephi envisioned other nations as well, nations not sprung from Israel, each with revelations, each with a record. "For I command all men, both in the east and in the west, and in the north, and in the south, and in the islands of the sea, that they shall write the words which I speak unto them." Every people had its revelation and its record. "I shall also speak unto all nations of the earth and they shall write it."[15] World history was creating a river of bibles cascading down through time from the diverse peoples of the earth.

The ultimate value of this great library of records went beyond their use by each individual people. In time the records would come together just as the people themselves would be gathered. The ritual of exchanging histories practiced in miniature by Limhi, Mosiah, Alma, and Ammon would be replicated on a grand scale. Nephi gave it as a general principle that "when two nations shall run together the testimony of the two nations shall run together also." At the concluding gathering at the end of the earth, all of these various records would be joined, and each people would learn the others' histories. "The Jews shall have the words of the Nephites, and the Nephites shall have the words of the Jews; and the Nephites and the Jews shall have the words of the lost tribes of Israel; and the lost tribes of Israel shall have the words of the Nephites and the Jews." It would be a complicated and time-consuming ceremony, but Nephi insisted that the exchange of histories among the various peoples must be complete. Each must know the history of the others as part of the final assemblage of Israel. Just as the Lord's peoples were to become one, so his "word also shall be gathered in one."[16]

Records, then, in the Nephite conception of the world, were in effect surrogates of peoples. They encompassed their revelations and their experience, and when Providence in the end assembled and united all peoples, bringing history to a conclusion, the records stood for the people. At that final day, their records would give the Nephites a part in the grand orchestra of the nations.[17]

The central place given records at the end grew out of their function all through the course of history. We have seen how peoples exchanged records when they met, whether in the course of events or at the final restoration. The ritual was important: the records were powerful forces shaping and directing their culture. Consider the poor people of Zarahemla who left Jerusalem in the days of Hezekiah without records, no one having had the foresight to wrest them from a Laban. When they met Mosiah, all they could offer by way of history was a genealogy, recited from memory by their leader Zarahemla. Without a record, within three or four hundred years their language was corrupted, and they had lost their religion, not even believing in God anymore. When they met Mosiah, they yielded at once to the superior culture of the Nephites, learning their language and making Mosiah king in place of Zarahemla.[18]

Something of the same sort was true for the Christian church. Nephi saw the apostasy of Christianity in his wilderness vision and explained why the church stumbled. They began with the record of the Jews containing "the fulness of the gospel of the Lord." People fell after there were "many plain and precious things taken away from the book." The perversion of the scripture record brought on apostasy. "Because of these things which are taken away out of the gospel of the Lamb, an exceeding great many do stumble, yea, insomuch that Satan hath great power over them." Records guided and sustained culture; without a true record, religion and the social order fell apart. Within the world of the Book of Mormon, it was perfectly consistent for the resurrected Christ to examine the Nephite records and require their amendment when an omission was found. The maintenance of culture depended on accurate records.[19]

If poor records led to the deterioration of culture, by the same token, true records had the power to revive and redirect a people. Since the loss of plain and precious truths from the record of the Jews caused the gentile Christian church to stumble, what better means to restore it than a true and accurate record? In fact, what other means? Without a true record there was no hope for a true religion. The ultimate role of Nephi's record was to "make known the plain and precious things which have been taken away" from the Jewish record and thus bring people back to Christ. The Nephite record was to speak from the dust especially to the Lamanites, establishing their true identity as the covenanted people of Israel.[20]

What was true for the Lamanites was true for all of Israel. One of Nephi's central themes, taking its cue from Isaiah, was the ultimate restoration of Israel. And by what means was God to accomplish this great recovery? "He shall bring forth his words unto them," the words recorded truly in the Book of Mormon. The great work of God in restoring lost Israel was to be accomplished by the production of a record, the written history and revelations of an ancient people. Confidence in the power of words in the world of the Book of Mormon far exceeds the comparable faith of our own supposedly literate culture.[21]

So we can see that records wind their way in and out of Nephite culture, not superficially but profoundly. They lay at the foundation of the Book of Mormon world as depicted by its prophets. The practice of exchanging histories suggests the Nephite assumption that every people must have its record, and that one people relates to another by presenting its testimony, that is to say its history. The exchange of records facilitates relationships from time to time in the course of ordinary events, but also at the culmination of world history when all people will come together and join in one, exchanging histories and testimonies as part of the concluding restoration.

Beyond the articulation of relationships among the nations, in the Book of Mormon world, records sustain the identity and culture of a people. Without records a people degenerate, lose their religion and their language, and forget their covenants with God. By the same token, records have the power to revive culture, to restore religion, and to reaffirm a people's identity and remembrance of covenants. Records are the primary instrument of restoration. Hence the Book of Mormon's mission to inform Israel of the covenant of the Lord and to convince Jew and Gentile that Jesus is the Christ. Within the world of the Book of Mormon, an historical record was the natural instrument to accomplish these grand purposes.

The Book of Mormon works out this schema of world history down to the brass tack details and the practical problems of making the system work. From a practical standpoint, the recovery and exchange of diverse records entails serious technical difficulties. Multiple languages require translations from one tongue to another. Otherwise how are people to understand one another at the last day? Rather than finesse the technical problems, leaving them to be settled in some vague, unspecified fashion, the Book of Mormon focuses on them. It brings forward the issue of multiple languages, exalts translators, and makes translation a holy process.

From the very outset, record-keeping and the problem of language were joined. In the same opening statement where he announced himself as a record-keeper, Nephi informed his readers of the characters in which he wrote—Egyptian. At the end of Nephite history, Moroni again raised the language question, mentioning that the record-keepers used reformed Egyptian.[22] How was a record in reformed Egyptian to be read? Moroni believed that "none other people knoweth our language," leading to problems when the Nephite records written in a lost language reached the Gentiles and the latter-day Lamanites. That, of course, is all worked out in the story. God had long before foreseen the need and given the Brother of Jared stones for interpreting language.[23] But that was not all. The interpreters were associated with a person and a calling. A new religious office emerges in the world of the Book of Mormon, one to my knowledge unknown in other religious cultures, the office of translator, a person granted the "high gift," as Ammon said, of translating records. The first Mosiah, the father of King Benjamin, was the first man in the record to actually exercise the gift when he translated the engraved stone that told of Coriantumr, the Jaredite. Although not commonly exercised thereafter, the translating powers of the seers were nonetheless well known. When Ammon heard about the twenty-four gold plates, he knew at once how to get them interpreted. "I can assuredly tell thee, O king, of a man that can translate the records." Ammon knew that King Mosiah, grandson of the previous translator, could perform the task because Mosiah had the interpreters. The power of seership and thence of translation passed with the records and the interpreting stones. Even Ammon, a soldier and explorer who counted himself unworthy to baptize, was aware of the gift. It was likely part of common lore, known to Ammon and many others, that whoever possessed the stones "is called seer, after the manner of old times."[24]

Which brings us at last to Joseph Smith and the modern Church of Christ. I wrote at one time that the Book of Mormon had peculiarly little influence on Mormonism considering the great effort that went into the book's translation. I now see I was mistaken. In the early years of the church, Joseph Smith was to a surprising degree absorbed into the world of the Book of Mormon. The Book of Mormon had a peculiar power to draw readers into its world. Its authors continually turn from the world in which they themselves lived, toward their modern readers. "I have seen your day," one said, and virtually all wrote in that spirit, looking us right in the eye. Moroni carries this connection with the modern world to an extreme. He acts like the explorer in the Woody Allen movie *Purple Rose of Cairo*. He steps off the screen into the audience, shows up in the bedroom of Joseph Smith, and invites him to join the story going on inside the movie.

And Smith did, in one portion of his life, become a character in the Nephite drama. The mission to the Lamanites was part of the story, but not all. Hints of Joseph's role appear in the book itself, in the prophetic description of the modern Joseph. He is there defined primarily as a seer, and as one who would bring forth records. The modern revelations to Smith picked up that theme. They made clear that his great gift, the one first to define his religious vocation, was the gift of translation. Prominent among the titles given him at the organization of the church were those of "a seer, a translator." It did not suffice at the beginnings of the church for Smith to receive revelations like the prophets who preceded him. He was also to translate, the role given him by prophecy in the Book of Mormon.[25]

Naturally the title fit because Smith's first great call was to translate the Book of Mormon. But his license to translate did not lapse once he completed the book. In the world the Book of Mormon created, translation had lasting importance. It was not a fleeting assignment that ended when a single job was done. The Book of Mormon filled history with sacred records, all requiring translation to complete the work of restoration and the unification of the earth's peoples. Though the gift of translation might lie dormant, as it did periodically in the Book of Mormon itself, the gift could never lapse completely while records in diverse tongues yet remained. Especially at the end of the world, in the time of restoration, the seer must repeatedly exercise his powers. In keeping with the requirements of the age, the revelations assigned the title of translator to Smith to the end of his life, and permanently attached it to the office of President of the High Priesthood.[26]

In Smith's own time, the powers of translation did not remain dormant. The modern revelations took up where the Book of Mormon left off with intimations of additional ancient records to be translated. At one point a revelation promised Oliver Cowdery the prized gift of translation. When he failed to translate from the Book of Mormon plates, a revelation told him not to worry. He would have another chance with "other records" yet to come forth. The revelations referred to "all those ancient records which have been hid up, that are sacred." Although Cowdery remained on the margins of the work, Smith soon was deeply immersed in the recovery of such records. The Book of Moses revealed through the latter half of 1830 contained scriptures "lost because of wickedness" from Moses's original record. Soon after, Smith began retranslating the Bible, and in 1835 started on the Book of Abraham. In the midst of organizing the church, sending out missionaries, establishing Mormon settlements, and directing migrations, Smith did not forget his crucial role as translator. Though harried with demands of every kind, for days at a time he worked away on one record or another to fulfill his divine calling.[27]

There is not then a gap between the Book of Mormon and the early latter-day church, as I once thought. Jan Shipps has argued that the Book of Mormon was one of the great foundation pillars of early Mormonism, and I agree.[28] Far more than the folk magic that soon receded into the background, the translation of ancient records was Smith's central religious vocation from 1827 until the organization of the church. He was in 1830 above all a seer and a translator. The work of translation occupied much of his time, the gift of translation attracted followers, and the role distinguished him. And the role, the gift, and the underlying conception of historic peoples keeping sacred records to be recovered in the last day all emerged from the world of the Book of Mormon.

The Book of Mormon in fact gave to the word restoration its peculiar Mormon flavor. Restoration was more than the recovery of true doctrine, or even the bestowal of priesthood keys. Restoration in the Book of Mormon sense meant the recovery of the entire experience of all the world's peoples through the translation and absorption of their histories. Nothing less than the restoration of world history was the charge given to Joseph Smith when he accepted the responsibilities of seer and translator prophesied of him in the Book of Mormon.

NOTES

Richard L. Bushman, *Joseph Smith and the Beginnings of Mormon-*

ism (Urbana and Chicago: University of Illinois Press, 1984), 128–31, 140–42; Grant Underwood, "The Earliest Reference Guides to the Book of Mormon: Windows into the Past," *Journal of Mormon History* 12 (1985): 69–89; Grant Underwood, "Book of Mormon Usage in Early LDS Theology," *Dialogue: A Journal of Mormon Thought* 17 (Autumn 1984): 56–61.

The best Book of Mormon analysis has always done this, of course. A recent excellent example is John L. Sorenson, *An Ancient American Setting for the Book of Mormon* (Salt Lake City: Deseret Book Co., 1985).

John L. Sorenson makes astute and revealing comments about Book of Mormon record-keeping in *An Ancient American Setting for the Book of Mormon*, 50–56.

1 Nephi 1:1–3, 16–17, Book of Mormon (subsequent references are to the Book of Mormon unless otherwise noted).

1 Nephi 4:13, 17.

Mormon 1:1–4; 4:23; 6:6; 8:1.

Jacob 7:27; Omni 11, 25; Mosiah 25:13.

Omni 8–12. For an analysis of the motives of these record-keepers, see John W. Welch, "The Father's Command to Keep Records in the Small Plates of Nephi," unpublished typescript, Foundation for Ancient Research and Mormon Studies, 1984.

From time to time records came to the fore in Israelitish history as in 2 Chronicles 34:29–30 and 35:26–27 in the reign of Josiah. Emphasis on records was not inconsistent with events in the Bible; records simply received much more attention in the Book of Mormon.

Mosiah 7:1, 2, 17–33; 8:1, 3–4.

Mosiah 22:14; 25:1–6.

Mosiah 25:7–12.

Mosiah 28:12, 18.

1 Nephi 22:3–5. See also 3 Nephi 15:20.

2 Nephi 29:11–13. See also Alma 29:8. The "all nations" must have had some qualifications, as John Sorenson has pointed out to me, since the people of Zarahemla and the Lamanites were known not to keep written records.

2 Nephi 29:8, 13, 14.

Ezekiel 37:15–20 is one passage in the Old Testament suggesting a similar process. For comments on this passage from a Latter-day Saint point of view, see Keith H. Meservy, "Discoveries at Nimrud and the 'Sticks' of Ezekiel," *Newsletter and Proceedings of the Society for Early Historical Archaeology* 142 (November 1978): 1–10; Hugh Nibley, "The Stick of Judah," *The Improvement Era* (January 1953): 16–17, 38–41; (February 1953): 90–91,

123–27; (March 1953): 150–52, 191–95; (April 1953): 150, 267; (May 1953): 331–32, 334, 336, 338, 341, 343.

18. Omni 14–19.

19. 1 Nephi 13:24, 28, 29; 3 Nephi 23:7–13.

20. 1 Nephi 13:35–40.

21. 2 Nephi 25:17, 18; 3:12; 29:2; 30:3–6; Mormon 5:14–15; 7:1, 9, 10, 19.

22. 1 Nephi 1:2; Moroni 9:32. Since an altered form of Hebrew was the vernacular language of Nephite society, according to Moroni, the record-keepers had to learn a second language. Benjamin taught his sons language, presumably Egyptian, to enable them to read the prophecies (Mosiah 1:2). All of the record-keepers must have received the same instruction. Moroni said the reformed Egyptian was handed down from generation to generation to the very end (Moroni 9:32). Assumption of responsibility for the records included mastery of a priestly language. Apparently the high place afforded record-keeping in the culture sufficed to sustain this arduous requirement over a thousand-year period.

23. Mormon 9:34; Ether 3:23.

24. Mosiah 8:13–14; 28:13–16; Omni 20. The Nephites believed the stones were "prepared from the beginning, and were handed down from generation to generation, for the purpose of interpreting languages." Alma the younger received the interpreters as did his son Helaman (Mosiah 28:20; Alma 37:21). Although the gift went unused for generations, Alma said the "gift of translation" was one of the gifts granted to the Nephites (Alma 9:21). Moroni, for example, translated the Jaredite record anew, rather than going back to Mosiah's previous translation (Ether 1:2). For the seers who possessed the interpreters, the translation of ancient records was a matter of course.

25. 2 Nephi 3:7, 12, 19; Doctrine and Covenants (hereafter cited as D&C) 1:29; 3:11–12; 10:1–3, 46–53; 20:8.

26. D&C 107:91, 92; 124:25.

27. D&C 6:25, 26; 8:1, 11; 9:2; Moses 1:23. On the translation of other texts, see Richard P. Howard, *Restoration Scriptures: A Study of Their Textual Development* (Independence, Mo.: Department of Religious Education, Reorganized Church of Jesus Christ of Latter Day Saints, 1969); Robert J. Matthews, *"A Plainer Translation:" Joseph Smith's Translation of the Bible, A History and Commentary* (Provo, Utah: Brigham Young University Press, 1975); and James R. Clark, *The Story of the Pearl of Great Price* (Salt Lake City: Bookcraft, 1955).

28. Jan Shipps, *Mormonism: The Story of a New Religious Tradition* (Urbana and Chicago: University of Illinois Press, 1985), 25–39.

"Walls, Grates and Screeking Iron Doors": The Prison Experience of Mormon Leaders in Missouri, 1838–1839

Dean C. Jessee

The last day of October 1838 was a moment when all-out war seemed inevitable between Mormon and non-Mormon forces confronting each other at the approaches to the little town of Far West in Caldwell County, Missouri. Under the presumption they had been invited to discuss ways of defusing the volatile situation that had developed there, five Mormon leaders approached the camp of Missouri militia commander, Samuel D. Lucas, under a flag of truce. The five were Joseph Smith and Sidney Rigdon, members of the church's First Presidency; Parley P. Pratt, an apostle; and George W. Robinson and Lyman Wight, Mormon militia officers. Far from entering into discussions, however, General Lucas had the five Mormons taken into custody and placed under heavy guard. "Judge of my surprise," wrote the Prophet, "when instead of being treated with that respect which is due from one citizen to another, we were taken as prisoners of war, and treated with the utmost contempt."[1] According to Pratt they were marched into the enemy camp "surrounded by thousands of savage looking beings, many of whom were dressed and painted like Indian warriors. These all set up a constant yell . . . mocking, railing, raging and foaming like a troubled sea."[2] Thus began an ordeal of confinement that was to last through the coming winter.

The circumstances that gave rise to the imprisonment of the Mormon leaders began with a revelation to Joseph Smith in July 1831 designating Jackson County, Missouri, as the place "consecrated for the gathering of the saints" and the building of "the city of Zion." The directive specified Independence as "the center place" where a temple would be built, and almost immediately Latter-day Saints began migrating from Ohio to western Missouri.[3] But for reasons attendant upon the influx of a large group of outsiders with differing social, religious, and economic values and practices, tension soon developed between the Mormons and old settlers, increasing until the Saints were violently driven from Jackson County in 1833. After remaining in Clay County a short time, they moved on, hoping to establish their Zion in the newly formed counties of Caldwell and Daviess; but antagonism erupted there too, at places that have become symbols of misunderstanding and inhumanity: Gallatin, DeWitt, Crooked River, and Haun's Mill.[4]

The morning after the arrest of the Mormon leaders at Far West, Joseph Smith's brother, Hyrum, and Amasa Lyman were added to the group of prisoners. "We spent this day, which proved to be rainy, on a small spot of ground snugly inclosed by a guard of ninety men," noted Wight. The day was marked by an attempt by militia officer Moses Wilson to bribe Wight to turn state's evidence and testify against Joseph Smith. Asked to tell what he knew of the Prophet, Wight replied that as far as he was acquainted with Joseph Smith, he "knew no man more honest or more philanthropic, having a greater zeal and love for his country and its laws, or one who would strive more for the peace and happiness of mankind than Joseph Smith." Hearing this, Wilson told Wight he had no further use for him and ordered him placed back with the other prisoners.[5]

At a "court" held by officers of the militia, General Lucas ordered a subordinate officer, Alexander Doniphan, to "take Joseph Smith and the other prisoners into the public square at Far West, and shoot them" at nine o'clock the next morning. Doniphan's bold refusal not only saved the lives of the prisoners, but endeared him ever after to the Latter-day Saints. "It is cold blooded murder. I will not obey your order. My brigade will march for Liberty tomorrow morning, at 8 o'clock, and if you execute those men, I will hold you responsible before an earthly tribunal, so help me God!" he is reported to have said.[6]

John B. Clark, major general of the 1st Division of Missouri Militia, who had been appointed by Governor Lilburn Boggs as field commander of the state militia forces confronting the Mormons in

Caldwell County, had not yet arrived at the scene of conflict before the Mormon leaders were taken into custody by General Lucas. Apparently motivated by his reverence for strict military etiquette, professional jealousy toward General Clark, and pride at having "captured" the Mormon leaders in the absence of his superior officer, General Lucas ordered the Mormon prisoners taken to Independence, his 4th Division headquarters of Missouri Militia.

After a tearful departure from their families, the men headed south, arriving at Independence during a heavy downpour on Sunday, 4 November, and were immediately confined in a comfortable log house with a "noble fire" on the north side of the public square. In a letter dated the day of arrival, Parley P. Pratt stated they had been "treated with every kindness and respect which we could desire. It is true I anticipated anything but kindness and hospitality when we fell into the hands of this brigade, knowing the long hostility which had existed; but we are happily disappointed." He noted that the Jackson County officers and troops had

> behaved with that respect, honor and kindness towards us which we would have expected from Brethren; and which has in a great measure atoned for their former trespasses, and has restored the best of feelings between us and them. We fared even better on the way than their own troops. Our meals were served to us in the best manner with plenty of coffee and sugar. We had the privilege of sleeping in a tent with the officers, while many of the troops slept in the open air. No person was suffered to insult us or treat us with disrespect in the least.

As the cortege moved through the countryside, crowds thronged the wayside to see the Mormon prisoners. "General Wilson often halted the troops to introduce us to them. Many of both sexes shook us warmly by the hand." In their comfortable surroundings people continued to flock to see them. At mealtime they were taken to a hotel.

> A splendid supper was set before us. After refreshing ourselves we were guarded back to our house and provided with paper and writing materials and candles; and Br. Smith, Br. Robinson, and myself now sit at the same stand scribbleing each to our respective families while Brs Wight, Rigdon, Hyrum Smith, and Br. Lyman are in conversation with the visitors and guards; and indeed were it not for the absence of our families we should almost forget that we are prisoners. We believe that

this journey saved our lives from the hands of furious men and will result in good.[7]

Seated at the same table with Pratt, Joseph Smith also wrote of high spirits and good treatment. "We have been protected by the Jackson County boys in the most genteel manner, and arrived here in the midst of a splendid parade. . . . Instead of going to jail we have a good house provided for us, and the kindest treatment." He noted that as they arrived at the Missouri River crossing the previous evening, an express had come from General Clark claiming his right to command, and ordering the Mormon prisoners back to his jurisdiction. But the injunction was disregarded and the company continued on to Independence. "There is some feelings between the officers. I do not know where it will end. It is said by some [that] General Clark is determined to exterminate. . . . What God may do for us I do not know but I hope for the best always in all circumstances. Although I go unto death, I will trust in God." Paramount in Smith's mind was his family: "Those little children are subjects of my meditation continually. Tell them that Father is yet alive. God grant that he may see them again. Oh Emma for God sake do not forsake me nor the truth but remember me. If I do not meet you again in this life may God grant that we may meet in heaven. I cannot express my feelings, my heart is full."[8]

While at Independence the prisoners were allowed to walk the streets without a guard and were soon transferred from the house in which they were first placed to a "respectable" hotel, where they were entertained "in the best style of which the place was capable." Pratt noted that they were free to come and go as they pleased, "a certain keeper being appointed merely to look to us." At one point Pratt "walked out of town and visited the desolate lands" formerly inhabited by the Latter-day Saints and also the place dedicated seven years previously for the building of a temple, "it being a beautiful rise of ground, about half a mile west of Independence. When we saw it last it was a wilderness, but now our enemies had robbed it of every stick of timber, and it presented a beautiful rolling field of pasture, being covered with grass." The prisoners were also invited to dine with General Wilson and other officers. There was much "politeness and attention on their part, and much cheerfulness and good feeling on our own," wrote Pratt.[9]

After three days of serenity in Independence, the prisoners were ordered to Richmond. The Jackson County authorities encountered difficulty obtaining a guard to accompany them, but three men finally came forward and the company proceeded northward by carriage and horseback. Pratt wrote, "Sometimes we were sixty or eighty rods in front or rear of our guard, who, by the by, were three sheets in the wind, in the whiskey line." Noting the ease with which they could have escaped, he explained that they did not take advantage of the opportunity because they "were not guilty of any crime." At one point, after crossing the Missouri River, the guards all went to sleep, leaving their pistols with the prisoners to defend themselves in case of an attack, as they were in a "very hostile neighborhood."[10]

Arriving on the outskirts of Richmond on 9 November, the company was met by a contingent of Clark's soldiers who escorted them military fashion with great pomp, "like Bonaparte and his body guards," into town.[11] With the arrival of Clark's troops, the laxness that had characterized the jaunt into Jackson County ceased. The prisoners were thrust into an "old log house" in Richmond where, with three trace chains and seven padlocks, they were chained together by their legs at two-foot intervals.[12] "Brother Robinson is chained next to me," wrote Smith, "He has a true heart and a firm mind; Brother Wight is next, Br. Rigdon next, Hyrum next, Parley next, Amasa next, and thus we are bound together in chains as well as the cords of everlasting love."[13]

On 12 November a court of inquiry was held at Richmond before Judge Austin A. King in which Joseph Smith, his fellow prisoners, and some fifty other Mormons were charged with alleged crimes connected with the conflict of the previous summer. The prisoners whose cases were not bailable (including Joseph Smith and Parley Pratt) were ordered confined until the sitting of the local circuit court the next spring. On the day the Richmond inquiry opened, Joseph weighed his prospects in a letter to his wife: "Although there has been things that were unbeknown to us, and altogether beyond our control, that might seem to the mob to be a pretext for them to persecute us . . . on examination, I think that the authorities will discover our innocence and set us free. But if this blessing cannot be obtained, I have this consolation, that I am an innocent man, let what will befall me." Much of his letter reflected concern for his family at Far West.

Beside his thirty-four-year-old wife, Emma, his family consisted of an adopted daughter, Julia, seven; Joseph, six; Frederick, two; and five-month-old Alexander. "Oh God grant that I may have the privilege of seeing once more my lovely family in the enjoyment of the sweets of liberty and social life. To press them to my bosom and kiss their lovely cheeks would fill my heart with unspeakable gratitude." He told Emma to tell the children he was alive and expected to see them before long.

> Tell little Joseph he must be a good boy. Father loves him with a perfect love. He is the eldest [and] must not hurt those that are smaller than him, but comfort them. Tell little Frederick Father loves him with all his heart. He is a lovely boy. Julia is a lovely little girl. [I] love her also. She is a promising child. Tell her Father wants her to remember him and be a good girl. Tell all the rest that I think of them and pray for them all. . . . . Little Alexander is on my mind continually. Oh my affectionate Emma, I want you to remember that I am a true and faithful friend to you and the children forever. My heart is entwined around you forever and ever. Oh may God bless you all, Amen.[14]

While confined at Richmond, Sidney Rigdon became so ill from exposure that he fell into a state of delirium. In this condition he was still chained to the other prisoners when his daughter Athalia, who was also the wife of another of the prisoners, George W. Robinson, a "young and delicate female" with an infant child, was admitted to the crude prison. Parley Pratt observed that the young woman broke into tears as she greeted her sick father and her husband "amid the clank of chains and the bristle of weapons."[15]

During the confinement at Richmond, the circumstance of Joseph Smith's rebuke of the guard took place. One night after listening to the usual vulgarity and abuse, Smith suddenly arose, according to Pratt, and commanded the guards in the name of Jesus Christ to be still, "or you or I die this instant!" Later reflecting upon the event, Pratt noted that "dignity and majesty have I seen but once, as it stood in chains, at midnight in a dungeon, in an obscure village in Missouri."[16]

At the conclusion of the Richmond hearing, Joseph Smith, Hyrum Smith, Lyman Wight, Alexander McRae, and Caleb Baldwin were charged with "overt acts of treason in Daviess county," and Sidney

Rigdon, with the same offense, in Caldwell County. However, in the absence of a jail in those two counties, these six men were committed to the Clay County jail to await trial the following spring. In addition, Parley Pratt, Norman Shearer, Darwin Chase, Luman Gibbs, and Morris Phelps were accused of the murder of Moses Rowland at the Crooked River fight the previous October and committed to the Ray County jail in Richmond to await their trial. Numerous others, charged with lesser offenses of robbery, burglary, arson, and larceny, were eventually freed upon payment of bail.[17]

The Mormon prisoners committed to the Clay County jail arrived in Liberty, the county seat, on 1 December 1838, in a heavy wagon accompanied by an armed escort. Except for their heads and shoulders, the men in the wagon were hidden from view by the high wagon box. As the procession crawled through town, curious onlookers gathered at the jail, saw the wagon disgorge its occupants, and the men disappear inside. The jail, a sturdy structure, built in 1833 at a cost of $600, was two stories, with an outside wall of rough-hewn limestone two feet thick, and an inside wall of twelve-inch hewn oak logs, the two walls separated by a twelve-inch space filled with loose rock. Combined, the walls made a formidable barrier four feet thick. The interior of the building measured 14 by 14 1/2 feet divided into an upper and lower room. The lower, or "dungeon," where the prisoners were kept, was lighted by two narrow windows grated with heavy iron bars. Access to the jail was through a single door that opened into the upper room, and, from there, a trap door into the dungeon.[18] An eyewitness, who saw the prisoners arrive, said that Joseph Smith was the last to enter the jail. He "looked at the curious multitude that had gathered . . . lifted his hat and said in a distinct voice, 'Good afternoon, gentlemen,' and disappeared behind the heavy iron door."[19]

It is impossible to reproduce the human drama that unfolded in the Liberty jail between 1 December 1838 and 6 April 1839 — a drama that lies hidden behind the phrases of those who languished there: "grates and screeking iron doors," "dirty straw couches," the "nauseous" smell, the "grimace of the guard night and day," "weary joints and bones," and "this hell surrounded with demons." To those who had not had the experience, it was said "pen, or tongue, or angels" could never describe what took place there.[20]

The first reaction of the prisoners to the jail is contained in a letter Joseph Smith wrote his wife the day he arrived: "My dear companion I take this opportunity to inform you that we arrived in Liberty and [were] committed to jail this evening but we are all in good spirits."[21] It is difficult to tell whether his reference to "good spirits" reflected his true feelings, or whether it was merely a ploy to guarantee delivery of his letter since the mail carrier was Samuel Bogard, the mob leader who confronted the Mormons at Crooked River earlier in the year.

One of the main sources of satisfaction to those confined at Liberty was the visits and letters of relatives and friends. During the first two months of confinement family members of all the prisoners visited the jail. The wives of Joseph and Hyrum, their brother Don Carlos, Lyman Wight's wife and four boys, and Alexander McRae's wife and two boys all came. On one occasion Emma brought six-year-old Joseph III with her, who remembered staying all night with his father and receiving a blessing from him. In February 1839 Hyrum's wife brought their infant son to the jail where his father saw him for the first time. Other visitors included Edward Partridge, Brigham Young, and Heber C. Kimball—the latter having promised to supply Joseph with clean clothes. Benjamin Covey brought each of the prisoners a new pair of shoes; Porter Rockwell came many times with food; Jane Bleven and her daughter brought cakes and pies and handed them in at the windows. And lawyers Peter Burnett, Alexander Doniphan, Joel Turnham, and Andrew S. Hughes, visited the jail as legal counsel for the prisoners.[22]

Shortly after his call to the Council of Twelve in 1839, Joseph's cousin, George A. Smith, came to the jail in company with Brigham Young and Heber C. Kimball. Waiting until the evening meal was served, the visitors spent an hour locked in with the prisoners. George A. recalled that although the Prophet spent most of the time conversing with the two older apostles, he "always regarded it as a blessing" that he had the privilege of being locked up with those men, even if it was but for an hour.[23]

By February 1839, the flow of visitors and mail to the prison had dwindled due to the exodus of the Saints from Missouri. The smallest kindness or greeting was received as a sweet morsel. On 20 March letters from his wife, his brother Don Carlos, and one from Bishop

Edward Partridge, all breathing "a kind and consoling spirit," elicited from Joseph Smith his most profound response from the jail. "We had been a long time without information and when we read those letters they were to our souls as the gentle air is refreshing . . . the flood gates of our hearts were hoisted and our eyes were a fountain of tears. But those who have not been enclosed in the walls of a prison without cause or provocation can have but a little idea how sweet the voice of a friend is. One token of friendship from any source whatever awakens and calls into action every sympathetic feeling."[24]

Not all who came to see the Mormon prisoners were friendly. Some came to taunt, jeer, and accuse. Alexander McRae said some were angry with Joseph and accused him of killing a son, a brother, or some relative at Crooked River, which seemed strange to him since the Missourians had reported only one man killed there.[25]

As word of the occupants of the jail spread, the place took on some aspects of a zoo. Hyrum Smith was exasperated at the curiosity seekers who crowded the place. "We are often inspected by fools who act as though we were elephants or dromedarys or sea hogs or some monstrous whale or sea serpents. We have never had our teeth examined like an old horse, but expect [to] every day when . . . a new swarm come[s] that have never seen us." He noted that they were "frequently saluted . . . by the children of the streets banging against the door" yelling "come out here damn ye, I'll kill you," and cursing and profaning and taunting, "prophesy you damned rascals."[26]

A source of anguish to those in the jail was the suffering of the Saints, and the knowledge that their situation came in consequence of traitors within the church itself, who had perpetrated "frauds, secret abominations, and evil works of darkness."[27] Another trial was the poor food. McRae recalled that the food was "very coarse, and so filthy that we could not eat it until we were driven to it by hunger."[28] Wight added that the "mercies of the jailor were intolerable, feeding us with a scanty allowance, on the dregs of coffee and tea, from his own table, and fetching the provisions in a basket on which the chickens had roosted the night before, without being cleaned." Hyrum Smith testified that the food "was anything but good and decent"; and that poison was administered to them on three or four occasions. "The effect it had upon our system was, that it vomited us almost to death, and then we would lay some two or three days in a torpid, stupid state, not even caring or wishing for life."[29] McRae confirmed the poisoning, which he supposed was administered in either tea or coffee; but since he did not use either, he was not affected. Those that were, however, "were sorely afflicted, some being blind two or three days, and it was by much faith and prayer that the effect was overcome."[30] Both Hyrum Smith and Lyman Wight testified that at one time the prisoners were fed human flesh. Hyrum said none of them partook of it except Wight, and he explained that "extreme hunger" had driven him to eat it.[31] So far as the menu was concerned, the only fare mentioned by the prisoners was coffee, tea, and cornbread; hence, it was a noteworthy occasion three days before leaving the jail when Hyrum wrote in his diary, "We had some rice today for dinner for the first time since we have been confined." He added, "Our food has been very poor and unwholesome."[32]

From the standpoint of physical comfort, the Liberty jail had little to recommend it. Joseph wrote a friend that it was a "hell surrounded with demons if not those who are damned . . . where we are compelled to hear nothing but blasphemous oaths and witness a scene of blasphemy and drunkenness and hypocracy and debaucheries of every description."[33] He wrote another correspondent: "We are kept under a strong guard, night and day, in a prison of double walls and doors, proscribed in our liberty of conscience, our food is scant, uniform, and coarse; we have not the privilege of cooking for ourselves, we have been compelled to sleep on the floor with straw, and not blankets sufficient to keep us warm; and when we have a fire, we are obliged to have almost a constant smoke."[34] Elsewhere, he noted, "Our souls have been bowed down and we have suffered much distress . . . and truly we have had to wade through an ocean of trouble."[35]

In terms of the physical and emotional impact, the toll was heavy. James E. Ford, one of the jailers, recalled that the place was so dark the prisoners all got sore eyes.[36] On the last day of March, Hyrum wrote that he was "sick with earache," and the swelling in his ear was "very painful." He noted that Joseph was also unwell, and added, "we feel wearied of this prison. Our beds are worn out."[37] The Prophet added, "My nerve trembles from long confinement," as he apologized for "imperfections" in his handwriting. He lamented, "If I could tell you my tale, I think you would say it was altogether enough for once, to gratify the malice of hell that I have suffered."[38]

Hyrum later summarized his experience in Liberty jail, noting that he had "suffered much for want of proper food, and from the nauseous cell in which I was confined." He talked of his anxiety for his family, left without a protector and unable to help themselves. "My wife was confined while I was away from home, and had to suffer more than tongue can tell." Nor were the Missourians his only oppressors. "Those with whom I had been acquainted from my youth, and who had ever pretended the greatest friendship towards me, came to my house while I was in prison, and ransacked and carried off many of my valuables." These circumstances were almost overwhelming. "I traversed my prison house for hours, thinking of their cruelty to my family, and the afflictions they brought upon the saints . . . but how inadequate is language to express the feelings of my mind. . . . From my close and long confinement, as well as from the sufferings of my mind, I feel my body greatly broke down and debilitated, my frame has received a shock from which it will take a long time to recover."[39]

On 25 January 1839, after petitioning to have their case heard on a writ of habeas corpus, the prisoners were brought before Clay County Judge Joel Turnham at the Liberty courthouse. Rigdon said that there, for the first time since his arrest, he heard the evidence upon which he had been charged with treason.[40] During these proceedings, the prisoners were defended by Alexander Doniphan and Peter Burnett, except for Sidney Rigdon, who pled his own case. Doniphan later said he had never heard such a masterful plea as Rigdon's. His performance so touched the antagonistic crowd of "Mormon eaters" packed into the courthouse that many were melted to tears, and after the verdict was announced to free Rigdon, they collected a large sum for his benefit.[41] According to Joseph Smith, the others should have been freed at the same time Rigdon was, "had not our own lawyers interpreted the law contrary to what it reads against us, which prevented us from introducing our evidence."[42]

Following this hearing it became apparent to the five prisoners remanded to jail that justice would be difficult to obtain in that part of Missouri, and they concluded to try other means to obtain their freedom. Having noticed that the jailer who brought their food was occasionally lax in his security procedures, it was decided to make a break for freedom at the time of the evening meal on 6 February. The opportunity that evening seemed particularly good because the guard entered alone, left the door open behind him, and went to a corner of the jail and engaged himself in reading a book. But because Wight had pled for a day's delay, no effort was made to escape that night.

The situation the next night, agreed upon for the escape, was much different. The jailer entered the cell accompanied by a heavy guard, and six other men who had come to visit the prisoners: Erastus Snow, William Huntington, Cyrus Daniels, David Holeman, Alanson Ripley, and Watson Barlow. The jailer took every precaution to guarantee security. "It looked like a bad chance to get away," wrote McRae, who left the most detailed account of events. "But we were determined to try it; so when the jailor started out, we started too." By taking two of the guards with him, Cyrus Daniels got out of the jail, but the jailer and another guard slammed the door shut before the rest could free themselves. Seeing the others had failed to escape, and losing hold of the guards he had carried into the street, Daniels began a sprint for cover, but tripped and fell just as a bullet passed over his head. McRae wrote that the commotion aroused the local citizens, and the ensuing scene at the jail became very ugly. The entire town and many from the surrounding country gathered at the jail. "Every mode of torture and death that their imaginations could fancy, was proposed for us, such as blowing up the jail, taking us out and whipping us to death, shooting us, burning us to death, tearing us to pieces with horses, &c. But they were so divided among themselves that they could not carry out any of their plans, and we escaped unhurt."[43]

The second attempt of the prisoners to free themselves occurred less than a month later, after they had bored a hole in the four-foot-thick wall with crude tools apparently smuggled into the jail. They had planned to leave the jail on 3 March "without fail," but after working hard all that day were unable to succeed. "We will do it tomorrow if the Lord will," wrote Lyman Wight; but again they were disappointed. Word of the impending break had been confided to a friendly outsider who inadvertently let slip a hint of his secret, and just as the prisoners were ready to go, ten guards appeared on the scene.[44] Joseph Smith attributed the failure to "imprudence," and shrugged off the incident. "We should have taken a habeas corpus before the high judge and escaped the mob in a summary way; but unfortunately for us, the timber of the wall being very hard, our auger handles gave out, and hindered us longer than we expected; we applied to a friend, and a very slight incautious act gave rise to some suspicions, and before we could fully succeed, our plan was discovered." He added that everything was ready except the last stone and they could have "succeeded admirably" had it not been for a little "over-anxiety on the part of our friend. The sheriff and jailor did not blame us for our attempt. It was a fine breach and cost the county a round sum."[45]

Following these attempts to escape, security at the jail was increased. According to one account, Sam Tillery, the jailer, was about to have the prisoners placed in irons and chained to the floor, but the threat did not materialize.[46] To discourage further attempts of escape, occasional inspections were made of the jail and a close watch placed over the prisoners. On 17 March the jailer found an auger handle, and called twenty-five men to make a thorough search. "The jailor appeared to be offended [and] threatened to put us in chains," but "soon calmed down and agreed to call again and settle the matter," wrote Hyrum Smith.[47] Presendia Huntington visited the jail on 15 March, accompanied by her father William, Heber C. Kimball, Joseph B. Noble, and Alanson Ripley: "When we arrived at the jail we found a heavy guard outside and inside the door. We were watched very closely, lest we should leave tools to help the prisoners escape. I took dinner with the brethren in prison; they were much pleased to see the faces of true friends; but I cannot describe my feelings on seeing that man of God there confined in such a trying time for the saints."[48]

Others who visited the jail were refused entrance. On 4 April, Stephen Markham and William Huntington were turned away. "This bringeth painful sensations to our minds to think that our beloved Brethren take pains to come to see us and then they are forbidden and have to go away grieved with the treatment they received," wrote Hyrum.[49] It is evident that much of the strictness at the prison was motivated by public opinion and threats that if the prisoners escaped, the jailer would be held accountable. Joseph noted that the jailer was "a very jealous man, for fear some one will have tools for us to get out with. He is under the eye of the mob continually, and his life is at stake if he grants us any privilege. He will not let us converse with anyone alone."[50]

Although it is difficult to detail events at Liberty jail between 1 December 1838 and 6 April 1839, available sources give some insight to what took place there. On the eve of their departure, Hyrum wrote in his diary, "We pray God that when we are taken from this place we shall fall into better hands. May God give us our liberty is our prayer daily."[51] The same day, Joseph writing to Emma reflected upon his experience in his letter from the prison:

> I sit down just as the sun is going down, as we peek through the grates of this lonesome prison, to write to you, that I may make known to you my situation. It is I believe . . . now about five months and six days since I have been under the grimace of a guard night and day, and within the walls, grates and screeking iron doors of a lonesome dark dirty prison. With emotions known only to God, do I write this letter. The contemplations of the mind under these circumstances defies the pen, or tongue, or angels to describe or paint to the human being who never experienced what we experience. This night we expect, is the last night we shall try our weary joints and bones on our dirty straw couches in these walls, let our case hereafter be as it may. . . . We cannot get into a worse hole than this is. We shall not stay here but one night besides this, if that, thank God. We shall never cast a lingering wish after liberty in Clay County, Missouri. We have enough of it to last forever.

Although a change in location seemed imminent, the outcome of the prisoners' case was clouded. Joseph wrote of their anticipated change of venue to one of the "lower counties," but wondered about their chances for protection under the law, "from beings" who had conducted themselves as some of the inhabitants of that part of the state had already done. He added, "we lean on the arm of Jehovah, and none else for our deliverance, and if he don't do it, it will not be done, you may be assured, for there is great thirsting of our blood in this state." He wrote that his thoughts were of his wife and children continually. "I would gladly walk from here to you barefoot, and bareheaded, and half naked, to see you and think it a pleasure, and never count it toil." He besought his wife to "not let those little fellows forget me. Tell them Father loves them with a perfect love."

In closing his letter, he urged Emma to "teach them all you can, that they may have good minds. Be tender and kind to them, don't be fractious to them, but listen to their wants. Tell them Father says they must be good children and mind their mother. . . . There is great responsibility resting upon you, in preserving yourself in honor, and sobriety before them, and teaching them right things, to form their young and tender minds that they begin in right paths and not get contaminated when young by seeing ungodly examples."[52]

On 6 April 1839 the prisoners were taken from the Liberty jail and hurried to Daviess County guarded by about fifteen men. After a tedious journey, "for our long confinement had enfeebled our bodily powers," they were delivered to the custody of Daviess County Sheriff William Morgan on 8 April. Two days later a grand jury, presided over by Thomas C. Burch, judge of Missouri's Eleventh Judicial Circuit, convened at the house of Elisha B. Creekmore, near Gallatin, and brought indictments of riot, arson, burglary, treason, and receiving stolen goods against the five Mormon prisoners, and denied them bail.[53] Objecting to a trial in Daviess County on grounds of extreme prejudice in that part of the state, and that the judge had been counsel in the case, the prisoners were granted a change of venue to Boone County. Sheriff Morgan was directed to deliver the prisoners to Columbia, along with the warrant or process by which they were being held.[54]

The five prisoners left Gallatin in a two-horse wagon accompanied by the sheriff and four men. At Diahman the prisoners bought two horses from the guard, paying for one with clothing and giving their note for the other.[55] A short time later, while traveling near Yellow Creek in Chariton County, the Mormon prisoners escaped. They later testified that Judge Burch and ex-Sheriff William Bowman, who had provided transportation for the prisoners, had connived in the escape. Hyrum Smith said that three days out of Gallatin they bought a jug of whiskey, that three of the guard "drank pretty freely" and went to bed. Sheriff Morgan showed the prisoners the mittimus committing them to prison, that it was illegal because it was "without date or signature," and said, "I shall take a good drink of grog and go to bed, and you may do as you have a mind to." According to Wight, the sheriff said the people of Daviess County "would be surprised that the prisoners had not left them sooner."

Then with the aid of the remaining guard, the prisoners changed the direction of their course, heading instead to Illinois. Joseph Smith wrote, "We thought that it was necessary for us, inasmuch as we loved our lives, and did not wish to die . . . to deliver ourselves from our enemies. . . . Accordingly, we took advantage of the situation of our guard and departed."[56]

After pursuing their course night and day, avoiding main roads, and "suffering much fatigue and hunger," Joseph Smith arrived in Quincy, Illinois, on 22 April 1839. Although little is known of the journey to Illinois after their escape,[57] Orange Wight, Lyman's son, later recorded an incident told by his father that showed the cross-country ordeal of the escapees was not without its lighter moments. As soon as they departed from their captors, the men changed their names and posed as land seekers from the east hunting a place to settle. At one point they came to a ranch in an out-of-the-way place and asked for a night's lodging. Having given the proprietor their fictitious names, the "land seekers" arose the next morning and were casually walking about the premises—all except Alexander McRae, who was in the house talking with the proprietor. In the course of conversation the farmer asked McRae his name, as he had forgotten it. The query hit McRae like a bolt of lightning when he realized he did not remember the name he had been assigned. "It had the effect to cause Bro. McRae to take a terrible cramp in the stomach. It came near throwing him into spasms." Whereupon, the farmer ran out where his companions were and told them their friend was very ill. They came rushing in and said, "Mr. Brown, what is the matter with you; what have you been eating?" This "relieved Mr. Brown to such an extent that he began to get better right away. In the meantime, the proprietor had brought in a jug of whiskey . . . and recommended Mr. Brown to take a glass—thought it would help him. He done so; and the others—those that were disposed that way which was nearly all—[also] took some for fear the disease was contagious." Orange Wight added that whenever the Liberty jail veterans thereafter partook of a beverage of any kind they would jokingly recommend that Bro. McRae be served first in case he should get a cramp and "not be able to remember his name."[58]

If there were redeeming qualities in the experience of those

Mormons confined in Missouri prisons in 1838–39, they are found in inspired instructions given there, the strengthening of virtues of love and friendship, and the literary contributions that have survived. Nearly twenty years later, Lyman Wight, writing from Texas, fondly recalled the months of instruction he received from Joseph Smith. "Joseph blessed me many times while in jail and prophecied much on my head and gave me much good instruction which is long to be remembered."⁵⁹ Joseph Smith traced increased feelings of sensitivity to his jail experience: "No tongue can tell what inexpressible joy it gives a man to see the face of one who has been a friend, after having been inclosed in the walls of a prison for five months. It seems to me my heart will always be more tender after this than ever it was before. . . . For my part I think I never could have felt as I now do if I had not suffered the wrongs which I have suffered. All things shall work together for good to them that love God."⁶⁰

Beyond this, both the participants and those who have read their story have gained insight to the meaning of suffering and adversity in human experience. In March 1839, following the failure of the Liberty jail escape attempt, while languishing in his miserable surroundings, Joseph Smith pled with his creator, "O God! where art thou? And where is the pavilion that covereth thy hiding place? How long shall thy hand be stayed, and thine eye, yea thy pure eye, behold from the eternal heavens, the wrongs of thy people, and of thy servants, and thine ear be penetrated with their cries?" In answer, these thoughts, since incorporated into the canon of LDS scripture in Doctrine and Covenants Sections 121, 122, and 123, came from his lips as he dictated to McRae:

> My son, peace be unto thy soul; thine adversity and thine afflictions shall be but a small moment; and then, if thou endure it well, God shall exalt thee on high; thou shalt triumph over all thy foes; thy friends do stand by thee, and they shall hail thee again, with warm hearts and friendly hands; thou art not yet as Job; thy friends do not contend against thee, neither charge thee with transgression, as they did Job. . . . If thou art called to pass through tribulation . . . and . . . if the very jaws of hell shall gape open the mouth wide after thee, know thou, my son, that all these things shall give thee experience, and shall be for thy good. The son of man hath descended below them all; art thou greater than he?⁶¹

NOTES

Unless otherwise indicated, manuscript sources are located in the LDS Church Archives, Salt Lake City, Utah. Spelling and punctuation have been modernized.

1. "Extract from the Private Journal of Joseph Smith, Jr." *Times and Seasons* 1 (November 1839): 5.

2. Parley Parker Pratt Jr., ed., *Autobiography of Parley Parker Pratt* (Salt Lake City: Deseret Book Co., 1970), 228–29.

3. Doctrine and Covenants 57:1–3.

4. The complex issues that gave rise to the expulsion of the Latter-day Saints from Missouri have been dealt with in the following scholarly studies: Warren Jennings, "Zion is Fled: The Expulsion of the Mormons from Jackson County, Missouri," (Ph.D. diss., University of Florida, 1962); Leland Gentry, "A History of the Mormons in Northern Missouri from 1836 to 1839," (Ph.D. diss., Brigham Young University, 1965); Max Parkin, "A History of the Latter-day Saints in Clay County, Missouri, from 1833 to 1837," (Ph.D. diss., Brigham Young University, 1976).

5. Diary of Lyman Wight, cited in Heman C. Smith and Joseph Smith III, eds., *History of the Reorganized Church of Jesus Christ of Latter Day Saints*, 4 vols. (Independence, Missouri, 1951), 2:260–61. The original Wight diary no longer exists.

Another version of this incident occurs in "History of Lyman Wight," *Deseret News* 8 (25 August 1858): 109: "During the evening, Gen. Moses Wilson took him [Wight] out by himself, and tried to induce him to betray Joseph Smith, and swear falsely against him; at which time the following conversation took place. Gen. Wilson said, 'Col. Wight, we have nothing against you, only that you are associated with Jo Smith. He is our enemy and a damned rascal, and would take any plan he could to kill us. You are a damned fine fellow; and if you will come out and swear against him, we will spare your life, and give you any office you want; and if you don't do it, you will be shot tomorrow at 8 o'clock.' Col. Wight replied, 'Gen. Wilson, you are entirely mistaken in your man, both in regard to myself and Joseph Smith. Joseph Smith is not an enemy to mankind; he is not your enemy; but is as good a friend as you have got. Had it not been for him, you would have been in hell long ago, for I should have sent you there, by cutting your throat, and no other man but Joseph Smith could have prevented me, and you may thank him for your life. And, now, if you will give me the boys I brought from Diahman yesterday, I will whip your whole army.' Wilson said, 'Wight, you are a strange man; but if you will not accept my proposal, you will be shot tomorrow morning at 8.' Col Wight replied, 'Shoot and be damned.' "

6. *History of Caldwell and Livingston Counties, Missouri* (St. Louis, 1886), 137.

7. Parley Pratt to Mary Ann Pratt, 4 November 1838. Ms. In a later recollection of the trip to Independence, Hyrum Smith wrote, "on our way to Jackson county we excited great curiosity; at our stoping places, people would flock to see us, from all quarters; a great number of whom would rail upon us, and give us abusive language, while a few would pity us; . . . When we arrived at Independence . . . the citizens flocked from all parts of the county to see us. They were generally very abusive, some of the most ignorant gnashed their teeth upon us." (Hyrum Smith to the Saints Scattered Abroad, December 1839, as cited in *Times and Seasons* 1 [December 1839]: 22.) And an 1840 history noted: "After we arrived at Independence . . . we served the same purpose that a caravan of wild animals would for a show, as hundreds of people called to see us. We were put into an old house and left to sleep on some blankets we had with us." ("A History of the Persecution of the Church of Jesus Christ, of Latter Day Saints in Missouri," *Times and Seasons* 1 [September 1840]: 161.)

8. Joseph Smith to Emma Smith, 4 November 1838. Ms. RLDS Church Archives.

9. Parley P. Pratt, *History of the Late Persecution Inflicted by the State of Missouri upon the Mormons* (Detroit: Dawson and Bates, Printers, 1839), 46–47.

10. En route to Independence on 3 November, General Lucas had received an express from General Clark ordering him to march the prisoners to Richmond, disband his forces, and report to Clark's camp, but Lucas ignored the order because he "could not, under any circumstances, be commanded by a junior Major General." Not until the weight of the commander-in-chief was added to Clark's order did Lucas start the prisoners for Richmond on 6 November. (Missouri, General Assembly, *Document Containing the Correspondence, Orders, &c., in Relation to the Disturbances with the Mormons* [1848], 71.)

11. Ibid., 48.

12. Wight, 297.

13. Joseph Smith to Emma Smith, 12 November 1838. Ms. RLDS Church Archives.

14. Ibid.

15. Pratt, *History of the Late Persecution*, 52–53.

16. Pratt, *Autobiography*, 228–29.

17. "State of Mo. vs. Jos. Smith Jr. et al." Daviess County Circuit Court Papers, Ms. State Historical Society of Missouri, Columbia, Missouri; also, U.S., Congress, Senate, Document 189, *Testimony given Before the Judge of the Fifth Judicial Circuit of the State of Missouri, on the Trial of Joseph Smith, Jr., and others, for High Treason, and other Crimes against that State*, 26th Cong. 2d Session (15 February 1841).

In considering the charges made against the Mormon prisoners at the Richmond hearing and the context in which they were made, there is evidence to conclude that Mormon blame in upper Missouri may not have been as blatant as the Richmond charges would indicate. General H. G. Park writing to Governor Boggs on 25 September 1838 said that upon his arriving at the scene of conflict he found a large body of men from adjoining counties "armed and in the field, for the purpose . . . of assisting the people of this county against the Mormons, without being called out by the proper authorities." (Parks to Boggs, 25 September 1838, cited in Missouri, General Assembly, *Document Containing the Correspondence, Orders &c.*, 32–33.) General David Atchison wrote Governor Boggs on 27 September, "I have no doubt your Excellency has been deceived by the exaggerated statements of designing or half-crazy men. I have found there is no cause of alarm on account of the Mormons." (Atchison to Boggs, 27 September 1838, ibid., 34.) Atchison and Alexander Doniphan, in a request for arms from the federal garrison at Fort Leavenworth, wrote that citizens of the northern counties had "raised mob after mob for the last two months for the purpose of driving a community of fanatics, (called Mormons) from those counties and from the State. Those things have at length goaded the Mormons into a state of desperation that has now made them aggressors instead of acting on the defensive. This places the citizens of this whole community in the unpleasant attitude that the civil and decent part of the community have now to engage in war to arrest a torrent that has been let loose by a cowardly mob." (Atchison to Mason, Commanding at Leavenworth, 27 October 1838. Ms.) Later, Atchison wrote the U.S. adjutant general that "the imprudent conduct of a part of the citizens in the upper counties, have brought about the present difficulties; goading the Mormons to acts of desperation; even bloodshed and plunder, laying waste and devastating a whole county." (Atchison to Jones, 6 November 1838. Ms.)

According to Joseph Smith's history, their treason consisted of "having whipped the mob out of Daviess county and taking their cannon from them." ("A History of the Persecution of the Church of Jesus Christ of Latter Day Saints in Missouri," *Times and Seasons* 1 [September 1840]: 164; Joseph Smith, *History of the Church of Jesus Christ of Latter-day Saints*, ed. B. H. Roberts, 7 vols. [Salt Lake City: Deseret Book Co., 1957], 3:212.)

18. Joseph and Eunice McRae, *Historical Facts Regarding the Liberty and Carthage Jails* (Salt Lake City: Utah Printing Co., 1954), 48, 50; Andrew Jenson, *Autobiography of Andrew Jenson* (Salt Lake City: Deseret News Press, 1938), 163–64; Floyd C. Shoemaker, "Clay County," *The Missouri Historical Review* 52 (October 1957): 28.

19. Lyman Littlefield, *Reminiscences of Latter-day Saints* (Logan, Utah, 1888), 79–80.

20. Joseph Smith to Emma Smith, 4 April 1839, Ms. Yale University.

21. Ibid., 1 December 1838.

22. Diary of Lyman Wight, 309, 315. "Memoirs of Joseph Smith III," *The Saints' Herald* 81 (October 1934): 1414. Alexander McRae, "Incidents in the History of Joseph Smith," *Deseret News* 4 (2 November 1854): 1; "Recollections of the Prophet Joseph Smith," *The Juvenile Instructor* 27 (1 July 1892): 398.

23. "Memoirs of George A. Smith," 123–25. Ms.

24. Joseph Smith to the Church and Edward Partridge, 20 March 1839. Ms. A letter dated 6 March 1839 notified Joseph and Hyrum Smith that their father's family had all left the state of Missouri. (Don C. Smith and William Smith to Hyrum and Joseph Smith, 6 March 1839, cited in Joseph Smith, Letter Book 2, pp. 38–39. Ms.)

25. McRae, "Incidents," *Deseret News* 4 (2 November 1854): 1.

26. Diary of Hyrum Smith, 18 March and 3 April 1839. Ms.

27. Joseph Smith to the Church in Caldwell County, 16 December 1838. Ms.

28. McRae, "Incidents," *Deseret News* 4 (2 November 1854): 1.

29. "Missouri vs. Joseph Smith," *Times and Seasons* 4 (15 July 1843): 254, 269.

30. McRae, "Incidents," *Deseret News* 4 (9 November 1854): 1.

31. "Missouri vs. Joseph Smith," *Times and Seasons* 4:269. In a list of those who had traveled with Zion's Camp in 1834, George A. Smith wrote, opposite the name of William Weden, "afterwards killed and fed to Joseph and others in prison," evidently referring to this incident. ("Memoirs of George A. Smith," 45. Ms.) Alexander McRae recalled that the prisoners were presented human flesh for food five days in succession. "We did not know at the time what it was, only that it was meat of some kind that we . . . did not eat," except for Lyman Wight, who ate of it. McRae added that they learned afterwards "by one of the guards who told it to one of our friends" that it was human flesh. (Alexander McRae, Autobiographical sketch, 22nd Quorum of Seventy Record, Ms.) Hyrum Smith said that the prisoners were "subjected to the necessity of eating human flesh for . . . five days or go without food," and that they overheard the guard make fun of them, "saying they had fed us on Mormon beef." Hyrum afterwards described the appearance of the meat to "several experienced physicians and they . . . decided that it was human flesh." (Smith, *History of the Church*, 3:420.)

When interviewed by Andrew Jenson and Joseph S. Black in September 1888 during a visit to church history sites in Missouri, James H. Ford, the Clay County deputy sheriff in charge at the jail when the Mormon prisoners were there, said he had "on many occasions," taken the men out one at a time for walks around the town, in order to give them an opportunity "to enjoy the fresh air and get better meals than the jail fare allowed." He said he never looked upon Joseph Smith and his friends as "real criminals" but ascribed their incarceration mainly to "the excitement and bigotry of the times." Ford added that he took the best care of the prisoners he could, and "it was a lie that they had been fed on human flesh." (Andrew Jenson, *Autobiography*, 163–65; Diary of Joseph Smith Black, 18 September 1888, p. 40. Ms. BYU Archives.)

32. Diary of Hyrum Smith, 3 April 1839. Ms.

33. Joseph Smith to the Church and Bishop Partridge, 10 March 1839. Ms.

34. Joseph Smith to Isaac Galland, 22 March 1839. Ms.

35. Joseph Smith to the Church in Caldwell County, 16 December 1838. Ms.

36. Diary of Joseph Smith Black, 18 September 1888, p. 40. Ms. BYU Archives.

37. Diary of Hyrum Smith, 31 March 1839. Ms.

38. Joseph Smith to Emma Smith, 4 April 1839. Ms.

39. Hyrum Smith to the Saints Scattered Abroad, December 1839, as cited in *Times and Seasons* 1 (December 1839): 22–23.

40. "Missouri vs. Joseph Smith," *Times and Seasons* 4 (1 August 1843): 277.

41. *The Saints' Herald* 31 (2 August 1884): 490; F. Mark McKiernan, "Sidney Ridgon's Missouri Speeches," *BYU Studies* 11 (Autumn 1970): 90–92. Burnett did not mention the Rigdon defense, but regarded Doniphan's closing argument as "one of the most eloquent and withering speeches I ever heard." Peter H. Burnett, *Recollections and Opinions of an Old Pioneer* (New York, 1880), 32–33.

42. Joseph Smith to the Church and Edward Partridge, 20 March 1839. Ms.

43. McRae, "Incidents," *Deseret News* 4 (2 November 1854): 1. Diary of Erastus Snow, January 1838–June 1841, pp. 38–49. Ms.

44. Diary of Lyman Wight, 2:317.

45. Joseph Smith to the Church and Edward Partridge, 20 March 1839. Ms.

46. Caleb Baldwin threatened the jailer with violence if anyone tried to chain him. (Obituary of Caleb Baldwin, Journal History of the Church of Jesus Christ of Latter-day Saints, 11 June 1849.)

47. Diary of Hyrum Smith, 17 March 1839. Ms.

48. Edward W. Tullidge, *Women of Mormondom* (New York, 1877), 209.

49. Diary of Hyrum Smith, 4 April 1839. Ms.

50. Joseph Smith to Presendia H. Buel, 15 March 1839. Ms.

51. Diary of Hyrum Smith, 4 April 1839. Ms.

52. Joseph Smith to Emma Smith, 4 April 1839. Ms. Yale University. Agnes Smith wrote to Joseph and Hyrum a week later and told them to "be comforted" concerning their children, "for they are not cast down and sorrowful as we are; their sorrows are but momentary . . . ours continual."

(Agnes M. Smith to Hyrum and Joseph Smith, 11 April 1839, retained copy in Joseph Smith, Letter Book 2, pp. 39–40. Ms.)

53. Smith, *History*, 3:309.

Hyrum Smith wrote that as they arrived in Gallatin they "found a large concourse of people gazing and gaping, straining their eyes to see us. They seem the most ignorant of all Adam's race and more, the most savage race that dwells on the earth. May God grant that we may be delivered out of their hands." (Diary of Hyrum Smith, 8 April 1839. Ms.)

James Ford, who had helped guard the prisoners, recalled that at Gallatin Joseph Smith was challenged to wrestle by one of the strong men of the county. After repeated solicitations Joseph finally consented on grounds that there would be no hard feelings. After several attempts to throw the Mormon leader proved unsuccessful, the challenger found himself upon his back in a pool of water. "This made the fellow mad, although he had agreed not to get offended if thrown, and he wished to fight, but the guard interfered." (Jenson, *Autobiography*, 164–65.)

54. "State of Mo. vs. Jos. Smith Jr., et al." Ms. Daviess County Court Papers, Missouri Historical Society Mss., Columbia, Missouri.

55. A note in the Joseph Smith papers, with the signatures removed, dated 16 April 1839, promises to pay John Brassfield $150 "one day after date." On 28 February 1843 Joseph Smith's diary reports that "Mr. Brassfield who helped Joseph to escape from the Missourians came and spent the day and night."

The transaction involving the horses evidently took place at William Bowman's. According to Hyrum Smith, after leaving Gallatin on the 12th, they went to Diahman where they were treated kindly by Bowman who occupied the house originally built by Lyman Wight. (Diary of Hyrum Smith, 12 April 1839.)

56. Smith, *History*, 3:320–21, 448–49.

There is some evidence that the prisoners may have paid the guard to effect their escape, which occurred on 15 April 1839. In a letter to his wife two weeks after the prisoners escaped, William Phelps mentioned the incident and a report that Joseph had "bribed the guard with six thousand dollars." At the time of this writing Phelps was out of the church. (William Phelps to Sally Phelps, 1 May 1839.) In 1875 *The Chicago Times* reported Alexander Doniphan as saying he had learned from Alanson Ripley, who had been sent to Missouri in 1839 to dispose of Mormon property, that on the eve of the departure of the prisoners from Gallatin, he (Ripley) had given Joseph Smith $900 and that Joseph had bargained with the sheriff and guards for $1100, that he had paid $700 down and reserved $200 for traveling expenses, and gave Sheriff Morgan a note for the remaining $400. (*The Chicago Times*, 7 August 1875, p. 1.) And yet, Hyrum Smith's diary, the only contemporary account, does not mention any of this. He does mention on 14 April that "all things tend to be favorable to us; the guard

[are] very lenient and kind." (Diary of Hyrum Smith, 14 April 1839. Ms.)

Following the escape of the Mormon prisoners, the people of Gallatin charged Sheriff William Morgan and ex-Sheriff Bowman with complicity in the escape; they "rode the sheriff on a rail," and the ex-sheriff was dragged through the town square "by his hair."

Clay County later submitted a bill of $400 to Daviess County as costs for guarding the Mormon prisoners, which Daviess regarded as exorbitant. The matter was finally arbitrated in court and Daviess ordered to pay $480 to Clay County. (*History of Daviess County* [Kansas City, 1882]:205–6, 247, 249.)

57. Reflecting upon the incident, Joseph Smith later noted the haste and determination connected with their escape. "When we escaped I was the worse off. Hyrum got one of my boots and I jumped into the mud, put on my boots without working [them on] and when I got to water after going over 15 miles [of] prairie my boots were full of blood." (Joseph Smith Diary, 30 December 1842. Ms.)

Hyrum Smith noted that Caleb Baldwin became separated from the others without a horse, but after wandering two days and traveling all one night he "providentially" rejoined the group as they were resting with a family of Mormons living on the banks of the Big Chariton River on the 18th. (Diary of Hyrum Smith, April 1839. Ms.)

Dimick Huntington, the first to meet Joseph Smith after his arrival in Quincy, Illinois, on 22 April 1839, described him as unshaven and pale, dressed in an old pair of worn boots, pants torn and tucked inside his boots, a blue cloak with collar turned up, and a wide-brimmed black hat. (D. B. Huntington's statement of Joseph's landing at Quincy. Ms.)

58. Orange L. Wight, "Reminiscences," 15–17. Ms.

59. Lyman Wight to Wilford Woodruff, 24 August 1857. Ms.

60. Joseph Smith to Presendia H. Buel, 15 March 1839. Ms.

61. Joseph Smith to the Church, 20 March 1839. Ms.

"A New and Everlasting Covenant": An Approach to the Theology of Joseph Smith *

THOMAS G. ALEXANDER

Even the casual observer will understand that the idea of covenants has long been important within the Judaeo-Christian tradition; that the concept could be understood as the central organizing principle of Joseph Smith's theology is the argument of this essay. Covenants can be agreements entered into between God and man or between man and man at particular times and under particular conditions. The covenant can be initiated by God, or, in the nineteenth-century conception, by man. Moreover, the concept of covenant has varied in importance in various theological systems over time. Puritans, for instance, clearly perceived it as more important than did Universalists.[1]

The idea of a covenant between God and man and man and man are both present in the biblical accounts. Genesis 17, for instance, tells of God's "everlasting covenant" with Abraham that he would be "father of many nations," and that he would receive "all the land of Canaan for an everlasting possession." In return Abraham was to serve Jehovah as his god. As a token of the covenant, God instituted the ordinance of circumcision.[2] In I Samuel, we read of the covenant that David and Jonathan made with each other because of their love for one another.[3]

Implicit in the idea of a restoration of the gospel through Joseph Smith was the concept that the old covenant had been broken and

* A version of this paper was presented at a symposium on Joseph Smith and Mormonism at Indiana University on 4–5 December 1981 and at the Sunstone Theological Symposium in August 1982. The author expresses appreciation to those at the symposia for their comments on the paper, and particularly to James B. Allen and Scott Kenney for their critiques.

that a new covenant was necessary. Indeed, the concept can be seen in the words of Moroni to Joseph Smith that the Lord would "plant in the hearts of the children the promises made to the fathers, and the hearts of the children shall turn to their fathers. If it were not so, the whole earth would be utterly wasted at his coming."[4] This is so particularly if one reads the statement as Joseph Smith would have understood it in 1823 when the visit took place, or even in 1838 when the account was written, since work for the dead as we know it today had not yet been revealed.

Nevertheless, the concept became explicit in April 1830 shortly after the Church of Christ (soon to be officially known as Church of Jesus Christ of Latter-day Saints) was organized. At that time, converts began to apply for membership. With a formal church organization, the restoration became much more than a series of relationships which had developed between Joseph Smith and the Lord. It was now a public organization, and some basis for membership in the church and commitment to the being who commanded its establishment was necessary.

As a consequence of asking about applications for membership, Joseph Smith received a revelation outlining the basic relationship between the members, God, and the church. Applicants were told "that all old covenants have I caused to be done away in this thing; and this is *a new and an everlasting covenant, even that which was from the beginning.* Wherefore, although a man should be baptized an hundred times it availeth him nothing, for you cannot enter in at the strait gate by the law of Moses, neither by your dead works. For it is because of your dead works that I have caused this last covenant and this church to be built up unto me, even as in days of old."[5]

The concept of the centrality of the new covenant was further explicated in a revelation given to Joseph Smith in March 1831. Joseph was told that "unto as many as received me gave I power to do many miracles, and to become the sons of God; and even unto them that believed on my name gave I power to obtain eternal life. And even so I have sent mine everlasting covenant into the world, to be a light to the world, and to be a standard for my people, and for the Gentiles to seek to it, and to be a messenger before my face to prepare the way before me. Wherefore, come ye unto it, and with him that cometh I will reason as with men in days of old." The revelation then discussed in the same context Enoch and the people who followed him and who were promised they should find a way to separate themselves from the world. The discussion then moved to the second coming of Christ, and the establishment of the New Jerusalem.[6]

On the surface, it may appear impossible to find an organizing principle to reconcile these disparate elements. In order to recognize the significance of these developments, it might be well to turn to Perry Miller's work on the New England Puritans, largely because Miller recognized the broad range of types of covenants in Puritan theology. In his discussion of the New England Puritans, Miller identifies a number of covenants that seemed pervasive in the society. Among those most important was the Covenant of Grace, by which God agreed to save those who joined in "covenant with any who will not resist Him," and who would agree "to accede to the divine proposal" to grant salvation to them. As one New England divine put it: "Therefore goe on boldly, God hath promised to heare you, hee cannot deny you."[7]

Miller then identifies other covenants that go to make up the important aspects of "federal theology." These included the Social Covenant, or agreements between citizens within the church and civil society. In society, for instance, rulers were expected to enforce God's law and provide for the common welfare, and the citizens were to obey the law or accept just punishment. He identifies also a church covenant that was a covenant with God, a covenant with each other, and a covenant with civil magistrates.[8]

For Latter-day Saints, the idea of covenants was, if anything, more pervasive than for the New England Puritans. It is precisely because the concept of covenant was so important to Mormons and that it was used in so many different ways that it seems legitimate to perceive it as the central organizing principle of early Latter-day Saint theology.

A careful reading of early LDS church literature reveals a number of ways in which the term covenant is used. It is used to mean consecration of property to the church for use within the Law of Consecration and Stewardship. In this case, the covenant was, in part at least, a civil covenant between the member and the bishop.[9] The Book of Mormon is referred to as a covenant. Organizations within the church are spoken of as having been created by a covenant. The Doctrine and Covenants speaks also of a covenant of fellowship between the Saints.[10] The first issue of *The Evening and the Morning Star*, the church's first periodical, contained "The Articles and Covenants of the Church of Christ," which Joseph Smith received in April 1830 and which now appears in a somewhat altered form as Section 20 of the Doctrine and Covenants.[11] That same revelation became Section 2 of the first edition of the Doctrine and Covenants in 1835. There it followed a special introduction that had been given in November 1831, and that also speaks of establishing an everlasting covenant. In addition, the use of names like "Doctrine and *Covenants*" and "Articles and *Covenants*" (italics added) reveals a concern of Joseph Smith and the early Latter-day Saints with the idea of covenants as central to their system of belief.

Perhaps the most pervasive use of covenant is within the general concept of sanctification—the belief that a person through the atonement of Christ could become worthy to enter into God's presence. Each person who accepted the covenant and lived faithfully could receive sanctification. They could be separated from the world as Enoch's people were, they could be saved from destruction at Christ's second coming and become "the sons of God," and they could obtain "eternal life."[12]

The Latter-day Saints called their agreements with God the "new and everlasting covenant," restored in the fulness of times. Under this covenant, the scattered remnants of Israel were to "come to a knowledge of the truth, believe in the Messiah, and be redeemed from oppression." Under this covenant the Saints were to be gathered prior to the second coming into a community of the elect serving God and following his ways: under this covenant as it was elaborated in Nauvoo, the family was perceived to endure eternally and mortal men and women were eligible to become gods and goddesses to rule and reign forever. In line with those aspects of covenant doctrine revealed by the early 1830s, Jackson County, Missouri, was designated as the New Jerusalem or as Zion for the gathering of part of the Children of Israel, including the Latter-day Saints.[13]

Unlike God's covenant with the ancient Israelites, the new covenant was universal. As the title page of the Book of Mormon put it, the book was written "unto the remnant of the House of Israel . . .

that they may know the covenants of the Lord, and that they are not cast off forever—And also to the convincing of the Jew and Gentile that Jesus is the Christ, the Eternal God." Thus all people were invited to enter the new covenant through baptism and the laying on of hands. In Kirtland those under the covenant were eligible to receive an endowment which included some rituals, but most especially included the actual visitation of beings from the realm of God and the infusion of Pentecostal gifts.[14] In Nauvoo, those under the covenant were invited to serve as proxies for their kindred dead and as participants in rituals by which they gained a more thorough understanding of the purpose of life and of Christ's mission. In these rituals, they made further covenants in which they committed themselves more fully to the work of God and Christ on earth and to the eternity of the family.[15]

If the concept of a new and everlasting covenant was central to the understanding of Latter-day Saint theology in Joseph Smith's time, why has that generally not been the case today? There are, of course, some exceptions, such as Bruce R. McConkie's discussion of the concept of covenants in *Mormon Doctrine*.[16] In general, however, the term *covenants* has taken on a special rather than general meaning in the everyday language of the Latter-day Saints. After the promulgation and general acceptance of the revelation on eternal marriage, the Saints increasingly began to think of covenants in the more restricted sense of marriage for eternity rather than in the general sense of agreements with God.

It is nevertheless important to an understanding of the system of theology as the early Saints perceived it to go back beyond this present-day usage and to look into the centrality of the idea of covenants in the 1830s and 40s. Saints of the 1830s would, for example, sometimes sign letters with such phrases as "in token of the new and everlasting covenant."[17] Nor is it surprising that the first major missionary tract published by the church, Parley P. Pratt's 1837 *A Voice of Warning*, discussed the importance of the concept of covenants between God and mankind. It is significant, however, that Pratt began his discussion not with the concept of the covenant itself, but with the idea of prophecy and prophets, probably because the concept of prophecy provided legitimacy for the idea that God revealed a new and everlasting covenant.[18]

In fact, the idea of prophecy and prophets is one of the concepts which a superficial examination might label as extraneous, but which in fact is related to the central theme of covenants. One could argue, for instance, that the first revelation to Joseph Smith came because of a covenant of God who promised in James 1:5 to give wisdom "to all men liberally," were they simply to ask. Even though he may not have called it such at the time, Joseph Smith made implicit use of the concept of covenant in receiving his first revelation. By the same token, on a more general level, asking for information and receiving revelations from God may be understood to result from his covenants with man. In a similar way, other principles of the gospel such as restoration, priesthood, and the kingdom of God, are all bound up in covenants either between God and man or one man and another.

In this connection, it is most important for anyone who tries to understand the theology Joseph Smith expounded and the covenants he revealed to see that he and his followers perceived him as a prophet in both the Old and New Testament mold. For them and for himself, he played those roles we associate with biblical prophets.[19] Again, Joseph Smith's role as prophet provided legitimacy in the legal and theological sense for the teachings and obligations he laid on the Latter-day Saints.

First, he was an unquestioned leader of his people. Disciples such as Brigham Young and Heber C. Kimball, even when they questioned his views, followed his teachings and admonitions explicitly. Those who refused to accept this role either left the church as David Whitmer and Oliver Cowdery did or turned against Joseph Smith as did William Law and John C. Bennett.

Second, he was a moral critic of state and society. He felt no compunction against criticizing political leaders like John C. Calhoun for his views on states' rights or Martin Van Buren for his unwillingness to redeem the Saints from their tormentors in Missouri. His writings abound with denunciations of licentiousness and adultery, and he played the role of political and military leader on occasion.

Third, he was a predictor of things to come. Mormons cite as prophetic of the Civil War the 1832 revelation reproduced as Section 87 of the Doctrine and Covenants that the rebellion of South Carolina then taking place would eventually divide the northern and southern states, that slaves would rise against masters, and that war would eventually be poured out upon all nations.

Fourth, he was a spokesman for God. Theologically this is probably the most important prophetic role Joseph Smith played. Latter-day Saints, then and now, view this doctrine as the foundation of their religion. He perceived himself and was perceived by his followers as the representative of God, holding the keys of the kingdom and authorized to reveal God's will and covenants to his people on the earth.

Any approach to Joseph Smith's theology must begin with an understanding of this concept. Like Christ and like the Old Testament prophets, he "taught them as one that had authority, and not as the scribes."[20] For Latter-day Saints, then, Joseph's pronouncements are to be seen as fundamentally different from the exposition of ministers or priests or even of other Latter-day Saint leaders: when he spoke as a prophet, the doctrines he expounded were perceived as authoritative statements of the will of the Lord.

According to revelation those ordained with specific authority could speak the will of the Lord and what they said under inspiration would become scripture. In November 1831, Joseph Smith revealed that those things spoken "when moved upon by the Holy Ghost shall be scripture, shall be the will of the Lord, shall be the mind of the Lord, shall be the word of the Lord, shall be the voice of the Lord, and the power of God unto salvation." In this connection, revelations for the entire kingdom were to come through Joseph Smith since "no one shall be appointed to receive commandments and revelations in this church excepting my servant Joseph Smith, Jun., for he receiveth them as Moses."[21]

In approaching the role as prophet and the relation of this role to covenant theology, it is important to keep in mind a number of things about the doctrine of continuous revelation. First, most of Joseph Smith's revelations are written in a rather matter-of-fact style. They are generally not in the highly allegorical language often associated with the apocalypse of John or some passages of Isaiah, Ezekiel, or Jeremiah.

Second, most of the revelations seem to have come in answer to particular questions. Joseph Smith would inquire about the will of the Lord on particular matters under consideration and receive a revelation on that question. Section 5 of the Doctrine and Covenants, for instance, came in response to a question raised about the desire of Martin Harris for a witness that Joseph Smith had the plates from which the Book of Mormon was translated. The revelation confirmed the existence of the plates and gave other instructions. In many cases, revelations came in answer to questions about the meaning of specific passages of scripture. In some cases, the context in which the question arose is not apparent from the revelation itself, but others who have spoken about the events have filled in the story. This was the case, for instance, with Section 89 of the Doctrine and Covenants which produced a set of dietary rules for church members.

Third, Joseph Smith was often led to inquire and to receive revelation on particular points because he was at work on a collateral problem. It is not at all surprising, for instance, that most of the revelations accepted by the Latter-day Saints as canonical were received during the early 1830s. During that period, Joseph Smith was engaged in a revision—or what he referred to as a translation—of the Bible. What that meant essentially was that he sought the will of the Lord as to the original intent of the writers of biblical texts. He wrote the corrections on manuscript pages to correspond to marks placed in a copy of the King James version.[22]

In revelations received while working on collateral topics, Joseph Smith proposed the germs of some of the doctrines that seem most heretical to orthodox Christians. In spite of appearances, many of these doctrines are interpretations of concepts found in the Bible. Among these are doctrines relating to the plurality of gods and the potential godhood of human beings. It must be understood that Joseph Smith went to the biblical text without the usual background of training in theology and philosophy that a minister or priest might have had. As a result, he exhibited a tendency to a particular type of biblical literalism that the average Protestant or Catholic would undoubtedly find unusual.[23]

Perhaps the most doctrinally influential work that Joseph Smith did was in his revision of the gospel of John. It was while revising that book that he was led to the beginnings of some of the most important doctrines in Mormon theology. Contemplation of John 5:29, for instance, from the background of a belief that "if God rewarded everyone according to the deeds done in the body, the term 'Heaven', as intended for the Saints' eternal home, must include more kingdoms than one," led Joseph Smith and Sidney Rigdon to the revelation recorded as Section 76 of the Doctrine and Covenants. The revelation outlines a program of salvation that provides a degree of glory for everyone except a small number designated "sons of perdition" who have sinned against the Holy Spirit by assenting to the crucifixion of Christ after having received the light.[24]

Contemplation of the opening passages of John's gospel led to another revelation of importance. This is the doctrine of the antemortal presence of human spirits as entities coexistent with God. The Latter-day Saints today read the passages of this revelation—Doctrine and Covenants Section 93—particularly verses 29 through 38 to mean that the doctrine of the church as understood in 1833 was that human beings were coeternal with God. The major problem with this interpretation is that this passage is one of the occasions when the text of the revelation yields a quite esoteric allegorical quality. The current reading of this passage, I believe, comes from the influence of succeeding doctrinal development, and as I indicated in an earlier article, the First Presidency as late as 1911 was unwilling to grant man and God's coeternity.[25]

Fourth, beyond the understanding of the central nature of continuous revelation itself in Joseph Smith's theology, it is important to understand the relatively utilitarian purpose of revelation. This has already been alluded to in connection with the discussion of Joseph Smith's revision of the Bible. It is, nevertheless, something that deserves some considerable emphasis.

The practical purpose of revelation is one of the reasons that such a large number are dated during the earliest years of the church's history and why the number declines after 1833. It is also part of the reason why revelations increase in number again during 1843 in and around Nauvoo, Illinois. In a practical sense, revelation was perceived as an aid to the human mind in accomplishing particular tasks. In fact it was often seen as a means of confirming something already worked out in the mind. This is apparent in an admonition given to Oliver Cowdery through Joseph Smith and recorded as Section 9 of the Doctrine and Covenants. "Behold, you have not understood; you have supposed that I would give it unto you, when you took no thought save it was to ask me. But, behold, I say unto you, that you must study it out in your mind; then you must ask me if it be right, and if it is right I will cause that your bosom shall burn within you; therefore, you shall feel that it is right. But if it be not right you shall have no such feelings, but you shall have a stupor of thought that shall cause you to forget the thing which is wrong; therefore, you cannot write that which is sacred save it be given you from me."[26]

In this context, the reason for the decline in canonical revelations after 1833 is evident in a passage found in Section 102 of the Doctrine and Covenants. There, in minutes of the Kirtland High Council revised by Joseph Smith and accepted as authoritative, it was written that "In case of difficulty respecting doctrine or principle, if there is not a sufficiency written to make the case clear to the minds of the council, the president may inquire and obtain the mind of the Lord by revelation."[27] Thus, new revelation became necessary only in the absence of previously revealed directions or principles.

Fifth, Joseph Smith often found physical artifacts useful in receiving revelations. Early in his career, he used a seerstone and the Urim and Thummim.[28] Revelations in the Doctrine and Covenants indicate that he used biblical texts to concentrate his mind on particular problems.[29] Later, he seems to have used some Egyptian papyri for the same purpose.[30] It seems evident, however, that the necessity for the use of such physical aids declined over time until, late in the Nauvoo period when he preached some of the most far-reaching doctrines, they were used seldom if at all.

Finally, it should also be apparent that Joseph Smith's approach to knowledge recognized no division between natural and supernatural means of obtaining information. That does not mean that he did not recognize the supernatural. The revelation instructing Oliver Cowdery mentioned above recognized the need to use natural faculties and then to call upon the Lord for supernatural help. This approach might be labeled Baconian since, like Francis Bacon, Joseph Smith believed that both the supernatural and the scientific were compatible. Except for Joseph Smith's belief that as a prophet he could receive new canonical scripture through supernatural revelation, his approach was in this sense similar to that of nineteenth-century Evangelical Protestants.[31]

With this background of the concept of revelation, it is now possible to investigate the implications of the idea of the new and everlasting covenant as understood by Joseph Smith and his contemporaries. The best way to understand the broad implications of covenants to Joseph Smith and his contemporaries is to explore the relationship between the concept of the new and everlasting covenant and specific doctrinal topics. The following discussion will do that by looking at the doctrines of millennialism and of the atonement and sanctification first as they were understood in the early 1830s and as they were perceived in the 1840s.

On the surface, it seems evident that the millennial doctrine as understood by most church members in the early 1830s was quite similar to the dispensational premillennialism usually associated with Protestant fundamentalism.[32] Thus William W. Phelps could write for the dedication of the Kirtland Temple, "How blessed the day when the lamb and the lion / Shall lie down together without any ire, / And Ephraim be crowned with his blessing in Zion / As Jesus descends with his chariot of fire." Parley P. Pratt could write in 1840 of the days when the Saints might dwell with the Lord in peaceful bliss burdened only by the necessity to "tune the lyre."[33] A conception of the millennium and of the spirit world as a place and time to help the dead prepare themselves for salvation seems to have been absent in the early years; vicarious work for the dead was first introduced in Nauvoo in the 1840s.

It is clear from the revelations published in the Doctrine and Covenants that Latter-day Saints during the 1830s expected the second advent and millennium to come soon. A number of passages in the Doctrine and Covenants repeat such words as "the Lord is nigh," or "I come quickly."[34] There is some evidence that Joseph Smith recalled the Twelve from England in early 1841 because war between the United States and England seemed imminent, and the heightened millennialist fervor led the Saints to believe that the second coming was near at hand.[35]

This dispensational aspect of Mormon millennialism is extremely important. As the revelation given only four months after the organization of the church in 1830 said, this was the "dispensation of the gospel for the last times; and for the fulness of times, in the which I will gather together in one all things, both which are in heaven, and which are on earth." As a result, Joseph Smith and his associates received the ministration of God's messengers from previous times who conferred the keys of their dispensations on the prophet.[36]

As with the doctrine of millennialism, the concept of the atonement especially as it relates to individual sanctification as taught by Joseph Smith and his associates during the pre-Nauvoo period was quite exclusivist, and quite consonant with the understanding of the general membership of the church on salvation. Most thought salvation available only for those under the new and everlasting covenant who accepted Christ, received baptism in the name of the Father, Son, and Holy Ghost through the constituted authority of the church, and remained faithful. In 1838, for instance, Joseph Smith and Sidney Rigdon were asked, "Will everybody be damned but Mormons?" "Yes," they responded, "and a great portion of them unless they repent and work righteousness." Even though Section 76 of the Doctrine and Covenants had been given in 1832 and published in 1835, the conception of differential salvation and degrees of glory seems not to have been generally accepted in the church until the 1840s at Nauvoo.[37] In fact, even a stalwart like Brigham Young with his Methodist background had a great deal of difficulty accepting the idea.[38]

The fate of all not members of the Church of Jesus Christ of Latter-day Saints was made most explicit in 1832 in a revelation designated as "the olive leaf . . . plucked from the tree of Paradise." Joseph wrote, in words reminiscent of John's apocalypse,

> And another angel shall sound his trump, saying: That great church, the mother of abominations, that made all the nations drink of the wine of the wrath of her fornication, that persecuteth the saints of God, that shed their blood — she who sitteth upon many waters, and upon the islands of the sea — behold, she is the tares of the earth; she is bound in bundles; her bands are made strong, no man can loose them; therefore, she is ready to be burned. And he shall sound his trump both long and loud, and all nations shall hear it. And there shall be silence in heaven for the space of half an hour; and immediately after shall the curtain of heaven be unfolded, as a scroll is unfolded after it is rolled up, and the face of the Lord shall be unveiled; and the saints that are upon the earth, who are alive, shall be quickened and be caught up to meet him. And they who have slept in their graves shall come forth, for their graves shall be opened; and they also shall be caught up to meet him in the midst of the pillar of heaven — They are Christ's, the first fruits, and they who shall descend with him first, and

they who are on the earth and in their graves, who are first caught up to meet him; and all this by the voice of the sounding of the trump of the angel of God.

The revelation then goes on to discuss the judgment of the dead who receive the gospel after death, though there is no intimation of vicarious work, and then to talk of a third group who were to be judged and condemned.[39]

The concept of a great and abominable church representing all those who do not belong to the Church of Jesus Christ found in Section 84 is found also in the Book of Mormon. There, Nephi wrote that "there are save two churches only; the one is the church of the Lamb of God, and the other is the church of the devil; wherefore, whoso belongeth not to the church of the Lamb of God belongeth to that great church, which is the mother of abominations; and she is the whore of all the earth."[40]

Perhaps it is unnecessary at this point to pursue this early understanding of doctrines any further. It seems that Timothy Smith and Marvin Hill were fundamentally correct when they proposed the view that the early traditions of church members were quite close to those of contemporary Protestant denominations.[41]

If that was the case, then, one might fairly ask what was it that attracted people to Mormonism. It was, I believe, the perceived authority of both the teachings and the teachers. Here, I believe that Mario DePillis has hit on the key.[42] People were searching not only for the message of the primitive church and the imminence of the second coming, but they also sought some certainty that those who preached the gospel had authority. In the Book of Mormon they had a volume of scripture that they could examine and in the person of Joseph Smith they had a prophet who revealed the word of the Lord with authority. They were admonished to test both the book and the prophet by turning to the Lord for the confirmation of the Spirit, and they were promised as Moroni put it in the Book of Mormon, "by the power of the Holy Ghost ye may know the truth of all things."[43] Thus, doctrinally, they were encouraged to receive a personal witness or revelation of the authority of Joseph Smith and the truth of his teachings.

At this point, it seems best to turn to the Nauvoo period, which was when the various doctrines were drawn together within new covenant theology in what most people see today as the unique and important in Mormonism. First we can look at the transformation of millennial doctrine.

In a revelation given to Joseph Smith in 1843, the Saints learned that the millennium was not as close as they had assumed. The event was thereafter perceived to be at least forty-seven years in the future, and perhaps even longer.[44] Under those conditions it became necessary to provide an earthly organization to govern in place of the millennial organization Christ himself would establish upon his second advent. Thus the Council of Fifty was organized and Joseph was crowned king.[45] The organization continued sporadically until the 1880s, though in practice it was never particularly important except in the immigration to Utah.[46] It provided nevertheless a bridge between anticipation of the imminence of the millennium implicit in the early understanding of the new and everlasting covenant and the current tendency to perceive it as an event far in the future. In an address to stake leaders at Brigham Young University, Bruce R. McConkie of the Council of the Twelve said he did not expect the second coming in his lifetime or perhaps even in the lifetime of his children and grandchildren.[47]

The revelation of this idea of the establishment of the Kingdom of God on earth preparatory to the coming of Christ has led some recent observers to view Mormon millennialism as having been transformed from pre- to postmillennial in Nauvoo. On this, however, I believe that recent research by Grant Underwood is correct and that Mormon millennialism must still be perceived as premillennial.[48] Following the analysis of essays in the volume by Robert G. Clouse,[49] Underwood argued that the prime factor in typing millennial doctrine is not the presence of features such as the development of the Kingdom of God on earth prior to the coming of Christ, but rather the idea of whether the earth has reached a millennial state before Christ comes. Since Latter-day Saints still talked of burning and destruction immediately prior to his coming and since they perceived the Kingdom and gathering of the Saints as a means of establishing a place of refuge from the world, I believe that Mormon millennial doctrine, even with the changes, must be seen as premillennial.

With the doctrinal development at Nauvoo, perhaps the most important aspect of the New and Everlasting Covenant was the transformation of the doctrines of the atonement and salvation and the role of the covenant as a vehicle providing for the eternal unity of the family. As early as the Kirtland period, all members of the church having received baptism as a token of the covenant were eligible for a personal revelation given through a patriarch that designated their lineage within the House of Israel and foretold their individual destiny. In Nauvoo, with the introduction of a temple ritual different from that at Kirtland, all worthy members were encouraged to receive their personal endowments, to make certain additional covenants, and to be sealed in a marriage that promised an eternal family, contingent upon faithfulness.

Some observers who have had difficulty in understanding the significance of the temple in Mormonism have failed to ask the most searching questions about it. While it may be interesting to speculate on the relationship between the Masonic ritual and the Latter-day Saint temple, such speculation ignores the central purpose of the temple.[50] That purpose is not found in the signs and tokens learned in the temple, which, while bearing some similarity to Masonic rituals, are set in a much different context. Rather, from a doctrinal point of view, the temple is an expansion of the new covenant theology revealed early in the church's history. The covenants made in the temple provided a basis for sanctification through the atonement of Jesus Christ and for entrance into the presence of God as heirs of his kingdom with the potential of becoming gods and goddesses.

In this connection, it is a fundamental misunderstanding of Mormon doctrine as taught by Joseph Smith to see it as radically Pelagian, that is, in seeing salvation as possible without the intercessionary atonement of Jesus Christ.[51] Christ's atonement plays a central role in the temple ceremony, and the temple itself is perhaps the only place in Mormondom that all Mormons would perceive as sacred space. It is there that they return to times of the beginning in the way in which Eliade has outlined that idea.[52] In the temple ceremony time and space are telescoped as the story of mankind and of the human relationship with Deity are unfolded.

It was at Nauvoo that these doctrines achieved the form in which they are best known today. While it required three-quarters of a century for church members fully to accept the doctrines Joseph Smith taught in Nauvoo, those doctrines were the culmination of a development that had gone on over his entire active ministry. Initially, doctrines such as millennialism and the atonement were similar to those that might have been found in many contemporary Protestant denominations. There were, of course, differences, some of which we have indicated here, but it is noteworthy that many of those who broke with Joseph Smith cited doctrinal changes, departures from the common beliefs, as the reason. John Corrill, David Whitmer, Sidney Rigdon, and William Marks come readily to mind as otherwise faithful members who seemed unwilling to accept doctrinal innovations even though they had joined the church in part because of its doctrines and because of the authority with which they saw Joseph Smith clothed.

The culmination of this doctrinal development and the revelation of the ultimate significance of the new covenant theology was the King Follett discourse given slightly more than two and one-half months before Joseph Smith was murdered.[53]

It is perhaps most significant that although the King Follett discourse was presented at general conference, it was a funeral sermon. As with most funeral sermons, it was designed for the benefit of the family and mourners. They, not the dead King Follett, needed the reassurance that there was a purpose in what had happened and that God and Christ offered salvation for them as well as for the deceased. Joseph Smith provided this reassurance by announcing that God had once stood in their shoes, that he had once been a man, and that like other men he had died, and had been resurrected. This doctrine is based on a literal reading of the gospel of John, particularly John 5:19, which reads, "The Son can do nothing of himself, but what he seeth the Father do: for what things soever he doeth, these also doeth the Son likewise." Thus, if Christ, who was human, had laid down a mortal body and taken up an immortal body, then God the Father must have done the same thing.

From there, Joseph moved to a discussion of the creation and of the relationship between God and man. For Joseph Smith, as he announced that doctrine in Nauvoo, creation did not originate *ex nihilo*. It meant rather the organization of the universe through the agency of the Gods—in the plural. Beyond this, Joseph said in the creation of man, God took "the mind of man—the intelligent part—" a part "as immortal as, and . . . [a part] coequal with, God Himself," and placed it in a body fashioned from earthly elements. This exposition provided the basis for the current explication of Doctrine and Covenants Section 93, though the church membership required a long time to accept Joseph Smith's views.

After considering the idea of the eternity of man, Joseph moved to the eternity of the family unit, again a fit subject for a funeral discourse. Citing Hebrews 11:40, Joseph said that "they [that is, our ancestors and our children] without us should not be made perfect." Again, reading the passage literally, he argued that it was necessary to seal the family together in one eternal unit before salvation was possible for any part of the unit. From there, he elaborated on the idea of universal salvation, insisting that all sins except the sin against the Holy Ghost would be forgiven in this world or the world to come. Thus, for people like King Follett and others who were faithful, the rewards were great, including the continuation of the family as a unit throughout eternity, and even potential godhood.

Thus we find in the thought of Joseph Smith a theology at once traditional and unique. It is at base a new covenant theology, finding at its source a set of agreements between God and man. It is a theology based on the elaboration of ideas found in the Bible, interpreted in an extraordinarily untraditional way. It is a theology of dispensational premillennialism, yet again quite untraditional because of the addition of the concept of a preadventist temporal Kingdom of God established to prepare the way for Christ's coming. It is a theology accepting fundamentally the atonement of Christ, yet reserving for the family of human beings the eternity of the family and potential godhood with God and Christ. It is a theology that sees God as creator, but rejects the concept of *ex nihilo* creation.

Mormons are wont to see Joseph Smith as the unlettered plowboy who translated the Book of Mormon through the gift of God. While he was that, he was also an enormously gifted and creative thinker who brought together and elaborated a new covenant theology that Latter-day Saints find at once reverential toward God and Christ and uplifting in its concept of the potential of mankind.

NOTES

1. Perry Miller, *New England Mind: The Seventeenth Century*, Book 4 (New York: Macmillan, 1939) discusses Puritan thought as a covenant theology.

2. Genesis 17:1-14. It is, of course, possible to read this as an unconditional covenant imposed upon Abraham by God with righteousness the consequence not the predicate of the covenant. Since it seems unlikely to me that early nineteenth-century Latter-day Saints would have read it this way, and since I am interested in interpreting the biblical precedents the way they would have seen them, I would insist on the reciprocal nature of the Abrahamic covenant. In practice it does not matter that God initiates the covenant, it is still between him and a particular person or people, even though it may not require any reciprocal obligation on the part of the people. See for instance Genesis 9:8-17. Moreover, the New England Puritans interpreted covenants in the same sense as similar to agreements between people as in a business transaction. Miller, *New England Mind*, 375.

3. I Samuel 18:3.

4. Joseph Smith—History 1:39.

5. Doctrine and Covenants (hereafter cited as D&C) 22:1-3 (emphasis added).

6. D&C 45:8-10.

7. Miller, *New England Mind*, 395-96. See all of chapter 13 for a discussion of the covenant of grace.

8. Ibid., 428-31 and 461-62, but see also chapters 14 and 15.

9. See for instance D&C 52:2-3 and 104:52.

10. D&C 84:57; 78:11; and 88:133.

11. *The Evening and the Morning Star* 1 (June 1832): 2.

12. D&C 66:2; 78:11; 84:40; 98:14; 109:66-78; 132:19; and 45:8.

13. Ibid., 109:67; 38:20; 42:13, 30; 104:4-5; 132:2-4, 19-20; 76:57-58; and 57:1-3.

14. Stanley B. Kimball, *Heber C. Kimball, Mormon Patriarch and Pioneer* (Urbana: University of Illinois Press, 1981), 37.

15. For a discussion of the substance of the Nauvoo temple ordinance see: James E. Talmage, *The House of the Lord: A Study of Holy Sanctuaries Ancient and Modern* (Salt Lake City: Deseret Book, 1968), chapter 4.

16. Bruce R. McConkie, *Mormon Doctrine* (Salt Lake City: Bookcraft, 1958), 154-56.

17. Joseph Smith, *History of the Church of Jesus Christ of Latter-day Saints*, ed. B. H. Roberts, 7 vols. (Salt Lake City: Deseret Book Co., 1957), 1:367, 387, 451, 456.

18. Parley P. Pratt, *A Voice of Warning*, 9th ed. (Salt Lake City: Deseret News, 1874), chapters 1 and 2, pp. 38-40, and passim.

19. The following categories are based on Lowell L. Bennion, "The Hebrew Prophets," *Sunstone* 5 (July-August 1980): 41-42. For one view of

the office of prophet see Hugh Nibley, *The World and the Prophets* (Salt Lake City: Deseret Book, 1954). The examples in the following discussion are drawn from well-known incidents in church history.

20. Mark 1:22.

21. D&C 68:4 and 28:1–11.

22. For a full discussion of Joseph Smith's revision of the Bible see: Robert J. Matthews, *"A Plainer Translation": Joseph Smith's Translation of the Bible, A History and Commentary* (Provo, Utah: Brigham Young University Press, 1975). On the notation system see especially pp. 56–95.

23. For a discussion of this matter see Thomas G. Alexander, "The Reconstruction of Mormon Doctrine: From Joseph Smith to Progressive Theology," *Sunstone* 5 (July-August 1980): 102–5.

24. See D&C 76: headnote, 28–42, and passim.

25. Alexander, "The Reconstruction of Mormon Doctrine," 30, 33.

26. D&C 9:7–9.

27. Ibid., 102:23.

28. Donna Hill, *Joseph Smith: The First Mormon* (Garden City, New York: Doubleday, 1977), 65–67, 71.

29. See especially headnote to D&C 76; D&C 93:6 and 130:10; and Matthews, *Plainer Translation*, 257–61.

30. Hill, *Joseph Smith*, 193.

31. See George M. Marsden, *Fundamentalism and American Culture: The Shaping of Twentieth-Century Evangelicalism: 1870–1925* (New York: Oxford University Press, 1980), 55–62 for a discussion of the Baconian tradition in Protestantism.

32. For a discussion of dispensational premillennialism see Marsden, *Fundamentalism and American Culture*, 51–54.

33. Grant Underwood, "Seminal Versus Sesquicentennial Saints: A Look at Mormon Millennialism," *Dialogue* 14 (Spring 1981): 35. See also Underwood, "Early Mormon Millennialism: Another Look," (M.A. Thesis, Brigham Young University, 1981), 16–18.

34. D&C 1:12; 43:17; 106:4; 33:18; 34:12; 35:27; and 39:24.

35. Thomas G. Alexander, "Wilford Woodruff and the Changing Nature of Mormon Religious Experience," *Church History* 45 (March 1976): 64.

36. D&C 27:13 and 110:11–16.

37. Underwood, "Mormon Millennialism," 16–18, and "Seminal Versus Sesquicentennial Saints," 32–44.

38. Ronald Esplin, talk on Brigham Young and succession, 19 November 1981.

39. D&C 88: headnote, 94–99, and passim.

40. I Nephi 14:10.

41. Marvin S. Hill, "The Shaping of the Mormon Mind in New England and New York," *BYU Studies* 9 (Spring 1969): 363–65; Timothy Smith, "Righteousness and Hope: The Biblical Culture that Nurtured Early Mor-

mon Faith," paper presented at the annual meeting of the Mormon History Association, Canandaigua, New York, 2 May 1980.

42. Mario S. DePillis, "The Quest for Religious Authority and the Rise of Mormonism," *Dialogue* 1 (Spring 1966): 68–88.

43. Moroni 10:5.

44. D&C 130:15–17.

45. Klaus J. Hansen, *Quest for Empire: The Political Kingdom of God and the Council of Fifty in Mormon History* (East Lansing: Michigan State University Press, 1967), 7–8, 66.

46. D. Michael Quinn, "The Council of Fifty and Its Members, 1844–1945," *BYU Studies* 20 (Winter 1980): 172–74.

47. "Elder McConkie Addresses BYU Stakes," *Seventh East Press* 1 (18 November 1981): 1.

48. Grant Underwood, "Seminal vs. Sesquicentennial Saints: A Look at Mormon Millennialism Then and Now," (paper presented at the Mosaic of Mormon Culture Symposium, October 1980), 19–22. This is an expanded version of the *Dialogue* article cited above.

49. Robert G. Clouse, ed., *The Meaning of the Millennium: Four Views* (Downers Grove, Ill.: InterVarsity Press, 1977).

50. See Jack Adamson and Reed C. Durham Jr., *Joseph Smith and Masonry, No Help for the Widow's Son: Two Papers on the Influence of the Masonic Movement on Joseph Smith and His Mormon Church* (Nauvoo, Ill.: Martin Publishing Company, 1980).

51. See Sterling McMurrin, *Theological Foundations of the Mormon Religion* (Salt Lake City: University of Utah Press, 1965), 67, 57–58.

52. Mircea Eliade, *The Sacred and the Profane: The Nature of Religion* (New York: Harcourt, Brace and Company, 1959), especially chapters 1 and 2.

53. For this discussion of the King Follett discourse, I have relied upon Stan Larson, "The King Follett Discourse, a Newly Amalgamated Text," *BYU Studies* 18 (Winter 1978): 193–208.

The "Articles of Faith" in Early Mormon Literature and Thought

DAVID J. WHITTAKER

Almost anyone familiar with Joseph Smith has heard of the letter he wrote to John Wentworth, editor of the *Chicago Democrat*, in 1842. He was answering a specific request from Wentworth to supply Wentworth's friend, George Barstow, information on the history and beliefs of the Latter-day Saints. Wentworth told Smith that Barstow was writing a history of the state of New Hampshire and that he wished to include information about the Mormons.[1]

Joseph Smith's letter is a masterpiece of succinctness: in just a few short pages he summarized his own religious experience and reviewed the first decade of the church's history. At the end of the historical sketch, Joseph attached a list summarizing the "faith of the Latter-day Saints," later titled the "Articles of Faith." Barstow never published the Wentworth letter,[2] but it was printed in March 1842 in the church's periodical, the Nauvoo *Times and Seasons*. In 1851, Franklin D. Richards, then president of the British Mission, assembled for that mission a pamphlet which contained a variety of documents that had earlier appeared in LDS publications. Among the items he selected was the "Articles of Faith." Reflecting the composite nature of his collection, he titled the work the Pearl of Great Price. In 1880, a general conference of the church voted to add this "gem" to the standard works of the church.[3] Along with the Bible, Book of Mormon, and Doctrine and Covenants, it thus achieved the status of canonized scripture.

Even before 1880, the "Articles of Faith" had been a standard reference for those seeking a concise list of LDS beliefs, and after the 1880 canonization, their position was assured. Thus when James E.

Talmage was asked by the First Presidency in 1891 to "prepare a work on theology, suitable as a text book for our Church schools," it was no surprise that he would use the "Articles of Faith" as the outline for his work.[4] Finally published in 1889, his *Articles of Faith* further cemented in the minds and hearts of LDS students the thirteen statements from the Wentworth letter.

Just how does the list of beliefs from the Wentworth letter fit into the larger body of LDS literature which contained similar lists of faith? Did Joseph Smith author them, or did he borrow from other early LDS authors who compiled similar lists? What was intended by these lists? In spite of his anticreedal attitude, did Smith intend to give the church a creed in these statements? How did the early church use and understand lists of belief? How have these listings changed over the years? This essay attempts to deal with these questions by examining the printed literature generated during the formative years of the Mormon movement. The approach will be primarily chronological, focusing on three periods of the "Articles of Faith": origin, popularization, and canonization.

Even before the church was organized, Joseph Smith felt the need to formulate a statement that would briefly summarize the major beliefs of the religious movement he had been commanded to give institutional embodiment. As early as 1829, he and Oliver Cowdery were committing to paper the beginnings of the "Articles and Covenants" of the church, later published as Doctrine and Covenants Section 20. The textual development of that section thus provides a starting point for our discussion.

The dating of Doctrine and Covenants 20 has never been precisely established. Today, the headnote suggests April 1830 as the date of its composition. The Manuscript History of the Church simply gives the general date of 1830.[5] The *History of the Church*, which generally prints the sections of the Doctrine and Covenants in chronological order, places Section 19 *after* Section 20, which suggests a pre-March 1830 dating.[6] Some authors even proposed that Doctrine and Covenants 20 was revealed on 6 April 1830, the day the church was organized.[7] But what appears to be the earliest effort to enumerate or summarize the main beliefs of the restoration, perhaps an urtext to Doctrine and Covenants 20, is an unpublished document in Cowdery's handwriting dated 1829 — possibly as early as June.[8] A revelation to Cowdery, which he himself recorded, the document bears strong similarities to Doctrine and Covenants 20. Specifically it commands Cowdery to write "the articles of the Church of Christ," and contains a number of specific items now found in Doctrine and Covenants 20. In addition to several quotations from Doctrine and Covenants 18, the document cites 3 Nephi 18:29–32 concerning the sacrament and the central role of the atonement of Christ.[9]

Doctrine and Covenants 20 is a much fuller elaboration of items in the Cowdery document. In their first printed form, Doctrine and Covenants 20 and 22 were combined and entitled "The Articles and Covenants of the Church" in the June 1832 issue of the *The Evening and the Morning Star*.[10] It seems clear that both Smith and Cowdery were responsible for the final version, a fact that helps to understand the background of the argument over Cowdery's insistence that Smith change the wording of verse 37.[11] Doctrine and Covenants 22 was later deleted from Doctrine and Covenants 20 and verses 66 and 67 were added. Even a superficial study of Doctrine and Covenants 20 reveals its composite nature. But it also reveals an orderly structure that led B. H. Roberts to call it "a declaration of fundamental doctrines," and to use its structure to outline and discuss the basic beliefs of the early church in his *Comprehensive History of the Church*.[12]

On 9 June 1830, during the first conference of the church, Joseph Smith read Doctrine and Covenants 20 to those assembled and the contents were accepted by the "unanimous voice of the whole congregation."[13] Thus Doctrine and Covenants 20 became the first revelatory item canonized in the early church. Surviving records indicate that this document was read as a regular item of business during succeeding conferences. Its importance to the church would have been reinforced by the practice of making copies for early missionaries to carry with them into their fields of labor.[14] Its prominence in early LDS thought is further emphasized by its place in the 1835 to 1869 editions of Doctrine and Covenants: it was the second document printed in those compilations of modern revelations to the church.

Briefly, Doctrine and Covenants 20 enumerated the following doctrines: the existence of God, the creation and fall of man, the roles of Jesus Christ, the Holy Ghost and the Trinity, justification and sanctification, falling from grace, baptism, the manner of baptism and confirmation, the duties of members, the sacramental prayers, duties of members respecting children, duties of the officers of the church, and the need for conferences. It was, of course, a redacted series of brief revelations on key concepts necessary for the infant church. It made no claim to completeness, and it seems that it was never taken as comprehensive by early members. It was a constitution, a basic charter of the new church, not a *Summa Theologia*. Doctrine and Covenants 20, then, functioned as a kind of creedal statement during the first decade of the church.

At least one other item that appeared in the early LDS scriptures also helped members to formalize the beliefs of the young church. During the winter of 1834–35 a series of seven theological "Lectures on Faith" were presented to elders in Kirtland, Ohio.[15] These lectures consisted of a series of propositions, each of which was supported by scriptural citations, logic, and short catechisms designed for a classroom presentation. The seven lectures lead to a final conclusion by the last one; their content and direction suggested to early members that any position on theological matters could be logical and systematically prepared and published.

The fact that these lectures were placed in the 1835 edition of the Doctrine and Covenants and remained until 1921 suggests their potential for systematically approaching the topic of faith. The School of the Prophets at which these lectures were presented was to instruct its members "more perfectly in theory, in principle, in doctrine, in the law of the gospel, in all things that pertain unto the kingdom of God."[16] The whole standardizing that school lectures implied could have furthered the early Mormon attempt to create a uniform and standard list of Articles of Faith.[17]

Joseph Smith indicated in the preface to the 1835 edition of the Doctrine and Covenants that the volume contained "the leading items of the religion which we profess to believe." Further, he and his colleagues reasoned:

> There may be an aversion in the minds of some against receiving any thing purporting to be articles of religious faith, in consequence of there being so many now extant; but if men believe a system, and profess that it was given by inspiration, certainly, the more intelligibly

they can present it, the better. It does not make a principle untrue to print it. Neither does it make it true not to print it. . . . We have, therefore, endeavored to present though in few words, *our* belief, and when we say this, humbly trust, the faith and principles of this society as a body.[18]

While it was not specifically intended to be a creed, the publication of the Doctrine and Covenants was another step in the standardizing of Mormon faith.[19]

It is significant that the first attempt to give a listing of "our principles" in early Mormon periodical literature was made by Oliver Cowdery. In the first issue of the *LDS Messenger and Advocate* in 1834, Cowdery listed eight items, all of which had their roots in his early draft of Doctrine and Covenants 20.[20] Writing that "our principles may be fully known" he enlarged upon those doctrines mentioned in Doctrine and Covenants 20:

> We believe in God, and his Son Jesus Christ. We believe that God, from the beginning revealed himself to man; and that whenever he has had a people on earth, he always had revealed himself to them by the Holy Ghost, the ministering of angels, or his own voice.
>
> We do not believe that he ever had a church on earth without revealing himself to that church: consequently, there are apostles, prophets, evangelists, pastors, and teachers, in the same.
>
> We believe that God is the same in all ages; and that it requires the same holiness, purity, and religion, to save a man now, as it did anciently; and that He is no respector of persons, always has, and always will reveal himself to men when they call upon him.
>
> We believe that God has revealed himself to men in this age, and commenced to raise up a church preparatory to his second advent, when he will come in the clouds of heaven with power and great glory.
>
> We believe that the popular religious theories of the day are incorrect; that they are without parallel in the revelations of God, as sanctioned by him; and that however faithfully they may be adhered to, or however zealously and warmly they may be defended, they will never stand the strict scrutiny of the word of life.
>
> We believe that all men are born free and equal, that no man, combination of men, or government of men, have power or authority to compel or force others to embrace any system of religion, or religious creed, or to use force or violence to prevent others from enjoying their own opinions, or practicing the same, so long as they do not molest or disturb others in theirs, in a manner to deprive them of their privileges as free citizens—or of worshiping God as they choose, and

attempt to the contrary is an assumption unwarrantable in the revelations of heaven, and strikes at the root of civil liberty, and is a subversion of all equitable principles between man and man.

We believe that God has set his hand the second time to recover the remnant of his people Israel; and that the time is near when he will bring them from the four winds, with songs of everlasting joy, and reinstate them upon their own lands which he gave their fathers by covenants.

And further: We believe in embracing good wherever it may be found; or proving all things, and holding fast that which is righteous.

This in short, is our belief, and we stand ready to defend it upon its own foundation, when ever it is assailed by men of character and respectability. And while we act upon these broad principles, we trust in God that we shall never be confounded.

Neither shall we wait for opposition; but with a firm reliance upon the justice of such a course, and the propriety of disseminating a knowledge of the same, we shall endeavor to persuade men to turn from error and vain speculation; investigate the plan which was devised for our salvation; prepare for the year of recompense, and the day of vengeance which are near, and thusly be ready to meet the Bridegroom.

Cowdery referred to these as "broad principles" and invited all to further investigate the church. In later issues, he wrote more detailed essays on Mormon doctrines as he tried to fulfill his assignment as a "messenger and advocate" of the restoration.

Two years later Brigham Young's brother, Joseph, provided John Hayward in Boston with five creedal statements, all of which were suggested in Doctrine and Covenants 20 and in Cowdery's 1834 listing.[21] Referring to his list as "its principal articles of faith" Joseph Young wrote:

1. A belief in one true and living God, the creator of the heavens and the earth, and in his Son Jesus Christ, who came into this world 1800 years since, at Jerusalem; was slain, rose from the dead, ascended on high and now sits on the right hand of the Majesty in the heavens that through the atonement thus wrought out, all men may come to God and find acceptance; all of which they believe is revealed in the holy Scriptures.

2. That God requires all men, wherever his gospel is proclaimed, or his law known, to repent of all sins, forsake evil, and follow righteousness; that his word also requires men to be baptized, as well as to repent; and that the direct way pointed out by the Scriptures for baptism, is immersion. After which, the individual has the promise of the gift of the Holy Spirit; that this divine communication is absolutely

promised unto all men, upon whom "the Lord our God shall call," if they are obedient unto his commandments. This gift of the Holy Spirit, was anciently bestowed by the laying on of the apostle's hands: so this church believes that those who have authority to administer in the ordinances of the gospel, have this right and authority, through prayer; and without this authority, and this gift, the church is not now what it anciently was; consequently, cannot be recognized as the true Church of Christ.

3. That God will, in the last days, gather the literal descendants of Jacob to the lands anciently possessed by their fathers; that he will lead them as at the first, and build them as at the beginning. That he will cause his arm to be made bare in their behalf; his glory to attend them by night and by day. That this is necessary to the fulfillment of his word, when his knowledge is to cover the earth as the waters cover the seas. And that, as men anciently saw visions, dreamed dreams, held communion with angels, and conversed with the heavens, so it will be in the last days, to prepare the way for all nations, languages and tongues, to serve him in truth.

4. That the time will come when the Lord Jesus will descend from heaven, accompanied with ten thousand of his saints; that a mighty angel will lay hold on the dragon, bind him, cast him into the pit, where he will be kept from deceiving the nations for a thousand years; during which time, one continued round of peace will pervade every heart. And,

5. They believe in the resurrection of the body; that all men will stand in the presence of God, and be judged according to the deeds, or works, done in this life; that the righteous will enter into eternal rest, in the presence of God, but the wicked be cast off, to receive a just recompense of reward; and that to ensure eternal life, a strict obedience to all the commandments of God, must be observed, to the end.

The first book-length treatise on Mormon doctrine was *A Voice of Warning*, issued in New York in 1837 by Parley P. Pratt. Its influence in shaping Mormon thought during the nineteenth century cannot be overstated. Its structure, logical arguments, and well-written prose assured from its inception that it would be a powerful weapon in the cause of Mormonism.[22] Published in New York City in September 1837, *Voice of Warning* proved to be the most popular nineteenth-century LDS work outside the standard works. Its subtitle promised that the work would be "An Introduction to the Faith and Doctrine of the Church of Jesus Christ of Latter-day Saints." By discussing items ranging from the atonement of Christ to the establishment of Zion, Pratt provided the first full explication of the LDS faith. Its success would help shape other LDS doctrinal works as would Pratt's various pamphlets.[23]

In October 1839, Pratt issued in Detroit his *History of the Late Persecution.* Three months later, he published a second edition in New York titled *Late Persecution of the Church*, to which he added a new introduction containing another concise formulation of Mormon beliefs.[24] In part, Pratt enumerated eighteen first "principles and doctrines" of the church, phrases from which are echoed in the later "Articles of Faith."

Pratt included in his introduction:

> The first principle of Theology as held by this Church is Faith in God the eternal father, and in his Son Jesus Christ, who verily was crucified for the sins of the world . . . and in the Holy Ghost who bears record of them, . . . the second principle is Repentance towards God; . . . the third principle is Baptism, by immersion in water, in the name of the Father, Son and Holy Ghost, for remission of sins, with the promise of the Holy Ghost to all who believe and obey the gospel. The fourth principle is, the laying on of hands in the name of Jesus Christ, for the gift of the Holy Ghost.
>
> Fifth, it is the duty and privilege of the Saints thus organized upon the everlasting gospel, to believe in and enjoy all the gifts of revelation, prophecy, visions, the ministry of angels, healing the sick by the laying on of hands in the name of Jesus, the working of miracles, and in short all the gifts as mentioned in scripture, or as enjoyed by the ancient saints.

Referring to these statements as a "brief outline of the doctrine of this Church" he added additional items.

> We believe that the scriptures now extant do not contain all the sacred writings which God ever gave to man. . . . the Holy Ghost is a spirit of revelation and prophecy . . . we therefore believe in the Book of Mormon which is an ancient American Record, lately discovered. . . . we believe that God will continue to reveal himself to us until all things are revealed concerning the past, present and future. . . . We believe that the Jews and all the House of Israel will soon be gathered home to their own lands . . . and that they will become one nation in the land upon the mountains of Israel. . . . We also believe that Jesus Christ will come in person . . . and that he will destroy the wicked from the earth by terrible judgments. . . . We also believe that the saints will raise from the dead at his second coming, and that they will

live and reign on earth one thousand years. . . . We further believe that the restoration of Israel and Judah, and the second advent of Messiah are near at hand.

At the end of this short discussion, Pratt referred his readers to his *Voice of Warning*, "which is particularly designed as an introduction to our faith and doctrine."

In February 1840, Pratt reworked the doctrinal portion of the introduction of his *Late Persecution* into a separate four-page pamphlet which he titled *An Address by Judge Higbee and Parley P. Pratt . . . to the Citizens of Washington and to the Public in General*. As Peter Crawley notes, this was the first short LDS missionary tract outlining the basic Mormon beliefs.[25] By April 1840, Pratt was in England where he reprinted this work, and by 1843, *An Address* had been reprinted twice more in England and three more times in the United States.[26]

Pratt's pamphlet was written with an awareness "of the anxiety of the public mind in relation to the faith and principles of our society" thus "we cheerfully offer this address, in order to give some information of our real principles." He included as items belief in God the Father and the Son; the Bible; one true church; spiritual gifts; freedom of religion; repentance, baptism, and the gift of the Holy Ghost; perfectability of the Saints; morality; restoration of Israel to Jerusalem; the second coming and the millennium; and the veracity of the Book of Mormon. It was a listing specifically addressed to the larger, non-Mormon public. *An Address* seems to have set the pattern for other such addresses published in the 1840s. Erastus Snow and Benjamin Winchester published in Salem, Massachusetts, in September 1841 an *Address to the Citizens of Salem and Vicinity*,[27] which followed in general content Pratt's *An Address*. Much of the pamphlet was structured by "We believe" paragraphs.

Perhaps the best-known early list of items of belief appeared in a pamphlet published by Orson Pratt. Obviously drawing upon his brother's work, Orson Pratt enumerated at least fourteen clearly identifiable articles of LDS beliefs in his *Interesting Accounts of Several Remarkable Visions* published in Edinburgh, Scotland, in 1840. His listing appeared at the end of his pamphlet and contained the following as part of his "sketch of the faith and doctrine of this Church."

First, We believe in God the Eternal Father, and in his Son Jesus Christ, and in the Holy Ghost, who bears record of them, the same throughout all ages and forever.

We believe that all mankind, by the transgression of their first parents, and not their own sins, were brought under the curse and penalty of that transgression. . . .

We believe, that through the sufferings, death and atonement of Jesus Christ, all mankind, without one exception are to be completely, and fully redeemed, both body and spirit . . . from the endless penalty of the original sin. . . .

We believe that all mankind, in their infant state, are incapable of knowing good and evil. . . .

We believe that all mankind, in consequence of the fall . . . are capable of obeying and disobeying a law. . . .

We believe, that the penalty . . . can have no effect upon persons who have not had the privilege, in this life, of becoming acquainted therewith. . . .

We believe that all who have done evil, having a knowledge of the law . . . are under its penalty. . . .

We believe that the first condition to be complied with on the part of sinners is, to *believe* in God. . . . that the second condition is, to *repent* . . . that the third condition is, to be *baptized* by immersion in water in the name of the Father, Son, and Holy Ghost for *a remission of sins* . . . that the fourth condition is, to receive the *laying on of hands*, in the name of Jesus Christ for the gift of the Holy Ghost. . . .

[We] believe in and enjoy all the gifts, powers, and blessings which flow from the Holy Ghost.

We believe that there has been a general and awful apostacy from the religion of the New Testament. . . .

We believe that there are a few, sincere, honest and humble persons, who are striving to do according to the best of their understanding; but they err in doctrine, because of false teachers and the precepts of men.

[We believe that] the gospel in the "Book of Mormon," is the same as that in the New Testament. . . .

We believe that God will continue to give revelations by visions, by the inspiration of the Holy Ghost, until the saints are guided unto all truth. . . .

We believe that wherever the people enjoy the religion of the New Testament, there they enjoy visions, revelations, the ministry of angels, etc.

We believe that God has raised up this church, in order to prepare a people for his second coming in the clouds of heaven, in power, and great glory; and that then the saints who are asleep in their graves will be raised, and reign with him on earth a thousand years.

The general thrust, order, and content of this listing have suggested to several LDS scholars that the Wentworth list came from this pamphlet.[28] Such a conclusion is not totally unwarranted, and it may be possible that this was one of several texts Joseph Smith used to prepare the Wentworth list.[29] However, the primacy of the compilation by Parley P. Pratt, which provided the immediate background, and the earlier listings by Joseph Smith and Oliver Cowdery, which provided the more distant background for all the early lists of beliefs, must be considered. It should be obvious that by 1841 there were standardized lists of LDS beliefs in common usage. Two additional examples further illustrate how common the central core of Mormon beliefs was by the 1840s.

In 1841, Benjamin Winchester, a leader of the church in the Philadelphia area, listed seven items in the first issue of his *Gospel Reflector*.[30] Referring to these items as "some of the leading principles of our faith," he included (1) "the scriptures contain the words of God"; (2) the Godhead; (3) "the name of Jesus Christ is the only name given under heaven, whereby man can be saved"; (4) the Gospel of Christ is the only plan of salvation, and it includes faith, repentance, baptism, and the laying on of hands; (5) an organized church after the New Testament pattern, with authorized leaders and the gifts of the spirit; (6) the majority of the Christian world lies in apostasy; and (7) the key role of the Book of Mormon in the restoration, especially in underpinning the Mormon belief in modern revelation.

At least one more list appeared following, but without access to, the Wentworth letter: written by June 1841, but not published until 1842 in Germany, Orson Hyde published *A Cry from the Wilderness*. It probably appeared in August of that year. Chapter 4 of *A Cry* contained sixteen "Articles of Faith and Points of Doctrine recognized by the Church of Latter Day Saints." The section headings were:[31]

1. About the Godhead
2. About the Use and the Validity of the Scriptures of the Old and New Testament in our Church
3. Faith
4. Repentance
5. Baptism

  6. Confirmation by Laying on of Hands after Baptism
  7. The Sacrament of the Bread and Wine
  8. The Confession of Sins and the Method of Dealing with Members who Act Contrary to the Laws of the Church
  9. Children and the Church
  10. Revelations and Commandments God has Given to the Church
  11. The Livelihood and Sustenance of our Priests
  12. Baptism for the Dead
  13. Prayer and the Manner of Prayer
  14. Holidays
  15. The Washing of Feet
  16. Patriarchal Blessings and a Word about Marriage

Orson Hyde's listing reveals several things. First, it was one of the first lists that moved beyond mere doctrinal points to more administrative matters, and thus reveals the influence of Parley P. Pratt's *Voice of Warning.* Secondly, it shows a tendency to combine Doctrine and Covenants material, material from earlier LDS sources, and incorporate more recent doctrinal developments in the church (i.e., baptism for the dead). Hyde told Joseph Smith he had "written a snug little article on every point of doctrine believed by the Saints." It also shows the tendency in foreign mission fields to emphasize those items of Mormon beliefs that would contrast with local or national beliefs. The pamphlet appeared in German, and therefore would not have had a great influence on other LDS works.[32]

Thus it was in this larger context that in March 1842, Joseph Smith appended to his letter to John Wentworth a listing of the thirteen Articles of Faith as now canonized as the last item of the Pearl of Great Price.[33]

The background of the Wentworth letter, and the history of its early printing, have been discussed elsewhere and need not detain us here.[34] It must be concluded, given the material just presented, that nothing new appears in the Wentworth listing. Every item had been presented in Mormon literature before the time of its composing. From Joseph Smith's coauthorship role with Doctrine and Covenants 20 through the emerging literature of the church, through his compiling of the letter, he was active in shaping the spirit and mind of the early church and so he remains central to the doctrine, no matter who finally set pen to paper.[35] But questions still remain: What was the list in the Wentworth letter meant to accomplish? And was it really the product, as B. H. Roberts suggests, of one mind, produced at one sitting?

The Wentworth letter itself is a composite document. Joseph Smith's personal history came largely from material committed to paper in 1838. In early June 1838 Smith commenced to dictate his history to James Mulholland. This historical material was abridged for the Wentworth letter and it was published in the 1 March 1842 issue of the *Times and Seasons*.[36] Two weeks later the same periodical began serializing the "History of Joseph Smith," and Smith specifically commented: "In the last number I gave a brief history of the rise and progress of the Church. I now enter more particularly to that history." What this means is that if the historical part of the Wentworth letter had been written four years before it was published, i.e., that Smith drew on previously written material, then it might be more likely for him to draw on previously composed material containing lists of beliefs. It should not detract from Smith's work or calling to suggest he did not create the Wentworth list of LDS beliefs out of whole cloth. It should be remembered that he himself had been the key mind of early Mormonism, helping to give shape and content to early statements of beliefs such as Doctrine and Covenants 20. It should also be remembered that Smith was capable of taking the statements of his followers and issuing them as his own, as was the case with the list of thirteen political beliefs prepared for the editor of the *Chester County Register and Examiner* in January 1840. This list is predated by an earlier statement of Oliver Cowdery, first published in the *Messenger and Advocate* in 1835 and eventually added to the Doctrine and Covenants.[37]

The first Mormon historian to suggest that the thirteen Articles of Faith were written as the LDS response to the major religious questions of the day was T. Edgar Lyon. First proclaimed on the 110th anniversary of the Wentworth letter, Lyon's views were popularized throughout the 1950s and 1960s in both talks and in various publications.[38] His view has been echoed by others and it remains the main theoretical explanation for the Articles of Faith.[39]

There is, however, no reason to accept this position as definitive. As far as is known, the only early Mormon writer who prepared a list of beliefs for particular response to other religious points of view was Parley P. Pratt. The last chapter of his *Voice of Warning* (1837) contains a parallel listing of "A Contrast Between the Doctrines of Christ and the False Doctrines of the Nineteenth Century."[40] Pratt also did the same kind of comparison (zeroing in on Methodism) in the final pages of his *Mormonism Unveiled* (New York, 1838).[41] While Pratt reveals his great abilities as a pamphleteer in the classical sense of the word there is little evidence that Joseph Smith intended to do the same in the Wentworth list. While it is true that Mormons were beginning to prepare their lists for outsiders by 1840, it should be remembered that all the previous lists were primarily designed for use *in* the Church — *that* was the heritage and the influence of Doctrine and Covenants 20.

In his essays and talks, Lyon argued (1) that the "Articles of Faith" were written by Joseph Smith; (2) that Joseph "apparently geared the Articles to try to deal with the important issues that people at that time were facing"; (3) that Joseph was not writing for LDS consumption; (4) that "the Articles reveal an acute awareness of the strong currents of religion that were in the world at that time," hence Joseph selected topics that were controversial topics of the period; and (5) that up to this time (1842) "the Church had been so busy with its various pioneering and missionary ventures that no one had taken time to write . . . an exposition of the principles of the faith."

In his item-by-item analysis of the Wentworth listing, Lyon argued that Article 1 showed that the Mormons rejected the Unitarian belief in the godhead and thus revealed they were a Christian body. Article 2 showed that Mormons rejected original sin, infant baptism, and predestination. Article 3 put Mormons close to the Universalists, while 4 was Joseph's way of specifically contrasting the Mormons with the Campbellites. Article 5 was to show the LDS position on the issue of the question of religious authority, and Article 6 put Mormons in the same camp as the Restorationists. Article 7 was Smith's reaction to "spirit rappings," and 8 was a response to critics who argued Mormons had rejected the Bible. Article 9 showed that Smith was not a millenarian; Article 10 revealed that he was not expecting an imminent return of Christ; Article 11 was a reaction to early Mormon experience with intolerance and persecution; Article 12 stated the LDS position regarding the important contemporary questions concerning the relationship of the individuals to governmental bodies;

and Article 13 was a kind of summary of the open-ended Mormon approach to life.

It *is* possible to argue all of these points, but such logic fails to consider the larger textual context out of which the Wentworth listing came. In addition, since the Wentworth list seems to depend on earlier, lengthier statements, it is possible to more fully understand many of the articles that only appear in their most abbreviated form in the Wentworth list. If this comparative textual approach is taken, it is also possible to show not only that several of Lyon's positions are incorrect, but probably what the Wentworth listing more fully meant for Joseph Smith.

Just what Smith had in mind in publishing a list in 1842 may never be known. In the 1838 account of his early religious experiences, he said that he was told in his first vision that the creeds of Christendom were an abomination in the sight of God,[42] and it is clear from the Pelatiah Brown affair that he did not like creedal statements.[43] The closest Smith came to summarizing LDS beliefs, excluding the Wentworth letter, was his published answer in the *Elder's Journal* to the question "what are the fundamental principles of your religion?" to which he replied, "The fundamental principles of our religion are the testimony of the Apostles and Prophets, concerning Jesus Christ, that he died, was buried, and rose again the third day, and ascended into heaven; and all other things which pertain to our religion are only appendages to it."[44] It is not even known for sure that he himself composed the Wentworth list. Lyon noted traditions in the Orson Pratt family (that he, Lyon, heard when doing research at the University of Chicago) that Joseph Smith had asked Orson to prepare a shorter, more concise list than what had appeared in his own 1840 tract. There is so far no evidence to substantiate this, although while Pratt could be quite wordy in his publications, he could also be quite succinct and to the point. He had a mind of a mathematician, a mind for reducing things to their lowest common denominator.[45] The fact that Joseph Smith never again referred to this listing, and that Orson Pratt did and even felt free to add a few more items to it in later lists, possibly suggests he helped write them in the first place.

We probably will never know just who was finally responsible for the form the articles took in the Wentworth letter — there is no question about their beauty or their conciseness; but they were hardly definitive answers to the pivotal religious questions of the early nineteenth century—many of them are so worded that they invite questions and further discussion, not so as to close the door. Many were so broadly worded that both Catholics and Protestants could agree with them. Thus there is little indication in either the origin or structure of any of these first listings to suggest that their authors were responding to the religious controversies of the 1830s. At best they were minimal statements of Mormon doctrine intended primarily for a Protestant audience. They were primarily declarative, confessional statements offered in a missionary context.[46] This does not mean that as propositions they could not be called upon in a debate or argument; and it is possible that their structure was dictated by similar creeds that were well known in New England.[47] If what is suggested here is true, that the earliest listings we have can be traced to Doctrine and Covenants 20, then they were written first for insiders, for members, and only gradually were used in a missionary context. Why would converts who had rejected the contemporary denominations need to be reminded how their new faith differed from those they had rejected?

Lyon thus failed to see the evolutionary nature of the Articles prior to 1842, especially the role of Doctrine and Covenants 20 and the subsequent newspaper and pamphlet literature. He also failed to consider the obvious borrowing and coauthorship that went on in the early church. Finally, like so many other LDS authors, Lyon allowed the public visibility of Orson Pratt to obscure the greater contributions of his brother Parley.

What is suggested for the pre-1842 period continued to be true during the years thereafter. It was probably the continued diffusion of various lists that led church leaders in 1880 to canonize the Wentworth list as part of the Pearl of Great Price.

The listing attributed to Joseph Smith appeared in March 1842 and was again printed in a book edited by John E. Page and L. R. Foster, *Correspondence Between Joseph Smith, The Prophet, and Col. John Wentworth*,[48] and even though his position gave them an "official" status that encouraged others to reprint them, there continued to appear other lists or modifications of those already published. Several publications that appeared between 1842 and 1844 just reprinted the Wentworth listing.[49] After Joseph Smith's death in 1844, Orson Pratt again printed his 1840 listing (adding a fifteenth item dealing with the impending destruction of the nation) in the short-lived *Listen to the Voice of Truth*.[50] Parley P. Pratt continued to issue his more narrative descriptions of Mormon belief.[51]

An interesting list appeared in April 1849 in a pamphlet published under Orson Pratt's direction: James H. Flanigan, *Reply to a Sheet Entitled "The Result of Two Meetings between the L.D. Saints and Primitive Methodists" at Gravely, Cambridgeshire*. This seems to be the first printing of the well-known thirteen Articles of Faith, with one additional one, and includes all the canon with some few additions: "The Lord's Supper" is a fifth ordinance listed in Article 4; "inspiration" is named in Article 5 as the vehicle of men's calling, and being "duly commissioned" replaces "in authority." Included in Article 7 as gifts believed in are "faith" and "discerning of spirits," "wisdom, charity, [and] brotherly love." Article 8 includes "all good books" as possible sources of the Word of God, but fails to include the "as far as it is translated correctly" rider to the Bible's credibility. Article 9 adds "the Messiah's second coming" as an addition to the belief in prophecy, and 10 sets the messianic reign at a thousand years. A whole eleventh article affirms that "We believe in the literal resurrection of the body, and that the dead in Christ will rise first, and that the rest of the dead live not again until the thousand years are expired." Article 12 includes the term "unmolested" as a condition of worship claimed by the Saints, 13 adds "queens" to the rulers to which they are subject, and 14 adds "temperate" and "upright" as qualities sought after, with a final "looking forward to the 'recompense of reward.' "[52] All these additional items are suggested in Orson Pratt's 1840 pamphlet and the other, earlier lists discussed above. The same list was included in Flanigan's *Mormonism Triumphant!*[53]

The listing by Orson Hyde in *The Frontier Guardian*[54] is exactly the same fourteen statements, including the caption. Hyde did add one sentence to the end: "But an idle or lazy person cannot be a christian, neither have salvation. He is a drone and destined to be stung to death and tumbled out of the hive," a clear indication of the pioneer work ethic the Mormons were beginning. It was from one of these listings that Charles Mackay, a non-Mormon author, obtained his list.[55]

In 1850, Erastus Snow listed sixteen articles of faith in a pamphlet published in Danish,[56] and a short three-page tract appeared in Liverpool in 1851 which listed fourteen with "Parallel Scripture References to prove the Latter-day Saint Faith and Doctrine."[57]

Although Franklin D. Richards included the Wentworth listing in his compilation The Pearl of Great Price[58] (Liverpool, 1851), neither Mormons nor non-Mormons seemed bound to them alone. Charles Mackay's *The Mormons: Or the Latter Day Saints* reproduced the fourteen, and the great success of this volume assured that others would quote this listing. The numerous "belief" publications of the 1850s fail to show any signs of being bound to one list. In 1852 a broadside listing fourteen "Latter-day Saint Beliefs" appeared in England.[59] In 1853 Hugh Findlay published a pamphlet in Bombay, India, and on the last page reprinted, with some alterations, the Flanigan listing, adding scriptural references after several of the articles, apparently following the 1852 broadside.[60] Another printing was a pamphlet by Jesse Haven, published in South Africa. He listed a total of thirty-three "principal doctrines," including the thirteen given in the Wentworth letter, to which he added such items as baptism for the dead, the three degrees of glory, and plural marriage. Haven's entire pamphlet was a list of items of belief.[61]

The next year, 1854, at least three different prints containing articles of faith appeared. Perhaps the best known was the listing that appeared in Sydney, Australia. This listing followed the fourteen and gave expanded "scriptural proofs" following many of the articles.[62] Although the exact publication date is unknown, there appeared an exact reprinting in London that same year.[63] It is not known who copied whom. During the same year John Routledge reprinted the Flanigan list in England in his *A Companion for the Bible, or Important Scripture References, to Prove a few of the First and Leading Principles of the Church.*[64]

Other lists appeared in the next few years. John Taylor published one of the most imaginative. Containing nineteen "beliefs," his list follows in idea the earlier printed lists of the 1850s although it seemed to rely on Orson Pratt's 1844 list in *Listen to the Voice of Truth.*[65] In 1855 George A. Smith reprinted the Wentworth list from the *Times and Seasons* in *The Deseret News*, to which he added "we also believe in the Patriarchal order of matrimony."[66] In 1856, Samuel M. Smucker printed the Flanigan list of fourteen items.[67] In 1857 the Wentworth listing appeared again in the LDS *Millennial Star*.[68] In 1862 Richard F. Burton reprinted Orson Hyde's *Frontier Guardian* list of fourteen with explanatory notes provided by Burton himself.[69]

Although some of the aforementioned lists did appear in Mormon publications after 1860, the trend over the next two decades was to reprint the Wentworth listing as in George A. Smith, *Rise, Progress and Travels*.[70] This standardization was in large measure a product of the growing centralization of the Mormon press[71] and several periods of housecleaning revealed most clearly in the reformation movement of 1856–57 and in the catechisms of the 1850s and 1860s. It was in this setting that lists of beliefs could assume a more functional role in LDS society.[72]

Three years after Brigham Young's death in 1877, the Pearl of Great Price was canonized,[73] and because the Wentworth list of thirteen articles was included in this volume its priority was assured. At a general conference ten years after their canonization Wilford Woodruff asked Orson F. Whitney to read the Articles of Faith just prior to the announcement of the manifesto which rescinded church approval of plural marriage. At the same time, F. D. Richards formally proposed the individual acceptance of the Articles of Faith "as a rule of our faith and of our conduct" for the Latter-day Saints.[74] But as late as 1897, when members of the Salt Lake Stake Sunday Schools were to recite the Articles of Faith in the Tabernacle, leaders sought to advise all of the "correct form" to be used by printing the Wentworth list.[75] As early as the 1870s, young children in the Sunday School were being taught to memorize the "articles of our faith" and were being told that Joseph Smith was the author.[76] This standardizing procedure has been followed in the years since, and as to the present time, in the curriculum materials used by the church as well as in the publications of various Mormon authors.[77]

When he wrote that the Articles of Faith "were struck off by one mind at a single effort," B. H. Roberts had failed to see the evolutionary nature of this creedal statement in nineteenth-century Mormonism.[78] Others since Roberts, assessing the significance of the Wentworth list have likewise been unaware of the amount of sharing and borrowing that went on during this formative period, and its impact on the composing of that letter. That the Articles of Faith evolved gradually, and that their role as a creedal statement evolved along with their wording is evident from the documents here cited.

The early development of such statements of faith and belief, in Mormonism as in traditional Christianity, helped to articulate categories of thought. Hymns, prayers, beliefs expressed in rituals, and creeds have appeared in the literatures of most religious movements, Christian included. And while the New Testament contains no fully developed creed, it does suggest the early existence of basic confessions of faith, as in Matthew 28:10–20 and Acts 8:37. That Mormonism's restoration of the primitive faith included such a statement of faith is here evidenced.

Also delineated here is the centrality of a core of Mormon doctrines during its formative years. In spite of the variations among the various published lists, they show a remarkable consistency, not all of it accounted for by the extensive borrowing from one to another.

NOTES

1. For the full letter see B. H. Roberts, ed., *History of the Church, Period I*, 7 vols. (Salt Lake City: Deseret Book Co., revised ed., 1956), 4:535–41 (hereafter cited as HC); and Dean C. Jessee, ed., *The Personal Writings of Joseph Smith* (Salt Lake City: Deseret Book Co., 1984), 212–20.

2. George Barstow (1812–83) did publish a history of the state of New Hampshire in 1842, but he did not include the material Smith sent to Wentworth. Some biographical information is in Jessee, *Personal Writings*, 667, n. 2.

3. A good study of its contents and history is James R. Clark, *The Story of the Pearl of Great Price* (Salt Lake City: Bookcraft, 1955). See also Clark, "Our Pearl of Great Price: From Mission Pamphlet to Standard Work," *Ensign* 6 (August 1976): 12–17.

4. "Journal of James E. Talmage," 31 January 1893. MS in Special Collections, Brigham Young University, Provo, Utah.

5. See "MS History of the Church," Archives, Historical Department of The Church of Jesus Christ of Latter-day Saints, Salt Lake City, Utah. This repository hereafter cited as LDS Church Archives.

6. HC, 1:64–74.

7. Orson Pratt discourse of 10 October 1880 in *Journal of Discourses*, 26 vols. (Liverpool, 1854–1886), 22:32. Compare the comments of A. A. Ramseyer in *LDS Millennial Star* 60 (6 September 1900): 566.

8. While an exact dating is not possible, it could have been as early as

June 1829. On 14 June 1829 Cowdery wrote a letter to Hyrum Smith, MS in LDS Church Archives, in which he included material from Doctrine and Covenants 18 (hereafter cited as D&C), the same section cited in the "1829" MS by Cowdery. See also David Whitmer, *An Address to All Believers in Christ* (Richmond, Mo.: Author, 1887), 49, 64.

9. For a discussion of the relation of this MS to D&C 20, which includes a typescript of the Oliver Cowdery MS, see Robert J. Woodford, "The Historical Development of the Doctrine and Covenants" (Ph.D. diss., Brigham Young University, 1974), 1:286–93. The original Cowdery MS is in LDS Church Archives.

10. *The Evening and the Morning Star* (Independence, Mo.) 1 (June 1832): 1, 2. In most all the early MS copies, D&C 22 is not combined with D&C 20. A useful overview of the early printings and texts is Richard L. Anderson, "The Organizational Revelations (D&C 20, 21 and 22)" in *Studies in Scriptures, Volume 1: The Doctrine and Covenants*, ed. Robert L. Millet and Kent P. Jackson (Sandy, Utah: Randall Book Co., 1984), 109–23.

11. HC, 1:104, 105.

12. See Roberts, *A Comprehensive History of the Church*, 6 vols. (Salt Lake City: Deseret News Press, 1930), 1:189–98. Hereafter cited as CHC.

13. "Far West Record," MS, LDS Church Archives, 1.

14. Woodford notes the various MS copies of D&C 20 extant in the handwriting of such early Mormon missionaries as Orson Hyde, Wilford Woodruff, and Orson Pratt. See Woodford, "Historical Development," 1:293. Martin Harris provided a copy of the Articles and Covenants to the *Painsville Telegraph* (19 April 1831), p. 4.

15. A general overview of the lectures is presented in Leland H. Gentry, "What of the Lectures on Faith?" *Brigham Young University Studies* 19 (Fall 1978): 5–19. The Lectures on Faith had been a committee project. See Elinore H. Partridge, "Characteristics of Joseph Smith's Style and Notes on the Authorship of the Lectures on Faith," *Task Papers in LDS History*, No. 14 (Salt Lake City: The Historical Department of The Church of Jesus Christ of Latter-day Saints, 1976); and Alan J. Phipps, "The Lectures on Faith: An Authorship Study" (MA thesis, Brigham Young University, 1977).

16. D&C 88:78.

17. The authorship questions are treated in the sources cited in note 36 below.

18. Preface dated 17 February 1835, Kirtland, Ohio.

19. David Whitmer later argued that the D&C was a creed. See his *An Address to All Believers in Christ*, 51–52. See also the "Kirtland Council Minute Book," 17 August 1835, MS in LDS Church Archives. Here the D&C is specifically referred to as containing "the faith[,] articles and covenants" of the Latter-day Saints.

20. *LDS Messenger and Advocate* (Kirtland, Ohio) 1 (October 1834): 1–2. For another example of the understanding of the central tenets of

Mormonism, see the summary in the letter of William E. McClellin to Samuel McClellin, 4 August 1832. MS in LDS Church Archives.

21. John Hayward, *The Religious Creeds and Statutes of Every Christian Denomination in the United States and British Provinces* (Boston: John Hayward, 1836), 139–40.

22. Bibliographical material is provided in Peter Crawley, "A Bibliography of The Church of Jesus Christ of Latter-day Saints in New York, Ohio, and Missouri," *BYU Studies* 12 (Summer 1972): 516–18.

23. On the larger impact of Parley P. Pratt see Crawley, "Parley P. Pratt: Father of Mormon Pamphleteering," *Dialogue: A Journal of Mormon Thought* 15 (Autumn 1982): 13–26.

24. *Late Persecution of the Church of Jesus Christ of Latter-day Saints. Ten Thousand American Citizens robbed, plundered, and banished; others imprisoned, and others martyred for their religion. With a sketch of their rise, progress and doctrine.* (New York: J. W. Harrison, Printer, 1840), iii–xiii.

25. Crawley, "Parley P. Pratt," 16.

26. Full bibliographical information is in Chad Flake, ed., *A Mormon Bibliography, 1830–1930* (Salt Lake City: University of Utah Press, 1978), 520. Hereafter cited as Flake, with item number following.

27. *An Address to the Citizens of Salem and Vicinity* was first issued in Salem, Massachusetts. The work was dated 9 September 1841. A second printing was made within a week by Freeman Nickerson in Boston. A third printing appeared in the *Times and Seasons* 2 (15 October 1841): 574–76 and 3 (15 November 1841): 578–84.

28. Among them are T. Edgar Lyon, S. George Ellsworth, Leonard J. Arrington, and Dean C. Jessee.

29. The ordering of the historical and doctrinal material in both Orson Pratt's pamphlet and in Joseph Smith's Wentworth letter make it difficult to argue against the strong possibility that Joseph had a copy of Pratt's pamphlet in front of him when he composed the Wentworth letter. According to Orson's 24 September 1840 letter from Edinburgh to George A. Smith, this pamphlet was "at press" and he expected 2,000 copies for a 6 October conference. MS in LDS Church Archives. Flake, 6501–6505.

30. *The Gospel Reflector* (Philadelphia) 1 (1 January 1841): 2–3. Winchester was also influenced by Parley P. Pratt.

31. English translation by Justus Ernst. MS of translation in LDS Church Archives. In a letter to Joseph Smith from London, 15 June 1841, Hyde told of writing this pamphlet "to publish in the German language" and specifically mentioned Orson Pratt and Oliver Cowdery as his sources. Hyde also outlined the contents of the pamphlet. See *LDS Millennial Star* 18 (6 September 1856): 565. Cf. HC, 4:373.

32. Several years later, as editor of the *Frontier Guardian* (Kanesville,

Iowa), Orson Hyde would print one of the well-known lists of fourteen articles of faith. See note 54 below.

33. *Times and Seasons* 3 (1 March 1842): 709-10. Between this printing and the most recent edition of the Pearl of Great Price (1981) there have been several textual changes made to this list. See Walter L. Whipple, "An Analysis of Textual Changes in 'The Book of Abraham' and in the 'Writings of Joseph Smith, The Prophet,' in the Pearl of Great Price" (MA thesis, BYU, 1959), 126-33, 140; and Lyndon W. Cook, "The Articles of Faith," *BYU Studies* 17 (Winter 1977): 254-56 (Re: changes in wording in the Fourth Article). It could be argued that someone other than Joseph Smith authored the Wentworth letter. He did use clerks and scribes for his correspondence and his History. But the following must be considered: (1) Joseph commenced as editor with the 15 February 1842 issue, the same issue that contained the farewell remarks of Ebenezer Robinson, the retiring editor; and (2) in the issue (1 March 1842) that contains the Wentworth letter, Joseph specifically inserted a notice to subscribers: "This paper commences my editorial career, I alone stand responsible for it, and shall do for all papers having my signature henceforth" (p. 710). This notice followed Joseph Smith's signature at the end of the Wentworth letter. Joseph was in Nauvoo during the month the letter appeared in the *Times and Seasons* and if he did not personally write the Wentworth letter, he surely approved of its contents.

34. CHC, 2:130-33; Joseph Fielding Smith, *Church History and Modern Revelation*, 2 vols. (Salt Lake City: The Council of the Twelve Apostles, LDS Church, 1953), 2:284-94; George Q. Morris, "The Origin of the Articles of Faith," *Instructor* 91 (February 1956): 44, 45; Preston Nibley, "The Wentworth Letter," *Improvement Era* 65 (February 1962): 96-97, 114-18; Robert J. Matthews, "The Number and Text of the Articles of Faith," (Provo, Utah: n.p., n.d.); Edward J. Brandt, "The Articles of Faith: Origin and Importance," *Pearl of Great Price Symposium* (Provo, Utah: BYU Press, 1976), 68-75; John W. Welch and David J. Whittaker, " 'We Believe . . .' Development of the Articles of Faith," *Ensign* 9 (September 1979): 51-55; and Whittaker, "Early Mormon Pamphleteering," (Ph.D. diss., BYU, 1982), 308-11, n. 137.

35. See, for example, David J. Whittaker, "Orson Pratt: Prolific Pamphleteer," *Dialogue* 15 (Autumn 1982): 34-35; and Peter Crawley, "Parley P. Pratt: Father of Early Mormon Pamphleteering," ibid., 14. Also valuable is Crawley, "The Passage of Mormon Primitivism," ibid. 13 (Winter 1980): 26-37.

36. The historical material came from the early sections of the "Manuscript History of the Church," a project begun in 1838. See Dean C. Jessee, "The Writing of Joseph Smith's History," *BYU Studies* 11 (Summer 1971): 439-73; and Howard C. Searle, "Early Mormon Historiography: Writing

the History of the Mormons, 1830–1858," (Ph.D. diss., UCLA, 1979), 200–336.

37. The list of Joseph Smith's political beliefs, dated 22 January 1840 and addressed to "Mr. Editor," appeared in the *Chester* (Pennsylvania) *County Register and Examiner*, 11 February 1840. See Jessee, *The Personal Writings of Joseph Smith*, 455–58. An examination of Joseph's list shows its relationship to the material authored by Oliver Cowdery. Known today as D&C 134, the statement was approved by a church conference in Kirtland on 17 August 1835. It was published in the *LDS Messenger and Advocate* 1 (August 1835): 163–64, and also appeared as Section 102 in the 1835 edition of the D&C. While Joseph Smith was not present at this conference he later referred to this section as "the belief of the Church." See ibid. 2 (April 1836): 291. Joseph's 1840 list of political beliefs illustrates his practice of taking material from the early publications and using it for his own purposes. Compare the earlier and shorter "Political Motto" (March 1838) in Joseph Fielding Smith, comp., *Teachings of the Prophet Joseph Smith* (Salt Lake City: Deseret Book Co., 1938), 117. It is possible that a committee produced D&C 134, just as they did D&C 109: the dedication prayer for the Kirtland Temple, which Oliver Cowdery and others helped Joseph Smith write. See Leonard J. Arrington, "Oliver Cowdery's Kirtland, Ohio, 'Sketch Book,' " *BYU Studies* 12 (Summer 1972): 426.

38. T. Edgar Lyon, "The Origin and Purpose of the Articles of Faith," *Instructor* 97 (August–October 1952); "Joseph Smith — the Wentworth Letter and Religious America of 1842," *Twelfth Annual Joseph Smith Memorial Sermon*, 5 December 1954 (Logan, Utah: LDS Institute of Religion, 1955). Also in *The Herald Journal* (Logan, Utah) 26 December 1954; "The Articles of Faith: How they were Born," *LDS Millennial Star* 119 (November 1957): 330–33, 338; "What Is a Prophet of God?" (Address to the student body of Brigham Young University, 2 November 1960), 3–8; and "Doctrinal Development of the Church During the Nauvoo Sojourn: 1839–1846," *BYU Studies* 15 (Summer 1975): 445–46: "What [Joseph Smith] really did was list points of doctrine which were directed to the burning issues of the day. . . . "

39. See Leonard J. Arrington, "Charles Mackay and his 'True and Impartial History' of the Mormons," *Utah Historical Quarterly* 36 (Winter 1968): 26; and Milton V. Backman Jr., "Joseph Smith, Popularizer or Restorer?" *Improvement Era* 70 (March, April 1967): 58ff, 76ff. This was published in pamphlet form by Deseret Book Company in 1967. Backman repeats Lyon's position: "The Articles of Faith . . . indicate, in part, the LDS position on controversial theological issues of the early nineteenth century" (p. 5). Backman argued that the Wentworth list emphasized the LDS similarities with other Christian religions rather than the differences.

40. Parley P. Pratt, *A Voice of Warning* (New York: W. Sandford, 1837), 121–28.

41. Parley P. Pratt, *Mormonism Unveiled* (New York, 1838), 42–45.

42. Pearl of Great Price, Joseph Smith—History, 1:19.

43. HC, 5:40–41 (8 April 1843): "I did not like the old man being called up for erring in doctrine. It looks too much like the Methodists and not like the Latter-day Saints. Methodists have creeds which a man must believe or be asked out of their church. I want the liberty of thinking and believing as I please. It feels so good not to be trammelled. It does not prove that a man is not a good man because he errs in doctrine." In 1835 Almon W. Babbitt was accused by the Kirtland High Council of teaching that "we have no articles of faith except the Bible." "Kirtland Council Minute Book," 19 August 1835, MS in LDS Church Archives. Also HC, 2:252. On 1 January 1843, Joseph Smith provided some additional insights: "In reply to Mr. Butterfield, I stated that the most prominent difference in sentiment between the Latter-day Saints and sectarians was, that the latter were all circumscribed by some peculiar creed, which deprived its members the privilege of believing anything not contained therein whereas the Latter-day Saints have no creed, but they are ready to believe all true principles that exist as they are made manifest from time to time" HC, 5:215. Compare HC, 5:517. In his diary (kept by Willard Richards) for 31 December 1842, Joseph notes: "I have no creed to circumscribe my mind therefore the people do not like me." MS in LDS Church Archives. William W. Phelps, in a letter to William Smith in December 1844, echoed these sentiments: Mormonism is "the great leveling machine of creeds." *Times and Seasons* 5 (1 January 1844): 758. All of this underlies the key Mormon belief in the principle of continuing revelation and that a creedal statement suggests an end to development.

44. The question (#20) appeared in the *Elders Journal* (Kirtland, Ohio) 1 (November 1837): 29. The answer was in ibid. (Far West, Mo.) 1 (July 1838): 44.

45. See Whittaker, "Orson Pratt: Prolific Pamphleteer," 32–36.

46. See Steven P. Sondrup, "On Confessing Belief: Thoughts on the Language of the Articles of Faith," in Neal E. Lambert, ed., *Literature of Belief* (Provo, Utah: Religious Studies Center, BYU, 1981), 197–215.

47. In addition to Williston Walker, *The Creeds and Platforms of Congregationalism (1969)*, see Milton V. Backman Jr., *American Religions and the Rise of Mormonism* (Salt Lake City: Deseret Book Co., 1965), 446–56; Samuel Miller, *The Utility and Importance of Creeds and Confessions: An Introductory Lecture . . . July 2, 1824* (Princeton, N.J.: D. A. Boorenstein, 1824); John H. Leith, ed., *Creeds of the Churches* (Richmond, Va.: John Knox Press, rev. ed., 1973).

48. John E. Page and L. R. Foster, *Correspondence Between Joseph Smith, The Prophet, and Col. John Wentworth* (New York: J. N. Harrison, 1844), 6. This was published by John E. Page and L. R. Foster.

49. See, for example, Noah Packard, *Political and Religious Detector* (Medina, Ohio: Michael Hyee, 1842), 34; the 1842 edition of John Hayward, *The Religious Creeds*; and I. Daniel Rupp, *An Original History of the Religious Denominations, at present existing in the United States* (Philadelphia: Humphreys, 1844), 41 (2nd ed., 1849), 348.

50. *Listen to the Voice of Truth*, Vol. I, No. 1 (New York City: S. Brannan 1844), 1–4. According to *The Prophet* (New York) this tract was to be "the first of a series of cheap, comprehensive TRACTS illustrating the great truths we are contending for." *The Prophet* (15 August 1844). The title above the text reads "A Sketch of the Faith of the Church of Jesus Christ of Latter Day Saints Particularly for those who Are Unacquainted With Our Principles." The material is an exact reprint from the first American edition of Pratt's *An Interesting Account* (New York: Joseph W. Harrison, Printer, 1841), 25–34 (1842 ed.), 27–36.

51. See "What is Mormonism" *The Prophet* (New York) beginning with No. 46. Pratt's systematizing reached its fullest expression in *Key to the Science of Theology* (Liverpool: F. D. Richards, 1855).

52. James H. Flanigan, *Reply to a Sheet Entitled "The Result of Two Meetings between the L.D. Saints and the Primitive Methodists" at Gravely, Cambridgeshire* (Liverpool? 1849), 7–8. While this pamphlet is dated Bedford, 1 March 1849, Flanigan's Journal shows that on 3 April 1849, "I wrote the 'Reply' to the Ranters in Gravely Cambridgeshire." He received 300 copies on 21 April 1849, but he does not indicate who printed them. MS in LDS Church Archives. On 1 January 1849 Flanigan received word that Orson Pratt had appointed him to be the president of the Bedford Conference, and it was in connection with this assignment that Flanigan published several items defending Mormonism. It is probable that the source for the "printed 'Creed' " of the Latter-day Saints reprinted in the 1851 British Census for Religious Worship was this pamphlet. See *Census of Great Britain, 1851, Religious Worship, England and Wales, Report and Tables* (London: George E. Eyer and William Spottiswoode for Her Majesty's Stationery Office, 1853), cx–cxi.

53. James H. Flanigan, *Mormonism Triumphant!* (Liverpool: R. James, 1849), 32. James H. Flanigan's Journal reveals that he wrote this work in June and July, and that he finished it on 13 July 1849, the day he sent the MS to "O. Pratts press." He suggests that 6,000 copies were made, 500 of which he received on 22 September 1849, the remainder of which were presumably distributed by the LDS *Millennial Star* office in Liverpool. MS in LDS Church Archives. The pamphlet was advertised as "just published" in the *Millennial Star* 11 (15 August 1849): 256. Flanigan's letter to Orson Pratt was printed just inside the cover of the pamphlet.

54. *Frontier Guardian* 2 (20 February 1850): 1. It was published under the title "Latter-day Saints's Faith."

55. Between June 1851 and 1857 Charles Mackay's *The Mormons: Or the Latter-day Saints* (London) went through five editions. The 14 Articles appeared on pages 46–47 in the 1851 edition and pages 40–41 in the 1852 edition. The impact of this history is considered in Arrington, "Charles Mackay and his 'True and Impartial History' of the Mormons," 24–40. It was from Mackay that Wilford Wood obtained the list he included in his second volume of *Joseph Smith Begins His Work* (n.p.: Wilford C. Wood, 1962). Wood's volume is the source for the popular knowledge in the LDS Church of the list of fourteen "Articles of Faith."

56. See *En Sandheds-Rost* (A Voice of Truth) (Kjobenhavn, 1850), 14–16. English translation by Paul V. Johnson in Special Collections, BYU. Flake, 8169. Lorenzo Snow had earlier written a pamphlet that dealt with only the first four articles: *The Only Way to be Saved* (London: D. Chalmers, 1841).

57. *Invitation* (Liverpool, 1851). Flake, 1882a. This item containing fourteen articles of faith was reprinted several times.

58. The Pearl of Great Price (Liverpool: F. D. Richards, 1851), 55. In this first edition the caption read simply " 'Times and Seasons,' Vol. III, page 709." In a preface, Richards stated that he hoped "this little collection of precious truths" would increase the ability of true believers in the divine mission of the Prophet Joseph Smith "to maintain and to defend the holy faith by becoming possessors of it." The title caption "Articles of our Faith" was added to the 1878 edition (Salt Lake City: LDS Printing and Publishing Establishment), 63. This was reprinted in the 1879 edition (Liverpool: William Bridge), 79; and the 1882 edition (Liverpool: Albert Carrington), 79. The 1888 edition shortened the title to "Articles of Faith" (Salt Lake City: *Deseret News Company*), 121. This was not followed in the 1891 edition, where the caption returned to "Articles of Our Faith" (Salt Lake City: George Q. Cannon and Sons Co. Publishers), 79. The 1902 edition, which was divided into chapters and verses with added references by James E. Talmage returned to the 1891 caption "The Articles of Faith" to which was added "Of the Church of Jesus Christ of Latter-day Saints." In addition the reference to the *Times and Seasons* was eliminated in this edition (Salt Lake City: *The Deseret News*), 102. This remained the practice through the 1921 edition, which was the last major edition until the 1982 edition, which added after the title "History of the Church, Vol. 4, pp. 535–541."

59. "Latter-day Saint Beliefs" (Liverpool? 1852?). Original in BYU Archives. Flake, 4771a. A blank space was left at the bottom of the broadside where missionaries could add information regarding their preaching locations. This was probably the first use in Mormonism of the "missionary card" containing the Articles of Faith, although it was not until the 1870s and more fully after World War II that the individualized Articles of Faith cards became standard fare for Mormon missionaries. Examples of these include the following, most of which are in the LDS Church Archives: "The

Latter Day Saints' Belief," Broadside (Hull: Oliver's Printing Establishment, 1852?); "The Latter-Day Saints' Belief," Broadside (Liverpool? 1852?); "Articles of Faith," Broadside (n.p.: n.p., 187–?); "Latter-Day Saints" (Liverpool: Millennial Star Office, 1895). This broadside included a list of LDS publications, including "Articles of Faith, per 1000" 1 Shilling; "A Conference of Members of the Church . . . in the Sheffield Conference District will be held in the County Court Room, (Guild Hall,) Doncaster on Sunday, November 8, 1986." On the reverse side of this broadside were the "Articles of Faith"; similar conference announcements are extant which were issued in England in 1896, 1897, and 1900, all of which contain the Wentworth listing on the verso of the broadside. The Deseret Sunday School Union issued several printings of the Wentworth listing in the 1880s and 1890s. The smaller, wallet-size Articles of Faith cards seem to have become popular after World War II. They have since appeared in many languages, especially during the 150th anniversary of the church in 1980. Samples are in LDS Church Archives. The standardization of the translation is assured by *The Pearl of Great Price Translation Guide Fascicle 5, The Articles of Faith* (Salt Lake City: Translation Services, The Church of Jesus Christ of Latter-day Saints, 1978).

60. *The Mormons or the Latter-day Saints* (Bombay, India: Duftur Ashkara Press, 1853), 22: "The Latter-day Saints Belief." See also Hugh Findlay, *To The Marattas of Hindoostan, A Treatise on the True and Living God* (ca. March 1855), same listing on last page.

61. *Some of the Principle Doctrines or Belief of the Church* (Cape Town: W. Foelscher 1853), 1–6. This pamphlet was reprinted in David J. Whittaker, "Early Mormon Imprints in South Africa," *BYU Studies* 20 (Summer 1980): 410–16.

62. *Zion's Watchman* 1 (5 August 1854): 135–36. "The Faith and Doctrines of the Latter-day Saints, With Scriptural Proofs."

63. C. Armstrong, *"He that Readeth, Let Him Understand."* (Walworth: W. Aubrey, 1854?) under the title "The Faith and Doctrines of the LDS With Scriptural Proofs," 2–4. Flake, 201.

64. John Routledge, *A Companion for the Bible, or Important Scripture References, to Prove a few of the First and Leading Principles of the Church* (Liverpool, 1854), 20–21. He included the Flanigan listing (again from Mackay?) but without scriptural references under the title "Latter Day Saints Faith."

65. This list ran in every issue of *The Mormon* (New York City), beginning with Vol. 1, No. 1 (17 March 1855): 4. It also included the same material in French on the same page.

66. *Deseret News*, 5 September 1855.

67. *The Religious, Social and Political History of The Mormons* (New York: Miller, Orton's Mulliged, 1856), 61–63. This list clearly came from

Mackay's volume. Note the comments by John Taylor in *The Mormon*, 20 September 1856.

68. *Millennial Star* (21 February 1857): 120.

69. *The City of the Saints* (New York: Harper and Brothers, 1862), 387–98.

70. George A. Smith, *Rise, Progress and Travels* (Salt Lake City: Deseret News Office, 1869), 40–41.

71. See Whittaker, "Early Mormon Pamphleteering," 35–49.

72. The standardizing of LDS beliefs can be seen in the various published catechisms in early Utah. See Davis Bitton, "Mormon Catechisms," *Task Papers in LDS History*, No. 15 (Salt Lake City: Historical Department of The Church of Jesus Christ of Latter-day Saints, 1976). We have generally ignored here lists of beliefs issued by individuals or groups who broke with mainstream Mormonism. Examples would include William Smith, *William Smith on Mormonism* (Lamoni, Iowa: Herald Steam Book and Job Office, 1883), 29–32 (Seventeen Articles); *Articles of Faith, Published by Committee of the Church of the Firstborn, Organized in San Francisco, California, July 2nd, 1876* (San Francisco: n.p., 1887) (Thirteen Articles); and "Statement of Belief," mimeographed MS, 8 pp., copy in LDS Church Archives, Reorganized Church of Jesus Christ of Latter Day Saints; last two pages follow Wm. Smith's list: "Epitome of the Faith and Doctrines of the Church of Christ."

73. See Journal History for an account of the 10 October 1880 conference. Also Clark, *The Story of the Pearl of Great Price*, 205–7. As Clark suggests there must have been some question as to the exact place of the Articles of Faith in the standard works, as they were specifically recanonized in October 1890.

74. See *LDS Millennial Star* 46 (17 November 1890): 722. The date of the proposal was 6 October 1890. Wilford Woodruff had set the stage for the public reading of the Articles of Faith by Orson F. Whitney by counseling that an often asked question is "What do the Latter-day Saints Believe In?"

75. *Deseret Evening News* 30 (16 February 1897): 4.

76. *The Juvenile Instructor* 74 (1 January 1879): 5.

77. In publications between 1882 and 1985, the following authors and authorities contributed to the standardizing process: John Jaques, *The Church of Jesus Christ of Latter-day Saints: Its Priesthood, Organization, Doctrines, Ordinances and History* (Salt Lake City: Deseret Book Co., 1882), last page; Wilford Woodruff, in "Official Refutation of Slander," *LDS Millennial Star* 73 (9 and 16 March 1891): 145–49, 160–64, esp. 163; James E. Talmage, *The Articles of Faith* (Salt Lake City: Deseret Book, 1899); Arthur Price, "On Remembering the Articles of Faith," *LDS Millennial Star* 66 (10 November 1904): 732–33; Charles W. Penrose, "The 'Mormon' Creed

Explained," ibid. 64 (6 March 1902): 157–58; cf. the earlier listing in "The Character of the 'Mormon' People," ibid. 49 (1 August 1887): 491; First Presidency, Joseph F. Smith, Anthon H. Lund, John Henry Smith, letter of 6 February 1911, in ibid. 73 (2 March 1911): 137, refer to the Articles of Faith specifically as a "creed"; Heber J. Grant, in Address of 3 October 1919, in *Conference Reports* (October 1919), 27–34; also 5 April 1935 in *Conference Reports* (April 1935), 8–11; and Spencer W. Kimball, in Address of October 1975, in *Conference Reports* (October 1975), 117–19; and Bruce R. McConkie, *A New Witness for the Articles of Faith* (Salt Lake City: Deseret Book Co., 1985).

78. CHC, 2:131. Compare with HC, 4:535n.

PART TWO

The Church and the People, in Utah and Abroad

In its formative years, the Church of Jesus Christ of Latter-day Saints had few enough followers that the Prophet and a few intimates could govern them quite successfully. Even after the Nauvoo phase, when wards were devised and bishops appointed, there was a strong sense of central administration. By the time the Saints reached Utah, however, the numbers, now into the tens of thousands, demanded a distribution of administrative functions along with continued central decision-making. Throughout the early Utah period of Mormon history, various facets of Mormon life reflected the process.

The collection of tithes, for example, was affected by the geographical diffusion of the Saints. William G. Hartley, an associate of the Joseph Fielding Smith Institute at Brigham Young University, traces the evolution of the tithing system of church support in the 1847–56 period in his "Ward Bishops and the Localizing of LDS Tithing." Growing out of his wider interest in the temporal functions of priesthood administration in the nineteenth century, this study of one phase in the history of church revenue describes the transformation, under Bishop Edward Hunter's direction, from central adminstration to local collection and distribution.

Another approach to Mormon temporal affairs was the experiment, in the 1870s, known as the United Order of Enoch, treated here under title "Brigham Young and the Bishops: The United Order in the City," by Dean L. May of the University of Utah's Department of History. From its beginning in St. George in February 1874, the order, taunted by the *Salt Lake Tribune* as the "United Order of

Euchre," rose, largely failed, and then was abandoned in 1876. May details the responses of Salt Lake City bishops to the challenge.

To understand the history of the Utah years one must understand the unit through which most of the Saints found their connection to their church. The Mormon ward, a geographical area with fixed boundaries and a stable leadership, became the focus of their spiritual community. In " 'Going to Meeting' in Salt Lake City's Thirteenth Ward, 1849–1881: A Microanalysis," Ronald W. Walker, another associate with Brigham Young University's Smith Institute, provides a case study of Utah urban wards as they gathered their members to worship.

Also following a microcosmic approach, Gordon Irving, who heads the James H. Moyle Oral History Program for the Historical Department of the Church, examines in his "Coming of Age in a Western Farm Community: Union, Utah, 1900–1910" the changing life-style imposed on a rural Mormon community by advancing industrialization and urbanization. Working demographically on the generation following that of Walker's study, Irving gives insight into the lives of yet another group of Utah Mormons.

Although the major call to Latter-day Saint converts in the nineteenth century was to "gather to Zion," the history of the movement must also consider the activities of those converts who remained where missionaries converted them. R. Lanier Britsch, now vice president of Brigham Young University, Hawaii Campus, looks at "Latter-day Saint Education in the Pacific Islands" to trace church involvement with its members abroad. He summarizes major developments in church schools from their beginnings in the early 1850s, when the wives of missionaries kept school for the island children, to the present, when the church operates a university, a college, and twenty-four schools in Polynesia.

One of Leonard Arrington's most significant frontline contributions is his support for and involvement in the field of women's history. The two essays that follow are examples of the hundreds of studies of Mormon women's history to be published in the last decade.

As the nineteenth century progressed, Utah women were engaged in increasingly diverse activities. The 1896 restoration of the vote to women after its initial granting in 1870 and withdrawal in 1887 is a study in gains and losses of political power. As the Mormons accommodated themselves to American politics, Mormon women found themselves facing each other across partisan lines. From the vantage point of her long study of Emmeline B. Wells, Carol Cornwall Madsen, associate in the Smith Institute, looks at the impact on women of the events surrounding Utah's final bid for statehood.

Mormon women came into public power in Utah, in part at least, through the organization and reorganization of the Relief Society, initially founded in 1842 in Nauvoo. But as other nineteenth-century innovations altered in the move to bureaucratization of LDS temporal programs, so the charitable work of women through their society was gradually shifted to a centrally administered, staff operated department of social services. The transition from one mode to another and its impact on the personnel involved is traced in the essay "Changing Relief Society Charity to Make Way for Welfare, 1930–1944," by Jill Mulvay Derr. Once an associate in the History Division of the LDS Church, Derr is now completing, with Janath Cannon, a full history of the Relief Society, as well as a study of the church's Social Service Department.

It is the nature of huge organizations that smaller entities within the whole often find themselves buffeted about. Such is the case, Richard Jensen points out, in the final essay of this section, "Mother Tongue: Use of Non-English Languages in the Church of Jesus Christ of Latter-day Saints in the United States, 1850–1983." Jensen, an associate at Brigham Young University's Smith Institute, uses his background in Scandinavian and other European languages to investigate the experiences of various language groups migrating into Utah. The official response to languages, and the cultures they represented, shifted with changing demographic, political, and ecclesiastical needs. Jensen charts those changes over more than a century among Pacific as well as European immigrants.

Ward Bishops and the Localizing of LDS Tithing, 1847–1856

William G. Hartley

Tithing, the lifeblood of the Church of Jesus Christ of Latter-day Saints' financial system, has a history of its own. Although official tithing records are closed to research, Leonard Arrington and other scholars have written several chapters of tithing's history.[1] Chapter one, the Nauvoo beginnings, and chapter two, the exodus, are sketchy. The fourth and fifth chapters about tithing's connections with consecration and United Orders are well written. A later chapter about turn-of-the-century shifts to cash tithes awaits telling.

What follows is a chapter three, dealing with tithing between 1847 and 1856. During this period new Presiding Bishop Edward Hunter revolutionized the tithing system by making ward bishops, instead of the presiding bishop, responsible to receive tithes from, keep accounts for, and make annual tithing settlements with individual Saints.

A previously ignored, undated "Circular" from Hunter to ward bishops, which we can now date to late 1852, initiated the new program.[2] The new system took three years to implement fully and required printed instructions and forms, new record-keeping systems, trainers, and monitors, standardizing valuation lists, building local storehouses, and intermittent scoldings to help bishops and members turn tithepaying into a ward matter.

Once they had become established in their Great Basin communities, LDS pioneers were expected to pay three types of tithes: property, increase, and labor. Apostle Parley P. Pratt, on 7 October 1849, gave perhaps the first Utah discourse that details the triple tithe.

First, he said, "To fulfill the law of tithing a man should make out and lay before the [Presiding] Bishop [then Newel K. Whitney] a schedule of all his property, and pay him the tenth of it." That is, he should pay a one-time initiatory tithe on all *property* he possessed. "When he has tithed his principal once," Pratt continued, "he has no occasion to tithe again" on that property. But the next year he must pay one-tenth of his *increase* of "cattle, money, goods and trade." A member also owed "the tenth of his time" — a *labor* tithe of each tenth day of man, young man, and work animals and wagons for the days not devoted to producing income or increase.[3]

The first Mormon pioneers had no large scale "increase" to tithe until their first harvest in 1848. Albert Carrington's personal tithing book pinpoints 5 October 1848 as "the beginning of tithing in this valley" — months before any Utah wards were created.[4]

The exodus from Nauvoo had disrupted stake, ward, and quorum organizations. "Until now," First Presidency Counselor Heber C. Kimball said on 16 February 1849, our organizations "have all been kicked to pieces." To solve the problem, the First Presidency then called a stake presidency and high council, and divided Great Salt Lake City into nineteen wards, each with a bishop. Several country wards also were created.[5]

Newly appointed bishops met together as a quorum, beginning on 25 March 1849. Their meetings became bimonthly. At the initial meeting Daniel H. Wells, director of the church's public works projects, said he had "arranged the City into tithing wards and wish the Bishops with their men to be on hand when called upon." His term "tithing ward" referred to labor tithing only, and he soon assigned city wards one by one or in clusters to provide workmen for community projects.[6]

Presiding Bishop Whitney continued to receive, record, and disburse cash and commodity tithes from Salt Lake Valley Saints. When LDS settlements rooted beyond the Salt Lake Valley, bishops in distant wards acted as his agents, funneling tithes and keeping simple records of receipts and disbursements. Bishop Whitney conducted no tithing settlements in 1849 or 1850. He lacked a good storehouse for the commodities/tithes. During 1850 he handled tithing business in a room in the State of Deseret statehouse, in the mint, and in a joiner's shop. Meanwhile, he eagerly watched the rise of walls for the new tithing storehouse. But he died in September 1850 before the place was finished.[7]

In 1851 a series of actions worked together to systematize tithe-handling. First, during April conference Bishop Edward Hunter, a skilled businessman, became the new presiding bishop six months after Whitney's death. Second, that spring a central tithing store-house finally opened, with one apartment to store grain, others for a store, and a mechanic's shop, and cellars for vegetables.[8] Third, in April leaders announced plans to build the Salt Lake Temple, a project requiring tithing food to feed workmen and tithing materials with which to build.[9] Fourth, during fall conference Bishop Hunter received as helpers two traveling presiding bishops, Nathaniel H. Felt and John Banks, whom he assigned to visit outlying wards and "settle with the several Bishops from time to time and report the same to the Presiding Bishop."[10]

Finally, with the tithing office open and capable men called to manage the tithes, Brigham Young shocked conference attenders on 10 September 1851. He required them to covenant by raised hand and voice vote to tithe faithfully and to again pay their initiatory tithe on "all they have got." He asked Saints to "commence anew the tithings and consecrations, and that within thirty days, each Saint should make a consecration of one-tenth of his property, and one-tenth of his interest or income ever after."[11] After the covenanting conference, Bishop Hunter and his staff opened for tithing settlement "business," which lasted until the next March.

A *Deseret News* editorial on 29 November 1851 invited all Saints to settle their tithing accounts. The General Tithing Office, it said, wanted to close up accounts not settled since the fall of 1848. Many had tithed, the paper said, but had never made settlement since reaching the valley. Only those who settled their tithing could have their names entered in the church's sacred financial record, The Book of the Law of the Lord, and could receive certificates proving they were full tithepayers. They received one of four tithing certificates: for initiatory property tithes paid prior to 10 September 1851; for labor tithes; for increase tithes; and for property tithes paid in accordance with the 10 September 1851, covenant. "Each person ought to be able to show these four separate certificates to his Bishop this present season." After 1852, the editorial added, only the produce and labor tithing certificates would be required.

Saints, after covenanting, sent a stream of tithing that brought Hunter and staff new problems. The increase tithe and the labor tithe posed no challenge, but the property tithes on such things as a horse or a house did. "We have got to take one kind of property to pay tithing of another," a bishop pointed out. Hunter said that "When a man is industrious, and has only a span of horses and a cow, we don't want to cripple him. In such cases we will take hewed timber, Poles, wood, lumber, or labor."[12]

But how many feet of lumber was a horse worth? How much tithing labor was an adobe house worth? How many peaches was a cast-iron stove worth? In bishops meetings and by correspondence, the portly Bishop Hunter set standardized valuation and exchange rates. "Cows should be estimated from twenty to thirty dollars," Hunter advised, and oxen at $60 to $80 per yoke. He warned bishops not to appraise low. "When you find a first rate piece of property, put on a first rate price, and a poor piece of property in a decreasing rating." Tithing office clerks could not appraise properties, he announced; only he could.[13] By posting valuation and exchange rates, Hunter opened the door for all ward bishops to soon become tithing appraisers and receivers.

To aid the 1851 tithing settlement at church headquarters, Church Recorder Willard Richards issued a "Tithing Circular" on 15 November to tithing handlers in Utah and abroad. It called for full and accurate tithing records that listed when payments were received, by whom, and where, and also how, when, and to whom disposed. By October conference each year, it instructed, all tithing accounts should be submitted to the tithing office. Saints wishing to make tithing settlements must bring receipts from bishops to whom they paid tithes. Utah bishops should make semiannual reports of their tithing books at conferences. Bishop Hunter and his staff were "to see that all Bishops and agents do their duty, and report according to this circular." A year later, however, the historic 1852 circular cancelled these instructions.[14]

Hunter's office, lacking ward rosters and master lists of church members, had no way to know how well Saints were paying tithes. So, on 20 January 1852, he asked bishops to help him find out if their people paid tithing. This reversed roles. Previously, bishops wanting to know which ward members paid tithes would ask the General Tithing Office. But now Hunter asked bishops for that information. How could a ward bishop know who paid tithes at the central office? Only by asking each member. Hunter also pressed bishops to give him lists naming people unwilling to pay tithing. This act involved virtually every ward bishop for the first time in the tithing settlement process.[15]

In February 1852 ward bishops learned they soon would receive tithing ledgers, and that Bishop Hunter planned to build regional tithing storehouses, "with a cellar and upper Story." Hunter's assistant, Bishop Felt, advised bishops to obtain tubs for storing tithing butter, pork, eggs, and other perishables.[16]

Hunter finished settling the 1851 tithes on 25 March 1852. The First Presidency judged the year successful. "The brethren generally have been prompt in paying in one-tenth of their property according to their vote of last September Conference," they said, "and never before has the Lord's storehouse been so well supplied with wheat, meat, butter, eggs, vegetables, and other useful articles, and His pasture with cattle, as at the present time." However, church needs exceeded tithes received, forcing the church to pay one-fourth of its annual expenses from nontithing sources.[17]

After April 1852 conference the First Presidency published a rare disclosure of tithes. It shows that between November 1848, the last tithing settlement, and 27 March 1852, tithepayers paid property tithing in accord with the 10 September covenant of one-quarter million dollars.[18]

Capping the tithing push, the First Presidency made Edward Hunter's trial appointment permanent by ordaining him as presiding bishop at April conference in 1852. They also appointed five men as assistant presiding bishops: Seth Taft, David Pettigrew, Abraham Hoagland — three city bishops who retained their offices — and David Fullmer and Daniel Spencer of the Salt Lake Stake's presidency.[19]

Tithing merely trickled during the summer of 1852, stopping public works for want of materials and food. By fall the plan to make tithing a ward matter was finalized. No October conference talks of which we have record discuss the change, but during conference week Brigham Young told high priests of a "future plan" of bishops keeping their own books and of members settling their tithes with their bishops. At conference Bishops Nathaniel Felt, John Banks, and Alfred Cordon became traveling presiding bishops to assist Hunter.[20]

In November or December 1852, Bishop Hunter issued the historic circular instructing ward bishops to handle, record, process, and forward tithes at the ward level and hold annual tithing settlements with members—tasks his office had handled until then. The two-page, printed, undated circular is addressed "to bishop_____," is signed by Hunter, and includes a "postscript" by Brigham Young. "Hereafter, all the settlements of Tithing with those living in your branch or ward, will be made at your office" is the key phrase of the letter to the bishops.[21]

This major policy statement has been overlooked by historians because, somehow, a library cataloger mistakenly labeled it as an 1860s document. Not only does the context of tithing history date this document to 1852, but we also find a tithing instruction in 1859 that refers to a time when people settled tithing with the General Tithing Office "previous to the Bishops being authorized to do so in 1852."[22]

Tithepaying was being localized, the circular said, because a "rapid increase" in population meant that "our settlements have extended themselves for hundreds of miles on every side." Because of such growth, tithing management required that "some new arrangements" be created to produce "uniformity in all the branches."

The circular next discussed four tithing matters: bookkeeping, appraising, annual settlements, and disbursements.

Bookkeeping. Bishops were warned to "keep an accurate account of all tithing deposited with you" by using a daybook and a ledger. In the daybook "every item of tithing paid, should be plainly and distinctly entered to the credit of the individual." The daybook should be preserved until deposited in Hunter's office. The daybook accounts should be posted in the ledger book. "The necessary forms of Bookkeeping, settlements, reports, etc." accompanied the circular. Bishops should spell names properly and fully and should preserve and file away "all your receipts, orders, and due bills, with the names and dates endorsed on the back, as these will all be required in the settlement of your accounts."

Appraising. The circular gave bishops skimpy advice on how to assign values to donated tithing items. Regarding labor tithing, bishops should be governed "by your own judgment, taking the circumstances of the several cases into consideration." As a general rule bishops "will allow at the rate of a month for tilling 2 acres of land, and charge four dollars labor tithing per month for the residue of the year; eight dollars a year for tithing on team work for a yoke of oxen, span of horses, or mules, when the owner is not engaged in teaming for wages."

From cows either labor, butter, or a fee was expected: "When a tenth of butter is not paid, you will charge two dollars per annum for each cow." Bishops were told to state on their tithing settlement reports any reasons "why a man's labor tithing is less or more than the usual or general amount," and "if there are any reasons why any man's produce tithing is not as large as would ordinarily be expected."

Hunter inserted a reminder, humorous today but serious then, about quality tithing: "And we wish the Bishops in no wise to countenance nor receive old worn out oxen, kicking cows, scabby sheep." Young's postscript to the circular asked for good materials but insisted that tithes should be paid in the product produced, not with substitutes:

> The individual who neglects to pay a tenth of his butter, eggs, wool, stockings, cloth, &c, but pays the value thereof in wheat, potatoes, squashes, &c.; (while those who employ all their time and means, in rearing the Temple, and building up the Kingdom, are living with their families upon bread and water, and are destitute of the necessaries of life, or clothing to shield them from the inclemency of the weather,) has not fulfilled the law of tithing. Neither has that person who turns out the old broken-down horse, ox, or cow, while he retains the young and healthy stock, available property, or money in his own possession.

Annual tithing settlements. The circular gave most attention to settlements matters. At least once each year, or oftener, "a full settlement should be made, the books balanced, and the report made to this office, where the General Records are kept" so that "the same may be put upon the record in their proper places, and the individuals may receive a certificate from this office." Bishops and any clerks they employed should sign the reports because "you will be held accountable for all property put into your hand, as also for the correctness and safety of your books."

The circular listed sample questions for bishops to use during settlement interviews:

> Had you any property when you came into the valley, on which you had not paid tithing?
> Had you any money on hand?
> In what were you engaged during the year after you arrived?
> How much land did you till?
> How many teams had you?
> Did you pay a tenth of your Produce?
> Did you pay a tenth of your Hay?
> Did you pay a tenth of your Butter?
> Did you pay a tenth of your Eggs and Chickens?
> Did you make any thing by trading?
> How much did your property increase in your hands?
> Had you any increase of stock?

Disbursement. Regarding the distribution of collected tithes, the letter asked that "All the heavy articles of tithing" be forwarded "as heretofore" to the "General Tithing Store House," where receipts would be issued "which you will enter to their several accounts." Lighter items and "smaller articles of domestic production, such as butter, cheese, eggs, &c., you will receive and credit, and forward as circumstances will admit."

Bishops must not take lightly these new tithing duties, the letter warned: "We shall charge you here as Bishop, with the total amount of tithing received by you, from each person, and it will stand against you until you account for the manner in which the produce and other property have been disposed of." To supervise and train local bishops, "Traveling bishops" would visit the wards, inspect the tithing books, "audit all the accounts of your Ward, and assist in continuing a uniformity of system, and valuation of property."

Should nontithepayers be disciplined? No, Hunter advised, "It is your duty to see that your wards fulfill the Law of Tithing, or let it alone, and in accordance to their works, let their accounts be rendered to the General Office. As this is a matter between them and their

God, to us, it matters little whether they pay, or do not." Young's postscript underscored the point: "there is no compulsory or arbitrary power to be exercised over this brethren, in order to coerce the payment of tithing."

Closing the epistle, Bishop Hunter expressed his hopes for the new ward tithing plan: "A strict adherance to the instructions herein contained, will render the business throughout the Territory easy, safe, and uniform."

Although bishops' quorum minutes record no mention of the circular, several entries show that bishops knew of the ward tithing plan by the end of 1852. Hunter probably had the circular's instructions in mind at the 7 December meeting when he "remarked upon the multiplicity of business which was increasing upon the hands of the bishops and which before long will call for their whole time to be devoted to it." Also, the bishops gave tithing reports at the 21 December meeting, showing they were busily engaged by then in gathering tithes. In the Tenth Ward, for example, men "were fast settling up their labor tithing." Another bishop said that "none in his ward had refused to pay their tithing." Traveling Bishop Felt advised reluctant bishops that "twas not oppressive in a bishop in demanding the tithing."[23]

Trying out new tithing roles, some bishops encountered problems. In January 1853 Bishop Philip Klingonsmith of Cedar City sent Hunter a report but said he knew it was inadequate because he lacked account books and had never seen a correct form before. He also said he needed a storehouse, tithing office, and larger record books. Some people there claimed they had paid part of their tithes at Hunter's office, which Klingonsmith complained he had no way to verify.[24]

Bishop Abraham Hoagland of Salt Lake's Fourteenth Ward, responding to Hunter's circular, began a "Day Book for Tithing" on 11 December 1852.[25] The book has three hand-ruled columns in which Hoagland recorded daily tithing transactions during 1852 and 1853 by name, credits, and debits. A handful of women and 35 of the ward's 100 males are listed as donors. His busiest tithing month was March 1853, the last month for settling 1852 tithes. By categories, his March tithing transactions were:

Received:	Sent to Tithing Office:
Eggs 22.5 dozen	19 dozen eggs
Butter 5.5 lbs	4 lbs pork
Soft soap 20.5 lbs	2.75 lbs butter
pork, 4 lbs	basket
cloth, 5.5 yds.	garden seeds
coffee, .5 lb.	5.5 yds. cloth
garden seeds, 7 donations	
socks, 2 pr.	**Given to Ward Members:**
wood, 2 load	Sister Clement: 5 lbs soap,
basket	1.25 lbs sugar
blanket, potatoes	Mother Taylor: 5 lbs butter
sugar, 2 donations	Mother Snyder: Wood
	Bro Voorhees: Wood

His daybook lists only one tithing settlement—the others no doubt were entered in his missing ledger book, not now extant.

Utah tithepayers, including the 1851 covenanters, made 1852 a good tithing year despite the slack summer—whether or not ward bishops grasped their new tithing tasks. Late in 1852 the general storehouse contained fifteen thousand bushels of grain—a quantity so great that many felt Utah could never have a grain shortage (it did three years later). Bishop Elias Blackburn of Provo reported in November 1852 that: "The produce tithing is coming in well except the Wheat which has not yet been thrashed but I expect it ere long. There has been but few cattle paid in yet upon Property Tithing by the new comers Yet I believe they all manifest good disposition to pay up."[26] By mid-February 1853, Hunter observed that there was never a better spirit of tithepaying.[27]

Just before the April 1853 settlement deadline, Bishop Hunter reminded bishops to handle tithing settlements themselves rather than expecting his staff to do it. Ward bishops, he said, "know better how the brethren stood . . . than the clerks in the general office." Bishop Felt, liking the new ward tithing system, said he believed that the "time was just at hand when the whole temporal business of the church would devolve upon the bishops." The *Deseret News* reminded bishops that tithing returns were due at general conference. On 5 April, Traveling Bishop Cordon said that along his way to Provo he gave bishops forms to fill out and bring to conference.[28]

Tooele Bishop John Rowberry's postconference letter to Hunter shows some complications that distant bishops faced.[29] Rowberry, while settling tithing accounts at Richville and E T City, found some brethren who, because they maintained accounts with the General Tithing Office, refused to settle with him. His books therefore showed more unpaid tithing than was so. Produce tithing, he said, was lower than seemed right for their acreage, but their farms were new and lacked adequate water.

During April conference in 1853 Hunter's staff labored long hours to close the 1852 tithing books. Meanwhile, the church's need for tithes became visible on 6 April when Saints witnessed the laying of cornerstones for the Salt Lake Temple. Capitalizing on the occasion, several leaders called for tithes and consecrations to flow into the tithing house to "untie" leaders hands, overcome church indebtedness, and support the workmen. President Young wanted tithepayers to "be as prompt in paying, as you are in feeding your family," so the temple could rise quickly.[30]

The 1852 tithing season ended quietly in April 1853. Conference sermons, bishops' quorum minutes, and the First Presidency's 13 April general epistle neither laud nor berate the new ward tithing method. The epistle does note that "storehouses generally are in the various settlements."[31]

Hunter found it remarkable that during the weeks and months after the conference, surprisingly little was said from pulpits regarding tithing.[32]

New church programs, even then, required more time to implement than leaders expected. It took the ward tithing system three years to root firmly. Bishops' quorum minutes for 1854–55 show that some bishops adapted well, while others seemed confused and hesitant. Some Saints disliked paying and settling tithes with their own bishop. Current events, such as the 1854 consecration movement, the 1855 drought, changes in bishoprics, and moves by ward members hampered tithing operations.

The biggest problem plaguing the ward tithing system was bad bookkeeping. During the new system's first year, many bishops discovered their accounting inadequacies. To help them, General Tithing Office clerk Howard Coray gave the bishops' quorum bookkeeping instructions on 30 August.[33]

The bishops' second tithing settlement season lasted from the fall of 1853 to April conference in 1854. That winter Bishop Hunter and staff devoted "constant attention" to "heavy business" at the General Tithing Office. Early in 1854 Bishop Edwin Woolley predicted that recent "smooth doings" regarding tithing matters would soon change into a "storm." Look well to your wards, he advised bishops, "and have the tithing as straight up as possible."[34]

On the eve of the April conference, some tithepayers seemed confused about how to settle their accounts. Bishop Cordon, who was both a traveling bishop and General Tithing Office clerk, reported that "a question arised with many, where shall we settle our tithing? Some said settle with your bishop, but some said at the general office."[35]

That April conference brought no tithing "storm," but, instead, the First Presidency reintroduced the law of consecration. Consecration, however, was a second option for members, and the tithing system continued in place. In fact, some members "over Jordan" chose not to consecrate but salved their consciences by "overpaying their tithing."[36]

Tithing storm clouds billowed in July 1854 when the First Presidency urgently called for tithes to keep public works crews working. Bishops should immediately send to Bishop Hunter all tithing products within a 100–mile radius of Salt Lake City. The First Presidency asked bishops to compile and send in names of all who should pay tithing, and opposite each name bishops should note "the amount of wheat and all other grain, and of potatoes, and all other vegetables he raises this season as fast as it can be ascertained; also the amount of stock owned by each person, specifying the yearly increases; and in short, state all the items upon which a saint should rightfully pay tithing, keeping each item in a separate column." Bishop Hunter advised that ward teachers help bishops compile the lists.[37]

Neither tithes nor lists funneled properly into church headquarters, finally unleashing the storms Woolley had predicted in the form of heated reprimands. One struck that fall, another the next spring, and a final one the next fall during the fiery Mormon Reformation. Together the storms produced a fully baked ward tithing system from a half-baked one.

The first storm struck during Sunday tabernacle services on 5 November 1854 when President Brigham Young preached both morning and afternoon about tithing. He knew not one bishop who understood tithing, he said, criticizing specifically those who thought consecration was an extension of tithing, not tithing's predecessor. People needed picks and wedges, he said, to open their eyes to tithing. "It is the Tithing Office that has built up this city and territory," he asserted, and warned that "if the people do not observe the law of tithing, they will dwindle & be cursed. You cannot play with it. It will make you bleed."[38]

His fiery sermon brought almost instant results, as Heber C. Kimball, his counselor, reported on 26 November: "Since President Young and others have dwelt upon tithing, it is coming in first rate." Kimball then poked fun at Bishop Hunter: "Bishop Hunter has become frightened; 'Good heavens' says he, 'what shall we do with the tithing. We have not got room to put it.' 'Why,' says I, 'stretch out, Bishop.' "[39]

Brigham Young issued a second blast during the April 1855 conference.[40] He told forty bishops assembled in quorum meeting to "wake up and learn to do their duty." "The bishops must be corrected," he continued, "must be striped." He then chided them about poor records. "You do not seem to understand your office," he accused, "there never has been a bishop yet who has made a report that would give me any knowledge of the condition of his ward." "It is the bishops' duty to prepare an account book, and in the beginning of the year to know every man, woman, and child in his ward, and should know their occupation, and how they employ their time." He ordered bishops to "Make a schedule of your wards, make a return sheet so that Bishop Hunter can read it right; and know how many Oxen, Horses, Cows, Sheep, Lambs, Pigs, Fowls of all Kinds, Eggs, Butter, and Cheese, Produce of every kind, and money; also the profit on their goods." Only with such information could bishops know that tithing was properly paid.

Some bishops, he said, complained that such a job required their full time, something they could not give. "Well let it take up all your time," he said, "and trust in the Lord for a living." Bishops unwilling to do their duty should resign. "The Bishops should be business men," he warned. "Go to now and make a book; it is as simple as A.B.C." Bookkeeping could be learned "in five minutes." "Make a schedule of every man's property, and see that the tithing is paid" and "that it is put to proper use." Bishops should visit those who refuse to tithe and work with them. "The tithing belongs to the Lord," he concluded, "and there wants to be a concentration of faith, and a uniformity in business transactions."

Bishop Hunter, as chief trainer of bishops, pledged that "We will try until we get a report that will be accepted by our President." Keeping his word, Hunter told bishops on 15 May 1855 that "We got a few reproofs at Conference," and then he called for reform: "I would like the bishops to feel this storm, and arouse themselves, for they have been lukewarm. I want the Bishops to make out faithful reports—we will have a form printed and distributed among the bishops."[41]

To bishops who had not accepted the new ward tithing system he bluntly said: "It is intended that the Bishops settle with their own wards." A big discussion followed about how "to settle properly with ward members," including the need to visit members in their homes. One bishop rejoiced at the instructions given, "even though we do get a lashing now and then."[42]

Bookkeeping reform was in the wind that summer—along with deadly grasshoppers and a withering drought. Bishop Hunter sent out a new trainer, a Brother Hutchinson, to teach bishops bookkeeping. In June, Hunter informed bishops that instructions about how to settle tithes, as well as printed forms, were being mailed to them. On 31 July he "had an interview with Br. Hutchinson, who is instructing the Bishops on the method of settling with their wards, and how to keep their books. I was much pleased with his ideas on the subject of tithing. I am pleased he is with us." Hutchinson visited the city bishops and planned to revisit. He urged bishops to obtain competent clerks "which would be a great help to them, and prevent much confusion."[43]

The church's tithing bookkeeping system changed dramatically in 1855. Ledgers in the LDS Archives show that "in 1855 the General Tithing Storehouse began a system of ledgers for each ward."[44] In these books "the ward clerk or bishop would enter the donations received from the member of the ward. Then when the bishop brought the goods to the General Tithing Storehouse, the clerk in the Tithing Office entered them into the Bishops' Ledgers." Brother Hutchinson apparently designed the new record system. One researcher noted: "Probably he (Hutchinson) took the economic census form and adapted it to fit the Church's need. The columns listed almost everything possible the person could own (excluding household items) or produce. In the early schedules the bishop listed not only the tithing paid, but also everything the person owned, but very quickly the bishop listed only the tithing paid."[45] Starting in 1855, records show, ward tithing schedules first were sent into the General Tithing Office. At that office the schedules were later bound into three volumes: one for Salt Lake City, one for wards south of the city, and one for wards north.[46]

Drought and insects dried up the 1855 tithing flows. At October 1855 conference Brigham Young, sensing guilt among those who had nothing to tithe, told bishops that "it [tithing] is not required if a man has labored faithfully to produce, and his crops have failed." Hunter, anxious that bishops adopt the new bookkeeping system, added that "he wished the bishops clerks to be diligent, and to practice writing and accounts so as to make themselves proficient for their duty."[47]

Bishop Joseph Harker's experience in Butterfield Ward in southwest Salt Lake Valley illustrates how those first ward tithing settlements were conducted. His diary notes that on 9 December 1855 he "gave some instruction on tithing settlement" at a ward meeting. Several days later he "took two horses on tithing." Christmas Eve day he went to Salt Lake City "to get some council on tithing matters." On Christmas Day he "made some tithing settlements." The next day he "went to Harriman to make tithing settlements, 3 days." On 29 December he "came home via Mill Branch and made some tithing settlements." Two days later he settled more tithing. On 4 January he wrote that some members disliked having him press them for their tithes: "I was making tithing settlements, some of the members said they should settle tithing when they pleased." He spent a week until 12 January at Mill Creek settling tithing. He next mentioned tithing on 13 February when he "was settling my tithing books." Two weeks later he was "settling my tithing books" with a Brother Bennion. He then turned in his tithing records at Hunter's office, and "took Bishop Hunter's council in relation to deficits in the ward."[48]

Public works director Wells lamented that 1855 and early 1856 had been "financially disastrous" for the church because of drought. Compassionately, leaders did not chastize members for the small tithing totals for 1855.[49]

The 1856 tithing year began in famine but ended with a good harvest. That fall the purifying Mormon Reformation produced the third storm that scorched bishops about tithing, including Bishop Hunter. "There has been too much mere talking" about tithing, First Presidency Counselor Jedediah M. Grant warned him. "Talking so much and not doing is one of the grand evils; it is not for the Bishop to merely talk about people's paying their tithing, and say that they are good fellows, &c., but we want him to *know* that the people pay their tithing, and that they are right." He challenged Hunter to bring those facts to Brigham Young, "reporting faithfully the situation of all the Bishops in the Church, and how they stand in their accounts with the General Tithing Office." Grant told Hunter to call in the tithes in outlying settlements and not wait until April conference by which time cats, goats, ducks, rats, mice, geese, and rot would reduce the stored grain.[50]

By late 1856 Latter-day Saints and bishops knew that paying and settling tithing was a ward matter. During subsequent years Bishop Hunter, through sermons, circulars, and personal contacts, reminded and updated bishops about how to collect, record, store, and disburse tithes.

The success of annual ward tithing settlements varied year by year due to current events and bishops' talents. In 1857, for example, men on winter military duty in the Utah War could not settle their tithing accounts properly. In 1858 the "move south" disrupted tithing storehouses, payments, and bookkeeping. The year 1859 was the first full tithing year which might be termed "normal" for the ward tithing system—not disrupted by consecration movements, famine, reformation, or war.

The ward tithing system started in 1852 and was fully implemented in 1855. Since then, the church has adopted many procedural changes to upgrade accounting methods, improve storage, guide disbursements and uses of tithes, and switch from tithing in kind to a cash system. Despite such changes, the plan established in 1852, requiring ward bishops to be the primary tithing agents of the church, continues to be the basic administrative system for managing "the Lord's Tenth."

NOTES

1. Leonard J. Arrington, *Great Basin Kingdom* (Lincoln: University of Nebraska Press, 1966); Arrington, "The Mormon Tithing House: A Frontier Business Institution," *Business History Review* 28 (March 1954); Arrington, Feramorz Y. Fox, and Dean L. May, *Building the City of God* (Salt Lake City: Deseret Book, 1976); D. Gene Pace, "Changing Patterns of Mormon Financial Administration: Traveling Bishops, Regional Bishops, and Bishop's Agents, 1851-88," *BYU Studies* 23 (Spring 1983): 183-95; Dale Beecher, "The Office of Bishop," *Dialogue* 15 (Winter 1982): 103-15; Richard O. Cowan, *The Church in the Twentieth Century* (Salt Lake City: Bookcraft, 1985), 16-18, 294-97.

2. Edward Hunter, "Circular," (186-?), Library, Historical Department, Church of Jesus Christ of Latter-day Saints, Salt Lake City, Utah, cited hereafter as LDS Church Library. Date should read 1852.

3. Journal History, 7 October 1849, Archives, Historical Department, Church of Jesus Christ of Latter-day Saints, Salt Lake City, Utah, cited hereafter as LDS Church Archives.

4. Albert Carrington Journals, Tithing Accounts, 1848-1854, microfilm of holograph, LDS Church Archives.

5. Council Meeting, Minutes, Brigham Young Collection, 13, 14, and 16 February 1849, LDS Church Archives; Journal History, 14 and 16 February 1849.

6. Presiding Bishop's Meetings with Bishops, cited hereafter as Bishops Minutes, LDS Church Archives, 25 March 1849.

7. Journal History, 27 September 1850 and 14 December 1850.

8. First Presidency Fifth General Epistle, 7 April 1851, in James R. Clark, ed., *Messages of the First Presidency*, 6 vols. (Salt Lake City: Bookcraft, 1965), 2:65.

9. Journal History, 7 April 1851.

10. First Presidency Sixth General Epistle, 22 September 1851, in Clark, *Messages*, 2:90.

11. Journal History, 10 September 1851.

12. Bishops Minutes, 28 September 1851.

13. Ibid.; Journal History, 29 November 1851.

14. *Millennial Star* 14 (1 April 1852).

15. Bishops Minutes, 28 January and 11 February 1852.

16. Ibid., 25 February 1852.

17. First Presidency's Seventh General Epistle, 18 April 1852, in Clark, *Messages*, 2:92; Brigham Young Sermon, 9 April 1852, in *Journal of Discourses*, 26 vols. (Liverpool: F. D. Richards, 1855), 1:51–52.

18. First Presidency Seventh General Epistle, 18 April 1852, in Clark, *Messages*, 2:95–97.

19. Ibid., 97.

20. Journal History, 7 and 8 October 1852.

21. Edward Hunter, "Circular," (186–?) [1852].

22. Presiding Bishopric, "Instructions to the Bishops," booklet, 23 November 1859, LDS Church Library, 6.

23. Bishops Minutes, 21 December 1852.

24. Bishop Philip Klingonsmith to Edward Hunter, 12 January 1853, Hunter Incoming Correspondence Folder 4, LDS Church Archives.

25. Abraham Hoagland Daybook, holograph, LDS Church Archives, entries for December 1852 to April 1853.

26. Elias H. Blackburn to Hunter, 19 November 1852, Hunter Incoming Correspondence Folder 4, LDS Church Archives.

27. Bishops Minutes, 15 February 1853.

28. Bishops Minutes, 15 March 1853; Journal History, 19 March 1853; Alfred Cordon to Hunter, 5 April 1853, Hunter Incoming Correspondence, Folder 4, LDS Church Archives.

29. John Rowberry to Hunter, 25 April 1853, Hunter Incoming Correspondence, Folder 4, LDS Church Archives.

30. Journal History, 6 April 1853.

31. Bishops Minutes, 9 April 1853; First Presidency's Ninth General Epistle, 13 April 1853, in Clark, *Messages*, 2:113.

32. Bishops Minutes, 7 June and 19 July 1853.

33. Ibid., 30 August 1853.

34. Ibid., 8 October and 20 December 1853 and 14 February 1854.

35. Ibid., 28 March 1854.

36. Ibid., 25 April 1854.

37. Journal History, 20 July 1854.

38. Thomas Bullock Minutes, Tabernacle Meeting, 5 November 1854, in Brigham Young Papers, LDS Church Archives.

39. Sermon by Heber C. Kimball, 26 November 1854, in *Journal of Discourses*, 2:157–158.

40. Bishops Minutes, 7 April 1855.

41. Ibid., 7 April and 15 May 1855.

42. Ibid., 15 May 1855.

43. Ibid., 19 June and 31 July 1855.

44. Ronald G. Watt, "Church Financial Records in the Nineteenth Century," research paper in Watt's personal files.

45. Ibid.
46. Ibid.
47. Bishops Minutes, 8 October 1855.
48. Joseph Harker, Journal, film of holograph, LDS Church Archives.
49. Journal History, 11 March 1856.
50. Bishops Minutes, 8 October 1856.

Brigham Young and the Bishops: The United Order in the City*

DEAN L. MAY

Contemporary Latter-day Saints are prone to think of the United Order movement of the 1870s as a spontaneous effort at economic reform undertaken on their own initiative by a few extremists in southern Utah. As with most folk perceptions, the image is not entirely devoid of truth. Commitment to the United Order was stronger in rural areas and perhaps especially so in the southern part of the Mormon domain. And the southern Utah town of Orderville, founded in 1875 for the express purpose of living the United Order of Enoch in its most communal form, has tended for most people to symbolize the whole Mormon experience with communitarian reform.

Yet, far from being a momentary enthusiasm of a fringe group, the movement had its beginning and received its main impetus from central church leaders, especially Brigham Young and George A. Smith. It was as general a program among Mormons of the late 1870s as "correlation" was in the 1970s, with broadsides delineating the "Rules of the United Order" posted prominently in meeting-houses, advocacy in sermons at both general and local gatherings, and a wave of rebaptisms signifying commitment to the Order. Over two hundred United Orders were organized, with officers chosen and bylaws adopted, in communities the length and breadth of Mormondom.[1]

* This paper was prepared for a lecture series titled "Salt Lake City: Cross-roads of the West," sponsored by the Utah State Historical Society under a grant from the Utah Endowment for the Humanities. Lisa Viperman assisted in the perusal of newspaper files and Margaret Mower in typing the manuscript.

It is interesting that the limited present-day perception of the movement might reflect not only ignorance of the past but general subsequent adoption of a contemporary Salt Lake City urban view of the Order—as if Salt Lakers of the 1870s had been the nearly unchallenged perceivers and purveyors to subsequent generations of attitudes toward the United Order of Enoch now characteristic of Mormons generally. Certain it is that in 1874 Salt Lake City Latter-day Saints were cool towards the Order, taking it up slowly and halfheartedly and giving it up with alacrity. The story of the fate of the United Order in the city offers insights into the movement generally, while at the same time giving an instructive glimpse into the nature of Salt Lake City's church at the time. Moreover, Salt Lake City's reception of the United Order offers an occasion for worthwhile broader reflections on the fate of efforts to reform through voluntary means long-established economic systems.

The United Order of Enoch was officially launched in February 1874 at St. George, Utah, the aging Brigham Young's winter retreat and center of the cotton settlement mission begun in 1861. Sermons urging greater economic cooperation had been common since the late 1860s, when the cooperative movement leading to establishment of Zion's Cooperative Mercantile Institution was launched. They became more persistent and direct during the fall and winter of 1873–74. On 14 February 1874, after private meetings with local leaders, Brigham Young called an extraordinary general priesthood meeting for Mormon men from the St. George area. There he announced that "the time had arrived when we should conform to the Revelations . . . to be one. To enter into this friendly, brotherly, labor is the present duty of the Saints. . . . The question," he continued, "is are we ready, and are we willing? The answer is with the people themselves." At Sunday meetings the next day the call to a more inclusive cooperative program was made to the general public. Though the minutes do not reveal what details might have attended the call, three hundred people signified their commitment by signing a United Order Roll.[2] The St. George census precinct in 1874 had approximately 1,239 total inhabitants, which would indicate about 245 households. Evidently the St. George Saints were nearly all willing to make an initial pledge, at least, to the new program.[3] Moreover, enrollments continued to increase over the next two weeks.

Delighted with the response, Young shortly announced the plan to his counselors in Salt Lake City, Daniel H. Wells and Albert Carrington. His telegram, dated 28 February, read:

> We have organized six companies after the order of Enoch, two in St. George, one in Clara Settlement, one in Washington, one in Harrisburg, and one in Leeds and we go up the river next week to organize the settlements. The Brethren and Sisters all seem ready to go into the order of oneness, heart and hand, and all the settlements are pressing us to come and organize them preparatory for the spring work. Thank the Lord, the people are so prepared for it. With the fire of the gospel burning thus brightly, we need not fear the efforts of our enemies.
>
> We hope that some of the brethren in the city will feel like organizing some companies there before our return. We would like you brethren to meet and adjourn conference from sixth April to first Thursday in May. What do you think of this?
> B.Y. [Brigham Young]
> G.A.S. [George A. Smith][4]

The telegram reveals some of what lay behind Brigham Young's decision to launch the Order. First, there is evident in the message something of a siege mentality (note the reference to "our enemies") that is common in Young's other writings and sermons of the time as well. It arose partly from a fear that Latter-day Saint influence would be diminished by the great tide of Gentiles that had flowed into Utah in the pursuit of mining and commercial opportunities since completion of the railroad in 1869. Concerns raised by these important changes were heightened by the onset of a general depression following the panic of 1873. Records of local Mormon bishops at the time make frequent reference to the great increase in the number of families requiring assistance. The two phenomena were linked in Young's mind — the suffering brought by the depression being a consequence of the degree to which the Utah economy had become intertwined with that of the nation. As Young saw it the United Order would weaken that interdependence and thus insulate Mormons from national cycles of boom and bust.

Also evident in the telegram is relief that the movement seemed to be generally acceptable to the people. Young's earlier doubts of 14 February that his followers were ready for the reform had been belied by his experience in the St. George area and he seemed enormously pleased with the enthusiastic response of the Saints there.

Apparently Young attached great importance to the United Order both as a culmination of Joseph Smith's short-lived Consecration and Stewardship program of the 1830s and as a foil against gentile influence among the Saints. There is an almost audible sigh of relief in his triumphant announcement to the Salt Lake brethren: "Thank the Lord, the people are so prepared for it."

Finally, the instructions to the city dwellers are of importance. Expressing the hope that some companies of the Order would be organized before his return, Young nonetheless took the highly unusual step of suggesting that the church's semiannual general conference be postponed until he could be on hand personally to launch the new reform.

The United Order of Enoch was not to follow precisely the Law of Consecration and Stewardship that Joseph Smith began teaching in 1831. Smith announced his call to communalism in a revelation called "The Law of the Church" received on 8 February of that year. The revelation required the faithful to "consecrate of thy properties . . . with a covenant and a deed which cannot be broken." These consecrations "shall be laid before the bishop of my church," who then would assign "stewardships" or assignments of homes, supplies, and materials needed for the communicant to make a livelihood in his chosen profession. For this property "every man shall be made accountable unto me, a steward over his own property, or that which he has received by consecration, as much as is sufficient for himself and family." Any surplus was to be "kept in my storehouse, to administer to the poor and the needy, as shall be appointed by the high council of the church and the bishop and his council; and for the purpose of purchasing lands for the public benefit of the church, and building houses of worship, and building up of the New Jerusalem."⁵

This surplus was to be gathered systematically in an annual voluntary "consecration" or donation of whatever the steward might produce above what was necessary for the support of his family. The exact amount of the donation was to be worked out through negotiation with the bishop in an annual stewardship interview — a vestige of which remains among the Mormons in their annual tithing interview.

Though the entire system was attempted only during the early 1830s in Jackson County, Missouri, efforts were made at later times to identify and collect a surplus from the Saints. Brigham Young recalled that one such campaign, undertaken at Far West, Missouri, in 1838 met with less than satisfactory results.

> I found the people said they were willing to do about as they were counselled, but, upon asking them about their surplus property, most of the men who owned land and cattle would say, "I have got so many hundred acres of land, and I have got too many boys, and I want each one of them to have eighty acres, therefore this is not surplus property. . . ."
>
> Some were disposed to do right with their surplus property, and once in a while you would find a man who had a cow which he considered surplus, but generally she was of the class that would kick a person's hat off, or eyes out or the wolves had eaten off her teats. You would once in a while find a man who had a horse that he considered surplus, but at the same time he had the ringbone, and was broken-winded, spavined in both legs, and had the pole evil at one end of the neck and a fistula at the other, and both knees sprung.[6]

Despite such disappointments the communal ideal continued to nag at the Mormon consciousness. One consequence was the almost spontaneous outburst of enthusiasm for consecrating property to the church between 1854 and 1858, a period when several thousand heads of household recorded deeds assigning all their property, real and personal, to Brigham Young as trustee for the church. Though the church never took possession of property thus subscribed, the incident testifies eloquently to the fact that Joseph Smith's call to a communal economy had by no means been forgotten. The same impulse was manifested again in the cooperative movement of the late 1860s that led to the founding of dozens of producers' cooperatives in addition to nearly one hundred fifty retail cooperative stores, most part of the Zion's Cooperative Mercantile Institution (ZCMI) system founded at that time. The sermons urging establishment of these cooperative enterprises in fact merge with those of the early 1870s urging a more complete form of cooperation and finally in 1874 calling the Saints to live the United Order of Enoch.

As Brigham Young proceeded to organize the Order in virtually every Mormon settlement in southern and central Utah, church leaders in Salt Lake City seemed hesitant to act. General conference was convened on Monday, 6 April, and one address was given by Apostle Orson Pratt. Pratt's speech was carefully designed to present a general rationale for a more even distribution of wealth and division of labor. He stressed that continuous revelation provided Mormonism constant guidance and inspired adaptation of God's general principles to changing specific circumstances. He identified maldistribution of wealth as the great cause of class consciousness and divisiveness in the world. Economic equality was God's will, he explained, but this did not imply uniformity; on the contrary, he said, "God delights in variety." He then admitted quite openly that he did not know any specifics as to what the United Order was to mean for Salt Lake City. "I would tell you as much as I thought was wisdom, if I understood it myself, but I do not; I have had but very little information about it."[7] His only firm information was that it would not be precisely the same as Consecration and Stewardship had been in Missouri, because circumstances were different in 1874, and that it would be voluntary. After the speech, conference was adjourned, to be convened again on 7 May, as Brigham Young had proposed in his telegram.

Pratt's sermon could have done little to help dispel rumors that had been flying through the city since Brigham Young first began the program in St. George on 14 February. Daniel H. Wells had preached on the subject in Salt Lake City by 6 March, according to Sixteenth Ward bishop Frederick Kesler, and the next day an evening meeting was held at the city hall "where we heard something in relation to cooperatives in the southern portion of our territory."[8] The *Deseret News*, a Mormon-controlled newspaper, was surprisingly hesitant to comment on the United Order, at least until Young arrived in Salt Lake City late in April to launch the movement officially.[9] The non-Mormon *Tribune*, on the other hand, was quick to note and comment on the Order, offering, from early in March, an almost continuous series of articles on the subject. Notices from their correspondent in Beaver, Utah, were published on 7 March, reporting that Young had "browbeat" nearly every property owner in St. George into joining the United Order and deeding all their property to the church. "Only about a dozen hold out against him," the report said, "and he has probably persuaded those into it by this time, or cut them off." The early *Tribune* articles stressed that the movement was an effort on the part of Young to consolidate his power over Mormons by taking control of their property. Some Mormons in Beaver, the 7 March report read, "say that he wishes to get hold of their property, then he can compel them to do anything he orders or excommunicate them. May this order of Enoch be the enterprising wedge that shall rend the fabric of priestcraft and bestiality, is the prayer of all non-Mormons in this vicinity."

A letter also published in the 7 March *Tribune* reviewed Mormon communal efforts in the past, concluding that while people in southern Utah seemed to be enthusiastic about the Order, "the Lord (i.e. Brigham) cannot enforce . . . [its acceptance] where Gentile influences prevail . . . hence the necessity for taking the initiatory step at St. George, where the 'D----d Gentiles' cannot interfere. This ecclesiastical communism will be beautiful for Brigham and his pals, if they can carry it, but not quite so lovely for their dupes."[10] The overall effect of these reports must surely have been to raise fears among the more affluent Salt Lakers that the United Order, whatever it might prove to be, threatened to alter their economic status for the worse. The *Tribune* was fomenting rumors certain to fill city dwellers with doubt and reluctance long before Brigham Young was on hand to offer his own rationale for the movement. Moreover, those most likely to read and hear of the *Tribune* pieces would be the more affluent, including the bishops, whose support would be vital to the success of the Order.

The *Tribune* writers went beyond their portrayal of the United Order as a threat to the pocketbook, however. Probably equally effective was a campaign to discredit and destroy the movement through ridicule. In early March they suggested a logo for the United Order: "A man, (Brigham), holding a bag, and crowds of the brethren rushing up to fill it—the priests, elders and teachers in the distance in ecstacies over the scene." On 11 March they described meetings held in a Provo ward, noting that "after dwelling at length upon the merits of freeing yourselves from all earthly encumbrances, by conveying the same to Brigham, who is able to bear them," the local leaders concluded by "promising the over-burdened people of Provo that they, as well as the inhabitants of St. George, should soon be blessed with that privilege." Part of a ten-stanza poem printed on 12 March went:

Poor, innocent Mormons, this Order have joined;
Their souls and their bodies, away they have signed;
Their houses and lands, with their chattels combined!
In Heaven, expecting, on record to find,
The *deeds* of the 'Order of Enoch.'

Tribune writers had a field day with a suggestion the church president made in Fillmore that wooden-soled shoes would reduce dependence upon outside manufactures. "The 'United Order' wooden shoes have more than cheapness to recommend them," they gibed. "They persuade polygamous wives into subjection, and mothers-in-law stand in awe of them. They are also good for trampling bugs in the garden." The rotund George A. Smith preached on the United Order in Provo. *Tribune* writers claimed that after his sermon, Smith jumped from the podium, the impact causing his wooden shoes to fall to pieces. "George is now wearing imported brogans," they concluded. By 27 March, the *Tribune* pieces were referring to the movement as the United Order of "Euchre," equating it with a notoriously risky card game popular in saloons and gambling halls. From that time on their editors used the word routinely in place of Enoch. For example, they expressed doubt that merchants William Hooper and William Jennings, "would turn over their large and valuable property to the Euchre, without a sign or tear. . . . Taking an 'outsider' view of this, we would advise the brethren to wait until those gentlemen walk up to the captain's office and 'turn over.' "[11] On 19 April they quipped, "A countryman coming into the city, felt somewhat anxious about the Euchre business, and thus interrogated Bishop Hunter [Presiding Bishop of the LDS Church]: 'Say, Bishop, what dost thou know about Enoch?' 'Enoch, Enoch,' replied the Bishop, 'don't know, don't know any man that does know.' How is that for Euchre?"

Thus from mid-February through April, while the city Mormons waited for a reconvened conference to give them authoritative word on the reform, rumors and ridicule were bandied about the city and attitudes formed and set. Though meetings were held in some wards to organize before Young's return, and numerous preachments were made on the subject, it was clear that during all this time no one knew for sure what the United Order would actually mean to the ordinary citizen. Of a meeting in Provo, the *Tribune* reported that though the local leaders were "always willing to obey the commands of Brigham," none seemed to know much about the Order. They were nonetheless willing to embrace the movement, for "Brigham was the Profit."[12]

Young reached the city late in April and began immediately a campaign to overcome the Salt Lakers' reluctance to accept the United Order. Regular Sunday meetings in the Tabernacle on 26 April were devoted almost entirely to the reform.[13] The next Wednesday, 29 April, Young organized the Twentieth Ward (between South Temple and Seventh Avenue and C and H streets, adjacent to his own ward on the east) and a slate of officers was elected. The *Deseret News* gave a terse report of this first United Order founding in Salt Lake City, thus lending some credibility to the more elaborate report of the *Tribune*. The church president, *Tribune* writers maintained, had modified his program to request consecration (or donation) of time, talent, and industry, but not necessarily of money. "If they have not faith to put in their means they are welcome to retain it in their own hands." Even with this considerable concession only thirty of approximately six hundred raised their hands in support of the Order. This "visibly chagrined Brigham but he used control rather than fury until there were fifty hands raised. He said that would be enough for a start."[14]

Again on 3 May, Sunday meetings at the Tabernacle were devoted to the United Order. When the delayed general conference convened on 7 May, Young set the agenda by asking those who would be speaking "to give us their instructions and views for or against this general co-operative system, which we, with propriety, may call the United Order." He avoided any discussion of the specific workings of the program however, emphasizing its broader aims in abstract terms. "I ask of my brethren who may address the congregations, to give us their views for and against union, peace, good order; laboring for the benefit of ourselves, and in connection with each other for the welfare and happiness of all, whether in the capacity of a family, neighborhood, city, state, nation or the world." Most of the world, he maintained, was like the man, who, asking a blessing on the food, prayed, "O Lord, bless me and my wife, my son, John, and his wife, we four, and no more. Amen." The United Order, Young insisted, did not presage "any new system, order or doctrine. . . . Our object is to labor for the benefit of the whole, to retrench in our expenditures; to be prudent and economical; to study well the necessities of the community, and to pass by its many useless wants; to study to secure life, health, wealth, and union, which is power and influence to any community." Noting the benefits to be gained by sharing farm equipment and becoming more self-sufficient, Young again asked subsequent speakers to voice their opinions for or against the Order.[15]

It is no surprise that the high church officials present stood up in turn to endorse the program Young had announced. Young's counselor in the First Presidency, George A. Smith, tied the reform to Mormon millennial expectations, maintaining that "the establishment of the United Order, is another step towards the triumph of that great and glorious work for which we are continually laboring, namely the dawning of the Millennium and the commencement of the reign of Christ on the earth." John Taylor, of the Quorum of Twelve Apostles, saw the Order as the culmination of a long tradition of Latter-day Saint cooperative practices. The Saints, he said, had long prayed for this moment, "yet when it comes along it startles us, we are confused and hardly know what to think of it." The movement, he maintained, would build unity, free Mormons from dependence on goods brought by the railroad, and make them self-sustaining. Apostle Erastus Snow emphasized that "The Order proposed before us affords the utmost freedom and liberty. All things shall be done by common consent." It would counter a trend of the last dozen years, during which "this people have been going on in the way that our fathers and the world generally walk in; and instead of building up Zion have been after their personal and individual interests."[16]

The conference seemed for the moment to stir up general enthusiasm for the Order of Enoch. Bishop Frederick Kesler wrote in his diary that ten thousand attended the meetings on 9 May, "nearly all voting in favor of the U.O."[17] By 3 June all but the Eighteenth and Fourth of Salt Lake City's nineteen functioning wards had held meetings to form branches of the United Order and elect officers. (The Sixth Ward was not organized at the time and Third Ward advocates of the Order joined the Eighth Ward Order.)[18] Yet, there seemed still to be no general understanding of what precisely the urban

Orders were to do, beyond electing officers. In the rural communities of southern Utah, where the ward and the town were virtually the same, and where nearly everyone was a farmer, the process of organizing production and consumption under a central administration was relatively simple and manageable. Salt Lake City, in contrast, had developed a more modern and complex economy, with most church members being wage earners whose economic livelihoods could not readily be subsumed under the Order. Given these fundamental differences, how was the United Order to function in the urban setting? Young seemed to offer no clear answer to that question.

When Young organized the Twentieth Ward Order he is reported to have concluded the meeting by saying that the Saints would have "a thousand and one questions to ask but there would not be time to reply to them." Neither the conference sermons nor the preachments accompanying ward organizations seemed to answer those questions. After three efforts were made to found an order in the Third Ward (south of Sixth South and East Temple to Third East), the bishop, Jacob Weiler, finally concluded, "He had been a good Mormon and wanted to continue being a good Mormon, paid his tithing and his donations, but would not join the U.O. or anything else he did not understand."[19] As noted above, Third Warders favoring the reform joined the Eighth Ward Order. On Wednesday, 3 June, Ninth Ward Bishop Samuel A. Woolley (the ward extended from Third South to Sixth South and from Third East to Sixth East) confided to his diary that the Order "seems to annoy about everybody for we do not understand it."[20]

The failure of church leaders to think out carefully how the United Order was to be applied in an urban setting no doubt was a major factor inhibiting wholehearted acceptance of the reform. The evidence would in fact seem to indicate that the city Saints, while quite willing to organize on paper and elect a set of officers for each Order, were notably reluctant to join the order themselves and commit their energies to its success. When the United Order was organized in the Ninth Ward, Bishop Woolley wrote with what seems deliberate precision, that there was "not a dissenting vote on the officers." He does not say whether there were dissenting votes on other matters affecting the Order or how fully his congregation supported the effort. Visiting the Third Ward during one of its organizational meetings, he noted that "a very few joined the order."[21] Wishing to appear upbeat, the editors of the *Deseret News* reported each ward's organization, with such comments as "Officers were elected unanimously," or "The utmost unanimity prevailed and the following officers were elected." It may be significant, however, that only once did they report membership, which in the First Ward was a reasonable 115. Bishop Alonzo Raleigh of the Nineteenth Ward (covering the west Capitol Hill area from Second North to Fifth North and from First West to the hill), himself a strong supporter of the movement, recorded that eighty-five joined in his ward. However, only ten or eleven of the four-hundred-member Eleventh Ward joined the Order. The vote for the reform in the Tenth Ward, *Tribune* writers reported, was "painfully light—the dupes in the Tenth Ward are by no means numerous." In the Seventeenth Ward "only fifteen joined the fraud."[22]

Though Young was no doubt unhappy to see that no groundswell of support for the Order was materializing he may have been less disappointed by the poor support than *Tribune* reporters imagined. In a set of instructions telegraphed to Salt Lake City before he left St. George, Young asked the apostles to begin holding ward meetings,

> to see who wishes to take hold of this order of Zion. Take the names of such brethren both male and female as wish to enter into this order of their own will and choice for we do not wish any one to enter upon this holy order against their own choice. . . . If there are not more than a dozen in a ward, whatever there is, organize them. . . . Such as do not wish to join, treat them with all kindness and·fellowship as though they were in the Order for many will wish to wait and see what the result of our acts will be.[23]

As the summer of 1874 wore on many seemed still to be waiting, and confusion continued as to what the Order was to be and how its goals were to be realized. A bewildering variety of tradesmen's organizations, retail associations, and manufacturing establishments seem simply to have changed their name to incorporate the words, "United Order." Young tried to enlist the cooperation of high church officials and wealthy Mormon merchants in his organization of the Central United Order of Zion on 9 May and the United Order of Salt Lake City No. 1, on 4 August. Neither met for more than a few times or conducted meaningful activities. A Farmer's and Carpenter's United Order was organized in mid-June. A month later a Tailor's United Order was formed.[24] Yet all of this seems to have been an ad hoc effort bridging earlier cooperative movements with the United Order.

Perhaps taking the tradesmen orders and the well-known Brigham City cooperative as models (its name, typically, changed from the Brigham City Mercantile and Manufacturing Association to the Brigham City United Order), Presiding Bishop Edward Hunter gave direction and some momentum to the ward organizations in October. At a regular meeting with all the Salt Lake City bishops he suggested that "each ward should try to start some kind of industry and then sustain it, a tannery, butcher's shop or shoe and boot factory."[25] Thus offered the possibility of a concrete project towards which the cooperative impulses of the ward congregations might be directed, bishops set about making plans for such enterprises. The Twentieth Ward began a shoe and boot manufacturing project, as did the Eighth Ward. The Fifteenth Ward decided to produce hats. Bishop Woolley's Ninth Ward made plans for the manufacture of washboards. The First Ward began to promote the production of sugarcane and molasses as well as knitting machines. The Thirteenth Ward United Order opened a butcher shop and the Nineteenth Ward a soap factory. Pleased with the new direction, *Deseret News* writers noted on 28 November that "the plan of a United Order organization taking hold of one particular branch of business and making that a specialty and a success appears to be much better than 'having too many irons in the fire.' " Shortly ads began to appear in the *Deseret News* for such establishments as the Bountiful UO Brickyard, the Tailor's UO Association, the Eleventh Ward General Store, and for Nineteenth Ward UO Soap.[26]

Had these organizations survived and proliferated they might indeed have helped to effect a general self-sufficiency among city wards similar to that Young had hoped would be achieved within the country wards—each ward specializing in a product which through barter and exchange would provide economic autonomy. Yet only the soap factory and tradesmen associations survived an appreciable length of time. Compiling his manuscript histories of each ward just after the turn of the century, Mormon historian Andrew Jenson commented briefly but eloquently upon the efforts of each ward. Of the

Tenth Ward, he wrote, "Nothing whatever was done under this organization." "Nothing was done, however, by that order in the sixth ward." The Eighth Third Ward Order "organized a hat factory that did not pay." The Thirteenth Ward butcher shop "ran for a number of years," but closed, "not being a success, the stockholders had only a small portion of their money returned to them."[27] Bishop Woolley never mentioned the washboard factory after buying lumber for it on 10 November.[28]

Still another effort was made to breathe new life into the flagging movement during the winter of 1874–75. Church authorities encouraged members to be rebaptized "for the remission of your sins, the renewal of your covenants, and the observance of the rules of the holy United Order."[29] Though many hundreds of Latter-day Saints complied, many did not, and as late as November 1875, Apostle George Q. Cannon was chastizing city bishops who had not been rebaptized.[30] The wave of baptisms was insufficient to revive the movement. There are occasional passages in diaries that indicate a lingering of some aspects of the city orders for a considerable time. Emily Dow Partridge Young, one of Brigham Young's wives, wrote on 12 May 1875 that "I have got a woman to wash for me today she lives in the united order. I sure . . . pity her."[31] The diary does not indicate whether the washwoman was pitied for her being in the Order or having to do the laundry of others. As late as January 1878 the same Mrs. Young complained of having been overcharged by the tailors of the United Order.[32] Yet, as we shall see, such references in all probability refer to lingering use of the name after the movement generally had died. For all practical purposes the United Order had ended throughout the city by the end of 1875.

In September 1876 Brigham Young provided his own epitaph to the movement he had launched. Perhaps recalling his optimism at St. George early in 1874 and his fears, also expressed there, that the people were not ready, he assured a gathering of Salt Lake bishops, who apparently had some question on the matter, that he "had been inspired by the Gift and power of God to call upon the saints to enter into the United Order, or order of Enoch, and that now was the time, but he could not get the people to enter into it. He had cleared his skirts if he never said another word about it."[33]

It is evident that in terms of the goals of changing the economic structure and of increasing unity among the Mormons the United Order was a failure in Salt Lake City. The reasons seem clear. Perhaps most fundamentally, the size of the city and the character of its economy did not favor the reform. Salt Lake City was near sixteen thousand in population in 1874 — and a commercial hub of a rapidly growing agricultural and mining region. Previous efforts to transform a liberal, capitalistic society into a communal one had been successful only among very small populations of self-selected persons. The Amana colonies numbered less than two thousand souls during their communitarian period; the Oneida Perfectionists barely more than two hundred. The populations of all the Shaker colonies combined never totaled more than seven thousand.[34] There was, quite simply, no precedent for transforming the population of a well-established city with its economy fully functioning and integrated into national patterns by voluntary means into a communal society.

Equally important was the fact that many of the bishops, whose leadership positions made their support essential to the success of the reform, were among those most heavily involved in the capitalist economy of the city. Ninth Ward Bishop Samuel Woolley, for example, was a hard-driving entrepreneur. Typical entries in his diary discuss business dealings and prospects: 8 May 1874, "Sold some hay, attended conference"; 27 May, "Work fixing ditch on lot. Sold some lumber. . . . Had a meeting in the ward, & organized in the united order"; Sunday, 31 May, "Went to Townsend house & got a check of Mr. Harkness for $105.60. Went to Tabernacle to meeting"; 3 September, "Loaned $200 to Wm. Chivrell for four (4) months at two Per cent Per month. Took a mortgage on his house & lot in 20th Ward"; 30 November, "Went up town & signed a Paper to throw W. Showells into bankruptcy. He owes me about ($1000). I perhaps will get a couple hundred." On his fiftieth birthday (1 September 1875) Woolley made a point to list his material assets, "Good lot with two houses worth $8,000; 42 1/2 acres field land worth $6500; a lot in 13th ward worth $600; five wagons worth $400; eight oxen worth $330; two cows worth $50; & $6250 money on interest, with $250 in bank and debt due me of over $900; coop stock $600 and 357 sheep worth $1071; horse & equip. worth $60; harnesses worth $110 and

interest due of $20 and am in debt to hired men, tithing, etc. $350."
Woolley would hardly seem the man to lead his congregation into a
communal economic system.

It thus may not be surprising that Woolley reported on 20 June
"At a meeting of the officers of the United Order Prest. B. Young
made a few very cutting remarks to me after meeting," or that on 10
September, "At Bishop meeting in evening the Prest. was there &
called a vote on the United Order. I did not vote."[35] The minutes of
that meeting recorded that Young had "said the UO was a subject in
which every Bishop should be entirely devoted to, instead of being
so entirely absorbed by their own private affairs." Again, on 3 June
1875, Young commented "on the way in which the Bishops and
other leading men treated the united order when it was preached to
them." On 1 July, John Taylor felt it necessary to remind the bishops
that "We are not here to build up individualism and get personally
rich." George Q. Cannon added, in the same meeting that "As a
City we are far behind many other settlements in making an effort to
unite the people, and unless we turn round and carry out the United
Order God will withdraw his spirit from us and raise up the Lamanites
to take the lead."[36]

There were bishops, such as Alonzo Raleigh, who seemed less
involved in worldly matters, and who remained committed to the
United Order throughout. And it is not surprising to note, as in the
case of Raleigh, that Order projects seem to have fared better in
these wards. Yet the church leaders' complaints about the material-
ism of the bishops would seem to indicate that Samuel Woolley was
not all that atypical, and that the bishops as a group—chosen in part
because they had distinguished themselves in the community—had
considerable interests in the burgeoning capitalistic economy of Salt
Lake City in the 1870s and would seem the least likely to give strong
leadership in reforms that would change their accustomed patterns
of economic activity.

There was yet another factor inhibiting full-hearted participation
in the Order by the bishops. Even those bishops not heavily involved
in business suffered enormous demands upon their time as part of
their ecclesiastical calling. A fairly typical week for Bishop Alonzo
Raleigh began on Sunday with meetings occupying a good portion
of the day. On Monday he participated in temple ceremonies at the

Endowment House and attended a theological school. On Tuesday he made out the report of a committee on premiums of the Deseret Agricultural and Manufacturing Society. Wednesday was spent clearing snow, reading, and posting accounts. Thursday he met with the teachers quorum of his ward, handling two church court cases, "one of apostacy and one of indebtedness." Friday was devoted to making out a general report of the Brighton Ward tithing for 1873. (His calling as bishop seemed to extend to Brighton where he was involved in the lumber business.) On Saturday he ordered coal for the poor, met with a prayer circle and with the directors of the Deseret Agricultural and Manufacturing Society. The next day, Sunday, 22 March 1874, was the first mention in his diary of the United Order: "I spoke in the afternoon upon our condition as a people as to preparation for an advanced step in the order by which the will of God might be done on earth as it is in heaven."[37]

One cannot help wondering how the bishops—all heavily involved in a hectic schedule of meetings, civic affairs, caring for the poor during depression years, attending temple services, mediating disputes, and providing for multiple wives and families—could have found time to organize and administer so sweeping a reform as the United Order promised to be. It would not be surprising if some, though supportive of the new program, simply did not have time to commence organizing it in a systematic way. The press of long-standing everyday concerns and commitments would certainly place the United Order on the periphery of their attentions.

Moreover, in commencing the United Order bishops had to fight against a set of attitudes and prejudices formed by rumor and an unsympathetic press during the two and one-half months that elapsed since news of the reform was first communicated to Salt Lake City and Brigham Young arrived to take the lead in initiating it. The bishops, being men of affairs, were perhaps more likely than most of their congregations to be exposed to views hostile to the United Order. George Q. Cannon in September 1876 specifically "exhorted the Bishops to discountenance the patronage and perusal of that scandalous sheet, the 'Tribune' which abounded in misrepresentations and falsehood." Earlier Cannon had complained of their "sending children to sectarian schools," urging that bishops not do this.[38]

The momentum lost by the piecemeal way in which the United Order began being discussed and organized in Salt Lake City might have been overcome had Brigham Young given clear direction when he finally arrived in the city in late April. He did not, however, partly because he apparently had no clear model of how the Order was to operate in an urban setting, and partly because he insisted that in participation and form the Orders be products of local support and initiative. He wanted participation in the Orders to be voluntary with no prejudice against those not joining and he was willing to countenance cooperative endeavors of any form that the people would find acceptable. This put the burden squarely on the bishops who in every case but one were elected presidents of the United Order in their wards, but who, for reasons noted above, were not likely to be the most avid or effective leaders of the reform.

Paradoxically, their stature as bishops was in this case not as useful an asset in their role as United Order directors as one might think, because the very distinguishing traits which led to their episcopal callings—their prominence in civic and business affairs—helped to diminish their enthusiasm for the Order. It is interesting to note, in addition, that the form of United Order organization which finally did evolve in the city—the sponsorship of cooperative manufacturing enterprises—was almost precisely the form of endeavor church leaders turned to in the economic crisis of the 1930s. This system of cooperative producing and manufacturing enterprises, owned and managed by local church units, continues to the present day to sustain the widely acclaimed Church Welfare System.

Once wards did begin to form United Order cooperative establishments they were caught up in a classic bind of communitarian reformers—the problem of how to raise capital without strings attached leading back to the old system. Most raised capital by selling stock in denominations small enough for even the very poor to own a share. Yet, when enterprises were successful, these shares, held mainly by the more wealthy even from the start, drifted more and more into the hands of the well-to-do, the enterprise eventually losing altogether its cooperative character.

The Nineteenth Ward, for example, under Bishop Alonzo Raleigh, sold $5,000 in stock which they used to launch their soap factory in December 1874. Though troubled by lawsuits the factory seems to have flourished. Raleigh was heavily engaged in United Order business and his diary indicates strong ward support for it and for the United Order movement generally. However, in January 1878 a new board of directors was organized. Raleigh wrote on that occasion that "there had been gotten up an opposition ticket by dissaffected men & the Adversary labored hard through them to carry his points but failed." A few days later, however, Raleigh's optimism had dimmed. "Met with the Directors of what is called the United Order of the 19th Ward, . . . which order, however, exists only in name, the spirit of it having fled away and the spirit of the world taken the place thereof." A year later, Raleigh, though still a member of the board of directors, did not bother to attend their meeting. "I was not present," he wrote, "but understood that the same old Spirit was there though kept more quiet and private than at the previous election a year since."[39] It was Raleigh's last mention of the United Order. Apparently Raleigh was recording with dismay the loss of company control to men who did not share his communitarian values and chose to run the soap factory as a private enterprise. When this happened, Raleigh, though originally a major investor, lost all interest in a factory managed in "the spirit of the world."

Finally, it should be noted that the United Order movement suffered from Young himself failing to set an example by committing his own considerable assets to the Order. It is perhaps significant that Young's own Eighteenth Ward was one of but two for which no record exists of even an attempt to organize a United Order. Though there is ample evidence that Young regarded all his wealth as church property and thus perhaps did not feel it necessary formally to consecrate it to the church, his failure to do so was taken up quickly by the *Tribune* and certainly noted by others as well. It may be that if Young's bishops found it difficult to commit their own wealth and affairs to the United Order, Young, for the same reasons, found it even more difficult to do so, however much he may have committed to its principles in the abstract. Had he consecrated his possessions to the Order, as he had done by deed during the consecration movement of the 1850s, his example might have weighed strongly with the more wealthy Mormons and given momentum to the movement. As it was, neither Young nor other high church leaders set an example by committing their own wealth to the Order.

Given that the United Order was a failure in terms of its explicitly stated goals at the time, were there long-term consequences of importance to the Mormons? A journal entry by Third Ward Bishop Jacob Weiler's wife suggests that there were. Writing two years after his death she offers a summary of his forty years as bishop.

> Jacob Weiler was Bishop and presided over the third ward and its people for nearly forty years. He was greatly beloved by the members of his ward and always had enjoyed the confidence of the authorities with a slight exception; there was a time when President Brigham Young was over persuaded by someone who was over zealous, and who wanted to get in favor with the Pres. It was when Pres. Young wanted to inaugurate the United Order. Bishop Weiler freely expressed himself, that when the authorities would take the lead by dedicating all they possessed, he would be ready to follow. This did not suit some and they tried to nominate another Bishop, but the people would not, and did not vote for him: After President Taylor was elected Pres. he came and repaired the wrong by having Bro. Weiler reconfirmed by the people. Thus his enemies were frustrated and the United Order failed for that time to be a success.[40]

The United Order proved a searing experience for Bishop Weiler and his family, the pain of it clearly evident in a recollection twenty years later. It caused the one blot on a lifetime of dedicated service, and her husband's stand on the reform required justification, in Mrs. Weiler's judgment, as a closing addendum to his life story. Yet there seems profound significance in Mrs. Weiler's admission that the United Order failed *for that time*. However bitter her memories of Bishop Weiler's experience with the Order, she nurtured a belief that at some future time the Mormons, perhaps in happier circumstances, would be asked to live the United Order again.

Many thousands of Mormons living today can recall being catechized by the question, "Could you live the United Order if asked to?" Though most have only a vague idea of what the United Order would be, Mormons still regard being asked to enter into a more just and equitable economic system as the ultimate test of faith and one they will be required to live before Christ's return. In the early 1950s, Mormon bean farmers in Ramah, New Mexico, when asked what a perfect society would be like, reported to a team of Harvard researchers that part of their affairs would be under the United Order. "There would be just one people, all of one belief, where they treat everybody equal, no injustice to any of them, each looking out for the other's welfare. I think that used to be done in years back."[41] This statement, described by the researchers as a typical response of the Mormons, contrasted sharply with the materialistic and highly individualistic response of other Americans questioned as part of the same study.

In recent years, apostle and counselor in the First Presidency, Marion G. Romney, has several times enjoined Mormons to observe principles that will prepare them to live the United Order. On one occasion he wrote, "The procedural method for teaching Church Welfare has now changed, but the objectives of the program remain the same. Its principles are eternal. It is the gospel in its perfection—the united order, toward which we move."[42] Finally, Mormons who participate in temple services make, just prior to the highest point of the ceremony, a strong covenant, to consecrating all their resources, material and personal, to furthering Christ's work. The frequent repetition of this oath of consecration serves as a persistent reminder of the continuing nature of obligations required under the United Order.

The point, hopefully, is clear. It is much easier to file and forget an incomplete blueprint than a partially finished structure. Mormons, through their painful experience of attempting to live the United Order in the 1870s were endowed with a collective memory of a half-finished structure that continues to enjoin subsequent generations to live a more communal life. The United Order still nags at the Mormon conscience as it would not have had they not attempted it in the 1870s. It is possible to imagine, in an age when many of our brightest minds anticipate certain eventual worldwide catastrophe, a time when cooperation would be necessary to survival. In such circumstances their past experience would almost certainly be recalled and Mormons would commence again the labor that seemed so utterly derelict at the end of the 1870s.

NOTES

1. A history of the broader movement is found in Leonard J. Arrington, Feramorz Y. Fox, and Dean L. May, *Building the City of God: Community*

and Cooperation Among the Mormons (Salt Lake City: Deseret Book Company, 1976).

2. St. George Stake Manuscript History, 14 February 1874, Church Archives, Church of Jesus Christ of Latter-day Saints, Salt Lake City, Utah, hereafter cited as LDS Church Archives.

3. The St. George population is calculated by straight-line estimation between the 1870 and 1880 federal census counts of St. George precinct. Households in southern Utah at the time averaged close to five persons. See Dean L. May, "People on the Mormon Frontier: Kanab's Families of 1874," Journal of Family History 1 (Winter 1976): 173.

4. Brigham Young and George A. Smith, Brigham Young Telegrams to D. H. Wells, et al., 28 February 1874, LDS Church Archives.

5. Doctrine and Covenants 42:30–35.

6. George D. Watt, ed., Journal of Discourses 26 vols. (1855–1886; repr. ed. Salt Lake City: Bookcraft, 1966), 2:306–7.

7. Ibid., 17:32, 35.

8. Frederick Kesler Diary, 6–7 March 1874, Western Americana, Marriott Library, University of Utah, Salt Lake City.

9. I have been able to find few specific references in the Deseret News to the United Order before April 1874.

10. Salt Lake Tribune, 7 March 1874.

11. Ibid., 21 and 24 April, 18 June, and 8 April 1874.

12. Ibid., 17 March 1874.

13. Frederick Kesler said of the meeting, "I have not seen or felt more of the Spirit of the Lord at a meeting for years." Kesler Diary, 26 April 1874.

14. Deseret News, 2 May 1874; Salt Lake Tribune, 30 April 1874.

15. Journal of Discourses, 17:56–58.

16. Ibid., 62, 66, 75, 77.

17. Kesler Diary, 9 May 1874.

18. A list of United Order organizations is in Building the City of God, 407–19.

19. Salt Lake Tribune, 30 April and 23 June 1874.

20. Samuel A. Woolley Diary, 3 June 1874, LDS Church Archives.

21. Ibid., 27 May and 6 May 1874.

22. Deseret News, 23 and 26 May 1874; Alonzo Raleigh Diary, 19 April 1874, LDS Church Archives; Salt Lake Tribune, 20 May, 2 June, and 29 May 1874.

23. Brigham Young to D. H. Wells, et al., telegram of 11 March 1874, Brigham Young Telegrams, LDS Church Archives.

24. Building the City of God, 221–22; United Order Number One Minutes, LDS Church Archives; Deseret News, 13 June 1874; Presiding Bishopric, Bishops' Meeting Minutes 1862–1879, 16 July 1974, LDS Church Archives.

25. Bishops' Minutes, 22 October 1874.

26. Accounts of the founding of ward industries are in the Manuscript Histories for the various wards, LDS Church Archives, and in *Deseret News*, 1 July and 5 September 1874, and 1 January 1875; see also 15 June and 6 July 1874.

27. Manuscript Histories of the various wards, LDS Church Archives.

28. Samuel A. Woolley Diaries, 10 November 1874 and passim.

29. The prayer is recorded in St. George Stake Manuscript History, 31 July to 5 September 1875.

30. Bishops' Minutes, 4 November 1875.

31. Emily Dow Partridge Young Diary, 30 January 1878, LDS Church Archives.

32. Ibid., 12 May 1875. Maureen Ursenbach Beecher kindly brought these references to the author's attention.

33. Bishops' Minutes, 21 September 1876.

34. The Salt Lake City population is calculated by straight-line estimation between the 1870 and 1874 federal census counts.

35. Samuel A. Woolley Diary for the dates indicated in text.

36. Bishops' Minutes, 10 September, 3 June, and 1 July 1874.

37. Alonzo H. Raleigh Diary, 15–22 March 1874, LDS Church Archives.

38. Bishops' Minutes, 21 September 1876 and 8 November 1875.

39. Alonzo H. Raleigh Diary, 9 September and 7 and 9 December 1874 and passim, esp. 31 October 1876, 14 January 1878, and 18 January 1879.

40. Jacob Weiler Autobiography, LDS Church Archives.

41. Evan Z. Vogt and Ethel M. Albert, eds., *People of Rimrock: A Study of Values in Five Cultures* (Cambridge: Harvard University Press, 1966), 28.

42. *Ensign* 5 (November 1975): 127. This reference was brought to the author's attention by Bruce D. Blumell.

"Going to Meeting" in Salt Lake City's Thirteenth Ward, 1849–1881: A Microanalysis

RONALD W. WALKER

The Mormon past can best be understood by a variety of approaches, including the intensive study of a topic on a small scale. For instance, a microanalysis of the pioneer meeting patterns of Salt Lake City's Thirteenth Ward tells a great deal about early Mormonism. During the tenure of its first two bishops, 1849–81, local worship routines were surprisingly complex. While this conclusion may startle some historians who have assumed a later date for local and ward worship, there are even broader insights to be gained. Such a study suggests new dimensions to events such as the Mormon Reformation and the "move south," when in 1858 the Mormons abandoned Salt Lake City in the face of advancing U.S. troops. We also learn how the Saints worshipped and the process by which local, ward initiative slowly passed to centralized authority. Clearly, the church was rapidly changing during the middle decades of the nineteenth century. The open, fluid, and informal procedures of the early church were giving away to the more intricate and formal structure of our own time.[1]

During the middle of February 1849, while the Saints were still cramped in their pioneer fort, President Brigham Young directed the organization of the Saints into nineteen Latter-day Saint (LDS) wards or congregations. Five days later, as the people began leaving the fort to settle on their homesites, Young was quick with additional instructions. Two-man teams should be organized to visit regularly each ward family. Young also directed that ward schools be built. And in a move both practical and symbolic, he required each congregation to fence its boundaries. That way meandering cattle might be controlled, and wards could begin to develop within their boundaries a neighborhood feeling.[2]

From the beginning, the Thirteenth Ward lay at the center of things. Its nine-block area was bounded on the east and west by Third East and State streets, with South Temple and Third South streets serving as meridians to the north and south. It therefore was squarely positioned in downtown Salt Lake City, adjacent to Young's office and the humming beehive of church headquarters.

The Thirteenth Ward population reflected its geography. Several years after its founding, it claimed seventy-six families or about six hundred members. These figures doubled by 1858, and two years later the ward had one hundred sixty families or about thirteen hundred people. During the 1860s it added twenty more families. Throughout the pioneer period, the congregation was the largest not only in Salt Lake City but probably in Mormondom as well.[3]

Among its members were some of the most prominent men in the territory. In 1856 they included Jedediah M. Grant, Salt Lake City mayor and counselor in the First Presidency; Daniel H. Wells, soon to succeed Grant in both offices; Ezra T. Benson, Orson Hyde, and Erastus Snow, members of the Quorum of the Twelve Apostles; Dustin Amy, William Howard, William Nixon, Enoch Reese, Thomas Williams, prominent merchants and land investors; Truman Angell, Almon W. Babbitt, Reynolds Cahoon, Asa Calkins, Hiram B. Clawson, George Goddard, Christopher Layton, Jesse C. Little, Alexander Neibaur, Joseph B. Noble, Orson Spencer, Zerubbabel Snow, and Hosea Stout, prominent church and civic leaders of the first or second rank.[4] As Mormon settlements multiplied in the territory, many left the ward. Nevertheless, the congregation retained a remarkable level of talent during its first three decades of history.

Symptomatic of its human resources, the ward's first two bishops were among pioneer Utah's ablest. The first, Edward Hunter, served almost five years until his concurrent duties as presiding bishop required him to resign his ward position in 1854.[5] Edwin D. Woolley, a kindly but blunt and contrary-minded merchant, took his place and served twenty-seven years until his death in 1881.

The Thirteenth Ward's vocational and economic profile mirrored its talent. By the middle of the 1850s, contemporary accounts divided its working men into three groups: farmers, craftsmen, and mechanics or shopkeepers. Common laborers were noticeably absent, the congregation having "fewer labouring men, than . . . the least ward in the City."[6] While the ward had its poor, landholders and merchants more than balanced accounts. "The 13th Ward," observed one resident in 1863, "was richer than all the Saints at Kirtland when the Temple [there] was built." Indeed, it probably enjoyed the highest income level of any neighborhood in the church.[7]

The ward's wealth brought cultural diversity. By the 1870s the neighborhood boasted three of the Saints' most conspicuous buildings, all of which a contemporary visitor might encounter within a single city block. By walking south down State Street, he first would see on the left the Social Hall. A boxlike structure of little architectural distinction, it housed more Salt Lake City "parties . . . than in any other place."[8] Schools and religious meetings were also held there. On the other side of the street a half block south sat the imposing Salt Lake Theatre. During pioneer times, it attracted both local and national drama companies and substantial and appreciative audiences. Finally, the Seventies' Council Hall lay several buildings further down State Street. During winter months, popular weekly lectures were held there.

These citadels of approved Mormon culture did not go unchallenged. Early in the 1870s the ward also contained a billiard parlor, eight liquor taverns, and another eight saloons that served beer. Five hotels catered primarily to the gentile trade, while Methodists, Episcopalians, and Catholics each had a church within ward boundaries.[9] More disturbing to the LDS faithful was the Liberal Institute. This lecture hall, probably the most commodious in the city, was erected in the early 1870s by Mormon dissenters led by William S. Godbe. It sponsored a stream of nationally and internationally prominent spiritualists whose freewheeling lectures were anathema to Mormon traditionalists.[10]

Clearly, the Thirteenth Ward was not cut from ordinary cloth. By virtue of its large, able, and flourishing membership, its proximity to church headquarters, and its early and close experiences with non-Mormons, its congregation practiced what might be described as an "ideal" Mormonism. Its worship more closely reflected what general church leaders intended than the activities of outlying units that labored without sufficient resources or supervision. At least, this was the view of some churchmen who found rural congregations to be generally less structured, less governable, and not as free with their time and donations in support of the church.[11] Moreover, the Gentile challenge forced the Thirteenth Ward and other city congregations to respond creatively in a classic Toynbeean manner, alternatively producing defensiveness, innovation, adaptation, and at times accommodation. The result was nineteenth-century Mormonism on the cutting edge.[12]

In July 1849, five months after the organization of the Thirteenth Ward, its members gathered with the other Saints at the recently built "Bowery" on Salt Lake City's Temple Square to commemorate their coming to Utah. The day-long ceremonies were elaborate, with the firing of cannon, speeches, toasts, hosanna shouts, and—apparently in a mix of anger and humor—orchestrated, community wide "deathly groans" to mark the Saints' past persecutions. Like other congregations, members of the Thirteenth Ward marched to the square as a unit, sat and ate together, and hoisted their own ward flag.[13]

The celebration, combining community and neighborhood activity, drew on the Saints' previous experience. First in western New York and later at Kirtland, Ohio, and in the western counties of Missouri, members had often gathered for town- or citywide amusement and worship. "Ward" activity, however, began in Nauvoo, Illinois, when civil wards, or precincts, became the boundaries for religious organization. These church wards were presided over by bishops; they levied quotas for church building projects, conducted neighborhood or ward visiting to resident families, and oversaw the needs of the poor.[14] While at first spasmodic, local or ward meetings became increasingly important during the Mormon trek west. Camped in Winter Quarters, near present-day Omaha, Nebraska, church leaders once again organized wards and instructed bishops to hold schools and maintain, at least during the winter months, regular worship services.[15] Following the Nauvoo pattern, the summer season meetings were held in the open air for the entire community.

In Utah these patterns continued. At first the Temple Square community worship services were paramount. Following the Mormons' long-standing custom, the entire settlement was expected to congregate each Sunday at 10:00 A.M. and 2:00 P.M. These citywide assemblies, however, preserved some ward identity. Like other congregations, members of the Thirteenth Ward sat in a specially reserved area. In addition, on a rotating basis with other wards, their bishopric and teachers might prepare the hall for worship, provide water for the congregation, and prepare and pass the sacrament.[16]

In the winter months worshipping on Temple Square could be forbidding. The pioneer Bowery was a shaded, open-to-the-elements meeting area, and its Old and New Tabernacle successors afforded only slightly better protection from the cold. Consequently, as early as the Thirteenth Ward's first winter, the devout worshipped in homes and warmer buildings. While its earliest records were lost, the ward's meetings were undoubtedly similar to others being held in the city.[17] "Blessing" meetings were periodically held at President Young's request to confirm the baptized or rebaptized. More frequently, Sunday afternoon "worship" services were held. These followed the pattern of Temple Square: an opening prayer and singing, followed by several hours of male preaching that might be interrupted in mid-discourse by the blessing and passing of the sacrament.[18]

Prayer meetings, whose antecedents probably reached to the church's founding, were perhaps the most characteristic gathering of the time. Spontaneous and democratic, these meetings allowed men and women to participate together, often with an abundant display of the primitive gifts of the spirit. While no record of a Thirteenth Ward's prayer meeting apparently survives, its worship activity was undoubtedly similar to sessions held elsewhere in the city. "Meeting at E. M. Saunder's [?] house," read the minutes of one of the more dramatic prayer meetings held in the Nineteenth Ward, "filled to overflowing[.] Pres John Young opened the meeting by singing and prayer[.] [He] made some remarks, ex[h]orted the brothern to use their privelages in ocupying the time[.] Was followed by the Brotheren in quick sucession[.] Brotheron and sisters delivered their testimony concerning the work of the Lord. [Many] spake in toungs, and prophsied[.] [The] spirit of God was with us to the rejoiceing of all present[.]" The meeting, which followed a worship meeting of several hours in the afternoon, began at 6 P.M. and ended three and one-half hours later at 9:30.[19]

By the middle of the 1850s, the Thirteenth Ward meetings assumed a regular schedule. From April conference to sometime beyond the church's general conference in October, activity centered at Temple Square. However, by winter the routine was reversed. While some Saints might still brave an off-again, on-again Tabernacle service at 11:00 A.M., most meeting-goers gathered at the ward, where "two, three, and four meetings . . . [each week], for both old and young" were held.[20] The Sunday worship service was most important, which by the 1850s had a surprisingly "modern" aspect. From the pulpit Bishop Woolley typically welcomed ward members to the meetings. Members then might sing a favorite hymn like "Redeemer of Israel" or "Come Let Us Anew." An opening prayer, a choir selection, preaching, and a closing prayer then followed in succession.[21]

There was, in fact, a plethora of meetings. For example, the ward boasted a "singing school" that required attendance. It also permitted private neighborhood gatherings, a possible explanation for Bishop Hunter's 1851 comment that "many on the West line of the Ward do not attend our meetings." While priesthood quorums generally met on a multiward basis, special male meetings were periodically held within the congregation to aid immigration, levy taxes, or oversee road, canal, school, or chapel construction. Moreover, popular culture lyceums were common, teaching young women on one occasion the folly of placing in water "genteel table knives, handled with wood or any kind of horn."[22]

Given the "alluring paths into which many had been drawn," youth became a special object for meetings. Bishops and "other leading spirits" were told to reclaim them by "amusing and instructive" activities, which President Young prescribed should be held at least monthly. Sometimes the result was spectacular. "On the 17th Feby in a youth's meeting in the 13th Ward," recorded one 1854 diary, "three angels were seen by Duncan F. Cook, clothed in white, and [they] ascended up on high."[23]

By the summer of 1854, the Thirteenth Ward ladies also had their own gatherings. Earlier in the year, some Salt Lake City women had organized themselves into a Relief Society to aid the territory's impoverished Indians. Brigham Young quickly took hold of the idea, whose origins lay with an 1842 Nauvoo society of the same name, urging the sisters to meet in their local wards to assist not only the Indians but the Mormon poor as well. Thus the Thirteenth Ward Relief Society was born, with a slate of officers that included Matilda Dudley, president and treasurer; Augusta Cobb and Sarah A. Cook, counselors; and Martha Jane Coray, secretary. The women covenanted to forsake "evil speaking" among themselves, divided themselves into pairs for monthly "block" visits to the congregation, solicited donations for the poor, and met each Wednesday to process the gifts and to receive instruction from their women leaders.[24]

Next to Sunday, Thursdays were clearly the most important worship day. During the 1850s the prayer meetings, once impromptu and irregular, increasingly became a weekly Thursday evening staple, their format only slightly less rigid than that of the Sunday preaching service. In addition, the Saints met on the first Thursday afternoon of each month for a two- or three-hour fast and blessing meeting. Hunter reminded that these services should not be ladened by formal preaching from the stand. Instead, they were intended to bless the rank-and-file with the "gifts of the spirit," which included spontaneous "testimony bearing" by members and occasional glossolalia. Toward the end of the service, Woolley or other priesthood leaders might consecrate oil for the blessing of the sick, christen infants, or confirm the recently baptized—functions taken from the earlier blessing meetings. As part of the ritual, members often donated to the poor the food that their fasting had left unconsumed. A decade or so later, the practice was systematized by sending boys into the ward to make formal collections.[25]

These and other meetings imposed heavy demands on the conscientious. For example, Thirteenth Ward member George Goddard attended over forty church-related meetings in the month of March 1857. Goddard worshipped each Sunday at both the Tabernacle and the ward. His weeknights were no less occupied. On Mondays he attended the Seventies' lectures. Wednesdays found him at the Old Tabernacle rehearsing for the choir. The ward's prayer service filled Thursday evenings. And on Fridays he was at Nathaniel Felt's prayer circle. On other nights he visited his assigned teaching blocks, and attended his teachers' meeting, the high priests' meeting, and the lesser priesthood meeting. Finally, there was the afternoon fast meeting, the bimonthly bishops' meetings, occasional lyceums and parties, and a miscellaneous meeting with President Young himself. He was at home only two evenings the entire month.[26]

In reality, few members had Goddard's stamina and sociability, church leaders admitting as much. "Suppose I should appoint a meeting for tonight," President Young complained in 1851, "about a dozen [members] would come, [and] without any candles." Social activity brought a different response. "If I were to say—level this stand for the band that we may have a dance, they would bring the stoves from their wives' bedsides, and would dance all night, and the house would be filled to overflowing." Such behavior had Young alternating between wanting to "cuff every elders ears" to weeping "over their follies."[27]

The Thirteenth Ward's lack of attendance bore out the president's complaint. Bishop Hunter acknowledged that ward meetings were "not so well attended as they might be." In fact some were hardly attended. Within several years after its organization, the Relief Society had as few as five sisters at its meetings and seldom more than a dozen. The situation was apparently pervasive. "The non-attendance at meetings," observed the peripatetic Goddard whose widespread activities must have given him an unparalleled view, was "about as much neglected as any other duty."[28]

By the middle 1850s, then, the ward's meetings presented something of a paradox. In sharp contrast with the ward's starkly low attendance figures lay its impressive organizational achievement. Drawing on Nauvoo and Winter Quarters' precedents and following the general pattern of other major Salt Lake City wards, the neighborhood had created within less than a decade an intricate web of meetings. These included youth meetings, women's meetings, men's meetings, Quaker-type meetings that allowed broad-based participation, and preaching meetings that were held during the winter season as often as three times per week. Such development was all the more remarkable given the lack of specific guidelines issued by headquarters. "It is required that preaching be Kept up in the Wards," the leadership had typically advised in 1852.[29] Church leaders gave little instruction as to how often the Lord's Supper might be administered, when meetings should be scheduled, or even the specific nature of the meetings themselves.

The wide gap between the ward's worship structure and the reality of its members' nonattendance may have been one of the contributing factors to the Saints' periodic malaise. Beginning in the middle 1850s and continuing for at least twenty years, Thirteenth Ward preachers seemed continually beset with introspection and pessimism. Mormonism, in their view, seemed constantly in jeopardy.

The 1856–57 Mormon Reformation, the first of these crises of spirit, thoroughly aroused the congregation. Jedediah Grant, its leading crusader, preached several gritty sermons to his Thirteenth Ward neighbors.[30] But Bishop Woolley surpassed him in sharpness of tongue. "It is often the greatest whore that preaches loudest about purity," he observed. "I want the people to stick as far as they go [with the Reformation], and not get to the top of the tree, and then fall."[31]

Woolley's formula for deliberate and permanent improvement did not focus on inner feelings or personal sanctification. Like elsewhere in the territory, the Thirteenth Ward preachers stressed cleanliness, sexual purity, honesty, sobriety, prayer, obedience to authority, and— if the Reformation's famed "Catechism" was applied in the ward— attendance at meetings. "Do you labor six days," it asked, "and [then] rest, or go to the house of worship, on the seventh?" Another of the Catechism's twenty-seven questions made the point explicit. "Do you and your family attend Ward meetings?"[32]

The Catechism may have begun the process, so important in the twentieth century, of linking meeting attendance to Mormon "activity" or orthodoxy. But the main means of determining Mormonness during the Reformation was rebaptism and reconfirmation. The congregation's ordinance book listed 563 rebaptisms in 1857—virtually everyone over eight years of age who wished a continuing identification with the religion.[33] The reconfirming process, in turn, dominated the ward's fast and prayer meetings on 5 March 1857. "About 150 were reconfirmed under the hands of twelve brethren divided into six couples," reported Goddard. The ordinances began at 10 A.M. and concluded at 9 P.M., with only a few hours respite in the late afternoon.[34]

While the Reformation stimulated good works and probably raised church attendance, the 1858 "move south" had disastrous results. Amid rumors of Mormon disloyalty that later proved untrue, President James Buchanan had dispatched a federal army to the territory.

The Saints saw the approaching troops as yet another persecution. While first preparing to fight, they later avoided confrontation by abandoning Salt Lake City and moving en masse forty miles south. Eventually the crisis was resolved, but upon returning to their homes, the Saints seemed afflicted by an "awful spirit." Church officials estimated that at best 20 percent of the settlers attended to their prayers. Still fewer "carried the Spirit." The payment of tithing and the attendance of meetings flagged. Drunkenness, stealing, and even prostitution seemed on the rise. Some Saints were disrespectful of church authorities. "Many of the people don't care a damn about the Bishops," despaired Hunter, "and if a Bishop's Court, . . . meet to decide a case, the very parties will insult you before they leave the place."[35]

Perhaps the flames of the Reformation and the later talk about war had emotionally spent the people. But there were also tangible factors creating discontent. The Saints' military preparations and the move south brought severe economic dislocation. With even the weather appearing to grow more severe and few jobs on hand, many Mormons packed their belongings and left the territory.[36]

These forces impacted heavily on the Thirteenth Ward. "More meanness" could be found there, thought one churchman, than in any other congregation in the city. Indeed, Woolley acknowledged "the coldness of the people." Instead of tending to their souls, ward members were "gone to the kanyons for wood, or over [the] Jordan [River] hunting [lost] stock."[37] Certainly they were not near a house of God. Since their return from the south, Woolley found it "impossible to get up meetings." The Relief Society had disbanded. Thursday evening prayer sessions were suspended — and never revived. For over a year, even fast and worship meetings were rare. The best the bishop could do was wring his hands and instruct his "block" teachers to try and persuade the people to worship at the Tabernacle.[38]

Nor did a new regimen of meetings quickly materialize — either in the Thirteenth Ward or apparently elsewhere. Bishop Hunter, who continued his leadership of the other bishops, at first mildly entreated the ward leaders to recommence their meetings. "It argues [for] an unhealthy state of mind when Meetings are neglected," he advised. Bishop L. D. Hardy, his counselor, was more pointed. "Good meetings and good preaching," he insisted, "will resurrect the people and bring them back again to their former experience and feeling in the Kingdom of God." When six months of such cajoling failed to produce any results, President Young sharply announced that weekly ward meetings would begin *immediately*. Apparently due the small number of attenders, the Thirteenth Ward was assigned for a time to worship with the Twelfth.[39]

Meeting attendance, however, gradually recovered, and the ward embarked on a major building project. Since the 1850s the neighborhood had met in two successive school buildings and occasionally in the Social Hall. But on New Year's Day, 1861, the congregation dedicated the Thirteenth Ward Assembly Rooms. Planned since 1854, the $10,000 chapel was by all accounts Mormondom's most richly appointed. Its pulpit and windows were draped in crimson, two bronze chandeliers hung from the ceiling, and a "very fine" stucco cornice framed the interior. Although financed by ward members who purchased stock at $25 per share, the building was not intended solely for ward activity. Its shareholders promised to make the building available for any worthwhile civic purpose.[40]

Perhaps the resplendent chapel helped to soften the frontier folk, whose Tabernacle and ward decorum was sometimes lacking. While worshipping at the Tabernacle, they might engage in loud laughter and foot stomping.[41] When one Thirteenth Ward meeting was disrupted by a turmoil, the responsible men were forcibly removed and guards posted to hoist them down the stairs if they attempted to return.[42] Sacrament behavior was a particular problem. Church leaders complained that dirty children drank from the common cup, while some fathers failed to remove their hats or, worse, slept. The men who blessed the Lord's Supper (they sometimes stood rather than knelt), offered prayers that might only slightly resemble their scriptural models. Moreover, when partaking of the water some drank too deeply, quenching a physical instead of a spiritual thirst.[43]

And then there was Bishop Woolley. Charitable, well meaning, and firmly dedicated to his religion, he could also be summary in his acts. During one worship service, he "spoke warmly" of those who accused him of failing to act "the part of a Father" and urged his critics to air their feelings. When William Capener did so, Woolley peremptorily cut him off from the church. Members debated the action during the following week, with half the congregation refusing to sustain the excommunication. Woolley, however, refused to budge. Railing "about the whoredom and the wickedness" of the ward, the bishop ended the discussion by vowing "by the help of the Lord and the brethren" to cleanse it.[44]

While his personal feelings seldom influenced his ecclesiastical judgment, Woolley's words often made for lively meetings. In 1865 he mounted a ward reformation aimed at the Gentiles who were rapidly transforming his neighborhood, and his language was severe.[45] We shall attempt to "break up the low, vile dens which infest this ward," he announced. "They who come here from California, Oregon, Idaho and Nevada to teach us civilization, the low, *dirty, miserable, scraping rabble of the earth*, why do they come here? What brings them here? . . . They have tried for 34 years to wipe us off the face of the earth. . . . I will give all the evildoers time to reform, and we will *clean, purify* and *wash* the *13th Ward* of all *damnable* sinners."[46]

Woolley might denounce them, but the Gentile challenge was not easily turned aside. Utah's non-Mormons in fact were partly responsible for reviving the ward's appetite for meetings. The problem came not so much from the unsavory Gentile, but from "those of Educated and refined manners [who] are able to exercise great influence." These, with their newly established Protestant denominational schools, were drawing away an increasing number of LDS youth, who as a result mixed with the children of "apostates and traitors."[47]

To defuse this new Gentile threat, church leaders turned to the Thirteenth Ward. Brigham Young, George A. Smith, Daniel H. Wells, George Q. Cannon, and other prominent churchmen met with ward officers on 30 March 1867 and resolved to form a Sunday school.[48] During the organizational spate of the 1850s, several congregations had begun short-lived Sabbath schools, and the middle 1860s brought several more. But Woolley's proposed school was the first since the city's bishops had agreed, in a major policy decision, to counter the denominational academies with LDS Sabbath schools.[49] Woolley had moved with untypical dispatch — probably at the nudging of his priesthood leaders, who hoped to make the Thirteenth Ward's school an example for other wards to follow.

The project began impressively. On 7 April 1867 leading churchmen George A. Smith and George Q. Cannon called a "large assembly of children" to order and named A. Milton Musser as superintendent. Also present were Bishop Woolley, most ward officers, and even Mormondom's "first lady" Eliza R. Snow, who penned for the occasion a poem, "In Our Lovely Deseret." The succeeding weeks were as notable. The school soon acquired a library of 150 books and, more importantly, the services of such leading LDS intellectuals as William S. Godbe, William H. Shearman, E. L. T. Harrison, and Eli Kelsey. In addition, Mormon general authorities Ezra T. Benson, Orson Hyde, George A. Smith, and President Brigham Young himself periodically taught the "scholars." Such talent quickly attracted an average attendance of over two hundred youth and produced a model that other wards copied. Before a year had expired, President Young was acknowledging the "happy results arising from our Sabbath schools."[50]

The Sunday school movement was a watershed. For the first time since the move south, the Mormons regained their organizational momentum and even began to innovate. Previously the bishopric and block teachers, about twenty men, shouldered the ward's leadership and performed its labor. In contrast, the Sabbath schools sharply increased opportunities for lay service, particularly for women. The Thirteenth Ward organization required a staff of twenty-one women and twenty-three men, who were charged not only with the school's supervision and teaching, but soon were asked to attend a monthly training meeting run by the Salt Lake Stake.[51] The latter suggested another significant change. The ward's autonomous ways were slowly being surrendered to centralized control.

The chief beneficiaries of the Sabbath school, of course, were the children themselves. A typical Sunday might find them meeting at the Assembly Rooms, where as a group they listened to short talks, sang, and recited inspirational prose and poetry. Leaders might also catechize the youth with questions drawn from the Bible, Book of Mormon, or LDS church history, liberally awarding prizes for both correct answers and proper conduct. To these general activities, Superintendent Musser and his staff soon added classes based on age and apparently sex. There were less formal times, too. The school sponsored concerts and a series of parties, the logistics of which must have been staggering. On one occasion thirty "omnibuses, coaches, [and] wagons" conveyed over five hundred children, teachers, and other Thirteenth Ward members to Calder's [now Nibley] Park.

Another ambitious excursion took the school to Ogden on the recently built Utah Central Railroad "in the Mormon Car on a Mormon R. R."[52]

As in Victorian England, Mormons used their Sabbath schools for both moral and social uplift. At first without didactic teaching materials, the Thirteenth Ward school taught academic subjects such as astronomy. But its fare quickly turned to proper and moral conduct. The boys and girls were taught scripture study, Sabbath observance, propriety, honesty, family solidarity, and especially the inviolability of the Mormon "Word of Wisdom." When eleven-year-old "Master" Heber Grant repeated the health code "very correctly," he personified the purpose of the school. Later to become Mormonism's long-tenured twentieth-century president, Grant and his fellow scholars were being "refined." By internalizing the school's Victorian behavior codes, they could rise above their parents' rough frontier society.[53]

Finally, Sabbath schools changed the old patterns of worship. The Sunday morning Tabernacle service was an early casualty. Children and Sabbath workers often failed to leave their wards for the additional Temple Square meeting, and in 1872 President Young suspended the citywide morning service.[54] This, however, brought no diminution in meeting activity. A First Presidency circular asked ward leaders to take a more active role in their Sabbath schools. It also directed, with great specificity, that the children attend the ward's afternoon worship service, hitherto an adult preserve. During the afternoon meeting, ward leaders should place the boys and girls next to their Sunday School teachers in a special section of the meeting hall. Water should be made available for their refreshment and their seats made "very comfortable, so that the children will not get uneasy." Moreover, ward officers were to see that the youth received the sacrament during both the morning and afternoon services.[55]

Thus the Sunday school greatly increased lay (and especially women's) church service, established the precedent for centralized or stake direction, and infused within the ward Victorian values. More importantly, the Sabbath school success brought other ward "auxiliaries" into being, making the Thirteenth Ward's meetings increasingly diverse and specialized. On 18 April 1868 Woolley revived the ward's Relief Society, which had been defunct for ten years. Like the organization of the Sunday School, it owed its revival to the Gentile specter. With the coming of the transcontinental railroad and the arrival of eastern values and commodities, local female societies, church leaders reasoned, could preserve such traditional Mormon values as frugality, self-sufficiency, and simplicity. Furthermore, the sisters' charity might do "great good and much relieve the hands of the Bishop and his Council."[56]

For Thirteenth Ward Relief Society "presidentess," Woolley picked Rachel R. Grant, whom he "ordained, blessed and set apart." The bishop told the women at their organizing sessions that "it was not his habit to be in a hurry in his movements" and he wished the society to be likewise "cool and deliberate." Their leaders, he cautioned, should be obedient in carrying out "such measures as he should suggest from time to time." Woolley's words of caution and his obvious delay (the Thirteenth Ward Relief Society was one of the last in the city to organize) were perhaps due to what Woolley described as the "forever wrangling" by the members of the ward's first society in the 1850s.[57]

The ladies followed the pattern of the earlier society, meeting weekly and undertaking the neighborhood's various tasks of charity. Notwithstanding "often having to endure insults," the Relief Society block teachers monthly scoured the congregation to discover the needy and to secure measures for their relief. While occasionally getting a cash donation, the sisters were usually more successful in procuring yarn, thread, calico pieces, rugs, and discarded clothing which they transformed into stockings, quilts, and rag rugs. The Relief Society women also braided straw, fashioned hats and bonnets, stored grain, and sewed underwear, buckskin gloves, and burial and temple garments. On these items the poor had first claim; the remainder were sold with most of the proceeds going to charity.[58]

As it did in the Sabbath school, a strong Victorian current flowed in the Society's doings. "We all have trials to pass through," Rachel Grant consoled her sisters, "but if living up to our duty . . . [these challenges] are sanctified to our best good." Her tendency was to see only the good in life. She called for obedience to authority and the avoidance of faultfinding. God's hand and his rewards were omnipresent. "I am a firm believer in our being rewarded for all the good we do," she insisted, "and everything will come out right with those who do right." By propounding duty, goodness, obedience, toil, and sacrifice, the Relief Society reflected the spirit of the times.[59]

During the 1870s the ward added three additional auxiliaries. The Young Ladies Retrenchment Association began its Thirteenth Ward meetings in March 1875. With General Relief Society President Eliza R. Snow and her Thirteenth Ward counterpart, Rachel Grant, in frequent attendance, the meetings partook of the reigning feminine ideal.[60] For instance, Sister Snow pointedly noted how the Farmington young ladies had insured proper conduct. By pledging themselves against such recent innovations as the waltz and polka, they brought an end to these dances. President Snow also revealed that the Farmington women had refrained from associating with those of persistently bad habits. When "a few rowdy young men rode through the town calling on the girls, and proposed to give them a sleigh ride, the girls staunch to their purpose, withstood the temptation and refused the invitation."[61]

The Thirteenth Ward Young Men's Mutual Improvement Association (YMMIA) could be equally high-toned, though once it peremptorily refused a member's suggestion to take the "round dance" pledge.[62] When organized in August 1875, the congregation's YMMIA became the first in the church. Like their Retrenchment friends, the men sponsored activities that included short addresses, readings, essays, music, lectures, and answering questions on religious and cultural topics.[63] Moralizing was frequent. "Bro. M. B. Young . . . felt sorry to see so many of the Young Brethren in Zion violating the Word of Wisdom," the minutes of one session read, "and he hoped that the young Brethren in the Thirteenth Ward would set an example to others worthy of imitation." During 1875 both the Retrenchment Society (soon rechristened the Young Ladies MIA) and the YMMIA met weekly. Thereafter their sessions became sporadic until the two began "conjoint" sessions in 1879.[64]

The Thirteenth Ward's final auxiliary was the Primary Organization, a weekday organization for small children. On 2 April 1879 the ubiquitous Eliza Snow first called the children to order. She not only required her young congregation to select an opening hymn, but if the early minutes are accurate, their officers as well. "Sister

Snow then addressed the children asking them a few simple questions requiring short answers," a pattern that would characterize many later Primary meetings.[65]

In summary, two years before Bishop Woolley's death, the ward completed its early organizational development. On Sundays it hosted two meetings, and during some winter months, three meetings: a morning Sunday School, which adults increasingly attended; an evening preaching session; and when frigid weather prevented Temple Square attendance, an occasional afternoon meeting. The Young Men and Young Ladies organizations met every seven days at various times. The Primary children and the Relief Society sisters also met weekly, the first usually on Wednesday afternoons and the women on the following morning. Moreover, there were many specialized meetings: choir meetings, block teachers meetings, priesthood meetings, and the monthly Fast and Testimony meeting held on the first Thursday of the month.

Though the Assembly Rooms housed many meetings, ward members remained careless attenders. From a congregation of twelve to fourteen hundred in the 1870s, the men's Mutual Improvement Association averaged a mere fifteen youth at its meetings. Rachel Grant repeatedly complained of her Relief Society's meager few sisters, while Fast Meeting attendance was so poor that Woolley at one point urged the meetings be suspended.[66] The broader picture was as gloomy. According to an 1870 statistical summary, one hundred eighty-one Mormon families lived in the ward. Bishop Woolley declared over half of these to be "perfectly indifferent" to any kind of church activity. While about 30 percent financially supported the ward or paid tithing, only thirty-one families, about one in six, regularly worshipped at the chapel.[67] With even the faithful not attending every meeting, no more than 10 to 15 percent of the congregation came to the main preaching service on a given Sunday—far below the 43 percent attendance achieved by the present-day church at comparable meetings.[68]

Without the Thirteenth Ward's fine chapel, talented membership, and urban setting, other wards probably drew even thinner crowds. "Going to meeting" clearly was not a popular nineteenth-century pastime. Part of the problem lay with economics. Frontier scarcity restricted leisure time and therefore church attendance, especially during crisis years like the period after the move south. Moreover, humdrum meetings contributed to the lack of attendance. During the two- and sometimes three-hour worship services, impromptu speakers often preached interminably, often without the virtue of edifying. Nor is there evidence that President Young's precise instructions for the care and seating of youth made meetings interesting to children or encouraged family participation.

There was a still more fundamental reason for lack of worshippers at the Assembly Rooms. Nineteenth-century Mormons simply refused to regard meeting attendance as a serious religious obligation. While the linking of "going to meeting" with religiosity surfaced as early as the 1850s, the idea obviously failed to take hold. Instead of gathering at the chapel, the pioneers declared the faith by adopting a life-style that set them apart from the world and put them to work "building the kingdom." After their conversion and baptism, they had typically abandoned "father and mother for the Gospel's sake," migrated and settled in Zion, raised families, and periodically resubmitted themselves to baptism and confirmation during one of their church's reoccurring nineteenth-century "reformations" or crusades.[69]

More than indicating the Saints' activity patterns, the early Thirteenth Ward gatherings revealed the new religion's evolving spirit and structure. At first, ward meetings were informal, spontaneous, erratic, and frequently blessed with the ecstatic spiritual gifts. Democratic or homogeneous in tendency, the meetings were led by a minimum of officers who experienced only limited bureaucratic dictation. There were home and neighborhood meetings, singing schools, educational lyceums, blessing and fast meetings, youth and women's meetings, and the main prayer and worship services held on Thursday and Sunday evenings. While evidence is limited, it appears that temporal and spatial boundaries were fluid. Meetings were held at the convenience of the worshipper who at times crossed ward lines to satisfy individual needs.

These tendencies were rapidly changing by Woolley's death. In a pattern conforming to Emile Durkheim's model for maturing social entities, the loose and homogeneous manner of the early ward gave way to a systematized and complex organizational dynamic.[70] Meetings became structured, well defined, and closely supervised. The relationship between members increasingly mirrored their ward role as lay offices, some staffed by women, were greatly expanded to meet the needs of the new auxiliary organizations. Finally, the congregation's central worshipping focus shifted from individual homes, the scene of many early meetings, to the Assembly Rooms. There, formal moral and ethical pedagogy replaced the ecstatic gifts as a meeting staple and specialized meetings assumed a life and meaning of their own.

In this evolution the move south was a watershed. Its severity erased many of the Thirteenth Ward's organizational precedents and possibly hastened the inauguration of a more complex meeting pattern a decade later. The coming of the Gentile in the late 1860s and early 1870s was equally significant, forcing the ward to expand and upgrade its programs. The Gentile also introduced Victorian sentiment, which by stressing proper conduct and outward observance softened and refined Mormon meetinghouse manners and led to the renewed preaching of the Word of Wisdom.[71] Lastly, there was another factor at work, perhaps more fundamental than the rest. All enduring religions inexorably travel a common road of organic growth, trading simplicity for complexity, social equality for diversity, spiritual gifts for indoctrination, and diffuse energy for structured behavior—behavior such as "going to meeting."[72] If the Thirteenth Ward proves an accurate microcosm, Mormon meeting patterns during the nineteenth century assumed a momentum of their own, as the new religion "put away childish things" and reached for maturity.

NOTES

1. While microanalysis is used increasingly by American scholars to discover the rich texture of national life, it has enjoyed its most success in Mormon studies among geographers and demographers. Few narrative historians have made much use of it.

2. Journal History, 13, 14, 16, 19, and 22 February 1849, Library-Archives of the Church of Jesus Christ of Latter-day Saints, Salt Lake City, Utah, hereafter LDS Archives.

3. Pioneer leaders multiplied families by a factor of eight to secure population totals. For the Thirteenth Ward number of families, see Leonard J. Arrington, *From Quaker to Latter-day Saint: Bishop Edwin D. Woolley*

(Salt Lake City: Deseret Book Company, 1976), 325, 361; and Minutes of Bishops' Meetings, 22 November and 6 December 1860 and 1 September 1870, Presiding Bishopric Papers, LDS Archives. Arrington's book contains able and generous passages describing Thirteenth Ward events.

4. Thirteenth Ward Freight Book and Assessment Roll, 1855–56, LDS Archives. Unfortunately, early records do not list the ward's women.

5. Journal History, 8 January 1854.

6. Minutes of Bishops' Meetings, 6 December 1860, Presiding Bishopric Papers, LDS Archives. The division of trades is provided in Arrington, *From Quaker to Latter-day Saint*, 325.

7. Zerubbabel Snow, Thirteenth Ward General Minutes, 12 May 1863, LDS Archives; Arrington, *From Quaker to Latter-day Saint*, 325.

8. George Goddard Journal, 27 January 1881, George Goddard Papers, LDS Archives.

9. Minutes of Bishops' Meetings, 1 September 1870, Presiding Bishopric Papers.

10. Ronald W. Walker, "The Liberal Institute: A Case Study in National Assimilation," *Dialogue: A Journal of Mormon Thought* 10 (Autumn 1977): 74–85.

11. Minutes of Bishops' Meetings, 12 May 1857, 18 July 1861, and 17 December 1863, Presiding Bishopric Papers. Obviously such a conclusion requires additional research, comparing the worship activity of rural wards with the practices of such Wasatch Front congregations as the Thirteenth Ward.

12. D. W. Meinig, "The Mormon Culture Region: Strategies and Patterns in the Geography of the American West, 1847–1964," Association of American Geographers, *Annals* 55 (June 1965): 191–220, argued a similar thesis for Mormonism's "core area" lying along Utah's Wasatch Front. Others have ably taken issue. See Charles S. Peterson, "A Mormon Town: One Man's West," *Journal of Mormon History* 3 (1976): 3–12.

13. Historical Record, 5 July 1849, Tenth Ward Papers, LDS Archives.

14. Douglas D. Alder, "The Mormon Ward: Congregation or Community?" *Journal of Mormon History* 5 (1978): 66; and Dale F. Beecher, "The Office of Bishop: An Example of Organizational Development in the Church," *Task Papers in LDS History*," No. 21 (Salt Lake City: Historical Department of the Church of Jesus Christ of Latter-day Saints, 1978), 2–9.

15. Winter Quarters Stake High Council Minutes, 13 December 1846, LDS Archives.

16. Ward Seating: Minutes of the Bishops' Meetings, 4 June 1863, Presiding Bishopric Papers; Hall Preparation: ibid., 28 September 1851; Water: ibid., 24 June 1869; Sacrament: ibid., 6 December 1860. Apparently the bishop and his counselors blessed the sacrament while the mature "acting" teachers passed it. Youth participated little if at all in the activity.

17. These meetings were soon commonplace. Journal History, 17 Feb-

ruary 1850 records: "Ward meetings and Quorum meetings were also held as usual during the day."

18. Blessing Meetings: ibid., 2 June 1850 and Seventh Ward Historical Record, 12, n.d., LDS Archives; Worship Meetings: Nineteenth Ward Book A, 11 January 1852, LDS Archives; Thirteenth Ward General Minutes, 12 March 1854, LDS Archives.

19. Nineteenth Ward Book A, 18 January 1852. Prayer meetings occupy a prominent place in most of the minutes of the early Salt Lake wards. In contrast with the informal activity of the wards, the church leaders' prayer sessions seem more structured, using ceremonial clothing and ritual prayer forms.

20. Heber C. Kimball to William Kimball, 21 December 1854, Journal History.

21. Thirteenth Ward General Minutes. See the especially full and detailed minutes for the middle 1850s.

22. Singing School: Thirteenth Ward General Minutes, 9 March 1854; Neighborhood Meetings: Minutes of the Bishops' Meetings, 25 February 1852 and 9 December 1858, Presiding Bishopric Papers; Priesthood Activity: Thirteen Ward General Minutes; Lyceums: Deseret News, 8 February 1851.

23. Minutes of the Bishops' Meetings, 24 June 1851 and 19 January 1860, Presiding Bishopric Papers; Orson Spencer Journal, 18 February 1854, Deseret News Office Papers, LDS Archives.

24. Thirteenth Ward Indian Relief Society Minutes, 1854–57, LDS Archives. For an overview of these early Relief Society meetings, see Richard L. Jensen, "Forgotten Relief Societies, 1844–1867," Dialogue: A Journal of Mormon Thought 16 (Spring 1983): 105–25.

25. Thirteenth Ward General Minutes. For specific items such as Hunter's comment: Minutes of the Bishops' Meetings, 10 August 1876, Presiding Bishopric Papers; Consecration of Oil: Thirteenth Ward General Minutes, 3 September 1868; Fast Offering Collection: Minutes of the Bishops' Meetings, 8 August 1878, Presiding Bishopric Papers. B. H. Roberts, A Comprehensive History of The Church of Jesus Christ of Latter-day Saints, 6 vols. (Salt Lake City: Deseret News Press, 1930) 4:108–12 certainly errs in stating that LDS fast offering procedures began as a result of the famine of 1855–56. The practice commenced in Kirtland and was a part of the worship routine of the Thirteenth Ward prior to the pioneer famine.

26. George Goddard Diary, George Goddard Papers.

27. Deseret News, 11 January 1851, reporting a sermon of 29 December 1850.

28. Hunter: Minutes of the Bishops' Meetings, 11 February 1852; Relief Society: Thirteenth Ward Relief Society Records, 1854–57, June 1856, LDS Archives; Goddard: Minutes of the Bishops' Meetings, 18 December 1855, Presiding Bishopric Papers. Unfortunately, with the exception of the Relief

Society, statistical totals for ward meetings were not kept.

29. Minutes of the Bishops' Meetings, 7 January 1852, Presiding Bishopric Papers.

30. For example Thirteenth Ward General Minutes, 9 November 1856.

31. Minutes of the Bishops' Meetings, 25 November 1856, Presiding Bishopric Papers. Woolley's remarks were to the assembled city bishops.

32. "Questions to Be Asked the Latter-day Saints," 1856[?], manuscript, LDS Archives. Paul H. Peterson, "The Mormon Reformation" (Ph.D. diss., Brigham Young University, 1981) affords an excellent survey of the Reformation.

33. Thirteenth Ward General Minutes, 1857. More than a few members chose to be rebaptized and reconfirmed several times.

34. George Goddard Diary, 5 March 1857, George Goddard Papers.

35. Minutes of the Bishops' Meetings, 11 November 1858, 7 and 21 July, and 27 October 1859, Presiding Bishopric Papers.

36. Military Expenditures: ibid., 17 March 1859; Weather: ibid., 23 June 1859; Emigration: ibid., 12 May 1859.

37. Meanness: ibid., 21 July 1859; Coldness: Thirteenth Ward General Minutes, 9 July 1859; Hunting: Journal History, 24 July 1859.

38. Minutes of the Bishops' Meetings, 7 July 1859, Presiding Bishopric Papers.

39. Ibid., 3 March, 7 July, and 4 August 1859.

40. *Deseret News*, 9 January 1861.

41. Minutes of the Bishops' Meetings, 8 April 1864, Presiding Bishopric Papers.

42. *Union Vedette* (Salt Lake City), 7 January 1865.

43. Minutes of the Bishops' Meetings, 7 April 1857, 15 June 1865, 30 April 1868, 2 September 1869, and 17 March 1870, Presiding Bishopric Papers.

44. Thirteenth Ward General Minutes, 21 and 25 December 1856. According to Woolley, Capener had previously agreed their long-standing dispute would be settled privately. The disgruntled communicant, however, refused to come forth.

45. Arrington, *From Quaker to Latter-day Saint*, 413–15, treats Woolley's anti-Gentile crusade in detail.

46. *Union Vedette*, 7 January 1865.

47. Minutes of the Bishops' Meetings, 30 November 1865 and 7 March 1867, Presiding Bishopric Papers. Thomas Edgar Lyon, "Evangelical Protestant Missionary Activities in Mormon Dominated Areas," (Ph.D. diss., University of Utah, 1962) treats the rise of the Gentile schools.

48. Thirteenth Ward General Minutes, 30 March 1867; "Minutes of the Thirteenth Ward Sunday School Jubilee," Thirteenth Ward Teachers' Report Meetings, 1891–1907, 17 December 1899, LDS Archives.

49. Earlier Schools: Seventeenth Ward Bishop's Record, January 1854,

p. 51, LDS Archives; Arrington, *From Quaker to Latter-day Saint*, 459; and Minutes of the Bishops' Meetings, 8 March 1866 and 7 March 1867. Sabbath School Decision: ibid., 7 March 1867.

50. Minutes of the Thirteenth Ward Sunday School Jubilee, 17 December 1899 and Thirteenth Ward Sunday School Minute Book, 1867–1880, 7 April 1867, LDS Archives. For Young's statement, Minutes of the Bishops' Meetings, 12 February 1868, Presiding Bishopric Papers.

51. Thirteenth Ward Sunday School Minute Book, 1867–1880, and Minutes of the Bishops' Meetings, 10 January 1878, Presiding Bishopric Papers.

52. Thirteenth Ward Sunday School Minute Book, 1867–1880, especially 14 July 1869 and 22 May 1870.

53. Ibid., especially 26 April 1868. For the social ramifications of Victorian reform, see George Kitson Clark, *The Making of Victorian England* (Cambridge: Harvard University Press, 1962), 147–205.

54. Minutes of the Bishops' Meetings, 7 November 1872 and 14 August 1873, Presiding Bishopric Papers. For a while the Thirteenth Ward Sunday school was rescheduled for 8:30 a.m., one-half hour earlier than normal. However, the innovation apparently brought no greater attendance to the Tabernacle.

55. "Circular of the First Presidency . . . to All the Officers and members of the Church," 11 July 1877, in James R. Clark, ed., *Messages of the First Presidency*, 6 vols. (Salt Lake City: Bookcraft, 1965), 2:289.

56. Bishop L. S. Hardy, Minutes of the Bishops' Meetings, 2 January 1868, Presiding Bishopric Papers. The revival of the Relief Societies is treated by Leonard J. Arrington, *Great Basin Kingdom: An Economic History of the Latter-day Saints, 1830–1900* (Cambridge: Harvard University Press, 1858), 251–54.

57. Thirteenth Ward General Minutes, 7 May 1857; Thirteenth Ward Relief Society Minutes, Book A, 18 April 1868, pp. 1–2, LDS Archives.

58. Thirteenth Ward Relief Society Minutes, Book A, 4 December 1873, p. 164; "Rachel Ridgway Grant," memorandum dated 28 March 1903, Box 176, fd. 22, Heber J. Grant Papers, LDS Archives; *Woman's Exponent* 4 (1 December 1875): 98, 5 (1 June 1876): 5, and 14 (15 June 1885): 13–14.

59. Thirteenth Ward Relief Society Minutes, Book A, 5 March 1874, 4 June 1874, 2 September 1875, and 13 January 1898, pp. 175, 188–89, 244, and 633; Thirteenth Ward Relief Society Minutes, Book B, 13 March 1902, pp. 97–98; Lucy Grant Cannon, "Recollections of Rachel Ivins Grant," *Relief Society Magazine* 25 (May 1938): 293–98; Rachel R. Grant to Heber J. Grant, 7 May 1905, Family Correspondence, Heber J. Grant Papers.

60. Barbara Welter, "The Cult of True Womanhood: 1820–1860," *American Quarterly* 18 (Summer 1966): 151–74.

61. Thirteenth Ward Young Ladies Mutual Improvement Association Minutes, 3 March 1875, LDS Archives.

62. Thirteenth Ward Young Men's Mutual Improvement Association Minute Book, 1874–76, 20 September 1875, LDS Archives.

63. First MIA: Thirteenth Ward Manuscript History, LDS Archives. Activities: Salt Lake Stake Historical Record Book, 1876–1880, 5 April 1878, LDS Archives. A year prior to the Thirteenth Ward's formal organization, some of the young men had met informally for "mutual improvement" and literary study. See Thirteen Ward General Minutes, 25 January 1874 and 15 February 1874.

64. Word of Wisdom: Thirteenth Ward Young Men's Mutual Improvement Association Minute Book, 1874–76, 27 September 1875. Conjoint Sessions: Salt Lake Stake Historical Record Book, 1876–1880.

65. Thirteenth Ward Primary Minute Book, 1879–1902, 2 April 1879, LDS Archives.

66. Thirteenth Ward Young Men's Mutual Improvement Association Minute Book, 1874–76; Thirteenth Ward Relief Society Minutes, Book A, 28 April 1870, 5 August 1875, 29 June 1876, 26 May 1880, pp. 66, 240, 260, and 337; and Minutes of Bishops' Meetings, 1 March 1860, Presiding Bishopric Papers.

67. Minutes of Bishops' Meetings, 1 September 1870, Presiding Bishopric Papers.

68. "Church News Section," 9, *Deseret News*, 4 March 1981. The figure is for churchwide sacrament meeting attendance.

69. The thesis that pioneer temporal activity was a religious expression is argued by Jan Shipps, "In the Presence of the Past: Continuity and Change in Twentieth-Century Mormonism," in Charles Redd Monographs in Western History, No. 13, ed. Thomas G. Alexander and Jessie L. Embry, *After 150 Years: The Latter-day Saints Sesquicentennial Perspective* (Provo, Utah: Charles Redd Center for Western Studies, 1983), 3–35. While Shipps may be correct that the crises of the late nineteenth century forced Mormons out of their "sacred space," making them practitioners of outward behavior and church attenders par excellence, these tendencies were clearly present earlier than she suggests. Her argument also seems to neglect important nineteenth-century economic and cultural currents and the organic development of the church.

70. Emile Durkheim, *The Division of Labor in Society*, trans. George Simpson (New York: Free Press, 1964), esp. 174–229.

71. Of course the reemphasis of the LDS Word of Wisdom came as a result of other factors as well. Leonard J. Arrington, *Great Basin Kingdom*, 250, argues the case for economic causation.

72. There is of course a large body of literature dealing with this process, including John G. Gager, *Kingdom and Community: The Social World of Early Christianity* (Englewood Cliffs, N.J.: Prentice-Hall, 1975), esp. 32–37.

Coming of Age in a
Western Farm Community:
Union, Utah, 1900-1910*

GORDON IRVING

Recent studies of late nineteenth- and early twentieth-century America give much attention to social transformations wrought by urbanization and industrialization. Such works generally deal with social and economic change in large cities, even though most Americans during the period lived in small towns or on farms, places also subject to sweeping changes. Given major increases in agricultural productivity because of scientific and technological innovation, as well as the pressure of a growing rural population on a relatively fixed amount of farmland, agricultural America after 1900 was ripe for change. The resulting adjustment has brought a continuing reduction in the number of farm families over the past seventy-five years, with the excess rural population either migrating to the cities or staying at home but moving into nonfarm occupations.

Historians have written about the impact of the new agricultural surpluses,[1] but little has been said about the concomitant rural population surpluses. Of value in this regard are a number of studies of colonial New England towns. In his examination of conditions in eighteenth-century Kent, Connecticut, Charles Grant argues that fifty years after settlement economic opportunity was on the decline

---

* This essay was prepared in early 1983 as a seminar paper at the University of Utah, under the direction of Dr. F. Alan Coombs. A preliminary version was written for a course in quantitative methods taught by Dr. Edward J. Davies II. Appreciation is expressed to both Professors Coombs and Davies for their suggestions. The author is presently working on an expanded study of Union's young men.

because the community's population had grown too large for its agricultural land base. This is also the finding of Kenneth Lockridge, who notes that in Dedham, Massachusetts, the phenomenon manifested itself in a sharp decline in the average size of farms, greater cultivation of marginal lands, and rising land prices. Gordon W. Kirk's *The Promise of American Life* makes the same general case regarding a nineteenth-century Michigan community fifty years after settlement. Kirk finds a decline in occupational mobility, largely because only half the sons of farm operators themselves became independent farmers, while fewer agricultural laborers moved up to farm operator status than had been the case earlier. With Grant and Lockridge, Kirk argues that the crucial factor was the fall in the amount of agricultural land per capita as the community became older, which forced young men to leave the farm to take urban blue-collar jobs.[2]

The most detailed and solidly researched exploration of the dynamics of the population/land squeeze is Philip Greven's *Four Generations: Population, Land, and Families in Colonial Andover, Massachusetts.* Greven's principal focus is the changing relationship between fathers and sons over time, with the nature of his evidence leading him to approach the matter from an economic point of view. He argues that as the land filled up, sons continued to depend on their fathers for a start in life, but that fathers increasingly saw their ability to provide such assistance decline, with the result that sons were forced to become more independent. Signs of such a change included the increasing proportion of sons who left crowded Andover; the twin tendencies of young men to marry earlier and to buy family land, rather than waiting to inherit before establishing their own households; and the shift from farm work into manufacturing or service occupations within the community.[3]

A central issue in all of these studies is the declining prospects of those coming of age in overcrowded farm communities. With that background in mind, the present essay examines the experience of young men living in Union, Utah, a rural Western community, during the first decade of the twentieth century. While a study covering only ten years cannot hope to do justice to all the changes occasioned by rural population growth, it can describe the coming-of-age process in Union and then use that information to determine what kinds of change, if any, were occasioned by the pressure of population on land.

Union on several counts is a suitable place in which to investigate such matters. By 1900 it had been settled for half a century, a period long enough for the farmland in Kent, Connecticut, and Holland, Michigan, to fill up. Also, Union's population increased 38 percent between 1900 and 1910, rising from 757 to 1,045. While Salt Lake County's population rose a much larger 69 percent over the same period, Utah's population grew a similar 35 percent and the number of persons living in the county's rural sector increased only 24 percent, indicating that Union experienced more rapid growth during the decade than did most other comparable places in the same general area. Finally, Union Precinct was one of Salt Lake County's smaller communities, encompassing some six square miles of land, all of which had passed from the federal government into private hands by the early 1890s.[4]

Lying some ten miles south of Salt Lake City, Union differed from many other Utah farming communities in that it was, first, so close to a major city and, second, because it was contiguous to Murray, Midvale, and Sandy, small towns then emerging as smelting, railroad, and secondary commercial centers. Union's location may well give the coming-of-age process there a dimension absent in more isolated towns, both because its farms had such excellent access to urban markets and because Union's young men who did not find work in farming occupations had the options of remaining in the community and seeking nonagricultural work in neighboring towns.

The primary sources of information used here are the manuscript schedules of the 1900 and 1910 federal censuses of Union Precinct, copies of which were provided by the National Archives. The schedules contain information regarding age, household and marital status, occupation, property ownership, and so on. Supplementary information regarding family relationships and places of residence for more than 80 percent of the group under study was found in the family reconstitution forms collection of the LDS Church's Genealogical Department Library. Additional data have been drawn from the 1900 tax assessment roll for Union and from Salt Lake County marriage records.[5]

The 1900 census of Union lists eighty-three male residents ages fifteen to twenty-four, young men born between 1875 and 1885. Of this group, three died before 1910, while another young man was determined to be older than twenty-four. The exclusion of these four leaves seventy-nine individuals for study, to whom have been added the thirty-one other young men of the same age listed in the 1910 census of Union, for a total of 110 persons whose status and experience are considered here.[6]

Successful establishment of a young man in a farm community like Union involved (1) acquiring sufficient farmland to make a living; (2) working on one's own account as a farmer, rather than working for someone else; and (3) establishing one's own household, which in Union almost always involved marrying and starting a family. Since an individual might be successful in none, one, two, or three of these categories, a scoring system has been devised whereby a young man's various achievements can be "added up." Points have been assigned, on the basis of information given in the 1900 and 1910 census schedules, according to the following scheme:

Household status:	0 - Not head of household
	1 - Head of household
Occupational status:	0 - Not farm owner or operator
	1 - Farm owner or operator
Property status:	0 - Owned no real property
	1 - Owned a house, but not a farm
	2 - Owned a farm

Individual scores range from 0 to 4. A score of 0 indicates continued dependence upon parents, while 4 reflects successful completion of the establishment process outlined above. Scores of 1, 2, or 3 may result from various combinations, but generally 1 represents a married person renting a house, 2 a household head who owned a home, and 3 a householder who owned a farm but was employed in some other occupation than farming. This system is simple and direct enough that scores so calculated reflect social and economic realities, rather than being artificial constructs without any real meaning or possibility of interpretation.

Not all of the young men included in the study were "successes" in terms of these criteria, nor was it expected that they would be, but the experience of both those who were and those who were not throws light upon the social processes at work as Union's land became more crowded. Among the matters investigated are geographical mobility, the role of family assistance in the establishment process, the impact of family wealth, what became of young men who did not become farmers, and how the experience of those studied compared with that of their fathers and older brothers.

Before considering the fortunes of young men who came of age after 1900, it may be helpful to look briefly at the community's entire adult male population. Of males fifteen and older who were present in 1900 and presumably still living in 1910, 57 percent remained in Union, which is a very high proportion of "persisters." Young men were more likely to be geographically mobile than were older persons—only 48 percent of those ages fifteen to twenty-four in 1900 remained in Union ten years later, while the corresponding figure for those twenty-five and older was a remarkably stable 63 percent. However, it should be noted that the decade also witnessed a considerable influx of new people—of 303 Union males fifteen and older who appear in the 1910 census, 124 were persisters from 1900, but 179 others were newcomers. And these men were only the newcomers who remained until 1910. If Union was like other American communities, large numbers of other persons may have resided there briefly between the two census enumerations.[7]

The period under study was a time of change in the community's overall occupational structure. While there were actually more males age twenty and over engaged in farm occupations in 1910 than there were in 1900 (152 vs. 130, an increase of 17 percent), the blue-collar work force had grown so much more rapidly (81 vs. 44 individuals, an increase of 84 percent) as to cause a significant change in the relative standing of the two groups. As a result, farm occupations declined from 72 to 60 percent of all jobs, while blue-collar positions rose from 24 to 32 percent.[8] The change was particularly marked among the younger men—among those who were in their early twenties, the farm occupation sector declined both absolutely (a decrease of 29 percent in the number so employed) and relatively (from 83 to 50 percent of the workers of this age group), while the number of such young men in blue-collar positions jumped by 180 percent and the proportion increased from 17 to 41 percent.

Also of interest is a change in the makeup of the blue-collar segment of the Union work force. Taking into account all males fifteen and over who held blue-collar jobs, in 1900 60 percent were employed in either the railroad-smelting-mining industries or in the building trades. A decade later only 41 percent of blue-collar workers were listed as being employed in these two fields. This shift was the result of the growth of the proportion of blue-collar workers who were day laborers from 29 to 47 percent. It would probably be wrong to make too much of this, since many of those employed in 1900 by the smelters or railroads were working as laborers, but it would appear that by 1910 a larger proportion of Union's unskilled had to seek work on a day-to-day or at least a temporary basis.

One way to evaluate the coming-of-age process in Union is to compare the position of fifteen- to twenty-four-year-old males who appear in the 1900 census with the position of males age twenty-five to thirty-four listed in the 1910 census—in other words, to examine the changes in the aggregate status of the community's young men as they grew ten years older. The comparison is a rough one, as it is evident that the group was not made up of the same individuals in both years. Subsequent sections will sharpen the analysis by tracing the experience of individuals over time.

Before considering the social and economic establishment of young men in a farm community, it is worth noting that in 1910 there were *fewer* members of the age group under study living in Union than there had been a decade earlier. Excluding the three young men present in 1900 who died, there were ten fewer individuals in this age cohort in 1910 than there had been in 1900, a drop of 13 percent, during a period when the general population of the community increased by 38 percent. Had all males living in Union in 1900 remained in the community, a decade later there would have been 389 men age ten and older. Instead, the net result of deaths and migration into and out of the community was a decrease of twenty-four individuals relative to the 1900 base population. Those contributing most to this decline were young men ages ten to nineteen in 1900 (with those in their late teens, of course, being part of the group under study here) and men sixty and older in 1900. Presumably death thinned the ranks of the latter group, but low persistence figures for the young men show that they moved away faster than they were replaced by newcomers of the same ages, suggesting that there was less "room" for them in Union than there had been a decade earlier.

Turning now to the various measures of status involved in the establishment process, the decade saw a move from a situation of almost total dependence of the young men upon their parents to one in which most were now heading families of their own. The percentage of household heads rose from 11 in 1900 to 74 in 1910, although it also bears noting that 22 percent of the group were still resident in their parents' homes in the latter year. A similar trend is evident in the percentage who were single, which dropped from 86 in 1900 to only 25 in 1910. Both changes are manifestations of the same "leaving-the-nest" phenomenon, since none of the fifty-one who headed households in 1910 were single. Except for two men who lived in the households of older brothers and one boarder (a schoolteacher), all the single men in Union in 1910 lived under the parental roof, most of them in households headed by their fathers or stepfathers.

There was also a marked shift in occupational profile in connection with the coming of age of Union's young men. In the summer of 1900, nearly 20 percent were still schoolboys, while among those who did have an occupation, 80 percent were involved in farming (almost all of them as farmhands). A decade later, 54 percent were working in the farm sector, with 45 percent holding other types of jobs, most of them blue-collar. Only 38 percent of the young men were farm operators in 1910, representing 70 percent of the group in farm occupations generally.

With regard to property ownership, in 1900, with most young men still dependent upon their parents, only one of them actually owned any land—a mortgaged farm—although eight others were renting houses or farms. Ten years later the situation had changed considerably, with 68 percent of young householders owning some kind of real property. At that point 35 percent of Union's young men owned a farm. With an additional eight of them renting farms, nearly half the group controlled farmland. Among property owners, 40 percent reported mortgages, the rate for homes (55 percent) being much higher than for farms (33 percent).

TABLE 1
ESTABLISHMENT SCORES OF UNION YOUNG MEN, 1900–1910

SCORE	1900 SCORE (Ages 15–24)		1910 SCORE (Ages 25–34)	
0	66	84%	14	20%
1	9	11%	16	23%
2	3	4%	15	22%
3	—	—	6	9%
4	1	1%	18	26%
Total	79	100%	69	100%
	(Mean = 0.2)		(Mean = 2.0)	

Source: 1900 and 1910 federal manuscript census schedules for Union Precinct

Having examined in turn each of the criteria of social and economic establishment, it is now possible to discuss the overall position of Union's young men in 1900 and 1910. Table 1 shows a considerable change in the distribution of establishment scores over the decade, with the percentage of young men scoring 0 declining from 84 in 1900 to only 20 in 1910. The preceding discussion has shown that this decline was primarily the result of young men marrying and establishing their own households. Marriage by itself did not result in the full economic establishment of the individual, however, as evidenced by the fact that in 1910 fully 45 percent of the young men scored either 1 or 2, low scores that generally mean that they were married and living in either a rented or mortgaged house, although some were operating rented farms. Only 26 percent of the group scored 4, indicating full establishment as independent farmers, in accordance with the criteria used in this study.

The discussion to this point has treated the young men of Union as a body. If the group is divided between those who were in their late teens in 1900 and their late twenties a decade later, on the one hand, versus those who were in their early twenties at the turn of the century and in their early thirties in 1910, the older group had a head start in 1900 (having a mean score of 0.6, as opposed to a mean of 0.0 for the younger group) and maintained that lead over the decade (with a mean score of 2.3 in 1910, as compared to the younger group's average score of 1.7). Interestingly enough, some 20 percent of both age groups were still dependent on their parents in 1910. The older group, however, had been far more successful than their younger brothers and neighbors in terms of establishing themselves as farmers, with 52 percent of males in their early thirties who had left their parents' homes scoring 4, as contrasted with only 17 percent of householders in their late twenties.

These differences suggest that coming of age was a process of several years' duration rather than an event that took place all at once when a young man reached a certain age. For those young men present in Union in 1910 who were then married, the mean age at marriage was 23.1 years. The data in this section, while not by any means conclusive, suggest that among those who became independent farmers, the ownership of farmland often did not come until they were in their early thirties, approximately a decade after marriage.

Based on this description of the general status of young men as they came of age in Union, what follows will extend and deepen the analysis by identifying the circumstances that led to greater or lesser degrees of success in the establishment process.

As noted earlier, the young men age fifteen to twenty-four who resided in Union in 1900 split on a nearly fifty-fifty basis with regard to geographical mobility, 52 percent having left the community by 1910. Sociologists studying contemporary communities have argued that migration is a selective process—that is, that there are differences in the socioeconomic characteristics of migrants and non-migrants, with the differences usually favoring those who leave. Historians, on the other hand, have found that persistence and wealth usually tend to be linked, since those who owned most of a community's resources had more reason to remain than did others.[9] This section deals with possible differences in the backgrounds of persisters and outmigrants from Union, as well as examining in a preliminary way what became of the forty-one young men who left the community.

One possible difference might be the existence of family ties for some and not for others. Of the seventy-nine individuals under consideration, all but the lone boarder and three young heads of house-

TABLE 2
INFLUENCE OF FAMILY POSITION ON PERSISTENCE/MIGRATION

| | FAMILY POSITION IN 1900 | | | | | | | |
	1	2	3	4	5	6	7	TOTAL
PERSISTER SONS	3 33%	29 50%	4 80%	1 33%	--	1 50%	--	38 48%
OUTMIGRANT SONS	6 67%	29 50%	1 20%	2 67%	1 100%	1 50%	1 100%	41 52%
N =	9	58	5	3	1	2	1	79 100%

Column headings: 1 = head of household; 2 = son (head = father); 3 = son (head = widowed mother); 4 = son (head = step-father); 5 = son-in-law; 6 = brother or brother-in-law; 7 = boarder

Source: 1900 and 1910 federal manuscript census schedules for Union Precinct

holds were either sons or sons-in-law of Union families. Given the extreme preponderance of sons living in their fathers' homes (with an exact fifty-fifty division between persisters and outmigrants in that category), family ties per se explain little. (See Table 2.) Thirty-four of the forty-one young men who left the community were sons of Union families. Among this group, there was a further fifty-fifty split, this time between those who struck out on their own, leaving parents and siblings behind in Union, and those who moved away with their entire families. Seven of the eight young men with no parental ties in Union had left by 1910, suggesting that the *absence* of such ties was strongly related to migration.

Family ties do, however, help to explain migration decisions if the economic status of families in the community is also taken into account. Sons of farmers and of skilled or semiskilled blue-collar workers were somewhat more likely to remain in Union than the typical young man, while the few sons of farm laborers and unskilled blue-collar workers (as well, again, as those without fathers in Union at all) were more likely to leave. Consideration of the fathers' 1900 farm establishment scores, calculated from the information in the census on the same basis outlined earlier, yields a similar result.

Unfortunately, the fact that two-thirds of the young men were sons of Union farmers makes the interpretation of such findings difficult. What is needed is a way of examining differences within the group of farmer-fathers. An obvious approach is through parental wealth, with data on total assessed wealth (mainly in the form of land and improvements) being drawn from Union's 1900 tax roll.[10] Table 3 examines the influence of family wealth on filial persistence in Union. With the exception of the fourth column in the table, there is a positive relationship between high levels of wealth and high persistence rates. The chi square value for Table 3 indicates that this is definitely not a distribution that would occur by chance, while the contingency coefficient shows a moderately strong relationship between parental wealth and persistence. If the categories are collapsed, as in Table 4, the relationship becomes statistically stronger, as indicated by the very high Yule's Q of 0.85.[11]

Although confirmation of the point awaits examination of the county land records, it seems reasonable to believe that the wealthier fathers were in a better position to provide economic assistance to their sons, in many cases enabling those sons to remain in Union, than were fathers endowed with fewer resources. Since the relationship between wealth and persistence does not show a one-to-one correlation, it may be expected that other noneconomic considerations also played a role. For instance, the high persistence level for sons in the third column of Table 3 is largely due to the fact that all the sons in this study (three in each family) of Willard Burgon, a brickmason and farm owner who became Union's Mormon bishop in 1900, Robert Milne, a locomotive engineer who owned a farm, and Philip Stone, a farmer, remained in the community. The low persistence rate in the next column, by the same token, is largely the result of the decision of somewhat more wealthy farmers Alfred Ball and Niels Lundberg to take their families (including five sons in this study) to other communities. And the already high percentage of persistence in the last column might have been fifteen points higher had not three of the four sons of well-to-do farmer John Oborn included in the study chosen to move away, leaving the rest of the family behind them. While it remains to be seen why these individuals acted as they did,

TABLE 3
FATHER'S WEALTH IN 1900 AND PERSISTENCE/MIGRATION OF SONS

	FATHER'S WEALTH IN 1900						
	NONE*	$1-500	$501-1000	$1001-1500	$1501-2000	$2001+	TOTAL
PERSISTER SONS	1 8%	1 17%	20 74%	4 27%	1 100%	11 65%	38 49%
OUTMIGRANT SONS	11 92%	5 83%	7 26%	11 73%	– –	6 35%	40 51%
N =	12	6	27	15	1	17	78

*Includes cases where father not present in Union in 1900 as well as cases where father was Union resident but is not listed in tax list

Chi square = 23.2 (five degrees of freedom), p = .001
Contingency coefficient = 0.48

Source: Wealth data—1900 tax assessment roll for School District 23; persistence data—1900 and 1910 federal manuscript census schedules for Union Precinct

TABLE 4
FATHER'S WEALTH IN 1900 AND PERSISTENCE/MIGRATION OF SONS
(COLLAPSED TABLE)

	FATHER'S WEALTH IN 1900			
	$0-500*	$501-1500	$1501+	TOTAL
PERSISTER SONS	2 11%	24 57%	12 67%	38 49%
OUTMIGRANT SONS	16 89%	18 43%	6 33%	40 51%
N =	18	42	18	78

*Includes cases where father not present in Union in 1900 as well as cases where father was Union resident but does not appear in tax list

Chi square = 13.8 (2 degrees of freedom), p = .001
Contingency coefficient = 0.39
Yule's Q for persister/outmigrant vs. 0–500/501+ = 0.85

Source: Table 3

on the whole it seems clear that family wealth played a role in the question of migration.

Another question requiring further research is whether those young men who left Union after 1900 fared better in their efforts to establish themselves in life than did those who remained behind. Since family wealth has been shown to be positively related to persistence, it might be supposed that they did not. However, the matter cannot be addressed with any great certainty until outmigrants can be traced in the 1910 federal census schedules. In the meantime, the family reconstitution forms and other records have been used to determine the probable residence of 76 percent of the individuals in question, based on the birthplaces of their children born closest to 1910. Half of the outmigrants who could be traced remained in Salt Lake County, while just over two-thirds stayed in Utah. A half-dozen moved to Salt Lake City and presumably became part of the urban work force, while those who moved to Sandy or Murray might have also moved out of farm work. But, surprisingly enough, the attraction of urban economic opportunities was rather weak, as most of Union's outmigrants (or their fathers) selected new places of residence characterized by an agricultural lifestyle.[12]

In the absence of information regarding the property and occupational status of outmigrants in 1910, the only comparisons now possible between the young men who left Union and those who persisted are those discussed above. However, the presence of young men between ages twenty-five and thirty-four who were in Union in 1910 but who had not lived there a decade earlier provides an opportunity for contrast and counterpoint of persisters and newcomers.

The family reconstitution forms and county marriage records indicate that of the thirty-one newcomers, seven were sons—or in one case a grandson—of parents either present in Union's 1900 census or listed as landowners in the community's 1900 tax roll. Another nine had no such parental ties themselves but had married daughters of Union families. Thus 52 percent of the newcomer group had some familial tie in the community. The remaining fifteen individuals were neither returning sons nor sons-in-law of Union families, although two of them were brothers of Union residents of 1900.

The same sources, or the census itself in some cases, provide clues about the previous whereabouts of 61 percent of Union's newcomers of 1910. Of those traced, few came from very far away, with almost two-thirds having moved to Union from nearby communities in Salt Lake County and about three-fourths having been Utah residents a decade earlier. Almost all the sons-in-law came from Salt Lake County homes, with none coming from out of state. Even among those without family ties, about 60 percent had Utah roots, the remainder having come from other states to work or from Europe as converts to Mormonism.

Earlier the components of the group's farm establishment scores were used to sketch a general picture of the position of Union's young men in 1910. We now turn once more to those indicators, this time contrasting the status of persisters and newcomers in order to determine the influence of persistence and family ties on the establishment process. It should be borne in mind that all but one of the persisters were sons of Union families, the one exception being a son-in-law.

In all four subgroups most young men were heads of households. All of the sons-in-law and 80 percent of the newcomers without previous family ties in Union headed independent households. There was apparently little reason for unattached males to come into the community (other than to marry Union girls), as indicated by the presence of only three unmarried newcomers, one of them a boarder and two other young men who had come to Union after 1900 with their families. Among both persisters and returning sons, about 30 percent were unmarried and still living under the parental roof. As indicated earlier, marital status closely paralleled family position among Union's young men. Obviously all the sons-in-law were married, while the three newcomers without previous family ties who were not heads of household were the only single members of that subgroup.

Before discussing the occupational profiles of the various subgroups of 1910, a related question needing attention is the extent to which returning sons and persisters followed their fathers' occupations. This issue is treated in Table 5, which provides striking evidence of the intergenerational transmission of occupational status. As can be seen, 78 percent of the sons of farmers were themselves employed in farm occupations a decade later (two-thirds of them as owners or operators of farms), while 85 percent of the few sons of

TABLE 5
INTERGENERATIONAL TRANSMISSION OF OCCUPATIONAL STATUS, 1900–1910

SON'S OCCU- PATIONAL STATUS IN 1910	FATHER'S OCCUPATIONAL STATUS IN 1900					
	FARMER	FARM WORKER	WHITE COLLAR	BLUE COLLAR[a]	BLUE COLLAR[b]	TOTAL
FARMER	16 52%	--	--	--	1 100%	17 42%
FARM WORKER	8 26%	1 100%	--	--	--	9 22%
WHITE COLLAR	--	--	1 100%	1 14%	--	2 5%
BLUE COLLAR skilled or semi-skilled	3 10%	--	--	5 71%	--	8 20%
BLUE COLLAR unskilled	4 13%	--	--	1 14%	--	5 12%
N =	31	1	1	7	1	41

[a] = skilled or semiskilled
[b] = unskilled

Source: 1900 and 1910 federal manuscript census schedules for Union Precinct

skilled and semiskilled blue-collar fathers were also employed in some type of nonfarm manual labor in 1910. In the single cases of sons of farm laborers and white-collar workers, both had the same occupational status as their fathers. Of course, before concluding that occupational status transmission was almost total, it should be remembered that nearly half the sons of Union fathers, including the sons of farmers, had left the community by 1910.[13]

Turning again to the total group of persisters and newcomers, Table 6 indicates that persisters were considerably more likely (66 percent) to be working in farm occupations than were any of the categories of newcomers, family ties notwithstanding. If the comparison is based on the figure for persister sons and returning sons of Union farmer-fathers given in the previous paragraph (78 percent), the contrast is even more striking. However, it is also noteworthy that while no sons-in-law came into the community to work as farm-

TABLE 6
OCCUPATIONAL STATUS, BY PERSISTENCE CATEGORY,
OF UNION YOUNG MEN OF 1910

OCCUPATIONAL STATUS IN 1910	PERSISTERS	RETURNING SONS	SONS-IN-LAW	NEWCOMERS*	TOTAL
NO OCCUPATION	--	1 14%	--	--	1 1%
FARMERS	17 45%	1 14%	4 44%	4 27%	26 38%
FARM WORKERS	8 21%	1 14%	--	2 13%	11 16%
WHITE COLLAR	2 5%	--	1 11%	2 13%	5 7%
BLUE COLLAR[a]	7 18%	2 29%	2 22%	2 13%	13 19%
BLUE COLLAR[b]	4 11%	2 29%	2 22%	5 33%	13 19%
N =	38	7	9	15	69

[a] = skilled or semiskilled
[b] = unskilled
*Newcomers without previous family ties in Union

Source: 1900 and 1910 federal manuscript census schedules of Union Precinct

hands, the percentage of farm operators among them was as high as it was among persisting sons. Turning to the blue-collar occupations, 58 percent of returning sons were employed in such work, as compared to only 29 percent of their persisting brothers. Nearly half of the sons-in-law and the newcomers without family ties were also blue-collar workers. The proportion of all newcomers employed as day laborers, depending upon the category of newcomer being considered, ranged between double and triple the corresponding figure for persisters.

While nearly half of the persisters owned no real property, according to the 1910 census, returning sons and newcomers without family ties were even less likely to be property owners. Surprisingly enough, the group with the highest proportion of property ownership, by a small margin, was the sons-in-law. Obviously these figures are affected

TABLE 7
PROPERTY OWNERSHIP STATUS, BY PERSISTENCE CATEGORY,
OF UNION YOUNG MEN (HEADS OF HOUSEHOLD ONLY) IN 1910

PROPERTY CATEGORY	PERSISTERS	RETURNING SONS	SONS-IN-LAW	NEWCOMERS*	TOTAL
OWNED NO REAL PROPERTY	5 20%	--	4 44%	5 42%	14 27%
OWNED HOUSE, BUT NOT FARM	5 20%	2 40%	2 22%	4 33%	13 25%
OWNED FARM	15 60%	3 60%	3 33%	3 25%	24 47%
N =	25	5	9	12	51

*Newcomers without previous family ties in Union

Source: 1900 and 1910 federal manuscript census schedules of Union Precinct

by the relatively high number of persisters who were not heads of household. Table 7 sharpens the analysis considerably by looking only at the property status of those who headed their own households in 1910. Viewed in this way, sons of Union families had a clear advantage over sons-in-law and newcomers without family ties. While more than 40 percent of the latter two groups owned no real property, only 17 percent of persisters and returning sons heading their own households found themselves in such circumstances. Sons of Union parents particularly had an advantage over other young men in terms of farm ownership, with 60 percent of them owning farms, as compared to only 33 percent of sons-in-law and 25 percent of newcomers without family ties. Although the supposition needs to be checked in the land records, presumably the three newcomer sons-in-law listed in the census as farm owners had received land from their wives' families, strengthening the relationship between family assistance and farm ownership. The importance of family assistance is also implied by differences in the percentages of farms and houses that were mortgaged—for example, among persisters and returning sons the figures were 33 percent and 40 percent, respectively, while among newcomers without family ties the corresponding figures were approximately double—67 percent and 75 percent.

With regard to property ownership, an additional point worth making relates to the timing of succession to family land. Among sons of Union families, 40 percent in 1910 had deceased fathers. Of household heads whose fathers had died, 91 percent owned farms. On the other hand, among householders whose fathers were still alive and residing in Union, only 35 percent were farm owners, even though 94 percent of them were sons of farm-owning fathers. This suggests that the rather lengthy establishment process might even last until the death of a young man's father. The sons' ages also played a role, though. Of householders who were sons of living and deceased Union fathers, the percentages of those in their early thirties who were farm owners were 60 and 83 percent, respectively. The corresponding figures for those in their late twenties were 0 and 27 percent. Thus both life and death seem to have favored, by a substantial margin, the older group of young men over those in their late twenties.

Having reviewed the various elements of the process of coming of age from the point of view of persistence, we now turn to the composite establishment scores, which are presented in Table 8. The mean scores for each subgroup indicate that Union's typical young man had taken two steps in the process of establishing himself socially and economically as an adult—the setting up of his own household and the acquisition of title to a house and lot. While this is the central tendency of the figures in the table, it is somewhat misleading, as the actual cases are dispersed across the whole range of scores, with a concentration at the bottom of the scale in all categories except that of sons-in-law. In no case had more than one-third of the young men achieved full establishment, as defined in this study.

A slightly different pattern emerges if the group of young men is divided between those in their late twenties and those in their early thirties. As was noted earlier, the percentage of the older group achieving full establishment as farmers is triple the corresponding figure for the younger group. The difference is almost entirely due to the fact that older persisters attained that status more than five times

TABLE 8
ESTABLISHMENT SCORES, BY PERSISTENCE CATEGORIES,
OF UNION YOUNG MEN OF 1910

	PERSISTERS	RETURNING SONS	SONS-IN-LAW	NEWCOMERS*	TOTAL
0	9	2	– –	3	14
	24%	29%		20%	20%
1	7	2	3	4	16
	18%	29%	33%	27%	23%
2	7	– –	3	5	15
	18%		33%	33%	22%
3	4	2	– –	– –	6
	11%	29%			9%
4	11	1	3	3	18
	29%	14%	33%	20%	26%
N =	38	7	9	15	69
Mean =	2.0	1.7	2.3	1.7	2.0

*Newcomers without previous family ties in Union

Source: 1900 and 1910 federal manuscript census schedules of Union Precinct

as often as their younger counterparts. Apparently few fathers were prepared to divide family land with adult sons under the age of thirty.

Whether age is considered or not, it is consistently the sons-in-law who have the highest mean scores, no doubt because all of them headed households, while in the other categories 20 to 29 percent of the young men were still dependents in their parents' homes. This is a rather paradoxical situation, since older persisters who had established their own households scored much higher than did household heads in the other categories, as can be seen in Table 9. Persisters show up as highly successful, as do the few returning sons and sons-in-law, although at a slightly lower level. When the data are viewed in this way, the disadvantage of the newcomers without family ties becomes particularly apparent. Yet the paradox remains, for many of the sons of Union families were still dependents in 1910, which kept them at the bottom of the establishment scale.

One further matter remains to be treated in this section—whether sons of more well-to-do fathers fared better in the coming-of-age

TABLE 9
ESTABLISHMENT SCORES, BY PERSISTENCE CATEGORIES, OF UNION YOUNG
MEN (OLDER GROUP: AGES 30–34, HEADS OF HOUSEHOLDS ONLY) OF 1910

	PERSISTERS	RETURNING SONS	SONS-IN-LAW	NEWCOMERS*	TOTAL
1	1	1	– –	2	4
	8%	33%		29%	16%
2	2	– –	1	3	6
	15%		50%	43%	24%
3	1	1	– –	– –	2
	8%	33%			8%
4	9	1	1	2	13
	69%	33%	50%	29%	52%
N =	13	3	2	7	25
Mean =	3.4	2.7	3.0	2.3	3.0

*Newcomers without previous family ties in Union

Source: 1900 and 1910 federal manuscript census schedules of Union Precinct

process than did those who were sons of fathers with fewer resources. It has already been established that sons of fathers with medium or high levels of wealth were far more likely to stay in Union than were those whose fathers had little or no wealth. With regard to the group of young men living in Union in 1910, Table 10 takes the analysis a step further by examining the relationship between fathers' farm establishment scores in 1900 and the scores of their sons a decade later, with 1910 residents who were not sons of Union families serving as a control group.

The differences between those with parental ties and those without are not large, if viewed in the aggregate—for instance, 45 percent of both groups had scores of 0 or 1—but at the higher end of the scale, sons of Union families had some advantage, with the proportion of scores of 3 or 4 being 38 percent for sons, versus 26 percent for the others. When the fathers' status is taken into account, however, it becomes clear that sons of high-scoring fathers were the only ones who achieved full establishment, doing so nearly half again as often as young men who had come from outside Union.

The division of the young men into younger and older age groups again shows that age played a part in the establishment process.

TABLE 10
ESTABLISHMENT SCORES OF FATHERS IN 1900 AND SONS IN 1910

SON'S SCORE IN 1910	FATHER'S SCORE IN 1900				TOTAL	NOT IN UNION	GRAND TOTAL
	1	2	3	4			
0	– –	2 100%	– –	8 26%	10 25%	4 15%	14 21%
1	– –	– –	1 14%	7 23%	8 20%	8 30%	16 24%
2	– –	– –	4 57%	3 10%	7 18%	8 30%	15 22%
3	– –	– –	2 29%	3 10%	5 13%	1 4%	6 9%
4	– –	– –	– –	10 32%	10 25%	6 22%	16 24%
N =	0	2	7	31	40	27	67*
Mean =		0.0	2.1	2.0	1.9	1.9	2.0

*Excludes two cases where fathers were former Union residents who had died by 1900

Source: 1900 and 1910 federal manuscript census schedules for Union Precinct

Among those in the younger group, only 12 percent of the sons of high-scoring fathers had achieved full establishment by 1910, as opposed to 21 percent of those in their late twenties without parental ties in the community. For the older group, the corresponding figures are 60 and 29 percent. It is noteworthy that the older sons of high-scoring fathers, with one exception, were either fully established as farmers or were still dependent upon those fathers, while those of the same age who had no parental ties in Union are scattered along the whole range of scores.

Table 11 expands Table 10 by taking into account the variations in wealth of fathers with an establishment score of 4 in 1900. Not only were the sons of Union's most well-to-do farmer-fathers nearly twice as likely to be successful as were the sons of fathers of middling wealth (the few sons of fathers with little or no wealth having left the community en masse), but it is also striking that those who remained under the parental roof in 1910 were almost exclusively sons of men of medium wealth. This suggests that the timing of

TABLE 11
ESTABLISHMENT SCORES OF FATHERS (INCLUDING LEVEL OF WEALTH FOR FATHERS WITH SCORES OF 4) AND OF SONS IN 1910

SON'S SCORE IN 1910	FATHER'S SCORE IN 1900							NOT IN UNION	GRAND TOTAL
	1	2	3	4ª					
				LOW	MED	HIGH	TOTAL		
0	– –	2 100%	– –	– –	7 41%	1 8%	10 26%	4 14%	14 20%
1	– –	– –	1 14%	– –	4 24%	3 23%	8 21%	8 29%	16 23%
2	– –	– –	4 57%	– –	1 6%	2 15%	7 18%	8 29%	15 22%
3	– –	– –	2 29%	– –	1 6%	1 8%	4 10%	1 4%	6 9%
4	– –	– –	– –	– –	4 24%	6 46%	10 26%	7 25%	18 26%
N =	0	2	7	0	17	13	39*	28	69**

*Two cases are excluded because of problems in interpreting wealth data in tax list regarding fathers
**Includes all cases
ªDivided by level of wealth: low = $0–500, medium = $501–1500, high = $1501 +

Source: 1900 and 1910 federal manuscript census schedules for Union Precinct; 1900 tax assessment roll for School District 23.

land transfer was tied not only to the ages of the fathers and sons, as well as whether the father was still living, as noted earlier, but also to the family's level of wealth. Once sons of middle-level families established their own households, however, they were nearly as successful as the sons of the more wealthy (40 percent with scores of 4, versus 50 percent), although it would appear that the circumstances of their families might have required them to wait a great deal longer to achieve that independence.

The relationship between family wealth and sons' occupations in 1910 is also revealing. Among sons from middle-level families, 52 percent were working in nonagricultural jobs in 1910, the figure for sons of the wealthiest families being only 8 percent. Even among sons of farmers the difference is striking, with 68 percent of sons of middle-level families working in farm occupations, versus 92 percent of the sons of the wealthiest families. The corresponding figures for sons who were farm operators are 37 and 77 percent, respectively, reinforcing the point that parental wealth had a significant impact on a son's prospects even within the farm sector. A similar situation prevailed with regard to the related matter of land control. Only 56 percent of householders whose fathers had middling wealth owned or were renting farms in 1910 (with only 60 percent of that number listing farming as their principal occupation, the rest being in blue-collar positions), while 89 percent of householders who were sons of the most well-to-do farmers either owned or were renting farms (with 88 percent of them actually operating those farms).

None of this is particularly surprising. Wealth in Union was generally a function of the amount of land owned, and if a farm were small it seems unlikely that a father would endanger his family's economic survival by dividing his land with grown sons. If sons in such families chose neither to leave Union nor to marry and seek nonfarm work, their only alternative was to live with their parents and hope to inherit the family farm at the death or retirement of their fathers. Still, for a young man reared in a farm family, the reward to be gained might have appeared worth the wait, since the alternative was a change in lifestyle, as evidenced by the fate of many of the newcomers without family ties — renting, manual labor done at the pleasure of someone else, and probably moving from community to community in search of better prospects.

Analysis of the coming-of-age process provides a way of assessing the changes brought by growth of population on a fixed agricultural land base. Studies of other farm communities fifty to a hundred years after settlement suggest that two prime consequences of rural population growth in Union would be accelerated movement of young men out of the community and a concomitant movement of persisters out of farm occupations. Does what has been learned about the establishment process in Union provide support for this view?

Most young men living in Union in 1910 had achieved only very modest success in establishing an economic base for themselves. The great majority had married and set up their own households, and of those who had done so, just over two-thirds owned property. However, in most cases such property was a house and lot, rather than a farm. Only one in four young men living in Union had attained full economic establishment as a farmer. However, low levels of achievement by themselves prove nothing about declining opportunities for young men, as the question of change requires comparisons over time.

With regard to persistence levels, only 48 percent of young men present in 1900 were still in Union a decade later, as compared to 63 percent of older males. Also, the size of the group under study declined over the period, even though the overall population of Union grew rather rapidly. Both findings are consistent with a narrowing of opportunity for young men, but neither measure offers a comparison over time. A stronger approach takes time into account by comparing the situation of young men after the turn of the century with that of young men who lived in the community twenty years earlier. The estimated ten-year persistence rate for young men living in Union in 1880 is 52 percent. A drop of four points over twenty years might be held to be evidence of declining opportunity, but the difference is a very small one. Of greater significance is the widening gap between persistence rates for young men and older males over the twenty years, rising from eight points (52 vs. 60) in the 1880s to fifteen points (48 vs. 63) in the first decade of the twentieth century.[14]

The argument for declining opportunity is strengthened by noting a change in the nature of migration from Union. In the 1880s those young men who left almost without exception moved away with their parents, often going to unsettled areas in northern Utah or southeastern Idaho in search of unoccupied land. Of the young men resident in Union in 1900, some outmigrants also left with their families, but fully half the single males who moved away left parents and siblings behind. Where Union could once provide economic opportunities to all the youthful members of its more stable families, a generation later even these families were frequently split, with some members staying in Union and others seeking economic opportunity elsewhere.

The data regarding persistence agree in a general way with the findings of other scholars, although there is not the major acceleration of migration that one might have expected to find. This may be in part due to Union's peculiar location, as noted earlier. With regard to the other sign of declining opportunity—lower rates of success in the farm establishment process for young men living in Union in 1910—the evidence supports in a stronger and less equivocal fashion the basic thesis Philip Greven and others have advanced.

The comparison of the statuses of young men and their fathers suggests a certain amount of intergenerational economic decline, but it is likely misleading to compare the position of a group of young men with the status achieved by older men after a lifetime of work.[15] A better comparison, entailing additional research, would contrast the position of Union's young men in 1910 with that of their fathers thirty years earlier, but for the time being something less than that will have to do. If the growth of population did indeed result in declining prospects for young men ages twenty-five to thirty-four in 1910, it seems reasonable to expect that their farm establishment status would be lower than that of their older brothers and neighbors—Union residents ages twenty-five to thirty-four in 1900 —when they were the same age.

Figures based on the 1900 and 1910 census schedules show that young men in their late twenties were 14 percent more likely to be heads of households in 1910 than were their counterparts a decade earlier. There was a 21 percent decline in the proportion of real property ownership, coupled with a 14 percent drop in the proportion of farm ownership. Viewed only in terms of heads of households, 44 percent of such young men in their late twenties had owned farms in 1900, compared with only 33 percent in 1910. Comparing the groups that were in their early thirties in the two years, it can be

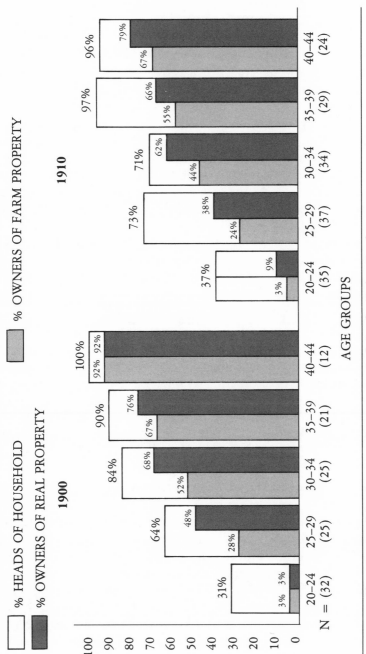

PERCENT OF SELECTED AGE GROUPS OF UNION MALES IDENTIFIED AS HEADS OF HOUSEHOLD AND OWNERS OF REAL PROPERTY IN 1900 AND 1910 FEDERAL CENSUS SCHEDULES

☐ % HEADS OF HOUSEHOLD   ▨ % OWNERS OF FARM PROPERTY

■ % OWNERS OF REAL PROPERTY

1900

1910

AGE GROUPS

Source: 1900 and 1910 federal manuscript census schedules for Union Precinct seen that a considerably lower proportion (down 15 percent) were household heads in 1910 than had been the case in 1900, while the proportions of property owners and farm owners had also declined (down 9 and 15 percent, respectively). When viewed in terms of *householders* who were in their early thirties in the two years, however, the percentage of farm ownership actually remained the same, 62 percent.

These figures also show a relative decline in the position of men who were in their late thirties and early forties, the proportion of householders in their late thirties who owned farms declining from 74 percent in 1900 to 57 percent in 1910, with the corresponding figures for household heads in their early forties dropping from 92 to 70 percent. Thus the decline in the position of those whose progress has been followed in this study, Union's young men, was not out of line with the patterns for their older brethren. All these figures support the view that as population increased and Union's farmland became crowded, economic opportunity in its traditional form declined.

Table 12 gives an overall picture by comparing the establishment scores of young men who were twenty-five to thirty-four in 1900 with those of the group who were that age in 1910. The differences are not major ones, the mean scores for the young men of 1900 and the young men of 1910 differing by only 0.2. Not surprisingly, by now, the major variations between the two sets of distributions appear to be the rise in the proportion of young men in their early thirties who remained in their parents' homes (up 83 percent) and the rise in the proportion of those in their late twenties who chose *not* to stay home, but rather to marry and establish their own households (up 58 percent). The percentage of young men who achieved full farm establishment fell over the course of the decade, with the decline being 23 percent for the total group, 7 percent for the older subgroup, and 30 percent for the younger subgroup. Consideration of both farm ownership and the broader measure provided by the farm establishment score suggests that a prime component of economic decline in Union was the deterioration of the position of the younger men vis-à-vis that of their slightly older brothers.

It would appear from this discussion, in conjunction with various points raised earlier, that as opportunity for farm ownership and

TABLE 12
ESTABLISHMENT SCORES OF YOUNG MEN AGES 25–34 IN 1900 AND YOUNG MEN AGES 25–34 IN 1910

	1900 GROUP, 25–34*	1910 GROUP, 25–34**	CHG. IN PCT.	1900 GROUP, 25–29*	1910 GROUP, 25–29**	CHG. IN PCT.	1900 GROUP, 30–34*	1910 GROUP, 30–34**	CHG. IN PCT.
0	9 18%	14 20%	+2	6 24%	7 19%	−5	3 12%	7 22%	+10
1	8 16%	16 23%	+7	5 20%	12 32%	+12	3 12%	4 13%	+1
2	13 26%	15 22%	−4	7 28%	9 24%	−4	6 24%	6 19%	−5
3	4 8%	6 9%	+1	2 8%	4 11%	+3	2 8%	2 6%	−2
4	16 32%	18 26%	−6	5 20%	5 14%	−6	11 44%	13 41%	−3
N =	50	69	(−9%)	25	37	(−6%)	25	32	(−12%)
Mean =	2.2	2.0		1.8	1.7		2.6	2.3	

*1900 establishment scores
**1910 establishment scores

Source: 1900 and 1910 federal manuscript census schedules for Union Precinct

operation declined in Union, there were two responses to the change. Among those residing in Union in 1900 who would be in their late twenties a decade later, nearly 60 percent left the community. Those of this age group who were still in Union in 1910 chose, or were forced, in large part to turn their backs on the declining possibility of farm succession by marrying and seeking work in blue-collar occupations, often of an unskilled nature, rather than waiting at home to inherit family farmland. Among the group who were five years older, just over 40 percent of those present in 1900 moved somewhere else. Those young men in their early thirties who had family ties and were still residing in the community in 1910 had either received family land and become farmers or had delayed marriage and continued working on the family farm while waiting for something that might never come.[16]

The differences between the two groups are a matter of degree, of course, as there were younger farmers and older blue-collar workers, but there appears to be a clear difference in the trend for each age group. Older brothers responded to declining opportunities by waiting for the old familiar patterns to work, while their younger fellows took a position at once more radical and more pragmatic, acknowledging the new economic facts of life by seeking nonfarm work. For many this was no doubt more a matter of necessity than it was a question of personal preference. Those forced to cut their ties with the traditional lifestyle of their families—for farming is a way of life as much as it is an occupation—became in a very real sense displaced persons faced with the need to make a considerable adjustment in their activities and their view of the world.

The study of conditions in Union also demonstrates that the decline in opportunity was not spread evenly across the whole group of young men. In this community, as would likely be the case in most rural settings, family wealth was a mediating factor, determining who could continue in the old traditional ways and who would have to change. Young men without family ties in Union in 1900 almost without exception left the community, while sons of fathers with little or no wealth also moved away en masse. For those who remained, as well as among those newcomers who had joined them by 1910, family ties had much to do with which young men became farmers, 88 percent of the young farm owners at the end of the decade being sons or sons-in-law of Union families. But here too family wealth played a significant role, with young men from the community's wealthiest families becoming fully established as farmers twice as often as were sons of Union's middling families. Lack of family resources thus forced young men in both the poor and middling groups into the increasingly urban-oriented, nonagricultural employment patterns of the twentieth century, while outsiders coming into the community had almost no chance of establishing themselves in the farm sector. Some of the less fortunate who had grown up in Union responded by moving, usually with their parents, to marginal agricultural areas in Utah or Idaho. But for the many who struck out on their own, the principal alternative to blue-collar work in Union appears to have been blue-collar work in nearby communities in Salt Lake County.[17]

The course of social and economic development in Union is very much in line with patterns observed in other American agricultural communities farther east in earlier times. This is hardly surprising; the outcome would almost seem to be inevitable. As population increased in an area, only part of the residents could be farmers; the rest would have to move on or do some other kind of work. In the eighteenth and nineteenth centuries the result was a surplus population that could settle the West, where the process would be repeated again. In the early twentieth century the introduction of expensive farm machinery, new crop varieties, chemical fertilizers, and so on, meant that fewer farmers were required to produce food for both local needs and distant markets. One result was an acceleration of the flow of people out of agriculture and into urban centers, or at least urban types of occupations. In Union, and probably in many other rural communities, population growth worked in tandem with the forces of modernization, breaking up the agricultural land base and providing a pool of former farm workers for manufacturing, mineral-processing, and service-sector jobs. These were necessary preconditions for subsequent, even more far-reaching social and economic transformations.

NOTES

1. Examples of such works are Theodore Saloutos and John D. Hicks, *Agricultural Discontent in the Middle West, 1900–1939* (Madison: University of Wisconsin Press, 1951); James H. Shideler, *Farm Crisis, 1919–1923* (Berkeley and Los Angeles: University of California Press, 1957); and Gilbert C. Fite, *American Farmers: The New Minority* (Bloomington: Indiana University Press, 1981).

2. Charles S. Grant, *Democracy in the Connecticut Frontier Town of Kent* (New York: Columbia University Press, 1961); Kenneth Lockridge, "Land, Population and the Evolution of New England Society, 1630–1790," *Past and Present*, No. 39 (April 1968): 62–80; Gordon W. Kirk Jr., *The Promise of American Life: Social Mobility in a Nineteenth-Century Immigrant Community, Holland, Michigan, 1847–1894* (Philadelphia: The American Philosophical Society, 1978).

3. Philip J. Greven Jr., *Four Generations: Population, Land, and Family in Colonial Andover, Massachusetts* (Ithaca, N.Y.: Cornell University Press, 1970).

4. U.S. Census Office, *Census Reports, Vol. 1; Twelfth Census of the United States, taken in the year 1900; Population, Part I* (Washington: U.S. Census Office, 1901). 392; U.S. Department of Commerce, Bureau of the Census, *Thirteenth Census of the United States, 1910; Population by Counties and Minor Civil Divisions, 1910, 1900, 1890* (Washington: Government Printing Office, 1912), 531. The 1910 population of Union comes from the manuscript census schedule. In 1904 Salt Lake County's twenty-seven precincts were consolidated to form ten civil precincts. Steven K. Madsen, *A Union, Utah, History* (Union: Union Fort Chapter, Sons of the Utah Pioneers, 1981), 94–95. However, Union continued as a voting precinct and in the 1910 census is enumerated apart from other communities. Information on disposition of government lands is from the Tract Books of the Salt Lake City office of the U.S. General Land Office, on microfilm at the Bureau of Land Management office in Salt Lake City.

5. For each of the 110 individuals, a search was made in the collection of family reconstitution forms. These forms provide dates of birth, marriage, and death, as well as information about parentage, places of residence, and church membership. For 58 percent of the individuals, forms were found on which they appear as husbands, while for 74 percent forms were located on which they appear as children in their parents' families. An additional five individuals were found listed as sons-in-law on forms for their wives' parents. Only twenty individuals (18 percent of the group) could not be located at all in the collection. Supplementary information regarding five of them was found in the Salt Lake County marriage records or in the membership records of the LDS Church. Thus for only 14 percent of the individuals included in the study are the census schedules the sole

source of information. The tax roll and county marriage records are available on microfilm, the former at the Utah State Archives and the latter at the LDS Church Genealogical Department Library.

6. It was originally planned to study males ages ten to nineteen in 1900 and twenty to twenty-nine in 1910. A quick survey of the 1900 and 1910 censuses was proof enough that the establishment process had barely gotten under way for males twenty to twenty-four in both years. It thus seemed more reasonable to study the group mentioned in the text. Philip Greven has been criticized by Maris Vinovskis for dealing only with the descendants of Andover's original settlers, which probably biases his study's outcome in favor of society's most prosperous members. That is, while Greven found evidence of economic decline, he perhaps greatly understates the case. Maris Vinovskis, "American Historical Demography: A Review Essay," *Historical Methods Newsletter* 4 (September 1971): 141–48. The present study of Union has sought to avoid this problem by including all members of the age group involved, whether rich or poor, from old families or new.

7. A convenient review of recent studies on geographical mobility, although slanted toward large cities, is Stephan Thernstrom and Peter R. Knights, "Men in Motion: Some Data and Speculations about Urban Population Mobility in Nineteenth-Century America," in *Anonymous Americans: Explorations in Nineteenth-Century Social History*, Tamara K. Hareven, ed. (Englewood Cliffs, N.J.: Prentice-Hall, 1971). Thernstrom's view that urban Americans in the nineteenth century were extremely mobile has been challenged by Donald H. Parkerson in "How Mobile Were Nineteenth-Century Americans?" *Historical Methods* 15 (Summer 1982): 99–109. For examples of studies dealing with persistence and mobility in rural communities, see James C. Malin, "The Turnover of Farm Population in Kansas," *Kansas Historical Quarterly* 4 (November 1935): 339–72 and Merle Curti, *The Making of an American Community: A Case Study of Democracy in a Frontier County* (Stanford, Cal.: Stanford University Press, 1959). In studying persistence in five areas of Kansas for the periods 1895–1905 and 1905–1915, Malin found rates ranging between 40 and 50 percent for farm operators.

8. The term "laborer" was used ambiguously by census enumerators in Union, or at least so it seems from the vantage point of the 1980s. There is no problem with specific references such as "laborer at smelter," but in cases where the place of employment is unspecified, one wonders what type of work such persons did. The term "farmhand" is used in the census, but almost always in reference to persons living with and apparently working for farm-owning parents. The case might be made that day laborers in Union were as likely working for farmers as in more strictly blue-collar areas, where "blue collar" is taken to mean "nonfarm." The approach taken in this paper has been to view day laborers as persons who did manual labor on an ad hoc basis, without implying that they were factory workers or mill

hands. Even if such men spent part of their time in farm work, their positions were insecure and their status no doubt the lowest in the community.

In discussing the general occupational situation in the community, males between fifteen and nineteen were excluded, since the 1910 census was taken in April (earlier censuses were enumerated in June); many teenagers who in the summer would have probably been farmhands were thus listed as schoolboys. To have included them would have supported the interesting but questionable conclusion that Union fathers in 1910 were in less need of agricultural help and were therefore keeping their sons in school longer than had been the case a decade before.

9. For studies by sociologists, see Jon H. Rieger, "Geographic Mobility and the Occupational Attainment of Rural Youth: A Longitudinal Evaluation," *Rural Sociology* 37 (June 1972): 189–207; Harry K. Schwarzweller and James S. Brown, "Social Class Origins, Rural-Urban Migration, and Economic Life Chances: A Case Study," *Rural Sociology* 32 (March 1967): 5–19; and Seena Kohl and John W. Bennett, "Kinship, Succession, and the Migration of Young People in a Canadian Agricultural Community," *International Journal of Comparative Sociology* 6 (March 1965): 95–116. For the view of historians, see Richard S. Alcorn, "Leadership and Stability in Mid-Nineteenth-Century America: A Case Study of an Illinois Town," *Journal of American History* 61 (December 1974): 685–702 and David Gagan and Herbert Mays, "Historical Demography and Canadian Social History: Families and Land in Peel County, Ontario," *Canadian Historical Review* 54 (March 1973): 27–47. An essay that links wealth and persistence in nineteenth-century Utah is J. R. Kearl, Clayne L. Pope, and Larry T. Wimmer, "Household Wealth in a Settlement Economy: Utah, 1850–1870," *Journal of Economic History* 40 (September 1980): 477–96.

10. Four of the parents listed in the census do not appear in the tax records and are here presumed not to have owned property in Union. Another case is excluded because the father in question apparently held property jointly with others of his own father's heirs and it is thus not possible to determine what his own level of wealth was. It should also be noted that terms such as "wealthy" and "rich" are only meaningful in a comparative sense; the most well-to-do father in 1900, with an assessed wealth of $3,600, would have been viewed as a person of middling or perhaps even insignificant means had he moved to certain neighborhoods in Salt Lake City.

11. Historians interested in quantification can generally show that a relationship exists between two variables, but such findings are generally made meaningful only if the *strength* of the relationship can be determined. Yule's Q is an easily calculated measure that can be used with 2 x 2 contingency tables, with values ranging between 0 (no relationship between variables) and 1 (a total and direct relationship).

12. Studies of geographical mobility based on urban populations, such as those done by Thernstrom and Knights, have implied that mobility was

a symptom of rootless transiency. In his "Migrants in the Nineteenth Century: Fugitives or Families in Motion?" *Journal of Family History* 6 (Fall 1981): 257–77, sociologist A. Gordon Darroch, after assessing several historical studies of geographical mobility, argues that migration was not necessarily the disruptive, negative force that Thernstrom sees it to be, since much of it occurred under family auspices and within "apparently well-defined and relatively narrow cultural and geographical limits," thus representing a commonsense adjustment to changing circumstances. Migration into and out of Union conforms more to Darroch's view than to Thernstrom's, with movement being confined within a very small geographical area — largely rural Salt Lake County, although some young men ranged further afield, moving as far as Idaho or even southern Alberta.

13. Examples of sociological studies of occupational and ownership transmission are W. A. Anderson, "The Transmission of Farming as an Occupation," *Rural Sociology* 4 (December 1939): 433–48 and "Transmission of Farming as an Occupation, II," *Rural Sociology* 5 (September 1940): 349–51; Mark Lancelle and Richard D. Rodefeld, "The Influence of Social Origins on the Ability to Attain Ownership of Large Farms," *Rural Sociology* 45 (Fall 1980): 381–95; and Robert T. McMillan, "Farm Ownership Status of Parents as a Determinant of the Socioeconomic Status of Farmers," *Rural Sociology* 9 (June 1944): 151–60. The inclusion of a time dimension makes these articles useful not only for the models offered, but also as historical studies.

14. The persistence rate for the period 1880–90 is at best approximate, the 1890 census having been destroyed several years ago in a fire. The list of Union residents is from the 1880 census, on microfilm at the LDS Church Genealogical Department Library. Which males were still present a decade later was determined by using the 1890 Union tax roll, on microfilm at the Utah State Archives, and the Genealogical Department Library's collection of family reconstitution forms. For further information on the social and economic history of Union prior to 1900, see Gordon Irving, "Land, Families, and Population Turnover in Union, Utah, 1849–1900: First Approximations of Nineteenth-Century Mormon Social Patterns" (unpublished paper presented at the annual meeting of the Mormon History Association, May 1982; copy in author's files).

15. On the methodological difficulties inherent in comparing the status of fathers and sons, see Kirk, *The Promise of American Life*, chapter 5.

16. The fate of the five sons in their early thirties who in 1910 were still dependent upon their parents is a rather sad footnote. Three of them never married, one had been married but by 1910 was divorced and never remarried, and one did not marry until age forty-one, when he married the widow of his younger brother. Three of the five were employed in 1910 as farm laborers, suggesting that they were indeed waiting to inherit, one was an unskilled laborer, and one had a position in the skilled/semiskilled

blue-collar sector. The experience of these five men highlights a perplexing feature of quantitative/social-science history, of which this essay is an example. It has been argued here that these individuals had failed to marry by 1910 for economic reasons, but there is no way of determining whether, or to what extent, personal considerations of a noneconomic nature (such as social backwardness or lack of ambition) affected their decisions. In a study of a small group, where the idiosyncrasies of one or two members of the group can shift the results fairly dramatically, at the very least the historian ought to offer his conclusions with a fair degree of humility.

17. Much of what has been reported in this essay is tentative, in the sense that census schedules yield only "snapshots" of the situations of Union's young men in 1900 and 1910, with explanations of the changes occurring between those two points being based on inference. It has been assumed, for example, that if a young man in 1910 had both land and family ties in Union, then he must have received the land from his family. This seems a reasonable view, but additional research in county land records will doubtless reveal much more about the dynamics of the process of coming of age, especially as regards the mechanism (or mechanisms) used in Union for the actual transfer of family wealth from one generation to the next. Some factors have been identified here that apparently affected the nature and timing of the transfer process, such as the ages of fathers and sons, whether the father was living, and the family's economic position, but much remains to be done to establish the study on more solid evidentiary ground. For thoughts on the ways in which studies of social processes based solely on information from one or two points in time can be misleading, see Lutz K. Berkner, "The Use and Misuse of Census Data for the Historical Analysis of Family Structure," *Journal of Interdisciplinary History* 4 (Spring 1975): 721–38.

Latter-day Saint Education in the Pacific Islands

R. LANIER BRITSCH

It would be impossible to calculate the money or man-years the Latter-day Saints have expended on educational ventures in the Pacific Islands. But the amounts are very large and the chronological commitment long. Today in the Pacific the church operates one university, one college, six high schools, ten middle schools, and eight elementary schools. In addition, over 11,500 students were enrolled in seminaries and institutes in 1981.[1] The church is thus a substantial presence in the nine island groups that comprise Polynesia with its three million plus population.

Of the many kinds of social efforts in which the church could have been involved—medicine, politics, industry—missionaries and church leaders consistently chose education as the most important to its Polynesian members. It is not surprising that missionaries involved themselves in education at an early date, for learning of all kinds has been a hallmark of the Mormons since the early days of the restoration. LDS scriptures aver the importance of learning and church leaders regularly emphasize its value.[2] In the early days of LDS missions in the Pacific the need for basic literacy was so evident that almost all missionaries, no matter how rudimentary their own skills, recognized that they could help. Over the decades the need became complex, but recognition of basic literacy as essential to the growth of the individual has never diminished in the minds of missionaries or their leaders.

LDS schools in the Pacific have proven useful to members in another way than providing educational opportunity. Elementary, secondary, and collegiate schools have opened many doors to the

Polynesian community at large. They are a means of influencing nonmember students and a focus for public relations. In American Samoa, for example, the brass band from the LDS school frequently played at government functions and made many influential friends for the church. In Tonga, Liahona High School has been the means of inviting Tongan royalty to campus many times. Liahona High School has also been the means of conversions to the gospel and of helping the church to enter another island group — Kiribati — that had formerly been closed to LDS missionary work. Whatever the motive, the story of Latter-day Saint education in the Pacific spans 130 years and an accelerated shift from independent initiative to survival through sophisticated cooperation.

LDS educational activity in the Pacific began in the mid-nineteenth century almost as soon as the Mormons began settling the Great Basin. When Louisa Barnes Pratt and Caroline Barnes Crosby found themselves among the illiterate children of Tubuai, French Polynesia, in 1850–51, they desired to teach them how to read and write so as to at least understand the scriptures.[3] Mary Jane Dilworth Hammond in Lahaina, Hawaii, was motivated by similar concerns at about the same time. In addition to her work, in 1853 and for several years after that, LDS male missionaries operated schools on Oahu, Kauai, Maui, Molokai, and Lanai. Their purpose was similar to that of Pratt, Crosby, and Hammond, but they also wanted to provide LDS children an alternative to Protestant- and Roman Catholic-dominated institutions where Mormonism might be discouraged. Although all of these LDS schools closed in 1858 (perhaps because of the Utah War, when Brigham Young recalled all missionaries), an elementary school was reopened in Hawaii in 1865.

Later Mildred E. Randall operated two small schools in Laie — one for *haole* (white) children and one for Hawaiians, the differences in the children's language abilities being the reason given by the mission president for the separate schools.[4] The Laie schools were created because there was no other school there. It was an on-again, off-again proposition until 1887, then operated continually until 1927, when the Territory of Hawaii took it over.[5]

In New Zealand LDS missionaries did not open small chapel schools until the 1880s. As a rule these schools were short-lived, entirely dependent on the teaching abilities and length of stay of the various missionaries. A number of the schools were operated until around 1913, when the mission turned its attention and resources to the new Maori Agricultural College, a small residential high school. While they lasted, the New Zealand chapel schools served to provide basic literacy in areas where no government schools yet existed and, less successfully, to lure LDS children away from older and generally better Protestant schools.[6]

The most unusual early schools operated by the church in the Pacific were the German schools in Samoa. Following the German takeover in 1899, German colonial policy demanded that all schools for Samoan children be conducted in the German language, with only a few exceptions made for vernacular schools and those for non-Samoan children. Since one of the principal subjects in LDS schools had been English, this policy made LDS education efforts very difficult. Nevertheless, in an effort to continue to influence Samoan children, the mission opened several schools in which German was the medium of instruction. The First Presidency supported this effort by assigning German-speaking missionaries to Samoa. Unfortunately, the quality of instruction fell short of the German governor's expectations and these schools were discontinued in 1905. In 1913 a second attempt was made to open German-language schools. This effort, however, came to an abrupt halt with World War I and the British takeover of Samoa on 28 August 1914. Almost immediately the mission began new English-language schools.[7]

None of these early schools were of the one-room log or brick variety found on the American frontier. The earliest were literally conducted under coconut trees. Soon more permanent schoolhouses were constructed of palm fronds, but most buildings were temporary and makeshift. Other materials to support the learning process were also hard to come by. While missionaries did their best to obtain books, paper, even sticks with which to write in the sand or dirt, their mission presidents could offer mostly hope and encouragement in the dual tasks of proselyting and teaching.

The twentieth century would see improvements. In fact, even before the turn of the century missionaries in Samoa were establishing central schools—larger elementary schools which attracted students from several villages and branches of the church. These offered larger classes, pooled resources, and better schooling. In 1904, missionaries and members in Samoa created a residential school in the newly founded Mormon village of Sauniatu. Here, LDS students primarily from the island of Upolu were brought together to be taught not only the "three Rs" but also appropriate Christian living. Boys and girls were housed in separate large *fales*, and adult chaperones who followed the traditional *matai* system (i.e., the chiefly, patriarchal way) directed the students' activities during out-of-school hours. Work on the church-owned plantation was a standard part of the regimen.[8] A similar school was organized at about the same time near Pago Pago in American Samoa, and in 1913 missionaries and members in New Zealand organized the Maori Agricultural College to help Maori boys learn modern agricultural methods.[9]

Yet even into the first half of the twentieth century there was no organized LDS school system in the Pacific. True, mission presidents, sometimes assisted by local boards of one configuration or another, usually oversaw the work of the schools. Moreover, many of the schools enjoyed the supervision of an appointed principal. But there was little coordination between schools within an island group and even less between countries or missions.

An exception was the R. E. (religious education) system in the Pacific that flourished between World Wars I and II. Although formal R. E. classes were not instituted until the late 1930s, at Kohala, Hawaii, religion was intertwined with the curriculum of most of the early schools from the very beginning. The scriptures were often used as reading textbooks, and the teachers themselves were almost always missionaries. When the Territorial Legislature of Hawaii allowed students one hour per week of free schooltime to attend classes taught by the denomination of their choice, LDS religious instruction in the Pacific was made official. Once underway, this program expanded rapidly. Religion classes were also offered at the Maori Agricultural College, Makeke School in Tonga, and the advanced schools in Samoa, all before World War II. By 1941 there were eighty-five R. E. classes being offered in seventy-one different schools in Hawaii, with an average weekly attendance of 1,468 (approximately half not members of the church).

But the bombing of Pearl Harbor crippled the R. E. program. During the war years it limped along due to lack of missionaries. Then, in 1948, the U.S. Supreme Court dealt another blow by decreeing unconstitutional any religious classes held in public schools. Although other arrangements were made, this drastically curtailed the R. E. program in Hawaii,[10] concluding a century of LDS educational efforts in the Pacific, a century characterized by persistent yet sporadic and isolated programs subject to the winds of political change.

After World War II the casual, time-honored pace of LDS schools in the Pacific began to change. Until the 1950s, though extensive and with deep historical roots, the "system" had developed with no master plan. Mission presidents, missionaries, and local Saints in each area had responded independently to immediate, local needs. Now a new pattern emerged. For the first time, church leaders in Salt Lake City began to take responsibility for schools in the Pacific missions.

President David O. McKay played an especially important role in the consolidation of efforts, feeling an unusual closeness to the peoples of Polynesia from the time of his first visit there in 1921. He would oversee the radical transition from mission- to church-operated schools, with all the ensuing complications. Probably the most important development in the evolution of the administration of Pacific schools was the building of two church colleges. The first of these was the Church College of New Zealand, whose genius was initially not President McKay.

Following his call as an apostle in 1946, Elder Matthew Cowley regularly encouraged members of the Council of the Twelve to support the construction of a new residential school in New Zealand. It would replace the old Maori Agricultural College, but it would be different because it would be coeducational, with European children as well as Maoris welcome there. When President George Albert Smith set apart Gordon C. Young as mission president in 1948, he told him to look for land for another school.[11]

Young found land and construction of a new school, the Church College of New Zealand, began in 1951. But progress was slow until the Hui Tau (all-New Zealand LDS conference) of April 1952. At that time New Zealand Saints voted to support volunteer laborers with food and money until the school was completed. Within a few days of the Hui Tau, forty laborers reported to the building site. (A similar volunteer system had previously worked successfully in Tonga.)[12] Through the combined efforts of the mission president,

Sidney J. Ottley, the construction supervisor, George Biesinger, who had been sent from Salt Lake City, and Wendell B. Mendenhall, who initially had no official role in the project but who took an interest in the construction of the school while he was visiting his missionary son in New Zealand, the project got under way. Mendenhall worked with Biesinger for about two months trying to get the buildings started and then returned to his home in California where, with the support of President McKay, he arranged for seven skilled craftsmen to go to New Zealand on construction assignments. These men became supervisors of crews of builders. They trained Maoris, Samoans, Tongans, and other volunteers to be carpenters, brick masons, cabinetmakers, electricians, concrete workers, and so forth. By May 1954, part of the school was ready for visitors and the annual Hui Tau was held there. Thus the school opened four years before it accepted students.

President McKay's role in the creation of the Church College of Hawaii was more pivotal, for the story of what would become the Brigham Young University, Hawaii Campus, had begun not in the 1950s when the Twelve Apostles approved a proposal to create a college in Hawaii, but in 1921 when Apostle McKay visited Laie and envisioned a college to serve the needs of the many races of people who lived in and surrounding the Pacific. Over the next thirty years he often spoke with church leaders in Hawaii concerning his school in Laie.

When he became president of the church in 1951, McKay took immediate action. In 1954 plans for the school were made public and a year later McKay traveled to Hawaii to preside at the ground breaking.

The missionary purpose of the college was a priority with the president. In his prayer consecrating the land to the college he said, "We dedicate our actions in this service unto thee and unto thy glory and to the salvation of the children of men, that this college, and the temple, and the town of Laie may become a missionary factor, influencing not thousands, not tens of thousands, but millions of people who will come seeking to know what this town and its significance are."

The new school—originally named the Church College of Hawaii—opened its doors on 26 September 1955, much of it still housed in temporary war surplus buildings. From that humble beginning with 153 students, the college has grown to a student body of two thousand. The current campus is a beautiful multimillion-dollar facility. Although it was originally a two-year junior college, almost as soon as it received accreditation in 1959 it was expanded to a four-year teacher-trainer institution. Since then the number of courses has expanded considerably.

From 1951 on, President McKay backed the building of other modern schools. He encouraged mission and local leaders in Samoa and Tonga in construction of the new Pesega and Liahona High Schools. Under his direction skilled craftsmen were called from the United States to serve as builders in the islands until new concrete block buildings replaced the frame and frond structures of past decades. The completion of these new campuses emphasized the size of the church's commitment in the islands and brought to everyone's attention the costs of creating and operating schools.

But the comprehensiveness and complexity of the new building program was not as overwhelming as the new administrative tasks. The problems of staffing, maintaining, and directing all that would go on in the new schools was staggering. One change was from missionary to professional teachers. Another was the adjustment in the nature and mission of the school system consequent to development of junior and senior high schools. Earlier schools had generally served the needs of students who lived close to them. But the new high schools were larger than earlier schools and, for some students, were residential as well. The resulting capital outlay was far greater than in earlier years and those costs signalled the need for trained, full-time administration.

In January 1955, President McKay toured the island missions. He had previously approved a new high school for American Samoa, but while there he decided that the plans were far too small for the need. He was right; at that time only a small percentage of high school-age youth could be accommodated by the one small high school. Elsewhere on the tour President McKay approved new buildings at Pesega, Liahona, and the Church College of New Zealand, and also selected the temple site in New Zealand. The magnitude of what was happening was clear to him. Mission presidents would find it difficult to handle the prodigious amount of work necessary to direct both the schools and the proselyting efforts. It would be necessary to create a different kind of system.

Wendell B. Mendenhall, who served as chairman of the Church Building Committee from 1955 to 1965, helped in the transition to that system. Under his direction the labor missionary system flourished in the Pacific. Hundreds of buildings—chapels, school buildings, dormitories, shops, houses, and the New Zealand Temple—were constructed by participants in this program. Because the building missionary program was so substantial in the islands, Elder Mendenhall spent considerable time there directing the work. President McKay trusted him and relied on his observations.

Mendenhall suggested that the schools be removed from the jurisdiction of mission presidents, and that the principals of the schools be responsible to the First Presidency or whomever they designated. That separation was made in 1957. He also suggested that missionary teachers be selected from among the proselyting missionaries, but be called directly as teacher-missionaries.[13] That suggestion was followed only briefly. By 1959 all missionary teachers had been phased out and a professional force had been hired in the missionaries' place.

Mendenhall's suggestions were an appropriate beginning, but it was soon recognized that the separate schools could be administered more efficiently if they were combined into a system. To achieve this objective, the First Presidency and Council of the Twelve formed the Pacific Board of Education on 21 June 1957. "The Church schools in the Pacific," wrote the Pacific Board of Education in 1961, "fitted with perfect naturalness into an integrated system of education, made homogenous by Church membership, geography, similar administration problems and a student body predominantly Polynesian. Such a system under centralized control would relieve the First Presidency of supervisory detail while remaining directly responsible to their authority."[14]

Predictably, Mendenhall was appointed chairman of the Pacific Board, with four other men completing the organization. The board would be both a policy-making and an administrative body, in this respect differing from most boards of education. Besides formulating policy, it directly administered the Pacific schools of the church, hiring, firing, and supervising the administrative personnel, staff, and faculty for the system. All this was done without forfeiting the missionary emphasis of earlier times, for the board was an ecclesiastical as well as managerial body. In 1961 board members wrote: "Teachers have been selected first of all for spiritual worthiness. . . . Each has assumed his appointment in the South Pacific in the spirit of a missionary."[15]

One of the first problems the Pacific Board faced was not spiritual but temporal: that of equity in salary schedules. The question of how to pay teachers has been a problem ever since. While missions operated the schools, salaries had not been a problem: missionaries were supported from home. But after 1957, when the Pacific Board began to make the rapid change from missionary teachers to professionals, church education leaders had to grapple with the problem. The trickiest issue was how to set salaries for Americans versus salaries for local teachers. It was impractical to expect American teachers to live on the local pay scale of Samoa or Tonga. (Probably very few Americans would have accepted such conditions unless the assignment came as a mission call.) On the other hand, if native teachers were paid on an American scale they would be so much wealthier than their peers that serious problems could result. Yet it was inequitable to assign locals to a low island pay schedule while paying Americans a higher salary for the same work.

As the ensuing years have shown, there is no satisfactory answer to this problem. Probably the best solution is to eliminate American teachers from the island schools altogether, but some outside teachers have always been needed to help the quality of various faculties. The Pacific Board decided to adopt the New Zealand Government Salary Scale for teachers who were native to the islands, but raised the salary amounts somewhat. Thus they used the precedent established by a major national educational system as parity for islanders' salaries. They did what they were legally bound to do while supporting the American teachers on a scale similar to what they would have earned in the States.[16] Clearly, a suitable answer had not been found, but it was the best anyone could devise.

The Pacific Board directed church schools in the Pacific for eight significant years. From 1957 to 1965 the growth of the system was rapid. The Church College of New Zealand was completed and dedicated in April 1958, its final cost near seven million dollars. Then in January 1961, the new Mapusaga High School in American Samoa was dedicated. It initially offered high school education to two hundred young people, many of whom otherwise would have gone without schooling. In 1963, the Pacific Board opened a primary school in Papeete, Tahiti, the first LDS school in French Polynesia since World War I. In addition, the board supervised numerous additions to classroom and administrative buildings, dormitories, and teacher dwellings. Virtually all of these buildings were constructed by labor missionaries of the church, even the early buildings at the Church College of Hawaii (Brigham Young University, Hawaii Campus).

Synchronous to the development of an LDS educational system in the Pacific was an updating of the religious instruction classes so badly curtailed in 1948. An early-morning, nonreleased-time seminary program was introduced in Hawaii in 1953. Ten years later 927 seminary students were attending various programs in Hawaii, with slow growth to 1,100 by 1975. From its Hawaii renewal, the program ranged to all the Pacific islands. Religion classes are required of all students attending LDS middle and high schools, while in such distant places as New Caledonia and Vanuatu (formerly the New Hebrides) home study courses are offered.

Institute courses for college students were also first offered in Hawaii, at the University of Hawaii in 1959. In the late 1960s New Zealand institutes were founded at universities in Auckland and Wellington. Even a small college in Apia, Western Samoa, now enjoys an LDS Institute for religious study by college youth.

Expansion in LDS education efforts in the Pacific in the 1960s coincided with exploding growth throughout the church, particularly in seminaries and institutes and at Brigham Young University in Provo, Utah. Church authorities determined to bring all church schools together under a centralized organization. Effective 1 January 1965, the church created the Unified Church School System with Harvey L. Taylor as administrator of all schools but Brigham Young University, Provo, which was administered by Ernest L. Wilkinson. The Church Board of Education consisted of the First Presidency and the Council of the Twelve Apostles.[17] With the church as a whole, LDS schools in the Pacific completed the transition to a modern era.

The years of the Pacific Board had seen buoyant growth. Schools had been constructed at comparatively low cost, with the total financial outlay to operate the system less than two million dollars in

1960.[18] But the cost of building and operating schools inflated rapidly during the late 1960s and through the 1970s. The challenge faced by administrator Taylor and his successors was to help the system survive. This required efficiency and sophistication.

In 1970 the First Presidency changed the name of the school system to the Church Education System (CES), with Neal A. Maxwell as commissioner of education. Under his direction the church world was divided into zones, and administrators were put in charge of seminaries, institutes, and schools within these zones. (The church university and colleges were administered more directly.) A direct ecclesiastical relationship was also added with members of the First Quorum of the Seventy acting as zone advisors. Area administrators were appointed to direct CES affairs within the zones. With minor changes the system has followed this pattern to the present.

It became clear that growing numbers and diversity among church members meant the CES could not meet the demands of every group of Saints in the world. Priorities must be set for the system to continue to achieve anything at all. With this in mind the Commissioner's Office formulated some guiding principles for the operation of the system. The policies put into effect in 1971 state: (1) Literacy and basic education are gospel needs. (2) Church programs will not duplicate otherwise available opportunities, especially in higher education. (3) Ultimately, all high school- and college-age Latter-day Saints should have access to weekday religious education in tandem with secular education.[19]

The first policy reaffirmed the LDS commitment to provide schooling for its members where secular education was not available. Accordingly, most church schools in the Pacific continue to operate and several new schools have been founded. An example may be seen in Kiribati (formerly the Gilbert Islands).

In 1972 school and mission leaders in Tonga and Fiji received letters from the headmaster of a small Kiribati school asking admittance of some of his students to Liahona High School. Though not LDS, twelve of his graduates were accepted at Liahona in 1972 and twelve more in 1973. Most of these students joined the church, and more enrollees were to follow in subsequent years. This proved the beginning of both educational and proselyting efforts by the Mormons in Kiribati, for prior to this the church had been shut out of these islands by a "catch-22" regulation that required any church wishing to proselyte to have a minimum fifty members already on the islands. Before long the Kiribati graduates of Liahona High School were returning to their homes as both high school graduates and native LDS missionaries. By 1976 there were enough local members in Kiribati to organize the church there, and since then the church has become involved in a small middle school there.[20]

Another school founded in response to unmet educational needs of church members is the LDS Technical High School in Fiji. Established in 1975, this institution was created to prepare students for vocations and represents an entirely new type of church school.[21]

Policy in 1971 made it clear that the church would not duplicate educational efforts of governments or other systems. Changes in local conditions require continual evaluation of the need for LDS schools. For instance, during the 1960s and 1970s the U.S. government expended many millions of dollars improving the public education system in American Samoa, making Mapusaga High School a serious duplication of "otherwise available opportunities." The school was accordingly closed in 1975.

The LDS Primary School in Tahiti was closed in June 1982 for somewhat different but related reasons. Because the church operated no high school in Tahiti, LDS children attended a government-supported secondary school. To enter, they were required either to graduate from the public elementary school or to pass an examination proving equivalent achievement. Because some students were not passing the examination, LDS parents had begun taking them out of the church school and registering them in the public elementary school to insure their preparation for secondary school. Church education leaders could either improve the LDS Primary School or, since fine alternate schooling was available, abandon it. So many students withdrew during the several years prior to its closing that the latter choice was fairly painless, and the school property served as the site for the new Tahitian Temple.[22]

One of the most difficult administrative decisions has been to keep the Church College of New Zealand open even though it clearly cannot be justified by present policy guidelines. Recently Bruce M. Lake, zone administrator of the New Zealand area, had his staff study the cost and implications of closing the Church College of New Zealand. He presented four options to the Church Education System Board: Option one was to continue on the present basis. Option two was to close the school, there being considerable precedent in Tahiti, Samoa, Mexico, South America, and so forth. The third option was to accept the government education grants received by all other private schools in New Zealand. The fourth was to accept the conditions of the Private Schools Conditional Integration Act of 1977, which provides for the government to take over the school, paying for salaries, books, maintenance, etc. The school would be run by a local committee and could have continued to hire only LDS teachers and teach religion classes. That option was declined because the Church Education System Board does not believe in such close arrangements with governments. The decision was made to continue to operate the school on the present basis.

Why was the Church College of New Zealand not closed? All students in New Zealand have access to fine free public education. The school obviously represented a gospel need other than education alone. To close the school would have closed the community of Temple View. It would have dissolved a stake and affected the New Zealand Missionary Training Center. Even though costs to operate the school will double in the next several years, the school is the flagship of the church in New Zealand. It, along with the temple and the village of Temple View, has become a public landmark and the focal point of the church in that land.

Church Education System administrators have worked toward total rationalization of the Pacific school system. Nevertheless, significant problems continue to occur. Government education policies change constantly, as do local goals and needs. Keeping abreast of such changes and responding appropriately has been an ongoing challenge. Within the LDS system some problems continue to cause concerns. For example, the home study seminary lessons in the French language do not adequately serve the children of French Polynesia who speak Tahitian as a first language. But the lessons are not available yet in Tahitian. Another problem has been finding the right people to serve as superintendents of the systems in Tonga and Samoa. Some have strong spiritual attributes and some administrative skills, but finding both combined has been difficult. For this reason administrators in Salt Lake City have found it necessary to appoint outsiders in top positions from time to time.

A Tongan student wondering why her school is closing, or a Maori boy greeting his new teacher from America, might tell stories seemingly unrelated to the administrative tale related in this essay. Yet clarity in seeing the big picture is increasingly important to the development of LDS education in the Pacific. And through the three phases of growth—the long first century of frond and *fale* classrooms, the postwar transition period during which the Pacific islands came of age, and the economic pressures of the past two decades—LDS educational efforts there have been guided by individual needs and one overriding principle: Knowledge is essential to the growth of each member of the church. In the Pacific the church will continue to be a resource in obtaining that knowledge.

NOTES

1. Church Education System, Yearly Seminary Summary for 1981, composite total from area reports.

2. For example, Doctrine and Covenants (hereafter cited as D&C) 93:36, "the glory of God is intelligence"; D&C 130:18, "Whatsoever principle of intelligence we attain unto in this life, it will rise with us in the resurrection"; 2 Nephi 9:29, "But to be learned is good if they hearken unto the counsels of God"; and D&C 131:6, "It is impossible for a man to be saved in ignorance." Joseph Smith said in April 1842, "A man is saved no faster than he gets knowledge."

3. Louisa Barnes Pratt, "Journal of Louisa Barnes Pratt," Kate H. Carter, comp., *Heart Throbs of the West* (Salt Lake City: Daughters of Utah Pioneers, 1967), 8:245–46.

4. George Nebeker to Brigham Young, 17 October 1865 and 19 November 1866, Archives, Historical Department of the Church of Jesus Christ of Latter-day Saints, Salt Lake City, Utah; hereafter cited as LDS Church Archives.

5. Andrew Jenson, "Manuscript History of the Hawaiian Mission," passim, 1927, LDS Church Archives.

6. Andrew Jenson, "Manuscript History of the New Zealand Mission," 2 April 1904, LDS Church Archives.

7. Andrew Jenson, "Manuscript History of the Samoan Mission," passim, 1892–99, Samoan Mission Historical Record, passim, LDS Church Archives.

8. Mission Financial and Statistical Reports, Samoa, 31 December 1930, LDS Church Archives. The Sauniatu residential schools remained open until after World War II.

9. Brian W. Hunt, "History of the Church of Jesus Christ of Latter-day Saints in New Zealand" (M.A. thesis, Brigham Young University, 1971), chapters 6 and 7.

10. Roscoe E. Cox, "Religious Education in Hawaii," *Improvement Era* 44 (December 1941): 728; William E. Berrett, interview, 23 June 1976; Frank W. McGhie, "Religious Education in the Hawaiian Islands," (typescript in possession of author); Leon R. Hartshorn, "Mormon Education in the Bold Years," (Ed.D. diss., Stanford University, 1965), 120.

11. Gordon Claridge Young Oral History, interviews by Lauritz G. Petersen, 1972, typescript, 12, 23, Oral History Program, LDS Church Archives.

12. See David W. Cummings, *Mighty Missionary in the Pacific* (Salt Lake City: Bookcraft, 1961), chapters 2–12; see also Jeannette McKay Morrell, *Highlights in the Life of President David O. McKay* (Salt Lake City: Deseret Book Company, 1966), chapter 20.

13. Pacific Board of Education, Report to the First Presidency, 1 December 1961, Part I, p. 13. Copy in possession of the author.

14. Ibid., Part I, p. 15.

15. Ibid., Part II, p. 3.

16. Ibid., Part II, pp. 4–5.

17. Harvey L. Taylor, "The Story of L.D.S. Church Schools," bound typescript, 2:174, in LDS Church Archives.

18. Pacific Board, Report, Part III, p. 1.

19. Commissioner of Education, Report for 1971, p. 1, LDS Church Archives.

20. R. Lanier Britsch, "On the Pacific Frontier: The Church in the Gilbert Islands," *Ensign* 11 (October 1981): 28–31.

21. Bruce M. Lake, interview, 2 November 1982, Salt Lake City, Utah.

22. Ibid., 28 September 1982.

Schism in the Sisterhood: Mormon Women and Partisan Politics, 1890–1900

Carol Cornwall Madsen

Utah's long struggle to become the forty-fifth state in the Union featured conflict, concession, and eventual conciliation, a process which has been characterized as "the Americanization of Utah."[1] Objection to Utah's entry focused on the Mormon political hegemony, inherent in the numerical dominance of Mormons in the territory, and the more sensational Mormon practice of plural marriage. The resolution of both of these controversial impediments to statehood bore heavily on the political, legal, and social status of women in the future state. The Woodruff Manifesto of 1890, which disestablished plural marriage as a religious practice, disrupted the family and social order of its adherents and required extensive legal and social adjustment for plural wives and their children extending well into this century. But the implementation of a national two-party political system, which broke the Mormon political unity, also altered the topography of Mormon life by generating dramatic new configurations of political and social alignments among Mormon and Gentile women, as well as among men.

Gentile (non-Mormon) women had long been antagonistic toward Mormon women over the issue of polygamy, and passage of a woman's suffrage bill by the Utah legislature in 1870 only exacerbated the discord.[2] It was clear to Gentiles in Utah that contrary to the supposition of easterners, Mormon women would not use their new voting power to eliminate polygamy. Rather, local non-Mormons regarded this extension of political power as a means of sustaining Mormon religious domination and thus perpetuating the practice of plural marriage. To counter this situation, Gentile women organized the

Anti-Polygamy Society in 1878, which sought local and federal means to eradicate polygamy, beginning with the disfranchisement of Mormon women, even at the expense of losing their own political rights.[3]

The first major legal challenge to the statute occurred in 1880 when members of the Gentile Liberal party filed suit for a writ of mandamus compelling the voting registrar in Salt Lake County to strike from the registration list the names of all women. Their challenge was based on the claim that the law granting the vote to women was discriminatory because the 1859 statute on elections provided that only men who were taxpayers could vote while the 1870 law extending the vote to women contained no such requirement. The writ of mandamus was denied and in a test case the following year the court found the taxpayer distinction neither illegal nor unconstitutional but against the "policy of the law" and ordered it struck from the statute.[4] Several other unsuccessful local attempts to disfranchise women followed. When local efforts failed, the Anti-Polygamy Society enlisted the help of militant Protestant reform women who were equally anxious to extirpate polygamy, which they considered an affront to Christian womanhood. In October 1884, more than two hundred fifty thousand signatures were gathered from all over the country memorializing Congress to withdraw the vote from the women of Utah. Whatever their own antipathy to polygamy, eastern suffragists deplored this move to disfranchise such a large body of voting women and did not join in the antipolygamy movements.[5]

Congressional approval of the Edmunds Bill in 1882, which disfranchised all polygamists, reflected the growing national concern over affairs in Utah. While not solely responsible for passage of the Edmunds Bill, the Anti-Polygamy Society had been instrumental in creating enough agitation and public sympathy to its cause to require some kind of congressional response. More stringent antipolygamy legislation was proposed thereafter, most of which included the disfranchisement of all Utah women, and in March 1886, responding to the latest congressional proposals, Mormon women held a mass rally in Salt Lake City to protest the imprisonment of polygamists, removal of the legal immunity of plural wives to testify against their husbands, and the proposed repeal of woman suffrage. Suffragists

Emmeline B. Wells, editor of the Mormon woman's newspaper, the *Woman's Exponent*, and Dr. Ellen B. Ferguson carried a memorial to Congress soliciting reconsideration of the Mormon question. A more convincing voice was heard, however, that of Angie Newman of Lincoln, Nebraska, a Methodist social reformer who had joined the cause of the antipolygamists. She carried her own memorial to Congress, endorsed by organizations representing three hundred thousand women. Passage of the Edmunds-Tucker Bill the following year, which disfranchised all Utah women, vindicated her efforts.[6] With a diminished Mormon electorate, the non-Mormon Liberal party began winning local elections for the first time.

In the meantime, Mormon women were gaining political experience by serving as members of the central committee of the Mormon People's party and as delegates to the 1882 and 1887 constitutional conventions. Some of these women, Emmeline B. Wells, Emily S. Richards, Isabella M. Horne, and Sarah M. Kimball, later played significant roles in public politics until after statehood was achieved in 1896.[7]

With a view toward eventual statehood, Mormon suffragists made plans, with the encouragement of church leaders, to organize suffrage associations throughout the territory.[8] A preliminary meeting was held early in January 1889, attended by several church authorities and the general presidency of the Relief Society, Zina D. H. Young, Jane Richards, and Bathsheba Smith, the two general secretaries, Sarah M. Kimball and Emmeline B. Wells, and board member Emily S. Richards. An organizing meeting was scheduled for the following week. President Woodruff then appointed Emily S. Richards to attend the annual National Woman's Suffrage Association convention later that month since she was "posted in these matters and had previously reported the labors of the Ladies of this Territory at Washington." An effort to enlist the support of Gentile women proved ineffectual when Wells and Richards called on Jennie Froiseth, author of the antipolygamy volume, *Women of Mormonism*, and also first vice-president of the National Woman's Suffrage Association for Utah. Not surprisingly, she refused to assist and the work of organization was left almost exclusively to Mormon women.[9]

At the organizing meeting, Margaret N. Caine, wife of Utah's congressional delegate, John T. Caine, was elected president. Most of the major officers were monogamous Mormons in an effort to avoid associating the nascent franchise movement with polygamy. Several Gentile suffragists joined the association: Corinne Allen, wife of C. E. Allen, who became Utah's first congressman; Emma J. McVicker, coworker of Emmeline Wells in the territorial kindergarten association; Isabella E. Bennett, wife of Judge Charles W. Bennett and member of the territorial silk committee; and Mrs. Lillie R. Pardee, a prominent Utah educator.[10] Seventeen county associations were organized that same year. Territorial conventions were to be held annually in Salt Lake City. The next year, 1890, veteran suffragist Sarah M. Kimball was elected president with Emmeline B. Wells, who would ascend to the presidency in 1893, as vice-president.

Meanwhile, Utah demonstrated its willingness to concede to public demand in its sixth attempt at statehood, following the Edmunds-Tucker Act in 1887. The proposed constitution included sections prohibiting polygamy, restricting suffrage to male citizens, and insuring political separation of church and state. Its failure to receive a favorable hearing in Congress, even with these provisions, coupled with the punitive measures of the Edmunds-Tucker Act, led inevitably to the more dramatic conciliatory gesture by the church, the Woodruff Manifesto of 1890, suspending plural marriage as a church practice. This major religious capitulation, followed by the termination of Utah's local political parties, opened the way to statehood.

Efforts to dissolve the People's party and realign church members with the national political parties began early in 1891.[11] Throughout this early transformation period, the major thrust of church counsel was directed not toward political doctrine but toward numerical balance of the parties. It was essential to create political symmetry in the new state, not only to reassure non-Mormons but to meet the political imperatives of securing statehood. Since virtually all repressive measures against the church had been initiated by Republicans, beginning with their 1856 vow to obliterate the "twin relics of barbarism"—slavery and polygamy, Mormon sympathy had largely been with the Democratic party. Southern Democrats, remembering their own experience with Republican-directed reconstruction, had empathized with what they saw as a parallel infringement on state and territorial rights during the antipolygamy "raids" of the 1880s. Southern congressional Democrats had thus resisted some of the more stringent legislation proposed against the Mormons. However, when Utah's attempt at statehood failed during Grover Cleveland's first administration, the first Democratic administration since pre-Civil War days, there was a natural disillusionment among many Mormons.[12] In the meantime, an active campaign by the Republicans to win favor with Utahns by promising support for their statehood efforts, a gesture successful in bringing in several other territories under the Republican banner, bore fruit when President Woodruff, Counselor Joseph F. Smith, and several apostles privately affirmed their Republican preference. Because of the predominant Mormon allegiance to the Democratic party, those who espoused Republicanism were urged by church leaders to solicit converts to their party.[13]

By May 1891 both Democrats and Republicans had effected organizations in Salt Lake City, and in June the People's party formally disbanded.[14] A large faction of the Gentile Liberal party, supported by the *Salt Lake Tribune*, continued as a third party, unable to accept the "good faith" of the Mormons. It finally disbanded in 1893 after a heavy election defeat, many of its members moving into the Republican party. The *Tribune* followed them into the Republican camp.

The new political divisions among a heretofore politically united Mormon electorate created "considerable feeling and some pettiness," Emmeline B. Wells observed. L. John Nuttall, secretary to the First Presidency of the church, noted the anxiety felt by many: "I fear the results of these measures of uniting on party lines as some of our people will carry their party feelings into their church membership."[15]

These new alignments, which teamed Mormons and Gentiles in the same political parties, created an ambiguous future for woman's suffrage. "Which party will recognize women?" Emmeline B. Wells queried in a *Woman's Exponent* editorial in June 1891. Perhaps neither, she feared, for "wherever suffrage for woman is spoken of in public gatherings," she wrote, "there are only a few who dare speak for Utah upon this question."[16] It was still too soon to determine which if either party would favor the vote for women or whether woman's suffrage would be expedient or even possible for Utah. "It does not yet appear to be the time of women's choosing in political issues," Wells wrote, "until further developments of difficult questions now pending are made in this Territory."[17] Women's exclusion from a federal amnesty act in July 1893, restoring the vote to disenfranchised male polygamists, intensified her resolve to regain the vote for women at statehood.

At this time, most women had not publicly declared a party preference, keeping woman's suffrage a bipartisan issue as they had been advised by national suffrage leaders. Moreover, most women, like Ruth May Fox, who later became an active Republican, preferred to do "further study of the parties" to determine their choice.[18] At a meeting of the Utah Women's Press Club to which many Mormon suffragists belonged, President Emmeline Wells, anticipating the divisive influence of partisan politics, set the limits of political expression. "These meetings," she said, "are simply for literary improvement and devoted to the press and similar things, and not for the discussion of religion or politics as we can secure these things in other places. No subject should be presented here upon which we are likely to conflict or that will create unpleasantness."[19]

Occasional infractions occurred, however. Shortly before the ratification election of 1895 Ruth May Fox, giving a paper on current political affairs to the Reaper's Club, another popular literary association, criticized a statement of prominent Democratic Judge Orlando Powers. She "immediately withdrew it," as the club was "divided in politics and some of the ladies thought we should take no note of it on that account." At the next meeting, however, a Democratic member of the club found opportunity to defend Judge Powers, before she was presumably silenced also.[20]

The surface unity of the suffrage association, like other women's groups, also rippled with waves of dissension created by a growing acknowledgment of basic political differences and individual ambitions. A predictable rivalry developed early between Ellen Ferguson, able president of the influential Salt Lake County Suffrage Association, and Emmeline Wells, president of the territorial association. Wells had unsuccessfully sought to block Ferguson's nomination for chairman of the organizational meeting of the Salt Lake County Suffrage Association, preferring Ruth May Fox to have the position.[21] Marshalling the force of her county organization, Ferguson retaliated by drafting a letter objecting to unfair treatment by the territorial officers and questioning the legality of the recent territorial elections that had given Wells a second term as president. The effort failed, but among other names, the letter carried the concurring signature of Emily S. Richards, Wells's vice-president.[22] Though these three women had not yet publicly announced their party preferences, their political differences were already generating differences within the otherwise unified suffrage effort. The political rivalry between Emmeline Wells and Emily Richards intensified in the following months when these two capable leaders chose opposing political parties.

Concerned about a movement within the suffrage ranks to establish independent women's political leagues, President Wells warned Mary A. White, president of the Beaver County Suffrage Association, about these "unwise women who would push the Association to the extreme and antagonize all the men in the country." Referring to three or four unnamed women who were "trying to form a League — and go ahead and have said to me they would write to the County Associations and get them to join in this League," she advised White not to ally herself with either political party, though there were many suffragists who were beginning to do so. These are "smart women," she wrote, "who are very dangerous and have to be guided if they will submit, and if not then one must be on the watch for breakers."[23] Throughout the letter her major fear was of those women whose zeal and aggressiveness might jeopardize five years of careful spadework for the restoration of the ballot to women. Confident in the men who controlled the political future of the women in the state, she wrote, "I rather trust men than *distrust* them by far . . . most of our leading brethren I believe think the woman element in politics at this present crisis will be a *saving* power." Nevertheless, the letter conveyed an apprehension as she suggested strategies in case of defeat.

Despite internal squabbles, the diligent efforts of the suffragists resulted in the inclusion of woman's suffrage in both party's platforms, though not all of the individual delegates were enthusiastic.[24] Enough declared their support that on the eve of the constitutional convention in March 1895, the suffragists, the press, and the general public acknowledged confidence that woman's suffrage would be part of the new state constitution.[25] Favorable reports from the governors of Colorado and Wyoming of its effectiveness in their states reassured many doubters.[26]

A warning note from Susan B. Anthony, which accompanied her letter of congratulations on impending statehood, proved to be timely: "I am sure that you, my dear sisters, who have not only tasted the sweets of liberty, but also the bitterness, the humiliation of the loss of the blessed symbol, will not allow the organic law of your state to be framed on the barbarism that makes women the political slaves of men. . . . Demand justice now. Once ignored in your constitution you'll be as powerless to secure recognition as are we in the older states. And more, the men of your convention should not allow the question to be separately voted upon, either."[27] These became the very issues on which the suffragists would wage their unexpected battle for the vote in the weeks ahead.

Soon after the convention began, the territorial and several county suffrage associations submitted memorials. Their rather perfunctory reception by the delegates seemed to verify the general confidence in the measure's passing. Thus Democratic delegate B. H. Roberts's unexpected challenge caught both delegates and suffragists off guard and prolonged what had been thought to be a "rubber-stamp" measure into a two-week debate.[28] Arguing that a suffrage clause might jeopardize congressional approval of the constitution, Roberts ignored the intent of the Democratic platform on which he ran, garnering widespread disapproval from many of his constituents. He was countered in the convention not only by those Republicans who, regardless of their private convictions, held firmly to their party platform, but also by fellow democrats, Orson F. Whitney and Franklin S. Richards, whose persuasive oratory was equal to his.[29] But Roberts managed to create doubts about the advisability of including woman's suffrage in the constitution, and a proposal to submit the articles on woman's suffrage separately to the voters in November was made in the convention, as Susan B. Anthony had anticipated. Two informal straw polls indicating a majority of women against equal suffrage added momentum to a *Salt Lake Tribune* campaign to urge separate submission of the woman's suffrage section.[30]

On 2 April, a mass political meeting was held in Ogden that concluded with a recommendation for separate submission and a call for petitions favoring it. Three days later a similar meeting, called by Gentile women for "those who do not hold suffrage above statehood" was held in the Grand Opera House in Salt Lake City. Several Mormon women were called out of the general church conference to observe the proceedings.[31] A resolution in favor of separate submission was drawn up and signed by twenty-nine women, many of them suffragists such as Jennie Froiseth. Conspicuously absent were the names of Gentile members of the Utah Woman's Suffrage Association, Corinne Allen, Emma McVicker, Isabella Bennett, Lillie Pardee, and Margaret Salisbury.[32] While both parties were split over this measure, suffragists were divided more visibly along the old Mormon-Gentile lines.

At the request of Emmeline Wells, Relief Society President Zina Young turned the morning session of the general Relief Society conference to a consideration of the separate submission proposal. Both Emmeline Wells and Emily Richards spoke. To Emily Richards's request for a standing vote of those in opposition to a separate proposal, the entire congregation of women in the assembly hall stood.[33] Armed with this support Mormon women mobilized to counter the growing tide of separate submission sympathy.[34] On 5 April the Utah Women's Press Club abandoned its planned program in order to talk about suffrage and voted to aid the cause by circulating petitions against separate submission. County suffrage associations joined in the effort.[35]

In the midst of the deluge of petitions both for and against separate submission, the proposed section on woman's suffrage was suddenly called up for vote in the convention and passed with a large majority.[36] According to a *Tribune* report, the petitions ultimately tallied 15,366 signatures for separate submission and 24,801 signatures for inclusion of woman's suffrage in the constitution.[37] Both the delegates and the people had given their endorsement to the principle of equal suffrage. With ratification of the constitution, the women of Utah would once again be voters.

The success of the suffragists infused the Rocky Mountain Woman's Suffrage Convention, held in Salt Lake City just a few days after the close of the constitutional convention in May, with jubilance. The presence of Susan B. Anthony and the Reverend Anna Shaw heightened the joy of success. But the constitutional convention proved to be only a preamble to the political attention women would continue to engender in the following months. It began with a proposition submitted by convention delegate Franklin S. Richards to allow women to vote in the November ratification election. It was defeated in the convention, but the issue had already been addressed by the papers in several articles that reviewed the legality of women exercising their newly acquired franchise before statehood. The controversy centered on the legal interpretation of an ambiguous phrase in the Enabling Act providing that "the qualified voters of said proposed state" should vote in November for or against the constitution. While the act seemed to be clear that only males could vote on the constitution, there seemed to be a legal possibility that women could at least vote for the new state officers. Opinions were divided on the intent of the Enabling Act regarding women.[38]

Recognizing the political potential of a female electorate in this important election, the Democrats issued a formal call to women to join their party. Their invitation was appealing: "The party now leads out in welcoming the women of Utah into their political organizations as full members, entitled to a voice in choosing delegates to the county and territorial conventions, and also to act as delegates themselves. . . . Whether they can vote or not in November, they have an interest in the choice of the proper persons for office in the new state."[39]

The propriety of publicly affiliating with the political parties became a topic of much concern to both the leading sisters and church leaders. Early in the morning of 15 June, Relief Society General President Zina Young visited her counselor Jane Richards and her husband at the home of Franklin S. and Emily Richards, Jane's son and daughter-in-law. Democrat Franklin S. explained to them the party's plan to have women join with men in the political societies, caucuses, and conventions and to become involved with the party on the precinct, city, county, and territorial levels. The Democrats wanted women to be part of the nominating process as well as to vote in the election. Later that day the three women attended the quarterly woman's conference of the Salt Lake Stake where discussion centered on steps to be taken toward dividing on party lines. At the conference, Zina Young, Jane Richards, and Salt Lake Stake Relief Society President Isabella Horne all declared for the Democratic party.[40]

Before the month was over, five women had been appointed to the Salt Lake County Democratic executive committee and a move to add women to executive committees in all the counties was well under way. When Bathsheba W. Smith, second counselor in the general Relief Society presidency also joined the Democrats, along with three prominent women doctors and suffragists, Martha Hughes Cannon, Ellen Ferguson, and Romania Pratt Penrose, the Democrats had reason to feel secure in the woman's vote.[41]

The political activity of these respected women and the assurance of the Democratic *Salt Lake Herald* that political participation would not require anything that would be "offensive to their true womanhood," that, indeed, government was a "great household and women [could] do much to keep it clean," helped assuage the fears of many women that their womanliness would be compromised by an interest in politics.[42]

Through most of the month of June, the Democratic *Herald* chided the Republican *Tribune* for failing to take the initiative in bringing women into its party's ranks. To the question, "What to do with the ladies?" the *Herald* claimed that the Republicans would wait until the courts decided whether the women could vote. The Democrats, on the other hand, the *Herald* was quick to point out, had wanted them in the party ever since they had been given the right to vote by the constitution. Moreover, it claimed, there were many "leading and influential" women who were desirous of aiding the party to carry the state elections in November. It concluded its recital of the party's program to include women with a challenge to the Republicans to copy them.[43]

The conservative *Tribune* countered with the question, "Who will care for mother now?" But the *Herald* had an answer: "The Democratic societies; so long as she has a vote and they a chance to get it." The *Herald* reminded the *Tribune* of the Republican opposition to woman's suffrage but thought the party would be quite willing to change its position if there were any possibility that women would be able to vote in the fall.[44]

Though the *Tribune* had frequently expressed its opinion that women would lose some of their womanliness if they joined in political activities, it noted, for the *Herald*'s benefit, that a woman was a delegate to the national Republican convention and that Republican women had organized their own Republican league. The *Herald* merely pointed out the party's inconsistency, suggesting that it had added one more change to its "chameleon journalistic colors."[45]

As the Democratic drive to enlist women gathered momentum, the Republicans recognized the political necessity to follow suit. Being reminded by the persistent *Herald* that the Republican-controlled convention had caused the problem by defeating the Richards amendment to the constitution that would have entitled the women to vote by legislative decree, the Republicans reiterated their view that women were not eligible before the constitution was ratified. They did, however, acknowledge that political expedience necessitated the inclusion of women in the party. At bottom, the *Herald* rightly asserted, was the fear of Republicans that if women were somehow permitted to vote in November, their party would be "swamped" and the Democrats would carry the day.[46]

Determined to "fight the thing out on the lines proposed by the Democrats," the Republicans urged the organization of women's Republican clubs, modeled after the national Woman's Republican League. The greatest advantage of the Republicans in this effort was the decision of Emmeline B. Wells to join their party in early July. Except for the aged Sarah Kimball she was initially the only prominent Mormon woman to declare for Republicanism. Many Mormon women were reluctant to join the party because of its large Gentile membership. As Ruth May Fox rationalized, "When the women who had been ardently working for suffrage arrayed themselves for the political battle, most of them [Mormons] seemed to be Democrats while Aunt Em Wells stood almost alone, a Republican. To even things up a bit, I joined hands with that great leader."[47]

Wells's decision to separate herself politically from most of her Mormon associates and join with her Gentile friends is not immediately apparent. The male political influence in her family, on which most women depended, was varied. Without a living husband or son, she did not have the natural persuasion toward a political affiliation that the Richards women did. One son-in-law, John Q. Cannon, son of George Q. Cannon, was a Democrat.[48] But another son-in-law, Septimus Sears, was a Republican. Her close confidante, friend, and relative, and champion of woman suffrage, Orson F. Whitney, was a popular Democrat.[49] Daniel H. Wells, her third and last husband, who had died four years earlier, was considered "the father of Republicanism" in Utah and his political influence may have lingered. Her family loyalties were thus divided. But Emmeline Wells was fiercely independent and undoubtedly made her decision for her own purposes. Though she indicated in a political speech that she had "turned from a Democrat to a Republican," she did not articulate her reasons, which were undoubtedly based on her own appraisal of the parties and her personal political aspirations. Even her daughter Annie's disapproval did not dissuade her.[50]

Just days after joining the party, Emmeline Wells was chosen permanent chairperson of the territorial Republican Women's League. Though both men and women of the party deliberated at some length before deciding on a separate organization for women, the *Herald* quickly ridiculed the plan:

> While the Democratic women are thus enjoying equal political privileges, . . . a handful of Republican women will be endeavoring to devise some means of carrying on a sort of afternoon tea and sewing circle style of politics separate from the regular organization, which does not want them and is content that they shall get off in one corner and do what they like, so long as they do not interfere with the plans of the men. What a spectacle for gods and men.[51]

In reality, women were included in both the party organizations as well as their own clubs, Emmeline Wells and Corinne Allen having been appointed to the territorial executive committee, and Lillie Pardee elected as permanent secretary. The party sent a letter signed by Wells, Pardee, and Allen to Republican women throughout the territory, announcing its intention to organize individual clubs and advising the women to prepare "at once for the possible exercise of your franchise in November." The *Tribune* was less hopeful. While supporting the move to organize women's clubs, it asserted its opinion that "under the law women have no more rights to vote this year than have boys of twenty years of age."[52] But the work of organizing went on. Besides the help of two young Mormon women, not yet prominent in community or church affairs, Ruth May Fox and Clarissa Williams, Wells was assisted in organizing Republican clubs by her Gentile suffrage associates, Corinne Allen, Emma J. McVicker, Isabella Bennett, and Lillie Pardee.

Throughout the summer of 1895 the *Herald* continued to attack the Republicans for their hesitancy to admit women, their reluctance to endorse a favorable position toward woman's vote in November, and their decision to organize independent women's clubs. The Republican *Tribune* continued to justify the party's caution and its separate organizations. As membership grew in the Republican women's league, the *Herald* warned of the impending contest: "Now the Democratic women have a foe in sight," the *Herald* warned. "They see that the game of politics for them has begun in real earnest."[53] If the women themselves did not yet perceive the political schism in military terms, the warring "morning contemporaries" as the newspapers were known, would keep the battle cry ringing from their paper columns throughout the campaign.

The extent to which women had been rapidly absorbed into the Democratic party was evident in the third annual convention of the Democratic societies held in the Salt Lake Theatre on 13 July 1895. Three days before, the *Herald* trumpeted the news that women would be a part of all its deliberations. Many of the delegates were leading ladies of the community, it commented, and others would attend "to see how their sisters comport themselves in a public political meeting." Some of these "leading ladies" were from the Fourteenth (political) Ward in Salt Lake City, which elected Amelia Folsom Young and seven other women as delegates, forming a majority of the fifteen-member delegation from that ward. Four women were named to the executive committee of the ward, also comprising a majority. Other wards and precincts had also elected women to various party committees. "The ladies are better hustlers," than the men, one Democrat reported, and he wanted them "on all the committees."[54]

At the Democratic convention it was estimated that one-third of the delegates were women. Featured on the stage beside Governor Caleb West, congressional delegate J. L. Rawlins, former delegate John T. Caine, and other prominent Democrats, were Zina D. H. Young, Jane S. Richards, Bathsheba W. Smith, Mary Isabella Horne, Martha Hughes Cannon, and "others not known to the Newsman." Judge Henderson, who presided, congratulated the convention on the fact that "women had been taken in as an auxiliary aid, to mingle their wisdom and advice with the men." He opined that if they were allowed to vote in November, they "would aid in giving party prin-

ciples clearness and strength." At the convention Zina D. H. Young
was elected first vice-president of the party's executive committee
and Euretha LaBarthe and Electa Bullock were elected secretaries.
Several women were appointed to the committee on resolutions, and
Zina Young, Euretha LaBarthe, and Isabella Horne were invited to
address the twelve hundred delegates. The convention endorsed the
right of women to vote in November if the Enabling Act permitted.[55]

However much the *Herald* ridiculed the organization of Republican women's clubs, Democratic women were not above forming their
own separate organizations. A number of Salt Lake City women,
under the chairmanship of Euretha LaBarthe, combined into "a special political education and work society" with the intention of meeting regularly for their own political edification and assistance to the
party. Other groups followed that eventually included most of the
prominent women Democrats in the city.[56]

The expanding political activity of Mormon leaders, particularly
women, became a matter of concern. The problem was aired at a
meeting on 30 July attended by the First Presidency of the church,
five apostles, the Salt Lake Stake presidency, and John T. Caine,
Samuel R. Thurman, Judge William King, and clerk George F. Gibbs.
Caine voiced the fear of some Gentiles that "the Church was using
the women to help it accomplish things they desired in a political
way," and that the Democrats had capitalized on the leading sisters
who had joined their party with the result that Salt Lake Stake President Angus Cannon, a Republican, had asked them "to resign their
[Church] positions or cease mixing in politics." Such church interfer-
ence, he felt, would create "discord and bitterness on the part of
Gentiles." After a lengthy discussion in which all viewpoints were
aired, from nonparticipation to total political freedom, President
Woodruff expressed regret as to "the course the sisters had taken,
but now that they have gone so far," he concluded, "it will be better
to let them finish this campaign on the lines which have been marked
out for them."[57] In the future both men and women in high church
positions would be counselled not to take "a very active part" in
political affairs. George Q. Cannon further suggested that the sisters
and all others should be restrained from declaring the politics of
"our dead leaders," an obvious allusion to Isabella Horne's and Amelia

Folsom Young's impassioned speeches invoking the "democratic political beliefs" of Joseph Smith and to some political literature circulated by both parties making similar assertions in support of their own political philosophies.[58]

Afterwards, the general Relief Society presidency, Isabella Horne, and Emily S. Richards were called before the First Presidency and counselled "as to the course they should pursue in their political relations and labors as suffragists and as Democrats. Very clear, pointed & energetic instructions as to political principles and as to practice," were given to them, according to Apostle Franklin D. Richards. Republican Emmeline B. Wells was pleased with the outcome of the meeting, when she heard about it, and was confident that "Sister Young, Smith and Horne will be more moderate."[59]

In August, the voting eligibility of women was finally decided by the territorial supreme court. A test case had been brought in Ogden by Sarah N. Anderson, who was refused when she applied for registration on 6 August. Anderson sought a writ of mandate to compel Deputy Registrar Charles Tyree to register her. Judge H. W. Smith of the Ogden district court found for the plaintiff and ruled that women were eligible to vote not only for state officers at the next election but also on adoption or rejection of the state constitution. Tyree immediately appealed to the territorial supreme court.[60]

On 22 August, while the case was being deliberated, Republicans held their Salt Lake County convention. Emmeline Wells was named temporary chairman of the convention and applauded the delegates for the honor conferred upon the "women of Utah" through that gesture.[61] When Charles S. Varian was elected permanent chairman, she was elected one of the permanent vice-chairmen. On the second day of the convention nominations were made for the new state legislature, twenty-nine persons nominated for ten seats. Emmeline Wells was nominated for the house and Lillie A. Pardee for the senate by Ruth May Fox. Both became official candidates of their party along with Emma J. McVicker, nominated for state superintendent of schools a week later at the territorial convention.[62]

The Democratic county convention assembled on 31 August. At the same time, the supreme court delivered its ruling on Anderson vs. Tyree, reversing the judgment of the lower court. Democratic convention chairman James H. Moyle concluded that the decision denying women the right to vote in the coming election also denied them the right to run for office, though the ruling was not explicit. Thus, no women were nominated by the Democrats. The Republicans, however, already had three women candidates on their ballot. At their ratifying meeting on 2 September, speaker Arthur Brown, who had successfully represented Tyree in the supreme court case, interpreted the ruling differently from Moyle. "The right of women to vote has been questioned," he said. "Her right to hold office after the adoption of the constitution has never been questioned. I have never questioned that. The whole question is one of time. After the proclamation is issued women may hold office. . . . If you believe in woman suffrage, here is the only ticket with women upon it."[63]

In a curious reversal of positions, the Republicans were now defending the right of women to run for office. Though women were not entitled to vote in the election, a decision Brown had helped obtain, there was nothing to prevent them from being elected to office, he reasoned, as they would be qualified voters and legal officeholders before they took their seats. In an overtly hostile attack, the *Herald* now lambasted the Republicans for favoring women:

> Of course now that the supreme court has decided that women cannot vote this fall, the ambition of Mrs. Emmeline B. Wells and Lillie Pardee must be nipped in the bud. They must be taken down from their high pedestals, the salaries of $100 per month which they have been receiving as the prices for relinquishing their previous Democratic ideas, and carrying on the evangelical and organization work of the Republicans, will be stopped and they will be relegated to a condition of innocuous desuetude into which the hum of ambition will penetrate but weakly.
>
> It is truly a mournful spectacle. Here were two distinguished women who have always been understood to be Democrats until the time for organization of the Democratic women. Then neither happened to be invited to take a very high position in the Democratic ranks. The Republicans held out promises of honor and emolument, and they followed.[64]

Public pressure mounted against the Republican women candidates, and doubts about their eligibility were raised in a Republican planning meeting. Republican lawyers could not agree, but while they were conferring Emma McVicker declared her own ineligibility.

By the end of September Lillie Pardee, while still holding that women had the right to run for election, acknowledged lack of support from members of her own party and thus felt the necessity to withdraw.[65]

Emmeline Wells held back on principle. "I suppose there is really no alternative but to withdraw," she reflected. But "I believe it is wrong. . . . I do not believe it would really affect the party or statehood or cut any figure in the matter whatever, and I think moreover I have a right to be elected to the legislature — as also other women — I yield unwillingly to the pressure brought to bear against the name of women on the Ticket."[66]

While she deliberated, the problem developed into a source of antagonism between Emily Richards and Emmeline Wells. On 7 October, the *Herald* began printing Richards's four-part reply to *The Republican Catechism*, a pamphlet Wells prepared for distribution to women explaining the Republican platform. In her reply, Richards made a pointed reference to Wells's assertion that Governor West, a Democrat, did not favor equal privileges for women because he failed to appoint any to territorial boards. His refusal, Richards pointed out, resulted from the restrictions of the Edmunds-Tucker Act (prohibiting women from voting or holding office). That he was correct in his conclusion, she continued "is demonstrated fully for Republicans in the resignations of Mrs. Pardee and Mrs. McVicker . . . for the reason that the decision of the court withholding from the women the right to vote disqualified them for holding office."[67] The implication was clear that Emmeline Wells should also resign. On the day the first installment of the Richards criticism was published, Wells and Richards met together in a woman's suffrage meeting. Emmeline Wells found it "a very unpleasant affair with Mrs. Richards, who made up her mind to have some changes made."[68] While not detailing the difficulties, Wells recorded that at the afternoon meeting "came the struggle with the faction from the county" (meaning the Salt Lake County association), another manifestation of the ongoing conflict between the county and territorial suffrage leaders with Emily Richards, territorial vice president, supporting Ellen Ferguson, Salt Lake County president. "I suffered very much in my feelings," Emmeline Wells recorded. This was but another incident in the political rivalry between Emily Richards and Emmeline Wells, following a similar unpleasant episode in a Relief Society board meeting a week earlier.[69] Despite their efforts, they could not contain their differences within the political arena.

As the pressure for her resignation continued to mount, Wells's resolve to remain firm weakened. On 17 October she decided to resign against her own "better and best judgment." Convinced that her name on the ballot would not adversely affect either her party or statehood, or make any difference, except to "make a test of the principle of woman's equality," she unwillingly submitted a letter of resignation. While acknowledging the legal doubts of women's eligibility to run for office, she did not relinquish her own opinion on the matter. She gave credit to the Republican party for "expressing their appreciation of this new element in politics . . . by placing the names of women in nomination for offices of emolument and trust, expecting them to take an active part in the affairs of the new State."[70]

Despite her resignation, she continued to campaign for her party, as did her Democratic counterparts. The overwhelming acceptance of the constitution in November pleased them all. That the Republicans made a sweep of state offices was especially satisfying to her. After writing to Susan B. Anthony and Carrie Chapman Catt, national officers of the suffrage association, she expressed to her diary her personal feelings about the election: "It seems almost too good to be true that we have equal suffrage . . . Junius [a nephew] has been in and several others of my friends, and all seems secure and no permanent ill feelings I trust."[71]

Her hopes that this first experiment in partisan politics would not produce an enduring schism among the politically active women of the church at first seemed to be premature. A Leap Year Ball, planned by the suffrage association as a fund-raising event in connection with the statehood celebration in January 1896, created another opportunity for disagreement with Emily Richards. After much preparation, the event turned out to be "a fine affair" though inexplicably none of the Richards family attended. The next day, however, as Wells noted in her diary, "Mrs. Richards [Emily] was on hand to know all about the party—and was very disagreeable when she learned that no more [money] had been made." She then suggested that if Emmeline Wells, who had supervised the affair, had not been so involved in planning the annual birthday celebration for Relief Society President Zina Young, set for a few days later, she "might have succeeded better," a curious criticism from a sister Relief Society worker.[72]

But Wells was yet to suffer a greater disappointment. On 18 December 1895, the suffrage association nominated a delegation of twelve to attend the celebration of Utah's statehood and the achievement of woman's suffrage at the National Woman's Suffrage Association convention in Washington the next January.[73] As president of the territorial suffrage association, Wells was naturally expected to attend. In fact, Margherita Hamm, correspondent of the *New York Mail and Express*, described the coming celebration: "From far-off Utah will appear Mrs. Emmeline B. Wells, who has toiled thirty years for her principles, and now sees them triumphant in her own home. She will receive an ovation because long ago she foresaw and foretold what happened in the Great Basin last November. In fact, five years ago she laughingly said: 'Women will vote and hold office in my poor little mountain State before they do in the rich and powerful states of the seaboard.' "[74]

Only two of the nominees, however, actually attended as official delegates, Emily Richards and Sarah Boyer. Unable to raise the funds for her own expenses and evidently unable to obtain church or Relief Society financial support, as she had done in the past, Emmeline Wells found it necessary to forgo the grand celebration. "I can scarcely believe I am not going to Washington," she wrote on the day Richards and Boyer left for Washington. She may have been somewhat mollified by the expressions of regret proffered by many church leaders. President Woodruff indicated that his preference had been for Relief Society President Zina Young and Emmeline Wells to represent the suffrage association, but since President Young would not go without her and she was unable to go without financial assistance, the honor fell to Richards and Boyer.[75] Despite her own keen disappointment, she enthusiastically reported in the *Woman's Exponent* the details of the festivities in Washington, including the victory speech of Emily Richards.

In Washington, both Anna Shaw and Susan Anthony paid tribute to Utah which had joined Wyoming and Colorado as "the crown of our Union, those three states on the crest of the Rockies." Corinne

Allen, wife of Utah's new congressional representative, Sarah Boyer, and Emily Richards all responded to the speeches of congratulations. A special tribute to Emmeline Wells, "whose influence had been paramount in securing the franchise for the women of Utah," was heartily applauded and a telegram of congratulations sent to her.[76]

In the following months both of these leaders repeatedly appealed to women to maintain the best of feelings toward each other, despite party difference, and to put aside "intense partisanship" in the interest of the public good. As evidence of the sincerity of her own appeal, Emmeline Wells, on the last day of December 1896, recommended Emily Richards as a new member of the Reaper's Club, a conciliatory conclusion to their political conflicts.[77]

It is not improbable that most Mormon women shared the sentiments of Ruth May Fox as they encountered the divisive experiences of partisan politics. "I do hope they will not engender bad feelings in their divisions on party lines," she wrote. "As for my part I care nothing for politics. It is Mormonism or nothing for me."[78]

Capitalizing on her shared political affiliation (and family relationship) with the new governor, Heber M. Wells, son of Emmeline's sister-wife, Martha, Emmeline immediately lobbied to create opportunities for women in the new state government. A week after the election, at the suggestion of a party member, she wrote to each member of the senate and house proposing that they elect a woman as chief clerk of the senate, nominating Lillie R. Pardee for the position. Her efforts were successful, and she felt well pleased to think "that the Certificate of the new senators had to be signed by a *woman* as well as a man." Nor was she slow to complain to the inauguration committee that "it was noticeable women were not considered in the proceedings or in any way recognized as a part of the new state."[79] She lobbied for a state-sponsored silk commission, passage of a kindergarten bill, the building of a public library, and the appointment of women to various state boards. She was determined that woman's voice would be heard in the affairs of the new state.

By summer of that first year of statehood, interest was again focused on the coming election, the first one to include women since 1887. Both Emmeline Wells and Emily Richards had maintained active association with their respective parties. Both were nominated for the state senate, although Richards declined to run. Republican state chairman George M. Cannon claimed that Wells's name on the ticket "would strengthen the ticket to the extent of 6000 votes."[80] Alas, it proved to be empty rhetoric. From a field of ten candidates for the senate, five were elected. Emmeline Wells came in last. It was a clear-cut Democratic victory. Dr. Martha Hughes Cannon trailed the Democrats of the ticket for state senator but she garnered more votes than any of the Republicans, including her husband, Salt Lake Stake President Angus Cannon, who had decided to enter the political field himself, after advising the women who held church office in his stake to withdraw the year before.[81]

After three successful years, the Republicans went down to defeat. How decisive a factor the women's vote was in the election suggested by a Republican appraisal from the year before. "The Gentile women don't register," the pollster complained, "the Mormon women do. That hurts us. The majority of Mormon women are Democrats. The majority of Gentile women are Republicans." Another Republican observed that "far from being converts to Republicanism, women are flocking to the Democrats."[82] These are only impressionistic appraisals but they suggest that the woman's vote may have made the difference in the 1896 election.

Three women, all Democrats, won legislative seats that year and eleven throughout the state were elected to the position of county recorder. While congratulating the women who won, Emmeline Wells expressed her own very personal disappointment that "all the women [who were candidates] were not elected, for it would have been a much truer test of women's power had there been some women from each party." Her fighting spirit not entirely extinguished, she concluded, "women as well as men must content themselves as best they can until another election, when things may be different."[83]

Though women had established a foothold in the political affairs of the new state, they had not been given a clear mandate for continued widespread involvement. Only two years after statehood the active Utah County Woman's Suffrage Association denounced the "informal understanding" between the two political parties "eliminating women from the state and county tickets at the next election" and refuted the charge that women were "a weakness upon the ticket" because they lacked executive ability and could not draw the votes of other women. While the charge may not have been universally supported, it indicated the association's awareness of the persistence of social and psychological barriers to women's full political participation: the reluctance of men to integrate women into the political system, and the ambivalence of women toward the propriety and capability of women entering politics. Utah would never replicate the events of 1895 or 1896 when women were at center stage in the political drama.[84]

In their transition from the Woman's Suffrage Association to the political parties, however, women lost both power and autonomy. The year 1895 was an exceptional year for Utah women, not a portent of a continued pattern of political attention and involvement. The campaign to put woman's suffrage in the Utah state constitution had been a woman's campaign, planned and executed by women who had to convince the majority of 104 men that woman's suffrage, which the legislatures of forty-two other states opposed, was good for Utah. In leaving their suffrage association and moving into the political parties, these same women, capable, experienced, energetic, moved back into traditional organizational relationships with men. They were often vice-chairpersons, but seldom permanent chairpersons. They were delegates but not strategists. Their experience and ability were useful in the parties but not to lead them, conduct the campaigns, or develop political philosophies. And in that one exceptional year, 1895, it is not difficult to appraise the attention they received from both the press and the parties as exploitive.

Ultimately, while still participating in party organizations and continuing in small numbers to hold public office, they organized separate women's Republican and Democratic clubs. Separatism, they discovered, proved to be the most reliable strategy for achieving authority and recognition. But for one year, at least, the women of Utah commanded the political spotlight. It was a year that produced a unique chapter in Utah's political history.

NOTES

1. See for example, S. George Ellsworth, "Utah's Struggle for Statehood," *Utah Historical Quarterly* 32 (Winter 1963): 60–69; Richard

D. Poll, "A State is Born," *Utah Historical Quarterly* 32 (Winter 1964): 9–31; Gustive O. Larson, *The Americanization of Utah for Statehood* (San Marino, Calif.: The Huntington Library, 1971); Howard R. Lamar, "Statehood for Utah: A Different Path," *Utah Historical Quarterly* 39 (Fall 1971): 307–27. Grant Underwood, in his paper "Mormonism as a Historical Concept," presented at the annual meeting of the Western History Association in Salt Lake City, 13 October 1983, challenges the prevailing conceptual framework of this period that insists that statehood necessitated major shifts in Mormon life. Arguing that only a minority of Mormons practiced polygamy, that the communal economic systems were short-lived and ineffective, and that the majority of Mormons were basically "mainstream" Americans, he suggests that the "Americanization" view is too narrow a perspective. It focuses on religious, social, and economic concepts and principles rather than on actual practice, he maintains, and posits that for the majority of Mormons statehood necessitated no significant accommodation or adjustment.

2. Woman suffrage in Utah has been the subject of a number of historical studies. See T. A. Larson, "Woman Suffrage in Western America," *Utah Historical Quarterly* 38 (Winter 1970): 8–19; Beverly Beeton, "Woman Suffrage in the American West, 1869–1896," (Ph.D. diss., University of Utah, 1976); Thomas G. Alexander, "An Experiment in Progressive Legislation: The Granting of Women Suffrage in Utah in 1870," *Utah Historical Quarterly* 38 (Winter 1970): 20–30; Ralph L. Jack, "Woman Suffrage as an Issue in the Mormon and non-Mormon Press of the Territory, 1876–1877," (M.S. thesis, Brigham Young University, 1954); Carol Cornwall Madsen, " 'Remember the Women of Zion': A Study of the Editorial Content of the *Woman's Exponent,* A Mormon Woman's Journal," (M.A. thesis, University of Utah, 1977).

3. A full discussion of the organization and activities of the Anti-Polygamy Society can be found in Robert Joseph Dwyer, "The Gentile Ladies Hoist Their Standard," *The Gentile Comes to Utah: A Study in Religious and Social Conflict, 1862–1890* (Salt Lake City: Publishers Press, 1971), 190–214.

4. Another issue in the case concerned differing citizenship requirements for men and women, the 1870 law allowing alien women who were married to citizens the right to vote. A federal statute granted such women citizenship on the basis of their relationship to a citizen, but in the case of Utah the legality of alien plural wives obtaining citizenship in this manner created another Mormon-Gentile friction point until 1882 and the disfranchisement of all polygamists and their wives by the Edmunds Bill.

5. Dwyer, *Gentile Comes to Utah,* 201. Lucy Stone, editor of the Boston suffrage paper, the *Woman's Journal,* responded for many suffragists to these attempts at disfranchisement: "It is hardly possible that so bold an attempt to disfranchise citizens who have exercised the right to vote for

ten years can be accomplished. It would certainly never have been attempted if these citizens had not been Mormons." (9 October 1880), in Dwyer, *Gentile Comes to Utah*, 201–2.

6. See Orson F. Whitney, *History of Utah,* 4 vols. (Salt Lake City: George Q. Cannon and Sons Company, Publishers, 1893), 3:60–61. For a full account of the proceedings see "Mormon Women's Protest, An Appeal for Freedom, Justice and Equal Rights," Salt Lake City, Utah, 6 March 1886, Utah State Historical Society, Salt Lake City, Utah, hereafter cited as USHS. The Woman's Christian Temperance Union, the Woman's Home Missionary Society, and the Presbyterian Missionary Society, all prestigious and large women's associations, were among the organizations endorsing the memorial. The Newman memorial to Congress can be found in "Woman Suffrage in Utah," Misc. Doc. #122, 49th Congress, 1st Session, United States Senate, USHS.

7. Susa Young Gates Papers, USHS. See also *Woman's Exponent* 17 (15 June 1888): 10. The 1870 statute allowing Utah women to vote did not include a corresponding right to hold public office. A move in 1880 to amend the statute failed when the governor refused to sign the bill, which had passed both houses of the legislature.

8. General Relief Society President Zina D. H. Young, her counselor Jane Richards, and Jane's daughter-in-law and board member, Emily S. Richards, met first with John L. Nuttal, secretary to the First Presidency, in November 1888 and arranged a meeting for the following January. In attendance at the January meeting were President Wilford Woodruff, Apostles Franklin D. Richards, Brigham Young Jr., John Henry Smith, Heber J. Grant, and Secretary Nuttal, along with the Relief Society President Zina Young, Jane Richards, and Bathsheba W. Smith, Secretaries Sarah M. Kimball and Emmeline B. Wells, and board member Emily S. Richards. For details of the meeting see Emmeline B. Wells, Diary, 2 January 1889, Special Collections, H. B. Lee Library, Brigham Young University, Provo, Utah, hereafter cited as BYU Library; Zina D. H. Young, Diary, 2 January 1889, Archives, Historical Department of the Church of Jesus Christ of Latter-day Saints, Salt Lake City, Utah, hereafter cited as LDS Church Archives; L. John Nuttal, Journal, 2 January 1889, also 14 November and 31 December 1888, LDS Church Archives; and Franklin D. Richards, Journal, 2, 10, and 24 January 1889, LDS Church Archives.

9. *Woman's Exponent* 17 (15 February 1889): 138; *Salt Lake Tribune*, 11 January 1889.

10. Wells, Diary, 8 January 1899. These women signed the memorial to the constitutional convention in behalf of woman's suffrage along with a number of Mormon suffragists. See *Woman's Exponent* 23 (1 April 1895): 241.

11. L. John Nuttal, Journal, 25 February 1891.

12. Lamar, "Statehood for Utah: A Different Path." For other factors in a diminishing Democratic preference see Davis Bitton, "The B. H. Roberts Case of 1898–1900," *Utah Historical Quarterly* 25 (January 1957): 27; Richard D. Poll, "A State is Born," *Utah Historical Quarterly* 32 (Winter 1964): 9–31; Lamar, "Statehood for Utah: A Different Path"; Leo Lyman, "The Mormon Quest for Statehood," (Ph.D. diss., University of California at Riverside, 1981); and Larson, *The Americanization of Utah for Statehood*.

13. See Lyman, "Mormon Quest for Statehood," 323–83. See Jean Bickmore White, "The Making of the Convention President: The Political Education of John Henry Smith," *Utah Historical Quarterly* 39 (Fall 1971): 350–69.

14. *Deseret Evening News*, 7 May 1891; B. H. Roberts, *A Comprehensive History of the Church*, 6 vols. (Provo, Utah: Brigham Young University Press, 1965), 6:299–301.

15. Wells, Diary, 9 June 1891; Nuttal, Journal, 21 May 1891.

16. *Woman's Exponent* 20 (15 June 1891): 188.

17. "Women in Politics," *Woman's Exponent* 20 (15 August 1891): 28.

18. *Woman's Exponent* 23 (1 and 15 November 1895): 201.

19. *Woman's Exponent* 22 (15 August 1893): 21.

20. Ruth May Fox, Diary, 12 and 28 October 1895, Ms., Ruth May Fox Papers, USHS.

21. Ruth May Fox, "My Story," Ms., Ruth May Fox Papers, USHS. Wells, Diary, 29 June 1895.

22. Fox, Diary, 30 December 1894 and 9 January 1895.

23. Minutes of the Beaver County Woman's Suffrage Association, 14 January 1895, BYU Library.

24. *Woman's Exponent* 23 (1 and 15 February 1895): 233; Fox, Diary, 19 February 1895.

25. *Salt Lake Tribune*, 15 March 1895. The *Young Woman's Journal* ran a series of statements by prominent Utahns, Mormon and Gentile, men and women, expressing their views on the topic. All were, to varying degrees, favorable. See *Young Woman's Journal* 6 (February and March 1895): 224–37 and 279–86.

26. Journal History of the Church (hereafter cited as JH), 21 February, 19 March, and 5 April 1895, LDS Church Archives.

27. *Woman's Exponent* 23 (1 and 15 August 1894): 169.

28. For details of this debate, see Jean Bickmore White, "Woman's Place Is in the Constitution, The Struggle for Equal Rights in Utah in 1895," *Utah Historical Quarterly* 42 (Fall 1974): 344–69.

29. Orson F. Whitney, Diary, 6 April 1895; White, "Woman's Place Is in the Constitution."

30. *Salt Lake Tribune*, 31 March and 1, 2, and 3 April 1895. Orson F. Whitney explained to the convention the invalidity of one poll taken at the

Opera House in Salt Lake City. Tickets in favor and against woman's suffrage were issued to children who were told to deposit only those against the measure. JH, 5 April 1895.

31. Mary Ann Burnham Freeze, Diary, 5 April 1895, Mary Ann Burnham Freeze Papers, Special Collections, BYU Library.

32. Proceedings of the Constitutional Convention, 1:754–55, as quoted in White, "Woman's Place Is in the Constitution." See also *Salt Lake Tribune*, 7 April 1895. Charlotte Kirby, former corresponding secretary of the Utah Woman's Suffrage Association, submitted an article to the *Tribune* supporting both woman's suffrage and separate submission. While disclaiming the validity of Roberts's arguments against suffrage on its merits, she supported his arguments on expedience.

33. Wells, Diary, 4 April 1895; *Woman's Exponent* 23 (1 May 1895): 262. Church leaders were divided on this issue. Wilford Woodruff expressed a fear that the constitution would not pass if woman's suffrage were not part of it. He was supported in that view by Counselor Joseph F. Smith. Second Counselor George Q. Cannon, however, favored separate submission and argued so strongly for it that he succeeded in changing the mind of President Woodruff, though not that of Joseph F. Smith. See Abraham H. Cannon, Journal, 4 and 12 April 1895, Ms., USHS.

34. Fox, Diary, 3, 4, and 9 April 1895; Freeze, Diary, 4, 5, and 9 April 1895. An interesting sidelight involves suffragist Margaret Roberts, wife of B. H. Roberts. Before the debate on suffrage began, she frequently attended the convention with Mary Ann Freeze. After Roberts's speeches on 28 and 29 March, however, she no longer attended nor was she visibly present in the political campaigns that followed.

35. Utah Women's Press Club Minutes, 5 April 1895, USHS. For a humorous account of the name-gathering effort, see Cactus [pseud.], "Cactus Papers No. 2," *Woman's Exponent* 23 (15 May 1895): 267, 271–72.

36. Final tally was 75 for, 14 against, 13 absent, and 5 excused from voting. See White, "Woman's Place Is in the Constitution," 362. A later motion to reconsider was defeated, ibid., 363.

37. *Salt Lake Tribune*, 19 April 1895.

38. Jean Bickmore White, "Gentle Persuaders, Utah's First Woman Legislators," *Utah Historical Quarterly* 38 (Winter 1970): 40–41; *Salt Lake Tribune*, 1 April 1895.

39. *Salt Lake Daily Herald*, 2 June 1895.

40. Franklin D. Richards, Journal, 15 June 1895; Wells, Diary, 15 June 1895.

41. *Salt Lake Daily Herald*, 15–18 and 25–28 June 1895.

42. Ibid., 19 June 1895.

43. Ibid., 16 June 1895.

44. Ibid., 19 June 1895.

45. Ibid., 21 June 1895.

46. Ibid., 11 July 1895.

47. *Salt Lake Tribune*, 15 June and 2 July 1895; *Salt Lake Daily Herald*, 3 July 1895; Wells, Diary, 2, 3, 5, and 6 July 1895; Fox, "My Story," 26.

48. Her daughter, Annie Wells Cannon, was appalled when Wells became a Republican though she herself joined the party a few years later. Wells, Diary, 25 August 1895.

49. Whitney's grandfather, Newel K. Whitney, was Emmeline's second husband, but as a plural wife Emmeline was not Orson's grandmother. Whitney's support of suffrage in the constitutional convention endeared him to all the suffragists. His speeches in behalf of suffrage were printed in a separate pamphlet by the Utah Woman's Suffrage Association.

50. *Salt Lake Tribune*, 7 January 1896; *Salt Lake Daily Herald*, 28 July 1895; Wells, Diary, 25 August 1895.

51. *Salt Lake Daily Herald*, 13 July 1895.

52. Wells, Diary, 9 September 1895; Fox, Diary, 30 August and 15 and 23 September 1895; Wells, Diary, 6 and 9 July 1895; *Salt Lake Tribune*, 2 July 1895.

53. *Salt Lake Daily Herald*, 18 July 1895.

54. Ibid., editorial, 10 July 1895; *Salt Lake Tribune*, 9 July 1895.

55. JH, 13 July 1895, p. 6.

56. *Salt Lake Daily Herald*, 21 and 24 July 1895.

57. Abraham H. Cannon, Journal, 30 July 1895; Emmeline B. Wells, Diary, 26 July 1895.

58. *Salt Lake Tribune*, 9 July 1895; see also "Nuggets of Truth" and "Nuggets of Truth, Hear Ye the Whole Truth," pamphlets, USHS.

59. Franklin D. Richards, Journal, 30 July 1895. See also Jean Bickmore White, "Utah State Elections, 1895–1899," (Ph.D. diss., University of Utah, 1968), 81–85; Wells, Diary, 30 July 1895.

60. The Utah Commission had been approached to issue a directive to registrars concerning the eligibility of women to register, but the members had left the decision to the individual registrars initially. However, they later decided to instruct the registrars to register women in case they could vote in November. Since the legislature had not ruled, the issue would ultimately have to be decided judicially. Sarah Anderson's suit against Tyree was a deliberate effort to have the issue resolved. See *Salt Lake Daily Herald*, 14 and 20 July and 7, 9, and 11 August 1895. See also White, "Gentle Persuaders," 40–42.

61. *Deseret Evening News*, 22 August 1895.

62. Emmeline Wells had hoped for a senate nomination but a miscue in nominations gave that honor to Lillie Pardee. See *Salt Lake Daily Herald*, 24 August 1895.

63. *Salt Lake Daily Herald*, 3 September 1895; *Salt Lake Tribune*, 3 September 1895.

64. *Salt Lake Daily Herald*, 2 September 1895.

65. *Salt Lake Tribune*, 12 and 15 September 1895. See letter in *Salt Lake Tribune*, 29 September 1895.

66. Wells, Diary, 16 and 17 October 1895.

67. Emily S. Richards, *The Republican Catechism Criticized and Amended for the Benefit of the Women of Utah*, pamphlet, USHS, 40, reprinted from the *Salt Lake Daily Herald*, 30 August and 1, 6, and 21 September 1895.

68. Wells, Diary, 7 October 1895.

69. Ibid., 1 October 1895. The two women were also active members of the newly organized Federation of Women's Clubs, which provided another setting for their power struggles. As a member of the nominating committee in May 1895, even before the heated campaign of that election year began, Emmeline Wells and Emily Richards displayed their competitiveness. Discovering that the Ogden delegates "had been coached and were primed ready to vote for Mrs. F. S. [Emily] Richards" as the new president, Wells was "very determined" that she would not be and succeeded in making Emma McVicker's nomination to replace retiring president Corinne Allen unanimous (Wells, Diary, 22 May 1895).

70. Wells, Diary, 17 and 20 October 1895. See also *Salt Lake Tribune*, 20 October 1895.

71. Wells, Diary, 7 November 1895.

72. Ibid., 16 and 17 January 1896.

73. *Woman's Exponent* 24 (1 February 1896): 108; Wells, Diary, 18 December 1895.

74. JH, 23 January 1896, p. 8.

75. Wells, Diary, 11, 15, 19, 21, and 23 January 1896.

76. Susan B. Anthony, et al., *The History of Woman Suffrage*, 4 vols. (New York: Fowler and Wells, 1881–1922), 4:260–62; JH, 27 January 1896, p. 5; *Woman's Exponent* 24 (1 February 1896): 108–9.

77. *Woman's Exponent* 24 (1 March 1896): 122; 25 (1 and 15 November 1896): 68; Minutes, Utah Women's Press Club, 30 December 1896, USHS.

78. Ruth May Fox, Diary, 14 July 1895.

79. Wells, Diary, 13 and 17 November 1895 and 1 and 22 January 1896.

80. Annie Wells Cannon, "In Memoriam: Emily Sophia Tanner Richards," Utah State Historical Society, 25; *Salt Lake Daily Herald*, 8 October 1896.

81. *Salt Lake Tribune*, 14 November 1896 and White, "Gentle Persuaders," 31–49.

82. *Salt Lake Daily Herald*, 11 July and 25 August 1895.

83. "Woman's Work and Duty," *Woman's Exponent* 25 (1 and 15 November 1896): 69.

84. "The Women Resolve," *Woman's Exponent* 27 (1 September 1898): 33.

Changing Relief Society Charity to Make Way for Welfare, 1930–1944

Jill Mulvay Derr

"As one thinks over the work of the Relief Society during the past ninety years, the care of the sick, the poor and the needy of the Church is its most significant service," observed the Latter-day Saint Relief Society general presidency in 1932, upon the eve of the organization's ninetieth birthday. Charity work had been the group's "guiding star" since its organization in Nauvoo in 1842. The presidency was proud, too, of the Relief Society's more recent "constructive educational program," which made for "both an efficient relief agency and a strong practical educational institution."[1] However the charitable work of the LDS Relief Society, like that of many other private charity organizations in the United States, changed substantially in the wake of the Great Depression. Emergency federal aid, followed by a permanent federally funded system for welfare in the United States, curtailed the Relief Society's close cooperation with state and county agencies, and the organization's forceful community presence subsequently waned. After the introduction of a comprehensive churchwide Welfare Plan in 1936, the Relief Society gradually ceased to initiate and direct its own charity work, assuming an important but auxiliary role in the new welfare program of the LDS Church. As Relief Society discontinued collecting and disbursing relief funds and commodities within both the community and the church, it turned to its educational program and almost exclusively emphasized preventive social work—the strengthening of homes and families with the hope of eliminating the causes of poverty.

For nearly three-quarters of a century the Relief Society followed its original 1842 commission to "seek out and relieve the distressed" by collecting donations from its members, raising additional funds, regularly visiting families to ascertain need, and administering goods and services to the needy.[2] The first significant changes in the Relief Society's charitable work began a decade before the stock market crash of 1929. In 1919, with the support of Presidents Joseph F. Smith and Heber J. Grant, Relief Society general secretary Amy Brown Lyman established a department for social services at Relief Society headquarters in Salt Lake City, signaling the organization's growing interest in new scientific methods for helping families in need. From then until the early years of the Great Depression the Relief Society, through its local units and central department for social services, forwarded virtually every major aspect of the new social work: family casework, training of local leaders, cooperation among community social agencies, and legislative efforts for social reform.[3] This involvement essentially paralleled that of other private charitable organizations in the United States, which multiplied during the decade following World War I as private and voluntary institutions cooperated with expanding local and state welfare agencies in addressing the social problems intensified by urbanization.[4]

In the LDS Church, as in the nation at large, charity historically had been funded and distributed at the local level. In local church units or wards both bishops and Relief Society organizations collected donations and provided cash and commodities for the needy. This system had emerged during the nineteenth century when American men and women moved in essentially separate spheres. Though early church directives supported independent action on the part of either the ward bishop or Relief Society president, cooperation between the two clearly strengthened ward relief efforts. When insolvable conflicts occurred, sisters were instructed to defer to their bishops. During the early years of the twentieth century, as the political and economic spheres of American women and men merged, women entered male-dominated institutions where new roles and relationships were often defined for them. In the LDS Church during this period, extensive administrative reforms aimed at strengthening lines of priesthood authority, eliminating duplication of effort, and promoting efficiency resulted in a new official relationship between the Relief Society and the Presiding Bishopric. By 1913 the Relief Society general presidency and board were making their policies regarding charity work in connection with rather than independently of the Presiding Bishopric, the priesthood authority in temporal matters. During the 1920s, when Utah experienced an economic recession, the Presiding Bishopric and Relief Society general presidency worked closely together, meeting regularly to formulate and coordinate the relief policies to be implemented by bishops and Relief Societies at the ward level. They encouraged local bishops and Relief Society presidents likewise to meet frequently to coordinate the administration of ward charity.[5]

The new Relief Society Social Service Department was partially funded by the general board and partially through the Presiding Bishopric who endorsed the department's work with bishops of wards in Salt Lake City. Non-Mormon community agencies, with whom the department cooperated in the city's confidential information exchange and Central Council of Social Agencies, agreed to refer all LDS clients to the Relief Society department. A caseworker there then contacted a client's bishop or ward Relief Society president to work out a plan for relief, often some combination of aid from relatives, the county, and the church. Following this initial contact with the department, the responsibility for helping most LDS families fell to the bishop of the ward in which they resided. The department's relief funds were limited and it assumed direct responsibility only for transients, aggravated cases, and specialized cases such as adoptions. The Relief Society's Social Service Department, under Lyman's supervision from 1919 to 1934, also operated an employment bureau for women and, at the request of Salt Lake County, investigated and supervised LDS mothers' pension applicants and LDS cases from the community clinic, county infirmary, and juvenile court.[6]

While the procedures for Relief Society charity work changed considerably during the 1920s, charity remained the organization's central concern. The injection of monthly social service lessons into the curriculum for ward units, new institutes training stake leaders in social work history, theory, and methods, and sponsorship of legislation for maternal and child health and care of the feebleminded extended Relief Society charity work beyond ward neighborhoods.[7] At the same time the work in wards continued, with increased direction from the general board and Presiding Bishopric.

Updated instructions for ward charity work were issued by the Presiding Bishopric three months after the November 1929 stock market crash. The 40 percent drop in the price of stocks traded on the New York Stock Exchange triggered bank failures, mortgage foreclosures, and unemployment; but initial prospects for reversing the economic decline seemed good. Conservative leaders viewed growing unemployment as a temporary emergency that required short-term relief administered through the same private and volunteer charitable organizations so effective during the postwar decade. The February 1930 *Ward Charity* pamphlet issued by the Presiding Bishopric called for continued cooperation with county officials and included suggestions for stake and ward authorities in helping members secure employment. Relief Society sisters were to investigate and report all cases, utilizing modern social work methods, but the work was to be "entirely voluntary" and geared toward "help[ing] people help themselves."[8]

The role of Relief Society sisters formed a prominent part of the 1930 instructions that asked wards and stakes in larger towns and cities to organize employment committees: stake committees composed of "a man and a woman who are in touch with the sources of employment" and ward committees consisting of a member of each of the ward's three Melchizedek priesthood quorums "together with a member of the Relief Society." Procedures to be followed in a "typical charity case," where a family moved into a ward and sent word to the bishop that they were out of work, without means, and in need of immediate help, involved a representative of the local Relief Society at almost every step. At the bishop's request the representative was to visit the family personally to determine "by tactful and sympathetic inquiry" the family's work, medical, and church history, the extent of their need, and the availability of financial assistance through relatives. This last item was particularly important since many state laws made relatives primarily responsible for the care of those in need and counties secondarily responsible. County aid was to be secured through a man or woman designated to serve as the stake's liaison with county officials. The church recommended that every effort be made to secure financial assistance from these two sources before drawing church aid from tithes and offerings. Generally church officials preferred more permanent relief measures, such as securing employment or improving family health or home management. Unemployment cases were to be referred to ward employment committees, and where other services were needed the Relief Society representative and president were to work out a family plan in connection with the bishop. Free medical service and budgeting assistance came through the Relief Society, which also provided needy families with emergency supplies of food and clothing. Regular follow-up visits from Relief Society workers continued until the family became self-sustaining.[9]

In order to carry out these instructions effectively, local society officers needed to "secure training under the Relief Society General Board in the essentials of social service."[10] The board, in cooperation with the Relief Society Social Service Department, had sponsored social service training institutes between 1920 and 1928. These were recommenced during the summer of 1930 at the request of the Presiding Bishopric, who hoped the department would use its salaried workers less in the office, serving transients and special bishops' referrals, and more in the field, training workers at the local level where the administration of relief was supposed to take place.[11] The institutes would provide six weeks of intensive training for one representative from each stake, specifically "a sister who is able to give the time, not only to the study course itself, but one who will carry the work back and put it into effect in the stake."[12]

One delegate from each of twenty-five stakes assembled at the Relief Society offices in the Salt Lake City Bishop's Building for the 18 August through 27 September 1930 institute. The training included fieldwork with non-Mormon social agencies in Salt Lake City who were "greatly interested in the project." Laura A. Watkins represented the Logan Stake at this institute and found it "the most profitable six weeks I ever spent from an educational viewpoint." The group discussed methods of dealing with people and then went out and made "direct contact with the problems of disease, poverty, neglect, [and] delinquency." Watkins noted that "preventative rather than curative methods were stressed," and left the training course with a commitment to develop her own powers, to "preserve the finer elements of family life," and "help others make a more harmonious adjustment to life."[13]

Through the 1920s, effective utilization of women trained at social service institutes had posed a challenge for both the general board and local leaders who were unclear about the exact role these women should assume in Relief Society charity work. With firmer direction from the Presiding Bishopric about the importance of home investigations, in October 1930 the Relief Society general presidency and board presented to stakes a comprehensive outline of the duties of stake workers completing the institutes, or "social service aids." Aids were to give up all other church positions and devote their time exclusively to local social work, assisting ward presidents or other ward workers with making investigations, budgets, and general plans for needy families. When possible, aids were to hold special meetings with the stake priesthood and Relief Society presidencies to report on their training in social work methods. Meetings with bishops were encouraged, as well as training for sisters at stake leadership or union meetings. Sometimes the social service aid represented the Relief Society on the stake employment committee or served as the official liaison with the community. Aids were to become acquainted with local officials and heads of community agencies in order to help Relief Society ward presidents utilize community resources.[14]

Granite Stake Relief Society President Emmaretta G. Brown reported her stake president's enthusiasm for working with the stake's social service aid and learning social work methods. With his support, and feeling "that our brethren should understand as we understood," the stake Relief Society arranged to have a staff member of the Relief Society Social Service/Family Welfare Department come and conduct a training course at night so the men could be present. Granite Stake President Hugh B. Brown admonished his bishops to cooperate closely with their Relief Society presidents, explaining "that the ward president was still responsible for the charity work of the Church." He asked ward presidents to handle casework within each ward, discussing individual case problems with the stake social service aid. Emmaretta Brown was delighted to have a supportive stake president to "tell the bishops what they should do. We cannot expect to tell them ourselves," she observed, "they do not take it from us women."[15] She viewed the Relief Society as "an auxiliary to the Priesthood" in welfare matters, reflecting official instructions that assigned ward bishops responsibility "for the care of the worthy poor," with "the Relief Society labor[ing] under their direction."[16]

The Relief Society general board in connection with the Social Service Department sponsored another training institute for twenty-five stakes from 4 January to 14 February 1931, and another from 4 October to 13 November 1931 with ten women attending from Utah, six from Idaho, three from Wyoming, one each from Nevada and California, two from Arizona, and three from Alberta, Canada. The three institutes provided training for approximately seventy-five stake workers, representing a significant percentage of the church's 104 stakes.[17]

Some stakes and missions lacked women with training in social work methods or chose not to utilize separate social service aids. Almira Cozzens Rich, president of the Mt. Ogden Utah Stake Relief Society from 1922 to 1936 was actively engaged in welfare work, but her 1929–36 personal journal makes no mention of an aid assisting her. During 1931 Rich served as a member of the Ogden Central Committee, "investigating cases, and directing others in the distribution of food and clothing," an effort which in a year's time had helped eighteen hundred Ogden families. Her journal entry for 7 March 1932 notes that she "went down to Community Service to receive clothing gathered by Scout boys . . . called 15 charities to meet Tuesday at 4 o'clock p.m. on planning distribution of clothing."[18]

With or without social service aids, Relief Society cooperation with community agencies and officials was a conspicuous part of Relief Society work during the early years of the Great Depression, even in the missions. Pearl C. Sloan, president of the Northwestern States Mission Relief Societies reported in April 1933 that some of the groups there had "cooperated very closely with the welfare agencies," one of the presidents contributing one full day each week to the local welfare bureau. Likewise, presidents of Relief Societies in the Southern States Mission and Central States Mission reported working with community agencies who sought their counsel and advice concerning the poor.[19]

Nowhere was the Relief Society's cooperation with community agencies more apparent than in Salt Lake City where the Relief Society Social Service Department had served for more than a decade as the connecting link between the LDS Church and community social agencies. This role was strengthened as church leaders intensified their cooperation with civic officials. In the fall of 1930 — at President Herbert Hoover's suggestion that mayors organize broad-based committees to address local unemployment — Salt Lake City Mayor John T. Bowman met with church representatives and others to determine which families would be in need of supplies during the coming winter. The church helped to make a house-by-house survey of unemployment in the Salt Lake district and then contributed over $12,000 in cash plus some 420,000 pounds of fruits and vegetables to be delivered to the needy in Salt Lake City that winter. The next fall this plan was continued and expanded. A warehouse, funded by the county charity department, the church, and the community chest, was stocked with food, clothing and donated coal. Each of the three groups issued orders on warehouse supplies, with the Relief Society Social Services Department representing the church and issuing about one-half the total orders. A ward member who obtained a note from his bishop or Relief Society president indicating need could present the note to the Relief Society Social Service Department in person or have a social service aid present it so his eligibility could be cleared through a citywide confidential information exchange (to prevent duplication), his needs assessed, and an order issued for supplies.[20]

Salt Lake County Commissioner of Health and Charities B. F. Quinn reported that during 1930 "Relief Society trained workers" investigated needy families for Salt Lake County and distributed a total of $20,176 in commodities. "If we did not cooperate with the Relief Society," he commented, "it would mean that within Salt Lake City, Salt Lake County would have to maintain five or six additional workers, so we make full use of your organization and your trained workers."[21] However, Joseph A. Geddes, a professor of sociology at Utah State Agricultural College in Logan, argued in 1933 that there were limits to the effectiveness of this cooperative system, particularly in rural settings where volunteer workers lacked the training of professional caseworkers such as those employed in the Social Services Department. Most charitable agencies such as the Relief Society were carrying a double burden, "its own load for which it was organized and, (2) the carrying of a part of the county load, over which it does not have full control and for the handling of which its organizational mechanism was not designed." Geddes maintained that counties needed more paid help.[22]

The Relief Society concurrently both helped community agencies and carried forward its traditional charity work. As part of their monthly visits to members' homes, visiting teachers collected funds and commodities, reporting both collections and assessed needs to the ward Relief Society presidency who decided how the society's charity fund should be disbursed. Local Relief Societies were asked to keep on hand for emergencies a supply of food, clothing, bedding, and layettes. Such a supply was urgently needed in 1931 in West Frankfort, Illinois, a mining district where most of the men were out of work. The Relief Society there collected and distributed six boxes of good clothing first to needy branch members and then to nonmember families.[23] Granite Stake Relief Society women helped supply and staff the stake's small storehouses for food and remodeled clothing, available to members who came with notes from their bishops.[24] In addition to these local efforts, the general board maintained its own small charity fund and storehouse of used clothing and furniture for emergency use by its Social Service Department in Salt Lake City.

The total of Relief Society funds "spent for charitable purposes" decreased slightly in 1929 and then rose dramatically as unemployment increased, as reflected in the following statistics: 1928 — $100,836.76; 1929 — $98,925.02; 1930 — $109,493.19; 1931 — $116,448.17[25] These figures reflect nationwide trends. When it seemed that the economic slump would be short-lived, the government continued to view relief as a local problem and tried to stimulate private contributions. In the fall of 1931, community chests across the country raised approximately 10 percent more funds than in the previous year.[26] Relief Society donations increased 11 percent between 1929 and 1930, and an additional 6 percent between 1930 and 1931.

By the end of 1931, however, Relief Society leaders expressed concern that while conditions worsened and demand for relief increased, "welfare agencies throughout the country, including the Relief Society, are facing a shortage of funds." Due to unemployment some faithful contributors found themselves "less able to give, and others, through fear and apprehension, are cutting down their contributions, even though their circumstances have not changed,"

General Treasurer Emma A. Empey wrote in December 1931.[27] Between 1931 and 1932 nationwide community chest donations declined 22 percent and Relief Society donations declined 24 percent between 1931 and 1933, with the second year showing the greatest drop.[28]

The traditional sources of relief, including local tax revenues and charitable donations, were strained to the utmost by unemployed Americans, whose numbers increased eightfold between 1929 and 1933, from 1,499,000 to 12,634,000. Evelyn Hodges, a Relief Society Social Service Department caseworker, recalled that "the wards were using all their funds and we had secured all the county funds and all the widow pension funds we could possibly get. . . . Most bishops were very eager for federal participation in the relief program, because they weren't able to meet the needs."[29]

In May 1932 Amy Brown Lyman told members of the Relief Society general board that "it was the feeling now and general among the agencies as well as lay people, that the only source of relief in the future will be through federal channels as the States and local communities have just about exhausted their resources," noting that "the attitude of social workers had changed materially upon this subject."[30] The Children's Bureau had already gathered statistics on public and private relief and in 1931 and 1932 congressional committees in Washington, D.C., received testimony regarding the extent of national unemployment and the paucity of state and local funds.

President Hoover reluctantly signed the federal Emergency Relief and Construction Act in July 1932. Through the Reconstruction Finance Corporation (RFC), a state could be loaned federal money for relief following certification that its public resources and private contributions were inadequate to meet its relief needs.[31] In the late summer and early fall of 1932, at the request of Salt Lake City and County governments, Amy Brown Lyman and the staff of the Relief Society Social Service Department made a survey of unemployment and relief cases in Salt Lake City, taking their statistics and selected case histories to the state capitol "for hearings there to prove federal relief [to Utah] was necessary."[32]

RFC funds, first available in Utah in August 1932, were channeled though state hands and provided 68 percent of the funds spent on relief in the state during 1932–33.[33] A five-member committee appointed by Governor George H. Dern determined relief needs, planned work relief projects, and administered relief activities through county governments working in connection with private agencies. During the winter of 1932–33 Salt Lake County opened a commodity warehouse similar to the one it had operated the previous winter, but subsidized by the RFC. The Relief Society Social Service Department, like other local charitable agencies, helped administer the federally augmented county relief by assessing the eligibility and needs of applicants and filling out monthly orders for emergency food and clothing. In many cases the department simply cleared the names on orders submitted by ward bishops whose Relief Society workers had already assessed needs. The county delivered goods either directly to needy individuals or to stake storehouses where they existed. In other counties inside and outside Utah local Relief Societies often assisted in distributing public relief commodities.[34]

The RFC's impact on the traditional charity work of the Relief Society served as a harbinger of changes imminent with permanent federal relief. In November 1932, for example, the Relief Society general board decided to discontinue its support of the Salt Lake City Schools' annual drive for Thanksgiving and Christmas baskets for the poor, "as the relief agencies through local and R.F.C. funds are able to be provided with supplies, and in many cases it has worked a hardship to collect these from the people."[35] Granite Stake's storehouses for food and clothing were permanently closed in 1933 because, according to stake Relief Society President Emmaretta Brown, "the people seemed to like federal relief better."[36] The Relief Society's total charitable disbursements declined in 1932, beginning a downward trend that lasted until 1937.[37] This decline coincided with the introduction of RFC funds and paralleled a similar decline in general church relief after 1932.[38]

With the economic crisis deepening, RFC loans nearly depleted, and Relief Society donations and disbursements declining, the society's general officers questioned whether they were doing enough to help members in need. In February 1933 two board members proposed "putting into effect a program of relief by the General Board," but the board tabled their motion, objecting to "the lack of a plan or means by which such action could be Church-wide in its scope."[39]

The RFC, a one-year appropriation, was exhausted on 31 May 1933. Franklin D. Roosevelt's inauguration in March 1933 and passage of the Federal Emergency Relief Act during his first hundred days in office extended federal relief to the unemployed for two more years, but there was no indication this aid would be permanent. In August 1933 the First Presidency sent a letter to all stake presidents explaining that "while it seems our people may properly look, as heretofore, for relief assistance from governmental and perhaps other sources, it cannot now be certainly foretold either what or how fully sufficient this assistance will be, and we must therefore prepare ourselves to meet the necessities that may fall upon us." Anticipating that the church would soon shoulder a greater relief burden, the letter requested a survey of members to determine the church's effectiveness in meeting welfare needs, exhorting leaders not to let anyone suffer but to encourage "habits of thrift, economy, and industry."[40] Belle Spafford remembered how she and other Relief Society sisters in her Salt Lake City ward scrupulously followed church leaders' counsel to avoid unnecessary waste that fall, gathering windfall peaches and apples, sterilizing collected bottles "in great big tubs with boiling water," and putting up fruit all day long, which needy families lined up to receive "before the bottles were cool."[41]

At the end of June 1933, J. Reuben Clark, second counselor in the First Presidency, expressed his opinion that "it is to [Church] aid that the Church members must and should primarily look in these times of stress," and drafted his own "Suggestive Directions for Church Relief Activities," which, though not officially distributed, first signaled the priesthood leaders' move toward a new churchwide plan for relief.[42] A number of stakes had been experimenting with their own relief measures, including self-help programs, commodity warehouses, interstake cooperatives and exchanges, and work projects for the unemployed. Heartily endorsing this last measure, church officials asked that all those administering relief likewise "devise ways and means by which all able-bodied Church members who are in need, may make compensation for aid given them by rendering some service."[43]

Social workers, church leaders, and national leaders all agreed that relief ought to help people help themselves. Careful attention to a family's needs and resources could help assure, "that the *will to do for self* shall not be crushed by want," observed Annie D. Palmer, supervisor of casework at the Relief Society Social Service Department. Amy Brown Lyman repeatedly told women to "minister to the strength of people and not to their weakness," and social service aids came away from training institutes anxious to avoid "pauperizing" families by making them dependent upon others for relief and decision-making.[44]

Anxious to put America back to work, the Roosevelt administration expanded Hoover's Public Works Administration and organized the Civilian Conservation Corps (for unmarried men ages eighteen through twenty-five), the National Youth Administration (for school-age youth), and the Civil Works Administration, a crash program of extemporized public works intended to put a lot of people to work fast. The CWA employed some four million workers from November 1933 until it ended in the spring of 1934. Its successor, the longer lived Works Progress Administration, was instituted in connection with the Social Security Act of 1935.[45]

LDS women as well as men were actively engaged in federal work projects, with the blessing of church leaders.[46] Some Relief Society presidents such as Almira Cozzens Rich took the lead in involving local women in work relief. President of the Mt. Ogden Utah Stake Relief Society, Rich chaired the local CWA Women's Project Committee, which provided work to over one hundred women through the government's school lunch program for undernourished children. The committee also sponsored seventeen cooking classes held in school buildings and Relief Society halls where thirty-eight women were employed to demonstrate preparation of inexpensive, nutritious meals.[47] St. George women transcribed personal histories as part of a WPA writing project directed by stake Relief Society President Juanita Brooks. A spare room in her home provided office space for typing the handwritten histories of southern Utah pioneers. The thirty-dollar monthly wage was "a literal godsend" to the women employed.[48]

Church support for government work relief continued even after the Welfare Plan was initiated, though members were instructed to be "scrupulously careful to do an honest day's work for a day's pay."[49]

In addition to a comprehensive program for work relief, the New Deal offered direct relief totaling $500 million to be distributed as matching grants to states through the Federal Emergency Relief Administration (FERA). An August 1933 federal ruling required FERA funds to be administered through paid employees in public agencies. However, because Utah counties did not have enough trained social workers to process all relief applicants, during a sixteen-month transitional period they employed workers from private agencies to share their caseload until they could assume full responsibility for public assistance cases.[50]

Under this arrangement the Relief Society Social Services Department in Salt Lake City continued to distribute county relief, but because of the new federal requirements, as soon as it began to draw from FERA funds it was designated as District 7 of the Salt Lake County Department of Public Welfare, with some workers' salaries paid partly by federal funds. This "federalization" of a private agency was a temporary measure used in many states with a shortage of social workers. The government paid salaries, while the agency provided offices and experienced personnel, posting notices that it represented the federal government and administered relief according to FERA regulations.[51]

Caseloads grew exponentially during 1933–34 and the county's need for professional social workers drew away from the Relief Society Social Services Department several of its most experienced staff members, further increasing the caseload of those remaining. When Evelyn Hodges started working with the department in 1929, her load consisted of about seventy-eight cases. By the time she left in September 1934, the number had risen to "somewhere around 775 cases," many of them skilled and professional people. She still attempted to interview each of the families at least twice monthly, the average interview lasting only ten minutes, with ten or fifteen people waiting in the outside office for their turns in the private interviewing rooms. The staff often worked nights and weekends to keep confidential records updated. She relished her full fifteen-minute rest during the workday and took comfort in the large rolltop desk she closed each night "so that I couldn't see any more letters or papers."[52]

The staggering caseload of Evelyn Hodges and her coworkers can be explained largely by the fact that in Salt Lake City, where 40 percent of all church members on relief resided, a central application bureau referred all applicants with LDS heads of household to the Relief Society District 7 office.[53] In November 1933, hoping to keep church relief efforts ward-administered, the Presiding Bishopric requested that members see their bishops before applying for public assistance. Church leaders had asked each of Salt Lake City's six stake presidents to select a Relief Society-trained social worker to become a county-salaried employee at District 7, working under the supervision of a Relief Society-salaried worker. Bishops could decide whether to assume full care of a needy family or refer the family to the stake representative at District 7 for public assistance, still largely relief in kind.[54] Church members who went directly to the department were to be referred back to their bishops. In practice, however, under FERA, caseworkers such as Evelyn Hodges did not usually notify the bishop unless the client "wanted funds from the Church." Some clients "resented and resisted coming to the Church" for relief or "did not want the bishop to know."[55]

At the end of 1933 the Relief Society Social Service Department was divided into two sections in addition to its employment bureau for women: one, under the direction of Amy Whipple Evans, included the stake representatives working in cooperation with Salt Lake County; the second, directed by Amy Brown Lyman, focused on continued welfare training for Relief Society officers in all stakes and wards. The Presiding Bishopric maintained a strong emphasis on social service work by *local* Relief Society officers — unpaid workers "trained in the best methods of caring for the poor." In 1934 Lyman put together a new program of social service institutes and introduced a monthly newsletter to update workers. The real meat of the new course included principles and procedures for investigating homes and formulating family relief plans, with particular emphasis on the importance of helping families to become self-supporting rather than merely giving relief that was not necessarily constructive or helpful in and of itself.[56]

In December 1934, Utah completed the mandated transfer of cases from private to public agencies. District 7 was dissolved and the six stake social workers, who had been on the Salt Lake County payroll for a year, were transferred to county offices.[57] As the county permanently withdrew from its special cooperative arrangement with the church, the First Presidency again considered the possibility of an independent church relief program. Comparing county statistics provided by Amy Whipple Evans with their own church statistics, the Presiding Bishopric reported to the First Presidency that government relief expenditures in District 7 were three to four times the amount of church relief expenditures in the six Salt Lake City stakes during 1933 and 1934. Even in Pioneer Stake, which helped more of its members than any other Salt Lake stake, 470 members received public assistance while 243 received church relief.[58] While it seemed that church resources were insufficient to replace government relief expenditures for Latter-day Saints, the First Presidency told the Presiding Bishopric in April 1935 that they still desired "to develop some system by which the deserving poor of the Church now drawing federal relief [may] be taken over by the Church," stating that prolonged relief "was destroying the morale of the Latter-day Saints and developing humiliating situations."[59]

From her perspective as Relief Society general president, Louise Y. Robison saw many Saints with the old pioneering spirit "trying to get along without Federal aid," and she asked ward presidents "to see that these people are not allowed to suffer and are not forced to ask for Federal help if you can help them." She too questioned whether Saints were leaving relief "too much to the Government now."[60]

The government's emergency relief measures were replaced by a permanent federal program of jobs and social insurance for the unemployed and aged, established when Roosevelt signed the Social Security Act in August 1935.[61] While Relief Society women had lobbied for some of the act's major provisions, the new legislation unquestionably ushered in a new era that altered the welfare work of the society and similar voluntary organizations. The close cooperation with public agencies that had helped define Relief Society charity work for two decades was substantially reduced, as Utah and other states established departments of public welfare to administer increasingly complex and professional relief systems. On 5 February 1936 Relief Society general board members discussed how to adapt their charity program to the change, and it was their "consensus of opinion that we should go back to the work of previous years."[62]

Going back was not possible. In April 1936 the First Presidency publicly announced the organization of a centrally directed church Security Program which, as Louise Y. Robison predicted, would be "the beginning of a new epoch for the Relief Society."[63] The Security Program asked members to act upon principles already familiar to them — the payment of tithing and fast offerings, for example — but also provided a new framework for meeting the needs of the poor and the unemployed. The church was divided into large regions composed of four to sixteen stakes each. The regional unit insofar as possible was to work toward economic self-sufficiency, supporting the wards and stakes within its bounds in providing commodities to those in need and finding or creating employment for the unemployed. Hoping to re-enthrone work "as the ruling principle in the lives of our Church membership" and help men and women maintain their self-respect, relief would not normally be given as charity, but distributed for work or services rendered.[64]

The plan was created, introduced, and directed by a special church Relief Committee called for the purpose, and though both the Presiding Bishopric and the Relief Society were to assist in implementing it, neither had been involved in its formulation. Harold B. Lee, managing director of the new Security Program, stressed the importance of administering the plan through existing Church officers. Ward relief organizations were to consist of the bishop and the ward Relief Society president and her assisting social service workers. At the stake level the relief organization was to include among others the stake presidency and stake Relief Society presidency. Welfare regions, directed by an executive council of stake presidents also included some stake Relief Society presidents.[65]

Relief Society General President Louise Y. Robison was not a member of the Relief Committee, or the Security Committee as it came to be called, nor was her experienced first counselor Amy Brown Lyman, who left Salt Lake City in 1936 when her husband Richard was called to preside over the European Mission. Robison later confessed she had originally seen the new plan as a "priesthood activity" and in that light told sisters in October 1936 that there would be "no real change in our work, we will just take care of our own in the same way we have done, and as Latter-day Saints contribute to the Security Fund."[66] She admonished women to play a supportive role, though during 1936 the exact nature of that role was in the process of definition, a frustrating process for Relief Society leaders at all levels. Marian W. Snow recalled that in the St. George Stake, "There was much trial and error, many long meetings, and many opinions and interpretations; but in it all, the women were loyal and willing."[67]

In April 1936 every bishop was asked to accumulate by the following October "sufficient food and clothes to provide for every needy family in his Ward during the coming winter." Relief Society women were essential to this effort, helping to appraise needs of ward members and directing and assisting "the needy sisters of the Ward in drying and preserving fruits and vegetables, providing clothing and bedding, etc."[68] Sisters everywhere worked intensely. Some gave every tenth jar of their own home-bottled fruit. Others had city lots plowed so they could plant gardens and preserve the harvest. Converts in New Jersey who had never canned anything managed to get 410 cans completed, some containing whole kernel corn, which though they cost them "plenty of work . . . taste[d] good." In southern Utah the Relief Society put up 14,000 cans of peaches and ingeniously shelled their peas by running the pods through the "clothes wringers on [two] brand new Speed Queen washing machines" loaned by generous sisters for the purpose.[69]

Those "who required relief were to be given the opportunity to work in the sewing and canning projects," but in most localities the burden was shouldered by Relief Society officers, who Robison feared were being overworked. She noted with concern at the October 1936 Relief Society conference that "we have had more resignations of Ward Presidents this Fall than we have had at any other time." She hoped that once the new work was launched women "in need of help will be given pay for that work and relieve our splendid Ward Presidents."[70]

The burden added to the work of local officers by the new Security Program was one of several problems Robison discussed with members of the church Security Committee during the six-month interval between the Relief Society's October 1936 and April 1937 conferences. Requests from local priesthood leaders that sisters use their Charity Fund to help finance Security Program projects concerned her, and she wondered to what extent ward societies should maintain emergency supplies of food, clothing, and bedding now that commodity storehouses were being established through the Security Program. Robison hoped that "matters could be more clearly worked out between the Relief Society and the Church Security Program," and indeed during 1937 communication and cooperation seem to have increased substantially.[71]

Harold B. Lee, the Security Program's managing director, prepared for the March 1937 issue of the *Relief Society Magazine* a "chart showing Relief Society responsibility in directing and supervising in cooperation with the priesthood authorities, the varied operations of the Church Security Program." A later bulletin issued jointly by Robison and church Security Committee Chairman Melvin J. Ballard, a member of the Quorum of the Twelve Apostles, indicated that a member of the Presiding Bishopric as well as a member of the Relief Society general presidency would be present at weekly meetings of the Security Committee to harmonize the new program "in all its phases that the utmost of unity will result in the regions, stakes and wards of the Church." A special committee from the Relief Society general board would give direction to women in such matters as family investigations and relief planning, budgeting assistance, and home canning and sewing, working through regional committees of stake Relief Society presidents appointed by the board.[72]

This arrangement was most fully realized in the Salt Lake region. Even there implementation was slow, but some results of the increased cooperation with priesthood officials were immediately apparent. Questions about emergency supplies and the Charity Fund met with a quick response from priesthood leaders who instructed that both should be retained by the Relief Society.[73] For their part, Relief Society sisters gave "whole-souled" service to the Security Program during 1937, and at the following April conference Presiding Bishop Sylvester Q. Cannon praised them for producing, among other items on a long list, 4,097 quilts, 8,452 items of new clothing, 15,808 items of remodeled clothing, 102,585 quarts of fruit, and 134,585 quarts of vegetables, representing 40,850 total days of service.[74]

In April 1937, the Relief Society general board introduced a new plan to ease the load of sisters who had "worked beyond their strength" in the Security Program and at the same time move church members toward self-sufficiency. "Our call now," explained Robison, "is to see that every woman who is able and strong enough to knit, to sew, or to use her hands in any useful way, be taught how to do something." Those who had previously been given quilts would learn how to make their own, and those who had received canned fruit would learn how to put it up themselves. "We want to lift our women up," said Robison. "They have had a hard time, and it is our pleasure to help them get the joy that comes through meeting their own problems."[75]

During 1938 the society's monthly work and business day was devoted to improving homemaking and consumer skills. After surveying women to help them evaluate their work at home, stake and ward leaders planned instruction and demonstrations in bread-making, sewing, and laundry.[76] This simple program added considerable value to the Welfare Plan since even in 1940 90 percent of those receiving assistance were "from homes where the mother does not know how to bake bread."[77] Demonstrations could be held in connection with bishops' storehouses. At the Ogden Storehouse, the women's work director sponsored sewing classes in addition to directing women's production of welfare supplies. One popular class featured the remaking of old suits for men into new suits for women.[78] These projects reflected a national consciousness that some families suffered economically because they purchased services from agencies outside the home that an efficient homemaker could provide less expensively. Agricultural colleges and county agents offered pamphlets and demonstrations on basic skills, and popular magazines—like *Scribners* with its February 1937 article entitled, "The New Woman Goes Home"—emphasized the trend toward retrenchment. Additional financial incentive for developing homemaking skills was offered in April 1937 when the general board announced the opening of a new outlet for women's handwork. Mormon Handicraft was established to provide "mothers in the home an opportunity in their spare time for creating something beautiful, and also help to increase the family income." Work was to be submitted through stake and ward work and business supervisors who would insure "the highest standard of excellence." More than four thousand dollars was paid out to contributors the first year.[79]

The home investigations by Relief Society presidents and social service aids continued under the Security Program. Workers assessed a family's needs and reported them to the bishop along with their recommendations for helping the family.[80] The general board stressed the importance of family budgeting for all sisters, particularly those receiving assistance, and introduced a food budget to be used in connection with the home investigation to project relief needs. The food budget was also used to project the kinds and amounts of food supplies needed for a storehouse for a given period of time.[81]

With the appointment of a new Presiding Bishopric in 1938, special training for those conducting home investigations was again requested. In the spring of 1939 Amy Brown Lyman, who had recently returned from the European Mission, joined Amy Whipple Evans in a new training class for sisters, stressing confidentiality and methods of assessing needs and developing plans to move families toward self-sufficiency.[82] A Presiding Bishopric survey of those receiving church assistance indicated that some were receiving cash from their bishops "contrary to the spirit of the Church Welfare Program" and others were receiving both church and county assistance. Presiding Bishop LeGrand Richards reemphasized the need of clearing names with other community agencies, noting that in some cases the church might need "to supplement the help given by other agencies, but when we do so we ought to do it with their knowledge and our knowledge, so we know that what is being given is supplemental help, and each agency understands where its responsibility begins and where it ends."[83]

In April 1940 Harold B. Lee addressed the first Relief Society conference convened under the direction of the society's new president Amy Brown Lyman and listed the Relief Society's major responsibilities in the Welfare Program, including participation in weekly meetings with the ward welfare committee, distribution of storehouse commodities, home investigations, and special Relief Society welfare projects such as beautification, home nursing, canning and sewing for welfare plan production, and vocational training to qualify unemployed women for work in private industry.[84] In the four years since the program was first introduced the Relief Society had found a place, involving women as planners, participants, and recipients. Along with their work for the new program, however, local sisters had been using their Charity Fund and other monies to carry out welfare projects of their own. Many groups continued to work for the health of mothers and children. Clinics held in connection with state boards of health provided needy and handicapped children with the opportunity to see doctors, dentists, and optometrists. Even without clinics Relief Societies often paid for children's eyeglasses and dental work. The Snowflake Arizona Stake Relief Society opened a maternity home in 1939, truly a cooperative venture: the state furnished a full-time paid nurse and the county helped pay the rent; the ward Relief Society furnished the bedding and the linen; local women and the stake board the kitchen; and the state board of health new equipment for the delivery room; NYA helped with the housekeeping; and the county welfare department contributed layettes![85]

Because Relief Society women themselves often viewed these projects as part of the church Welfare Plan, even though they were financed at least in part by Relief Society funds, the line separating church welfare work from Relief Society welfare work became increasingly difficult to draw. In 1940 the general board suggested that the monthly work and business meeting be tied to the Welfare Program by using the time to make "a definite number of articles as assigned by the Region." Interest from the Relief Society Wheat Fund, established in 1918 from the sale of Relief Society wheat to the federal government, was used by local units for more than twenty years for child and maternity health work, while the fund itself was held in trust by the Presiding Bishopric until such time as the General Authorities advised the sisters to buy wheat. "That time has come," Amy Brown Lyman announced in October 1940, explaining that part of the fund had been used to buy wheat to be stored in an elevator near the bishops' storehouse for the Salt Lake region and that the church through its Welfare Committee had "proffered to carry all the expense connected with the storing and proper care of the wheat."[86]

In the gradual merging of its welfare work with that of the church Welfare Plan the Relief Society lost its Charity Fund. In 1942 the general board voted that wards be allowed to use their Charity Funds for maternal and child health care, emergency relief, and service-oriented Welfare Program projects. In 1943, quilting production projects were added to the list and in 1944 clothing for welfare assignments. That year the general board wrote to the Presiding Bishopric, questioning "whether the Relief Society should continue to collect donations from ward members through the medium of visiting teachers, particularly in view of the apparent lack of need for these funds."[87] That October the collection of charity funds by Relief Society visiting teachers was discontinued. Thereafter, the Relief Society participated in the larger Welfare Program as a "service agency" in the production of welfare commodities and the evaluation of family needs for bishops.

Changes in the Relief Society's traditional charity work during the Great Depression typify the adaptations volunteer charitable organizations and agencies made during this period. Unable, even in connection with state and county governments, to meet the relief needs of millions of unemployed Americans, organizations such as the Relief Society welcomed federal aid and initially cooperated in its distribution. When the government decided to dispense its relief only through professional social workers in public agencies, these organizations redirected their energies. Like many other private agencies, the Relief Society Social Services Department turned almost exclusively to direct services such as foster care, adoption, and counseling—drawing new clients from the middle and upper classes. The Relief Society abandoned its traditional collection and distribution of local charity funds because new standardized programs for government and church welfare provided material assistance more efficiently. The post-World War II Relief Society expanded and improved its educational program and, like similar women's groups in America, directed its major efforts not toward the community but toward the home. This was an easy philosophical transition because of the centrality of the family in Mormon doctrine, and also because social work theory itself acknowledged the overriding importance of preventive social work: strengthening individuals and families with the hope of eliminating the causes of both economic and emotional distress.

As charity work assumed a lesser role in the Relief Society, the Relief Society assumed a lesser role in the Welfare Plan of the church. The society's stature as an independent charitable organization peaked during the first third of the twentieth century when it served as a strong connecting link between the church and other private and public charity organizations. When the government established a new welfare system separate from private agencies and the church developed a plan to separate its people from the government system, the Relief Society's connecting role lost its significance. As it operated more exclusively within the context of the church organization, its independent stature was obscured because its own relief efforts became so closely identified with those of the new priesthood-directed Welfare Plan.

The new program stressed unity, renewing Mormon cooperative tradition. Members—rich and poor, male and female—united their efforts and resources to uplift the poor. Emphasis on unification through official priesthood channels lessened the possibility and efficacy of independent Relief Society action. At a philosophical level the Welfare Plan represented the church's commitment to combat societal trends toward secularization and to maintain the union of spiritual and temporal welfare. Relief Society charity since its Nauvoo beginnings had aimed "not only to relieve the poor, but to save souls."[88] If during the Great Depression Relief Society women directed their efforts toward physical relief, during the prosperous postwar years they intensified their focus on spiritual values, and indeed the new age posed significant spiritual challenges. It is not impossible, however, that there will be a return swing of the pendulum, giving the Relief Society responsibility once again for the temporal as well as spiritual well-being of church members.

NOTES

1. "Greetings By the Presidency of the Relief Society," *Relief Society Magazine* 19 (March 1932): 37.

2. The original commission is recorded in "A Record of the Organization and Proceedings of the Female Relief Society of Nauvoo," 17 March 1842, microfilm of holograph, Archives of the Historical Department of the Church of Jesus Christ of Latter-day Saints, hereafter cited as LDS Church Archives. A thorough analysis of the society's charitable work in the nineteenth century is needed.

3. Two excellent discussions of Relief Society welfare work during the 1920s are Bruce D. Blumell, "Welfare before Welfare: Twentieth Century

LDS Church Charity before the Great Depression," *Journal of Mormon History* 6 (1979): 89–106; and Loretta L. Hefner, "This Decade was Different: Relief Society's Social Services Department, 1919–1929," *Dialogue: A Journal of Mormon Thought* 15 (Autumn 1982): 64–73. Amy Brown Lyman authored two relevant accounts: "In Retrospect: Relief Society Welfare Work and Related Activities," *Relief Society Magazine* 29 (July 1942): 460–71 and "Social Service Work in the Relief Society, 1917–1928," typescript, LDS Church Archives.

    4. Charity organization societies and the Red Cross encouraged other private institutions to follow their lead in implementing modern social work methods and coordinating community efforts in order to avoid duplication. The Relief Society's initial exposure to modern social work came in 1917 through a Red Cross "home service institute" held in Denver to train volunteers in relief work for families of American military personnel. Four Relief Society women, including the organization's general secretary, Amy Brown Lyman, attended the six-week session, returning to Utah to direct home service work for LDS families in Salt Lake City, Ogden, Cache Valley, and Utah Valley. After additional training in Denver, Lyman set up the Social Service Department. See Hefner, "Relief Society's Social Services Department," 64–66. For a discussion of national trends see James Leiby, *A History of Social Welfare and Social Work in the United States* (New York: Columbia University Press, 1978), esp. chapter 8, "Charity Organization and Social Settlement, 1877–1920," and chapter 10, "The 1920s: Constructive Ideas." Clark A. Chambers, *Seedtime of Social Reform: American Social Service and Social Action* (Minneapolis: University of Minnesota Press, 1963) looks carefully at voluntary social service associations. An important analysis of LDS attempts to address social problems in the 1920s is Thomas G. Alexander, "Between Revivalism and the Social Gospel: The Latter-day Saint Social Advisory Committee, 1916–1922," *BYU Studies* 23 (Winter 1983): 19–39.

    5. Apparently regular meetings between ward bishops and Relief Society presidents were a long time coming in many wards. Blumell, "Welfare before Welfare," 102.

    6. See Lyman, "Social Service Work in the Relief Society," 1–2, 7–8, 12–14, 16. The Social Service Department is also called the Welfare Department or the Family Welfare Department.

    7. Amy Brown Lyman was a representative in the Utah Legislature in 1923 and introduced the bill providing for Utah's acceptance of the provisions of the Sheppard-Towner Act. She served on the board of trustees for the Utah State Training School from 1930 to 1941. Lyman, "In Retrospect," 468, 470. See also Loretta L. Hefner, "The National Women's Relief Society and the U.S. Sheppard-Towner Act," *Utah Historical Quarterly* 50 (Summer 1982): 255–67; Amy Brown Lyman, "Training School for the Feeble-Minded," *Relief Society Magazine* 17 (January 1930): 22–24.

8. *Ward Charity: Details of Administration* (Salt Lake City: Presiding Bishopric, 1930), 3.

9. Ibid., 3–6.

10. Ibid., 3.

11. Bruce D. Blumell, " 'Remember the Poor': A History of Welfare in the Church of Jesus Christ of Latter-day Saints, 1830–1980," 88, typescript, Library of the Joseph Fielding Smith Institute of Church History, Brigham Young University, Provo, Utah. This study of church welfare is the most complete to date, since Blumell had access to minutes and papers of church officials largely unavailable to other researchers. An earlier study of the Welfare Plan that explores church welfare in light of leaders' responses to New Deal programs is Leonard J. Arrington and Wayne R. Hinton, "Origin of the Welfare Plan of The Church of Jesus Christ of Latter-day Saints," *BYU Studies* 4 (Winter 1964): 67–85. See also Arrington, et al. "Taking Care of Their Own: The Mormon Welfare System, 1936–1975," in Leonard J. Arrington, Feramorz Y. Fox, and Dean May, *Building the City of God: Community Cooperation Among the Mormons* (Salt Lake City: Deseret Book Company, 1976), 67–85.

12. General Presidency and Board of Relief Society to Relief Society Stake Presidents, 21 July 1930, as reproduced in Minutes of the Relief Society General Board, 21 July 1930.

13. Laura A. Watkins, "What the Social Service Institute Means to Us," *Relief Society Magazine* 18 (January 1931): 34–36.

14. "Social Service Recommendations" as reproduced in Minutes of the Relief Society General Board, 8 October 1930.

15. Emmaretta G. Brown, conference address, *Relief Society Magazine* 18 (November 1931): 635; also, Emmaretta G. Brown, "History of Church Welfare Work in Granite Stake, Church of Jesus Christ of Latter-day Saints, 1929–1933," typescript, 4, LDS Church Archives. Within the Granite Stake ward social service aids seem to have been working well in the capacity of assistants to ward presidents in welfare matters, but a 14 November 1931 letter from the Relief Society general board had recommended the release of ward aids until their duties could be more clearly defined. Minutes of the Relief Society General Board, 18 November 1931.

16. *Ward Charity*, 3.

17. "Notes to the Field: Social Service Institutes," *Relief Society Magazine* 18 (April 1931): 225.

18. Journal of Almira Cozzens Rich. Excerpts courtesy of Janath R. Cannon, Salt Lake City, Utah.

19. "Notes from the Field: Northwestern States Mission," *Relief Society Magazine* 20 (April 1933): 231–32; Reports of Grace E. Callis and Charolotte T. Bennion, "Relief Society Conference," *Relief Society Magazine* 21 (May 1943): 278, 280.

20. Blumell, " 'Remember the Poor,' " 91–92.

21. B. F. Quinn, "Cooperation Between Salt Lake County Charity Department and L.D.S. Relief Society," *Relief Society Magazine* 18 (June 1931): 326–27.

22. Joseph A. Geddes, "Should the Rural Counties of Utah Employ a Trained Social Worker?" *Relief Society Magazine* 20 (February 1933): 88.

23. "Notes from the Field: Northern States Mission," *Relief Society Magazine* 18 (April 1931): 224.

24. Emmaretta G. Brown, "Church Welfare Work in Granite Stake," 5–7.

25. "Relief Society Annual Report, 1928," *Relief Society Magazine* 16 (May 1929): 283–85; "Relief Society Annual Report, 1929," *Relief Society Magazine* 17 (June 1930): 339–41; "Relief Society Annual Report, 1930," *Relief Society Magazine* 18 (May 1931): 289–91; "Relief Society Annual Report, 1931," *Relief Society Magazine* 19 (May 1932): 274–76.

26. Hugo B. Anderson, "Federal Relief," *Relief Society Magazine* 20 (May 1933): 273.

27. Emma A. Empey, "Let Us Be Charitable," *Relief Society Magazine* 18 (December 1931): 693.

28. On community chests, see Hugo B. Anderson, "Federal Relief," *Relief Society Magazine* 20 (May 1933): 273. Relief Society donations totaled $106,769.05 in 1931; $102,692.37 in 1932; and $79,371.05 in 1933. See "Relief Society Annual Report, 1931," *Relief Society Magazine* 19 (May 1932): 274–76; "Relief Society Annual Report, 1932," *Relief Society Magazine* 20 (May 1933): 303–5; "Relief Society Annual Report, 1933," *Relief Society Magazine* 21 (May 1934): 314–16.

29. Evelyn Hodges Lewis Oral History, interviewed by Loretta Hefner, 1979, typescript, 4, James Moyle Oral History Program, LDS Church Archives.

30. Minutes of the Relief Society General Board, 19 May 1932 and/or 30 August 1933 when Lyman again emphasized the trend toward public relief agencies.

31. State of Utah Department of Public Welfare, *First Biennial Report, July 1, 1936–June 30, 1938, With supplementary data January, 1935 through December, 1938 and a Review of Public Aid in Utah Prior to Establishment of the State Department of Public Welfare in May, 1935* (Salt Lake City: State of Utah, 1939), 3, 5.

32. Minutes of the Relief Society General Board, 19 October 1932; Lewis Oral History, 6.

33. John F. Bluth and Wayne K. Hinton, "The Great Depression," 485 in Richard Poll et al., eds., *Utah's History* (Provo, Utah: Brigham Young University Press, 1978).

34. Blumell, " 'Remember the Poor,' " 94–95, 101; Utah Public Welfare, *Biennial Report, 1936–1938*, 4; Lewis Oral History, 14.

35. Minutes of the Relief Society General Board, 16 November 1932.

36. Brown, "Church Welfare Work in Granite Stake," 15.

37. Statistics for Relief Society "cash disbursements paid for charitable purposes" reflect the decline: 1931 – $116,448.17; 1932 – $102,692.37; 1933 – $83,853.27; 1934 – $75,789.79 "cash and merchandise"; 1935 – $66,863.86; 1936 – $66,189.48; and 1937 – $78,839.50. See "Relief Society Annual Report, 1931," *Relief Society Magazine* 19 (May 1932): 274–76; "Relief Society Annual Report, 1932," *Relief Society Magazine* 20 (May 1933): 303–5; "Relief Society Annual Report, 1933," *Relief Society Magazine* 21 (May 1934): 314–16; "Relief Society Annual Report, 1934," *Relief Society Magazine* 22 (May 1935): 300–302; "Relief Society Annual Report, 1935," *Relief Society Magazine* 23 (May 1936): 302–4; "General Relief Society Consolidated Statement of Cash Receipts and Disbursements, 1936," *Relief Society Magazine* 24 (June 1937): 385–87; "General Relief Society Consolidated Statement of Cash Receipts and Disbursements, 1937," *Relief Society Magazine* 25 (May 1938): 356–58.

38. Church relief increased after the introduction of the Welfare Plan. See *Conference Reports* for April 1931 through April 1937; Blumell, " 'Remember the Poor,' " 102.

39. Minutes of the Relief Society General Board, 15 February 1933.

40. First Presidency letter, 28 August 1933, as quoted in James R. Clark, comp., *Messages of the First Presidency*, 6 vols. (Salt Lake City: Bookcraft, 1966–73), 5:331–33. Also Arrington and Hinton, "Origin of the Welfare Plan," 75.

41. Belle S. Spafford Oral History, interviews by Jill Mulvay [Derr], 1975–76, typescript, 14, James Moyle Oral History Program, LDS Church Archives.

42. J. Reuben Clark, draft of "Suggestive Directions for Church Relief Activities," 30 June 1933, J. Reuben Clark, Jr., Papers, Harold B. Lee Library, Brigham Young University, Provo, Utah, as quoted in D. Michael Quinn, *J. Reuben Clark: The Church Years* (Provo, Utah: Brigham Young Univeristy Press, 1983), 259.

43. First Presidency letter, 28 August 1933, in Clark, *Messages*, 5:332.

44. Annie D. Palmer, "The Social Worker in the Unemployment Emergency," *Relief Society Magazine* 19 (January 1932): 19; "Social Case Work Department," *Relief Society Magazine* 16 (June 1929): 306–10; Lalene H. Hart, "The Social Service Institute," *Relief Society Magazine* 19 (January 1932): 35.

45. See Leiby, *A History of Social Welfare and Social Work*, 227–30.

46. In 1934 bishops were instructed to refer "all able-bodied Church workers in need of employment" to the stake representative in charge of unemployment relief so they could register with a county or federal employment agency and "obtain unemployment relief preferably through make-work or public works projects." *Care of the Poor* (Salt Lake City: Presiding Bishopric, 1934), 4.

47. Journal of Almira Cozzens Rich, 6 January 1934.

48. Maureen Ursenbach Beecher and Kathryn L. MacKay, "Women in Twentieth Century Utah," in Poll et al., eds., *Utah's History*, 580.

49. Clark, *Messages*, 6:10.

50. Leiby, *A History of Social Work and Social Welfare*, 224–27; Utah Public Welfare, *Biennial Report*, 6; Lowry Nelson, "Federal Aid," *Relief Society Magazine* 21 (November 1934): 677–83.

51. Leona Fetzer Wintch Oral History, interview by Loretta L. Hefner, 1979, typescript, 2, James Moyle Oral History Program, LDS Church Archives; Lewis Oral History, 11; Blumell, " 'Remember the Poor,' " 106.

52. Lewis Oral History, 3, 7–9, 14.

53. Blumell, " 'Remember the Poor,' " 105–7.

54. Wintch Oral History, 2; Lewis Oral History, 8, 12; Blumell, " 'Remember the Poor,' " 105–6.

55. Lewis Oral History, 18–19.

56. *Care of the Poor*, 11; "Social Work: Outline Summary for Relief Society Social Service Institute," January 1934, mimeograph with handwritten marginal notes by Amy Brown Lyman, Topic 7, pp. 11–12, Amy Brown Lyman Papers, University Archives and Manuscripts, Harold B. Lee Library, Brigham Young University; Welfare Department Newsletters, 1934–35, Relief Society Papers, LDS Church Archives.

57. Utah Public Welfare, *Biennial Report*, 6; Blumell, " 'Remember the Poor,' " 117.

58. Blumell, " 'Remember the Poor,' " 119–20, 129.

59. Meeting of the Presiding Bishopric with the First Presidency, 22 April 1935, Presiding Bishop's Office Journal, LDS Church Archives, as quoted in Blumell, " 'Remember the Poor,' " 123.

60. Louise Y. Robison address, "Relief Society Conference," *Relief Society Magazine* 22 (May 1935): 272.

61. The new law also provided aid to dependent children, crippled children, and the blind and grants for maternity and child health, child welfare, and vocational rehabilitation. Its provisions were examined at length in the society's magazine. See Ruth McQuarrie Penrose, "Mother's Aid," *Relief Society Magazine* 23 (January 1936): 40–41; Vera W. Pohlman, "Public Welfare Provisions," *Relief Society Magazine* 27 (November 1940): 767–75.

62. Minutes of the Relief Society General Board, 5 February 1936.

63. Ibid., 15 April 1936.

64. The results of an October 1935 survey of members receiving government and church relief were reported in a special priesthood meeting on 6 April 1936. This "Important Message from the First Presidency" set forth the guiding principles of a new church relief plan still being developed. *Deseret News*, 7 April 1936, as quoted in Clark, *Messages*, 6:10–13. The plan was outlined for the general membership in the Church Section of the *Deseret News*, 25 April 1936. See Blumell, " 'Remember the Poor,' " 124–29. Heber J. Grant reemphasized the principles of the plan when he summa-

rized its accomplishments at the October 1936 general conference. *Conference Report*, October 1936, p. 3.

65. Church Section, *Deseret News*, 25 April 1936; *Improvement Era* 39 (May 1936): 305 and (June 1936): 333–38.

66. Louise Y. Robison, "Relief Society's Contribution to the Church Welfare Program," *Relief Society Magazine* 25 (November 1938): 765 and "The Church Security Program," *Relief Society Magazine* 23 (November 1936): 713.

67. *Relief Society Memories — A History of Relief Society in St. George Stake*, comp. Verna L. Dewsnup and Katharine M. Larson (Springville, Utah: Art Publishing Company, 1956), 34.

68. "An Important Message," 6 April 1936, in Clark, *Messages*, 6:11.

69. Louise Y. Robison, "Relief Society's Contribution to the Church Welfare Program," *Relief Society Magazine* 25 (November 1938): 765–66; "Notes from the Field," *Relief Society Magazine* 23 (November 1936): 775; *Relief Society in the St. George Stake*, 28.

70. Louise Y. Robison, "The Church Security Program," *Relief Society Magazine* 23 (November 1936): 713.

71. Minutes of the Relief Society General Board, 3 June, 19 August, 21 October, and 4 November 1936; Louise Y. Robison, "The Church Security Program," *Relief Society Magazine* 23 (November 1936): 712–14.

72. Harold B. Lee, "Place of the Relief Society in the Church Security Plan," *Relief Society Magazine* 24 (March 1937): 140–43; Melvin J. Ballard and Louise Y. Robison, "Bulletin describing relationship of Relief Society organization to women's activities throughout the regions and stakes in connection with the Church Security Program," mimeograph, 3 pp., LDS Church Library.

73. Minutes of the Relief Society General Board, 21 October and 4 November 1936. Church Security Committee member Henry D. Moyle told the Relief Society presidency that the committee was setting up a revolving fund to defray the expenses of operating projects and had determined that Relief Society funds "were not to be touched for Church Security projects." Ibid., 23 June 1937. At the society's conference in April 1937 Presiding Bishop Sylvester Q. Cannon said Relief Society "funds for specific purposes should not be diverted," and the organization's responsibilities "should not be hampered or restricted by Stake Presidents or Ward Bishoprics." Sylvester Q. Cannon address, *Relief Society Magazine* 24 (June 1937): 350.

74. Figures cited for 1937 represent 99 out of 118 stakes reporting. Sylvester Q. Cannon address, *Relief Society Magazine* 25 (May 1938): 348.

75. Louise Y. Robison, "Official Instructions," *Relief Society Magazine* 24 (May 1937): 306.

76. Donna D. Sorensen, "The Work and Business Project," *Relief Society Magazine* 24 (August 1937): 513.

77. Harold B. Lee, "The Church Welfare Program," *Relief Society Magazine* 27 (July 1940): 462.

78. Adelia Busch, "The Bishops Storehouse, Ogden, Utah," xerox of typescript, 4, bound in Busch's collection of photos and related documents, LDS Church Archives.

79. Kate M. Barker address, "Relief Society Conference," *Relief Society Magazine* 24 (May 1937): 307; Louise Y. Robison, "Relief Society's Contribution to the Church Welfare Program," ibid., 25 (November 1938): 766.

80. Presiding Bishop Sylvester Q. Cannon told bishops it "should be their pleasure to accept the Relief Society recommendations," since they did "not have the facilities at hand to investigate for themselves." He acknowledged that the final decision in a case rested with the bishop, who might choose not to follow Relief Society recommendations. Sylvester Q. Cannon address, "Relief Society Conference," *Relief Society Magazine* 25 (May 1938): 349.

81. Minutes of the Relief Society General Board, 23 June 1937; Robison, "Relief Society's Contribution to the Church Welfare Program," 766.

82. Joseph L. Wirthlin, "Social Welfare Institutes," *Relief Society Magazine* 26 (May 1939): 319.

83. LeGrand Richards, "The Place of the Relief Society in the Welfare Program," *Relief Society Magazine* 27 (May 1940): 312. The need for communication with county agencies was emphasized by Vera W. Pohlman, "Public Welfare Provisions," *Relief Society Magazine* 27 (November 1940): 774. Pohlman helped develop the Relief Society "Record of Family Under Care," a comprehensive form to be completed by local workers doing home investigations. The form included questions regarding church and public aid and was used through the 1940s.

84. Harold B. Lee, "The Church Welfare Program," *Relief Society Magazine* 27 (July 1940): 458–62. Lee included a new assignment for the Relief Society: the employment survey assigned to priesthood leaders four years earlier. The Welfare Committee, having decided they had "pleaded long enough with the brethren of the Priesthood," gave the assignment to the women.

85. Louise Y. Robison address, "Relief Society Conference," *Relief Society Magazine* 25 (May 1938): 355. "Church Welfare as Interpreted by The Relief Society," *Relief Society Magazine* 26 (June 1939): 388–89; Relief Society Participation in Church Welfare," ibid., 26 (July 1939): 452.

86. Amy Brown Lyman, "President's Report and Official Instructions," *Relief Society Magazine* 27 (November 1940): 754–55.

87. Minutes of the Relief Society General Board, 19 April 1944.

88. Nauvoo Relief Society Minutes, 9 June 1842. The phrase is from Joseph Smith.

Mother Tongue: Use of Non-English Languages in the Church of Jesus Christ of Latter-day Saints in the United States, 1850–1983

RICHARD L. JENSEN

For fifteen years after their Relief Society was organized, the Danish women of the Mantua Ward in northern Utah recorded minutes of their meetings not in English but in Danish, and in old Gothic script. Only in 1878, so that stake leaders and other visitors could understand the minutes, did they begin recording them in English,[1] and even then many of the proceedings were in Danish for at least two more decades. In 1895 their ward clerk of forty-two years was still taking notes for the general ward meetings in Danish, then painstakingly transcribing them in English for the official minute book. Sometimes the result was a rather odd mixture, as in 1894, when ward teacher "Elder A. M. Jensen havde ingen Report to give [had no report to give]."[2]

A century later Fatu and Puapuaga Matagi similarly grappled with language assimilation with only modest success. For fifteen years after immigrating from Samoa to America they faithfully attended church meetings in a Salt Lake City suburb. They sent most of a large family on church missions; Fatu held some church positions. But Puapuaga, who did not share her husband's everyday contact with the English language, bore her testimony in Samoan on Fast Sundays. As their home teacher, I often accompanied their family on the piano while they sang hymns in Samoan. In 1982 the Matagis, with two unmarried sons and two other sons and their families, transferred from the Hunter Sixteenth Ward to the Samoan Branch in Salt Lake City, where they were able to participate in their native language.[3]

The Matagis of Hunter and the Danish sisters of Mantua illustrate the complexity of language assimilation even among the Latter-day Saints, who have been notable for the rapidity of their integration of immigrants. As Lowry Nelson and William Mulder point out, census figures show that English became the primary language of Utah's immigrant peoples more rapidly than it did in other states.[4] The Latter-day Saint Church has effectively contributed to this process by its emphasis of assimilation. One distinguishing trend in Utah has been the extremely high proportion of immigrants' children who became proficient in English, generally at the expense of the mother tongue. But a minority of Mormons represent a dimension too easily overlooked, a world of personal struggle with language adjustments in which English did not always win out. Adult immigrants often continued to feel more comfortable with the mother tongues, and many of them lived productive lives focused around their native language for half a century or more after their immigration to Utah.

Immigrants were not the only Latter-day Saints in the United States who spoke their own languages. Within American territory were also native Polynesians, American Indians, and Hispanic peoples who converted to Mormonism in significant numbers. Their Latter-day Saint activities and those of non-English speaking immigrants have formed a rich mosaic within the larger Mormon experience. This essay is an attempt to focus on the patterns of that little-noticed mosaic.

Two ideals have governed LDS policy toward minority converts and immigrants like the Matagis and the Danish sisters of Mantua. The first is set forth in the Doctrine and Covenants: "Every man shall hear the fulness of the gospel in his own tongue, and in his own language, through those who are ordained unto this power."[5] Through the years, this has meant that Latter-day Saints have extended themselves to preach in various languages — among the Norwegians in the Fox River settlements of Illinois in the 1840s, among the Germans of New York and Pennsylvania and the Utes and Paiutes of Utah in the 1850s, the Scandinavians of the Midwest in the 1870s, the Germans of Cincinnati and Milwaukee and the Scandinavians and Germans of Chicago around the turn of the century,[6] and the Spanish-speaking peoples of the borderlands in this century. These efforts have been, of course, in addition to the greater concentration on proselytizing abroad.

The second ideal is expressed in Ephesians 2:19, in which new believers are considered "no more strangers and foreigners, but fellowcitizens with the saints." Since communication was a prerequisite to unity, in English-dominated areas and in an English-dominated church, Paul's ideal was translated into a policy of uniformity of language. Often for practical reasons, the cultural reaching out did not extend far beyond offering the gospel in native languages. Once transplanted or converted into American Mormondom, immigrants or converts generally have been encouraged to adapt to American Mormon culture by learning the English language as quickly as possible. In the last century George A. Smith, of the Council of the Twelve, reflected this idea of a new "mother tongue" in a conference address:

> It appears that God in His divine wisdom revealed the gospel in the English language, which is the native language of the majority of the Saints. . . . It is very desirable that all of our brethren who are not acquainted with the English language should learn it. We do not wish to blot out the original languages that they may have spoken, but we want them all — men and women, old and young — to learn the English language so perfectly that they will be able to thoroughly understand for themselves the teachings and instructions and the published works of the Church, as well as the laws of the country."[7]

In this century, President Harold B. Lee suggested that this approach should be extended throughout the world. At the area general conference in Munich in 1973 he told listeners from six different language areas that he looked forward to the day when a person could speak into some instrument and have all his listeners hear in their own languages, without the intervention of human translation. But, since that scientific Day of Pentecost was not immediately at hand, he pointed out that the general authorities could not all learn the seventeen languages in which the gospel was then being preached. "Think how helpful it would be if every one of you now speaking in your own native tongues would all learn to speak English," he suggested. "I would like to challenge you to do that; then you would be able to talk with us more clearly and we could understand you better than we have today."[8]

But there has often been a tension between these two ideals. On the one hand is the desire to reach out worldwide in a way each person can best understand; on the other the need to pull in, bonding converts to the larger church body. This tension has been felt most intensely by new converts. The emphasis on language uniformity, intended to facilitate their adjustment to a new culture, has stood at odds with their actual immediate needs and desire to retain their native heritage.

Youth and some adults of the past and present have tended to adopt a new language and culture readily. Early European converts to Mormonism had additional incentives. They were admonished to reject much of European society as a spiritual Babylon and turn to a whole new way of life, which included a new language. In the nineteenth century, European converts often had a running start at learning the English language in their native lands. Missionaries and others who had studied the language of Zion were enlisted as instructors, as in the case of C. C. A. Christensen, a Danish convert supervising missionary efforts in Norway, who in 1856 used church funds to pay for his own private instruction by an Englishman and simultaneously taught his fellow Mormons.[9] But for many, despite such preparation, the confrontation with Mountain West English posed obstacles then, as now.

It is not surprising, therefore, that once in Utah early immigrants from Europe sought at least temporary refuge in religious meetings conducted in their mother tongue. The first such efforts were foreign language meetings held in settlements throughout Utah Territory. As early as November 1849 Welsh immigrants met on Sundays in Salt Lake City, although at least some of the proceedings were in English. Some 1852 predecessors of the Mantua sisters, the first immigrants to arrive in Salt Lake City from Denmark, held church-related meetings in Danish, and that year Alexander Neibaur, who had earlier instructed Joseph Smith in German, held what was apparently the first German meeting in the city. Beginning in 1870, Dutch meetings were held in Ogden. By 1906 Scandinavian meetings alone were being held in thirty-four locations in Utah and three in Idaho.[10] Except in time of war, meetings of such groups continued into the early 1960s.

There is no indication what kind of official sanction the meetings received initially, but by 1860 Brigham Young was exercising some supervision over their organization, appointing Karl G. Maeser president of the German meetings in Salt Lake City. Those meetings were discontinued in the fall of 1861 after most of the Swiss and German immigrants moved to southern Utah. But in 1870, after more immigrants had settled in Salt Lake City, President Young responded to local requests for meetings by again naming Maeser to preside.

Then, beginning with the general reorganization of stakes in 1877, the Salt Lake Stake presidency was given responsibility for overseeing such minority-language meetings in the valley.[11] Later other stakes were given direct supervision over foreign language groups within their jurisdiction. One or more of the general authorities, probably by assignment, usually exercised a broader stewardship over all such groups, seeing that needs were filled and problems solved. Often these authorities had some language background themselves: Anthon H. Lund of the Twelve and later the First Presidency, a Danish immigrant; John A. Widtsoe, a Norwegian; and LeGrand Richards, once a mission president in the Netherlands.

The need for involvement by general authorities is demonstrated in the history of the Scandinavian meetings spanning more than three-quarters of a century. For several decades, conjoint Scandinavian meetings served Danish, Swedish, and Norwegian Mormon immigrants in the Mountain West. All three languages were used, since all were generally understood by most participants. However, Swedish separatism asserted itself by the turn of the century, partly because more recent immigrants from northern and central Sweden could not understand Danish as well as could southern Swedes, who predominated among the early immigrants from their country. Controversy plagued the Salt Lake Stake's Scandinavian meetings organization for years, beginning in 1898. Both stake and general church officials attempted to promote unity, but gradual concessions were made to separatist sentiments. For several years immigrants could choose between conjoint or separate meetings. Finally, in 1935, conjoint Scandinavian meetings were limited to semiannual gatherings in conjunction with churchwide conferences.[12]

There is no indication that early minority-language meetings were intended to supplant the English-language services of the regular local wards. As a young man, Swiss native Arnold Schulthess served concurrently as secretary of the deacon's quorum in the Salt Lake City First Ward and "acting Deacon for the German Meeting in the old City Hall."[13] Many immigrants probably enjoyed participating in both kinds of meetings, although in an era when consistent attendance at all meetings was not the general rule, some immigrants probably chose to attend the one or the other or no meetings at all.

By fostering a sense of community among minorities, the officially sanctioned "meetings" helped provide a springboard for the launching of other functions in the mother tongue. Annual reunions and conferences, all church-oriented, became the general rule for the various language groups. Scandinavian Relief Societies were established in Brigham City and other communities. Musical, political, and cultural organizations also thrived.

Newspapers were another significant aspect of immigrant language and culture. As William Mulder has pointed out, these facilitated assimilation in a broad sense, while providing a haven of linguistic and cultural continuity. The most enduring of these were openly and enthusiastically Mormon. Church leaders first gave their permission, then their encouragement, later financial support; and finally the church assumed responsibility for the management of four newspapers, in German, Danish-Norwegian, Swedish, and Dutch.[14] This support was maintained until 1935, when all four newspapers were discontinued.

In the late nineteenth century, editorials and sermons frequently called attention to the need for immigrants to maintain and teach their mother tongues. The demand for new missionaries proficient in foreign languages was usually the predominant reason given. In turn, from this time onward the proselytizing impulse was significant in injecting vitality into the effort to preserve the mother tongue. An example was the maintenance of Utah's Latter-day Saint periodicals in foreign languages, which critics called unnecessary and undesirable. In 1894 a *Deseret News* editorial advocated that such publications should continue because for Latter-day Saints "the cultivation of linguistic skill becomes part of their religion. Without it they cannot fulfill their mission to their fellow-men."[15]

Theoretically, the *News*'s argument made sense. Immigrants and their American-born children could maintain fluency in the mother tongue and at the same time be totally integrated into the larger English-speaking community. In practice, however, few of the youth became truly bilingual. The second generation, particularly among northern European immigrants, frequently returned as missionaries to ancestral homelands with little working knowledge of the mother tongue. The press benefited primarily the first generation in Utah. Abroad, Latter-day Saint newspapers from Utah in the various languages were considered important proselytizing aids, countering the overwhelmingly negative press Mormonism generally received in Europe. Non-English newspapers and organizations served the everyday needs of first-generation immigrants in the Mountain West who continued to use their native languages. Some never effectively mastered English; others could communicate more effectively in the mother tongue, even though they became proficient in English. Beyond language considerations alone, cultural affinities and the maintenance of ethnic identity were also involved in native-language activities.

Latter-day Saint ethnic organizations in the Mountain West were reinforced after the turn of the century by ethnic "home missionaries," whose responsibilities were similar to those of home missionaries to English-speaking congregations, but who were called by general church authorities. Hans J. Christiansen, editor of the Danish-Norwegian newspaper *Bikuben*, thus visited Scandinavian "meetings" throughout Utah and in Idaho, promoting the newspaper at the same time he encouraged the Saints to observe their religion and maintain their organizations.[16]

With such encouragement, some minority organizations took on a feeling of permanence in the years prior to World War I. German organizations constructed their own meetinghouses in Logan and Richmond, Utah, as did Scandinavians in Spring City. Significantly, the German-speaking meetings in Logan offered the sacrament once a month, beginning in 1902.[17] As long as the sacrament was withheld from participants in mother-tongue meetings, worshippers' primary responsibility was more clearly to local English-speaking wards, with ethnic organizations serving only as a supplement.

But during World War I pressure against the use of foreign languages mounted throughout the United States. While the tone of editorials in the church-sponsored *Deseret News* reflected a more moderate approach, local pressures forced discontinuation of some ethnic meetings, despite demonstrations of patriotism by the immigrants. Richmond's German Latter-day Saints offered the use of their meetinghouse to a local ward whose facilities were insufficient, only to have their own organization dissolved soon thereafter. Local public opinion was the only reason cited for discontinuing German Latter-day Saint meetings in Logan late in the war.[18]

After the armistice, ethnic organizations were generally revived. A relatively large influx of Latter-day Saint immigrants from Europe in 1923 inspired the establishment the following year of the first general church supervisory body for minority language affairs. This Committee on Latter-day Saint Meetings and Newspapers in Foreign Languages was chaired by John A. Widtsoe of the Council of the Twelve. A survey taken for the committee found that a total of thirty "foreign" meetings were being held in twenty-one stakes, with two in Swedish, thirteen "Scandinavian," two Danish, two Dutch, and nine German, in addition to four "Mexican" local organizations. These served a total membership of 3,014.

The committee recognized a significant point never before articulated by the church: "There are many thousands of true Latter-day Saints, who have gathered to this country, who will never become familiar with the English language." With that in mind, activities and publications were to be provided to help fill the needs of a minority that would not disappear into the "melting pot" of American language and culture. Still, the committee sought to guard against ethnic separatism by recommending that "there should be no unnecessary multiplication of [foreign-language] meetings; but there should be a sufficient number to meet the needs of the people concerned."[19] Attendees of these meetings were to give primary allegiance to regular English-speaking wards and stakes, where they were encouraged to attend sacrament meetings. However, there is no evidence of any attempt to make those meetings understandable for immigrants who were not conversant in English. Local stakes were to continue to have jurisdiction over the organizations for foreign-language meetings, except in larger centers such as Salt Lake City and Ogden, where there were several stakes.[20]

Meanwhile, other developments affected the vitality of Latter-day Saint immigrant organizations. Increasingly in the 1920s, church leaders advised against "gathering to Zion." With new federal immigration restrictions and the loss of economic incentives to immigrate, the stream of European Latter-day Saints to America slowed to a trickle. As older immigrants died and others became fluent in English, church-sponsored minority newspapers lost readership. All four were discontinued in 1935. As for the meetings and their sponsoring ethnic organizations, World War II was more devastating than the antipathies of World War I. A terse statement announced the decision made at a meeting of the First Presidency and the Twelve in the Salt Lake Temple on 12 March 1942: All foreign-language activities except those of the Mexican Branch in Salt Lake City would be discontinued "for the duration of the war, or until further instruction from the First Presidency." Their property was to be deposited with the First Presidency "to be used as authorized by them." In place of the fellowship and support the ethnic organizations had provided, local leaders were directed to enlist the help of ward teachers and stake missionaries to "give special attention to the needs of the members of the Church of foreign birth, and to encourage them to do their full duty in the Church."[21]

Indications are that church leaders intended the change to be temporary, as their announcement indicated. For example, the records of the German organization in Logan were deposited in the LDS Church Archives, and local leaders were given to understand that the records were to be returned when their organization was reestablished. But such reestablishment was far from automatic. In this instance, ten years passed before the Cache Valley Germans again met together. Then it was largely through the assistance of Oliver H. Budge, former mission president in Germany, that arrangements were made for them to meet in the basement of the Logan Tabernacle. In the meantime, their own meetinghouse had become unusable because of a decade of neglect and abuse.[22]

Assimilation was a more dominant theme in church policies for immigrants from northern Europe than for three other groups, considered by Latter-day Saints to be largely descendants of "Book of Mormon peoples." While theological imperatives from Latter-day Saint scripture moved Mormons to seek converts among native Americans, Hispanics, and Polynesians, they found the language and culture of these converts more persistent, less conducive to integration than that of European immigrants. Most of the American Indians and Polynesians, and many of the Hispanic converts, did not immigrate to America as Latter-day Saint converts, but remained within ethnic communities that were occupied by their ancestors long before America had annexed their territory.

While European Latter-day Saint immigrant organizations were considered auxiliaries for more than a century, local wards and branches serving each of the three Book of Mormon peoples enjoyed full organizational status, serving all ecclesiastical functions for their members. The Iosepa Ward, in Utah's Skull Valley, consisted of Polynesian immigrants. For twenty-seven years most of its activities were conducted in the Hawaiian language. But the construction of a temple in Hawaii led to the emigration of members of the colony back to the islands, and in 1917 the ward was discontinued.[23] Washakie Ward served the needs of Shoshoni Indians near Malad, Idaho; the Papago Ward near Mesa, Arizona, consisted of Pima, Papago, and Maricopa Indians. In both of the latter wards, Indian languages predominated at first, supplanted later by English as ward members generally acquired fluency in English. The Spanish-speaking branch within Salt Lake City's Liberty Stake, founded in 1921, continued. Each of these church units should be considered in the light of broader developments in the Latter-day Saint approach to Book of Mormon peoples.

A sustained proselyting effort among Spanish-speaking peoples of the borderlands states began in 1915. Rey L. Pratt, president of the Mexican Mission, had evacuated Mexico with his missionaries in 1913 during the revolution there. He was directed in June 1915 to supervise the establishment of missionary efforts to Hispanics under the jurisdiction of the Western States Mission. In 1918 this work was given separate status under the so-called Mexican Mission, actually a mission in exile.[24] With increasing numbers of missionaries available after World War I, proselytizing was expanded from its beginnings in Colorado, Arizona, and New Mexico, to Texas and then to California. This brought the organization of numerous Spanish-speaking branches that eventually outnumbered the northern European ethnic organizations in the Intermountain West. These branches, such as the Spanish-speaking branch in Salt Lake City, differed from Latter-day Saint ethnic organizations under the jurisdiction of stakes, in that they functioned as church units, with ecclesiastical jurisdiction over their members. Thus, at least this one minority language in the "mission field" was an integral part of local church organization, in much the same way as the predominant languages of foreign missions.

Mormon proselytizing of the American Indians, benefiting from sporadic bursts of enthusiasm over the years, had seen periods of numerous conversions in the 1870s and 1880s. However, church members generally failed to consolidate these gains by bringing Indian converts into meaningful participation on an ongoing basis. In the late 1880s responsibility for working with the Indians was generally left to local stake leaders in the vicinity of Indian reservations. In 1918 the Mexican Mission was given primary responsibility for proselytizing Indians in Texas, New Mexico, Arizona, Colorado, and California. However, with the exception of building a missionary dwelling and a schoolhouse on the Gila Reservation, there was little actual increase in efforts among the Indians.[25]

Responding to the plea of Mary Jumbo, a Navajo Latter-day Saint, that the church become more active on behalf of the Indian people, George Albert Smith of the Council of Twelve initiated an expansion of Indian programs, beginning with the establishment of the Navajo-Zuni Mission in 1944. Presidents Rufus K. Hardy and Antoine R. Ivins of the First Council of Seventy, and later Spencer W. Kimball and Matthew Cowley, helped supervise church efforts on behalf of the Indians. The committee construed its responsibilities broadly, to include concern for Indian peoples of Latin America and for Polynesians, as well as Indians of the United States and Canada. Under the committee's direction, Golden R. Buchanan as coordinator of Indian affairs worked closely with stake leaders.[26]

The late 1940s and early 1950s thus saw a three-pronged approach to proselytizing among Indian peoples and providing for their church participation: missions became active on reservations within their territory; stake Indian Relations Committees were formed to coordinate proselytizing and assist the Indian branches and auxiliaries that soon were created within stake boundaries; and work was greatly expanded in the Southwest Indian Mission, successor to the Navajo-

Zuni Mission. While overall stake and mission activity on behalf of the Indians tended to taper off, intensive efforts in the one specifically Indian mission continued, and were extended to include the northern Great Plains area. Indian languages, primarily Navajo, were used in numerous branches; but cultural needs and geography, more than language, dictated the creation of separate ecclesiastical organizations for native Americans.

Until recent decades, when a substantial number of conversions were made in Latin America, the most encouraging response the Mormons received from Book of Mormon peoples was in the Pacific. Here, too, a policy of encouraging ethnic integrity predominated. Use of the mother tongue among Mormons in Hawaii, despite annexation by the United States in 1898, was much like that of any "foreign-language" mission until the 1920s. Proselytizing focused almost exclusively on those of native Hawaiian ancestry, believed to have descended from immigrants from the American mainland. The church counted among its ranks more than one-fifth of the native Hawaiian population before the onset of World War I.[27]

Gradually Mormonism became in a sense a champion of Hawaiian language and culture. Although immigration made native Hawaiians a minority in their islands, church leaders continued to promote the use of the Hawaiian language in meetings and proselytizing. Many adults could not understand English, or could better understand the gospel in their native language. Missionaries found that their use of the Hawaiian language made a good impression, giving them advantages in proselytizing.

Young Hawaiians became increasingly fluent in English in the decade after American annexation. As early as 1904 Honolulu's Latter-day Saints had both English and Hawaiian choirs, and by 1906 some meetings for children featured a mixture of English and Hawaiian speakers.[28] The transition to English was most accelerated on the island of Oahu. But the trend toward the use of English was inspired less by church policy than by larger social and governmental influences, and Mormonism in the islands remained predominantly Hawaiian for several more decades.

Intentions were announced as early as 1919 to begin proselytizing among all the varied nationalities in Hawaii.[29] During a mission conference in April 1925 mission president Eugene Neff called to the stand "representatives of the different nationalities and mixed nationalities," which included "American, Hawaiian, Samoan, Tahitian, Maori, Japanese, Chinese, Norwegian, Swedish, Danish, German, English, Scotch, Welsh, Portuguese, Filipino, Canadian, New Zealand English, Dutch American, Irish Hawaiian, French American, Indian Hawaiian, Spanish Hawaiian."[30] But effective missionary work to non-Hawaiian ethnic subcultures did not actually begin until the 1930s. As late as 1932 adult church membership in Hawaii was reported to consist of "12,500 Hawaiians, 75 Japanese, 50 Chinese, some Filipinos, Koreans, and Negro families, 1 eskimo family, and a few hundred whites."[31] A fairly high proportion of the "whites" were Latter-day Saints from the continental United States.

Beginning in the 1930s, the Japanese language was utilized for proselytizing and church services in Hawaii for persons of Japanese descent. With the termination of missionary work in Japan, Hawaii became the home of the Japanese Mission in 1937, renamed the Central Pacific Mission in 1944. Just as with the Mexican Mission earlier, this mission in exile reinforced the maintenance of separate organizations and services for a sizeable minority, largely in the mother tongue. Perhaps one reason was that there was little inclination for the easygoing Hawaiians and the efficient, punctual Japanese to integrate for religious activities. But by the end of World War II most Japanese as well as Hawaiian church members were conversant in English, and both missions, as well as local church units, were merged in 1950. A Japanese Sunday School that persisted in Honolulu for many years was the only separate Japanese organization to remain. Although some of the Japanese were not fluent in English, they were able to function in their new setting. In fact, the Japanese Americans soon provided much of the leadership of local church units.[32]

Since the establishment of a church stake in Honolulu in 1935, non-Hawaiians had been placed in numerous stake leadership positions. But after 1951 many of the American mainland newcomers congregated at the Waikiki Ward, rather than dispersing among the geographically based wards to which they otherwise would have belonged.[33] Hawaiian leadership, and to some extent the Hawaiian language, thus persisted into the 1950s, until overwhelmed by the influx of outsiders.

While general use of the Hawaiian language faded into a smattering of local color among an English-speaking majority, Latter-day Saints continued to value the dying tongue. In 1955 mission president D. Arthur Haycock published a relatively comprehensive guide for the study of Hawaiian. He encouraged missionaries to "speak in Hawaiian with Hawaiian people at every possible opportunity." He hoped missionaries would become familiar with Hawaiian culture "and be able to warm their hearts by teaching them the gospel on occasion in their mother tongue." Latter-day Saints continued to take pride in the 1855 Hawaiian translation of the Book of Mormon, extensive excerpts of which were a main feature in an attractive 120-page history of the church in Hawaii, published in 1978.[34] Thus language was a significant part of the church's self-identification with Polynesian cultural heritage, an emphasis now most evident in the church-sponsored Polynesian Cultural Center at Laie, one of Hawaii's foremost tourist attractions since 1965.

The Latter-day Saint experience with language in Hawaii was similar to the relationship with the Maori language in New Zealand, but without parallel in the United States. The relatively high proportion of Pacific island natives who converted to Mormonism, the longstanding lack of converts from other ethnic groups, and the widespread identification of the church as a native movement, were factors in the unhurried transition to English. But as the indigenous minority as a whole became fluent in English, the transition within the church became complete, accompanied by the broadening of membership to include other ethnic groups.

Among these later additions were not only the Japanese, but also Filipinos, Chinese, and converts from other groups within Hawaii's diverse population. Generally, these were proselytized in English, although some were more fluent in the mother tongue. Samoans, Tongans, and other Polynesians, some of them Mormons who immigrated from their native islands, attracted by the Latter-day temple or educational opportunities, added further diversity.

Because of the language skills of its Mormon members, Hawaii thus became a rich source of missionaries to their native or ancestral lands, including Japan beginning in 1948, Hong Kong from 1949 onward, the Philippines from the 1960s, and Micronesia beginning in 1976.[35] The Philippines were initially proselytized in English, the other lands in their native tongues.

In American Samoa, a possession of the United States beginning in 1900, English appeared unlikely to become the predominant language. This was also true of Puerto Rico, where Mormon proselytizing began on a sustained basis in the 1970s. Thus in these areas there was as little thought of a Mormon transition to English as in any typical "foreign speaking" area outside the United States. However, the relatively numerous immigrants from these islands to the mainland United States or to Hawaii, including the Matagi family mentioned above, encountered the same language problems as other immigrants.

Perhaps these exceptions were made because the people they served were presumed unlikely to be easily assimilated into the predominantly northern European culture, and less likely to acquire the use of the English language quickly.

Closer to church headquarters, proselytizing was focused on minorities in Utah and Idaho for the first time in the mid-1950s. The influx of postwar immigrants, together with others already present, provided the basis for establishment of regional missions in the Salt Lake Valley and in Ogden, the Uintah Basin, and Pocatello, Idaho. Missionaries were called locally who were capable of teaching in one of more than a dozen languages. After numerous converts were made, Salt Lake Valley Regional Mission President Golden Buchanan called to the attention of the general authorities the fact that not only the new converts but also many longtime church members among the minorities were not having their needs met by English-speaking church units. Many had little contact with the church as a result. Although some minority groups continued to meet annually or semiannually in reunions or conferences, with church encouragement, "meetings" in the mother tongues were fewer and often less frequent than before.

The Salt Lake Valley Regional Mission responded by serving as the catalyst for the organization of new Sunday Schools in German and Norwegian. Buchanan recommended that full-fledged minority-language wards or branches be established and placed under the jurisdiction of local stakes. Beginning in 1962–63, several branches were thus organized in the Salt Lake Valley, under general church direction. These included the Dai Ichi Branch (Japanese), the Cumorah Branch (Spanish), and branches in German, Dutch, Swedish, Danish, and Norwegian, as well as two American Indian branches. In addition, French, Mandarin, and Cantonese Sunday Schools were organized under stake leadership. Longtime church members from the minority groups were encouraged to remain with their local geographically based wards if they felt at home there and could understand and participate; otherwise they were welcome to join the minority units. Response was enthusiastic: during the seven years one man served in a Spanish branch presidency in Provo, Utah, no one declined a call to serve in a church position.[36]

With the establishment of such ecclesiastical units, the church-sponsored European American minority organizations which had carried out reunions and "meetings" without providing basic church services were generally discontinued in a policy of eliminating exceptions. The Salt Lake Valley Regional Mission itself—by now an anomaly—was discontinued in 1966, and its proselytizing efforts were not immediately assumed by any other entity. However, many of the ethnic wards or branches have continued to the present, under the jurisdiction of the stakes to which they were assigned.

The growth of the church in areas outside the Intermountain West and the establishment of stakes throughout the United States and abroad led to a streamlining of the function of missions. Mission boards and other mission-based support services for church members were discontinued, and wherever possible mission branches were transferred to the jurisdiction of stakes. Generally, this resulted in an enhancement of leadership training and allowed mission leaders to concentrate their efforts on proselytizing. However, in the case of ethnic congregations, particularly Spanish-speaking branches, the change was sometimes a mixed blessing. There was often a tendency to disregard the language needs of the transferred individuals. Visiting branches in California and Arizona in 1958, Spencer W. Kimball confided concerns to his diary that reflected his commitment to filling the needs of minority peoples: "THE CHURCH MUST NEVER ASS[U]ME THE ROLE OF FORCING THE SPANISH SPEAKING PEOPLE TO LEARN ENGLISH. The Church is for the people and not the people for the Church."[37]

In talking with the Spanish-speaking people, Kimball found "rebellion against regimentation in the matter of language." Stake leaders spoke to Hispanic church members in English without interpreters because many in their audience did understand some English. Thus they proceeded "with what seemed total disregard to the few to whom their talk had no meaning whatever." And those conducting stake meetings disregarded language needs. "It appeared that there had been a disregard or a lack of understanding or an unsympathetic feeling toward this minority on the part of some of the stake people who seemed to assume the attitude of superiority and of lending their principal efforts to helping the anglos rather than the minority group who needs their help so much. The physician had come to the well instead of the sick."[38] Thus Kimball sought to encourage greater attention to the needs of minorities in an era of increasing interaction with Anglo Mormons.

Before its termination in 1967 the large Spanish-American Mission systematically had thirty-five branches placed under the jurisdiction of various stakes and missions in Colorado, Texas, Arizona, and New Mexico. At the time of redistribution, and in the following years, there was a strong tendency to integrate the Spanish-speaking units with English-speaking wards and branches. Speaking only English would ease the burden of stake leaders in training and supervising the units. Anglo members could participate and add strength and leadership that sometimes seemed an acute need. Travel and expense could sometimes be saved by combining Anglo and Spanish-speaking branches in localities where commuting had previously been necessary for either group. While civil rights groups nationally sought more complete integration, church leaders both locally and in Salt Lake City sought the same goals within the church. Moreover, it was deemed essential for church members in the United States to learn English, both for their own economic well-being and for the achievement of unity.

But integration brought other problems. Unless pursued with sensitivity to the wishes of minority members, it sometimes amounted to coercion in matters of language and culture, depriving some individuals of the opportunity to participate fully in church programs, and alienating others. Former members of the Pecos Spanish-American

Branch in Texas aired some of these problems in a 1963 letter to the general authorities of the church. They complained that administrative protocol had not been observed in the merger of their branch into the local Anglo branch, that they had not been consulted about the change, that the proceedings of the organizational meeting had been only in English, that the opinions of those who had not voted in favor of the change had not been sought. In view of the fact that they had sacrificed to pay for the local chapel, for which the English-speaking branch had paid nothing, they questioned the justice of allowing the other branch to take over the building. Implicitly challenging the claim they understood had been made, that the change "was a direct order from the Prophet and the Council of the Twelve," they appealed the decision.[39]

In Pecos, as in some other branches, adjustments were made to smooth over difficulties inherent in an approach that sometimes lacked sensitivity to the effects of such changes. Speakers and hymns in Spanish were to be allowed, presumably with translation. A Sunday school class would be held in Spanish for those unable to understand English. An Anglo family who had snubbed the Spanish Americans and opposed the merger were visited by the Texas Mission president, and the new branch presidency, including a member of the former Spanish-American presidency, visited the Spanish-speaking members and reported improved feelings.[40]

Spanish-American Mission president Melvin Brooks reported that the complete elimination of Spanish from branch meetings, where such was attempted, "has turned some of our older members away for lack of edification when they attend meetings." He noted, "We want to encourage our people to learn English, but it is evident that they need some of their services in Spanish until they can communicate or receive edification in English." Moreover, missionaries were converting more people who were not conversant with English. Marion G. Romney of the Council of the Twelve, Brooks's area supervisor, concurred that teaching in Spanish would need to be provided.[41]

But elsewhere in the church, other Spanish-language branches were converted to English during the late 1960s and early 1970s. The Cumorah Branch in the Salt Lake Valley, a leader in their stake in activity, was dissolved, apparently under the assumption that its members were capable of being assimilated into English-speaking wards.

Yet assimilation was not as thorough as leaders hoped. One local church leader of Hispanic descent, whose ancestor was converted to Mormonism in New Mexico in 1877, participated in both ethnic and integrated church units and concluded that he preferred not to be assimilated. Fluent in both languages, he felt an affinity for Hispanic Latter-day Saints and suggested that ethnic wards and branches fostered greater enthusiasm and fellowship. A regional representative of Hispanic descent found that Anglo church members still tended to regard him as a foreigner.[42] Others, feeling the same lack of belonging, stopped attending church after their minority branches were discontinued. Observers indicate that this was true of many members of discontinued ethnic branches. Those who continued to attend church were seldom called to serve in ward positions, and even those fluent in English frequently remained outside the social fold of the flock. In 1970 Spencer Kimball, acting president of the Council of the Twelve, recommended increased tolerance and training after finding few Hispanic leaders within the Corpus Christi Stake, although Hispanics made up nearly half of the stake population.[43]

After the discontinuation of minority branches there was major attrition in the ranks of Indians active in church even at Brigham Young University, where a 1975 survey indicated that of 586 Latter-day Saint Indian students only 262 were enrolled with student wards, 76 were considered active in those wards, and none held a position as an officer or teacher.[44] This merely paralleled, in exaggerated form, the plight of other minorities in English-speaking Latter-day Saint congregations. Rarely called to positions of leadership, minority members often distinguished themselves in missionary service to their homelands or those of their ancestors but experienced little fellowship at home. As in the nation at large, integration of minorities in the church often brought disillusionment because it failed to provide full and meaningful participation.[45]

The situation in the church as Spencer W. Kimball assumed the presidency was thus one of increased frustration on the part of minority members. Efforts to streamline administration of the far-flung branches, wards, and stakes, so that central leaders could keep abreast of the needs throughout the church and more effectively manage those needs, seemed to have intensified rather than reduced the problem of neglect of minorities. The nationwide emphasis of the 1960s on integration, sharpened by civil rights crusades, had led to many achievements, only to be supplanted in minority consciousness by a renewed ethnic pride. The American Indian Movement and the Chicano movement helped focus attention on the needs of particular minorities nationwide, and may have served some of the same purpose for the church. On the other hand, concerns about the Chicano movement may have provoked the reactive merger of some Spanish-speaking branches in the Southwest with local English-speaking units.[46] The whole issue was complicated by increased immigration from Latin America and, beginning in 1975, an influx of refugees to the United States from Southeast Asia which was to test church minority programs.

Church headquarters responded with increased attention to minority needs, a point of view long held by President Kimball. Total integration continued to be the ultimate goal of church leaders responsible for minority programs, but the methods by which that goal was pursued, and the ways in which minorities were accommodated, varied. Changing signals from Salt Lake City reached the local stake and mission leaders; beginning at about the time Spencer Kimball became president of the church, fewer minority branches were discontinued. The time prior to President Kimball's revelation granting of priesthood to blacks was a period of productive ferment in formulation of the church's approach for other minorities. The Lamanite and Other Cultural Groups Committee, an expanded version of the Indian Relations Committee, was at work developing ways to implement ideas President Kimball had advocated for decades.[47]

Two keys to church administration attributed to President Kimball were simplification and flexibility. His advocacy of a greatly simplified church curriculum and organization overall began as a response to the needs of the Indian people, whom he saw overwhelmed by earlier church programs. The Basic Unit approach, which focused on the most urgent agenda for small church units, provided flexibility in local organization, limiting church positions to the capabilities of available personnel. Adopted in 1978, it removed small groups of Latter-day Saints from dependency on larger congregations and from administrative overload. Church branches with only a handful of members could carry on basic functions, and could move into auxiliary activities when their growth made that advisable.[48]

Proselytizing among ethnic minorities by regular geographically based missions in the United States, begun in the 1960s, accelerated in the mid-1970s. This was facilitated by language training for missionaries before they arrived in their assigned proselytizing areas. By 1983 more than six hundred full-time missionaries focused primarily on minorities within the United States. Additional help was provided by local part-time missionaries with essential language skills. A variety of options were developed to help local church units serve the needs of minority converts and visitors. Two sound systems, one with cordless headsets and the other a plug-in system with cords, were suggested to make simultaneous translation of church services available within chapels.[49] Or language groups might meet separately in the same building as English-speaking units, either functioning separately or integrating those who could understand English into one or more of the English meetings. For example, after a basic sacrament service in their native language the youth and children might attend English-language classes, while adults remained for instruction in their own language.

While English-based wards and branches thus served the needs of many minority worshippers, the number of separate units for minority groups multiplied rapidly in the late 1970s and early 1980s, with more than four hundred functioning in the United States and Canada by 1983 — the great majority of these being in the United States. The most recent listing available, for April 1982, showed 162 Spanish units in the United States, 112 Indian units, 58 Asian units, and 36 other units. The Asian units included 13 Laotian, 9 Chinese, 8 Cambodian, 7 Vietnamese, 6 Hmong, 5 Korean, 4 Asian, 3 Thai, 2 Indo-Chinese, and 2 Japanese. "Other" units included 15 American Sign Language (for the deaf), 9 Tongan, 6 Samoan, and 1 each of French, Polish, Russian, Danish, Norwegian, and German. Thus 56 percent of the Spanish units were located in California and Texas, 53 percent of Indian units in Arizona and New Mexico, and 52 percent of all minority units were found in those four southwestern states. Washington and Oregon accounted for 36 percent of Asian units, and Utah had 11 percent of the total minority units.[50] Only 2 of the

Spanish units, 1 Samoan, 1 Tongan, 1 German, and 11 Indian units were designated as wards, which would indicate that they had achieved size, local leadership, and presumed permanence beyond that of the others.[51]

A significant indicator of the church's willingness and ability to provide for the needs of its linguistic minorities was its arrangements for non-English languages in its temples. Although Latter-day Saints believed that temple ordinances were essential for full realization of the individual's eternal potential, it was not deemed essential that participants receive those ordinances in their own languages. Thus, like Roman Catholics attending mass in Latin, their involvement was often more on a strictly sacramental than on an emotional or intellectual level. For a century after the introduction of the temple ceremonies, the fact that English was the language of the temples was considered to be axiomatic. That in itself was an important factor in encouragement to learn English. Early participants at the temples who were not fluent in English may have had the ordinances briefly explained before or after receiving them. As temple rites were not to be discussed outside the temples, such explanations would generally have taken place during their visit to the temple.

Temple ordinances were received by a number of Indians presumably not fluent in English in the Endowment House in Salt Lake City in the 1870s and 1880s. Polynesians from the Iosepa colony participated in the dedication of the Salt Lake Temple in 1893, which featured an address to them in Hawaiian by George Q. Cannon. However, there is no indication that translation of the ceremonies was available for their subsequent visits to the temple, which for many had been a primary motivation for their immigration.[52]

At the time of the Hawaiian Temple's dedication in 1919, most of the adult Hawaiian Latter-day Saints were fluent only in the Hawaiian language. However, no indication has been found that temple ceremonies were translated into that language. Not until 1945 were temple rites translated. That year saw the first use of Spanish temple sessions in the Arizona Temple.[53] Mexican Latter-day Saints residing in Mexico, as a group, were apparently not expected to learn English in the foreseeable future. Thus, provision for fuller participation in the higher ordinances of the church by members outside English-speaking areas benefited not only them but also a corresponding minority within the United States.

European immigrants were the first to benefit from temple ceremony translations into their particular native languages, beginning in 1951. Construction was begun soon afterward on three temples outside the United States, in Switzerland, England, and New Zealand. These were the first to utilize film for the presentation of temple ceremonies, a procedure that reduced manpower needs and helped make participation in their native tongues possible for even small groups of temple patrons. Finally, beginning in the mid-1970s, numerous small temples were constructed in such locations as Brazil, Japan, Samoa, Tonga, Tahiti, Chile, Mexico, and East Germany. This was accompanied by further expansion of the use of temple translations in film. By mid-1970 temple ceremonies were available in twenty languages. With all but two temples in the United States using film, most temples could theoretically offer any of the twenty languages required. Translation to Navajo was in process, as was film in American Sign Language.[54] Benefiting from translation aimed primarily at temples abroad, minority Latter-day Saints in the United States thus had broad access to ceremonies in their mother tongues.

The ultimate goal of church leaders—total integration of minorities—tended to recede into the background in the late 1970s and early 1980s as local leaders were encouraged to concentrate on the most effective ways of filling needs of minority members. Yet there were still limitations. Renewed emphasis on uniform lines of local responsibility meant that language and ethnic functions crossing stake boundaries were exceptional, usually limited to occasional sociocultural gatherings. Minority units were discouraged from renewing their vitality by recruiting young families whose needs were filled in English units. While President Kimball and others encouraged parents to teach their children the mother tongue—usually with eventual missionary work in mind—many children preferred English-speaking wards and branches. Thus many families experienced tension over their choice of congregations. Since most decisions concerning minorities were made at the local level, attitudes of individual bishops and stake presidents were a crucial factor. Some were impatient with the maintenance of separate programs for minorities. In their insistence that "English is the language spoken here," they perpetuated what one articulate Hispanic observer called "a strategy of assimilation that smacks of cultural imperialism."⁵⁵

Beginning in 1975, the influx of refugees to the United States from Southeast Asia provided a test of church minority programs. While the refugees included a few Latter-day Saints, most had no prior acquaintance with the church. Proselytizing among them was often carried out in close conjunction with local church-sponsored efforts to help initiate the refugees into the nuances of everyday life in America. Such proselytizing was often highly successful. Many Latter-day Saints opened their homes and their hearts to refugees. Mormons were reminded of the Book of Mormon prophecy that "there shall none come into this land save they shall be brought by the hand of the Lord."⁵⁶ Latter-day Saints were often provincial and had frequently heretofore bolstered their ethnocentrism with the thought that their own ancestors had been led by the Lord to America. Now they found in their own scriptures about the divine mission of America the basis for wholehearted acceptance of immigrants with vastly different origins. Church guidelines for proselytizing among and assimilating minorities stressed meeting the converts on their own terms. Home teachers were even encouraged to learn the language and the culture of minority families to whom they were assigned.⁵⁷

Spencer Kimball's general conference address of 1 April 1979 was a call for major new progress in the church, focusing on the role to be played by individuals. "We have paused on some plateaus long enough. Let us resume our journey forward and upward. Let us quietly put an end to our reluctance to reach out to others—whether in our own families, wards, or neighborhood. We have been diverted, at times, from fundamentals on which we must now focus in order to move forward as a person or as a people."⁵⁸ A substantial measure of how well Latter-day Saints would fulfill these expectations would be their success in accommodating minorities within their midst.

Prejudice among the Latter-day Saint people has long been a major obstacle to successful proselytizing and assimilation of minorities. Brigham Young called upon Utah settlers in 1854 to overcome their aversion to associating with neighboring Indian peoples, that they might teach and aid them. Attitudes that contributed to wartime difficulties for European and Asian minorities in the

Intermountain West did not die with each armistice. Hispanic Latter-day Saints in recent times were still confronted with the stereotype of being lazy and dirty. Many Mormons joined the flight of white Anglo-Saxon Protestants from residential areas whose minority population was increasing. However, President Kimball's revelation on priesthood for blacks and his emphasis on proselytizing and fellowshipping minorities marked a turning point not only in church policy but also in the behavior of church members. With their prejudices undermined, their proselytizing urge awakened, Latter-day Saints had much to learn about being good neighbors, but seemed anxious to proceed. The initial response seemed encouraging, in that the hand of welcome was extended to minorities more warmly and far more frequently than before.[59]

The question remained what shape the overall process of assimilation would take. What contributions by the ethnic minorities would the English-speaking Latter-day Saints value? Church leaders expressed the hope that a Latter-day Saint culture would emerge from the interaction of its component peoples worldwide, benefiting from what was good in each. But minority languages, often a catalyst for the preservation of ethnic culture, seemed destined to play a relatively transitory role.[60] To what extent would important elements of culture survive the demise of minority languages and still retain sufficient vitality to affect the majority culture? On the other hand, perhaps minorities speaking fluent English would have more cultural influence on the majority than speakers in the mother tongue, whether in America or in other homelands.

In 1983 church leaders expected Southeast Asian refugees, generally eager to find a place in American society, to be assimilated relatively quickly. This expectation seemed justified by the efforts of many immigrants, despite frequent nativist harassment in Utah, particularly at times of high unemployment.

With the exception of northern Europeans and Hawaiians, the experience of the Latter-day Saints with successful assimilation of minorities into English-speaking congregations remains limited. The feasibility of the ideal of complete unity in language and culture remains as yet largely unknown. Assimilation into the Latter-day Saint community as a whole has been most effectively achieved when minorities have been provided access to church programs in their native tongue. When use of minority languages has been overruled in order to promote integration, many have dropped out of church activity and thus lacked the benefit of the church's assistance. On the other hand, whether through church-sponsored newspapers and supplementary organizations in an earlier period or through Relief Society and priesthood quorums in the 1980s, practical information in the native tongue has helped minorities fit more comfortably into American society.

For at least some minorities, language may well be only the most visible tip of an iceberg, only one element of a surprisingly solid ethnicity that plays a greater role in many lives than one might expect. Occasionally, when the church has built upon ethnic attachments, even provided opportunities for the development of self-esteem through ethnic enthusiasm, remarkable vitality has manifest itself among people who were otherwise relatively unproductive.

Latter-day Saint Americans who were members of minority groups have frequently benefited from church concerns that often focused elsewhere. Interest in proselytizing abroad led to emphasis on maintaining use of the mother tongue by immigrants. Belief that the church had special responsibilities toward descendants of Book of Mormon peoples led to benefits for other minorities as well. Translations primarily for the benefit of church members in their motherlands were also made available to immigrants. Most recently, church coordination of concerns for minorities on a worldwide basis may benefit from a broader perspective. For example, lessons may be gained from interaction with minorities in Canada, where preservation of ethnic language and culture is legally mandated.[61]

In the past eight years, with intensified attention to proselytizing and accommodating minorities, the Latter-day Saints have invested more effort in communicating in native languages within the United States than before. This has reemphasized the diversity characteristic of the church from its beginnings. It has also combined with the expansion of the church outside the United States to raise important questions about how best to reach the goal of becoming a people in which all are "no more strangers and foreigners, but fellowcitizens with the saints."[62] Creating a climate of acceptance, in which helping fill individual needs is paramount, may be not just a first pragmatic step toward reaching that goal, but the main step.

With the institutional support for minority programs in place, Spencer Kimball's perception in 1979 was that the most significant burden lay with individual church members. But his own encouragement had provided much motivation. By 1986, with his voice no longer heard, the vitality of the kind of outreach and accommodation he had inspired would be dependent both upon individual attitudes and efforts and upon church leadership at all levels.

NOTES

1. Mantua Ward Relief Society Minutes, 1874–1881, Historical Department Archives of the Church of Jesus Christ of Latter-day Saints, hereafter cited as LDS Church Archives.

2. Mantua Ward Acting Teachers Record Book C, 1886–95, entry in Danish for 6 January 1895 with notation "Recorded," and entry for 16 September 1894, LDS Church Archives.

3. By 1986 Fatu and Puapuaga and nearly half of their immediate family had returned to American Samoa, where Fatu served in the key position of Matai, or chief, for a large extended family.

4. William Mulder, *Homeward to Zion: The Mormon Migration from Scandinavia* (Minneapolis: University of Minnesota Press, 1957), 346, n. 3.

5. Doctrine and Covenants 90:11.

6. Mulder, *Homeward to Zion*, 7–17. New York City *The Mormon*, 5 September 1857. Richard L. Jensen, "Clothing the Indians and Strengthening the Saints: Organized Activity of Mormon Women During the 'Lapse' of the Relief Society, 1844–1867," *Task Papers in LDS History*, No. 27 (1979): 4–11. Salt Lake City *Bikuben*, 11 October 1877, 20 February 1879, 19 June 1879, and 2 December 1880. George Reynolds to Joseph Morrell, 25 November 1902, in James B. Clark, ed., *Messages of the First Presidency of the Church of Jesus Christ of Latter-day Saints*, 6 vols. (Salt Lake City: Bookcraft, 1965–75), 4:48. *Bikuben* published extensive correspondence from Scandinavian missionaries regarding their proselytizing in the Chicago area, 30 April 1896–19 January 1899.

7. Sermon by George A. Smith, 9 October 1867, *Journal of Discourses*, 26 vols. (London: Latter-day Saints' Book Depot, 1854–1886; reprint ed., 1967), 12:138.

8. Harold B. Lee address, 26 August 1973, *Conference Reports*, Munich Area General Conference, 110–11. See also Lee address of 25 August, p. 6.

9. C. C. A. Christensen Diary, 21 July 1856, Danish holograph and English translation by Orson B. West, LDS Church Archives.

10. Historian's Office Journal, entries for 11, 18, and 25 November, 2, 16, and 23 December 1849, and 3 February 1850, LDS Church Archives. Initial meetings were at the house of Thomas Bullock, an English-born church clerk. Andrew Jenson's historical sketch of Scandinavian meetings, Salt Lake City *Deseret News*, 28 November 1935. Alexander Neibaur Journal, 41, cited in Journal History of the Church, Ms., entry for 15 August 1852, LDS Church Archives. "Record of the Holland Dutch Meetings," Weber Stake, 1911–1935, 2 vols., LDS Church Archives. Information about early meetings is found in introductory comments, vol. 1, *Bikuben*, 11 Oct. 1906.

11. Historical sketch in *Der Salt Lake City Beobachter*, 12 February 1899.

12. Minutes of Scandinavian Meetings in Salt Lake City, 1898–1907, recorded in Danish and Swedish, LDS Church Archives. Mulder, *Homeward to Zion*, 251–55. Andrew Jenson historical sketch, *Deseret News*, 28 November 1935.

13. Arnold H. Schulthess Autobiography, LDS Church Archives.

14. William Mulder, "Utah's Nordic-Language Press: Aspect and Instrument of Immigrant Culture," (M.A. thesis, University of Utah, 1947).

15. Salt Lake City *Deseret Evening News*, 15 February 1894.

16. Hans Jacob Christiansen diary, 10 October 1905–8 November 1906, LDS Church Archives. In Danish. *Bikuben*, 10 October 1907.

17. Cache Stake German Organization Minutes, 1901–1963, entry for 2 March 1902, LDS Church Archives. In German. The sacrament was administered in the Logan German meetings monthly, on fast days, until at least as late as 1925. Further study is needed to determine how widespread this practice may have become in non-English meetings in the early twentieth century.

18. Logan, Utah, *Republican*, 21 June 1917; *Deseret Evening News*, 20 July 1918.

19. Committee on L. D. S. Newspapers and Meetings in Foreign Languages, Circular Letter, 5 November 1924, Presiding Bishopric Circular Letters, LDS Church Archives.

20. John A. Widtsoe to O. H. Budge, 28 January 1924, and John A. Widtsoe, Rulon S. Wells, and Serge F. Ballif to First Presidency, 28 June 1924, copies in Church Records Resource File, LDS Church Archives. Presiding Bishopric Circular Letter, 30 October 1924, in Presiding Bishopric Circular Letters, LDS Church Archives. Committee on L. D. S. Newspapers and Meetings in Foreign Languages, Circular Letter, 5 November 1924, Presiding Bishopric Circular Letters, LDS Church Archives.

21. "Foreign Language Meetings Banned," *Improvement Era* 45 (1942): 220.

22. Cache Stake German Organization Minutes, entries for 1(?) and 2 June, 6 July, and 2 November 1952, LDS Church Archives.

23. Mexican Mission Manuscript History and Historical Reports, entries for 23 June and 28 July 1915 and 6 April and 19 May 1918, LDS Church Archives.

24. Joseph F. Smith, Anthon H. Lund, and Charles W. Penrose to Rey L. Pratt, 13 and 17 April 1918, typescript, LDS Church Archives.

25. Mexican Mission Manuscript History and Historical Reports, entries for January 1889, 19 May and 31 May 1918, and 23 April 1921, LDS Church Archives.

26. Golden R. Buchanan Oral History, interviews by William G. Hartley, 1974–75, 5 vols., typescript, 2:70–111; 5:2–4. "Brief History of Indian Committee and Related Programs," 5, typescript at office of Coordinator of Indian and Minority Affairs, copy in possession of author. "Indian Committee Organized," *Improvement Era* 51 (September 1948): 580.

27. J. Bryan Barton, "The Hawaiian Mission Headquarters," *Improvement Era* 16 (April 1913): 568.

28. Hawaiian Mission Manuscript History, 20 April 1904, 25 March 1906, and 6 October 1907, typescript, LDS Church Archives.

29. *Liahona The Elders Journal* 17 (October 1919): 151.

30. Salt Lake City *Deseret News*, 23 May 1925.

31. Journal History of the Church, 19 March 1932, LDS Church Archives.

32. Edward L. Clissold Oral History, interviews by R. Lanier Britsch, 1976, typescript, 6–16, James Moyle Oral History Program, LDS Church Archives.

33. Ibid., 16.

34. *Hawaiian Language Study Course* (n.p.: Hawaii Mission, 1955). "Excerpts from The Book of Mormon in Hawaiian and Modern American English," in Joseph H. Spurrier, *The Church of Jesus Christ of Latter-day Saints in the Hawaiian Islands* (Honolulu: Hawaii Honolulu Mission, 1978).

35. Spurrier, *The Church . . . in the Hawaiian Islands*, 26–27.

36. Golden R. Buchanan Oral History, 5:64–147, esp. 126, 139, LDS Church Archives. Arturo Martinez Oral History, interviews by Gordon Irving, 1975, typescript, 28–30, 80, Oral History Program, LDS Church Archives. Fred Nelson interviewed by Mark Grover, 22 October 1981, cassette copy of recording in possession of the author.

37. Spencer W. Kimball Diary Extract, typescript and holograph, 5–18 March 1958, entry for 5 March 1958, LDS Church Archives. Capitalization in the original source.

38. Ibid., 16 March 1958.

39. Emeterio Porras, Aurelio L. Acosta, and Leandro Alba to "the General Authorities of the Church of Jesus Christ of Latter-day Saints," 6 June (a note indicates actual date must have been 6 July) 1963, typescript of translation, Spanish-American Mission Presidents Correspondence, LDS Church Archives.

40. Melvin R. Brooks to Marion G. Romney, 23 July 1963, Spanish-American Mission Presidents Correspondence, LDS Church Archives.

41. Brooks to Romney, 23 July 1963, Spanish-American Mission Presidents Correspondence. This is a separate letter from that of the same date cited above. Romney to Brooks, 29 July 1963, Spanish-American Mission Presidents Correspondence, LDS Church Archives.

42. Samuel V. Miera Oral History, interviews by Gordon Irving, 1975–76, typescript, 3–4, 63–66, 236, Oral History Program, LDS Church Archives. Arturo Martinez Oral History, interviews by Gordon Irving, 1975, typescript, 14, Oral History Program, LDS Church Archives.

43. Arturo Martinez Oral History, 261–63. Golden R. Buchanan Oral History, 5:9–11, 56. Fred Nelson interview. Edward L. Kimball and Andrew E. Kimball Jr., *Spencer W. Kimball* (Salt Lake City: Bookcraft, 1977), 388–89.

44. Golden R. Buchanan Oral History, 5:9, 57. Buchanan gave a figure of 76 active, p. 9, but only 32 on p. 57. This apparent contradiction has not been explained.

45. Orlando A. Rivera, "Mormonism and the Chicano," in F. LaMond Tullis, ed., *Mormonism: A Faith for All Cultures* (Provo, Utah: Brigham Young University Press, 1978), 120–25.

46. Arturo Martinez Oral History, 295–96, 301. Stewart Durrant Oral History, 20. Rivera, "Mormonism and the Chicano," 123.

47. Golden R. Buchanan Oral History, 5:13–14, 24–63, 177–91. Stewart Durrant Oral History, interviewed by Richard L. Jensen, 8 June 1983, typescript, 4–7, 9, James Moyle Oral History Program, LDS Church Archives.

48. Stewart Durrant Oral History, 4–7. Stewart Durrant, "Brief History of Basic Unit Program," typescript, copy in possession of the author. *Branch Guidebook* (Salt Lake City: Church of Jesus Christ of Latter-day Saints, 1977). *Branch Guidebook*, rev. ed. (Salt Lake City: Church of Jesus Christ of Latter-day Saints, 1980). *Priesthood Leader's Guidebook* (Salt Lake City: Church of Jesus Christ of Latter-day Saints, 1980). *Family Guidebook* (Salt Lake City: Church of Jesus Christ of Latter-day Saints, 1980). The three guidebooks listed above have been published in many languages and constitute the basic administrative instructions for small church units.

49. *Translation Equipment for Accommodating Language Minority Groups* (Salt Lake City: Church of Jesus Christ of Latter-day Saints, 1972).

50. Excerpt from report dated April 1982, from office of Coordinator for Lamanite and Other Cultures, copy of typescript in possession of author. It is impossible to determine from the report which Indian units used native languages; many used English while retaining their ethnic identity.

51. They include Spanish wards in El Paso, Texas, and Salt Lake City; a Samoan ward in the Torrance, California, Stake; a Tongan ward in Salt Lake City; a German ward in Salt Lake City; and the following Indian wards: Los Lunas Ward, Albuquerque Stake, New Mexico; Intermountain

School Indian Student Ward, Brigham City, Utah, Box Elder Stake; Rock Hill Ward, Charlotte, North Carolina, Stake; Ramah Ward, Gallup, New Mexico, Stake; Window Rock Ward, Gallup, New Mexico, Stake; Papago Ward, Mesa, Arizona, Lehi Stake; Tuba City Ward, Page, Arizona, Stake; Fifth Ward, Salt Lake Wells Stake; Taos Ward, Santa Fe, New Mexico, Stake; White Rock Ward, Santa Fe, New Mexico, Stake.

52. Harvey H. Cluff Journal, 9 April and 12 November 1893 and 2 April 1895, LDS Church Archives.

53. "History of the Translation of the Temple Ceremony," typescript, Translation Services Office files, Salt Lake Temple, Salt Lake City, Utah.

54. Information received from Alex Schmalz of Translation Services Office, Salt Lake Temple, and Steven Clawson, Temple Audiovisual Division, July 1983.

55. Rivera, "Mormonism and the Chicano," 124. Fred Nelson interview.

56. 2 Nephi 1:6. Stewart Durrant interview, 11–14.

57. *Guidelines for Proselyting Among Minorities* (Salt Lake City: Church of Jesus Christ of Latter-day Saints, n.d.), first published ca. 1978. *Accommodating Minority Cultures* (Salt Lake City: Church of Jesus Christ of Latter-day Saints, n.d.), first published ca. 1975.

58. Spencer W. Kimball, "Let Us Move Forward and Upward," *Ensign* 9 (May 1979): 82.

59. Richard L. Jensen, "Forgotten Relief Societies," *Dialogue: A Journal of Mormon Thought* 16 (Spring 1983): 108–11; Arturo Martinez Oral History, 12–13; Stewart Durrant Oral History, 10–13, LDS Church Archives.

60. Stewart Durrant Oral History, 15–17, LDS Church Archives.

61. I am indebted to Richard E. Bennett, an archivist from Winnipeg, Manitoba, for information about Canada's treatment of minorities.

62. Ephesians 2:19.

PART THREE

Mormon-Gentile Relations

The exodus in mid-nineteenth century from populated America to its Great Basin wilderness did not serve the Mormon intent of isolating the Saints from the Gentile world. However fortresslike their mountain valleys, they found themselves in Utah and the surrounding territories still neighbors with Gentiles in a Gentile nation. Coexistence must be worked out, year by year, threat by threat, opportunity by opportunity.

The late Eugene E. Campbell, professor of history at Brigham Young University, delineates some of the shifting ambivalent attitudes of the first-generation Great Basin settlers towards the federal government in his "Pioneers and Patriotism: Conflicting Loyalties." The present Mormon stance of fostered patriotism is easily understood in the light of Campbell's analysis.

To Campbell's study of the pioneer period of Utah-Mormon history, Richard Poll adds his analysis of the long sweep of the Mormon-Gentile coexistence in Utah. A former colleague of Campbell at Brigham Young University and for many years a vice president at Western Illinois University, Poll, now retired, looks at the diverse segments of Utah society as mutually beneficial in his analysis "Utah and the Mormons: A Symbiotic Relationship." He sees in the attitudes and actions of the Mormons three general stances: defensiveness, lasting until the end of official promotion of plural marriage; accommodation, a process continuing through the first half of the twentieth century; and finally, and still continuing, an international outreach in both internal church matters and concerns of universal brotherhood.

In "Beyond the Stereotypes: Mormon and Non-Mormon Communities in Twentieth-Century Mormondom," Jan Shipps, professor of history and religious studies and director of the Center for American Studies at Indiana University-Purdue University at Indianapolis, shows how diverse both groups actually are, and how understanding that diversity can aid in our understanding of events in which people of various stances in both groups have participated.

Pioneers and Patriotism: Conflicting Loyalties

EUGENE E. CAMPBELL

Patriotism has become a characteristic of dedicated Mormons, especially those living in the United States. Believing the Constitution of the United States to be divinely inspired and this land to be "choice above all other lands," some Mormon leaders stress loyalty to and love of this country to such a degree that it seems to be a basic tenet of their faith. Such an attitude seems to be widespread among the rank and file of Mormons during much of the twentieth century. But nineteenth-century Mormons, especially those who pioneered Utah, had conflicting loyalties and were considered to be less than patriotic by their fellow citizens. When Brigham Young asserted that willingness to leave the United States was a test of orthodoxy, and Orson Pratt published in his Mormon newspaper a call for all church members "to get out of this evil nation by next spring" and proclaimed that it was with "greatest joy that I forsake this republic,"[1] it is not surprising that Mormons were considered by many to be not only unpatriotic but actual enemies of the United States.

Yet these same leaders and others often expressed feelings of love for their country and demonstrated devotion to it in many ways. Such expressions of loyalty are certainly more numerous in the records than the disloyal ones. For example, resolutions in a letter addressed to President Polk, 9 August 1846, signed by President Young, indicated such attitudes. He wrote:

> Resolved, that should we locate within the territory of the United States, as we anticipate, we would esteem a territorial government of our own, as one of the richest boons of the earth, and while we appreciate the

constitution of the United States as the most precious among the nations, we feel that we had rather retreat to the deserts, islands, or mountain caves than consent to be ruled by governors and judges whose hands are drenched in the blood of innocence and virtue, who delight in injustice and oppression. . . . Resolved, That as soon as we are settled in the Great Basin, we design to petition the United States for a territorial government, bounded on the north by the British and the south by the Mexican dominions, and the east and west by the summits of the Rockies and the Cascade mountains.[2]

On 20 January 1846 the High Council issued the following circular:

We also further declare for the satisfaction of some who have concluded that our grievances have alienated us from our country, that our patriotism has not been overcome by fire, by sword, by daylight, or by midnight assassinations which we have endured, neither have they alienated us from the institutions of our country. Should hostilities arise between the government of the United States and any other power, in relation to the possession of the territory of Oregon, we are on hand to sustain the claims of the United States government to that country. It is geographically ours; and of right no foreign power should hold dominion there; and if our services are required to prevent it, these services will be cheerfully rendered according to our ability.[3]

In a spirited address by General Daniel H. Wells on 24 July 1852, the loyalty of the Saints by that date was reiterated in the following words:

Because demagogues have arisen and seized the reins of power, should we relinquish our interests in that country, made dear to us by every tie of association and consanguinity? Those who have indulged such sentiments concerning us have not read Mormonism aright; for never, no never, will we desert our country's cause; never will we be found arrayed on the side of her enemies, although she herself may cherish them in her own bosom. Although she may launch forth the thunderbolts of war, which may return and spend their fury upon her own head, never, no never will we permit the weakness of human nature to triumph over our love of country, our devotions to her institutions handed down to us by our honored sires, made dear by a thousand tender recollections.[4]

Such assertions of loyalty could be multiplied. However, despite such feelings for the United States, the Mormon leaders were often guilty of unpatriotic expressions and actions, and were at odds with federal officials during the last half of the nineteenth century. The reason for this apparent paradox was their loyalty to the Kingdom of God. In truth, they felt a dual loyalty, but when their loyalty to the United States came in conflict with their commitment to the Kingdom of God, they invariably chose the Kingdom. Such attitudes resulted in over fifty years of bitter conflict with federal officials, ultimately led to the loss of citizenship by many church members, and even threatened the existence of their organization.

Actually, there were many reasons for the Mormons to be loyal to the United States. A most important factor was their belief that:

> The American continent was to be the stage for the restoration of the Gospel of Jesus Christ and of the ancient liberties of mankind in the latter days. Hence God had purposely hidden the knowledge of its existence from the rest of the world until the time had ripened for the fulfillment of His purposes. When that time came, God's spirit sent Columbus to the promised land to open it to a new race of free men: "This land shall be a land of liberty unto the Gentiles, and there shall be no kings upon the land. . . . For it is wisdom in the Father that they should be established in this land and be set up as a free people by the power of the Father." Thus, the American revolution was part of a plan decreed by God to achieve the freedom of the New World, a freedom to be preserved through a constitution drafted by divinely inspired men specifically "raised up for this very purpose."[5]

Mormonism was to be the culmination of this grand design. "The United States of America," wrote Parley P. Pratt, "was the favorite nation raised up with institutions adapted to the protection and free development of the necessary truths. . . . No other country in the world provided the necessary conditions for the establishment of the Kingdom of God."[6] In fact, both Joseph Smith and Brigham Young asserted that the government of the United States differed very little from that of the Kingdom of God as they perceived it, even suggesting that "the Constitution and laws of the United States resemble a theocracy more closely than any government now on earth."[7]

A second factor encouraging patriotism was the fact that most of the early Mormon leaders were New Englanders with a long tradition of loyalty to their country. Perhaps Daniel H. Wells described this feeling most dramatically when he said, "Our devotion to her institutions was handed down to us by our honored sires, and made dear by a thousand tender recollections,"[8] but similar expressions were common in the writings and sermons of Joseph Smith, Brigham Young, Wilford Woodruff, Heber C. Kimball, and many others. In a letter to President Millard Fillmore, Young wrote: "Now sir, I will simply state that I know it to be true—that no people exist who are more friendly to the government of the United States than the people of this territory. The constitution they revere and the laws they seek to honor."[9]

In addition to their religious reasons and their patriotic upbringing, the Mormon leaders had a very strong motivation for patriotism—that of self-interest. Once the Treaty of Guadalupe-Hidalgo was ratified and the Great Basin region was ceded to the United States, it was imperative that the Mormons express their loyalty to the government of the United States if they hoped to be accepted into the Union as a state or at least be given territorial status.

They decided to apply for a "territorial government of our own" implying that the officers should be chosen from the Mormon leadership. An official petition was drawn up, and Dr. John M. Bernhisel was chosen to secure names on the petition and to carry it to Washington, D.C., for federal approval. When he left Utah on 3 May 1849, the document bore 2,270 signatures, including those of Brigham Young and many other Mormon leaders.

Two months later, the Council of Fifty, evidently fearing that a territorial form of government would probably result in the appointment of non-Mormon officials to govern the territory, decided to apply for admission as a state. Lacking time to go through the procedures of a constitutional convention and a bona fide democratic election, the council members wrote a constitution, formulated some minutes of a convention and a legislative session, and chose Almon W. Babbitt to carry the petition for statehood to Washington, D.C. He secured the cooperation of Bernhisel and the aid of Thomas L. Kane, who spoke out strongly against a territorial form of government.[10]

The petition became embroiled in the controversy that resulted in the Compromise of 1850, which created the Territory of Utah on 9 September 1850. Bernhisel's lobbying efforts were successful in securing the appointment of four Mormons as territorial officials, including Brigham Young as governor. While it was not quite a "territorial government of our own," it was a very favorable action on the part of both Congress and the president of the United States, and the Mormon leaders had good reason to feel loyal toward the federal government.

Brigham Young now experienced conflicting loyalties in a very real sense. As president of the church, he was the Lord's appointed director of the Mormon version of the Kingdom of God on earth, and as governor, he was the president's appointed representative of the federal government in Utah. But there was never any doubt as to his choice of loyalties in time of conflict—it was always the Kingdom of God. Within a few months such a choice became apparent when the first non-Mormon territorial officials arrived in Utah.

Before examining the events and conflicts that led to confrontations between the federal officials and the Mormon leaders, let us consider the factors that encouraged Mormon attitudes and expressions of disloyalty.

It should be remembered that the federal union under the constitution had been functioning less than fifteen years when Brigham Young was born, and antifederal union expressions were commonplace. Vice President Aaron Burr's attempt to create an independent empire in the Southwest occurred in 1804–05—about the time of Joseph Smith's birth. Radicals in the Hartford Convention in 1814 called for a secession of New England from the rest of the nation because of southern states' dominance of the federal government. Calhoun's famous Jackson Day toast in 1830 placed liberty ahead of the union when he said, "The Union, next to our liberty, the most dear," and South Carolina's nullification vote threatened the breakup of the Union in 1833. The Compromise of 1850, an attempt to stem the tide of anti-Union sentiment in the South, succeeded in nullifying the effectiveness of the prosecessionist Nashville Convention, but only created a temporary lull in such expressions. Brigham Young and other Mormon leaders thus grew up during a time when many citizens were counting the cost and questioning the value of the Union. Moreover, many of the early Mormon converts came from Great Britain and felt no deep-seated loyalty to the United States.

A second factor was the Mormon leaders' belief in the imminence of the second coming of Christ to usher in the millennium. Despite the fact that the Saints had been forced to leave Jackson

County, Missouri, before they could build a temple in which they would receive Christ, the millennial hope still remained strong in Mormonism. While the Saints were expending their energies to build communities in the Utah area, the leaders kept reminding them that their real purpose was to establish the Kingdom of God, and to live in such a way that they could "usher in" the millennium. In 1852, despite the obvious need for men to build the communities, church leaders sent missionaries to the "far corners" of the earth to warn them of the impending Parousia. These far corners included India, China, Ceylon, Palestine, as well as European nations and the Pacific islands. Brigham Young called on the people to "cease all evil and to prepare for the coming of the Son of Man."[11] He promised the members that if they would "stop their evil practices, thereby binding Satan, and if they would unite their hearts in the Church and Kingdom of God, rejecting diversification, they could be living in the Millennium."[12]

The following year, 1853, on the occasion of the dedication of the cornerstone of the Salt Lake Temple, a wave of millennial anticipation swept the Salt Lake colony. Asserting that a temple was necessary for Christ's advent, "for without it the Son of Man hath not where to lay his head," Brigham Young called on the people to rally behind the leaders and complete the building as soon as possible. Orson Pratt warned the people in 1855 that Christ's second coming "is nearer than this people are aware of,"[13] and the following year the "reformation" preaching was filled with millennial warnings.

The approach of a U.S. Army in 1857 set off a new wave of millennial prophecies. Charles C. Rich wrote in his diary in October 1857 that "I have been looking for the time of deliverance, but did not expect it so soon,"[14] while Brigham Young suggested that such activity by the United States was "hastening the work of the Lord." Wilford Woodruff believed that this action heralded the beginning of the decline and fall of the United States and that the Kingdom of God would rise to power. Heber C. Kimball prophesied that the Mormons, with God's help, would subdue any evil military force and would dictate terms of peace to the fallen political state. "The President of the United States will bow to us and come and consult with the authorities of this Church to know what is best to do for his people."[15]

Such optimistic predictions left the church leaders in an awkward position when a settlement was negotiated and the U.S. Army marched through the deserted streets of Salt Lake City and camped in Cedar Valley. "Many of the people are so grossly wicked, that were we to go out and fight," Young explained, "thousands of Elders would go into eternity and women and children would perish." He concluded that the Saints were "not yet righteous enough to receive and build up Zion in its purity."[16]

Millennial fervor died down for a time, but rose again with the outbreak of the Civil War. Mormon leaders saw the war as a punishment for the nation that had rejected the restored gospel, killed their prophet, and driven them from their homes. It was also seen as a fulfillment of Joseph Smith's prophecy made on 23 December 1833 and the beginning of the time when "war will be poured out on all nations" prior to Christ's second coming. Jackson County was being emptied of inhabitants, thus clearing the way for the return of the Saints and the building of the temple in preparation for Christ's return. Brigham Young talked frequently of the return to Jackson County, and on one occasion told a group of Saints that he expected to return to Jackson County in seven years.[17]

How could Mormons be loyal to their country when they believed it would soon collapse and be replaced by the Kingdom of God with Brigham Young in command? To the extent that expectations were for an imminent millennium, loyalty to the nation was at best tentative.

Another development that led to disloyal attitudes and expressions was the practice of plural marriage, especially after the 1852 public announcement and defense of the practice. John M. Bernhisel, Utah's representative in Congress, considered the public announcement a grievous error, for it revived the hostile feeling caused by the reports of the "runaway" officials circulated during the previous session of Congress. He asserted that "not one in a thousand will be convinced that the 'Doctrine' is at all consistent with chastity, or even morality, much less that it is a pure and righteous one."[18]

Bernhisel's apprehension was all too accurate. The LDS Church soon became the target of vilification and ridicule. Polygamy became the subject of a national debate when the passage of the Kansas-Nebraska Act in 1854 included the principle of popular sovereignty, which allowed a territory to choose whether it would tolerate slavery. Politicians were quick to see that the same principle could be applied to the practice of polygamy in a territory and used the Mormon control of politics in Utah as an argument against popular sovereignty. The Republican party, organized as a result of the Kansas-Nebraska Act, promised in its first presidential campaign slogan "to rid the nation of the twin relics of barbarism, Slavery and Polygamy." Democrats responded by condemning plural marriage even more vigorously than did the Republicans. Mormon leaders continued to defend the practice, adding to the growing public conception of the Mormons as disloyal, immoral, renegades, unworthy of citizenship.

One of the principal factors that alienated federal officials and convinced them that the Mormons were disloyal was the intemperate rhetoric used by Mormon leaders. Brigham Young, Heber C. Kimball, Jedediah Grant, and George A. Smith, all popular speakers in Mormon meetings, used excessive and sometimes violent language as they attacked their opponents and defended their doctrines and practices. Since preaching was a principal form of communication and entertainment in pioneer times, and since most of the leaders spoke extemporaneously, it should not be surprising that statements were made that offended non-Mormon officials.

This problem became apparent when the first non-Mormon territorial officials arrived in Utah and attended their first Mormon meeting. The occasion was the Twenty-fourth of July celebration, commemorating the fourth anniversary of the pioneers settling in Salt Lake Valley, and the speaker was Daniel H. Wells. General Wells, in reviewing Mormon history, asserted that the United States, which had required the Mormons to furnish a battalion of five hundred men to fight in the war against Mexico, "could have no other object in view than to finish by utter extermination, the work which had so ruthlessly begun."[19]

Brigham Young also addressed the assembly "in his usual interesting strain of intelligent eloquence" according to the chronicler of the occasion. The exact words of Governor Young are not extant, but the tenor of the speech was uncomplimentary about the late President Zachary Taylor and turned on the idea that those who worked against the Saints would die an untimely death and end up in hell. President Taylor was not a popular president even in Washington, but no one registered such pithy disapprobation of him as Young did when he said: "Zachary Taylor is dead, and in hell, and I am glad of it."[20]

Other speeches and religious services during the remainder of the summer included critical comments of governmental officials, while at the same time professing love for the Constitution and the government. These speeches often mentioned the second coming of the Savior and the political aspects of the Kingdom of God, which would replace the "corrupt" governments throughout the world. There is little wonder that the non-Mormon officials were upset.

They were not the only ones offended by Mormon rhetoric. The *Baltimore Sun* published excerpts from a sermon in which Governor Young was quoted as saying that he would remain in office "until the Lord Almighty says Brigham, you need not be governor any longer."[21] Bernhisel attached a clipping of this item to a letter and sent it to Young, gently scolding him for such remarks and urging him to tell the reporters and printers not to publish such statements as they were intended for the ears of the Saints only. "I have to meet all of these things here, face to face, and explain, palliate, contradict, deny as the case may be," Bernhisel complained, "and though the battle may be fought ever so successfully and victory perch on our banner, yet they leave a deep, black stain behind."[22]

In explanation of the statement, Governor Young gave something of his philosophy of life, which was essentially that God rules in the affairs of men. "Let small men or large men, officers of state, emperors, kings, or beggars say or do what they please, it is all the same to the Almighty. The king upon his throne, the president in his chair, the judges upon the bench and the beggar in the street are all overruled in their actions by the Almighty God of heaven and earth. Who can successfully fight against him?"[23] Later, commenting on his own remarks, he said,

> The newspapers are teeming with a statement that I said "President Pierce and all hell could not remove me from office." I will tell you what I did say and what I now say; the Lord reigns and rules in the armies of the heavens, and he does his pleasure among the inhabitants of the earth. He sets up a kingdom here, and pulls down another there at his pleasure. He walks in the midst of the people, and they know it not. He makes kings, presidents, and governors at his pleasure; hence,

I conclude that I shall be governor of Utah territory, just as long as he wants me to be; and for that time, neither the president of the United States, nor any other power, can prevent it. Then, brethren and sisters, be not worried about my being dismissed from office; for when the president appoints another man to be governor of Utah territory, you may acknowledge that the Lord has done it, for we should acknowledge his hand in all things. All people are in the hands of the Almighty, and he governs and controls them, though they cannot perceive, neither do they acknowledge, his handy work. He exalts the president to be head of the nation, and places kings upon their thrones. There is not a man that escapes his cognizance, and he brings forth his purposes in the latter days.[24]

This philosophy was expressed many times by Brigham Young.

Another case of inflated rhetoric that seemed less than enthusiastic about the national government is a letter sent to John M. Bernhisel when it became apparent that Brigham Young was not going to be reappointed as territorial governor:

Tell Mr. Franklin Pierce that the people of the Territory have a way, it may be a very peculiar way but an honest one, of sending their infernal, dirty, sneaking, rotten hearted pot house politicians out of the territory, and if he should come himself it would be the same. Talk about Democracy or Republicanism. How did our Fathers of 70 to 76 do when the Government of England . . . sent . . . Judges upon the country. . . . Were they right in doing as they did and shall we submit to their . . . cussed tyranny and not resist. No, by the means of our Defeated Fathers who bled for Liberty, No! . . . Tell Mr. Pierce this and that we ask no odds of him nor the Factious Blood stained rabble which seems to him such a high and mighty honor to preside over. When we have a president of the people and not of a party I shall feel that a representation has taken place in our country.[25]

Such intemperate statements had led earlier to an unfortunate verbal altercation with Associate Justice Brocchus in 1851 who felt sufficiently threatened that he decided to leave the territory, and was joined in this decision by Chief Justice Brandebury, Secretary Harris, and Indian Subagent Day. These "runaway officials" gave a very negative report about the loyalty of the Mormons, and such sentiments were subsequently echoed by others who were offended by Mormon rhetoric.

Some of these reports convinced President James Buchanan that the Mormons in Utah were in a state of rebellion against the federal government, and that the lives of federal officials as well as court records were in danger. He appointed a non-Mormon governor to replace Brigham Young and sent an army of 2,500 men to install the new officials and to control the rebellious Mormons. This led to the so-called Utah War, in which the Mormon leaders resisted and harassed the U.S. Army and defied the authority of the federal government.

They rationalized this defiance in two ways. First, in any conflict involving the interests of the Kingdom of God their religious loyalty always superseded their political loyalty. Second, they continually expressed their loyalty to the Constitution but questioned the administration of the government by the current officials. As Brigham Young expressed it, "I do not lift my voice against the great and glorious government guaranteed to every citizen by our Constitution, but against those corrupt administrators who trample the Constitution and just laws under their feet."[26]

His proclamation of martial law in September 1857 stated the Mormon position clearly:

> *Citizens of Utah*: — We are invaded by a hostile force who are evidently assailing us to accomplish our overthrow and destruction.
>
> For the last twenty-five years we have trusted . . . judges, governors, and presidents, only to be scorned, held in derision, insulted and betrayed. Our houses have been plundered and then burned, our fields laid waste, our principal men butchered while under the pledged faith of the government for their safety, and our families driven from their homes to find that shelter in the barren wilderness, and that protection among hostile savages which were denied them in the boasted abodes of christianity and civilization.
>
> The Constitution of our common country guarantees unto us all that we do now, or have ever claimed. . . . The government has not condescended to cause an investigating committee or other persons to be sent to inquire into and ascertain the truth, as is customary in such cases. . . .
>
> Our duty to ourselves, to our families, requires us not tamely submit to be driven and slain, without an attempt to preserve ourselves. Our duty to our country, our holy religion, our God, to freedom and liberty, requires that we should not quietly stand still and see those fetters forging around, which are calculated to enslave and bring us in subjection to an unlawful military despotism such as can only emanate (in a country of constitutional law) from usurpation, tyranny and oppression.[27]

Such rationalizations enabled the Mormon leaders to assert their patriotism while at the same time they were defying the fundamental authority of the federal government.

Church leaders saw the Civil War as a fulfillment of Joseph Smith's prophecy and the precursor of the millennium. The war was a divine retribution on the nation that had rejected Mormonism and killed their prophet, they claimed in their sermons, and they predicted the imminent downfall of the U.S. government. Church members were not encouraged to support the Union cause but to be thankful that they were far removed from the war. A few companies of the Nauvoo Legion answered President Lincoln's call for troops to guard the Overland Mail for a three-month period, but that was the extent of Mormon military participation in the war.

John Taylor, speaking at the Fourth of July celebration in 1861, set the tone of Mormon attitudes towards the conflict in the following words:

> It may now be proper to inquire what part shall we take in the present difficulties. We have been banished from the pale of what is termed civilization and forced to make a home in this desert place. . . . Shall we join the North to fight against the South? No! Shall we join the South against the North? As emphatically, No! Why? They have both, as before shown, brought it upon themselves, and we have had no hand in the matter. Whigs, Democrats, Americans, and Republicans have all in turn endeavored to stain their hands in innocent blood, and whatever others may do, we cannot conscientiously help to tear down the fabric we are sworn to uphold. We know no North, no South, no East, no West; we abide strictly and positively by the Constitution, and cannot, by the intrigues or sophisms of either party, be cajoled into any other attitude.[28]

Having decided that they would support neither group in the conflict the Mormon leaders continued to express their feelings that the war had been brought on by the wickedness of the people of the United States and more specifically by rejecting the gospel and permitting the death of the prophet of God and his colaborers to go unavenged. When they heard that Jackson County was a war zone, they concluded that Missouri was suffering the penalty for her former cruelties to the Mormons. Since Joseph Smith's prophecy had implied the imminence of the millennium and since Mormons expected to go back to Jackson County to help usher in that great event, it is understandable that they saw the destructions in Jackson County as a sign of the immediacy of the Second Coming.

An interesting summary of the teachings of the leaders of the church in regard to the Civil War and federal government in general was written by Governor Steven S. Harding, who arrived in Utah on 7 July 1862. After being in the territory about six weeks he wrote a letter to his superiors in Washington in which he summarized the preaching that he had listened to in the Tabernacle and other places where he heard the church leaders talk:

> The first and most important inquiry is, are these people . . . loyal to the government of the United States? I am compelled to answer in the negative and will state some of my reasons which determine my judgment.
>
> In the first place, Brigham Young and other preachers are constantly inculcating in the minds of the crowded audiences who sit beneath their teachings every Sabbath, that the government of the United States is of no consequence; that it lies in ruins; and the prophecy of Joseph Smith is being fulfilled to the letter—According to that prophecy, the United States as a nation, is to be destroyed—that the Gentiles—as they call all persons outside of their church will continue to fight with each other, until they perish and *then* the saints are to step in and quietly enjoy the possession of the land and also what is left of the ruined cities and desolated places and that "Zion is to be built up", not only in "The Valleys of the Mountains" but the Great Center of their power and glory, is to be in Missouri where the Saints under the lead of their prophet, were expelled many years ago.[29]

He also mentioned that the Mormons seem to delight in the fact that the Indians were to come into their share of the benefits after the cutting off of the Gentiles. Harding asserted that he had sat in the bowery Sabbath after Sabbath and listened to such declarations and heard hearty "Amens" in response to such statements as were made. He saw them wink and chuckle when some intelligence of disaster reached them concerning the great army of the Union now fighting for the rights of humanity and said "in all the meetings that I have attended not one word, not one prayer, has been uttered or offered up for the saving of our cause and for the restoration of peace, but on the contrary the God of the Saints has been implored to bring swift destruction on all nations, people and institutions that stand in way of the triumph of this people."[30]

As the war dragged on and casualties mounted, the Mormon leaders gradually changed their attitude, and began to express concern for their fellow citizens in the East. In 1863, Brigham Young said "The waste of life in the ruinous war now raging is truly lamentable,"[31] and a year later he had mellowed to a point where he expressed concern for the sufferings of the people in Jackson County. The Mormon leaders joined with the non-Mormon officials in celebrating Lincoln's reelection, and a few weeks later joined with them and a crowd of over three thousand citizens who met in the Old Tabernacle to mourn the death of the great Civil War president.

Unfortunately, this period of friendliness was only a brief interlude, and before many months had passed, the "Reconstruction" Congress was attempting to pass laws that would break the political power of the church and force the Mormons through a process of "Americanization." A quarter of a century later, the process was judged complete, and the Mormon-dominated Territory of Utah was finally accepted into the Union as the forty-fifth state.

Despite their unfortunate experiences in Missouri and Illinois, the Mormons had good reasons to be loyal to the United States. After all, it was state and local governments, not the federal government, that had persecuted them. True, the federal government had not intervened in their behalf, but such intervention should not have been expected, considering the traditional relationship of states and the federal government prior to the Civil War. The call of the Mormon Battalion had been motivated by a desire of President Polk to aid them in their trek west and to tie them to the country, and had been recognized as a favor by Brigham Young. Most of the church leaders were from New England and had been reared in an atmosphere of loyalty to their country with a special reverence for the Constitution. The Mormon leaders believed that the government of the United States was inspired by God to provide an atmosphere of freedom where his church could take root and grow. But, perhaps the most important factor that promoted loyalty on the part of the Mormons was self-interest. If they wanted to survive and grow in an area controlled by the United States they needed to express and demonstrate loyalty.

They did this in many ways, but they had a greater loyalty to their concept of the Kingdom of God and this loyalty was so overwhelming that for a few years their perception of reality was distorted to the point that they became disloyal in both thought and action. Their millennialism distorted their concept of time and negated some of their values. Their practice of polygamy made them easy targets for criticism and abuse. Their theocratic governmental patterns alienated the federal officials sent to work with the Mormons, causing these officials to send very negative reports concerning Mormon loyalty. These, in turn, led to the Utah War and the federal rejection of statehood for Utah on at least seven occasions during a forty-year period.

By the end of the early pioneer period in 1869, the Mormons in Utah were governed by increasingly hostile officials, and were threatened by a reforming Congress, determined to reconstruct the slaveholding South, and the polygamy-practicing Mormons.

Could it have been different? Certainly a little less rhetoric on the part of the Mormon leaders, and a more careful choice of territorial officials by those in charge of the federal government might have helped to avoid many misunderstandings and difficulties. But Mormon millennialism, theocracy, plural marriage, and devotion to the Kingdom of God made it difficult for them to survive and function in a society that questioned such beliefs and practices. During the next generation, however, after years of bitter experience and unfulfilled millennial hopes and with the advent of a more moderate leadership, the Mormons began to modify their concept of a political Kingdom of God and to accept the idea that the terms church and kingdom were synonymous. By the 1890s, they had developed an ecclesiastical organization that was no longer a political rival to the country. They still had divided loyalties, as do all people, but their loyalties were not in serious conflict. They could now follow Christ's admonition to "render unto Caesar the things that are Caesar's, and unto God the things that are God's." With that, the twentieth-century pathway to superpatriotism was opened.

NOTES

1. New York *Messenger*, 8 November 1845.

2. Leland H. Creer, *Utah and the Nation* (Seattle: University of Washington Press, 1929), 64.

3. Ibid., 64. Creer cites *Times and Seasons* 6 (20 January 1846): 1096.

4. Ibid., 65.

5. Klaus J. Hansen, *Quest for Empire* (Lincoln: University of Nebraska Press, 1970), 31.

6. Idem.

7. Ibid., 42.

8. Supra., 3.

9. Brigham Young to Millard Fillmore, Manuscript History of Brigham Young, 29 September 1851.

10. See Peter Crawley's *The Constitution of the State of Deseret* (Friends of the Brigham Young University Library Newsletter, Vol. 19, 1982), 16, for a detailed account of this deceptive action.

11. Brigham Young, *Journal of Discourses*, 1:201 (6 April 1852).

12. Ibid., 1:202-3.

13. Ibid., 2:29-30 (6 April 1853); 3:17 (20 May 1855).

14. Charles C. Rich, "Diary" (Typed copy of original in Brigham Young University Library), 7 October 1857.

15. Heber C. Kimball, *Journal of Discourses*, 5:93 (26 July 1857).

16. Young, *Journal of Discourses*, 7:42-45 (28 March 1858).

17. Journal History of the Church, 22 August 1862.

18. Gwynn Barrett, "John M. Bernhisel, Mormon Elder in Congress," (Ph.D. diss., Brigham Young University, 1968), 105.

19. Journal History, 24 July 1851.

20. J. Keith Melville, "The Infant Steps of Territorial Government in Utah, Or Getting Off On The Wrong Foot," unpublished manuscript in possession of author.

21. Barrett, "Bernhisel," 122.

22. Ibid., 123.

23. B. H. Roberts, *Comprehensive History of the Church* (Salt Lake City: The Deseret News Press, 1930), 4:186.

24. Ibid., 4:186-87.

25. Barrett, "Bernhisel," 124.

26. John A. Widtsoe, *Discourses of Brigham Young* (Salt Lake City: Deseret Book Company, 1961), 362.

27. Roberts, *Comprehensive History*, 4:273-74.

28. Salt Lake City *Deseret News*, 10 July 1861.

29. Gustive O. Larson, "Utah and the Civil War," *Utah Historical Quarterly* 33 (Winter 1965): 68. Emphasis in the original.

30. Ibid., 69.

31. Young, *Journal of Discourses*, 10:251 (October 1863).

Utah and the Mormons:
A Symbiotic Relationship*

RICHARD D. POLL

For all but the first seventeen of its one hundred fifty plus years the
Church of Jesus Christ of Latter-day Saints has been based in Utah.
The harried Mormon refugees from Kirtland, Far West, and Nauvoo
soon felt at home "in Deseret's sweet, peaceful land," and their heirs
by blood and adoption still sing:

> High on the mountain top
> A banner is unfurled. . . .
>
> For God remembers still
> His promise made of old
> That he on Zion's hill
> Truth's standard would unfold! . . .
>
> His house shall there be reared
> His glory to display. . . .
>
> For there we shall be taught
> The law that will go forth,
> With truth and wisdom fraught,
> To govern all the earth.[1]

For its entire history as a political entity, Utah has been Mormon
country. Not only have most of its inhabitants been members of "the
Church," but this is the single fact most likely to be known by non-
Utahns. People who have never heard of Alta, Bingham, or
Canyonlands know about the Tabernacle Choir and "This Is the Place."
Neophytes in LDS congregations hundreds of miles from the

---

* This paper is a revised version of the Second David E. Miller Lecture on
 Utah and the West, delivered at the University of Utah, 23 April 1980.

Wasatch Front still feel at a status disadvantage if they have no fore-bears who crossed the plains for the gospel's sake.

Symbiosis, however, is more than geographic coexistence or asso-ciation in the popular mind. It is, by one dictionary, "the intimate living together of two dissimilar organisms in a mutually beneficial relationship."[2] The fig wasp that inhabits and fertilizes the fig tree is a classic example. The tickbird on the rhino is another. Other defi-nitions encompass interaction in which the benefits are dispropor-tionate or one-sided—the cuckoo's egg in the robin's nest or the flea on the dog.

That the association between Utah and the Mormons is a symbi-otic relationship in the mutually interactive sense seems clear. Utah and the Mormons are what they are because their lives have been so intertwined—so interactive. Without the Mormons, Utah would be just another Wyoming or Nevada. And without its Utah experience Mormonism would be just another small denomination in American Protestantism.[3]

The symbiosis falls into four stages, each characterized by the nature and scope of Mormon initiative vis-à-vis Utah and the recip-rocal effect of Utah on the church and its people.

Period I extends from 1847 to 1890—from the Mormon arrival in the Great Basin until the Woodruff Manifesto. Utah was at least temporarily Zion, refuge for the gathered and beleaguered Saints, and its location and resources helped to shape the culture of the Kingdom. Church participation in the affairs of the territory was aggressive and comprehensive.

Period II covers the years 1890 to 1945—from Utah's acceptance of the conditions for statehood until the Second World War. Utah became "home" for most of the Saints as expectations of a return to Jackson County receded into the future. Intent on improving its image to facilitate peaceful coexistence with "the world," the church interacted with the state on a selective and primarily defensive basis.

Period III extends from 1945 to the present—the era of Mormonism's transformation from a regional to a national and then a world religion. An improving church image has remained linked to Utah's sheltering valleys, both in the perceptions of those who view from afar and in the perspectives of those sons and daughters of the pioneers who have gone beyond the mountains to preach and prosper in Babylon. The church behind the image, more confidently dominant in Utah than during Period II, has exerted its influence selectively but aggressively.

Period IV begins with the present. Since history and prophecy are separate callings—perceived by some, alas, to be at odds with each other—I shall deal only tentatively and briefly with the shape of things to come. The image and substance of Mormonism will, I believe, be less and less influenced by Utah-based events and attitudes. The influence of the church on the state will still be pervasive, but attention will be focused on the defense and enhancement of Mormonism's worldwide concerns.

The most studied aspects of this symbiotic relationship are from Period I, when most Mormons were Utahans and most Utahans were Mormons. The theocratic communitarian commitments of the Saints interacted with the physiographic realities of the Great Basin and Colorado Plateau to shape Utah Territory. An underdeveloped economy, embattled politics, and psychological isolation reflected both terrestrial distance and celestial aspirations. Even the Gentiles who came to Utah for the same reasons that brought miners to Montana and stockmen to Wyoming found their lives affected by the fact that they were in Mormon country.

It is arguable that the two most valuable contributions that Utah made to Mormonism in the nineteenth century were isolation and insufficient rainfall. They made it possible and necessary for the Saints to apply cooperative concepts received in the East successfully enough to become something more than a beleaguered community of followers of a charismatic leader.

The Mormon subculture took shape, not in New York, Ohio, Missouri, or Illinois, but in Utah, described in pioneer times as "a thousand miles from anywhere." Isolation was not complete, and Leonard Arrington pointed out years ago that the Gentile intrusions had their beneficial windfall aspects. But the preoccupations with building and defending Zion reinforced a doctrinally based "we-they" image of the world, and that perception has persisted among the descendants of the first Utah Mormons to the present day.

The "Americanization" of the tens of thousands of European converts who came to territorial Utah was hardly typical of the larger nineteenth-century assimilation process in the United States. A minority of the Mormon immigrants tarried long enough to sample life in New Orleans, St. Louis, Philadelphia, or New York, but most of the converts were shepherded straight through to the Great Basin. Never having voted in England, Scandinavia, or Germany, they cast their first ballots for church-nominated candidates in generally uncontested elections. They learned to venerate the American Constitution as a symbol, but they sometimes heard presidents and congressmen denounced as rascals and the government as a corrupt institution destined soon to fall. The "melting pot" for these newcomers was described in 1852 by Apostle Erastus Snow: "put all these parties through the furnace and run out a party of Saints for the Kingdom of God."[4] Helen Papanikolas notes that while there was some resistance to acculturation, "The logic of submerging national origins, languages, and customs to give strength to the new Church, reverence for English as the language in which the Book of Mormon had been translated, and the wholehearted acceptance of Utah's Zion as the immigrants' permanent home kept resistance low."[5]

In a recent paper on the demography of the Utah church, Dean May observes that the immigrants who comprised a large part of the adult population of many pioneer settlements had as role models the "Deseret Mormons" who had converted them and led them to their new world.[6] The consequences are still discernible. Trace elements of Old World culture like Sanpete's Scandinavian stories have foreign accents but one hundred percent Mormon Utah content.

Erastus Snow's furnace might have produced Saints of a different mettle if the Mormon country had not been so dry. Mark Leone has recently emphasized what others had earlier noted—that pioneer irrigation required an uncommon degree of cooperation and obedience to leadership, both reinforced by church sanctions. Building and rebuilding dams, cleaning ditches, and adjudicating water claims were acts of devotion to God. As Leone puts it: "Success happened by making economic and political decisions, which were often difficult and trying, calling them religious necessity, and defining the resultant material success as religious experience."[7]

If one sees in the Nauvoo period evidence that Joseph Smith had lost some of his enthusiasm for innovative economic schemes, then Mormonism's migration to Utah was critical for the survival of communitarian economics. "It was inevitable," according to Leone, "that the problem of learning how to farm a desert was handled through rituals."[8] Not everyone will be convinced by the interpretive super-structure which Leone builds on his evidence, but who will deny that the cooperative and authoritarian aspects of Mormonism were reinforced in meeting the Utah challenge?

Utah, of course, has always had non-Mormon minorities. In the territorial period their status was to a considerable extent a function of how they chose to relate to the majority. The Lamanite factor in LDS ideology had some impact upon the Indian story. The native Americans who begged or bargained were accommodated by a policy that it was "better to feed them than to fight them." Those who chose to fight were met, as Howard Christy has persuasively argued, with a strategy of defense and conciliation.[9] In the end the outcome for the Indians was not radically different from what came to pass in other parts of the American West.

Catholics and Jews, themselves subject to discrimination in nineteenth-century America, got along more or less amiably with the Mormons. Simon Bamberger would not later have become the first Jewish governor of an American state if Utah had not been comparatively free from anti-Semitism. On the other hand, Protestants and politicians who were more or less identified with the anti-Mormon crusade found minds and doors closed to them. The first women's club in Provo was formed by Gentile women as a response to social ostracism.[10]

Papanikolas and other students of Utah's ethnic minorities have shown that even the people who settled in towns and jobs outside the Mormon mainstream were involved in the symbiosis. Mormon mores shaped their perceptions of Americanism and local biases kept them at arm's length. The first who came to the mines and railroads prompted some Mormons to say: "If God had dipped them in once more, they'd have come out black."[11] The Joe Hills who came later with labor radicalism in their baggage found that the "right to work" concept had become a corollary of Mormonism. Still, the sons of the Swensons married the daughters of the Deniches and cultural accommodation was in time achieved.

The symbiosis presented different aspects in Period II, the interval from statehood to World War II. Anxiety to escape the old reputation and concern to develop the new Utah led the church to

move toward the American mainstream. Millenarian supranational-
ism gave way to circumspect, conservative, patriotic politics and institutional programs that emphasized gospel impact on individual lives.
But it is impossible to understand what happened to prohibition,
progressivism, social services, or Saltair without remembering that
Utah was the state of the Mormons.

Between 1890 and 1930, according to Thomas Alexander, the
church accepted, for the first time, the necessity of finding a way for
God's Kingdom "to coexist with Caesar's."[12] The process affected
politics and economics in many ways, but the net effect was far from
that total separation of church and state that Congress insisted on in
the 1890s. Several factors made it more difficult to determine the
direction and scope of church influence than before, whether one
were a Latter-day Saint looking for signs to follow or an anti-Mormon
seeking evidence that nothing had really changed.

One new factor was the transformation of the mechanism of church
leadership. Gone was the charismatic, intensely personal leadership
of Joseph Smith and Brigham Young, which sufficed for a movement
still relatively uninhibited by structures, norms, and precedents. Still
in the future was the bureaucratic church, managed by experts and
vesting the aura of leadership in the office of "the Prophet" rather
than the individual holding that position. Alexander characterizes
the interval between as the period of "collegiality." Policies were
worked out in councils in which presidents such as Joseph F. Smith
and Heber J. Grant were seen by many of their colleagues as merely
primus inter pares. The concept of "harmony" did not yet preclude
the public advocacy of minority opinions.[13]

Illustrations of maverick tendencies are not hard to find, from
Moses Thatcher's defiance of the political manifesto of 1896 to John
W. Taylor and Matthias F. Cowley's resistance to the second
antipolygamy manifesto after 1904. Apostle and editor Charles W.
Penrose felt free to oppose compulsory smallpox vaccination in the
Church News in spite of President Smith's favorable view of the
health measure. (A voluntary state program resulted.) Apostle Heber
J. Grant clashed openly with Smith on approaches to prohibition,
and Apostle-Senator Reed Smoot later disagreed publicly with Grant
over the League of Nations. Alexander notes that in the latter case
doctrine as well as politics was involved; Mormon foes of the League

tended to see it as futile because of the calamities that their premillennialism saw as imminent, while Saints who saw the achievement
of the millennium as partly a human enterprise thought of the League
as a useful tool.[14] This ambivalence about coming events has affected
Mormon concepts of civic responsibility to the present day.

A second factor complicating the Mormon-Utah relationship in
Period II was the decision that Mormons should identify with the
American political party system, and the implicit corollary that the
church would use the process to protect its interests. Apostle Joseph
F. Smith put it pragmatically in an 1891 letter: "We have nothing to
look for—nothing to hope for from the Dem's for the next two
years. The Repubs. are in power, and *can* help and have helped us.
And if we had more Repubs. among us, they would help us still
more."[15]

Given this stratagem and the fact that in the early twentieth
century the Mormon component in the Utah population dropped
below two-thirds for the one interval in history, it is not surprising
that the only Gentile U.S. senators and representatives and two of
the state's three non-Mormon governors were elected then. Thomas
Kearns was the last active anti-Mormon to represent Utah in Congress, however. His successor in 1905, Senator and later Supreme
Court Justice George Sutherland, was the unique non-Mormon in
the first class at Brigham Young Academy; his interpretation of the
Constitution has by now achieved semicanonical status among politically conservative Latter-day Saints.

In any event, implementation of the pragmatic policy contributed to the tacit understanding that Utah should have one Mormon
and one non-Mormon senator in the years before the Seventeenth
Amendment was adopted. It contributed also to the growth of Reed
Smoot's Republican machine and then to its derailing by disputes
about prohibition. The same pragmatism made church leaders quite
willing to work with Gentile officeholders such as Governors Bamberger
and George Dern. (J. Bracken Lee, Utah's most successful non-Mormon
politician, expressed the opinion that some LDS leaders preferred
working with officials who did not have to worry about appearing to
be church puppets. Dennis Lythgoe presents evidence that Governor
Lee enjoyed a "special relationship" with some church officials until
he had the temerity to veto Sunday-closing legislation in 1953.)[16]

It seems clear that Joseph F. Smith's editorial endorsement of William Howard Taft in 1912 had something to do with Utah's being one of only two states to approve a second term for the biggest man who ever occupied the White House. The decisive rejection of President Grant's endorsement of Alfred Landon in 1936, on the other hand, demonstrates that church influence was ineffective when it asked the Saints to go against what they perceived to be their secular interests. Since the same generation of Utahns and their predominantly Mormon legislators also rejected church counsel when they voted to repeal prohibition, it is arguable that the political *power* of the hierarchy reached its lowest ebb during the Great Depression.

Alexander and others have shown that in the first statehood decades church concern for the family influenced legislative action affecting public health, limiting child labor, and protecting women in the labor market. It also produced a temporarily successful campaign against "moonlight dancing" at Saltair and a short-lived legislative ban on selling cigarettes in Utah. Under the influence of Amy Brown Lyman and Arthur Beeley, the Social Advisory Committee introduced progressive social service concepts into LDS auxiliary programs and generated momentum for the establishment of the Utah State Welfare Commission.[17]

Mormonism's accommodation to American capitalism was another aspect of Period II that radically affected the Utah connection. Ronald Walker's vivid account of Heber J. Grant's going hat in hand from one New York banker to another to avert church bankruptcy in 1893 helps one to understand the subsequent thrust of Mormon policy.[18] As it worked its way out of debt, the church abandoned the effort to shape Utah's economy along the lines of consecration and stewardship. The revitalized tithing program was put on a cash basis, taking bishops' storehouses and tithing labor out of the market picture. Church-owned enterprises ranged from sugar factories to insurance companies and a hotel with a bar. At least as significant was a new posture toward Gentile enterprise; copper magnate Daniel Jackling, like Bamberger and Dern, was a business friend of the Mormon businessmen who were also church leaders.

This building of bridges helped to dethrone the American party in Salt Lake City politics and to convert the *Salt Lake Tribune* from what it was to what it has become. It also linked the secular policies of the church to the vicissitudes of regional economic colonialism and national business cycles, eventually giving rise to a new approach to gospel economics—the Church Welfare Plan. It is possible that if Utah had been less agrarian, less dependent and less severely wracked by the Great Depression, the plan would have been different in emphasis, scope, or timing. Certainly the plan is being reassessed by both leadership and laity as the focus of church programming moves from the Utah heartland.

An important fringe benefit of the welfare plan for Utah and Mormonism was the favorable effect it had on the popular image of both. According to Jan Shipps's recent analysis, media attitudes toward Mormons moved from negative to "slightly positive" for the first time with the publicity generated by the plan. (The graph trended upward to "extremely positive" in the early 1970s and then dipped a little with the controversy over E.R.A.)[19]

The spectacular growth of Mormonism during the post-World War II generation has changed but not ended the symbiotic relationship. Still Utah-based, with leaders shaped by the pioneer tradition, the church has reflected these conditioning factors in its approach to issues as disparate as the racial revolution and the Cold War. Its impact on social policy has extended from minibottles to Westminster College, from women's rights to the revitalization of downtown Salt Lake City. Its influence on the quality of life can be measured in the pedestrian traffic on Sunday mornings and in the vital statistics—birth and death rates—that put the state in a class by itself. Roots and retirement plans have produced a new kind of geriatric gathering, and as legions of missionaries have presented the gospel message in the accents of American Fork and Ephraim, Saints and sinners around the world have continued to think of Utah as Mormon country.

The political interaction between church and state in Period III has been at two levels. At the grass roots the fact that the Mormon component of the population has grown past seventy percent means almost inevitably that most of the candidates for public office have been members of the church. In a study of two recent elections for the legislature, Keith Melville expresses the opinion that "the necessity of being a Mormon is probably overrated," but then concludes:

"It appears that non-Mormons, women, and ethnic minority candidates may have no more, or possibly even less, chance of being elected today than when Utah first became a state."[20] The public perceptions supporting this conclusion are the same that lead most Mormon candidates to feature church affiliation in their campaign literature. The same perceptions have made statewide office a virtual Mormon monopoly for the last two decades and have produced majorities in excess of eighty percent in the state legislature. Stake presidents, ex-stake presidents, and former bishops make good candidates and often effective legislators; they "know the territory."

It would be a mistake, however, to identify every political position taken by a Mormon legislator as "the Church position." Knowledgeable people in both political parties make these points persuasively:

1. To the extent that the church has an institutional political orientation, it is a nonpartisan conservatism that stands some distance to the left of the John Birch faction of the Republican party. It is more moderate than ten or fifteen years ago, when President Hugh B. Brown used to jest about being the "token Democrat" in the hierarchy. Though most of the leaders are nominally Republican, they are at least as pragmatic as Joseph F. Smith about working with officeholders of both political parties.

2. Church intervention in governmental affairs is selective and infrequent, largely confined to areas of social policy and as likely to curb or temper legislation as to initiate it. Laws to protect battered wives and to fund bilingual education, for example, have benefitted from church support. The impetus for the tax limitation amendment did *not* come from the church.

3. The Special Affairs Committee follows the political scene and may make recommendations to the First Presidency. The committee is the channel through which political communication usually takes place. Legislators concerned about whether there is a "Church position" on a pending matter are likely to consult with a committee member or with its executive secretary.

4. On issues that the church leadership defines as moral—such as liquor control, parimutuel betting, pornography, and E.R.A.— the official LDS position is effectively communicated to legislators, and it is almost always decisive.

5. When the institutional church enters the open political arena, as with the "liquor by the drink" referendum in 1967 and E.R.A. ratification more recently, each congregation is a potential political action committee and the disciplined response is—depending on one's point of view—awesome or fearful.

6. Given its numerical base and authoritarian structure, it is not surprising that the church is often able to secure desired governmental actions—such as the right of eminent domain for Brigham Young University—and almost always able to block unwanted measures. Objections to this power come mostly from two groups—Mormons who object in particular instances and non-Mormons who object in general.[21]

Trapper Miles Goodyear was the first white Gentile who faced the prospect of living in Mormon Utah. He left. For two generations Utah's anti-Mormons tried to get the federal government to change the situation, but in the end what they changed was not the substance of power but the form of its exercise. Alfred Cumming is reported to have said at the close of the Utah War in 1858 that he was now governor of Utah Territory, "but Brigham Young is still governor of the people."[22]

Now, as in the past, non-Mormons have three options—to retreat, to resist, or to relax. The University of Utah—widely perceived among Mormons as a hotbed of resistance—has at least one persuasive spokesman for relaxation. In a delightful essay that circulates in mimeographed form, Noel de Nevers discusses how to cope with a society in which Mormonism is pervasive, active Latter-day Saints are too busy with church work to be social resources for Gentiles, children of the Gentiles are sometimes subject to social pressure at school, and they themselves "are occasionally the object of the vigorous Mormon proselyting effort." Of de Nevers's several constructive suggestions, which include taking advantage of the cultural and educational opportunities that abound, this is the fourth: "Conscientiously cultivate the attitude of a worldly Mormon-watcher. Anywhere else in the world when there's nothing to talk about one talks about the weather; in Utah . . . one talks about the Mormons. Mormon history, folklore, customs, and practices are extremely interesting and entertaining."[23]

An area of obvious recent church impact is Salt Lake City itself. According to Neal Maxwell, two interrelated considerations have led to an expanding institutional role in metropolitan affairs: the quality of life of the people and the vitality of the capital city of Mormonism. Impressions of these concerns are everywhere. The Salt Palace and more recently Symphony Hall and the Capitol Theatre would hardly have materialized without church support. When Obert Tanner took the chairmanship of the Ford Foundation challenge campaign in behalf of the Utah Symphony, it was with the understanding that President David O. McKay would give public support. He did. More recently Wendell Ashton's efforts with the orchestra were of both substantive and symbolic value. Other prominent Mormons and church instrumentalities have contributed to the opera and ballet.

That the church has a lot of money worries a lot of people, especially noncontributors. That some of that money has gone into rebuilding downtown Salt Lake City is clear to anyone who remembers where the city was trending a quarter century ago and who knows the functions of agencies like Bonneville Development Corporation, Deseret Management Corporation, and Zion's Securities Corporation. It may be anticipated that the combination of civic concern, image consciousness, business foresight, and seed money that has wrought such changes in the immediate environs of 47 East South Temple will continue to influence metropolitan development.

When federal pressure and financial necessity long ago led the church to abandon the idea of a parochial school system, the consequence was — and is today — a unique educational environment. It is hardly debatable that Mormonism is primarily responsible for the level of support for schools and the large and still increasing school-age population in Utah. (A recent projection of high school graduates in 1995 shows that the United States as a whole will be down 19 percent while Utah will be up 58 percent.[24])

Frederick Buchanan and Raymond Briscoe have documented the non-Mormon perception that Mormons dominate the public schools and that Mormon values are taught therein.[25] The commonest reported complaint — that the required junior high school course in Utah history is full of the Mormons — is as nonrational as a complaint that Irish history is full of Catholics. But other interrelationships are vulnerable to challenge. Knowing that a primary reference in the seminary class on the Old Testament is the LDS Pearl of Great Price, should anyone have been surprised that an ACLU lawsuit in Logan resulted in denying high school credit for the course?

An illustration of constructive symbiosis in the educational sphere is the role of the church in the late 1970s campaign to meet a financial crisis at Westminster College. When one recalls that the college originated in the nineteenth-century Protestant effort to fight Mormonism with Christian education, the fact that Nathan Eldon Tanner chaired the fund-raising drive is remarkable.

As one who finds demographic history rather tedious but is grateful that others are getting into it, I will close this observation of the Period III symbiosis with a reminder of what numbers can tell us about Utah and the Mormons.

1. Utah's birthrate has been higher than the United States for a century. For the state's Latter-day Saints it is now approximately double the national figure.

2. The state death rate is less than two-thirds the national figure and that for Utah Mormons is lower still.

3. Utah has a significantly lower infant mortality rate, death rate from cancer and heart disease, and a longer life expectancy rate than the United States. According to University of Utah medical researchers these differentials stem almost entirely from the active Mormon component of the populations.[26]

4. Obesity is a serious health problem, despite Word of Wisdom counsel that is apparently taken less seriously than that to which the favorable medical statistics are commonly attributed.

5. The marriage rate is about 10 percent higher and the divorce rate is almost exactly the same as the U.S. rate.

6. About 70 percent of teenage pregnancies—both in Utah and in the U.S.—are out of wedlock, and 70 percent of Utah's teenage brides are pregnant at marriage.

7. The rate of induced abortions in Utah is just over one-fourth the United States figure, and the rate of illegitimate births is just over one-third.

8. Utah County, where the world's highest concentration of active Mormons is probably to be found on the Brigham Young University campus, has the highest birthrate of any county in America. It has a

lower ratio of teenage mothers than the state as a whole. Births out of wedlock are at one-half the state rate and induced abortions are only one-fourth as common.[27]

If they do not exactly prove it, these statistics strongly suggest that Utah is as full as it is of vigorous oldsters, rambunctious youngsters, and hard-working in-betweensters because it is Mormon country.

As one looks back on the years since 1847, it seems clear that the most powerful symbiotic impact of Utah upon the Mormons has been the simple fact that it has been "home." For almost a century — the time span from Fort Sumter to Hiroshima — a majority of the Saints lived in Utah or the immediately contiguous Mormon communities. At its peak around the turn of the century the concentration exceeded 80 percent. The limited carrying capacity of Utah's dependent economy then contributed to the downplaying of the doctrine of gathering, but it did not change the geographic focus of the church. The net out-migration of population between 1900 and 1940 was mostly the surplus youth of Zion, leaving their homes but keeping their roots. They produced little outposts of Utah in California, New York, and Washington, D.C., but did not at first affect the way their kinfolks at home perceived the world beyond the mountains. At the outbreak of the Second World War there were more Mormons outside Utah than inside, but a generation later the members, leaders, and programs of the church still reflected the psychology of a "gathered" people — isolated and shaped by a historic experience in the valleys of the American West.

Dean May, whose demographic study has already been mentioned, points out that what he calls "Deseret Mormons" still command a numerical and cultural majority in the church, and he believes that their attitudes and values will continue to be imparted to converts around the world for a long time.[28] I believe that he underestimates the forces for change that are operating within Mormonism as it enters its fourth half-century.

From within the church come unmistakable signs that homogenizing converts into Deseret Mormons is not a policy objective. *Mormonism: A Faith for All Cultures*, the product of a 1976 conference at Brigham Young University, is one indication that total deculturizing is seen as neither feasible nor desirable.[29] In the sesquicentennial issue of *Ensign*, April 1980, Lavina Fielding Anderson reported on "The Church's Cross-Cultural Encounters" in terms that suggest that increasing effort is being made to separate gospel universals from historical particulars.[30] With missionaries from Utah now comprising less than 25 percent of the total proselyting force and with the number from outside the United States and Canada approaching 30 percent and rising, the prospects for cultural pluralism improve.

Even doctrinal emphases reflect the trend. "Sesquicentennially, we are a Church of multiple Zions," Neal A. Maxwell noted in the 5 January 1980 *Church News*. There are "no more treks to be made — except one last trek by those assigned to build the temple and establish a central presence in Missouri." Then he projected future growth in terms that clearly illustrate that premillennial expectations are not dictating church planning.[31] Priesthood manuals no longer interpret adoption into the gospel kingdom in ethnic terms, and speculation about what happens to the blood of converts is now largely confined to such people as assign theological significance to the administration of capital punishment by firing squad. The ban on priesthood for blacks possibly lasted as long as it did because traditional Mormons were valley dwellers. The splendid pictorial representation of Mormons from many lands in the April 1980 *Ensign* demonstrated a quick and remarkably painless adjustment to the concept of a polychrome church.

In a 1979 essay in *Sunstone*, Sterling McMurrin took favorable note of the trend. After reviewing some of the historic fetters that the church still wears, he said: "Mormonism has been the most successful American religious movement. Now that it is promising to become a world religion, it will encounter new and perhaps greater problems, but it has remarkable vitality and inventiveness and is capable of even radical adaptation and change. The Church has a powerful commitment and loyalty from its members and a strong tradition and habit of facing things head on." McMurrin added a judgment with which I fully concur: "I have nothing but admiration and appreciation for the breakthrough toward universality which the Church has made in the last three decades."[32]

Factors outside the church are likely to accelerate this universalizing trend and further weaken the symbiotic relationship with Utah. Two tendencies are illustrative:

1. That *close* families will continue to be a gospel ideal is much more certain than that *large* families will continue to be so. Dean May argues persuasively that "contemporary Mormon fertility [is] an artifact of their having been a frontier people and then being prevented by a provincial self-consciousness from dropping frontier values and habits, especially in those areas where doctrine and belief reinforce the frontier condition."[33] On the fragmentary evidence available, converts from other cultures have not—at least so far—assimilated this artifact. The birthrate among European, Japanese, and Korean Mormons is probably one-third less than for their Utah coreligionists. Even in prolific Latin America it is apparently lower than the Utah Mormon rate.[34]

2. That Deseret Mormons will continue to monopolize the church hierarchy is also unlikely, given the demographic realities. Projections of a membership of 11 million by the year 2000 may reflect an optimism born of faith, but the implications of the figures charted in the April 1980 *Ensign* are profound.[35] Thirty-six hundred stakes and 29,000 wards and branches will require and produce legions of leaders from the new converts. Administrative oversight, which has already found expression in area presidencies manned by general authorities, will almost certainly require the bureaucratization of the office of regional representative, and this new level of full-time leaders will likely have a relationship to Salt Lake City somewhat analogous to that between the non-Italian cardinal-archbishops of Catholicism and Rome. Must one look beyond the next half-century to see the day when Mormonism sustains a president with a name like Karol Wojtila?

As one reflects on the future of the Utah-Mormon symbiosis, it can confidently be predicted that the church—hierarchy and rank and file—will continue to influence the development of the state. It is more difficult to foresee how Utah will affect Mormonism as Salt Lake City becomes the center of a truly international church, led by men and women who as children never learned to sing "Land of the pioneers, Utah, we love thee."[36]

NOTES

1. Joel H. Johnson, words, and Ebenezer Beesley, music, "High on the Mountain Top," *Hymns of The Church of Jesus Christ of Latter-day Saints* (Salt Lake City: Church of Jesus Christ of Latter-day Saints, 1985), no. 5. At least eleven selections in this latest Mormon hymnal identify Mormonism with its geographic center.

2. *Webster's Seventh New Collegiate Dictionary* (Springfield, Mass.: G. & C. Merriam Company, 1967), 892.

3. Inferential support for this suggestion may be found in the current circumstances of such nineteenth-century radical groups as the Campbellites and Millerites, as well as the followers of Joseph Smith who did not follow Brigham Young into the West.

4. Quoted in Frederick S. Buchanan and Raymond G. Briscoe, "Public Schools as a Vehicle of Social Accommodation in Utah," in Clark Knowlton, ed., *Social Accommodation in Utah* (American West Center Occasional Papers, University of Utah, 1945), 99.

5. Helen Papanikolas, "Ethnicity in Mormondom: A Comparison of Immigrant and Mormon Cultures," in Thomas G. Alexander, ed., *"Soul-Butter and Hog Wash,"* Charles Redd Monographs in Western History, No. 8 (Provo, Utah: Brigham Young University Press, 1978), 102.

6. Dean L. May, "A Demographic Portrait of the Mormons: 1830–1980," *After 150 Years: The Latter-day Saints in Sesquicentennial Perspective*, Thomas G. Alexander and Jessie L. Embry, eds. (Provo, Utah: Charles Redd Center for Western Studies, 1983), 64–65.

7. Mark P. Leone, *Roots of Modern Mormonism* (Cambridge: Harvard University Press, 1979), 85.

8. Ibid., 87.

9. Howard A. Christy, "The Walker War: Defense and Conciliation as Strategy," *Utah Historical Quarterly* 47 (Fall 1979): 395–420.

10. I was so advised when I first talked to Provo's Nineteenth Century Club three decades ago.

11. Papanikolas, "Ethnicity in Mormondom," 92.

12. Thomas G. Alexander, " 'To Maintain Harmony': Adjusting to External and Internal Stress, 1890–1930," *Dialogue: A Journal of Mormon Thought* 15 (Winter 1982): 54. See also James B. Allen and Glen M. Leonard, *The Story of the Latter-day Saints* (Salt Lake City: Deseret Book Company, 1976), 486–88, 512–13.

13. Alexander, " 'To Maintain Harmony,' " 44–58.

14. Ibid., 52–53.

15. J. Keith Melville, "Political Conflict and Accommodation in Utah since Statehood," in Thomas G. Alexander, ed., *"Soul-Butter and Hog Wash,"* 140.

16. Dennis L. Lythgoe, *Let 'em Holler: A Political Biography of J. Bracken Lee* (Salt Lake City: Utah State Historical Society, 1982), 91–107.

17. Thomas G. Alexander, "Between Revivalism and the Social Gospel: The Latter-day Saint Social Advisory Committee, 1916–1922," *Brigham Young University Studies* 23 (Winter 1983): 19–39.

18. Ronald W. Walker, "Crisis in Zion: Heber J. Grant and the Panic of 1893," *Sunstone* 5 (January–February 1980): 26–34.

19. "Media attitudes toward Mormons," graph, *Church News*, 5 January 1980, p. 22.

20. Melville, "Political Conflict and Accommodation," 137, 152.

21. Conversations with many people contributed to these impressions; they include Leonard J. Arrington, Edwin B. Firmage, Willard H. Gardner, Brigham D. Madsen, Neal A. Maxwell, and S. Lyman Tyler.

22. T. B. H. Stenhouse, *The Rocky Mountain Saints* (New York: D. Appleton and Company, 1873), 445n.

23. Noel de Nevers, "Suggestions for Outsiders Moving to Utah." Unpublished ms. (n.d.), 1–5.

24. "Changing Numbers in High School Graduating Classes," *Chronicle of Higher Education*, 7 January 1980, p. 8.

25. As told to me by S. Lyman Tyler.

26. Joseph L. Lyon and Steven Nelson, "Mormon Health," *Dialogue: A Journal of Mormon Thought* 12 (Fall 1979): 84–96.

27. Statistical observations about contemporary Utah and the LDS Church are derived from information provided in 1980 by the LDS Church Historical Department, Salt Lake City; Utah State Department of Health, Bureau of Health Statistics, *Vital Statistics Summary: Utah, 1978–1979*, 1–4; "Family Planners Under Attack in Utah," *Macomb* (Illinois) *Daily Journal*, 20 February 1980, p. 28; *1979 Utah Statistical Abstract* and *1983 Utah Statistical Abstract* (Salt Lake City: Bureau of Economic and Business Research, University of Utah, 1979, 1983).

28. May, "A Demographic Portrait," 65–66.

29. F. Lamond Tullis, ed., *Mormonism: A Faith for All Cultures* (Provo, Utah: Brigham Young University Press, 1978).

30. Lavina Fielding Anderson, "The Church's Cross-Cultural Encounters," *Ensign* 10 (April 1980): 44–49.

31. Neal A. Maxwell, "The Church Now Can Be Universal with Priesthood Revelation of 1978," *Church News*, 5 January 1980, p. 20.

32. Sterling M. McMurrin, "Problems in Universalizing Mormonism," *Sunstone* 4 (December 1979): 17.

33. May, "A Demographic Portrait," 56.

34. Derived from partial 1979 LDS membership statistics by geographic area.

35. "A Statistical Profile: What Numbers Tell Us About Ourselves," *Ensign* 10 (April 1980): 15.

36. Evan Stephens, "Land of the Mountains High," *Hymns* (Salt Lake City: The Church of Jesus Christ of Latter-day Saints, 1948), no. 140. The 1985 LDS Hymnal does not include this hymn or O. P. Huish, "Utah, the Star of the West," no. 71, in the 1948 Hymnal.

Beyond the Stereotypes: Mormon and Non-Mormon Communities in Twentieth-Century Mormondom*

JAN SHIPPS

The story of modern Mormonism and its relationship to the non-Mormon world is often misunderstood because there is a tendency for persons with a superficial understanding of Mormonism to view the Latter-day Saints collectively, seeing them as a people subject to an ecclesiastical hierarchy whose control over their thoughts and actions is by and large absolute. Despite much negative publicity about the Saints that has been and is being purveyed in the "Godmakers" books and films and in other publications produced by militant anti-Mormons, it is likely that the prevailing Mormon image is still the stereotypical picture of persons who drink neither alcoholic beverages nor coffee and tea, who do not smoke, so they are very healthy, who, despite strange beliefs, are very nice people who "take care of their own."[1] They work very hard and by really trying often succeed in show business or "real" business (especially if their names happen to be Osmond or Marriott). Yet in the stereotypical portrait of the Saints, such successes are not regarded so much as personal triumphs as results of a certain "Mormonness," a commitment to an LDS lifestyle that includes acceptance of a powerful work ethic, as well as involvement in church activity. Within the stereotype, the LDS Church itself is seen as a monolithic institution whose authority Latter-day Saints rarely, if ever, question.[2]

In the popular mind, this prevailing misperception of Latter-day Saints is usually accompanied by a stereotypical image of the Gen-

* An earlier version of this essay was presented as the 1986 Dello Dayton Lecture at Weber State College, Ogden, Utah, 30 April 1986.

tiles (persons who are not Mormon) who reside in Utah and other geographical areas where significant numbers of Saints live. Probably originally drawn from fictional accounts of Mormon-Gentile struggle, this composite pictures non-Mormons as persons engaged in a perpetually adversarial relationship with the Saints. This is a misperception quite as divorced from reality as is the image of a monolithic LDS community and LDS culture. In reality, the world that the Mormons and non-Mormons have been inhabiting together since the 1850s has rarely, if ever, been a world as neatly divided as the popular press and many historical works about the Latter-day Saints have intimated.

If these stereotypes are to be stripped away, some means has to be found to make distinctions *within* the Mormon and non-Mormon communities. Here the census helps. But not much. Even though census takers at the turn of the century treated religion as a variable, their data reveal little aside from relative numbers of Latter-day Saints and Gentiles, and statistical information concerning the numbers of "Utah Mormons," as opposed to members of the Reorganized Church of Jesus Christ of Latter Day Saints, and marginally useful denominational breakdowns among the non-Mormon population.

As related in *Special Reports [on] Religious Bodies* (a Bureau of the Census publication published in 1910), at the turn of the century the population of Utah (where the great bulk of the Saints then lived) was 276,749. Of this number, 172,814 (a little over 62 percent) were reported as communicants of some religious body. If 62 percent of Utah's children under five years of age is added to this number, and if 62 percent of Utah's children ages five and six is likewise added, the total number of Utahns who might be described as religious communicants is 208,218, or a little over 75 percent of the state's population. Thus slightly less than a quarter of Utah's residents were not active enough in any church, whether an LDS church or some other, to have been counted as communicants. Utah citizens who fit into this category can appropriately be described as "unchurched."[3]

Not surprisingly, of the Utah residents who at the turn of the century were communicants of some church, more than 87 percent were Latter-day Saints. Communicants in various Protestant bodies made up 4.7 percent of the Utah citizens who fit in the "churched" category. A slightly higher percentage (4.8 percent) were Roman Catholics, while the remainder of those who counted themselves as communicants of religious bodies were Greek Orthodox and Jewish.[4] (About 0.2 percent of the Utah population, 550 persons, were included in a very small category described as "all other bodies.")

A number of historians have used such census data to work up valuable religious profiles of other geographical areas in the United States.[5] For purposes of such analyses, however, historians of American Protestantism usually make distinctions between so-called liturgical groups, such as Lutherans and Episcopalians, and evangelical groups, such as Methodists and Baptists. This conventional distinction did not really operate in Utah in the early part of the twentieth century, however. Not enough Lutherans lived there to merit a separate category in the census report, while the Episcopalians (one-fifth of all Utah Protestants) often cooperated so closely with Utah Baptists, Methodists, Congregationalists, and Presbyterians that this liturgical/evangelical difference that discriminated so nicely elsewhere had little significance in the Great Basin Kingdom. Moreover, from time to time, especially in the Utah political arena, the importance of the division between Mormons and non-Mormons was great enough to lead Roman Catholics and Protestants to make common cause together, a circumstance obtained nowhere else in the nation in 1900. In addition to allowing a dichotomous division of the Utah population into "churched" and "unchurched" categories, census data reveal that relative proportions of Utah's "churched" and "unchurched" people were not evenly distributed throughout the state. On the one hand, for example, in 1900 in such counties as Beaver County (in the southwestern part of the state, close to the Nevada border), 39.5 percent of the residents were unchurched; in Carbon County (including an important coal mining area), 50.7 percent of the population was unchurched; and in Summit County (including the silver mining area around Park City), 35.4 percent of the people were unchurched. On the other hand, in Cache County, (a fairly isolated valley area encircled by mountain ranges), originally settled by the Latter-day Saints, the proportion of unchurched was only 4 percent.[6] In Boxelder, Davis, Emery, Weber, and a number of other counties, the number of unchurched was less than 12 percent.

As for making distinctions among Latter-day Saints, elsewhere I have argued that by the end of the nineteenth century Mormon theological claims—in themselves not entirely unique, but put forward within a unique medium—and the experience of those who accepted these claims had created a people, a new ethnic group.[7] But the cohesiveness of this group was being severely strained at the turn of the century because the Latter-day Saints were living through the trauma that wracked the Mormon body in the wake of the dual demise of plural marriage and the LDS political kingdom. Consequently it would be possible to develop a categorical scheme locating Saints on a continuum based on rejection or acceptance of the changes that took place in Mormonism during the ecclesiastical administrations of Wilford Woodruff, Lorenzo Snow, and Joseph F. Smith. As for the non-Mormons, in a curious way it would also be possible to develop a continuum reflecting their attitudes about whether the Mormons had, or had not, accepted the changes they had been forced to make in the late nineteenth century.[8]

But here, categorizing both the Mormons and the Gentiles in a different manner is called for. With regard to the latter, categories need to be established that will separate non-Mormons according to whether any concerns they had about the Saints were mainly religious concerns, or whether their concerns were primarily political and economic. As necessarily inexact as such a division must be, rough categories can be established by making an assumption that those non-Mormons whose concerns about the Latter-day Saints were primarily religious are likely to have affiliated with one of the Protestant, Roman Catholic, or—much less likely—Jewish congregations in Utah.[9]

No matter how carefully the statistics gathered by the census bureau are examined and manipulated, however, they cannot reveal the relative numbers among the "unchurched" of those persons who had no particular interest in religious matters and might be described as truly secular and those persons who came to Utah as Mormon converts or the children of Latter-day Saints who, for one reason or another, were no longer officially counted as Latter-day Saints. In view of this lack of information, the safest strategy is to divide Utah citizens over seven years of age who fit into the unchurched category equally between the LDS and Gentile groups. If this is done, 23,416 non-Mormons (8.4 percent of the state's population at the turn of the century) were located in the "unchurched Gentile" category, while

21,782 persons (7.9 percent of the state's population) were located in the "churched" non-Mormon category. Even without a hard and fast determination of exactly which members of the non-Mormon community fit into these categories, this strategy allows the identification of two non-Mormon groups whose populations were basically equal: those who were essentially secular in their orientation, and a group of what might be called "religious" non-Mormons, many of whom had sentiments about the Saints not unlike those of the Protestant missionaries who, at the turn of the century, conceived of their task as the converting of Latter-day Saints away from "the heathen, pagan, 'Mohammedan-ish' heresy foisted onto the world by the so-called Mormon prophet."[10] Utah's Roman Catholics and Jews were never as hostile to the Saints as were the Protestants, and as the years of the twentieth century have passed, the division between liturgical and evangelical Protestants has asserted itself in the state. Such denominations as the Episcopalians and, to some extent, the Presbyterians and Methodists have settled into a much less adversarial relationship with the Latter-day Saints than is the case with most Baptist groups and other evangelical and fundamentalist Protestant organizations.[11]

Among the Saints, contrary to the perennially popular notion that Mormonism is, and has ever been, a monolithic movement in which internal conformity is rigorously enforced, diversity has never been entirely alien. During the pioneer period, the practicalities of the Mormon experience made universal suppression of dissident behavior and unconventional belief so difficult that, despite all the overblown stories of the refusal of LDS leaders to countenance dissent and notwithstanding all the fictionalized accounts of the terrible fate awaiting apostates, a surprising degree of multiformity was tolerated in the early years within the LDS Church itself. Moreover, there were yet other Mormons in the Utah LDS community who were not a part of the church over which Brigham Young presided. The claims of the "Brighamites," as the Saints who followed Young were sometimes called, were contested firsthand in Utah Territory by the "Josephites," members of the Reorganized Church of Jesus Christ of Latter Day Saints led by the Prophet's eldest son, Joseph Smith III.[12] And there were other Mormons, too, Saints who had first moved into and then back out of the church without following up their ecclesiastical exits (which were often, though not always, voluntary) with physical removal from the society of their former faithmates. Some of the persons in this interesting ex-Mormon category stayed in Utah for economic reasons.[13]

Others who, for one reason or another, were bitter toward the church seem to have functioned in the Mormon community mainly as thorns in the side of the "almighty hierarchy."[14] But many ex-Mormons stayed in the LDS community because, even as they rejected the legitimacy of the church organization and the authority of its leaders, or as they were rejected by the church, they continued in their own ways to affirm the truth of the LDS gospel.[15]

Disagreement about matters of faith was, then, not a novelty first making its appearance in the LDS community after that community was no longer effectively set apart from the larger world. Still, while intra-Mormon diversity was not new in the early twentieth century, developments across the years since 1890 have allowed that diversity to become more intense. Before 1890, even as they had occupied the same geographical space, Utah's Mormon and non-Mormon populations had lived in communities separated from each other psychologically. Each community had developed its own structures of internal governance and its own means of enforcing internal cohesion. Serving to counterpoise one another, each community had set limits on the degree of diversity tolerable in the other. But with the coming of statehood in 1896, interpenetration of the two communities occurred, and as the Gentile barrier around the LDS community grew progressively weaker, the latent diversity within the Mormon world began to make itself known.

Obvious differences in ethnic background had encouraged variety in the LDS population long before the pioneer era came to an end.[16] Lineage had made a difference historically, too. Distinctions between Latter-day Saints whose families had been long in the church and LDS converts new to the faith had been possible for decades, and distinctions between the members of the families of the Mormon elite, whose main business from the beginning had been running the church, and the members of ordinary, everyday Mormon families had likewise been felt for years.[17] But in the twentieth century, a different form of diversity started to cut across these more or less traditional LDS population categories. Perhaps it would be an overstatement to say that many LDS subcultures came into being during the first decades of the new century. Yet simply making distinctions between "true believers" and "cultural Mormons," as some students of modern Mormonism are prone to do, does not yield categories elegant enough to clarify the connections and relationship between what might be termed "modern Mormonism" and the secular establishment.

The general character of Mormondom became increasingly varied and complex after 1890, but because personal LDS behavioral patterns were not as set in the early years as they are now—and because behavioral patterns are notoriously difficult to tease out of the historical record in any event—a useful means of examining the variegated and catholic nature of the world of modern Mormonism is noting how Latter-day Saints are situated along an orthodoxy continuum, on the one hand, and, on the other, a dimension along which is measured levels of church activity and attitudes toward it.

Without making any effort at this juncture to determine the relative proportions of the LDS populations who fall into the various categories located along this belief-behavior continuum at various chronological points—a task that would be even more difficult than determining the relative number of non-Mormons in the secular and religious categories described above—the continuum itself can be described as follows:

1. At one extreme are those persons who regard themselves as the only true Mormons, but who are not recognized as Mormons by most Latter-day Saints, i.e., the Mormon "fundamentalists." In a sense, their beliefs are more than orthodox, in that they accept the Book of Mormon as a historical document, believing that this basic LDS scripture is precisely what it claims to be; they accept the LDS doctrinal formulations that were established during the lifetimes of Joseph Smith and Brigham Young, but reject the 1890 Manifesto proscribing plural marriage on the basis of its having been promulgated outside a "Thus saith the Lord" context, and they "live the gospel" as fully as they can by joining with like-minded Saints in isolated communities. In other words, at one of the continuum's extremities one finds, to use Eric Hoffer's term, the truest of true believers—the Saints who continue to practice plural marriage.

2. A second, less extreme category next to this "fundamentalist" one is the one in which is found active, almost superorthodox Saints.

These are the persons who seem to be certain that the Book of Mormon is historically accurate and who do not question the versions of LDS history long since canonized by the church. Saints in this category exhibit a very high level of church activity, not only in attendance at worship, but also in fulfilling church callings.

3. In a third category along this orthodox/active dimension are found Latter-day Saints who accept the truth of the LDS gospel, but concede that it might be held in "earthen vessels." These are persons who are not very worried about whether the Book of Mormon is history in the ordinary understanding of that term, as long as the book's narrative captures and represents truth in some abstract sense. They understand the principle of canonization and are inclined, as opposed to those in the very extreme categories, not to be threatened by academic approaches to the study of the past. They are generally active, not only in worship and in carrying out church callings, but they also tend to be active in quasi-official LDS organizations such as the Mormon History Association or the various Sunstone symposia.

4. Then there is a Mormon group that fits in the central category in this classification scheme. Their thought patterns were formed by their immersion in Mormon doctrine, but for one reason or another they do not themselves take much of a role in church activities, although they may send their children to Sunday School and sacrament meeting. They are not hostile to the institution or to other Saints. This category includes "cultural" and/or "ethnic" Mormons, large numbers of whom do not reside in Utah.

5. Moving further from the center is a category that might be described as mildly anti-Mormon. Popularly known as "Jack-Mormons," such Saints are located between the category that includes "cultural" or "ethnic" Mormons and a category that includes Saints hostile to the LDS Church and contemptuous toward its active members. This is a fairly heavily populated category that embraces inactive Mormons of many stripes, including those who are more amused than threatened by the actions of the members of the LDS ecclesiastical hierarchy.

6. A second "Jack-Mormon" category includes Latter-day Saints whose level of hostility toward the church as an institution is fairly high, who deny that in LDS scriptures might be repositories of truth, and whose attitude toward active and committed Mormons is gener-

ally one of contempt. This category often includes persons who have been disfellowshipped or even excommunicated, but who have not rejected their Mormon ethnicity.

7. Finally, at the opposite extreme from the Mormon fundamentalists is a category in which are found the ex-Mormons who are extremely antagonistic not only toward the LDS Church hierarchy, but toward anything Mormon. Truly anti-Mormon, the persons in this category believe that Mormonism is so dangerous that they expend an enormous amount of energy denigrating Mormon theology and opposing the LDS Church and its authority in the community.

Except for the subtle connotations that are sometimes attached to the terms "Gentile" and "non-Mormon," with the latter sometimes referring to persons unfriendly to the Saints, not many attempts have been made to identify and clarify distinctions within the non-Mormon community. But this present one is by no means the only effort that has recently been made to describe the variation within the Mormon community.[18] Whether these particular classification schemes or different ones are used to describe the structure of the "human landscape" in the world that Mormons and non-Mormons have been inhabiting together for more than a hundred years, discriminating descriptions of the two communities beyond the prevailing stereotypes point to the immense complexity of the history of Mormonism in the twentieth century. Such descriptions reveal, in fact, an intricate historical fabric that can be properly characterized only if the multiple strands in the pattern of the fabric are separated and considered in isolation, as well as together. While there are many fine threads in this fabric, three interwoven strands form the principal pattern. By identifying these, we can now begin to appreciate the relationship between the Mormon and the non-Mormon establishments. The first of these basic strands is the internal history of the Mormon community, the history of how Saints related to other Saints and how the community as a whole managed to negotiate the troubled times in which traditional LDS social, political, and economic arrangements were given up and new social, political, and economic arrangements instituted.[19] That story can never be fully and properly told, however, without paying attention to a second strand in the fabric of twentieth-century Mormon history, the strand that deals with the relationship between modern Mormonism and evangelical (later in the century, fundamentalist) Protestantism. Quite as clearly as the story of conflicts that can often be found within the Mormon community, this is a story of religious conflict in which the deeply held convictions of one group are more or less constantly challenged by the members of the other group.

The third prominent strand in the design of this historical fabric is the story of the Saints and the essentially secular Gentiles, those who, after the demise of plural marriage and the Mormon political kingdom, were far less concerned about Mormon religious beliefs than about the willingness of the Saints to permit Gentiles to participate fully in the creation of a modern society in the Intermountain West. To an amazing degree, as is shown in the history of Salt Lake City by James B. Allen and Thomas G. Alexander, this is not a story of unending conflict, but of surprising cooperation.[20] To be sure, a narrative of this strand of the Mormon-Utah story is by no means without conflict, but it generally includes accounts of healthy rather than destructive challenges. Often Latter-day Saints and Gentiles struggled together, not against each other. An unusually significant part of this strand covers the development of institutions that facilitated and continue to facilitate Mormon-non-Mormon interaction — the Alta Club, the Commercial Club, Rotary, the Salt Lake Kindergarten Association, the Ladies Literary Club, Art Institute, and Utah Symphony boards, and so on.[21]

Looking briefly at three historical examples will illustrate the value of separating out the various strands in the Mormon story. One of these examples is drawn from the early years of the twentieth century, one from the post-World War II years, and one is very current.

E. Leo Lyman and Henry J. Wolfinger, who have made close studies of the coming of Utah statehood, have described the deliberations that led up to the striking of an unwritten bargain between the Latter-day Saints and the national government in 1890. In return for Utah statehood, the Saints would give up the practice of plural marriage and enter into politics in the manner of other American citizens, dividing the LDS body politic, as it were, into national political parties.[22] As the new state came into existence, a second unwritten understanding was reached: Utah's congressional delegation would, as far as possible, be evenly divided between Saints and Gentiles, with the state's two senators always representing the two components of the Utah population.[23]

Nevertheless, after Reed Smoot, a member of the Quorum of the Twelve Apostles and prominent Utah Republican, was elected to the Senate in 1903, his right to hold the seat to which he had been elected was also challenged. In view of the fact that, with the blessing of the LDS Church hierarchy, non-Mormon Thomas Kearns was Utah's other senator at the time, this was a somewhat surprising turn of events, especially since the challenge was not based on any illegal act committed by Smoot.[24] It rested instead on the fact that he held a position of ecclesiastical authority in the LDS Church. Although the political situation in Utah was exceedingly complicated during this transition period and although the subtle partitioning that would separate non-Mormons into those primarily concerned about religious issues and those primarily concerned about secular matters was just beginning to occur, the challenge mounted against Smoot and the LDS Church is easier to comprehend if the story of the bitter adversarial relationship that existed between Mormonism and the non-Mormons concerned about religious issues is separated from the story of Mormonism's relationship with the secular establishment. Otherwise, the Smoot challenge, which upset the bargain that had been so carefully hammered out to insure fair play in the national political arena, appears to have been counterproductive for the challengers.[25]

A clearer picture of the complicated situation emerges if the role played in this drama by the Salt Lake Ministerial Association is kept in focus. The challenge to Smoot's right to occupy a seat in the U.S. Senate was penned by the Reverend W. M. Paden, pastor of the First Presbyterian Church of Salt Lake City; unsubstantiated charges about Smoot's having been a polygamist were added by the Reverend J. M. Leilich, superintendent of the Utah missions of the Methodist Episcopal Church; and a huge proportion of the petitions (that are supposed to have included four million signatures) against Smoot's being seated contained signatures gathered in evangelical Protestant congregations throughout the nation. Adding this dimension to our understanding of what happened lets us see that the Smoot investigation was one of the catalysts that helped to precipitate divisions *within* the non-Mormon community. This approach also clarifies the final outcome of the investigation, for it was, finally, the support of Theodore Roosevelt, probably the most prominent member of the secular establishment of the day, that led to the Utah senator being allowed to take his seat.

The Smoot investigation was an early example of cooperation between particular segments of the Mormon and the non-Mormon communities, i.e., between Gentiles, whose primary concerns about the Saints were/are religious concerns, and ex-Mormons, those former members of the LDS community who fit into the category that includes persons extremely antagonistic to the LDS Church and to everything Mormon.[26] Apostates in the eyes of the LDS Church, such individuals have made common cause with the Saints' evangelical Protestant opponents across the years. By the time of the Smoot investigation, Frank J. Cannon, one of the sons of LDS Apostle George Q. Cannon, was such a person. He provided information and even the wording for the initial attacks questioning the motives of the LDS Church and questioning the right of Reed Smoot to hold a Senate seat, and throughout the hearing he worked behind the scenes in opposition to Smoot. Wayne Stout, who wrote and (at his own expense) published a highly partisan multivolume history of Utah, portrays Julius Caesar Burrows, the senator from Michigan who chaired the Committee on Privileges and Elections, as another link between ex-Mormons and the non-Mormon antagonists of Senator Smoot and the LDS Church. Whether Stout was correct about Senator Burrows having been "a nephew of the notorious apostate, Sylvester Smith, who brainwashed Julius into a vehement Mormon hater," the public record shows the Smoot investigation to have been an early instance of cooperation between ex-Mormons and evangelical Protestants in fighting the LDS Church.[27]

Turning from cooperation among the opponents of Mormonism, a prime example of cooperation between the Latter-day Saints and the Utah secular establishment was the activities of an unusual "extra-political triumvirate" composed of Gustave P. Backman, John Fitzgerald, and David O. McKay who, as Backman recalled, met together every Tuesday morning in the coffee shop of the Hotel Utah to decide what needed to be done in Salt Lake City.[28] Composed of an inactive Mormon, one who would have fit nicely in the benign

Jack-Mormon category, a Gentile, whose primary concerns about the Saints (at least in his later years) had to do with finding ways to work together with them for the common good, and a very active LDS Church authority, this triad of unelected yet extremely powerful Salt Lake City leaders had started working together when they were all members of the Executive Committee of the Utah Centennial Commission which had been charged with planning the state centennial observance in 1947. For nearly a decade afterward, they continued meeting to consider social, political, economic, and religious issues that were of common concern to Utah's citizens—and particularly to Salt Lake City residents—and afterward communicated their ideas and tentative decisions informally to the business community and elected officials of the city, county, and state.

Persons who are suspicious of the secular power of the LDS Church would probably regard these weekly meetings of Backman, who was the executive secretary of the Salt Lake City Chamber of Commerce, Fitzgerald, who was editor of the *Salt Lake Tribune*, and McKay, who was president of the LDS Church, as evidence of the church's power and its desire for total control over Salt Lake City and the State of Utah. But Backman's informal memoirs suggest otherwise. These meetings seem, instead, to represent the visible working out of a pattern of cooperation between non-Mormons and Latter-day Saints (many of whom were/are very active and devoted to the LDS Church and many others who were/are inactive) which has functioned reasonably consistently all across the twentieth century. Keeping the historical strands separate, making it easy to differentiate between the cooperative relationship the Saints have maintained with the non-Mormon secular establishment and the adversarial relationship between the Saints and non-Mormons who are concerned about the LDS religious claims, makes a conspiratorial interpretation of the Backman, Fitzgerald, McKay meetings far less likely.[29]

In the religious arena, the Church of Jesus Christ of Latter-day Saints has never stopped dedicating its energies to proselytizing. Moreover, during the ecclesiastical administration of Spencer W. Kimball (1973–86), the church renewed its commitment to taking the message of the LDS gospel across the nation and throughout the world.[30] Appreciating the distinctions among Gentiles and keeping the exclusive nature of the LDS religious claims in mind helps to clarify the current success in evangelical and fundamentalist Protestant congregations of the "Godmakers" campaign in which, through professionally produced films and books, the LDS Church is being portrayed as a menace to the health of families and society, as well as a demonic threat to the salvation of humanity. Otherwise, this vocal anti-Mormon movement, now being conducted against the LDS Church by an alliance of ex-Mormons violently antagonistic to Mormonism and some very conservative Protestants, appears to fly in the face of the current existence of unusually cordial social, political, and economic relationships between Mormonism and the secular establishment in Washington, D.C., as well as in Salt Lake City and elsewhere. As curiously out of phase and out of place as this virulent campaign may appear to be, it has historical roots in the nineteenth century when bitter ex-Mormons joined forces with persons from Protestant and Roman Catholic churches across the country in a futile effort to deliver a death blow to the LDS Church.

As always, when one is dealing with the web of history, things are not as simple as the foregoing analysis would seem to make it. The multiple strands in the pattern of the LDS historical fabric cannot merely be identified in Utah, or even simply in the Mormon culture region in the Intermountain West. A separate and somewhat different story of twentieth-century Mormonism must be recounted for California, and for all the other areas in the United States that Saints in Indiana, Illinois, Georgia, and elsewhere often describe as "the mission field." And still other twentieth-century Mormon stories abound, in Europe, in Latin America, in the Orient, and in all the places where the Saints have carried the LDS gospel and established outposts of "the Kingdom."

Yet if all these separate stories differ one from another, much about them is continuous from one place to another. As the Mormon gospel takes root in different cultures, it takes on different forms. Always, however, there is the church and "the world," the Saints and the Gentiles. Wherever the LDS story plays itself out, its chroniclers and its interpreters would do well to remember that neither group is made up of ideal types.

NOTES

1. Currently "Saints Alive," which was formerly known as "Ex-Mormons for Jesus," is the most vocal and visible anti-Mormon group. "Saints Alive" leader Ed Dekker is the producer of the "Godmakers" films which the group distributes and is coauthor with Dave Hunt of *The Godmakers* (New York: Harvest House, 1984). A number of militant anti-Mormons are associated with the Modern Microfilm Company in Salt Lake City. Operated by Jerald and Sandra Tanner, this company produces a large number of publications that call LDS historical and theological claims into question. *Mormonism: Shadow or Reality*, one of the most elaborate of the Modern Microfilm publications, is distributed nationally by the Moody Press in Chicago. The *Utah Evangel*, a newsprint periodical, is distributed by the Reverend John Smith, who served as minister of a Utah Baptist congregation for more than fifteen years before moving to Texas to establish a ministry primarily devoted to converting Mormons away from Mormonism.

2. This description of the Mormon image is drawn from an examination of all the periodical articles on the Mormons and Mormonism indexed in *Poole's Index* and *Readers' Guide* between 1860 and 1960, as well as from impressionistic evidence developed from paying close attention to the treatment Mormons and Mormonism have received in both print and electronic media in the past quarter century.

3. Adding in those who were too young to be counted as communicants in order to develop a reasonably accurate religious profile of Utah called for a certain amount of guesswork. Counted in the total state population of 276,749 were 41,852 children under the age of five. Also, 38,128 children between the ages of five and nine were included in the census count. As no means exists to determine how many of these children were actually under age seven—the age when many churches start counting children as communicants—it seemed best simply to assume an equal number of children in each age category from five through nine—i.e., to divide by five and add two-fifths of the total (15,251) to the number of children under five to get a general notion of the number of children in Utah under seven years of age. This strategy was used to obtain a percentage of the Utah population under the age of seven and this percentage (20.6) was uniformly added to the numbers of communicants reported by the census takers whenever percentages were calculated throughout this essay.

4. At the turn of the century, the Reorganized LDS Church had 493 members in Utah. They were divided among five congregations. Exact numbers of Jews in Utah cannot be determined from the census data since only heads of households were reported under Jewish congregations.

5. See, for example, Linda Pritchard, "Another Look at Religion in Texas, 1845–1900," paper presented at the Spring 1986 meeting of the American Society of Church History, Ft. Worth, Texas, 5 April 1986. Both Paul Kleppner and Richard Jensen have used such religious profiles to expli-

cate political behavior in the Midwest: Kleppner, *Cross of Culture* (New York: Free Press, 1970); Jensen, *Winning of the Midwest* (New Haven: Yale University Press, 1967).

6. Since more than 99 percent of the churched population was LDS, this was a significant number.

7. This contention is crucial to the argument made in *Mormonism: The Story of a New Religious Tradition* (Urbana and Chicago: University of Illinois Press, 1985).

8. In a presentation made to clergy in the Idaho–Eastern Washington Conference of the United Methodist Church, such a scheme proved extremely helpful in clarifying where the LDS "fundamentalists," i.e., those Saints who continue to practice plural marriage, stand in relation to other Latter-day Saints. Shipps, "The Mormon Human Landscape," lecture presented to the Methodist "Circuit Rider Seminar," Boise, Idaho, April 1982. An extensive report of this lecture was published in the *Sunstone Review*.

9. This is not an unreasonable assumption since, in such an environment, personal identity was (and often still is) very much tied to religious affiliation. Because many non-Mormon children who grew up in Utah without some definite religious affiliation often moved over into the LDS camp, whether they became active participants, the members of non-Mormon family units generally identified themselves with some non-Mormon religious group.

10. This description is a composite taken from the published reports of Methodist, Baptist, Presbyterian, and Episcopal missionaries to Utah. See Shipps, "From Satyr to Saint: American Attitudes toward the Mormons, 1860–1960," a paper presented at the annual meeting of the Organization of American Historians held in Chicago, Illinois, April 1973. For the most complete description available of Protestant missionary efforts to convert Mormons away from Mormonism, see T. Edgar Lyon, "Evangelical Protestant Missionary Activities in Mormon Dominated Areas, 1865–1900" (Ph.D. diss., University of Utah, 1962).

11. This observation is based on personal discussions this author has had with members of various Protestant groups in Utah. To some degree the difference seems to be theological, reflecting a division among Protestants into so-called liberal and conservative camps. See also the editorials published in *The Utah Evangel*.

12. Altogether the RLDS Church had 40,851 members in 1900; they were concentrated in the upper Midwest, but, as indicated, there were five congregations in Utah.

13. Most of the Latter-day Saints who were involved in the "New Move" (the Godbeite movement), which was regarded as heresy, stayed in Utah following their excommunication from the church. However, as Ronald W. Walker indicates in his study of the career of T. B. H. and Fanny Stenhouse, apostates sometimes had difficulty collecting due bills in the LDS commu-

nity. For that reason, ex-Mormons who stayed in Utah for business reasons were more likely to be Saints who simply became less than fully involved in LDS endeavors, adopting a position somewhat analagous to that of inactive Mormons today. See Walker, "The Stenhouses and the Making of a Mormon Image," *Journal of Mormon History* 1 (1974): 51–72.

14. The most prominent ex-Mormon in the early years of the twentieth century was probably Frank J. Cannon, the author of *Under the Prophet in Utah: The National Menace of a Political Priestcraft* and many other exposes, who had once served as a U.S. senator from Utah.

15. The Godbeite "heresy" was presented as a form of *true* Mormonism. Other forms of Mormonism that existed alongside normative Mormonism are described in Russell R. Rich, *Those Who Would Be Leaders: Offshoots of Mormonism* (Provo, Utah: Brigham Young University Extension Publications, 1968).

16. In addition to large-scale immigration from England and Scandinavia, the LDS community included a significant German-speaking sector. The native Mormon population not only included Saints from all across the United States and Canada, but American Indians as well.

17. An analysis of the leadership of the LDS Church as a social elite is found in D. Michael Quinn, "The Mormon Hierarchy, 1832–1932: An American Elite" (Ph.D. diss., Yale University, 1976).

18. Such schemes are found in Robert Gottleib and Peter Wiley, *America's Saints* (New York: G. P. Putnam's Sons, 1984) and in James L. Clayton, "On the Different World of Utah," a presentation made 31 October 1985 at the National Collegiate Honors Council's Twentieth Annual Conference in Salt Lake City and printed in *Vital Speeches of the Day* (1 January 1986), 186–92.

19. The internal dynamics characterizing the relationships among those situated in various categories along the LDS belief-behavior continuum is a fascinating history in and of itself. Two recent works deal with this topic: Richard Cowan, *History of the LDS Church in the Twentieth Century* (Salt Lake City: Bookcraft, 1985) and Thomas G. Alexander, *Mormonism in Transition: A History of the Latter-day Saints, 1890–1930* (Urbana and Chicago: University of Illinois Press, 1986).

20. *Mormons & Gentiles: The History of Salt Lake City* (Boulder, Colo.: Pruett Press, 1984).

21. The records of most of these groups are housed in the Special Collections sections of the Marriott Library at the University of Utah. As an example of how these organizations worked to create arenas for Mormon and non-Mormon political, social, and economic intercourse, see especially the proposition of one of the founders of the Commercial Club, C. N. Strevell, who asked that the club be "a non-sectarian, non-political organization where Mormon, Jew, and Gentile could meet together." This club was organized in 1887 and, despite the need to guard against the develop-

ment of cliques, it became, in the words of a Mr. Armstrong (whose sentiments were recorded in the minutes of the Commercial Club Board for 19 January 1914), "the one place in Utah where open forum exists and where all men, regardless of race, color, creed, or previous condition of servitude can meet and be heard." O. N. Malmquist, *The Alta Club: 1883-1974* (Salt Lake City, n.p., n.d.). See also Leonard J. Arrington, *Service Over Self: A History of Salt Lake City Rotary Club No. 24* (Salt Lake City: Rotary Club, 1981).

Indeed, this is a story that cannot yet be fully told, for at this point there are more questions than answers. For example, (a) While there was a high level of cooperation between certain Mormons and certain non-Mormons in Salt Lake City, what level of cooperation existed in Utah's small towns where the Latter-day Saints outnumbered the non-Mormons by fifteen or twenty to one? (b) If such institutional avenues as the Commercial Club and the Federation of Women's Clubs existed to facilitate cooperative action in the public arena, did those institutional networks spill over into private arenas, so that pure socializing in which Mormons and non-Mormons came together simply for the pleasure of enjoying each other's company became commonplace? (c) Economics and politics, and such particular areas as that represented by the Irrigation Congresses all brought Mormons and non-Mormons into productive working relationships. Did such working relationships extend to the national level, or are such close working arrangements as that which developed between Senator Reed Smoot and President Warren Harding to be accounted for as personal friendships that might well have developed even if the overall relationship between Mormonism and the secular establishment had been primarily negative, rather than positive?

22. E. Leo Lyman, *Political Deliverance: The Mormon Quest for Utah Statehood* (Urbana and Chicago: University of Illinois Press, 1986); Henry J. Wolfinger, "A Re-Examination of the Woodruff Manifesto in the Light of Utah Constitutional History," *Utah Historical Quarterly* 39 (Fall 1971): 328–49.

23. Shipps, "Utah Comes of Age Politically: A Study of the State's Politics in the Early Years of the Twentieth Century," *Utah Historical Quarterly* 35 (Spring 1967): 94.

24. An earlier challenge to the right of a Latter-day Saint to hold a seat in the national congress had been based on that person's open defiance of the law forbidding the polygamous cohabitation. Brigham H. Roberts, an assistant to the LDS Church Historian and prominent Utah Democrat, was elected to Congress in 1900, but his right to occupy the seat to which he was elected was challenged and the challenge was upheld by the House of Representatives.

25. The official record of the Smoot investigation is contained in *Proceedings Before the Committee on Privileges and Elections of the United States Senate In the Matter of the Protest Against the Right of Hon. Reed*

Smoot, a Senator from the State of Utah, to Hold His Seat, 4 vols. (Washington, D.C.: Government Printing Office, 1904–6). The most recent and, without question, the best description of the Smoot election and investigation now in print is found in Alexander, *Mormonism in Transition.*

26. Such people fit in one of the extreme categories (category 7) in the classification scheme devised above to describe the "Mormon human landscape."

27. *History of Utah,* 3 vols. (Salt Lake City: 1965–71), 2:250.

28. Backman, unpublished memoirs in the files of the Salt Lake City Chamber of Commerce, Special Collections, Marriott Library, University of Utah. The characterization of these three as an "extra-political triumvirate" comes from Alexander and Allen, *Mormons & Gentiles,* 263.

29. In fact, a wider recognition of this part of the design in the Mormon historical fabric on the part of those who study the topic might make less likely the publication by respected presses of such broad conspiratorial interpretations of modern Mormonism as Ray Hinerman and Anson Shups, *The Mormon Corporate Empire* (Boston: Beacon Press, 1986).

30. The decision made by the highest LDS Church authorities to agree not to carry out a proselyting program in Jerusalem is important to understanding the development of Mormonism as a new religious tradition, since it indicates an implicit recognition of the limits of LDS expansion. But the assurances given to Israel should not be interpreted as an indication that Mormonism may be blunting its missionary thrust. Conference talks continue to emphasize the importance of missionary activity and young Latter-day Saint men and, increasingly, young Latter-day Saint women are still encouraged to accept missionary calls.

Part Four

Mormonism in the Larger Perspective

Most of the contributions to the present volume have been specific studies focusing on an incident, institution, or belief within Mormon history. While their significance may be large, they are typical of what historians do within the dimensions of a single article or chapter. Three of our scholars have chosen to position themselves somewhat differently, taking a comparative, philosophical, or bibliographical view.

D. Michael Quinn, professor of history at Brigham Young University, offers a comparison with one tradition of Christian belief in "Socioreligious Radicalism of the Mormon Church: A Parallel to the Anabaptists." Like all such comparisons, this one discloses both differences and similarities, but many readers, we suspect, will be surprised at the number of parallels between Mormonism and this strain of sixteenth-century Protestantism.

From a philosophical point of view, Paul M. Edwards, director of the Temple School of the Reorganized Church of Jesus Christ of Latter Day Saints, ponders the implications for various Mormon historians of their concept of man and God in time and space. Although not strictly historical, those concepts have large implications for studying the past.

On a more mundane level, James B. Allen, chairman of Brigham Young University's Department of History, assesses the contributions of the past thirty-five years of Mormon history writing in "Since 1950: Creators and Creations of Mormon History." The breadth of historical enquiry, he points out, has grown exponentially with the number of historians dealing with Mormonism in its many social, cultural, political, and economic manifestations.

Socioreligious Radicalism of the Mormon Church: A Parallel to the Anabaptists

D. Michael Quinn

Nineteenth-century Mormonism has traditionally been interpreted as a radical religious group within the context of American social ferment of the Jacksonian period.[1] Even two revisionist interpreters of Mormon radicalism, Klaus J. Hansen and Robert Bruce Flanders, have confined their analyses of Mormon radical and revolutionary characteristics primarily to the context of the American environment, although Flanders does acknowledge, "Without knowing it, Mormons thus stood somewhat in the same radical Christian tradition as the Donatists, the Montanists, the followers of Joachim of Fiore, the Anabaptists of Muenster, and a heritage with which they were more familiar, the Massachusetts Bay Puritans."[2] Although no religious or social movement can be understood independent of its immediate environment, similarities and differences between groups widely separated can be instructive to consider.

The nineteenth-century history of the LDS Church bears resemblances to the sixteenth-century Anabaptists of the Radical Reformation that neither group would be pleased to emphasize. Analogies between the Mormons and the Anabaptists have been suggested in 1838 by anti-Mormon LaRoy Sunderland, in 1873 by Protestant clergyman Joseph Parrish Thompson, in 1953 by American intellectual historian David Brion Davis, in 1959 by graduate student Robert S. McCue, in 1968 by Anabaptist historian Cornelius Krahn, and in 1982 by Graceland College professor William E. Juhnke.[3] Yet a comparison of the Anabaptists and the Mormons runs the risk, as historian Mario S. DePillis phrased it, of obscuring "historical time and place" to the point of distortion.[4]

To begin with, it must be acknowledged that no amount of similarity or parallel can eliminate the fundamental differences between sixteenth-century Anabaptism and nineteenth-century Mormonism. The religious ethos of their respective worlds was mutually exclusive. The Anabaptists arose as the Corpus Christianorum in Europe was disintegrating but still regarded as the ideal by various religious contenders; Mormonism arose in the American religious environment in which all churches could be classed as sectarian. In sixteenth-century Europe, religious toleration was generally considered destructive to the body politic; in nineteenth-century America religious toleration was axiomatic. In effect, Anabaptism and Mormonism arose in worlds in most respects alien to each other.

A further difference is the question of definition. Because Mormonism developed from the claims of priesthood and revelatory authority by Joseph Smith Jr. (1805–1844), Mormonism has focused in the concept of a single, monolithic church, whose doctrine and practice lay claim to precedents established by the founding prophet. Anabaptism, on the contrary, was disparate in leaders, precept, and practice. Claus-Peter Clasen has identified twenty distinct sixteenth-century Anabaptist groups in the southern Holy Roman Empire alone, and concludes: "It would be misleading, therefore, to single out a certain view as the central Anabaptist view just because it is held by the Mennonites today."[5] Despite this heterogeneity within early Anabaptism, some modern historians have persisted in trying to dismiss the Kingdom of Muenster and other "aberrant groups [which] have no claim to be considered as Anabaptists."[6] Although it is possible to distinguish between typical and atypical manifestations of sixteenth-century Anabaptism, it is inaccurate to impose legitimate versus illegitimate, genuine versus aberrant classifications upon the early Anabaptists. Concerning the Anabaptists of Switzerland, Germany, Austria, and the Netherlands, James M. Stayer notes: "They are members of sects practicing baptism of believers and forming religious groups on that basis." Any other general qualities, he adds, can be assigned only "on an *a posteriori* rather than *a priori*, basis."[7]

Nevertheless, the difficulties can be exaggerated unduly. In Mormonism, with all its uniformity, there were differences as well as development across time, which means one must recognize the difference between aberrations and the normative, between the temporary and the long standing. As for Anabaptism, to say that general qualities cannot be established *a priori* is not the same as denying that there did come to be some general characteristics. With all of its diversity, there were features readily associated with this branch of the Reformation that are found only there in the sixteenth century and not, for practical purposes, in the Christianity of the other ninety-nine-plus percent of the population. We need not enter into the dispute over what was legitimate and illegitimate; in other words, we notice features within Protestant radicalism of the sixteenth century that were notably absent from Catholicism and mainstream Protestantism but which reappeared like a Phoenix rising from the ashes in nineteenth-century America.

A starting point for the analogy is the Anabaptist practice of rebaptism, or more accurately, believer's baptism as contrasted with the baptism of infants in the sixteenth-century territorial churches, both Catholic and Protestant. To the Anabaptists the baptism of infants was a sham and perversion of the gospel taught and practiced by the primitive Christian church. The first rebaptism was performed in Zurich on 21 January 1525 by Conrad Grebel. This practice, which gave the movement its name, infuriated the secular and civil leaders of the rest of Christendom because rebaptism presupposed a rejection of Catholic and Magisterial Protestant (Lutheran, Zwinglian, Calvinist) concepts of salvation, the church, and the role of Christian magistrates. Although immersion was practiced in one instance by Conrad Grebel in the Rhine River, and was also characteristic of Anabaptism among the Polish and Lithuanian Brethren, conventional baptism by sprinkling or pouring was practiced by the Anabaptists throughout central Europe.[8] The age of baptism varied. The Hutterites baptized children at the age of twelve, while the English Familists, the Paulicians, the Servetians, and the followers of Hans Hut baptized believers at the age of thirty.[9] Anabaptist leaders regarded children susceptible to spiritual instruction and responsible for religious action between the ages of five and seven, whereas the Roman Catholic Canon Law had traditionally considered a person capable of mortal sin only after the age of seven.[10]

One of the first characteristics of Mormonism that drew the attention of a German Reformed pastor in 1830 was the Mormon emphasis upon adult baptism by immersion, a practice that also distinguished the major American denomination of Baptists.[11] Like medieval Catholics, Mormons believed that accountability for religious instruction and personal action began at age eight, but as early as 1830 the Book of Mormon condemned infant baptism as an abomination. This was a direct attack on Catholicism and mainstream Protestantism, which Joseph Smith reaffirmed specifically in 1831 by announcing a revelation that eight was the proper age for baptism.[12] Furthermore, from its outset as a church organization in April 1830, Mormonism repudiated even believers' baptism at whatever age in any Catholic or Protestant church, as announced in a revelation of Joseph Smith: "Wherefore, although a man should be baptized an hundred times it availeth him nothing, for you cannot enter in at the strait gate by the law of Moses, neither by your dead works."[13] The Mormons were Anabaptists in a way peculiarly their own, as alien and hostile to nineteenth-century Christendom as were their sixteenth-century counterparts.

Believer's baptism in the sixteenth century was, however, an outward manifestation of a theology that had far-reaching socioreligious consequences. Franklin H. Littell has identified the seminal ideology of Anabaptism as an effort to bring about the restitution of the true, primitive Christian church.[14] Other historians have pointed out that the theme of restitution was common also in the mainline Magisterial Reformation and therefore should not be regarded as peculiar to the Anabaptists.[15] It very much depended on how "restitution" was understood and implemented. The Anabaptist view amounted to a rejection not only of the rest of Christendom but also of the society which comprehended it. Permeating Anabaptist thought was the doctrine of the irreconcilable worlds of Satan and of God, which the Anabaptists transformed into a dichotomous world view. The choice was simple; it was either acknowledged compromise with sin or a radical rejection of Satan's realm.[16] Despite variation in method and manifestation, Anabaptism represented a radical rejection of the rest of Christianity.

Mormonism began as Joseph Smith's plea for forgiveness of personal sins and became a quest for divine, direct authority.[17] Claiming to have seen God and Jesus in 1820 and to have had communion with angels intermittently thereafter, Joseph Smith proclaimed himself as a prophet in no less a sense than Moses. Although still affirming the religious sanctity of the Bible, Smith introduced the Book of Mormon in 1830 as new scripture, and also began dictating and publishing new revelations that had ultimate religious authority for his adherents. Smith's revelations dealt with theology, ecclesiology, eschatology, economics, politics, and social relations.[18]

As Joseph Smith progressively unfolded the "Restoration of the Gospel" through public discourse and private instruction, he increasingly narrowed the correspondence between contemporary society and God's will for the Latter-day Saints. The revelations of God, both ancient and modern, had primacy for the Mormons over any customs, laws, and practices of a world they perceived within a dichotomy as radical as that of the Anabaptists. Like early Anabaptism, nineteenth-century Mormonism sought to reject or restructure characteristics of both religion and society that did not conform with ancient and modern revelation.[19]

Religiously and ecclesiastically, the Anabaptists saw themselves as isolated from the rest of Christendom. Rejecting the territorial church, they established the concept of the gathered church of believers withdrawn from the world. The withdrawal was at times physical as well as ideological, and some Anabaptists sought to establish strongholds in such places as Muenster and in Moravia. The resulting exclusiveness of voluntary Anabaptism in contrast to the encompassing religious community of Catholicism and mainstream Protestantism is consonant with Ernst Troeltsch's famous distinction between sect and church.[20] The Anabaptists reinforced the sense of exclusiveness by their frequent practice of holding secret night meetings.[21] Although required in large measure by persecution, the clandestine nature of Anabaptism only intensified opposition.

In nineteenth-century Mormonism, exclusiveness and separation were even more characteristic than among the Anabaptists. Driven by persecution or disaffection westward from New York, the Mormons established refuges of gathering respectively in Kirtland, Ohio (1831–37), Far West, Missouri (1838–39), Nauvoo, Illinois (1839–46), Winter Quarters, Nebraska (1846–47), and Salt Lake City, Utah (1847–1900). Although thousands of Mormons lived in scattered branches of the church throughout the world during the nineteenth century, they were urged to "flee Babylon" and settle in the areas of Mormon gathering. In Utah, the church established the Perpetual

Emigrating Fund to enable the Saints to make the journey to Zion in the mountains of the west.[22]

Equally prominent in Mormonism was secrecy. An 1830 observer noted that some Mormon activities were closed to non-Mormons.[23] Soon the congregation meetings were opened to the general public, but secret leadership meetings continued to be held. In 1844 Mormon leader Sidney Rigdon explained:

> The time has now come to tell why we held secret meetings. We were maturing plans fourteen years ago which we can now tell. Were we maturing plans to corrupt the world, to destroy the peace of society? No. Let fourteen years' experience of the Church tell the story. The Church never would have been here if we had not done as we did in secret. . . . Do not be astonished, then, if we even yet have secret meetings, asking God for things for your benefit.[24]

At Nauvoo, Joseph Smith institutionalized both exclusiveness and secrecy as permanent characteristics of Mormonism in the establishment of temple rituals and ordinances that were available only to the initiated, and by secretly introducing polygamy among his trusted adherents. Administratively, the presiding councils of the LDS Church and the parapolitical Council of Fifty met in absolute secrecy. Later even the members of the Schools of the Prophets (meetings of adult males for purpose of instruction and planning of economic strategy) were enjoined not to speak of the discussions outside the schools.[25] This heritage was reflected in the "Mormon Motto," often publicly proclaimed by church leader Joseph F. Smith (1838–1918): "Mind your own business."[26]

To reinforce their separatism and exclusiveness, the Anabaptists practiced discipline over their adherents even more rigorous than that of Calvinists and other mainline Christian churches. Of this Robert Friedmann has noted, "The Anabaptist church is also a 'church of order' in which the body determines the pattern of life for its members. In this it is radically different from the great established churches of the Reformation which always comprise both 'saints and sinners.' "[27] The means by which most Anabaptist groups exercised discipline was through the ban (excommunication). Menno Simons, for example, prescribed excommunication for persons living openly in sin, for those who caused divisions within the brethren, and for those teaching false doctrine. Some Anabaptist groups also extended the ban to include social and familial ostracism.[28] One group, the residents of the short-lived Kingdom of Muenster, used a far harsher form of discipline: summary execution by decapitation for persons guilty of adultery, profanity, perjury, and a host of other capital offenses.[29] Such discipline among the Anabaptists made their separatism more pronounced and radical.

Strict discipline was central to Mormonism even before Joseph Smith had organized the church. In the Book of Mormon, there were references to the names of persons being blotted out from the church for misconduct.[30] During the first four decades of the church, such discipline was especially common, and Mormons were excommunicated for such things as attending non-Mormon dances, failing to go on proselyting missions when assigned, using tobacco and intoxicating beverages, failure to pay tithing, gossiping, persistent swearing and Sabbath-breaking, patronizing non-Mormon businesses that competed with church-owned businesses, failure to follow the counsel of presiding authorities, and for the more serious crimes of theft, adultery, and murder.[31] During the periods when excommunication was used most broadly, rebaptism into the church upon confession of sins was readily attainable. During the 1840s and 1850s, however, some Mormon leaders preached that for grievous sins of apostasy, adultery, and murder, the sinner ought to suffer "blood atonement," in which the person's throat should be slit.[32] There is no evidence that this ideology was ever put into practice as a policy of church discipline, but the mere threat was sufficient to antagonize people within and without Mormonism.

Theologically, the sixteenth-century Anabaptists were regarded, often unjustly, as the worst of heretics by both the Catholics and mainline Protestants. Their belief in believer's baptism was used as grounds for employing capital punishment against them on the basis of the Justinian Code's strictures against the ancient Donatists.[33] The widespread Anabaptist affirmation of the freedom of will and the responsibility of man for the ordering of his life subjected them to the charge of the Pelagian heresy. Less representative beliefs, doctrines such as psychopannychism (death of the soul at physical death), and alterations of orthodox positions on the trinity and incarnation, could easily, although unfairly, make all Anabaptists suspect through guilt by association.[34] Catholics and Protestants felt theologically justified in suppressing Anabaptist heresy.

The theology of nineteenth-century Mormonism contained elements of heterodoxy that horrified orthodox Christians. Radical inspirationism, the claim that God had again chosen living prophets whose revelations had the force of scripture, seemed to open a Pandora's box. Official theology developed by Joseph Smith from 1830 to 1844 included a trinity comprised of three separate gods, two of whom had bodies of flesh and bone; creation of the world *nihil ex nihilo*; the rejection of the heaven-hell dichotomy of judgment and its replacement by a graded order of reward in which even adulterers and murderers would receive an eternal kingdom, albeit in the lower realms, of God's glory; and the assertion that men had within them the potential of godhood and might eventually become gods.[35]

As shocking as Mormon theology was to many orthodox Christians, it might have given Christian theologians an experience of déja vu. Aside from biblical texts that could be cited to support Mormon heterodoxy, many Mormon teachings were echoes of views expressed by ancient Greek philosophers, such classic Christian heresies as the Pelagians and Manicheans and late medieval dissenters. The King Follett sermon about God is reminiscent of a sermon by medieval mystic Meister Eckhart.[36] But Mormonism went medieval mystical theology one better by asserting not only that humans might ascend to God but that God the Father was once mortal and then became divine. Yet the Mormon maxim of "exaltation" (apotheosis) is "As man is, God once was; as God is, man may become." It is almost a restatement of the fourth-century Athanasian formula of the incarnation: "He was God, and then became man, and that to make us gods."[37] Far less within the tradition of Christianity was the speculative theology engaged in by Mormon leaders for two decades after Smith's death, in which they mused on such topics as the possibility of Adam being both God and the literal father of Jesus Christ, of the incarnation having occurred through a process of natural generation, and of Christ having sired children by one or more wives.[38] Even without such aberrations, which have not become central or normative in orthodox Mormonism, Christians of the nineteenth century regarded Mormonism as a dangerous heresy.[39]

Although Anabaptism was a religious movement, to sixteenth-century society the Anabaptists represented a social threat, perhaps most prominently with respect to government. Believing in a radical application of the doctrine of two worlds, most Anabaptist groups refused to participate in government, which by their definition exercised the sword (coercion) in the realm of Satan.[40] This refusal generally applied to any of the acts of citizenship, including the payment of taxes, holding of office, and participation in night watch. Within this context there were variations such as the Waterlanders and the followers of Pilgram Marpeck, who believed that Christians could participate in government, and the Hutterite communities which had a theocratic hierarchy of leaders over 1000, 100, 50, and 10.[41] The most notable departure from the general Anabaptist position concerning government occurred in the Kingdom of Muenster, where Jan of Leyden was anointed king of the whole earth and "king of the people of God in the New Temple; and . . . ruler of the New Zion."[42] However different the various Anabaptist groups were, their positions constituted either a reorientation or rejection of government.

Nineteenth-century Mormons regarded all secular government as a corrupt counterfeit of the order designed by God. More akin to Anabaptists like the Waterlanders and Pilgramites, the Latter-day Saints believed that they could with Christian conscience participate in government, and Joseph Smith publicly proclaimed LDS belief in support of all governments the Mormons might be subject to.[43] Nevertheless, as early as 1833, the official position was that whenever secular law failed to correspond to divine law, obedience to the latter superseded the former.[44] This distinction formed the basis for nineteenth-century Mormon civil disobedience, particularly with reference to laws against polygamy. Furthermore, the Mormons established a theocratic rule by the hierarchy of the church, which found presidents of the church serving as mayors, territorial governors, and candidates for the U.S. presidency, and other high ecclesiasts serving in municipal, county, territorial, and state legislative and judicial positions.[45] In March 1844, Joseph Smith organized a secret Council of Fifty to direct the political role of the LDS Kingdom of God, and by that body Smith and his two successors were secretly anointed "King Priest and Ruler over Israel on the Earth—over Zion & the Kingdom of Christ our King of Kings."[46] Mormon leaders not only ruled secular government in nineteenth-century Nauvoo, Illinois, and the Great Basin of the West, but they eagerly awaited the time when that rule would become absolute and independent of any secular authority. These characteristics of Mormonism, though within the law in almost every respect, caused secular leaders throughout the United States and the world to fear the establishment of a Mormon *imperium in imperio*.

Inseparable from the attitude of the Anabaptists toward government was their position regarding warfare. Most Anabaptists rejected the use of force and participation in warfare. Nevertheless, a few disparate Anabaptist groups did resort to force of arms, either in defense or in aggression. In Erfurt, Fulda, Waldshut, Hallau, Muenster, and the Netherlands, Anabaptists engaged in warfare with their secular and religious adversaries.[47] Moreover, common criminals such as Hans Krug in Thuringia and the Batenburgers in the Netherlands used their Anabaptist affiliation as a pretext for robbery, pillage, rape, and murder.[48]

Although nineteenth-century Mormonism was unified in a manner never characteristic of the Anabaptists, its position toward participating in warfare was ambivalent. For Mormons their prophet, commander-in-chief of the armies of modern Israel, would decide whether the Latter-day Saints would engage in any specific warfare. At times they suffered mobbings, expulsions, and even death pacifistically; at other times, the Mormons individually or in organized armies took up weapons in defense of home and kingdom. The will of the Lord as revealed through the prophet in given circumstances decided the issue. The Mormons engaged in virtual civil war with the anti-Mormon state militia in Missouri in 1838; pacifistically withdrew en masse from their capital, Nauvoo, in 1846, to flee from their enemies into the wilderness; formed a military battalion to aid the U.S. in the Mexican War; used all military means short of bloodshed to ward off a federal regiment invading Utah in 1857–58, only to prepare another pacifistic withdrawal into the wilderness when a scorched-earth policy failed; remained essentially neutral during the American Civil War; and enthusiastically engaged in the military activities of the Spanish-American War of 1898. I have called this a policy of "selective pacifism."[49]

Although not as widespread among the Anabaptist groups as the rejection of government and warfare, a rejection or modification of private property also characterized large segments of the Anabaptists. Peter J. Klassen has noted, "Common to Anabaptism, whether among the Swiss Brethren, the Dutch and South German Anabaptists, or the Hutterites, was the firm conviction that the church was composed of committed disciples who were united in a bond of love. In this relationship there could, in the strictest sense, be no individualism. . . . In this concept, where the welfare of others was always a compelling motive and concern, the Anabaptists were united."[50] This economic orientation manifested itself along various points between two poles. The "overwhelming majority" of Anabaptists maintained the concept and practice of private property while sharing generously of their means to aid less fortunate brethren. The Anabaptists of the Kingdom of Muenster practiced by compulsion total communism.[51] The Hutterites of Moravia established a thoroughly communitarian, voluntary society. The following prebaptism question was first asked by the Swiss Brethren: "Whether they would consecrate themselves with all their temporal possessions to the service of God and his people."[52]

Among the Mormons of the nineteenth century the communitarian impulse was ever present, but only intermittently active. In 1831, Joseph Smith revealed the basic outlines of the Law of Consecration and Stewardship, according to which all persons were to regard themselves as only stewards of any property they might acquire. Although private property and enterprise was the dominant practice among the Mormons of the nineteenth century, it was interspaced with communitarian practice. In the early 1830s efforts to implement the Order of Enoch in Missouri failed, but in 1838 it was reinstituted there. After brief success the communitarian society in Missouri was destroyed by mob action and expulsion from the state, and during the next thirty-five years the presence of Mormon communitarianism was kept alive by the practice of tithing and by the way church leaders periodically put faithful Mormons under covenant to consecrate their time, talents, and all their possessions for the building of the

Kingdom of God, by the organization of boycotts of non-Mormon merchants, and by urging the exclusive use of Mormon-produced goods. In 1869 Brigham Young instituted a "Cooperative Movement," in which Mormons of a community established firms for the production and merchandising of produce and goods. Some of these Mormon cooperatives were so successful as to provide 80 percent of the needs of the community. After this success and in the wake of a national depression, Brigham Young inaugurated the United Orders in 1874 to restore communitarian living and consecration of all property by those joining the orders. The conduct of the orders varied from community to community. One of the most successful, at Orderville, Utah, was the Mormon counterpart of the Hutterite communities in Moravia, with communal eating halls, identical clothing for members of the order, and identical shanties for homes. By the mid-1880s the communitarian practice of Mormonism had died, primarily a victim of the economic attack on the LDS Church by the federal government. The ideal is still expressed from time to time and had some influence on the Welfare Plan instituted in the 1930s.[53]

Within Anabaptism there was a reorientation of marriage by certain groups. The Hutterites of Moravia put their children in communal schools in order to weaken familial ties and anticommunitarian loyalties. Among other Anabaptists, the conjugal relation was strengthened by a reordering of the concept of marriage. George H. Williams has noted an emphasis of the status of wives. The religious significance of marriage was heightened by the Thuringian Anabaptists, who regarded marriage "as an eternal spiritual estate," and also by the erratic Anabaptist Nicholas Frey of Strasbourg, who defended spiritual marriage as the highest covenant of the church.[54] The most extreme departure from society's marriage norms was the practice of polygamy by Nicholas Frey, David Joris and the Batenburgers, Jan of Leyden and the Muensterites, and some Polish Anabaptists.[55]

Within Mormonism there was also a reordering of the concept and practice of marriage. Even prior to the organization of the church, the Book of Mormon had introduced the possibility of a restoration of polygamy by God among his people.[56] In 1835, an editorial in a Mormon periodical suggested that "we may prepare ourselves for a kingdom of glory; become archangels, even the sons of God where man is neither without the woman, nor the woman without the man in the Lord."[57] Soon thereafter, Joseph Smith introduced the practice of spiritual or eternal marriage, as well as polygamy, among the Mormons under the designation "Celestial Marriage" or "Marriage for Time and All Eternity."[58] Mormonism's Old Testament biblicism and emphasis on literal restorationism, as in the Kingdom of Muenster, predisposed the movement toward such developments within the family. Cornelius Krahn observes:

> In appraising the appearance of polygamy among the Muensterite Anabaptists, one must not lose sight of the Old Testament orientation of the leaders. The male member of the community was not only expected to give protection to the weaker sex, but through him the female member found access to the spiritual blessings of the Lord. . . . Developing this thought, the Muensterites, and later the Latter Day Saints, came to the conclusion that every woman must be attached to a man in order to be saved, just as a man is subject to Christ.[59]

Both the Muensterites and the Mormons believed that polygamy was as sacred as monogamous marriage; each prescribed severe penalties for adultery and other moral infractions.[60] Even after the Mormons established themselves securely in the mountain west of America, polygamy was a minority practice, involving perhaps 25 percent of the total population at its highest incidence.[61] Although polygamy was both a manifestation and an outlet for Mormon elitism, the practice of marriage for time and eternity to at least one wife was universal among faithful Latter-day Saints.

Virtually all the Anabaptist groups anticipated the imminent end of the world. Hans Hut predicted the end would come in 1528, whereas Melchior Hoffman and other Anabaptists chose different dates. Believing that they would live to see the events of the world's end, Anabaptists felt impelled to carry on the work of socioreligious reorientation with urgent dispatch.[62] In connection with this chiliasm, several Anabaptist groups developed an attitude described by James M. Stayer as "eschatological revenge." At its most unobtrusive this involved the expectation that when Christ returned he would wreak vengeance and death upon those who persecuted the faithful. More radical was the anticipation that the faithful (the Anabaptists) would be the ones to destroy the godless at the coming of Christ, and among some Anabaptists eschatological revenge was translated into the revolutionary view that since the end was so near they could begin the work of destruction now. This radical chiliasm was largely responsible for the isolated outbreaks of Anabaptist violence that occurred in Muenster, the Netherlands, and throughout the Holy Roman Empire.[63]

Chiliasm was also a dominant characteristic of those calling themselves the Latter-day Saints. Although continually affirming that the time of the coming of Christ and the end of the world is "near, even at the door," Mormon leaders have been wary of precise predictions. Joseph Smith came closest to naming a specific time when he drew attention to the year 1891 as having eschatological significance, but that was regarded by himself and his followers only as a possibility about which they adopted a wait-and-see policy. The year 1891 came and went among the Mormons without the wrenching syndrome of anticipation, unfulfilled prophecy, and resultant religious confusion described by Leon Festinger.[64] Nevertheless, chiliasm influenced the thinking of Mormons in all phases of their socioreligious lives.

That eschatological revenge was a dominant theme of nineteenth-century Mormonism is clearly demonstrated in such hymns as "Hope of Israel," "Praise to the Man," and "Up, Awake, Ye Defenders of Zion."[65] Like the Anabaptists, the Mormons endured persecution with the anticipation that destructive justice would be meted out by God upon their oppressors.[66] Occasionally church leaders of the nineteenth century mused upon the more radical possibility that the Latter-day Saints themselves might be the instruments of that eschatological revenge:

> President Young remarked that that was a vary nice point to distinguish between innocent Blood & that which is not innocent. Were we now Commanded to go & avenge the Blood of the prophets whare it wood reach infants from the Cradle to the third & forth generation would they know what to do in such a case? They would not. But there is one thing that is a consolation to me And that is I am satisfied that the Lord will not require it of this people untill they become sanctifyed & are led by the spirit of God so as not to shed innocent Blood.[67]

Some Mormons at Mountain Meadows, Utah, in September 1857, took upon themselves the revolutionary role of executing that vengeance upon their supposed enemies. That massacre of an emigrant train appalled Brigham Young, yet upon visiting the site of the massacre in 1861 and seeing the words of Romans 12:19 inscribed upon a marker, Young grimly remarked: "It should be Vengence is mine and I have taken a little."[68]

Although sixteenth-century observers commented on the piety, discipline, and Christian virtues of the Anabaptists, both Catholic and Protestant governments subjected the Anabaptists throughout Europe to unrelenting persecution. Anabaptists were expelled from cities and their property was confiscated, they were tortured for confessions, and many were disfigured by branding or having their tongues bored. Still others paid the maximum penalty of execution by decapitation, burning, strangulation, starvation, or drowning. Clasen has verified 835 executions in the southern Holy Roman Empire, but the actual number of Anabaptist executions throughout sixteenth-century Europe may have numbered several thousand.[69] Ultimately, as Anabaptists such as Menno Simons repudiated the most revolutionary Anabaptist manifestations, persecution waned. The extent to which they were harassed, let alone, or allowed to participate freely in society varied from country to country.

Compared to the persecutions of the Anabaptists (and certainly to the holocaust suffered by generations of early Christians and modern Jews), the persecution of nineteenth-century Mormons must remain barely a footnote in religious martyrology. Nevertheless, in the context of a society characterized by religious pluralism and toleration, the history of the Mormons is noteworthy. For varying reasons American society could tolerate or ignore the religious excesses of the Second Great Awakening, or even of a group as morally shocking to Victorian sensibilities as the Oneida Community. But America could not tolerate nineteenth-century Mormonism, a burgeoning society that appeared the antithesis of everything American. As Klaus Hansen observed, "Mormonism, from a cultural and ideological perspective, may well have been for nineteenth century Americans what communism became in the twentieth century."[70] Within fourteen years Mormons controlled a metropolis, and within twenty more years had established a political, economic, and social hegemony of a large portion of the American West.

During the first few years of Mormon history, persecution came in the form of scattered mobs, frequently led by ministers, who sought to plunder and terrorize Mormon missionaries and members for teaching and believing that which was regarded as heresy. In 1833, 1836, and 1838, Mormon communities in Missouri were expelled and plundered for reasons that were more social and economic than theological. As Mormons engaged in battle with the anti-Mormon mobs and state militia, nineteen Mormon men and boys were murdered at the Haun's Mill Massacre in Missouri in 1838. To resolve the conflict, which had transcended matters of faith, the governor of Missouri ordered that Mormons be expelled or exterminated. After an uneasy but extraordinarily important sojourn in Nauvoo, Illinois, during which time a radical transformation of Mormon theology, politics, and marriage was effected, Joseph Smith and his brother were murdered on 27 June 1844. Two years later the main body of Mormons left Nauvoo early in 1846 under threat of mob action; anti-Mormon mobs and militia lay seige to the nearly deserted city during the summer to drive out the remaining Mormons.[71]

Once the Mormons had established themselves in the Great Basin, the U.S. government itself sought to reverse their radical trend. A regiment of federal troops was sent to subjugate alleged Mormon rebellion in 1857–58, and troops returned in 1862 to keep the Mormons under surveillance. Ostensibly to coerce conformity to federal legislation against polygamy, but more precisely to destroy Mormon socioeconomic hegemony, the entire weight of the executive, legislative, and judicial branches of U.S. government was hurled against the authoritarian walls of the new Kingdom of God. The Mormon hegemony fell by attrition: the church was disincorporated by federal law in 1862, its judicial control of Utah Territory dismantled in 1872, its polygamous hierarchy subjected to disfranchisement and imprisonment in 1882, its financial assets confiscated in 1887, its members denied immigration and naturalization in 1889, and its entire membership threatened with unilateral disfranchisement in 1890. In September 1890, church president Wilford Woodruff bowed to federal authority by urging obedience to laws respecting polygamy. The social, economic, and political life of the Mormons began to mirror that of the rest of American society.[72] Predictably, the Mormons perceived their own group experience as a series of persecutions.

Since he owned a copy of Mosheim's *Ecclesiastical History*,[73] Joseph Smith could have had a textbook knowledge of the Anabaptists, but there is no indication that such awareness influenced the rise of Mormonism. Nor does a comparison of Anabaptism and Mormonism exhaust the comparative possibilities of either group. Analogies between the sixteenth-century Anabaptists and the nineteenth-century Campbellites and between the nineteenth-century Mormons and the second-century Montanists have been suggested elsewhere.[74] Other comparisons can also be illuminating. What the present essay does demonstrate is the many parallels between Anabaptism and Mormonism. Widely separated in time, they had deep structural affinities.

This essay stresses the radical kinship shared by two seemingly disparate religious groups that emphasized biblicism, chiliasm, and restorationism within a social context. Mormonism and Anabaptism are qualitatively, rather than causally, related as counterculture religious groups that sought to radicalize religion and society by reaffirming rejected practices of the past and by rejecting sacrosanct assumptions of the present. The fundamental relatedness of the two groups is perhaps best indicated by Cornelius Krahn's summary of sixteenth-century Anabaptism that, with a simple substitution of terms, can be applied verbatim to nineteenth-century Mormonism:

> It has become apparent that early Anabaptism was truly most radical in its break with the religious, social, economic, and political aspects of Christendom and the society of that time. It was even more than that. It made the most earnest effort to restore the potential of Christendom and its message in the world. A strong eschatological eagerness and missionary zeal characterized the movement. Dutch Anabaptism had its origin predominantly among the lower classes which responded uncompromisingly to the newly discovered Gospel. Ultimately, however, piety and industry led to respectability and prosperity which gradually dimmed the early vision and led to conformity with the environment.[75]

Obviously, in large terms the historical evolution of Anabaptists and Mormons has been similar.

The modern descendants of the Anabaptist groups and the present Latter-day Saints are viewed by themselves and by their contemporaries as anything but radical. There appears to be no discomfort with this among the Mennonites and Hutterites, but among some Mormons there is a subtle, if not explicit, longing for the radical past. Nineteenth-century Mormonism could not be lauded with the same enthusiasm as contemporary Mormonism is by the *Reader's Digest*, Norman Vincent Peale, and presidents of the United States. The differences are, in fact, so great that historian Klaus Hansen has asked if the Latter-day Saints have ceased to be Mormons.[76]

The Mormon and Anabaptist roads to social conservatism and acceptance have been quite different, however. Anabaptist groups, lacking a single authority structure, could disavow (as Menno Simons did in the sixteenth century) the Kingdom of Muenster and ultimately any characteristic that was considered too socially radical or revolutionary. Modern Anabaptists can thus see themselves as legitimate descendants of sixteenth-century Evangelical Anabaptism (to adopt George H. William's typology), and likewise repudiate the Revolutionary Anabaptists of Muenster and such Revolutionary Spiritualists as Thomas Muentzer, who played a prominent role in the Peasants' Revolt of 1525. For contemporary Mormons, however, it is not possible to dissociate themselves from their radical past. Although Mormonism had both evangelical and bourgeois characteristics throughout its nineteenth-century history, Joseph Smith instituted socioreligious radicalism on a pervasive scale. Subsequent Mormon leaders have relaxed or suspended many of these characteristics, but at the beginning radicalism was inextricably a part of the Mormon system of revelation, restoration, and authority. In this respect, Mormonism can never be less than a dormant socioreligious radicalism. Only time will tell whether the continued permeation of middle-class values within Mormonism will turn that dormancy into atrophy.

NOTES

1. See, for example, Alice Felt Tyler's treatment of Mormonism in *Freedom's Ferment: Phases of American Social History from the Colonial Period to the Outbreak of the Civil War* (Minneapolis, 1944).

2. Robert Bruce Flanders, "To Transform History: Early Mormon Culture and the Concept of Time and Space," *Church History* 40 (March 1971): 111; see also Klaus J. Hansen, "Mormonism and American Culture: Some Tentative Hypotheses," and Robert Bruce Flanders, "Dream and Nightmare: Nauvoo Revisited," in *Restoration Movement: Essays in Mormon His-*

tory, ed. F. Mark McKiernan, Alma R. Blair, and Paul M. Edwards (Lawrence, Kan., 1973), 10–11, 18–21, 149, 156, 165.

3. LaRoy Sunderland, *Mormonism Exposed and Refuted* (New York, 1838), 11; Joseph Parrish Thompson, *Church and State in the United States* (Boston, 1873), 138–39; David Brion Davis, "The New England Origins of Mormonism," *New England Quarterly* 26 (June 1953): 148–49, 156, 157, 165; Robert J. McCue, "Similarities and Differences in the Anabaptist Restitution and the Mormon Restoration" (M.A. thesis, Brigham Young University, 1959); Cornelius Krahn, *Dutch Anabaptism: Origin, Spread, Life and Thought (1450–1600)* (The Hague, 1968), 144; and William E. Juhnke, "Anabaptism and Mormonism: A Study in Comparative History," *John Whitmer Historical Association Journal* 2 (1982): 38–46.

4. Mario S. DePillis, "The Quest for Religious Authority and the Rise of Mormonism," *Dialogue: A Journal of Mormon Thought* 1 (Spring 1966): 83–84. The present essay was written with clear awareness of David Hackett Fischer's warnings about false analogy in *Historians' Fallacies: Toward a Logic of Historical Thought* (New York, 1970), 243–59.

5. Claus-Peter Clasen, *Anabaptism, A Social History, 1525–1618* (Ithaca, N.Y., 1972), xvii, 32. For similar evaluations of early Anabaptist divergence, see also Hans J. Hillerbrand, "Anabaptism and History," *Mennonite Quarterly Review* 45 (Spring 1971): 108; George H. Williams, *The Radical Reformation* (Philadelphia, 1962), passim, 853–54.

6. William Klassen, "The Relation of the Old and New Covenants in Pilgram Marpeck's Theology," *Mennonite Quarterly Review* 60 (January 1966): 99–100; for a similar view see Harold S. Bender, "The Anabaptist Vision," *Mennonite Quarterly Review* 18 (Spring 1944): 72–73.

7. James M. Stayer, *Anabaptists and the Sword* (Lawrence, Kan., 1972), 20. The complexity of Anabaptist origin has been emphasized in Stayer et al., "From Monogenesis to Polygenesis: The Historical Discussion of Anabaptist Origins," *Mennonite Quarterly Review* 49 (April 1975): 83–121.

8. Williams, *The Radical Reformation*, xxiv, 117, 649; William Echard Keeney, *The Development of Dutch Anabaptist Thought and Practice from 1539–1564* (Nieuwkoop, 1968), 83.

9. Clasen, *Anabaptism*, 278; Williams, *The Radical Reformation*, 788; Rollin Stely Armour, *Anabaptist Baptism: A Representative Study* (Scottdale, Pa., 1966), 95.

10. Hillel Schwartz, "Early Anabaptist Ideas About the Nature of Children," *Mennonite Quarterly Review* 47 (April 1973): 107; *New Catholic Encyclopedia*, 15 vols. (New York, 1967), 1:197.

11. D. Michael Quinn, "The First Months of Mormonism: A Contemporary View By Rev. Diedrich Willers," *New York History* 54 (July 1973): 331.

12. Moroni 8:19–22; Doctrine and Covenants (hereafter cited as D&C) 68:25.

13. D&C 22:2. The Mormons, however, surpassed the Anabaptists in the practice of rebaptism by baptizing living Mormons on behalf of deceased persons, and performing rebaptisms of Mormons for reinstatement to the church following excommunication, for the commission of serious sins, for restoration of health, for preparation to receive ordinances of the Mormon temples, for entering into the communitarian United Order of Enoch, and for the generalized purpose of "renewing the covenants" or original LDS baptism. Examples: Journal of Oliver Olney, 29 July 1842, Western Americana, Beinecke Rare Book and Manuscript Library, Yale University, New Haven, Conn.; Journal of Willard Richards, 27 April 1843, 22 May 1844, Archives Division, Historical Department of The Church of Jesus Christ of Latter-day Saints, Salt Lake City, Utah, hereafter cited as LDS Church Archives; *Journal of Discourses*, 26 vols. (Liverpool, England, 1854–1886), 1:324, 2:9, 18:160. See D. Michael Quinn, "The Practice of Rebaptism at Nauvoo," *BYU Studies* 18 (Winter 1978): 226–32.

14. Franklin H. Littell, "The Anabaptist Doctrine of the Restitution of the True Church," *Mennonite Quarterly Review* 24 (January 1950): 33–52.

15. Hillerbrand, "Anabaptism and History," 112–88; John H. Yoder, "The Hermeneutics of the Anabaptists," *Mennonite Quarterly Review* 41 (October 1967): 295.

16. Robert Friedmann, "The Essence of Anabaptist Faith: An Essay in Interpretation," *Mennonite Quarterly Review* 41 (January 1967): 9–10.

17. DePillis, "Quest for Religious Authority," 68–88; D. Michael Quinn, "From Sacred Grove to Sacral Power Structure," *Dialogue: A Journal of Mormon Thought* 17 (Summer 1984): 10–13; Richard L. Bushman, *Joseph Smith and the Beginnings of Mormonism* (Urbana, Ill., 1984), 56–61.

18. D&C, passim.

19. Hansen, "Mormonism and American Culture," 1–25; Lawrence Foster, *Religion and Sexuality: Three American Communal Experiments of the Nineteenth Century* (Oxford, 1981), 1–17, 125–39; Jan Shipps, *Mormonism: The Story of a New Religious Tradition* (Urbana, Ill., 1985).

20. Ernst Troeltsch, *The Social Teaching of the Christian Churches*, trans. Olive Wyon, 2 vols. (New York, 1930), 1:331–49. But see the revisionist view of Anabaptist origins in Hans-Jurgen Goertz, ed., *Umstrittenes Taufertum, 1525–1975* (Gottingen, 1975).

21. Clasen, *Anabaptism*, 73–75.

22. William Mulder, *Homeward to Zion: The Mormon Immigration from Scandinavia* (Minneapolis, 1957), 137ff, 142–45; Leonard J. Arrington and Davis Bitton, *The Mormon Experience: A History of the Latter-day Saints* (New York, 1979), xvii, 95–144.

23. Quinn, "First Months of Mormonism," 327.

24. B. H. Roberts, ed., *History of the Church of Jesus Christ of Latter-day Saints*, 7 vols., 2nd ed. (Salt Lake City, 1971), 6:290–91.

25. Examples: Klaus J. Hansen, *Quest for Empire: The Political Kingdom of God and the Council of Fifty in Mormon History* (East Lansing, Mich., 1967), 64; Minutes of the Salt Lake School of the Prophets, passim, LDS Church Archives; D. Michael Quinn, "Latter-day Saint Prayer Circles," *BYU Studies* 19 (Fall 1978): 79–105; Quinn, "The Council of Fifty and Its Members, 1844 to 1945," *BYU Studies* 20 (Winter 1980): 163–97; Andrew F. Ehat, "Joseph Smith's Introduction of Temple Ordinances and the 1844 Succession Question" (M.A. thesis, Brigham Young University, 1982).

26. *Proceedings Before the Committee on Privileges and Elections of the United States Senate In the Matter of the Protest Against the Right of Hon. Reed Smoot, A Senator from the State of Utah, to Hold His Seat*, 4 vols. (Washington, D.C., 1904–1907), 1:149.

27. Friedman, "The Essence," 13.

28. Keeney, *Development of Dutch Anabaptism*, 168; Frank C. Peters, "The Ban in the Writings of Menno Simons," *Mennonite Quarterly Review* 29 (January 1955): 20.

29. John Horsch, "The Rise and Fall of the Anabaptists of Muenster," *Mennonite Quarterly Review* 9 (April 1935): 133–34.

30. Alma 6:3.

31. Examples: *Journal of Discourses*, 6:196, 10:283, 285, 11:8, 22:311. A more recent perspective is Lester E. Bush Jr., "Excommunication and Church Courts: A note from the General Handbook of Instructions," *Dialogue: A Journal of Mormon Thought* 14 (Summer 1981): 74–98.

32. Ibid., 3:247, 4:49–50, 53–54, 7:20; Roberts, *History of the Church*, 5:296; Ogden Kraut, *Blood Atonement* (Salt Lake City, 1981); Paul Peterson, "The Mormon Reformation" (Ph.D. diss., Brigham Young University, 1981), 60–62, 92–93, 100–101.

33. Roland H. Bainton, "The Left Wing of the Reformation," *Journal of Religion* 21 (April 1941): 127; Williams, *Radical Reformation*, 239–40.

34. Williams, *Radical Reformation*, xxvi; Steven E. Ozment, *Mysticism and Dissent: Religious Ideology and Social Protest in the Sixteenth Century* (New Haven, 1973).

35. D&C 76:42–43, 70–103; 130:21–22; 132:19–20; Roberts, *History of the Church*, 6:308. The "unorthodoxy" of Mormon theology can be easily documented from Bruce R. McConkie, *Mormon Doctrine* (Salt Lake City, 1958); Sterling M. McMurrin, *The Theological Foundations of Mormonism* (Salt Lake City, 1965), 33–35, 66–67.

36. *Meister Eckhart, A Modern Translation*, trans. Bernard Blakney (New York, 1941), Sermon 28, "Blessed Are the Poor," 228–32.

37. "Four Discourses of S. Athanasius, Archbishop of Alexandria, Against the Arians," Discourse I, Chapter XI, Section 39, Paragraph 3, in *A Library of Fathers of the Holy Catholic Church*, Vol. 8 (Oxford, 1842). The most unorthodox expressions about God in the King Follett sermon were specifically attacked by Athanasius in the same discourse: Chapter VI, Section

21, Paragraph and Chapter V, Section 14, Paragraph 7. See also Athanasius, "On the Incarnation of the Word of God," Chapter 54, Paragraph 3, in *A Select Library of Nicene and Post-Nicene Fathers, Second Series*, 14 vols. (New York, 1890–1900) 4:65; also Stephen E. Ozment, "Luther and the Late Middle Ages: The Formation of Reformation Thought," in Robert Kingdon, ed., *Transition and Revolution: Problems and Issues in European Renaissance History* (Minneapolis, 1973).

38. *Journal of Discourses*, 1:50–51, 2:210, 4:217, 259–60, 5:331–32, 8:115, 218, 15:825. On this complex, esoteric topic, see Culley C. Christensen, *The Adam-God Maze* (Scottsdale, Ariz., 1981); David John Buerger, "The Adam-God Doctrine," *Dialogue: A Journal of Mormon Thought* 15 (Spring 1982): 14–58.

39. O. Kendall White, Jr., "Mormonism: A Nineteenth Century Heresy," *Journal of Religious Thought* 26 (Spring–Summer 1969): 44–55.

40. For extensive discussion of this complex issue in Anabaptism, see Friedmann, "Essence of Anabaptist Faith," 9–10; and Stayer, *Anabaptists and the Sword*.

41. Stayer, *Anabaptists and the Sword*, 326; Clasen, *Anabaptism*, 179, 246.

42. Horsch, "Rise and Fall of the Anabaptists," 140; Keeney, *Development of Dutch Anabaptist Thought*, 175.

43. Roberts, *History of the Church*, 4:541.

44. D&C 98.

45. Hansen, *Quest for Empire*, passim. But see the qualifications in Quinn, "The Council of Fifty and Its Members, 1844 to 1945," 163–97.

46. Hansen, *Quest for Empire*, 66, 155–58; Quinn, "The Council of Fifty and Its Members, 1845 to 1945," 186–88.

47. Stayer, *Anabaptists and the Sword*, 106–7, 109, 190, 197, 270; John S. Oyer, "Anabaptism in Central Germany: I. The Rise and Spread of the Movement," *Mennonite Quarterly Review* 34 (October 1960): 227, 241, 242.

48. Stayer, *Anabaptists and the Sword*, 198; Oyer, "Anabaptism," 242; and Williams, *Radical Reformation*, 381–82.

49. D. Michael Quinn, "The Mormon Church and the Spanish-American War: An End to Selective Pacifism," *Pacific Historical Review* 43 (August 1974): 342–66.

50. Peter J. Klassen, *The Economics of Anabaptism, 1525–1560* (The Hague, 1964), 26.

51. Ibid., 51, 83; Krahn, *Dutch Anabaptism*, 141.

52. Bender, "Anabaptist Vision," 85; Clasen, *Anabaptism*, 194–95, 210–98; Williams, *Radical Reformation*, 229–31.

53. Leonard J. Arrington, Feramorz Y. Fox, and Dean L. May, *Building the City of God: Community and Cooperation Among the Mormons* (Salt Lake City, Utah, 1976).

54. Clasen, *Anabaptism*, 34, 270; Williams, *Radical Reformation*, pp. 287–89, 506.

55. Williams, *Radical Reformation*, 287–89, 381, 414; Horsch, "Is Dr. Keuhler's Conception of Early Dutch Anabaptism Historically Sound?" *Mennonite Quarterly Review* 7 (January 1933): 50–51; A. L. E. Verheyden, *Anabaptism in Flanders, 1530–1650: A Century of Struggle* (Scottdale, Pa., 1961), 22.

56. Jacob 2:27–30.

57. *Latter Day Saints' Messenger and Advocate* 1 (June 1835): 130.

58. Roberts, *History of the Church*, xxix–xxxiii. On the origins of polygamy see Foster, *Religion and Sexuality*, 130–46; and Linda King Newell and Valeen Tippetts Avery, *Mormon Enigma: Emma Hale Smith* (Garden City, N.Y., 1984), 64–67, 95–101, 134–80.

59. Krahn, *Dutch Anabaptism*, 144.

60. Horsch, "Rise and Fall of the Anabaptists of Muenster," 137; *Journal of Discourses*, 3:247; D&C 42:80–81.

61. Stanley S. Ivins, "Notes on Mormon Polygamy," *Utah Historical Quarterly* 35 (Fall 1967): 311.

62. Clasen, *Anabaptism*, 33; Krahn, *Dutch Anabaptism*, 130.

63. James M. Stayer, "Hans Hut's Doctrine of the Sword: An Attempted Solution," *Mennonite Quarterly Review* 39 (July 1965): 188; Stayer, *Anabaptists and the Sword*, 106–7, 109, 190, 197, 270.

64. Roberts, *History of the Church*, 2:182, 5:338–39; Diary of Marriner W. Merrill, 5 October 1890, LDS Church Archives; Richard Lloyd Anderson, "Joseph Smith and the Millenarian Timetable," *BYU Studies* 3 (1961): 55–66; and Leon Festinger, *When Prophecy Fails* (Minneapolis, 1956); Grant Underwood, "Millenarianism and the Early Mormon Mind," *Journal of Mormon History* 9 (1982): 41–51.

65. *Hymns, Church of Jesus Christ of Latter-Day Saints* (Salt Lake City, 1948), 37, 64, 147. "Hope of Israel" is militant in the tradition of "Onward, Christian Soldiers," but the theme of eschatological revenge is the conclusion of W. W. Phelps's adulation of the martyred Joseph Smith, "Praise to the Man." The fourth verse reads, in part: "Earth must atone for the blood of that man. Wake up the world for the conflict of justice." More detailed in the revenge theme is Charles W. Penrose's "Up, Awake, Ye Defenders of Zion," as shown in the following excerpted phrases: "Remember the wrongs of Missouri; forget not the fate of Nauvoo. . . . Shall we bear with oppressions forever? Shall we tamely submit to the foe, while the ties of our kindred they sever And the blood of our prophets shall flow? No! the thought sets the heart wildly beating; Our vows at each pulse we renew: Ne'er to rest till our foes are retreating. . . . We'll scatter the troops at a glance. Soon 'the Kingdom' will be independent; In wonder the nations will view the despised ones in glory resplendent."

66. The best example of both the mood and content of that hope is perhaps unintentionally revealed in Nels B. Lundwall, comp., *Fate of the Persecutors of the Prophet Joseph Smith* (Salt Lake City, 1952).

67. Scott G. Kenney, ed., *Wilford Woodruff's Journal, 1833-1898 Typescript*, 9 vols. (Midvale, Utah, 1983-85), 4:410-11 (15 March 1856).

68. Ibid., 5:577 (25 May 1861). Juanita Brooks, *The Mountain Meadows Massacre* (Norman, Okla., 1962; 1st ed., 1950).

69. Clasen, *Anabaptism*, 143, 370.

70. Klaus J. Hansen, *Mormonism and the American Experience* (Chicago, 1981), 52.

71. Arrington and Bitton, *Mormon Experience*, 44-82.

72. Gustive O. Larson, *The "Americanization" of Utah for Statehood* (San Marino, Calif., 1971); Edward Leo Lyman, "The Mormon Quest for Utah Statehood" (Ph.D. diss., University of California at Riverside, 1981).

73. In 1844 he donated one volume of Mosheim's *Ecclesiastical History* to a library. See Kenneth W. Godfrey, "A Note on the Nauvoo Library and Literary Institute," *BYU Studies* (Spring 1974): 388.

74. Richard T. Hughes, "A Comparison of the Restitution Motifs of the Campbells (1809-1830) and the Anabaptists (1524-1560)," *Mennonite Quarterly Review* 45 (October 1971): 312-30; Sermon by Reverend J. B. Eddie, reported in *Salt Lake Herald*, 1 July 1901; and Flanders, "To Transform History," 111.

75. Krahn, *Dutch Anabaptism*, 262.

76. Klaus J. Hansen, "Are We Still Mormons?" *Dialogue* 4 (Spring 1969): 101-6; "Mormonism and American Culture," 22; and his fullest exposition, *Mormonism and the American Experience*.

Time in Mormon History

PAUL M. EDWARDS

Time is an essential concept in both theological analysis and historical perception. The goal of this inquiry is to provide a brief analysis of the theological concept of time that is held by the LDS Church and to take a look, however tentatively, at how this position is reflected in the writings of Mormon historians.

Human life, as it is lived biologically and through memory, is involved in the feeling (as well as the marking) of what we consider to be time. We assert that we are within time, as we might state that we are within a river moving with the current. As well we are aware of time conceptually; looking down on it — the ever-flowing river — as something different from our own presence. For most persons then, time is the most universal of all illusions.

As well, it is an illusion that is often seen in a struggle with space. Time and space, standing in juxtapositions, are the basis for describing all aspects of our existence. And within their interrelatedness resides both the whole of the finite realm in which we live and the promise of infinity through which we hope. Yet, while time and space are bound in an unavoidable manner, they also "stand in a tension with each other which may be considered as the most fundamental tension of existence. In the human mind, this tension becomes conscious and gets historical power. Human soul and human history to a large extent are determined by the struggle between space and time.[1]

The Greeks were preoccupied with eternity in a cosmos-centered world. They were caught in the dualism of a world with divine time on one hand, and a time of men on the other. For Aristotle time was circular, all things beginning and ending with the circle of motion. For Plato it was heuristic, a tool by which the imperfect world moved through change and process toward the perfect world of absolutes. The Greeks were never able to complete a concept of linear history or to identify a philosophy of history. This was because their spatial restrictions on time—its circular motion from cosmos to birth to death to cosmos—left history no other responsibility than simply to be a narrative of a portion of the process.

On the other hand in the world of the Hebrews, history was neither cyclic nor cosmological; rather it was anthropomorphic. It was a product of the reaction between man and God. Most often it was a narrative of events which were either rewards or punishments for human action. It was linear, that is a progression, and it was proceeding toward a fulfillment. By moving from a beginning to an end, which was not in itself a new beginning, history provided redemption. This redemption brought about through an apocalypse divinely decreed to be the end of human history. The Hebrew concept of history rested on the premise that history would come to an end, for in this context history without end would be basically meaningless. Berdyaev comments that endless progress as well as endless process means that death triumphs. "It is only the resurrection of all that have lived which can impart meaning to the historical process of the world."[2] The roots of linear progress are in the Hebrew scriptures which present a view of progression. This view, while maintaining an eschatology that spells out the end of human history, was sensitive to time, which moved forward and upward, taking men and the Jewish nation toward a positive goal.

We can see some of the relationship of time to space in Amos when God brought about the destruction of space—of the nation of his origin—without bringing about his own self-destruction. Such an action reflects on God's transcendence. The God of space becomes the God of time. His progression was not a history of a people in a specific place, but of all people throughout time "before whom the nations are like the sands of the sea."[3]

In this concept time is no longer under the control of space. As Tillich has suggested of the Jewish nation, the results of time's victory over space "represents the permanent struggle between time and space going through all times . . . it has a tragic fate when considered as a nation of space like every other nation, but as the nation of time, it is beyond tragedy . . . because it is beyond the circle of life and death."[4]

The God of time is the God of history. In such a view persons leave the natural world of creation and of control and become part of the prophetic progress which is where God is identified with the whole. Both the design of direction and the process of justice would belong to a God who acts in time. Moreover, humans mimic God in the balancing and regenerating nature of moving themselves, of leaving one space for another, taking themselves from epoch to epoch. Like God, humans are creating and enlarging from a definite beginning to a definite ending. For the Hebrews, however, it matters little where persons come into history, nor where they leave it, as long as they are aware that what *was* is no longer and what *was not*, now is.

The Hebrew dedication to time and the Greek view of a timeless eternity reach a paradoxical truce in Christianity. The problem — or perhaps it is only a dichotomy — is one of the perennial topics of Christian theodicy. The God of cosmological awareness is linked with the loving and involved deity of temporal involvement and duration. In his excellent book *Religion, Reason and Truth*, Sterling McMurrin, one of the original thinkers of our movement, asks,

How can a God whose ultimate nature is described primarily by a metaphysic of being which failed to provide for the movement of history, for whom there was no genuine historical telos, for whom the passage of time brought the world no nearer to the fulfillment of its purpose . . . how can such a God be related to the world of human history, the world of human striving, failures and fulfillments; how can he be involved with a world in which the urge to establish meaning in life and human endeavor centers in the cumulative event in history?[5]

The concept of the timeless, thus eternal, nature of God is well established in Christian thought. The Christian's quest for absolute, for unchanged and unchallenged power, has often had the effect of withdrawing God from time. God is seen as eternal and transcending by virtue of his power but is also seen as progression. Herein lies an orthodox denial of history, as well as a basis for some forms of determinism. It tends to lead humans to the awesome realization that their efforts are ultimately meaningless. As Snoopy would say, "the theological implications alone are staggering."

Equally as concerned are the many who assume God must be within time if in fact God relates to humanity. By insisting that God relates directly and personally, that he answers prayer, that he performs miracles, and that he loves, persons of this persuasion either accept God's limitations, in the fashion of Eldon Trueblood, or deny the eternal and ultimate nature of his being. If such a view had a clean answer, and it does not, it would be to deny the reality of time and with it any meaningful history.[6]

The classic metaphysic of Christianity has been that God is pure event. This classic position references God as having neither potential nor precedence, for he is outside of time and lives (is) in a state of divine omnipresentness. Time and event, process and space, are brought together because they are creations of this out-of-time first cause. Philo contended that there are no perimeters of time outside God, that past and future are within the present. God is present and nothing more is needed or necessary.

For the Christian of the Middle Ages awareness of one's own individual existence was not the result of a feeling of consciousness. Persons at this time were unable to draw any primary distinction between their awareness of duration and existence. Nor, it appears, between moments of distinction in time. For time served neither as a substitute for spatial consciousness nor as a formal condition of thought. The abstraction was beyond them so time was seen as a situation of incompleted permanence. In Aristotelian terms, the movement from actual to potential was recognized only in duration; time was the stream of direction, and existence was an identification of the moments of that stream.

It was for the Renaissance person to fully feel, and to articulate, the anguish as well as the joy of time. The anguish lay in the realization that one's birth is also the first second of one's death. The joy came from fulfillment by way of relationships past and present. Temporality was one's own unaided arena where despite one's mortality they could act out their divine characteristics. There they could taste, if not gain, immortality as cocreator of God's ultimate aim for history.

This idea of cocreation was brought to an end during the period of the Reformation. At that period persons were required to face the possibility of their fallen state. "For the first time in fifteen centuries . . . the creation no longer appeared the cardinal event in the history of the world. . . . human existence rested no longer in God-the-creator-and-preserver but in God-the-Redeemer."[7]

In the seventeenth century people found themselves less and less a part of things, and human thought was concentrated on distinguishing between self and other. Existence found its expression not in individuals but in the duration of a given moment (an event) that needed to be constantly reidentified—a creation that was both continuous and constant. "God's actions and man's action, grace and the knowledge of grace, are exclusively found within the span of the present moment."[8]

Through the eighteenth century the identification of existence was still a matter of identifying that which was being continuously saved from nonbeing. But this was no longer accomplished by divine creation. It was accomplished, rather, by feelings and sensations—or their causes—which d'Holbach defined as "an immense chain of causes and effects which proceed necessarily, one from another."[9] The multiplicity of sensations ensures duration. Thus the great implementation of the eighteenth century was its characteristic of memory by which one's existence was to endure between moments of identity. Time flows by reminiscence.

Continuity of experience is a product of Romanticism and of the nineteenth century. Within this continuity are the modern relations between human and cosmic time and the movement from personal to general memory (history) through which what is, is becoming. In the twentieth century this relationship was progression—a linear time encompassing both the future it creates and the past it reflects.

Any generalized statement concerning "Mormon theological beliefs" about time would be very difficult to construct and probably wrong. But theological assumptions are critically important to understanding a conception of time, and many Mormon historians reflect these theological ideas. The most critical, of course, and in the Christian sense the most heretical, is the Mormon position that God is in both time and space. The impact of this belief for both religion and history must not be underplayed. The position states that God is located within the confines of space and the flow of time. He is actually somewhere and sometime; even more important, he is somewhere at this time. As a being with a past, a present, and a future God lives within time. Thus he is structured by his involvement in history. God is involved in a time that reflects events, change, and most significantly, process.

What we identify as "this-worldliness" in Mormon theology—as well as in Mormon history—arises from a lack of distinctions between the secular and the sacred. Mormon theology accepts that the natural process of this world is orderly rather than chaotic and assumes the laws that govern us are stable. It also assumes that God's will is absolute but that it is not pantheistic. What exists then is not the sum of the parts, for the addition or the subtraction of any part does not necessarily disturb the total reality. The universalistic tendencies of Christianity, for example the concept of a trinity as one, are ignored by Mormons in their very particularized understanding of three personages in the Godhead.[10] There are some universal ideas, however, like the view of priesthood, which is seen as something that persons receive rather than a particular they have.

Persons as well are located within the framework of time and space. But while they are temporal they are not totally God's creatures nor creation. Persons are involved in a double creation of spirit and matter. This creation is not from nothing but rather from the existence of something—a sort of philosophical "stuff" from which all things have been created. The elements are in time and space and cannot begin, nor cease to exist, for they are eternal. The soul is preexistent,[11] probably existing from a more generalized act, but is also created from something. Man is existent, not by necessity, but as a given in history. Nothing is more original than the ultimate being of this person.[12]

Man's agency—his freedom to act—is without limitations. Nothing is able to compromise the freedom to act within the environment. B. H. Roberts states that, "through the fall, comes our present state of probation; our opportunities for gaining an experience in this life; . . . from which experience we shall learn on what basis rests the eternal felicity of intelligences, and how to perpetuate it throughout the ages yet unborn."[13] The nature of this freedom is found in the "capacity of the self to effect its choice as an uncaused cause."[14]

The full meaning of persons as free creatures within time is found in the human struggle to overcome evil just as God struggles with people in the endless effort to extend through them his dominion over the blind process of the material world. People and God participate in an endless and progressively creative process sometimes called "eternalism." It is God's limited power that makes him a partner in history. As Sterling McMurrin has written, "There can be no question of the theoretic strength of a finitistic conception of God in the structure of a theodicy, for it salvages faith in the supreme goodness of God and in the meaningfulness and worth of the moral experience of man."[15]

That the theological beliefs and concerns of Mormon historians are reflected in their writings seems to be too obvious to require additional commentary. These theological assumptions, however, do not necessarily reflect a long-awaited, but never articulated, philosophy of history for Mormonism. These historians tend to be aware of a cosmological setting for history — particularly in reference to time — and it is reflected in a variety of ways. This variety gives insight not only into the history also but into the historians of the movement.

In the main, Mormon historians are proponents of the idea of linear time and with it a concept of linear history. It is linear in that history is viewed as if it moved along a line from beginning to end. This view provides no circumstances within this structure where the end becomes the birth of a new beginning. Mormon historians discount the cyclical concept of time (history) held by the early Greeks.

There are some points, however, at which this is challengeable. Mormon historians have not dealt with the temporal implications of such concepts as "the dispensation of the fulness of time." Richard Bushman in "Faithful History" contends there is a continuity of diversity to Mormon historians that will provide no lasting history for the church until they (that is the historians) reach the dispensation of the limits of knowledge and of intelligence.[16] If such a dispensation is a moment in time, then it is a restorationist's moment. That is, it begins again without impact from the previous conclusion. And if that is the case it suggests that time is conforming to its more traditional design; that is, it is under control of space and thus is cyclical.

Looking at the Mormon theological position, we are drawn to the question of episodial history within the flow of time. Episodial history is an understanding of a time that varies in intensity rather than moving in equity along a line—a time of event not of mere chronology. In many Mormon historical writings there is a strong sense of episodial history. Historical time is conceived as something other than flow, with pockets, or voids, or even rapids on the river of time.

The flow of history, in other words, is not the same as the flow of time. This may best be seen in personal memory in which one can recall the significant points leading to some particular event but is confused as to the chronological order. The difficulty is not only that we forget as we get older, but that the temporal distance from the present is less significant to us than the causal relationship. In a sense the time between significant and causal events becomes a time that does not exist.

This distinction is recognized in the work of Mormon historians even while they are theologically (if not traditionally) committed to linear relationships. Thus they are faced with mutually exclusive propositions for which to write. On the one hand measurable time dissolves and is replaced by bundles of shaped time, which, when seen in a series, are an understandable basis for comprehension. On the other hand, the flow of time (linear and progressive) retains its significance insomuch as these epochs are connected. "Moments of significance" emerge from contexts where they are related to moments of previous cause, and to moments void of causes. The historian may conceptually withdraw into a time realm in order to be able to review the relationship that he anticipated.

In *The Credibility of Divine Existence*, Kemp Smith suggests events are never limited to the instantaneous present. Like the melody of a song they have a duration of their own that is recognized within the larger duration. As a rule, historians have it easier if they accept and identify events of shorter duration.

The concept of time implicitly employed among most Mormon historians, though I have not found it explicitly argued for, is that of a finite time found in an extensive series of moments. In this projection the universe, which had a beginning will, at some point, end. This will happen at a certain time though not at a certain place, since all space is at any moment concentrated. Mormon historians have chosen to walk the boundary between the two seemingly paradoxical views of chronological and episodial time. And they have often fallen victim to the uncritical acceptance of a translation from the property of flow to the content of flow, that is, they have conveyed to the historical process a concept of the whole and have granted it a progression that unfolds potentially toward a better future.

It is in the concept of linear time that we raise the questions of distinction between secular and sacred history. In Mormon historical writings the distinction between sacred and secular becomes nearly indistinguishable within linear process. Faith and history, as Richard Bushman suggests, are "immediately related only because of man's involvement in each, an involvement which does not discover history, but rather molds and shapes it."[17]

The Mormon view avoids the conception of classical Christian metaphysics—that God is totally event and thus not to be actualized. And they do so because time and process, just like man, come into existence at a beginning, a beginning that occurred in the eternal. "In contemplating the works of creation," Parley P. Pratt wrote in *Key to the Science of Theology*, "the student must not conceive the idea that space, or time, or element, or intelligence, was originated, but rather that these are eternal and that they constitute the energies which act, the things acted upon, including the place and time of action."[18]

It is in this act of creation from the eternal that God enters into a radical form of transcendence by joining with man in the control of uncreated elements. At the same time God remains the most effective and powerful factor in the victory of intelligence. Thus the sacred joins the secular in a linear progression "as knowledge grew into greater knowledge, by the persistent efforts of the will, his [God's] recognition of universal laws becomes greater until he attained at last a conquest over the universe which to our finite understanding seems absolutely complete."[19]

Certainly the intervention of any universal force upon the flow of time is a violation of the linear nature of time. If nothing else such an interruption breaks continuity and makes the normal relationship between cause and effect meaningless. If the significant events of history are neither the outcome of a series of determinable causes, nor themselves causes related to some discernible outcomes, then the conception of history as the flowing from one event to another is lost. In holding an "interventionist" view we must recognize that cause and effect are meaningful in linear time only by virtue of assuming a transcending umbrella. Such a transcending system would be outside of time and thus represent a force on history that is neither God nor man. Whichever it is, it stands in opposition to the Mormon insistence on God's residence and behavior within the confines of time.

For David Brion Davis, writing in "The New England Origins of Mormonism," Mormon history as written history differs significantly from that of the writers of the nineteenth and twentieth centuries. It differs because of God's involvement, and the fact this "personal God presides over the most minute happenings."[20] This seemed to be true, recognizing, of course, there are significant differences of opinion among Mormon scholars as to the degree of involvement. Davis Bitton represents a God in history who is active in time and space, not by intervention, but as the consequences of spatial laws of cause and effect.[21] Richard Poll, writing in "God and Man in History," makes the case for God's intervention in history at those points, and only at those points, where to do otherwise would violate his nature and the goals that he has for mankind. Atonement, as the prime example of this, had to be accomplished and to be accomplished miraculously.[22]

One must wonder at the extent such intervention provides foreknowledge. Poll suggests that the future is known to God only in the most general of terms. If God is in fact living in history, and if man does have some effect on the outcome of history, then God can only see the future moving ahead of himself. To Poll, God masters eternity—the timeless nature of totality—in his ability to understand and to use the historical process to bring about the sweeping goals, the final outcome.

William Mulder in looking at Mormon historians finds them much more closely aligned with those scholars of the Reformation who reaffirmed the role of providence, a "theology of history that prevailed in colonial New England and left its mark on American historiography, particularly on Mormonism." The "grand design" is seen in a series of "gospel dispensations in which God's purposes unfold as events in time . . . history written by historians faithful to the *a priori* assumptions of revealed religion."23

Sterling McMurrin represents the more traditional view that Jesus Christ intervened at that point where time and eternity met. In his own work *Religion, Reason, and Truth*, however, McMurrin raises the objection that eternity is timeless and thus only intersects outside of time. A metaphysical, thus metahistorical, event such as the arrival of Christ revolutionizes history for it lacks any explanation that is determined by history. While it frees history and liberalizes mankind it also states very clearly that time is not the only framework in which events impact. We seem to be thrown back again into eternal (timeless) significance. What matters if man can change history; he can never count on it nor lead it, when the timeless does not want to go.

For Heber C. Snell historical events, not dogma, were "the center of God's revelatory activity." Inasmuch as their actions cooperate with God's moral purposes, they too become the promoters of this revelation in history. There is no doubt that for Snell, as for later historians, history is not just a succession of happenings. Rather it is God's activity that takes place in cooperation with persons. Snell also assumes that there will be a confrontation with man's unwanted ramblings through time. This confrontation will effectively bring the Mormon theological assumptions of God's finity into serious question.24

In "To Transform History: Early Mormon Culture and the Concept of Time and Space" Robert Flanders suggests that Joseph Smith's prophetic activities had the effect of "foreshortening time for the Mormon mind." Within the prophetic framework Smith was able to tie past and present together in such a manner that it both filled time and fulfilled it. The message of time was not only made linear, but the intervention of God into this flow was discounted historically by pulling events together via prophetic understanding.25

The majority of Mormon historians deal with the confrontation of transcendentalism and time by asserting the immanent nature of God. The paradox of this time out of time has been a central theme in Mormon history and in its historiography. God lives in time and through him the future is discovered. But in an existential manner eternity cannot be related to time, for time is a condition of measurement. Eternity, which by definition has no end (and probably no beginning), is unmeasurable and thus is not *of* nor *in* time. Eternity is a word used to aid us in the understanding of something we conceive, but have never understood, unless we understand it as a quantum of certainty. Yet the Mormon historian's God lives within the confines of such time and is affected by, as well as affecting, the outcome. And the future is ahead of him. As Thomas F. O'Dea has written,

> It is a transcendentalism within the context of time itself. The apprehension of time, the experience of time, is of key importance here. Time is not a limitation from which man is to be delivered; it is a challenging vista. It is not experienced as a process of which we are integrally a part, but rather as one over which we are gaining mastery. The Mormon conception of time is an eschatological conception without an end. It is the prolonged moment of becoming—the moment of fruition never quite but always about to be realized.[26]

In this respect, however, God himself is controlled by the law and by time itself. Both the natural law and time existed prior to God and is transcended. The result is more and more a secularization of history through which the end resides in the process. This fulfillment of time within time, is an accomplishment found in becoming, a goal found in search of a goal. The conception may be true but, according to O'Dea, is rationally questionable, chronologically impossible, and logically invalid. "God is conceived as within the context of time, while man emerges from out of the context of history. The prospect of endless progression, a genuine development without a goal, a teleology without a *telos*."[27]

Over the years formulae have developed to explain the intricate relationship between the individual's life story and collective history. For Wilhelm Dilthey it was the elaborate binding of the individual to totalization. In every case the individual loses the inherent superiority which in turn is given to the universal. The universal supplies values and schema for understanding the direction of history. Endless progression is pertinent only to the universal and not, as it turns out, to the man who emerges from history into the time-less-ness that is his completion.

The acceptance of this view by Mormon scholars, who are also accepting of the temporality of God, involves them in a contradiction. According to Richard Poll, there are "many Mormons who want the security that comes from the concept of a supreme being who is apart from the temporal process and the feeling of kinship that comes from a Heavenly Father who is involved somehow in the same process as man." Like so many in the world, we "convey a strong suggestion that in this matter we can eat our cake and have it too."[28]

Temporal time-less-ness is strongly affected by the concept of freedom. Man is, we are to assume, free to affect history. Since freedom is one of the noncreated elements it seems to be akin to Boehme's *Ungrund*, the underlying will that proceeds the Godhead and that directs the outcome of history with its determining influence. Even God, it appears, is a part of this ontological freedom from the world process and within the world order. Mormonism, in order to avoid determinism, has made the choice of the primacy of being over the primacy of freedom.

Linear history is usually seen as progressive. This is the case with the Mormon use of time. Time in the Judeo-Christian tradition — no longer circular or spiral — proceeds toward actualization, toward the fulfillment of a goal. Time moves along a linear line from limited to complex, from beginning toward ending, in a manner that suggests growth, creation, progression, providence. And instead of revealing itself in miraculous intervention, the linear history is seen in a logical development. The assumption of the eighteenth century was that "the inevitable growth of human knowledge through the perpetual and unlimited argumentation of reasons will yield indefinite social progress and increase in human happiness."[29] This is the ideal of progress.

There is no doubt that for a significant segment of modern Mormon historians, history is related to providence. Some I am sure would agree with B. H. Roberts that history is more a moral judgment than a narrative of humanity in time. Like him, they would see "history as the unfolding of a vast Providential plan."[30] But there are other understandings as well. Robert Flanders, writing about, rather than within, the Mormon tradition suggests that Joseph Smith's response to the confrontation of space and of time in nineteenth-century America was to assert that history must be fully dynamic in both time and space: "Time from the restoration of the gospel . . . until the Parousia, was to be occupied in building the penultimate kingdom of God in this world and in history, a visible kingdom that would within the historical process begin to roll back sin and vanquish evil."[31]

The direction of time is a part of our concern as well, for without direction time is dominated by space, as in the cyclical understanding of history. Therefore it is the final success of time that its progression—and that of history—goes from birth to death, from growth to immaterialism, in a direction that for persons cannot be—or at least has not been—reversed.

The joining of goals within the temporal process, and their fulfillment in a beyond-time progression, is based on the assumption that the line between time and eternity is not clear. It is not clear because of its internal relation. This is not a new definition of eternity that has been designed to avoid the stigma of temporality; it is the paradox of temporal man who transcends time. Humans reaffirm the linear nature of progression, for persons are not allowed to *begin again* but rather they continue. The idea of historical progress—this act of being in process—is basically anti-Christian according to the classical framework. The idea also posed a problem for twentieth-century reflections because the loss of eternity and the assumed value of the trail from Eden to Hiroshima was not impressive. Mormonism, however, manages to maintain the ties of progress, using as the examples thereof the birth, growth, and contemporary "usefulness" of doctrines.[32]

The alignment of time and space at the crossroads of eternity is the object of mysticism. I use Dean Inge's definition of mysticism: "the attempt to realize in thought and feeling the imminence of the temporal in the eternal, and of the eternal in the temporal."[33] Mysticism has the effect of extinguishing time and space but, in so doing it must hold on to the contention that time cannot create something entirely new. As Tillich explained, "everything in time is subject to the circle of birth and death, and that no new creature can arise. Therefore salvation is beyond time, it is always independent of any stage of time. It is the eternal present above every temporal present."[34] Either way this sort of mysticism is one of the most subtle ways to deny the nature of history, for in a very real way it allows for the predominance of space. Turning once again to Tillich: "Mysticism is the spiritual form of the power of space over time, and therefore we can say that mysticism, in the sense of the great mystics, is the most sublime form of polytheism . . . a souring between space and the negation of space, but it was not the affirmation of time. Supernature as well as nature subjects time to space."[35]

In Mormon history there is a preoccupation with things of the world and with natural laws. These natural laws, which seem to be well into place before time and/or uncreated persons, are viewed by Mormons as inherent in the cosmos though not derived from God. God uses them, however, to work out his divine purpose. There is perhaps nowhere in Mormon historiography where this is so evident as it is in the naturalistic treatment in Arrington's *Great Basin Kingdom*, one of the few works that appear to me to be both good history and sound theology. The essence of God's revealed will, we come to understand, can only be accomplished in light of the natural formulation of laws, and known only by understanding the conditions that surrounded them and the symbolism in which they are couched. Historical events are internally related via law, as Bergson suggests, for "time is not an independent variable."

It is in Richard Poll's acceptance of God's laws that he finds his explanation of perceived inefficiency in the historical process. God's laws explain the existence of evil in life through the freedom of the historical process; a process in which God's commitment is determined by nature and by will. "Bound by His temporal nature and by the laws of the space in which He functions, God further restrains the arbitrary use of His knowledge of these laws in order that man may grow by learning those same laws and making wise choices based upon them. This is one reason why the historic process cannot be precisely plotted and why it is as inefficient, painful, and pathetic as it is."[36]

Nineteenth-century historical inquiry is primarily responsible for the acceptance of man's historicity: Man is in time and his internal relationship is to knowledge. It is there he found the grounds for the belief that time, as well as space, has creative power. Dilthey was perhaps the first to realize the full implications of this idea. He concludes that there are no "eternal truths" and accepts the burden of the relativity of human knowledge. To suggest, however, that time impacts on history, as many Mormon historians suggest, is to assume that there is within it, a priori, both a knowledge and a goal imposed upon the historical process. William Mulder asserts that Mormon history is written with the a priori assumptions of the believer, much like William Bradford's revealed religion. But he does not suggest, I believe, that this assumption comes from outside of time. Rather it is the product of time on man. Klaus J. Hansen in the preface to the Bison Book edition of *Quest for Empire*, asserts the logical irrelevancy, if not absurdity, of a view that a priori theological and religious assumptions (either the historian's, the god's, or time's) exist prior to history, man, or the process.[37]

If we follow the assumption of Mormon historians that man is free to effect what God knows, then it follows that the future is not yet fact. Man does make a difference in the outcome of history, for history is not yet written by God. Admittedly, such a view raises questions about predetermination (foreknowledge) which are standard within religious movements. "What we are presently engaged in," writes Richard Poll, "is not a drama without a point, or a fortuitous comedy of errors, a foredoomed tragedy, or a fully-scripted pageant in which we are all mimes. Fundamental to this concept is the conviction that God is the producer and Christ is the central actor in the play, but what happens on the stage depends significantly upon the choices of all members of the cast."[38]

William Mulder affirms the cognitive nature of history's own contribution, for "history itself may be seen as a witness alternatively supporting now one, now the other view."[39] But there is considerable evidence that historians do not accede to the contribution of history any more than they do to time itself. On the other hand the contribution is most evident in man's freedom and in the Mormon's somewhat obsessive concern for free agency. Works—man's activities in history—take on an epiphenomenological character of their own.

> It is this concept of man as uncreated and underived, a necessary being standing ontologically with God and the world, that constitutes the radical heresy of Mormonism against the traditional Christian faith. It is not only a fundamental departure from the established doctrine of man, for it entails the denial of the absoluteness of God and justifies also the denial of the doctrine of salvation by the divine grace only.[40]

The devotion to biography and testimonials is not just an affinity for the "faith of our fathers." It is the honest outcome of placing the necessity of works within a time tradition, and in doing so both releasing it from the transcending appeal of grace and conforming it to the daily activities of persons in contact with history.

To some extent the thesis described above drives us logically again to the question of the "transcendings" violation of time. Man is inherently — both theologically and historically — an uncreated member of existence. He has dignity and a seemingly inherent morality that liberate him from a determined evil if not from the reality of evil. All this rests, however, on each person's dependence on God for their present estate — a seeming violation of human will — and for the degree of their salvation. Paradoxically, persons work out their salvation as they prepare for the kingdom in the framework of grace — lying outside of history — where persons find their full salvation.

Mormon historians have been no more willing to seek a philosophy of history than most historians. Yet while there is little effort to write history according to some fully developed and acknowledged attitude about the nature of history, most of the writings of Mormon historians reflect their theological beliefs about the nature of time. To the degree that these beliefs are consistent with other late nineteenth- and early twentieth-century historians, Mormon historians are much like all other historians. But they are not the same. The difference is seen in the work of many historians as well as in their limited — but significant — discussions of the nature of history itself.

Most have not grasped the realization that a statement concerning time cannot be made from some point assumed to be outside the dimension of time. Remember it is not possible for any statement by man to be lacking temporal perspective. Nor is it possible for anyone to make such a statement eternally — that is timelessly. Thus I would suggest that the "generalizations" about movement and progression in the perspective of Mormon historiography are more likely to be effective because Mormon historians tend to write within the framework of time as it is acknowledged theologically. Latter-day Saints, like most persons, have difficulty with the nature of time and space and employ the words of infinity, timelessness, omnipresence, etc. to state something about their understandings of God. But in serious studies there is increasing indication of a willingness to foresee the meaning of the process, the media, and the direction of that we called time.

Parley P. Pratt, like so many fundamentalists of his age, saw history in terms of God's dealing through time with his chosen people. This is counter to the openness of Joseph Smith's mystic conceptions. B. H. Roberts was more reflective of the Romantics such as Prescott, whose response was emotionally tied to the past, feeling that the duty of the historian was not only to reflect a narrative but to serve as judge of time.[41] William Mulder, the Mormon historian, writes of history seen within the limits of divinely set thesis and design:

> He accepts the given of his faith like the net in tennis and plays his historical ball across that net, deriving his satisfactions from skimming the net and scoring inside the court and suffering anxieties when he does not. These gentlemen may be correct; it may be that history reflects the faith-oriented remembrance of events, but it does not reflect the tenets of the faith. No historian will ever be privy to God's purposes.[42]

That much is probably true; but it is too bad these historians do not respond in the writing of their history to their theological tenets.

Historians have the inalienable right to promote and provide any sort of history that pleases them; they have, so to speak, the constitutional right to be wrong in their own way.[43] But there seems to be validity in the comment by H. R. Trevor-Roper, Regius Professor of Modern History at Oxford: "A good historian, in my opinion, doesn't express his philosophy in philosophical terms. He allows it to emerge out of the long haul of writing. History is very complicated, and the philosophy of historians I respect is not expressed by them in brief tabloid form."[44] The historian, writing from a set of beliefs about the cosmology, will allow these to affect his or her interpretation of the relationship between time and event.

In the final analysis, truth is an eschatological concept. And historical truth appears to be no different. The serious historian, like the seriously religious person, is trying to finish the past in an acceptable—and often defined—direction. Thus there is an integration of the past and the present with the future, just as there is fusion of the cosmos and the event. These will force us back again and again to the human spirit and to the meaning humanity finds in its past. The form and the process of the past lies to a large extent, in the metaphysical formulization that we use to give order to the current, the past, and the transcendent.

There is a subtle joining in Mormon histories of the traditions of myth and of sacred history. In traditions Yahweh's purposes for man are revealed in the space-time form in which all persons live. The source of divine awareness remains cosmological, while the expression of it is in history. But in Mormonism the setting is no longer in the divine cosmos but in the mundane world of man and time.

NOTES

1. Paul Tillich, "The Struggle Between Time and Space," *Theology of Culture* (Oxford: University Press, 1959), 30.

2. Nicholas Berdyaev, *The Beginning and the End* (New York: Harper Tourchbooks, 1952), 229.

3. Tillich, "Struggle," 36.

4. Ibid., 31–39.

5. Sterling M. McMurrin, *Religion, Reason, and Truth* (Salt Lake City: University of Utah Press, 1982), 118.

6. Sterling M. McMurrin, "Religion and the Denial of History," *Sunstone* 7 (March–April 1982): 49.

7. As quoted in George Poulet, *Studies in Human Time* (New York: Harper Tourchbooks, 1956), 11.

8. Ibid., 17.

9. Ibid., 19.

10. Sterling M. McMurrin, *The Theological Foundations of the Mormon Religion* (Salt Lake City: University of Utah Press, 1965), 8–18.

11. This does not seem to be correct for it cannot exist prior to creation; but perhaps before material creation.

12. McMurrin, *Theology*, 3, 4, 25–26.

13. B. H. Roberts, *The Gospel* (Salt Lake City: Deseret Press, 1928), 27f.

14. McMurrin, *Theology*, 82.

15. Ibid., 105.

16. Richard L. Bushman, "Faithful History," *Dialogue* 4 (Winter 1969): 11.

17. This blending of the sacred and the secular Bushman calls "salvation history."

18. Parley P. Pratt, *Key to the Science of Theology* (Liverpool, 1855), 44.

406 / *Mormonism in the Larger Perspective*

19. John A. Widtsoe, *Rational Theology* (Salt Lake City: Deseret Press, 1915), 25.

20. David Brion Davis, "The New England Origins of Mormonism," *The New England Quarterly* 25 (June 1952): 166.

21. Davis Bitton, "Anti-Intellectualism in Mormon History," *Dialogue* 1 (Autumn 1966): 111.

22. Richard D. Poll, "Toward a Philosophy of Mormon History," *Dialogue* 7 (Spring 1977): 101.

23. William Mulder, "Mormon Angles of Historical Vision: Some Maverick Reflections," *Journal of Mormon History* 3 (1976): 15.

24. Richard Sherlock, "Faith and History: The Snell Controversy," *Dialogue* 12 (Spring 1979): 37.

25. Robert B. Flanders, "To Transform History: Early Mormon Culture and the Concept of Time and Space," *American Society of Church History*, 40:112-33.

26. Thomas F. O'Dea, "Mormonism and the American Experience of Time," *Sociology of Religion* (New York: Basic Books, 1979), 150.

27. Ibid., 40, 147.

28. Poll, "Toward a Philosophy," 104.

29. McMurrin, *Religion*, 125.

30. Davis Bitton, "B. H. Roberts as Historian," *Dialogue* 3 (Winter 1968): 43.

31. Flanders, "Transform," 108-11.

32. McMurrin, *Religion*, 141-44.

33. William Inge, *Christian Mysticism* (London: Methuen and Co. Ltd, 1948), 5.

34. Tillich, "Struggle," 34.

35. Ibid., 35.

36. Poll, "Toward a Philosophy," 107.

37. Klaus J. Hansen, *Quest for Empire* (Lincoln: University of Nebraska Press, 1974), xii, xiii.

38. Poll, "Toward a Philosophy," 107-9.

39. Mulder, "Mormon Angles," 16.

40. McMurrin, "Theology," 55.

41. Davis Bitton, "B. H. Roberts," 43.

42. Mulder, "Mormon Angles," 16.

43. David H. Fischer, *Historians' Fallacies* (New York: Harper and Row, Publishers, 1971), 64.

44. Caroline Seebolm, "Review of Hugh Trevor-Roper: History if Relevant," *New York Times Review*, 24 April 1977.

Since 1950: Creators and Creations of Mormon History

JAMES B. ALLEN

History is a social necessity. It is not only a tie with the past: it is a key to understanding the present. Nations and institutions look to their historians for insight on how existing conditions came to be, and as conditions change the questions society and its historians ask of the past also change. In addition, every newly discovered document has the potential of casting important new light on some old interpretation of the past. History thus becomes an ever-changing thing as the historians of each generation interpret and reinterpret for the time in which they write.[1] All this is true of history in general; it is equally true of the history of the Church of Jesus Christ of Latter-day Saints.

As part of Mormonism's centennial celebration in 1930, Brigham H. Roberts published his momentous six-volume work, *A Comprehensive History of the Church*, which even today is an essential reference for anyone seriously interested in Mormon history. But Bernard DeVoto still was scandalized at the dearth of scholarship on the Mormon past. The Mormon story, he wrote, "is probably the most important chapter in the history of the trans-Mississippi frontier, . . . and it is a treasure-house for the historian of ideas, institutions and social energies." Yet, he said, no qualified historian had written a comprehensive treatise on Mormonism, and very few had even written monographs on any of its aspects. Economists and sociologists had done even worse, and the general state of Mormon studies was so bad, DeVoto scolded, that "a complete bibliography of articles by qualified scholars will not fill this page."[2]

DeVoto was both right and wrong. In ignoring Roberts as a "qualified historian," he hardly did justice to the painstaking research and genuine attempt at balance that went into Roberts's work. Though the *Comprehensive History* clearly was written from the perspective of faith, Roberts did not ignore or hide important problems when he saw them. He was not professionally trained, but his ability to combine scholarly methods with religious commitment put his work a very long step ahead of anything previously produced within the church.[3] On the other hand, DeVoto was right in his general assessment of scholarly Mormon studies. His barbs were aimed chiefly at academia, where path-breaking, in-depth, interpretive studies were supposed to be produced but where, so far as Mormon history was concerned, they were almost nonexistent.[4] Some important studies were on the horizon, however, a few of which were well under way even while DeVoto was taking his potshots, and by 1950 his one-page bibliography might have been expanded to three or four.[5]

Then came the decade of the 1950s, in which an explosion of historical scholarship began. The availability of publishing outlets increased dramatically, as both the popular and the scholarly audience took greater and greater interest in Mormon history.[6] Hundreds of scholarly books, articles, theses, and dissertations appeared in the next thirty-five years, not to mention the myriad of publications aimed primarily at the popular Mormon audience.[7] At the same time, important things were happening in the secular world of scholarship and historiography, some of which would clearly affect the course of Mormon history.

In part the change was symbolized by the work of three young scholars who first became acquainted with each other in Logan, Utah, in 1950. S. George Ellsworth, who had just received his Ph.D. at Berkeley, was beginning his career in the history department at Utah State University; Eugene E. Campbell, a new associate director at the LDS Institute of Religion, would complete his doctorate at Southern California in 1952; and Leonard J. Arrington, a new faculty member in economics, was soon to complete his Ph.D. at North Carolina. These three, with some others, met frequently in a study group in which they read and critiqued each other's papers. Each of them was to have an important impact on what happened to Utah and Mormon history in the next thirty-five years.[8]

There were, of course, other young scholars fresh out of graduate school, or soon to be so, who were about to make important contributions to Mormon history.[9] Others were coming along — some undergraduates and some as yet not even in college — whose enthusiasm for history along with the influence of their mentors would soon lead them inevitably into the rising tide of Mormon history. There were also a number of established scholars whose excellent work had set the tone for the explosion to come, and who would continue to make new impressions on the Mormon history landscape. The scholarly footprints of Juanita Brooks, Gustive O. Larson, and Dale L. Morgan, for example, are apparent on both sides of 1950.

The richness of what was happening was enhanced by the close association of all these scholars, young and old, at historical conventions, at other special gatherings, and, after 1965, through the Mormon History Association. All this led to effective sharing of ideas and information, and to considerable encouraging of each other. In the thirty-five years since 1950 these scholars not only changed our understanding of many basic issues but also helped establish Mormon history in the American academic community as a respected and significant field of study.

What was happening was that the nature of Mormon history was about to change, for the nature of the *writers* of Mormon history was changing. The earlier generation of Mormon historians had been the first creators of the Mormon past; as such it was their task to lay out the major outlines, to develop the major images of the past appropriate for church manuals, and to build and support the faith of church members, to tie them to their foundations. Much of what they wrote was necessarily defensive in nature, for much, if not most, of what had been written about church history by non-Mormons consisted of bitter and often brutal attacks upon the church and its founders. Not unlike their scholarly successors, these early church historians selected their historical evidence carefully, with the honest intent of meeting the needs of the church as they perceived them in their time.

The new crop of professionally trained LDS historians, on the other hand, came to church history with different kinds of experiences behind them and different perceptions of contemporary needs. For one thing, they had not felt the barbs of anti-Mormon propa-

ganda quite so deeply, for non-Mormon scholars generally were beginning to take a more balanced and sympathetic view of Mormonism
than the debunkers who had preceded them. Since the young Mormon historians did not feel quite so defensive as they approached
their task, they could ask questions and deal with issues that went
beyond the matter of whether the church was true or false. Unlike
their predecessors, however, they were usually more well trained in
the process of investigation, comparison, and analysis of historical
documents. They were also trained to ask new kinds of questions,
seek for new perspectives, and to bring a much different kind of
interpretive analysis to bear on whatever they studied. Though philosophical frameworks differed, all had been schooled in the rigorous
methodology that required continuous reexaminations of old assumptions, painstaking care in seeking and examining historical documents, some kind of interpretive framework (more than just storytel-
ling) for every historical essay, and the feeling that history purely for
the sake of propaganda was, as David Hackett Fischer has said, "not
history at all."[10]

When the modern generation of Mormon historians began to
apply its professional training to the history of their own church, the
results were predictable. There were as many varieties of Mormon
history written as there were individuals. Some scholars continued to
provide works openly intended as defensive of the faith, only they
did it with considerably more professional skill than some of their
predecessors. Others took to exploring entirely new areas, often raising questions and delving into broader historical issues that seemed
never even to have been thought of before. Some saw certain broad,
general themes that, to them, were highly important, and they structured what they wrote to illuminate those themes. Some came away
from graduate school somewhat disillusioned with their history for,
as they delved into it on their own, they found so many seemingly
important topics that had been left out and others that seemed to
have been misinterpreted.[11] Perhaps some of the new historians were
too hard on their predecessors, not realizing fully enough what they
may or may not have been *prepared* to see in the record. And,
unfortunately, perhaps a few became so disillusioned that their questioning on the basis of secular assumptions led them even to deny
the foundations of their faith. I suspect, however, that such varieties

of responses are the same in every field, and that the incidence of spiritual disaster is really no greater as a result of professional historical training than it would be for some other cause had professionalism never been a factor.[12]

The year 1950, then, became a symbolic turning point in Mormon historiography. Among other things, that year saw the courageous publication of Juanita Brooks's *The Mountain Meadows Massacre*. This singular work of exceptionally painstaking scholarship cut through the myth, bias, and misinformation of generations and presented to the world a reasonable, balanced, highly readable account of one of the most tragic incidents in Mormon history. What made it especially significant within the context of Mormonism itself was that Brooks was an active Latter-day Saint and knew well the pressures within the church against dealing in that much depth with such a painful and potentially embarrassing topic. Yet her sense of historical integrity gave her no choice: she had to rescue the true story, as nearly as she could, from the mountain of misinformation that surrounded it. Her attitude typified that of many young Mormon scholars for whom she seemed to set an example: "Nothing but the truth," she said, "is good enough for the Church to which I belong."[13] Significantly, the story as she finally told it did nothing to hurt the church as an institution, and, more positively, it even helped rescue Brigham Young from the suspicion still in the air that he was an accessory to the murders. At the same time, it provided important enlightenment on the various church-related problems that led John D. Lee to make his fateful decision to cooperate with the Indians in the massacre, and it documented and clarified more fully than ever before the involvement of several other individuals. The work still stands among a small handful of essential books that have made a permanent, pivotal impact on Mormon history and are not likely to be replaced or lose their impact in any foreseeable future.

If Juanita Brooks exemplifies the established scholar whose contributions bridged the transition of 1950, then those three young scholars who met at Utah State University that year well represent the various kinds of contributions made by the new school of historians. George Ellsworth's Ph.D. dissertation, for example, still stands as the most significant analysis to date of the organization of missionary activity in the first thirty years of church history—a topic that had almost completely eluded church historians before his time. With him, it was not a matter of "setting the record straight," but, in reality, creating a history where there had been none before. At the same time, Ellsworth made an equally important contribution when he carefully plotted the early Mormon congregations and concluded that Mormonism was really not the "frontier" religion so often depicted by scholars but, rather, that its origins and early growth occurred in a maturing economic and social environment. [14] Here was an example of challenging old assumptions about church history without challenging the foundations of the faith, and this kind of significant contribution has been repeated time and time again in the recent annals of Mormon history. Beyond that, Ellsworth illuminated several specific incidents and developments in Mormon history, and, for me at least, his essay on early Mormons in the South Seas is still one of the classic pieces of Mormon historical literature. [15]

Eugene Campbell's studies concentrated on the Utah pioneer period in Mormon history, and in the process he discovered things that, he believed, simply had been reported wrongly. A number of his publications were devoted to "setting the record straight" by creating new and hopefully more correct images of past events. In one article he effectively questioned the validity of the idea that Brigham Young planned an "outer cordon"—a ring of colonies intended to encircle and protect the huge "empire" of Mormon settlements in the West. There he told a story that beautifully demonstrated how easily historical misimpressions can be created.

The settlement at Fort Lemhi, on Idaho's Salmon River, simply did not fit the "outer cordon" pattern, and all the research conducted by Campbell and his students demonstrated that Brigham Young did not really want a settlement there. Nevertheless, everyone, even professional historians, believed just the opposite. John D. Nash, one of Campbell's students, visited the site of Fort Lemhi and read the inscription on the historical marker that quoted Brigham Young as saying, "Go into the Salmon River Country, Oregon Territory. Many tribes converge upon that area to fish and hunt. Choose an appropriate location and found a mission. Teach them the arts of husbandry and peace according to our Gospel plan." Nash wondered why President Young had chosen such an uninviting, out-of-the-way place. In the course of his study he found that the church leader had actually instructed the colonists to settle near the Blackfoot River and, after visiting the Lemhi settlement, even publicly criticized their new location. As Campbell concluded the story:

> Puzzled by the apparent contradiction in Brigham Young's call as recorded on the monument and his reaction to the location after visiting it, Mr. Nash wrote to one of the leading historians in Idaho asking if he knew the documentary source for the quote on the marker. He was informed that there was no such statement in Brigham Young's journal, but that "the statement attributed to Brigham Young was written by me in the manner of 'poetic licence' for placement upon a plaque at the Salmon River monument. I think it conforms nicely with the spirit and intent of the mission call." A wonderful quote but very misleading. One is led to ask, "If you can't trust a historian, whom can you trust."[16]

Campbell's article typified the many contributions he and others have made to cleaning up such details of history. His death, which occurred as this volume was in preparation, leaves us all bereft.

Leonard Arrington's contributions were more diverse than those of any other living scholar, as will become apparent later in this essay.

While all this was going on, Mormon studies were being taken more seriously also by the non-Mormon world, as non-Mormon scholars were becoming less inclined to criticize the faith claims of the Mormons and more inclined to provide balanced and often empathetic studies of various aspects the Mormon community. Even as Arrington, Campbell, and Ellsworth were reading their papers to each other and preparing some of their most significant studies for publication, Thomas F. O'Dea, a Catholic sociologist, was preparing a sympathetic but detached analysis of the dilemmas faced by Mormons in the modern world. He spent a great deal of time in Utah, made friends with many members of the Mormon scholarly community, and in 1957 published his book, *The Mormons*. Though he relied heavily on Fawn Brodie for his description of Mormon origins, when it came to his personal analysis of modern Mormonism he did a commendable job of dealing with certain intellectual and social dilemmas with tact and understanding.

The list of other non-Mormon scholars whose well-balanced works helped illumine a wide variety of topics in Mormon history is long, but it includes Mario DePillis, who was one of the first to see the importance of the idea of divine authority in Mormon restorationism; David Brion Davis, who helped us see Mormon persecution in the larger context of nativism and persecution in the nineteenth century; Norman Furniss, who has provided the most important and well-balanced study of the Utah War to date; Lawrence Foster, whose book *Religion and Sexuality* is considered by most historians to provide the best analysis to date on the Mormon practice of polygamy, and is also especially important because of the comparative approach he makes by examining also the Shaker and the Oneida attitudes toward marriage; Mark Leone, an anthropologist, who provided a sympathetic analysis of life and institutions in certain communities along the Little Colorado; Keith Huntress, who provided important new insight into the circumstances surrounding the death of Joseph Smith by looking at it from the perspective of Governor Thomas Ford's need to avoid civil war in Illinois; and Lawrence Lee, who has published a fine article on Mormon settlement in Canada. The growing seriousness with which non-Mormon historians take Mormon history was significantly demonstrated when a recent major textbook on American history included a special section entitled "The Mormons as a Test Case." The section was part of a chapter dealing with the nature and limits of dissent in American society in the early nineteenth century, and its sympathetic treatment of the Mormons was used to illustrate the problems involved as the larger society tried to deal with a group that was considered to be different from the norm.[17] In addition, for the past several years the annual Tanner Lecture, funded by Obert C. and Grace A. Tanner, at the annual meeting of the Mormon History Association has featured a prominent non-Mormon scholar who has spent the previous year studying Mormon history in the light of his or her own field of specialty. Without exception, these excellent lectures have added an important dimension to Mormon history by putting one or more of its aspects in the context of broader American movements and ideas.

The most important non-Mormon contributions to Mormon history, however, have come from Jan Shipps. Since her first contact with the Mormons in 1960, she has participated eagerly in the process of creating Mormon history, including serving a term as president of the Mormon History Association, and has been particularly concerned with bringing Mormon studies into the mainstream of American religious studies. Her recent book, *Mormonism: The Story of a New Religious Tradition*, does just that. Perhaps the ultimate compliment to her efforts was paid her by a representative of the church's public communications department who wrote for the dust jacket of her book: "In *Mormonism* Jan Shipps combines the impressive skills of a distinguished historian, thorough researcher, and lucid writer with a quality rare among those who observe and write about the Church of Jesus Christ of Latter-day Saints. She understands us."[18]

There are numerous excellent examples in recent Mormon historiography of scholars who have investigated various questions and, in the process, provided the basis for some significant changes in our understanding of Mormon history. In addition, many of the areas investigated have reflected general trends in the broader historiographical scene, as changes in society, a variety of new research tools and techniques, and specialization have all affected the questions historians have asked.

Mormon economic history, for example, has been the focus of considerable attention since 1950, and Leonard Arrington became its most important pioneer. Between 1951 and 1958 he published at least forty articles on Mormon economics,[19] and in 1958 *Great Basin Kingdom* appeared. Arrington had asked searching questions about every aspect of Mormon economic activity in the nineteenth century. He was tenacious in seeking out every conceivable document, and was not afraid to go where his questions and sources led him. In a book that was a model of both thoroughness and scholarly integrity, he explicated as no one had before the intricate relationship between religious and secular concerns, demonstrating the church's deep involvement in economic planning, economic regulation, and a variety of specific economic enterprises. He dealt with both success and failure, and he added a dimension to Mormon history that could never again be ignored or dismissed by those who would take that history seriously.

Arrington was soon joined by several others who were asking a variety of economic questions, the answers to which deeply enriched our understanding of the totality of the LDS experience. What, for example, was the Mormon economy in Kirtland, Ohio, *really* like?

Using econometric techniques never before applied to Mormon history, Marvin Hill, Keith Rooker, and Larry Wimmer challenged a number of previous interpretations and demonstrated the economic viability of Kirtland, and the valid reasons for being optimistic about the area's economic growth at the time the Mormons settled there. One result of their study was to rescue Joseph Smith and other church leaders from previous interpretations suggesting that they were unthinking or irresponsible in their initial Kirtland investments and speculation. They also challenged the old assumption that the failure of the Kirtland bank could be blamed on the nationwide "Panic of 1837," demonstrating, in fact, that the panic probably prolonged the life of the Kirtland bank and that the lack of a charter was the real reason for its failure.[20]

Other economic questions were explored, even including the economics of the Word of Wisdom. The economic situation in western Illinois when the Mormons arrived was examined by Robert Flanders, providing readers with a better understanding of problems associated with the settlement of Nauvoo and the nature of Joseph Smith's activities as a buyer and seller of land. Dallin H. Oaks and Joseph I. Bentley looked in great detail at Joseph Smith's unsuccessful efforts to obtain discharge in bankruptcy in connection with his heavy Illinois debts, and clearly demonstrated that the prophet was not guilty of improper conduct, given the economic circumstances of the times, and that his intent in filing for bankruptcy was to give himself time to pay all his legitimate debts, not escape them. The economic problems involved in settling southern Utah were treated in greater depth by Juanita Brooks and others, particularly with reference to attempts to grow vineyards and cotton and to set up an iron industry. The nature of Mormon landholding before legal title was available in 1869 was examined by Gustive Larson. A popular stereotype that the Mormon pioneers were disappointed at finding a dry and desert place when they arrived in the Salt Lake Valley was questioned, and the resulting investigation by Richard Jackson demonstrated that their first perception was one of delight with a fertile valley that, with their effort, could produce bounteously. The Law of Consecration and the United Orders in Utah have long intrigued Mormons, and the recent scholarship of Leonard Arrington, Dean May, Dwight Israelson, and others has clarified not only the economic operation of these enterprises but also the various types of United Orders and other cooperative efforts in nineteenth-century Utah. Wealth patterns in nineteenth-century Utah were explored in detail by James Kearl, Clayne Pope, and Larry Wimmer, who provided important economic information for better understanding the Mormon community in general.[21]

Efforts were made to view Mormon economic problems in the light of national movements, and Ronald Walker discussed in detail the important role of Heber J. Grant in helping Utah and the church weather the panic of 1893. The historical relationship between Mormonism and labor unions was opened up by Kenneth Davies, who showed that, until about the 1880s, church members dominated the union movement in Utah and there was little tension between the church and the unions. After that time, however, possibly as part of the conservative position inherent in the church's growing involvement in major business enterprise and away from the cooperative values of the nineteenth century, church leaders tended to oppose the demands of organized labor. Members, nevertheless, were not enjoined from union membership, and they seemed to sign up in only slightly less proportion than other Americans. Twentieth-century economic activities were also plumbed, though not in as much depth as those of the earlier period. Some of the topics covered to date include the origins of the welfare program, the nature of church business holdings in modern times, the economic implications of the operation of many church institutions, and the intriguing changes in Mormon economic policy from a nineteenth-century emphasis on cooperative enterprise to a twentieth-century accommodation with corporate capitalism.[22] Much more remains to be done, but the amount of Mormon economic history now available to those interested is impressive indeed.

Another important trend in modern historiography has been demographics, or the statistical study of populations, and a number of recent studies in Mormon demography have made some significant contributions to Mormon history. The Family and Demographic Research Institute at Brigham Young University, for example, regularly sponsors research in Mormon population studies. Researchers there and elsewhere have, among other things, presented social profiles of early Mormon converts, provided more accurate estimates of the percentage of the Mormon population that moved west from Nauvoo, analyzed American-born versus foreign-born populations among the Mormons in Utah, described population growth rates, studied fertility patterns among the Mormons, made some conclusions regarding birth planning, demonstrated that the incidence of plural marriage in nineteenth-century Utah was higher than previously supposed, and provided an excellent index to the Utah census for certain years that are of inestimable value to other scholars seeking to incorporate demographic material into their work.[23]

One topic that cuts across many fields is community history. Since 1950 the Mormon village has been examined extensively in terms of settlement patterns, town planning, economic relationships within the towns and with surrounding communities, family patterns, social structure, community stress, and as a setting for cultural change. Dean May, for example, has led out in trying to establish techniques for studying Mormon towns. To put his research in context, he described the work of several historians who have applied the techniques of the so-called "new social history" to New England towns, and suggested that their research opens important possibilities for similar studies of early Mormon communities.[24] On the basis of such studies, May raised some important questions that scholars interested in community studies might ask as they look at Mormon communities.[25] The new availability of all kinds of records, including the genealogical records generated in Mormon communities and the other vast holdings of the church's Genealogical Society, as well as the development of new techniques related to psychology, sociology, econometrics, and demographic skills, have all contributed to this new social history. May used Kanab, Utah, for his own analysis of a Mormon community, but both before and after his important article was published a number of other Mormon communities were being studied.[26] Hopefully, the recent establishment of the Center for Family and Community History at Brigham Young University will greatly encourage the expansion of such studies.

The term "community," however, often refers to more than a town as defined by certain geographical boundaries. The sense of community among the Mormons as a people, no matter where they live, is an important aspect of Mormon studies. The Mormon ward can be identified as a special community within the larger one. In

1978, for example, Douglas Alder published a seminal article on the Mormon ward, in which he described many of its functions as a community but also challenged scholars to study the ward more deeply in order to find out what it really means to the Mormons in the twentieth century.[27] About 1984 Richard L. Bushman began an intriguing study of his own ward in Delaware that promised to produce some fascinating insights into the nature of the ward as a Mormon community outside Utah. The results are not yet published, but the project suggests the need to make similar and comparative studies of Mormon wards in the heart of Zion as well as in other locations throughout the world. Obviously, the possibilities for these and other kinds of community studies are almost limitless.

Though much more needs to be done, in recent years the history of Mormon women has received considerable attention in scholarly literature. As might be expected, the prolific Leonard Arrington gave one of the pioneer addresses on the subject, and it is significant that it came as his presidential address before the Western History Association in 1969. Not just the Mormon world, but the scholarly world at large was becoming interested in the topic, and received enthusiastically his paper entitled "Blessed Damozels: Women in Mormon History." Decrying the traditional male interpretation of Mormon history, he commented on the self-reliance, literary accomplishments, professional activity, and political involvement of Mormon women in the nineteenth century, interpreting it all as a "tradition of womanly independence and distinction [that] should inspire a later generation of women who are seeking their rightful place in the world."[28]

Since then a tremendous amount has been done, so that students of Mormon history can begin to feel that their image of and empathy with the women of the past is at least getting closer to historical reality. Like all the other topics we have mentioned here, the excellent studies are far too numerous to list, but suffice it to say that as the result of the scholarship of the last two decades we understand better than ever before such a variety of things as the changing role of women's organizations in the church, the lives and contributions of many of the most prominent leading women, the lives and everyday activities of the more common women (a topic that still needs a great deal more study, however), the feelings and problems of women involved in plural marriage, family life on the Mormon frontier, the literary contributions of women, Mormon women in the political life of Utah, and something about how attitudes toward women on the Mormon frontier compared with those in Victorian America in general.[29]

Much the same could be said for ethnic studies, politics, the family, Mormon biography, and a wide variety of other topics. All this only suggests the rich variety of insights that have been gained since 1950, and, as usually happens, each new study only opens up even more questions and more opportunities for eager scholars to plumb the depths even further.

Several historians, however, have pointed to the fact that the most significant studies will put their topics in a larger contextual framework.[30] But in recent years a number of studies have helped take church history out of a vacuum and demonstrate how it has been affected by, responded to, or even influenced the social, political, and economic movements around it. A provocative pioneering article was published by William Mulder in 1959, in which he briefly examined Mormon history against the background of several major movements or themes in American history, concluding that at times Mormonism was "a perfect epitome of its time and place," and at other times "a puzzling contradiction."[31] Since then numerous books and articles have dealt with the theme in one way or another. Some works are especially significant in the way they deal with topics that are of unique or special interest in and of themselves but, at the same time, also deal intellectually with larger themes that help illuminate the human experience. Gary Bunker and Davis Bitton, for example, have published a unique volume on the Mormon image from 1834 to 1914 as seen in the cartoons, caricatures, and illustrations of people who viewed them from the outside. The profuse illustrations attract the reader at first glance, but when he examines the text he will see that it is not just about cartoons—it is really, as the authors themselves explained, "a book about prejudice and the way prejudice became enthroned in stereotypes."[32] In the end, it becomes a highly important study not just of the Mormon image but also of the nature of American public opinion in the nineteenth century.

Numerous other pieces likewise illumine a variety of themes of broad general interest. A pathbreaking article by Alan Keele and

Douglas Tobler, for example, tells the story of a young German Mormon during World War II who found himself at odds with both his country and his local church as he opposed the Hitler regime even while his church leaders were telling him that it was his religious duty to be "subject to kings, presidents, rulers, and magistrates," and to obey, honor, and sustain the law. At its highest level, the article is a marvelous study in the profound and frequent human experience of divided loyalties.[33] Unfortunately, the two books whose titles most strongly suggest that they are going to deal in some comprehensive way with Mormonism and American history both deal only with a very few narrowly selected topics within the theme. Harper and Row published a volume edited by Marvin Hill and myself that contained eleven articles (mostly previously published) on various specific topics, and Klaus Hansen's important book, *Mormonism and the American Experience*, dealt with only a few major themes.[34]

The internationalization of the church has also received considerable attention, and at least six recent books provide some valuable insight into the story of Mormonism outside North America. These include Gilbert W. Scharffs, *Mormonism in Germany* (1970); Spencer J. Palmer, *The Church Encounters Asia* (1970); Spencer J. Palmer, *The Expanding Church* (1978), which provides some marvelous personal insights into the lives of Latter-day Saints in various parts of the world; F. Lamond Tullis, ed., *Mormonism: A Faith for All Cultures* (1978), which consists of a series of very important essays on a variety of topics; James R. Moss, et al., *The International Church* (1982), which is another fine collection of essays; and Lanier R. Britsch, *Unto the Isles of the Sea* (1986), a most interesting and valuable monograph on the expansion of the church in the Pacific. Many scholarly articles have also appeared in recent years, but this is one area that demands considerably more investigation. The various survey histories of the church are, unfortunately, notably lacking in any in-depth treatment of the church's activities abroad, and not until we get more individual studies such as those mentioned above can we expect to see a really adequate synthesis of this important topic.

With such a burgeoning of Mormon history, bibliographic guides have become more and more essential to the scholar. An idea of how extensive the task might become is seen in the fact that in 1959 Ida-Marie Logan published a bibliography of theses and dissertations on Utah and the Mormons completed *outside* the state of Utah, and her list included some 478 items.[35] Many of these dealt with agriculture, mining, geology, and other nonhistory items, but a significantly large portion were on Mormon history and the list only suggests the wide scholarly interest in the subject even that early. Since then considerably more help has been added. A number of journals, including the *Utah Historical Quarterly* and *Dialogue: A Journal of Mormon Thought*, have published cumulative indexes, though most are currently out of date. In 1958 Leonard Arrington's *Great Basin Kingdom* included an exhaustive and revealing bibliography of works on Mormonism up to that point. Other books also contain bibliographies, and one of the most complete, up to that time, was the bibliography in James B. Allen and Glen M. Leonard, *The Story of the Latter-day Saints* (1976). *Dialogue*, *BYU Studies*, and the Mormon History Association's *Newsletter* all frequently contain useful bibliographic updates and essays, as do some other books and journals. One of the most interesting of those dealing with specific topics is Davis Bitton's review essay on literature dealing with polygamy, published in the *Journal of Mormon History* in 1977, and a very worthwhile recent interpretive essay on general Mormon studies was published by Thomas G. Alexander in 1983.[36] On a more mammoth scale, in 1978 Chad Flake published an 825-page volume that listed books, pamphlets, periodicals, and broadsides relating to the church and published between 1830 and 1930. And at a different level, Davis Bitton provided an indispensable tool for researchers when he published his monumental *Guide to Mormon Diaries* in 1977. Finally, David Whittaker, university archivist at Brigham Young University, shows promise of becoming the most prolific publisher of bibliographies in the church. He has prepared several bibliographies on various specific topics for the *Newsletter* of the Mormon History Association, published a complete bibliography of Leonard Arrington's work (no mean task to complete), published other bibliographies on Mormon administrative history, Mormons and Native Americans, and church imprints in South Africa. The Leonard J. Arrington bibliography in this volume is his work. The mass of Mormon history rolling off the presses is overwhelming, and the bibliographers at least are making every effort to keep up.

In all this proliferation of scholarly publications on the Mormon past, what pieces shine out more brightly than the rest? Which do historians consider the best, most important works? Opinions vary widely, but at least we can report on what some people who have been responsible for making certain judgments have said at the time.

In 1977 S. George Ellsworth sent to several scholars an "Invitation to a Quest." "I invite you to help me arrive at a list of the *best books* of historical writing in the field of Utah and Mormon studies," he wrote, and he asked his potential respondents to name the ten best books in the field, as evidenced by "*sound scholarship and literary quality*." He also asked for the names of the authors of the "best ten (10) articles to appear in any periodical or journal in the field, ever."[37]

The results could hardly be interpreted as providing more than a guide to the thinking of one group of well-informed people, but they are nevertheless interesting. Thirty-five people responded, and those books that received the most votes for the "top ten" were, in order: first, Leonard J. Arrington, *Great Basin Kingdom*; second, Juanita Brooks, *Mountain Meadows Massacre*; tied for third, Fawn Brodie, *No Man Knows My History* and Klaus J. Hansen, *Quest for Empire*; tied for fifth, Robert B. Flanders, *Nauvoo: Kingdom on the Mississippi* and Thomas F. O'Dea, *The Mormons*; seventh, James B. Allen and Glen M. Leonard, *The Story of the Latter-day Saints*; eighth, B. H. Roberts, *A Comprehensive History of the Church*; tied for ninth, Nels Anderson, *Desert Saints*, William Mulder, *Homeward to Zion*, and Dallin H. Oaks and Marvin S. Hill, *Carthage Conspiracy*.

There were actually eleven books, then, on the list of the "top ten," because of tie votes. The list of the "second ten" was likewise affected by several tied votes, so that it was actually necessary to list fourteen. They were Juanita Brooks, *John Doyle Lee* and Charles S. Peterson, *Take Up Your Mission* (tied for twelfth); Gustive O. Larson, *The Americanization of Utah for Statehood* (fourteenth); Hubert Howe Bancroft, *History of Utah*, Leonard J. Arrington, Dean L. May, and Feramorz Y. Fox, *Building the City of God*, and Andrew Neff, *History of Utah* (tied for fifteenth); Joseph Smith Jr., *History of the Church*, edited by B. H. Roberts (eighteenth); S. George Ellsworth,

Utah's Heritage and Mark McKiernan, et al., *The Restoration Movement* (tied for nineteenth); Richard F. Burton, *City of the Saints*, Dean C. Jessee, ed., *My Dear Son*, Dale L. Morgan, *The Great Salt Lake*, Harold Schindler, *Orrin Porter Rockwell*, and Ray B. West Jr., *Kingdom of the Saints* (tied for twentieth).

If choosing the best ten books was complicated, the challenge to name the top ten articles ever to appear was even more so. Stanley S. Ivins, "Notes on Mormon Polygamy," and Lester E. Bush, "Mormonism's Negro Policy," were by far the overwhelming choices for first and second places. Beyond those two, however, the votes were so close that the list of the top ten had to include seventeen articles, and no more than two votes separated any of those behind Ivins and Bush. The remainder included: Mario DePillis, "The Quest for Religious Authority and the Rise of Mormonism"; D. Michael Quinn, "The Mormon Succession Crisis of 1844"; David Brion Davis, "Some Themes of Counter Subversion"; William Mulder, "Mormonism's Gathering"; James B. Allen, "The Significance of Joseph Smith's First Vision in Mormon Thought"; Thomas G. Alexander, "Wilford Woodruff and the Changing Nature of Mormon Religious Experience"; Mario DePillis, "Social Sources of Mormonism"; Marvin S. Hill, "Quest for Refuge"; Marvin S. Hill, "Secular or Sectarian History"; Gordon Irving, "The Law of Adoption"; Dale L. Morgan, "The State of Deseret"; Richard D. Poll, "The Political Reconstruction of Utah Territory, 1866–1890"; D. Michael Quinn, "The Evolution of the Presiding Quorums of the LDS Church"; Dean C. Jessee, "The Reliability of Joseph Smith's History"; and William Mulder, "Mormons in American History."

Ellsworth compiled some significant data relating to these books and articles. He classified fourteen of the book authors as Latter-day Saints (presumably active), four as "nominal" Latter-day Saints, two as Reorganized Latter Day Saints, and five as non-Latter-day Saints. Four of the authors were nonhistorians (West, Schindler, Burton, and Joseph Smith). More significant, however, was the fact that eight of the seventeen best articles were published by journals that were non-Mormon–oriented,[38] which demonstrates that Mormon history has received considerable attention outside traditional Mormon-oriented readers.

Two of the top twenty-five books (Joseph Smith and Richard Burton) were published in the nineteenth century, by nonhistorians, and will be considered important classics for generations to come. Three more (Roberts, Nels Anderson, and Dale Morgan) were published before 1950. The other twenty have all been published since then, and in a way, are significant bellwethers of what has happened in Mormon history generally.

No similar survey had been taken since 1977, but quality has been publicly recognized and rewarded. Each year since 1966 the Mormon History Association has given awards in various "best book," "best article," and other categories. The impressive list of awards given from 1966 to 1983 was compiled by Larry Porter and published in the Fall 1983 issue of *Dialogue: A Journal of Mormon Thought*. Each issue of the annual *Journal of Mormon History* also publishes a list of the past year's awards. In addition, in 1984 a new and prestigious award was announced through Brigham Young University: The David Woolley Evans and Beatrice Cannon Evans Biography Award. It consisted of an annual $10,000 prize for "a distinguished biography of any person significant in the culture or history of what may be called Mormon Country." Prizes have been awarded to Leonard Arrington for his *Brigham Young: American Moses*, Richard Bushman for *Joseph Smith and the Beginnings of Mormonism*, and Linda King Newell and Valeen Tippetts Avery for their highly significant work *Mormon Enigma: Emma Hale Smith*.

It would be difficult for me to announce my own nominee for the all-time "best book" or "best article" in Mormon history since 1950 — the criteria are too vague and the basis for judgment is too highly subjective. There are, however, a few items that stand out in my mind as having had a pivotal impact on Mormon historiography. A few books, for example, especially impress me as having made the kind of contribution that will affect the literature and our image of Mormon history for generations to come. They include, of course, Brooks's *Mountain Meadows Massacre* and Arrington's *Great Basin Kingdom*. They also include Klaus J. Hansen's *Quest for Empire*, for even though his research and interpretation has been significantly updated by Michael Quinn and others, he was the first to make the Kingdom of God concept widely known to scholars, and since then any adequate scholarly work has had to deal with the issue; Gustive O. Larson's *The "Americanization" of Utah for Statehood*, which was criticized by Tom Alexander for putting too much emphasis on church-state relations and not enough on polygamy as a concern of those national figures who were trying to reform the Mormons but nevertheless presented a concept of how the nation viewed the Mormons that will endure in the literature; Dean Jessee's two monumental edited works, *Letters of Brigham Young to his Sons* and *The Personal Writings of Joseph Smith*, which are not only the most outstanding examples available of how to edit and publish original documents, but which also make some pivotally important documents available to people who wish to study these two great church leaders; Dallin H. Oaks and Marvin S. Hill's *Carthage Conspiracy: The Trial of the Accused Assassins of Joseph Smith*, which, at least for me, placed the whole issue of the murder of the prophet and the subsequent acquittal of his accused murders in a most important thematic context; Leonard Arrington's *Brigham Young: American Moses*, which has received high praise not only for the depth of Arrington's research but also for the empathy and warmth which he interprets the great Mormon colonizer, and which, in my opinion, is his best work since *Great Basin Kingdom*; Richard Bushman's *Joseph Smith and the Beginnings of Mormonism*, which sets a fine example of both faith and scholarship and does the best job yet (at least of any book) of putting the origins of Mormonism in its broader historical context; and Jan Shipps's *Mormonism: The Story of a New Religious Tradition*, which stands as a monument to the fact that a non-Mormon scholar can get so well acquainted with the spirit of Mormonism, and which also places the history of Mormonism in the mainstream of American religious studies.

The great articles are so manifold that I will not even attempt a listing, but I must mention one that, for me, was an outstanding example of how a detailed study of just one idea can be of pivotal importance to our understanding of an era. Gordon Irving's "The Law of Adoption: One Phase of the Development of the Mormon Concept of Salvation, 1830–1890" approached a topic I had never thought of before it was published in *BYU Studies* (Spring 1974) but which permanently affected my understanding of and approach to certain aspects of the history of Mormon doctrine and practice.

The work goes on, and the richness and depth that has come to Mormon history since 1950 is only the beginning. I suspect that even Bernard DeVoto would have been impressed, though undoubtedly he would have something to say about the many works of dubious quality that also continue to appear. But even the Mormon History Association has not been above that, for one year it gave a "worst book" award to Stanley Hirshson for his less than adequate research and treatment of the great Mormon colonizer in his *Lion of the Lord: A Biography of Brigham Young*.

It is not my intent to say that "all is well in Zion" so far as the writing of its history is concerned. As of 1986 there are problems enough to concern us all. On the one hand, from outside the church we have witnessed a new generation of dedicated, professional anti-Mormons who use our own historical sources (often irresponsibly molded together) to create images of the past deliberately designed to undermine and destroy. On the other hand, from time to time we still see propaganda in its worst form (i.e., seemingly deliberate distortion, ignoring of evidence, and unsupported assertions about the past) issuing from well-meaning people even within the church. Both extremes are tragic and, as Fischer observed, "the fact that earlier generations and other ideological groups have committed the same wrong does not convert it into a right."[39] Propaganda plays tricks on the dead, deceives the living, and certainly is untrue to both.

But even among those whose work falls somewhere on the long scale between the extreme debunkers and the overzealous defenders, problems still arise. We still see shoddy research, conclusions not well thought out or not well supported, and poorly written, unimaginative history. Instead of having the impact of the well-written novel, some histories may well have the impact of a sleeping pill.

More importantly, at least for me, from time to time we also see types of history in which authors have insufficiently responded to that delicate need for balance that will make them pause several times before publishing in order to make certain that not only the documented facts but also the tone and empathy with which they portray the people of the past is indeed as true *to them* as they can make it, and whether that tone will, in reality, come across to their larger audience in the way that, deep down, they really intend. Some scholars may have become so enamored with the idea that we must show that the prophets were "human" as well as inspired that they have spent a disproportionate amount of time and space illustrating the human weaknesses, failings, foibles, and mistakes of the founders. The result may be that instead of the "balanced" view they profess to want to achieve, their very crusade has tipped the scales the other way.

In spite of its problems, however, I believe Mormon history is alive and well in 1986. Leonard Arrington and the other "transition scholars" of the 1950s laid excellent foundations. They along with their students and their students' students have explored in fascinating detail everything from the magnificent visions from the heavens to the pestiferous ironclads of the earth. They have laid the groundwork for broadening the Saints' understanding of and appreciation for their own history, and they have made Mormon history a significant and respected part of American history even as the church itself has gained new prestige and influence within its host society. But the work is by no means finished—in fact it has hardly begun. The thousands of books, monographs, and articles produced since 1950 have done more than illuminate the dark corners of the past. In the process, they have also raised more questions and opened more opportunities for new research than ever before. The work of creating our history has only begun, and new creators are appearing all the time.

NOTES

1. As Gerda Lerner remarked in her 1982 presidential address before the Organization of American Historians, "History is more than collective memory; it is memory formed and shaped so as to have meaning. This process, by which people preserve and interpret the past, and then reinterpret it in light of new questions, is 'history-making.' It is not a dispensable intellectual luxury; history-making is a social necessity." Gerda Lerner, "The Necessity of History and the Professional Historian," *The Journal of American History* 69 (June 1982): 10.

2. Bernard DeVoto, "The Centennial of Mormonism: A Study in Utopia and Dictatorship," *Forays and Rebuttals* (Boston, 1936), 82–83, as quoted in Rodman W. Paul, "The Mormons as a Theme in Western Historical Writing," *Journal of American History* 54 (December 1967): 512.

3. For a critical analysis of Roberts's work, see Davis Bitton, "B. H.

Roberts as an Historian," *Dialogue: A Journal of Mormon Thought* 3 (Winter 1968): 25–44. Bitton very deftly analyzes Roberts's historical writing in terms of both its weaknesses and its strengths. He concludes that in spite of much left to be desired, Roberts is still worth reading, even by professional historians.

   4. Until about 1920, most historical writings seemed to fall into the category either of anti-Mormon criticism or pro-Mormon apologia. Some of the latter was well-written and important, including works by Edward Tullidge, Orson F. Whitney, and B. H. Roberts, but none could qualify as truly scholarly studies. In the next decade a few more scholarly publications appeared. Morris R. Werner's *Brigham Young* (1925) was a transitional work in that it took a more detached position than most, but it suffered from poor documentation. Leland H. Creer's *Utah and the Nation* (1929) represented an even more important transition, for it became the first published work to analyze effectively the relationship between Mormonism and its larger American setting — a theme that has become especially important to scholars of Mormonism today. Also in this period, Ephraim E. Ericksen published his doctoral dissertation, *The Psychological and Ethical Aspects of Mormon Group Life* (1923), which was well received by scholars but frowned upon by certain church leaders because of its secular, naturalistic approach to Mormon institutions. For a sympathetic study of Ericksen, see Scott Kenney, "E. E. Ericksen Loyal Heretic," *Sunstone* 3 (July–August 1978): 16–27. A total of eleven Ph.D. dissertations, including Creer's and Ericksen's, were completed between 1900 and 1930, but beyond these items there was little of scholarly significance available to students of Mormon history. For further comment on early studies, see Leonard J. Arrington, "Scholarly Studies of Mormonism in the Twentieth Century," *Dialogue: A Journal of Mormon Thought* 1 (Spring 1966): 15–32, which includes a list of Ph.D dissertations on Mormon history and culture; Thomas G. Alexander and James B. Allen, "The Mormons in the Mountain West: A Selected Bibliography," *Arizona and the West* 9 (Winter 1967): 365–84; Thomas G. Alexander, "Toward the New Mormon History: An Examination of the Literature of the Latter-day Saints in the Far West," in Michael P. Malone, ed., *Historians and the American West* (Lincoln: University of Nebraska Press, 1983), 344–68.

   5. DeVoto himself made at least one important contribution when he discussed the Mormons as part of the larger American westering movement in his *Year of Decision* (Boston: Little, Brown, 1943). Among the other items of significance that might be included are the nineteen Ph.D. dissertations completed between 1930 and 1949, as listed in Arrington, "Scholarly Studies of Mormonism," as well as the following publications, some of which are the published versions of dissertations: John Henry Evans, *Joseph Smith, An American Prophet* (New York: MacMillan Co., 1936); Joel E. Ricks, *Forms and Methods of Early Mormon Settlement in Utah and*

the Surrounding Region, 1847–1877 (Ph.D. diss., University of Chicago, 1930, published in Logan, Utah: Utah State University Monograph Series, 1964); Clyde E. Buckingham, "Mormonism in Illinois," *Journal of the Illinois State Historical Society* 32 (1939): 173–92; Mark A. Pendleton, "The Orderville United Order of Zion," *Utah Historical Quarterly* 7 (1939): 141–59; Robert G. Raymer, "Early Mining in Utah," *Utah Historical Quarterly* 7 (1939): 81–88; Milton R. Hunter, "The Mormons and the Colorado River," *American Historical Review* 44 (1939): 549–55; Sharon McGarry, "Mormon Money," *The Numismatist* 63 (1940): 491–604, 698–706, 732–44, 830–40; Andrew Love Neff, *History of Utah, 1847 to 1869;* Leland Hargrave Creer, ed. (Salt Lake City: Deseret News Press, 1940); Chauncey D. Harris, *Salt Lake City: A Regional Capital* (Chicago: Privately printed, 1940), which is not on Mormonism as such but puts Mormon city building in an important perspective; Milton R. Hunter, *Brigham Young the Colonizer* (1940; 4th ed., rev., Salt Lake City: Peregrine Smith, 1973), originally prepared as a Ph.D. dissertation at the University of California, Berkeley; William John McNiff, *Heaven on Earth: A Planned Mormon Society* (Oxford, Ohio: The Mississippi Valley Press, 1940); Dale L. Morgan, "The State of Deseret," *Utah Historical Quarterly* 8 (April, July, October 1940): 65–239; Robert J. Dwyer, *The Gentile Comes to Utah: A Study in Religious and Social Conflict (1862–1890)* (1940; 2nd ed. Salt Lake City: Western Epics, 1971); Frank H. Jonas, "Utah: Sagebrush Democracy," Chapter 1 in Thomas C. Donnelley, ed., *Rocky Mountain Politics* (Albuquerque: University of New Mexico Press, 1940); Arden Beal Olsen, "Mormon Mercantile Cooperation in Utah," *Journal of Marketing* 6 (1941): 136–42, based on his excellent 1935 dissertation at the University of California, Berkeley, "The History of Mormon Mercantile Cooperation in Utah"; Nels Anderson, *Desert Saints; The Mormon Frontier in Utah* (Chicago: University of Chicago Press, 1942); Merrill D. Beal, *A History of Southeastern Idaho* (Caldwell, Ida.: The Caxton Printers, Ltd., 1942); Juanita Brooks, *Dudley Leavitt, Pioneer to Southern Utah* (St. George, Utah, 1942); G. Homer Durham, "Administrative Organization of the Mormon Church," *Political Science Quarterly* 57 (1942): 51–71; Austin E. Fife, "Popular Legends of the Mormons," *California Folklore Quarterly* 1 (April 1942): 105–56; Arnold M. Rose, "The Mormon Church and Utah Politics: An Abstract of a Statistical Study," *American Sociological Review* 7 (December 1942): 853–54; Juanita Brooks, "Indian Relations on the Mormon Frontier," *Utah Historical Quarterly* 12 (January–April 1944): 1–48; G. Homer Durham, "A Political Interpretation of Mormon History," *Pacific Historical Review* 13 (June 1944): 136–50; Alice Felt Tyler, *Freedom's Ferment: Phases of American Social History to 1860* (Minneapolis: University of Minnesota Press, 1944), which contains a chapter on the Mormons; Fawn M. Brodie, *No Man Knows my History: The Life of Joseph Smith, the Mormon Prophet* (New York: Alfred A. Knopf, 1945); M. Hamlin Cannon, "Migration of English Mormons to America," *Ameri-*

can Historical Review 52 (1947): 436–55; Leland H. Creer, *Founding of an Empire: The Exploration and Colonization of Utah, 1776–1856* (Salt Lake City: Bookcraft, 1947); Gustive O. Larson, *Prelude to the Kingdom: Mormon Deseret Conquest—A Chapter in Cooperation Experience* (Francistown, N.H.: Marshall Jones Company, 1947); Dale L. Morgan, *The Great Salt Lake* (Indianapolis: Bobbs-Merrill Co., 1947); Dale L. Morgan, "Salt Lake City: City of the Saints," in Ray B. West, ed., *Rocky Mountain Cities* (New York: W. W. Norton, 1949), 179–207. During this period the *Utah Historical Quarterly*, which began publication in 1928, published several Mormon history articles as well as a number of journals, journal extracts, and other documents that were of significance to scholars.

Within the church, the pages of such magazines as *The Improvement Era*, *The Juvenile Instructor*, *The Utah Genealogical and Historical Magazine*, and *The Relief Society Magazine* often carried significant historical articles. Books available, and in print, by 1950 that were written by Mormons and aimed primarily at the Mormon audience included Roberts, *Comprehensive History*; Andrew Jenson, *Latter-day Saint Biographical Encyclopedia* (4 vols.; Salt Lake City: Andrew Jenson History Co., 1901–1936); Joseph Fielding Smith, *Essentials in Church History* (26th ed.; Salt Lake City: Deseret Book Company, 1950); William Edwin Berrett, *The Restored Church* (6th ed.; Salt Lake City: LDS Church Department of Education, 1949), which was the standard church history textbook for the seminaries; Susa Young Gates, *Life of Brigham Young* (New York: MacMillan Co., 1930); Susa Young Gates and Leah D. Widtsoe, *Life Story of Brigham Young* (New York: MacMillan Co., 1930); Preston Nibley, *Brigham Young, the Man and His Work* (Salt Lake City: Deseret News Press, 1930), a biography especially notable for its lack of perception and balance; Joseph Fielding Smith, *Life of Joseph F. Smith* (Salt Lake City: Deseret News Press, 1938); Joseph Smith Jr., *History of the Church*, ed., B. H. Roberts (6 vols., Salt Lake City: Deseret News Press, 1904), sometimes referred to as the *Documentary History of the Church*; Matthias F. Cowley, *Wilford Woodruff* (Salt Lake City: Deseret News Press, 1909). For more references to publications before 1950, see the bibliography in Leonard J. Arrington, *Great Basin Kingdom* (Cambridge: Harvard University Press, 1958).

6. In 1950 publishing outlets for Mormon history were limited largely to the *Utah Historical Quarterly*, certain church magazines, notably *The Instructor* and *The Improvement Era*, Deseret Book Company, and Bookcraft. By the mid–1980s, however, the frequency and quality of historical articles in the *Ensign* magazine (which replaced *The Improvement Era*) had notably increased, and several journals regularly sought for and accepted articles related to Mormon history. These included *The Journal of Mormon History*; *Brigham Young University Studies*; *Dialogue: A Journal of Mormon Thought*; *Sunstone: A Journal of Mormon Scholarship, Issues, and Art*; *Exponent II*; *Utah Historical Quarterly*; and *The John Whitmer Historical*

Association Journal. Other journals more widely circulated to the national scholarly audience also showed frequent interest in Mormon studies, including such publications as *Church History* and *The Western Historical Quarterly*, *The Pacific Historical Review*, and several journals of regional interest such as *New York History*, *Idaho Yesterdays*, and *Arizona and the West*. In addition, a number of major publishing houses as well as university presses were not only willing but anxious to consider Mormon manuscripts. Both the University of Utah Press and the University of Illinois Press, for example, made Mormon history a major publishing commitment. Signature Press, located in Salt Lake City, was founded with Mormon history as its major commitment, and several other Utah presses, including Deseret Book Company and Bookcraft, regularly published significant books on Mormon historical topics. The Religious Studies Center at Brigham Young University also published several works of significant historical interest, and the Charles Redd Center for Western Studies regularly included Mormon history in its monograph series. In the 1970s Brigham Young University Press published a number of scholarly works on Mormon history but, ironically, by the mid–1980s it was no longer seeking such manuscripts.

7. As I was preparing this article, certain coworkers and I had compiled a list of over three thousand significant items published since 1950, and at least one thousand of these were scholarly items that I considered especially significant or important in some way.

8. Their influence came in various ways, including the classroom where, over the years, each had an important role to play in the training of at least some of the coming generation of Mormon historians. Ellsworth, for example, powerfully and methodically drilled into his students his own commitment to three important principles: the obligation of the historian to seek out and analyze every possible document that has anything to do with the topic of his research; the careful manner in which every document must be analyzed and compared with other documents in order to determine the degree to which it actually reflects what happened; and, the deep humility with which the historian must approach his task of finally presenting to the world some conclusions about his research. We must stand in awe before the task of recreating the past, he told his students, and none of us must be so vain as to think we have said the final word on anything. As a teacher in the Institute of Religion, it was one of Eugene Campbell's tasks—and he did it well—to help students find ways to reconcile the new and challenging ideas coming from their secular education with the fundamentals of their faith. His willingness—no, eagerness—to spend long hours outside the classroom exploring religious and intellectual concerns with his students, clarifying his commitment to the church, was exemplary. Later he became a professor of history at Brigham Young University, where he introduced literally thousands of students to the excitement of Utah history. Leonard Arrington became the great example of the enthusiasm that can come to a

person as he plows new fields, of the value of sharing ideas with others, and of the importance of trying to encourage other young people as they try to move up in the profession. Over his career, Leonard Arrington probably has done more cooperative research and writing with up-and-coming scholars, and actually giving several of them their start, than almost anyone else in the field of Mormon history.

9. These included Everett L. Cooley, who, in addition to publishing many significant items of his own, became editor of the *Utah Historical Quarterly* and in that capacity encouraged several younger historians in the early stages of their publishing careers; William Mulder, a young English professor at the University of Utah who made his name in Mormon history through his study of Scandinavian immigrants; and Richard Poll and Brigham Madsen, new professors of history at Brigham Young University.

10. David Hackett Fischer, *Historians' Fallacies: Toward a Logic of Historical Thought* (New York: Harper & Row, 1970), 314.

11. They would have agreed with one modern historian who said, "It is a truism, yet one easy to forget, that people see most easily things they are prepared to see and overlook those they do not expect to encounter." Anne Firor Scott, "On Seeing and Not Seeing: A Case of Historical Invisibility," *The Journal of American History* 71 (June 1984): 1.

12. This article is not, however, intended as another entry in the ongoing debate over the so-called "New Mormon History," as much of the recent scholarship has been dubbed. It is simply an attempt to evaluate certain general trends I see in the whole body of Mormon history since 1950, particularly in terms of what it has or has not done to help create better understanding, both in and out of the church, of the Mormon past. The term "New Mormon History" was apparently first coined by Moses Richins in "The New Mormon History," *The American West* 5 (March 1969): 49. The term has been used in a variety of ways, and the approach often implied by it has been both praised and vilified. For an early statement that tended to take the combined religious-scholarly attitude of many so-called "New Mormon Historians," see Richard L. Bushman, "Faithful History," *Dialogue: A Journal of Mormon Thought* 4 (Winter 1969): 11–25. For some specific positive assessments by non-Mormons of the "New Mormon History," see Robert B. Flanders, "Some Reflections on the New Mormon History," *Dialogue: A Journal of Mormon Thought* 9 (Spring 1974): 34–41; Lawrence Foster, "New Perspectives on the Mormon Past," *Sunstone* 7 (January–February 1982): 41–45. For an LDS historian's perspective, see Alexander, "Toward the New Mormon History." For some philosophical criticisms of the "New Mormon History," see Neal W. Kramer, "Looking for God in History," *Sunstone* 8 (January–March 1983): 15–17; David Earl Bohn, "No Higher Ground," *Sunstone* 8 (May–June 1983): 26–32; Gary Novak and Louis C. Midgley, "Remembrance and the Past: Jewish and Mormon Memory and the New History," unpublished paper presented at the

annual meeting of the Mormon History Association, 11 May 1984. For a response, see Thomas G. Alexander, "Historiography and the New Mormon History: A Historian's Perspective," *Dialogue: A Journal of Mormon Thought* 19 (Fall 1986): 25–50.

13. "God does not expect us to lie in his name," she continued and, she said, she owed it to her readers "to tell the truth, for the truth suppressed is its own kind of lie." Juanita Brooks to Dale L. Morgan, as quoted in Charles S. Peterson's "Introduction" to Brooks, *Quicksand and Cactus: A Memoir of the Southern Mormon Frontier* (Salt Lake City and Chicago: Howe Brothers, 1982), xxxii.

14. See S. George Ellsworth, "A History of Mormon Missions in the United States and Canada, 1830–1860," (Ph.D. diss., University of California, Berkeley, 1951).

15. S. George Ellsworth, *Zion in Paradise: Early Mormons in the South Seas* (Logan: Utah State University, 1959).

16. Eugene E. Campbell, "Brigham Young's Outer Cordon – A Reappraisal," *Utah Historical Quarterly* 41 (Summer 1973): 226–27.

17. Thomas F. O'Dea, *The Mormons* (Chicago: University of Chicago Press, 1957); Mario S. DePillis, "The Quest for Religious Authority and the Rise of Mormonism," *Dialogue: A Journal of Mormon Thought* 1 (Fall 1966): 68–88; David Brion Davis, "Some Themes of Counter-Subversion: An Analysis of Anti-Masonic, Anti-Catholic, and Anti-Mormon Literature," *The Mississippi Valley Historical Review* 57 (September 1960): 205–24; Norman F. Furniss, *The Mormon Conflict, 1850–1959* (New Haven: Yale University Press, 1959); Mark P. Leone, *Roots of Modern Mormonism* (Cambridge: Harvard University Press, 1979); Keith Huntress, "Governor Thomas Ford and the Murderers of Joseph Smith," *Dialogue: A Journal of Mormon Thought* 4 (Summer 1969): 41–52; Lawrence B. Lee, "The Mormons Come to Canada, 1887–1902," *The Pacific Northwest Quarterly* 59 (January 1968): 11–22; Bernard Bailyn, et al., *The Great Republic* (Lexington, Mass.; D. C. Heath & Co., 1977), 532–41.

18. For an impressive personal essay on her association with Mormons and Mormonism, see Jan Shipps, "An 'Insider-Outsider' in Zion," *Dialogue: A Journal of Mormon Thought* 15 (Spring 1982): 138–61.

19. See David J. Whittaker, "Bibliography of Leonard James Arrington," *Dialogue* 11 (1978): 33–47, which is appended to his article, "Leonard J. Arrington: His Life and Work," ibid., 23–32.

20. For some of the "old views" on the Kirtland economy, see Robert Kent Fielding, "The Growth of the Mormon Church in Kirtland, Ohio" (Ph.D. diss., Indiana University, 1957); Fielding, "The Mormon Economy in Ohio," *Utah Historical Quarterly* 27 (October 1959): 331–56; Roberts, *Comprehensive History*, 1:398, 402; Fawn M. Brodie, *No Man Knows my History*; and several other authors cited in various places in the following work. The most significant new research is brought together brilliantly in

Marvin S. Hill, C. Keith Rooker, and Larry T. Wimmer, *The Kirtland Economy Revisited. A Market Critique of Sectarian Economics* (Provo, Utah: Brigham Young University Press, 1977).

21. In this and notes to follow, there is space for only the most superficial sampling of the scholarly works available on the topics mentioned. See, however, Leonard J. Arrington, "An Economic Interpretation of the 'Word of Wisdom'," *Brigham Young University Studies* 1 (1959): 37–49; Robert Bruce Flanders, *Nauvoo Kingdom on the Mississippi* (Urbana: University of Illinois Press, 1965), esp. chapter 5; Dallin H. Oaks and Joseph I. Bentley, "Joseph Smith and Legal Process: In the Wake of the Steamboat *Nauvoo*," *Brigham Young University Law Review* 2 (1976): 735–82; Arrington, *Great Basin Kingdom*; *Utah Historical Quarterly* 29 (July 1961), special issue on Utah's "Dixie"; Gustive O. Larson, "Bulwark of the Kingdom: Utah's Iron and Steel Industry," *Utah Historical Quarterly* 31 (Summer 1963): 248–61; Gustive O. Larson, "Land Contest in Early Utah," *Utah Historical Quarterly* 29 (October 1961): 309–25; Richard H. Jackson, "Righteousness and Environmental Change: The Mormons and the Environment," in Thomas G. Alexander, ed., *Essays in the American West, 1973–1974*, Charles Redd Monographs in Western History, No. 5: 21–42; Leonard J. Arrington, Feramorz Y. Fox, and Dean L. May, *Building the City of God: Community and Cooperation Among the Mormons* (Salt Lake City: Deseret Book Company, 1976); Dwight L. Israelson, "An Economic Analysis of the United Order," *BYU Studies* 18 (Summer 1978): 536–62; James R. Kearl, Clayne L. Pope, and Larry T. Wimmer, "Household Wealth in a Settlement Economy: Utah 1850–1870," *Journal of Economic History* 40 (September 1980): 477–96.

22. Ronald W. Walker, "Crisis in Zion: Heber J. Grant and the Panic of 1893," *Arizona and the West* 21 (Autumn 1979): 257–78; J. Kenneth Davies, *Deseret's Sons of Toil: A History of the Workers' Movements of Territorial Utah, 1852–1896* (Salt Lake City: Olympus Publishing Company, 1977); Leonard J. Arrington and Wayne K. Hinton, "Origin of the Welfare Plan of The Church of Jesus Christ of Latter-day Saints," *BYU Studies* 5 (Winter 1964): 67–85; Arrington, et al., *Building the City of God*, chapter 15; Bill Beecham and David Briscoe, "Mormon Money & How It's Made," *Utah Holiday* 22 (March 1976): 4–11; Leonard J. Arrington and Davis Bitton, *The Mormon Experience; A History of the Latter-day Saints* (New York: Alfred A. Knopf, 1979), chapter 14; O. Kendall White Jr., "Mormon Resistance and Accommodation: From Communitarian Socialism to Corporate Capitalism," in Scott Cummings, ed., *Self-Help in Urban America: Patterns of Minority Economic Development* (Port Washington, N.Y.: National University Publications, Kennikat Press, 1980).

23. Lawrence M. Yorgason, "Some Demographic Aspects of One Hundred Early Mormon Converts, 1830–1837," (Master's thesis, Brigham Young University, 1974); Dean L. May, "A Demographic Portrait of the Mormons,

1830–1980," in Thomas G. Alexander and Jessie L. Embry, eds., *After 150 Years: The Latter-day Saints in Sesquicentennial Perspective* (Provo, Utah: Charles Redd Center for Western Studies, 1983): 37–70; Wayne L. Wahlquist, "Population Growth in the Mormon Core Area: 1847–90," in Richard H. Jackson, ed., *The Mormon Role in the Settlement of the West* (Provo, Utah: Brigham Young University Press, 1978): 107–35; James E. Smith and Phillip R. Kunz, "Polygyny and Fertility in Nineteenth-Century America," *Population Studies* 30 (1976): 465–80; Donald W. Hastings, Charles H. Reynolds, and Ray R. Canning, "Mormonism and Birth Planning: The Discrepancy Between Church Authorities' Teachings and Lay Attitudes," *Population Studies* 26 (1972): 19–28; 465–79; Phillip R. Kunz, "One Wife or Several? A Comparative Study of Late Nineteenth-Century Marriage in Utah," in Thomas G. Alexander, ed., *The Mormon People, Their Character and Traditions* (Provo, Utah: Brigham Young University Press, 1980), 53–74; Larry Logue, "A Time of Marriage: Monogamy and Polygamy in a Utah Town," *Journal of Mormon History* 11 (1984): 3–26; Lowell "Ben" Bennion, "The Incidence of Mormon Polygamy in 1880: 'Dixie' versus Davis Stake," *Journal of Mormon History* 11 (1984): 27–42; J. R. Kearl, Clayne L. Pope, and Larry T. Wimmer, comps., *Index to the 1850, 1860 and 1870 Census of Utah Heads of Households* (Baltimore: Genealogical Publishing Company, Inc., 1981).

24. See Dean L. May, "The Making of Saints: The Mormon Town as a Setting for the Study of Cultural Change," *Utah Historical Quarterly* 45 (Winter 1977): 75–92. Among the many useful models he points to are the studies of New England communities by John Demos, who studied family life in Plymouth Colony; Philip J. Greven Jr., who studied population, land, and family in colonial Andover, Massachusetts; Kenneth Lockridge, who studied another community during a 100–year period; and Richard L. Bushman, a prominent Mormon historian, who has achieved high praise for his work entitled *From Puritan to Yankee*, in which he used the techniques of psychology to study and help explain the changing social order in a Connecticut community.

25. They include questions about the relationship of family patterns to community stability; community growth and property holding; the nature of and reasons for community solidarity; the role of the family in community life; the role of the church, especially in Mormon communities; conflict within communities and the response to conflict. These and other questions have become important to historians who want to try to understand the nature of communities.

26. A pivotal and enduring early study, of course, was Nels Anderson, *Deseret Saints* (1944). For examples of more recent studies, however, see D. W. Meinig, "The Mormon Cultural Region: Strategies and Patterns in the Geography of the American West, 1847–1964," *American Geographers Asso-*

ciation Annals 55 (1965): 191–200; Charles S. Peterson, *Take Up Your Mission: Mormon Colonizing along the Little Colorado River, 1870–1900* (Tucson: University of Arizona Press, 1973); James B. Allen and Thomas B. Alexander, *Mormons and Gentiles: A History of Salt Lake City* (Boulder, Colo.: Pruett Press, 1984); Kerry William Bate, "Iron City, Mormon Mining Town," *Utah Historical Quarterly* 50 (Winter 1982): 47–58; Davis Bitton, "The Makings of a Community: Blackfoot, Idaho 1878–1910," *Idaho Yesterdays* 19 (Spring 1975): 2–15; Craig M. Call, "Discovering Chesterfield," *Sunstone* 6 (January–February 1981): 23–26.

27. Douglas D. Alder, "The Mormon Ward: Congregation or Community?" *Journal of Mormon History* 5 (1978): 61–71.

28. Leonard J. Arrington, "Blessed Damozels: Women in Mormon History," *Dialogue: A Journal of Mormon Thought* 6 (Summer 1971): 22–31; see also Leonard J. Arrington and Susan Arrington Madsen, *Sunbonnet Sisters: The Stories of Mormon Women and Frontier Life* (Salt Lake City: Bookcraft, 1984).

29. For a guide to the literature on women's history, see Carol Cornwall Madsen and David J. Whittaker, "History's Sequel: A Source Essay on Women in Mormon History," *Journal of Mormon History* 6 (1979): 123–45, and Patricia Lyn Scott and Maureen Ursenbach Beecher, "Mormon Women: A Bibliography in Process, 1977–1985," *Journal of Mormon History* 13 (1986): 113–27.

30. This is the burden, for example, of Bailyn's "History and the Creative Imagination."

31. William Mulder, "The Mormons in American History," *Utah Historical Quarterly* 27 (January 1959): 59–77.

32. Gary L. Bunker and Davis Bitton, *The Mormon Graphic Image, 1834–1914: Cartoons, Caricatures, and Illustrations* (Salt Lake City: University of Utah Press, 1983).

33. Alan F. Keele and Douglas F. Tobler, "The Führer's New Clothes: Helmuth Huebener and the Mormons in the Third Reich," *Sunstone* 5 (November–December 1980): 20–29. I like to think that my own article, " 'Good Guys vs. Good Guys': Rudger Clawson, John Sharp, and Civil Disobedience in Nineteenth-century Utah," *Utah Historical Quarterly* 48 (Spring 1980): 148–74, is a good example of something that deals with a similar larger theme.

34. Marvin S. Hill and James B. Allen, eds., *Mormonism and American Culture* (New York: Harper & Row, 1972); Klaus Hansen, *Mormonism and the American Experience* (Chicago: University of Chicago Press, 1981).

35. Ida-Marie Clark Logan, "A Bibliography of Theses and Dissertations Concerning Utah or the Mormons Written outside the State of Utah," *Utah Historical Quarterly* 27 (January 1959, April 1959): 85–100, 169–90.

36. Alexander, "Toward the New Mormon History."

37. Professor Ellsworth never published the results of his quest, but he has graciously shared his data with me, with permission to use it as it seemed appropriate.

38. These included *Western Humanities Review* (1); *Pacific Historical Review* (1); *Mississippi Valley Historical Review* (1); *Church History* (4); and the publications of the Reynolds Lecture Series at the University of Utah (1).

39. Fischer, *Historians' Fallacies*, 314.

Leonard James Arrington:
A Bibliography

COMPILED BY DAVID J. WHITTAKER

Abbreviations

AH	*Agricultural History*
AHR	*American Historical Review*
AW	*Arizona and the West*
BYU Studies	*Brigham Young University Studies*
BHR	*Business History Review*
Dialogue	*Dialogue: A Journal of Mormon Thought*
EHR	*Economic History Review*
Ensign	*The Ensign* (Salt Lake City)
Era	*The Improvement Era* (Salt Lake City)
HLQ	*Huntington Library Quarterly*
IY	*Idaho Yesterday*
JAH	*Journal of American History*
JEH	*Journal of Economic History*
New Era	*The New Era* (Salt Lake City)
PHR	*Pacific Historical Review*
PNQ	*Pacific Northwest Quarterly*
PUASAL	*Proceedings of the Utah Academy of Sciences, Arts & Letters*
SUP News	*Sons of Utah Pioneers News* (Salt Lake City)
UHQ	*Utah Historical Quarterly*
WHR	*Western Humanities Review*

1935

Article:

"Idaho Future Farmer Has Outstanding Project," *American Farm Youth* 1 (April 1935): 14.

1950

Review:

The Economics of Agriculture, by R. L. Cohen. In *Southern Economic Journal* 17 (October 1950): 209–10.

1951

Articles in Professional Publications:

"The Deseret Telegraph — A Church-owned Public Utility," *JEH* 11 (Spring 1951): 117–39.
"Economic Policy Crisis in Utah — 1869," *PUASAL* 18 (1951): 123 ff. Abstract.
"Iron Manufacturing in Southern Utah in the 1800s: The Iron Manufacturing Company of Utah," *Bulletin of the Business Historical Society* 21 (September 1951): 149–68.
"Property Among the Mormons," *Rural Sociology* 16 (December 1951): 339–52.
"Taming the Turbulent Sevier: A Story of Mormon Desert Conquest," *WHR* 5 (August 1951): 383–406.
"The Transcontinental Railroad and Mormon Economic Policy," *PHR* 20 (May 1951): 143–57. Reprinted in Thomas C. Cochran and Thomas B. Brewer, ed., *View of American Economic Growth: The Industrial Era* (New York: McGraw–Hill Book Company, 1966), 50–60.
"Zion's Board of Trade: A Third United Order," *WHR* 5 (Winter 1950–51): 1–20.

Article in Non-Professional Publication:

"Brigham Young and the Transcontinental Telegraph Line," *Era* 54 (July 1951): 510 ff.

Reviews:

Beckoning Frontiers: Public and Personal Recollections, by Marriner S. Eccles. In *WHR* 5 (Autumn 1951): 407–10. With Evan B. Murray.
Social Economy and the Price System: An Essay in Welfare Economics, by Raymond T. Bye. In *Southern Economic Journal* 17 (April 1951): 483–84.

1952

Articles in Professional Publications:

"Coin and Currency in Early Utah," *UHQ* 20 (January 1952): 56–76.
"The Institution of Private Property in Early Utah," *PUASAL* 29 (1952): 55. Abstract.
"The Mormon Debt Problem of the 1890's," *PUASAL* 29 (1952): 56. Abstract.
"Mormon Finance and the Utah War," *UHQ* 20 (July 1952): 219–38.
"Price Control in Early Utah," *PUASAL* 29 (1952): 55. Abstract.

"The Settlement of the Brigham Young Estate, 1877–1879," *PHR* 21 (February 1952): 1–20.

1953

Articles in Professional Publications:

"Early Mormon Communitarianism: The Law of Consecration and Stewardship," *WHR* 7 (Autumn 1953): 341–69. Reprinted without footnotes in Marvin S. Hill and James B. Allen, eds., *Mormonism and American Culture* (New York: Harper and Row, 1972), 37–58.
"The Provo Woolen Mills: Utah's First Large Manufacturing Establishment," *UHQ* 21 (April 1953): 97–116.
"Religious Sanction and Entrepreneurship in Pioneer Utah," *PUASAL* 30 (1953): 130. Abstract.

Review:

The Mormon Village: A Pattern and Technique of Land Settlement, by Lowry Nelson. In *PHR* 22 (May 1953): 181–82.

1954

Monograph:

Orderville, Utah: A Pioneer Mormon Experiment in Economic Organization (Logan: Utah State University Monograph Series, Vol. 2, Number 2, March 1954), 44 pp.

Articles in Professional Publications:

"Attitude of the Mormon Church Toward Mining, 1847–1900," *PUASAL* 31 (1954): 173–74.
"The Mormon Tithing House: A Frontier Business Institution," *BHR* 28 (March 1954): 24–58.

Articles in Non-Professional Publications:

"How the Saints Fed the Indians," *Era* 57 (November 1954): 800 ff.
"The LDS Hawaiian Colony at Skull Valley," *Era* (May 1954): 314 ff.

1955

Articles in Professional Publications:

"Banking Enterprises in Utah, 1847–1880," *BHR* 29 (December 1955): 312–34.
"Economic History of a Mormon Valley: Utah Valley, Utah," *PNQ* 46 (October 1955): 97–107.
"The Economic Role of Pioneer Mormon Women," *WHR* 9 (Spring 1955): 145–64.

"Utah's Coal Road in the Age of Unregulated Competition," *UHQ* 23 (January 1955): 35–63.

Article in Non-Professional Publication:

"Basic Economic Institutions of Pioneer Utah," *SUP News* 2 (August–September 1955): 6–7.

1956

Articles in Professional Publications:

"Agricultural Price Control in Pioneer Utah," *AH* 30 (July 1956): 104–13.

"The Deseret Agricultural and Manufacturing Society in Pioneer Utah," *UHQ* 24 (April 1956): 165–70.

The History of a Valley: Cache Valley, Utah-Idaho, edited by Joel E. Ricks. Logan, Utah: Cache Valley Centennial Commission, 1956. Chapters by Arrington: 7, "Life and Labor Among the Pioneers," 140–69; 8, "Transition to the Modern Era, 1880–1910," 205–39; 10, "Economy in the Modern Era," 240–74.

"The Mormon Cotton Mission in Southern Utah," *PHR* 25 (August 1956): 221–38. This article was awarded the Louis Knott Koontz prize of the Pacific Coast Branch, American Historical Association, as the best article published in *PHR* in 1956–57.

"Objectives of Mormon Economic Policy," *WHR* 10 (Spring 1956): 180–85.

"Role of the Mormon Church in the Economic Development of the Mountain West, 1847–1900," *PUASAL* 33 (1956): 193–94. Abstract.

"Taxable Income in Utah, 1862–1872," *UHQ* 24 (January 1956): 21–47.

Review:

A Mormon Chronicle: The Diaries of John D. Lee, 1848–1876 (two volumes), edited by Robert Glass Cleland and Juanita Brooks. In *PHR* 25 (August 1956): 405–7.

1957

Article in Professional Publication:

"Religion and Planning in the Great Basin, 1847–1900," *Proceedings of the Thirty-Second Annual Conference of the Western Economic Association, 1957* (Salt Lake City: University of Utah Press, 1957), 37–41. Reprinted in the Bobbs-Merrill Reprint Series in Economics.

Article in Non-Professional Publication:

"Mule Cars in Pioneer Utah," *SUP* 4 (July 1957): 15–16.

1958

Book:

Great Basin Kingdom: An Economic History of the Latter-day Saints,
1830-1900 (Cambridge: Harvard University Press, 1958), 534 pp. Published in paperback in the Bison Series (Lincoln: University of Nebraska
Press, 1966). This book won the Award of Merit of the American Association of State and Local History and was given the annual award of
the Pacific Coast Branch, American Historical Association, as the best
first book by a Western historian published in 1958-59. The book is
among those selected for the White House Library.

Articles in Professional Publications:

"An Economic Interpretation of the 'Word of Wisdom'," *BYU Studies* 1
(1958): 37-49.

"Planning an Iron Industry for Utah, 1851-1858," *HLQ* 21 (May 1958):
237-60.

"Religion and Planning in the Far West: The First Generation of Mormons
in Utah," *EHR* 11 (July 1958): 71-86. With Philip A. M. Taylor.

"The School of the Prophets," *PUASAL* 25 (1958): 145-46. Abstract.

1959

Book:

Introduzione alla Storia Economica delgi Stati Uniti (Genoa, Italy: Libraria
Mario Bozzi, 1959), 272 pp. Pages 241-60, "The American Economy
in the Age of the Atom and Automation," appear in English transla-
tion as Appendix E in Rebecca F. Cornwall, *From Chicken Farm to*
History: The Life of Leonard Arrington, 1917-1977 (Salt Lake City:
Privately Distributed, 1978), 406-21.

Articles:

"L'Economia Americana nell 'Era Atomica," *Civilta degli Scambi* (Bari) 4
(June 1959): 13-16.

"La Lotta Contro i Cicli Economici e l'Inflazione negli Stati Uniti," *Le Compere*
de San Giorgio (Genoa) 8 (February 1959): 3-8.

"Il Nuova Capitalismo negli Stati Uniti," serially in *Il Genovese* (Genoa) 12
July-6 September 1959.

Addresses and Duplicated Papers:

"L'Intervento Statale nella Vita Economica degli Stati Uniti," 1959, mimeographed, Bocconi University, Milan.

1960

Articles in Professional Publications:

"Crusade Against Theocracy: The Reminiscences of Judge Jacob Smith Boreman of Utah, 1872–1877," *HLQ* 24 (November 1960): 1–45.

"L'Economia Americana nell 'Era Atomica e dell'Automazione," in *Annali dell 'Universita degli Studi di Napoli* (Naples, Italy: Instituto di Storia Economica e Sociale, 1960), 35–47.

"Mormon Economic Organization: A Sheaf of Illustrative Documents," *UHQ* 28 (January 1960): 40–55. With Ralph W. Hansen.

Review:

The Mormon Conflict, 1850–1859, by Norman F. Furniss. In *Mississippi Valley Historical Review* 47 (December 1960): 509–11.

1961

Monograph:

From Wilderness to Empire: The Role of Utah in Western Economic History, Monograph No. 1, Institute of American Studies, University of Utah (Salt Lake City, 1961), 20 pp.

Articles in Professional Publications:

"Introduction" to "A World Divided in an Age of Space: A Symposium," *WHR* 15 (Summer 1961): 201–2. This symposium was held in October 1960 at Utah State University, Logan, Utah. It was part of the semiannual meetings of the Utah Academy of Sciences, Arts & Letters. Dr. Arrington was chairman of the Social Sciences section at the meeting.

"Religion and Economics in Mormon History," *BYU Studies* 3 (Spring–Summer 1961): 15–33.

"Utah and The Depression of the 1890's," *UHQ* 29 (January 1961): 3–18.

Address and Duplicated Paper:

"Economic Policies of the Mormon Church, 1847–1961," duplicated by Department of History, Brigham Young University, Provo, Utah, 1961. Address to Phi Alpha Theta and History Majors at Brigham Young University, 17 May 1961. 26 pp.

Review:

The Lamp in the Desert: The Story of the University of Arizona, by Douglas D. Martin. In *AW* 3 (Spring 1961): 91–94.

1962

Monograph:

The Price of Prejudice: The Japanese-American Relocation Center in Utah During World War II. Twenty-fifth Faculty Honor Lecture, Utah State University, Logan, 1962. 48 pp.

Articles in Professional Publications:

"From Panning Gold to Nuclear Fission: Idaho's Economic Development, 1860–1960," *IY* 3 (July 1962): 2–10.
"The Industrial Structure of the Mountain West, 1850–1950," in *Proceedings of the Thirty-Sixth Annual Conference of the Western Economic Association at Seattle, Washington, August 24–25, 1961* (Salt Lake City: University of Utah Press, 1962), 19–23.
"Utah's Emerging Metropolis: The Wasatch Front," in *Utah's Urban-Rural Revolution: Sixth Annual Agriculture and Industry Conference, Salt Lake City, February 6, 1962* (Logan: Utah State University, 1962), 9–20 plus tables. With George Hansen.
"Utah's Spectacular Missiles Industry: Its History and Impact," *UHQ* 30 (Winter 1962): 1–39. With Jon G. Perry.

Reviews:

The Charles Ilfeld Company: A Study of the Rise and Decline of Mercantile Capitalism in New Mexico, by William J. Parish. In *UHQ* 30 (January 1962): 92–94.
Our National Park Policy: A Critical History, by John Ise. In *AG* 36 (January 1962): 53.

1963

Books and Monographs:

The Changing Economic Structure of the Mountain West, 1850–1950 (Logan: Utah State University Monograph Series, Vol. 10, No. 3, June 1963), 64 pp. Reprinted in the Bobbs-Merrill Reprint Series in History.
"The Richest Hole on Earth": A History of Bingham Copper Mine (Logan: Utah State University Monograph Series, Vol. 11, No. 1, October 1963), 103 pp. Reprinted by Utah State University, 1969. With Gary B. Hansen.

Articles in Professional Publications:

"Abundance from the Earth: The Beginnings of Commercial Mining in Utah," *UHQ* 31 (Summer 1963): 192–219.
"Anchors Aweigh in Utah: The U. S. Naval Supply Depot at Clearfield, 1942–1962," *UHQ* 31 (Spring 1963): 109–26. With Archer L. Durham.

"Comparison of Income Changes in the Western States, 1929–1960," *Western Economic Journal* 1 (Summer 1963): 205–17. With George Jensen.
"They Kept 'Em Rolling: The Tooele Army Depot, 1942–1962," *UHQ* 31 (Winter 1963): 3–25. With Thomas G. Alexander.
"World's Largest Military Reserve: Wendover Air Force Base, 1941–1966," *UHQ* 31 (Fall 1963): 324–35. With Thomas G. Alexander.

Articles in Non-Professional Publications:

"Brigham Young and the Great Basin Economy," in *Seminar on Brigham Young 1962* (Provo, Utah: Brigham Young University Extension Publications, 1963), 79–96.
"Paying the Tenth in Pioneer Days," *The Instructor* 97 (November 1963): 386–87, 390.

Addresses and Duplicated Papers:

"The U. S. Army in Cedar Valley: Camp Floyd, Utah, 1858–1861," duplicated by Department of History, Brigham Young University, Provo, Utah, 1963. Prepared for the Special Tour of the Western History Association, meeting in Salt Lake City, 19 October 1963. 6 pp. With Thomas G. Alexander.

Reviews:

The Bonanza West: The Story of the Western Mining Rushes, 1848–1900, by William S. Greever. In *Northwest Historical Quarterly* 54 (October 1963): 177–78.
Mining Frontiers of the Far West, 1848–1880, by Rodman W. Paul. In *Mississippi Valley Historical Review* 50 (September 1963): 312–13.
The Progress of Economics: A History of Economic Thought, by Warren B. Catlin. In *AHR* 68 (July 1963): 1013–14.
Rebel of the Rockies: A History of the Denver and Rio Grande Railroad, by Robert G. Athearn. In *BHR* 37 (Autumn 1963): 293–94.

1964

Articles in Professional Publications:

"The Economic Value of Utah's Travel and Recreation Business: The Perspective of 117 Years," *Proceedings of the Third Annual Utah Travel Institute*, held in Salt Lake City, 1 February 1964, pp. 13–15.
Editor of "Experiment in Utopia: The United Order of Richfield, 1874–1877," by Feramorz Y. Fox, *UHQ* 32 (Fall 1964): 355–80.
"Origin of the Welfare Plan of The Church of Jesus Christ of Latter-day Saints," *BYU Studies* 5 (Winter 1964): 67–85. With Wayne K. Hinton.
"Sentinels on the Desert: The Dugway Proving Ground (1942–1963) and Deseret Chemical Depot (1942–1963)," *UHQ* 32 (Winter 1964): 32–43. With Thomas G. Alexander.

"Supply Hub of the West: Defense Depot Ogden, 1941–1964," *UHQ* 32 (Spring 1964): 99–121. With Thomas G. Alexander.
"Utah" in the *Encyclopedia Americana* (30 vols.; New York, Americana Corporation, 1964) 27:825–38. Revised and updated in 1969 edition.
"The Utah Military Frontier, 1872–1912: Forts Cameron, Thornburgh and Duchesne," *UHQ* 32 (Fall 1964): 330–54. With Thomas G. Alexander.

Addresses and Duplicated Papers:

"Cassandra in Pursuit of Clio; or, Why Economists Become Historians," duplicated by Department of Economics, Utah State University, Logan, Utah, 1964. Luncheon Address to the Pacific Coast Branch, American Historical Association, Los Angeles, California, 27 August 1964. 20 pp.
"The Commercialization of Utah's Economy: Trends and Developments from Statehood to 1910," duplicated by Department of Economics, Utah State University, Logan, Utah, 1964. Paper for the annual meetings, Utah State Historical Society, Salt Lake City, 12 September 1964. 40 pp.

Reviews:

Intermountain Railroads: Standard and Narrow Gauge, by Merrill D. Beal. In *AW* 6 (Spring 1964): 84–85.
John Doyle Lee: Zealot—Pioneer Builder—Scapegoat, by Juanita Brooks. In *Montana, The Magazine of Western History* 14 (April 1964): 114.

1965

Books and Monographs:

The Defense Industry of Utah (Logan: Department of Economics, Utah State University, 1965), Utah State Planning Program, Economic and Population Studies. 50 pp. With George Jensen.
A Study of the Impacts of Research and Development-Based Manufacturing in Utah. Prepared under contract C–394 with the National Science Foundation and subcontract No. 1 with Utah State University. Mimeographed by George Washington University, Washington, D.C., November 1965. 127 pp. With Reed R. Durtschi, Bartell C. Jensen, Charles T. Stewart, Don W. Thomas, and Thomas C. Anderson.

Articles in Professional Publications:

"Cooperative Community in the North: Brigham City, Utah," *UHQ* 33 (Summer 1965): 198–217.
"Launching Idaho's Beet Sugar Industry," *IY* 9 (Fall 1965): 16–27.
"The U.S. Army Overlooks Salt Lake Valley: Fort Douglas, 1862–1865," *UHQ* 33 (Fall 1965): 326–50. With Thomas G. Alexander.

"Utah's Biggest Business: Ogden Air Material Area at Hill Air Force Base, 1938-1965," *UHQ* 33 (Winter 1965): 9-33. With Thomas G. Alexander and Eugene A. Erb Jr.
"Utah's First Line of Defense: The Utah National Guard and Camp W. G. Williams, 1926-1965," *UHQ* 33 (Spring 1965): 141-56. With Thomas G. Alexander.
"Utah's Small Arms Ammunition Plant During World War II," *PHR* 34 (May 1965): 185-96. With Thomas G. Alexander.

Addresses and Duplicated Papers:

"The Economic Development of Utah," duplicated by Department of Economics, Utah State University, Logan, Utah, 1965. Address at the Annual Fellowship Banquet, Utah Academy of Sciences, Arts, & Letters, Logan, Utah, 16 April 1965. 15 pp.
"The Secularization of Mormon History and Culture," duplicated by Department of Economics, Utah State University, Logan, Utah, 1965. Paper for the annual meetings, Western History Association, Helena, Montana, 22 October 1965. 20 pp.

Reviews:

On the Mormon Frontier: The Diary of Hosea Stout, edited by Juanita Brooks. In *Utah Alumnus* 41 (April 1965): 12-14.

1966

Books and Monographs:

Beet Sugar in the West: A History of the Utah-Idaho Sugar Company, 1891-1966 (Seattle and London: University of Washington Press, 1966), 234 pp.
Water for Urban Reclamation: The Provo River Project. Utah Agricultural Experiment Station Bulletin, Utah Resources Series 29 (Logan, Utah, 1966), 35 pp. With Thomas G. Alexander.

Articles in Professional Publications:

"Camp in the Sagebrush: Camp Floyd, Utah, 1858-1861," *UHQ* 34 (Winter 1966): 3-21. With Thomas G. Alexander.
Editor of "Reappraisals of Mormon History," a 120-page "Special Section," in *Dialogue* 1 (Autumn 1966): 21-140.
"The Horn Silver Bonanza," in Gene M. Gressley, ed., *The American West: A Reorientation* (Laramie: University of Wyoming Publications, Vol. 32, 1966), 35-54. With Wayne K. Hinton.
"Inland to Zion: Mormon Trade on the Colorado River, 1864-1867," *AW* 8 (Autumn 1966): 239-50.

"Reclamation in Three Layers: The Ogden River Project, 1934–1965," *PHR* 35 (February 1966): 16–34. With Lowell Dittmer.
"Scholarly Studies of Mormonism in the Twentieth Century," *Dialogue* 1 (Spring 1966): 15–32.
"The U and I Sugar Company in Washington," *PNQ* 57 (July 1966): 101–9.
"Utah's Pioneer Beet Sugar Plant: The Lehi Factory of the Utah Sugar Company," *UHQ* (Spring 1966): 95–120.

Reviews:

The Mormon Establishment, by Wallace Turner, and *The Latter-day Saints: The Mormons Yesterday and Today*, by Robert Mullen. In *Dialogue* 1 (Winter 1966): 118–22.
Nauvoo: Kingdom on the Mississippi, by Robert Bruce Flanders. In *WHR* 20 (Autumn 1966): 356–57.

1967

Monograph:

Impact of Defense Spending on the Economy of Utah. (Logan: Department of Economics, Utah State University, 1967), Utah State Planning Program, Economic and Population Studies, 84 pp. With George Jensen.

Articles in Professional Publications:

"The Founding of the L.D.S. Institutes of Religion," *Dialogue* 2 (Summer 1967): 137–47. Dr. Arrington graduated from the LDS Institute of Religion, Moscow, Idaho, in 1939, and he taught occasionally at the Institute of Religion at Utah State University.
"Science, Government, and Enterprise in Economic Development: The Western Beet Sugar Industry," *AH* 41 (January 1967): 1–17.

Article in Non-Professional Publication:

"Gather Ye Together . . . Upon the Land of Zion," *The Instructor* 102 (April 1967): 148–49.

Reviews:

Claus Spreckels: The Sugar King in Hawaii, by Jacob Adler. In *AH* 41 (July 1967): 319–20.
The Company Town in the American West, by James B. Allen. In *AHR* 72 (January 1967): 721–22.
History of Wyoming, by T. A. Larson. In *AH* 41 (April 1967): 196.
Nevada's Twentieth-Century Mining Boom: Tonapah, Goldfield, Ely, by Russell R. Elliott. In *JAH* 53 (March 1967): 843–44.

1968

Articles in Professional Publications:

"Arizona in the Great Depression Years," *Arizona Review* 17 (December 1968): 11–19.
"Charles Mackay and His 'True and Impartial History' of the Mormons," *UHQ* 36 (Winter 1968): 24–40.
"Intolerable Zion: The Image of Mormonism in Nineteenth Century American Literature," *WHR* 22 (Summer 1968): 243–60. With Jon Haupt. This article was awarded the Mormon History Association Prize as best article on Mormon history published in 1968–69.
"The Search for Truth and Meaning in Mormon History," *Dialogue* 3 (Summer 1968): 56–66. This article was awarded the Mormon History Association Prize as best article on Mormon history published during the year 1967–68.

Addresses and Duplicated Papers:

"Mormon Economic Idealism," duplicated by the LDS Student Association, University of Utah, Salt Lake City, 1968. 10 pp. Address to the LDS Institute, Salt Lake City, Utah, 25 October 1968.

Review:

American Business History, by Louis Galambos. In *JEH* 28 (September 1968): 469–70.

1969

Books and Monographs:

Federally-Financed Industrial Plants Constructed in Utah During World War II (Logan: Utah State University Monograph Series, Vol. 16, Number 1, March 1969), 72 pp. With Anthony T. Cluff.
"Service Above Self:" A History of Logan Rotary Club, 1919–1969 (Logan, Utah, 1969), 42 pp.

Articles in Professional Publications:

"From Apache-hunting to 'Hosting' America: The Economic Development of Arizona, 1863–1950," *Arizona Review* 18 (August–September 1969): 1–5.
"Idaho and the Great Depression," *IY* 13 (Summer 1969): 2–8.
"Introduction" to *Rails from the West: A Biography of Theodore D. Judah*, by Helen Hinckley (San Marino, Calif.: Golden West Books, 1969), v–vi.
"The Intellectual Tradition of Mormon Utah," *PUASAL* (Salt Lake City, 1969), 45, Part 2, (1968): 346–65. An address to the Utah Academy in

St. George, Utah, on 13 September 1968, upon receiving the Charles H. Redd Award.

"The Intellectual Tradition of the Latter-day Saints," *Dialogue* 4 (Spring 1969): 13–26.

"Mormon Origins in New York: An Introductory Analysis," *BYU Studies* 9 (Spring 1969): 241–74. With James B. Allen.

"The New Deal in the West: A Preliminary Statistical Inquiry," *PHR* 38 (August 1969): 311–16.

"The Transcontinental Railroad and the Development of the West," *UHQ* 37 (Winter 1969): 3–15.

"Willard Young: The Prophet's Son at West Point," *Dialogue* 4 (Winter 1969): 37–46.

Article in Non-Professional Publication:

"Louisa Lula Greene Richards: Woman Journalist of the Early West," *Era* 72 (May 1969): 28–32.

Review:

The Rockies, by David Lavender. In *AHR* 74 (February 1969): 1075.

1970

Articles in Professional Publications:

" 'Divinely Tall and Most Divinely Fair': Josephine Donna Smith — 'Ina Coolbrith'," *Utah Libraries* 13 (Spring 1970): 8–14.

"James Gordon Bennett's 1831 Report on 'The Mormonites'," *BYU Studies* 10 (Spring 1970): 353–64.

"The Missouri and Illinois Mormons in Ante-bellum Fiction," *Dialogue* 5 (Spring 1970): 37–50. With Jon Haupt.

"The Mormons and the Indians: A Review and Evaluation," *The Record* 31 (Friends of the Library, Washington State University, 1970): 4–29.

"Western Agriculture and the New Deal," *AH* 64 (October 1970): 337–53. Presidential address to the Agricultural History Society at its annual luncheon held in Los Angeles, California, on 17 April 1970.

"Women as a Force in the History of Utah," *UHQ* 38 (Winter 1970): 3–6. This constitutes the "Introduction" to the special issue on the same topic.

Articles in Non-Professional Publications:

"Achievements of Latter-day Saint Women," *Era* 73 (April 1970): 61–62.

"How the Mormons Settled Idaho LDS Communities," *The Prospector*, No. 4, unpaged. This is the junior historical magazine of the Idaho Historical Society, Boise, Idaho.

"Why Did the Latter-day Saints Experience Persecution?" *Era* 73 (August 1970): 49–53.

Reviews:

AZn: A History of the American Zinc Company, by James D. Norris. In *JAH* 57 (June 1970): 191–92.
The Farm Boy and the Angel, by Carl Carmer. In *Dialogue* 5 (Summer 1970): 97–98.
The Lion of the Lord: A Biography of Brigham Young, by Stanley P. Hirshson. In *BYU Studies* 10 (Winter 1970): 240–45. Includes listing of manuscript material in LDS Church Archives on Brigham Young.
Silver and the First New Deal, by John A. Brennan. In *IY* 14 (Fall 1970): 31.

1971

Books and Monographs:

Kate Field and J. H. Beadle: Manipulators of the Mormon Past (Salt Lake City: Western History Center, University of Utah, 1971), 20 pp. Semi-annual American West Lecture.
William Spry: Man of Firmness, Governor of Utah (Salt Lake City: Utah State Historical Society and the Western History Center, University of Utah, 1971), 236 pp. With William L. Roper.

Articles in Professional Publications:

"Blessed Damozels: Women in Mormon History," *Dialogue* 6 (Summer 1971): 22–31. Presidential address to the Western History Association, given in Omaha, Nebraska, on 10 October 1969. Awarded Second Prize in *Dialogue*'s annual competition for the best article in the field of Mormon social literature.
"The 'First' Irrigation Reservoir in the United States: The Newton, Utah, Project," *UHQ* 39 (Summer 1971): 207–23. With Thomas C. Anderson.
"The 1921 Depression: Its Impact on Idaho," *IY* 15 (Summer 1971): 10–15. With Gwynn W. Barrett.
"Stopping a Run on a Bank: The First Security Bank of Idaho and the Great Depression," *IY* 14 (Winter 1970–71): 2–11. With Gwynn W. Barrett.

Articles in Non-Professional Publications:

"Background" to "The Order is Love" by Carol Lynn Pearson, *New Era* 1 (April 1971): 19–20. Also the "Introduction" to *The Order is Love* by Carol Lynn Pearson (Provo, Utah: Trilogy Arts, 1971), 7–9.
"The Human Qualities of Joseph Smith, the Prophet," *Ensign* 1 (January 1971): 35–38. Appears in Spanish translation in *Liahona* (Salt Lake City) 17 (July 1971): 7–10.

Address and Duplicated Paper:

"Highlights of Utah's Industrial History," duplicated and distributed by the Utah Manufacturers Association, January 1971. Address given at the annual membership luncheon of the Utah Manufacturers Association.

Reviews:

The *"Americanization"* of Utah for Statehood, by Gustive O. Larson. In *The American West* 8 (November 1971): 56.

The First 100 Years: A History of the Salt Lake Tribune, 1871–1971, by O. N. Malmquist. In *Ensign* 1 (October 1971): 66–67.

The Reminiscences and Civil War Letters of Levi Lamoni Wight: Life in a Mormon Splinter Colony on the Texas Frontier. Edited by Davis Bitton. In *Southwest Historical Review* 74 (April 1971): 565–66.

Wyoming: A Political History, 1868–1898, by Lewis L. Gould. In *Journal of the West* 10 (January 1971): 185.

1972

Articles in Professional Publications:

"Centrifugal Tendencies in Mormon History," in Truman G. Madsen and Charles D. Tate Jr., ed., *To the Glory of God: Mormon Essays on Great Issues* (Salt Lake City: Deseret Book Company, 1972), 163–77.

"Church History and the Achievement of Identity," *Commissioner's Lecture Series* (Salt Lake City: Church Education System, 1972).

"Church Leaders in Liberty Jail," *BYU Studies* 13 (Autumn 1972): 20–26.

"Crisis in Identity: Mormon Responses in the Nineteenth and Twentieth Centuries," in Marvin S. Hill and James B. Allen, eds., *Mormonism and American Culture* (New York: Harper and Row, 1972), 168–84.

"Joseph Fielding Smith: Faithful Historian," *Dialogue* 7 (Spring 1972): 21–24.

"Oliver Cowdery's Kirtland, Ohio, 'Sketch Book'," *BYU Studies* 12 (Summer 1972): 410–26.

Article in Non-Professional Publication:

"How Do You Know if You Have Received the Holy Ghost?" *New Era* 2 (October 1972): 40–41.

Addresses and Duplicated Papers:

"Achievements of Utah's Pioneer Businessmen," duplicated by Historical Department of The Church of Jesus Christ of Latter-day Saints, Salt Lake City. 13 pp. Address to Salt Lake City Rotary Club, 25 July 1972.

"How Relief Society Minutes Help Us in Writing Church History," duplicated typescript, Historical Department of The Church of Jesus Christ of Latter-day Saints, Salt Lake City. 8 pp. Address to Relief Society Conference, 5 October 1972.

"Joseph Fielding Smith: The Training of a Prophet," duplicated typescript, Historical Department of The Church of Jesus Christ of Latter-day Saints, Salt Lake City, 1972. 11 pp.

Reviews:

Hutterian Brethren: The Agricultural Economy and Social Organization of a Communal People, by John W. Bennett. In the *EHR* 25 (May 1972): 385–86.

Snake River Country, by Bill Gulick, photographs by Earl Roberge. In *IY* 15 (Winter 1972): 36.

Union Pacific Country, by Robert G. Athearn. In *UHQ* 40 (Winter 1972): 89–90.

1973

Book:

Bankers Extraordinary: A History of First Security Corporation, 1928–1973, 365 pp. Submitted to First Security Corporation, 1973. It has not been released to the public.

Articles in Professional Publications:

"Church of Jesus Christ of Latter–day Saints." In *Encyclopedia Britannica*, 1973 Book of the Year, 587–88.

"Community and Isolation: Some Aspects of 'Mormon Westerns'," *Western American Literature* 8 (Spring–Summer 1973): 15–31. With Jon Haupt.

"The Latter-day Saints in the Far West, 1847–1900," in F. Mark McKiernan, Alma R. Blair, and Paul Edwards, eds., *The Restoration Movement: Essays in Mormon History* (Lawrence, Kan.: Coronado Press, 1973), 257–71. With D. Michael Quinn.

"The Logan Tabernacle and Temple," *UHQ* 41 (Summer 1973): 301–14. With Melvin A. Larkin.

"Lorenzo Hill Hatch: Pioneer Bishop of Franklin," *IY* 17 (Summer 1973): 2–8. With Richard Jensen.

Articles in Non-Professional Publications:

"Delights of Church History," in *Know Your Religion Speeches: California, 1972–73* (Los Angeles: BYU California Center, 1973), 1–16.

"Latter-day Saint Women on the Arizona Frontier," *Henry Eyring Speakers' Series* (Tucson, Ariz.: LDS Institute of Religion, 1973), 1–17.

"Missionaries in Church History," *New Era* 3 (June 1973): 62–65.

"President Harold B. Lee: Eleventh President of the Church," in Joseph Fielding Smith, *Essentials of Church History*, 26th ed., (Salt Lake City: Deseret Book Co., 1973), 555–60.

Addresses and Duplicated Papers:

"A Pioneer Mormon Bishop and His Ward: Edwin D. Woolley and the Salt Lake City Thirteenth Ward," duplicated by Historical Department of The Church of Jesus Christ of Latter-day Saints, 1973. 24 pp. Address prepared for Mormon History Association Meeting, Fort Worth, Texas, 12 October 1973.

"The Confiscation of Church Properties Under the Edmunds-Tucker Act of 1887," duplicated by Historical Department of The Church of Jesus Christ of Latter-day Saints, 1973. 12 pp. Address prepared for Idaho Education Week, August 1973.

"History of Boise Stake," duplicated by Historical Department of The Church of Jesus Christ of Latter-day Saints, 1973. 22 pp. Address prepared for Idaho Education Week, August 1973.

"History of Bonneville Stake, Salt Lake City," duplicated by Historical Department of The Church of Jesus Christ of Latter–day Saints, 1973. 18 pp. Address prepared for High Priests and Wives, Bonneville Stake, 27 April 1973.

"History of Twin Falls Stake," duplicated by Historical Department of The Church of Jesus Christ of Latter-day Saints, 1973. 26 pp. Address prepared for Idaho Education Week, August 1973.

"History of University West Stake, Salt Lake City," duplicated by Historical Department of The Church of Jesus Christ of Latter-day Saints, 1973. 16 pp. Address prepared for High Priests and Wives, University West Stake, 8 March 1973.

"Mormonism and the Arts: An Historical Appreciation," duplicated by Historical Department of The Church of Jesus Christ of Latter-day Saints, 1973. 29 pp. With D. Michael Quinn. Address prepared for Mormon Arts Festival, Tempe, Arizona, 1 February 1973.

"Pioneer Mormon Midwives," duplicated by Historical Department of The Church of Jesus Christ of Latter-day Saints, 1973. 21 pp. Address prepared for Idaho Education Week, August 1973.

"Reflections on Pioneer History," duplicated by Historical Department of The Church of Jesus Christ of Latter-day Saints, 1973. 8 pp. Address prepared for the annual luncheon of Daughters of Utah Pioneers, Salt Lake City, 6 October 1973.

"Significance of the Mormons in American History," duplicated by Historical Department of The Church of Jesus Christ of Latter-day Saints, 1973. 21 pp. Address prepared for the LDS Institute at Stanford University, 1 March 1973.

"The Utah War," duplicated by Historical Department of The Church of Jesus Christ of Latter-day Saints, Salt Lake City, 1973. 23 pp.

Review:

Restless Strangers: Nevada's Immigrants and Their Interpreters, by Wilbur S. Shepperson. In *AHR* 78 (February 1973): 167–68.

1974

Book:

Charles C. Rich, Mormon General and Western Frontiersman (Provo, Utah: Brigham Young University Press, 1974), 386 pp. First volume in the "Studies in Mormon History" Series.

Articles in Professional Publications:

"The Commercialization of Utah's Economy: Trends and Developments from Statehood to 1910," in Dean May, ed., *A Dependent Commonwealth: Utah's Economy from Statehood to the Great Depression* (Provo, Utah: Charles Redd Monographs in Western History, No. 4, 1974), 3–34.

"Foreword" to *A Believing People: Literature of the Latter-day Saints*, Richard H. Cracroft and Neal E. Lambert, eds. (Provo, Utah: Brigham Young University Press, 1974), xv–xvi.

"General Editor's Preface," in *Letters of Brigham Young to His Sons*, Dean C. Jessee, ed. (Salt Lake City: Deseret Book Company in collaboration with the Historical Department of The Church of Jesus Christ of Latter-day Saints, 1974), vi–vii.

"Mormonism: Views from Without and Within," *BYU Studies* 14 (Winter 1974): 140–53.

Articles in Non-Professional Publications:

"All is Well," in *Mormon Pioneer Memorial Monument* (Salt Lake City, 1974), unpaged [pp. 5–13].

"Eleventh President: Harold B. Lee (1899–1973)," in Preston Nibley, *The Presidents of the Church* (13th ed., rev. and enl., Salt Lake City: Deseret Book Company, 1974), 427–57.

"Latter-day Saint Women on the Arizona Frontier," *New Era* 55 (April 1974): 42–50.

"The Many Uses of Humor," *Last Lecture Series* (Provo, Utah: Brigham Young University Press, 1974), 33 pp.

"Where Does the Term 'Jack-Mormon' Come From?" *Ensign* 4 (March 1974): 25.

Review:

The American West in the Twentieth Century: A Short History of an Urban Oasis, by Gerald D. Nash. In *JAH* 61 (June 1974): 233–34.

1975

Book:

David Eccles: Pioneer Western Industrialist (Logan: Utah State University Press, 1975), 294 pp.

Articles in Professional Publications:

" 'A Different Mode of Life': Irrigation and Society in Nineteenth-Century Utah," in *AH* 49 (January 1975): 3–20. With Dean May.

"Foreword" to *Latter-day Patriots: Nine Mormon Families and Their Revolutionary War Heritage*, by Gene Allred Sessions, (Salt Lake City: Deseret Book Company, 1975), xi–xii.

"Foreword" to *Brigham Young University: The First One Hundred Years*, Ernest L. Wilkinson, ed. (4 vols., Provo, Utah: Brigham Young University Press, 1975–1976), 1:vii–xii.

"Foreword" to *Mormon Democrat: The Political and Religious Memoirs of James Henry Moyle*, Gene A. Sessions, ed. (Salt Lake City: The James Moyle Genealogical and Historical Association, 1975), iii–iv.

"Panaca: Mormon Outpost Among the Mining Camps," *Nevada Historical Society Quarterly* 18 (Winter 1975): 207–16. With Richard Jensen. Originally duplicated by Historical Department of The Church of Jesus Christ of Latter-day Saints, 1973. 16 pp. Address prepared for the annual banquet of the Nevada State Historical Society, Las Vegas, 19 October 1973.

"Seven Steps to Greatness: Overview of the History of Brigham Young University," Commencement Address to the Graduates of Brigham Young University, 18 April 1975, published in *Task Papers in LDS History*, No. 3 (Salt Lake City: Historical Department of The Church of Jesus Christ of Latter-day Saints, 1975), 25 pp. Also in *BYU Studies* 16 (Summer 1976): 459–70.

Articles in Non-Professional Publications:

"History Is Then and Now: A Conversation with Leonard J. Arrington, Church Historian," *Ensign* 5 (July 1975): 8–13.

"The Looseness of Zion: Joseph Smith and the Lighter View," BYU Devotional Address, 19 November 1974, published in *Speeches of the Year: BYU Devotional and Ten-Stake Fireside Addresses, 1974* (Provo, Utah: Brigham Young University Press, 1975), pp. 291–300.

Addresses and Duplicated Papers:

"The Book of Mormon as an Influence in the Life of People," duplicated, 28 pp., 1975.

"Great Basin Queendom," address to the Salt Lake Retrenchment Society and the Utah Endowment for the Humanities, in Richfield and Salt Lake City, Utah, 18 and 25 September 1975. 21 pp.
"H.L.A. Culmer—First President of Salt Lake Rotary," address to Salt Lake Rotary Club, Salt Lake City, 22 July 1975, duplicated.
"Latter-day Saint Men at West Point," duplicated, 1975.
"The Marrow in the Bones of History: New Directions in Historical Writing," address for Western University Press Association, Salt Lake City, 12 October 1975. 14 pp.
"Reflections on Economics and the Church," address to the Conference on Economics and Mormon Culture, Brigham Young University, 7 October 1975, duplicated. 14 pp.

1976

Books:

Brigham Young University: The First One Hundred Years, Volumes 3 and 4 (Provo, Utah: Brigham Young University Press, 1976), 644 and 789 pp. Coeditor with Ernest L. Wilkinson.
Building the City of God: Community and Cooperation Among the Mormons (Salt Lake City: Deseret Book Company, 1976), 512 pp. With Dean May and Feramorz Y. Fox. Received the Best Book Award for 1976 from the Mormon History Association.
From Quaker to Latter-day Saint: Bishop Edwin D. Woolley (Salt Lake City: Deseret Book Company, 1976), 592 pp.
Tar Heels, Hoosiers, and Idahoans: A History of the Noah and Edna Arrington Family to 1933 (Salt Lake City: Privately Printed, 1976), 167 pp. With Rebecca F. Cornwall.

Articles in Professional Publications:

"Cache Valley's Bicentennial Heritage," address to Banquet for the George Washington Bicentennial Ball, Logan, Utah, 20 February 1976, published in Douglas D. Alder, ed., *Cache Valley: Essays on Her Past and People* (Logan: Utah State University, 1976), 1–12.
"Foreword" to *A School of Destiny*, by Ernest L. Wilkinson and W. Cleon Skousen (Provo, Utah: Brigham Young University Press, 1976), vii–x.
"Foreword" to *The Story of the Latter-day Saints*, by James B. Allen and Glen M. Leonard (Salt Lake City: Deseret Book Company, 1976), vii–viii.
"Mormon Beginnings in the American South," presented at the American Historical Association Convention, Atlanta, Georgia, 29 December 1975, published in *Task Papers in LDS History*, No. 9 (Salt Lake City: Historical Department of The Church of Jesus Christ of Latter-day Saints, 1976), 21 pp.
"Seven Steps to Greatness," *BYU Studies* 16 (Summer 1976): 459–70.

" 'This is the Place': The Mormon Trek to Utah," in *The American Destiny: An Illustrated Bicentennial History of the United States*, 10 vols. (New York: The Danbury Press, 1976), 5:94–114.

Article in Non-Professional Publication:

"Joseph Smith and the Lighter View," *New Era* 6 (August 1976): 8–13.

Addresses and Duplicated Papers:

"Agriculture and Mormonism: The Historical Perspective," address at Centennial Agricultural Week, Brigham Young University, 30 March 1976. 19 pp.
"Blessed Relief Society Sisters," prepared for Parley's First Ward Relief Society, 24 August 1976. 15 pp.
"A History [of sorts] of the Practice of Medicine in Utah," address to annual banquet of Western Anaesthesiologists, Salt Lake City, 21 February 1976, duplicated. 18 pp.
"The Importance of the Humanities," prepared for the Nevada Humanities Council, Lake Tahoe, 22 July 1976. 11 pp.
"John Tanner, His Children, and their Families Who Came West," prepared for the John Tanner Family, 13 September 1976. 26 pp.
"The Mormon Experience in Idaho," Summer School Lecture, Idaho State University, Pocatello, Idaho, 15 June 1976. 25 pp.
"Their Share and More: The Story of the Salt Lake Emigration Stake," prepared for Bicentennial Lecture Program, Emigration Stake, 30 September 1976. 32 pp.

1977

Book:

I'm Glad My House Burned Down: The Personal Story of Grace Fort Arrington (Salt Lake City: Privately Printed, 1977), 189 pp. Edited with Rebecca F. Cornwall.

Articles in Professional Publications:

"Building a Commonwealth: The Secular Leadership of Brigham Young," address for Statehood Day, St. George, Utah, 4 January 1977. *UHQ* 45 (Summer 1977): 216–32. With Ronald K. Esplin.
"George Albert Smith," in *Dictionary of American Biography, Supplement Five, 1951–1955*, John A. Garraty, ed. (New York: Charles Scribner's Sons, 1977), 639–40.
"Historian as Entrepreneur: A Personal Essay," *BYU Studies* 17 (Winter 1977): 193–209.
"Idaho's Benson Family," in *Idaho Heritage* 9 (1977): 18–19.

Howard D. Lamar, ed., *The Reader's Encyclopedia of the American West* (New York: Thomas Y. Crowell, 1977). Leonard Arrington is credited with the following entries: John Milton Bernhisel (p. 90); George Q. Cannon (p. 161); Patrick Edward Connor (p. 254); William Godbe (p. 445); handcart companies (p. 485); William Henry Hooper (p. 511); William Jennings (p. 598); Latter-day Saints (pp. 646–52); Logan, Utah (pp. 673–74); Ogden, Utah (p. 859); Joseph Smith Jr. (pp. 1112–24); Joseph Fielding Smith (p. 1124); Eliza Roxey Snow (pp. 1126–27); James E. Talmage (pp. 1155–56); John Taylor (p. 1161); uranium mining (pp. 1207–8); Utah (pp. 1208–11); Wilford Woodruff (p. 1287); Brigham Young (pp. 1299–1300); Mahonri Macintosh Young (p. 1301); and Zion's Cooperative Mercantile Institution (p. 1306).

"The Latter-day Saints and Public Education," *Southwestern Journal of Social Education* 7 (Spring–Summer 1977): 9–25.

"The Mormon Heritage of Vardis Fisher," *BYU Studies* 18 (Fall 1977): 27– 47. With Jon Haupt.

"The Six Pillars of Utah's Pioneer Economy," presidential address to Utah Academy of Sciences, Arts, & Letters, St. George, Utah, 25 March 1977, *Encyclia: Journal of the Utah Academy of Sciences, Arts & Letters* 54 (Part 1, 1977): 9–24.

Articles in Non-Professional Publications:

"Have the Saints Always Given as Much Emphasis to the Word of Wisdom as They Do Today?" *Ensign* 7 (April 1977): 32–33.

"Mississippi Saints," *Ensign* 7 (June 1977): 46–51.

"Vistas in Church History," *The First Annual Church Educational System Religious Educators Symposium*, held 19–20 August 1977, at Brigham Young University (Salt Lake City: Church Educational System, 1977), 17–21.

Review:

Massacre at Mountain Meadows: An American Legacy and A Monumental Crime, by William Wise. In *BYU Studies* 17 (Spring 1977): 382–84.

1978

Article in Professional Publication:

" 'In Honorable Remembrance': Thomas L. Kane's Services to the Mormons," *Task Papers in LDS History*, No. 22 (Salt Lake City: Historical Department of The Church of Jesus Christ of Latter-day Saints, 1978). Based on an address delivered at the Centennial Service, Kane Memorial Chapel, Kane, Pennsylvania, 2 June 1978. Reprinted in *BYU Studies* 21 (Fall 1981): 35–52.

Addresses and Duplicated Papers:

"Cedar City: The Building of a Community." Cedar City: Southern Utah State College and Iron Mission Days Committee, 1978. With Dean L. May. Originally prepared for 125th anniversary of the settlement of Cedar City, Utah, 11 November 1976.

" 'Clothe These Bones': The Reconciliation of Faith and History," address delivered at History Division Retreat, Ensign Peak, Salt Lake Valley, 23 June 1978. 16 pp.

"Fresh Insights into the Character of Brigham Young," presented at the annual banquet of the Utah Valley Historical Society, a chapter of the Utah State Historical Society, Provo, Utah, 14 November 1978.

"Mormon Colonization of the Great Basin Kingdom," address delivered at the Days of '47 luncheon, Salt Lake City, 24 July 1978. 12 pp.

"The Mormon Experience in Illinois," address delivered to a stake fireside, Urbana, Illinois, 15 April 1978. 18 pp.

1979

Books:

The Mormon Experience: A History of the Latter-day Saints (New York: Alfred A. Knopf, Inc., 1979), 404 pp. Published simultaneously in England by Allen and Unwin. Listed by the History Book Club. Awarded the Mormon History Association Best Book Award, 1980. Issued in paperback by Vintage Books of Random House, 1980. With Davis Bitton.

The Mormons in Nevada (Las Vegas: *Las Vegas Sun*, 1979). Originally appeared serially in *The Sun*, 15 and 29 April, 13 and 27 May, 10 and 24 June, 8 and 22 July, 5 and 19 August, and 2 and 16 September 1979.

Articles in Professional Publications:

"An Interview with Leonard Arrington and Davis Bitton," *Sunstone* 4 (July–August 1979): 38–41.

"Church of Jesus Christ of Latter-day Saints." In *Encyclopedia Britannica*, 1979 Year Book, s.v. Religion.

"The Mormon Settlement of Cassia County, Idaho, 1873–1921." *IY* 23 (Summer 1979): 36–46. Address delivered at Burley, Idaho, 18 October 1978. This was prepared for the Snake River Series under a grant from the National Endowment for the Humanities.

"Persons for All Seasons: Women in Mormon History," *BYU Studies* 20 (Fall 1979): 39–58. This appeared in modified form, translated into Dutch, as "Moeders, Zusters, Dochters: Aspecten van de Vrouw in de Mormoonse Geschiedenis," *Horizon: Tijdschrift over de Mormoonse Geneenschap* (Wilrijk, Belgium) 2 (May 1983): 58–66.

"The Role of the Council of the Twelve During Brigham Young's Presidency of The Church of Jesus Christ of Latter-day Saints," *Task Papers in LDS History*, No. 31 (Salt Lake City: Historical Department of The Church of Jesus Christ of Latter-day Saints, 1979). With Ronald K. Esplin.

"William A. ('Bill') Hickman: Setting the Record Straight," *Task Papers in LDS History*, No. 28 (Salt Lake City: Historical Department of The Church of Jesus Christ of Latter-day Saints, 1979). With Hope A. Hilton.

Articles in Non-Professional Publications:

"The Economics Past and Future of Utah," *Salt Lake Tribune*, Empire Edition, 17 February 1979.

"The John Tanner Family," *Ensign* 9 (March 1979): 46–51.

"Learning About Ourselves through Church History," *Ensign* 9 (September 1979): 6–8.

Addresses and Duplicated Papers:

"Achievements of Utah Women," paper presented at the annual luncheon of the Utah Federation of Women's Clubs, Salt Lake City, 27 January 1979.

"Early Idaho Personalities," presented at the annual banquet of the Idaho State Historical Society, Rexburg, Idaho, 5 March 1979.

1980

Book:

Voices from the Past: Diaries, Journals, and Autobiographies (Provo, Utah: Brigham Young University Press, Campus Education Week, 1980). Coedited with Thomas G. Alexander, Donald Q. Cannon, Richard H. Cracroft, and Neal E. Lambert.

Articles in Professional Publications:

"Can the Family Farm Survive?" In *The Future of Agriculture in the Rocky Mountains*, edited by E. Richard Hart (Salt Lake City: Westwater Press, 1980), 65–71. Address presented at the Conference on Western Agriculture sponsored by the Institute of the American West, Sun Valley, Idaho, 25 October 1979.

"Church of Jesus Christ of Latter-day Saints." In *Encyclopedia Britannica*, 1980 Year Book, s.v. Religion.

"Daniel Cowan Jackling." In *Dictionary of American Biography*, Supplement Six, 1956–1960, edited by John A. Garraty (New York: Charles Scribner's Sons, 1980), 316–17.

"The Mormon Family: A Historical Perspective." *World Conference on Records: Preserving Our Heritage* (Salt Lake City: The Church of Jesus Christ of Latter-day Saints, 1980), Vol. 3, Part 1, Series 331, 10 pp.

"Mormonism: From Its New York Beginnings," *New York History* 61 (October 1980): 387–410. Also published in *Dialogue* 13 (Fall 1980): 120–35. Originally presented at the Mormon History Association annual meeting, Canandaigua, New York, 3 May 1980.

"The Spirit of Mormon History," published weekly in the Church News section of the Salt Lake City *Deseret News*, 1, 8, 15, 22, and 29 March, 5, 19, and 26 April, and 3 May 1980.

Articles in Non-Professional Publications:

"Blessed Relief Society Sisters." In *Blueprints for Living*, edited by Maren M. Mouritsen (Provo, Utah: Brigham Young University Press, 1980), 2:14–24.

"Building Blocks of the Kingdom, 1830–1980," *Sidney B. Sperry Symposium*, 26 January 1980 (Provo, Utah: Brigham Young University Press, 1980), 15–26.

"Colonizing the Great Basin," *Ensign* 10 (February 1980): 18–22.

"The Faithful Young Family: The Parents, Brothers, and Sisters of Brigham," *Ensign* 10 (August 1980): 52–57. With JoAnn Jolley.

Addresses and Duplicated Papers:

"Across the Great Plains," presented at Brigham Young University Devotional, 22 July 1980.

"Economics of Cache Valley Agriculture, 1859–1900," 17 April 1980. Duplicated by Ronald Jensen Historical Farm, Logan, Utah. With Linda Wilcox.

"History of the Church in Utah Valley, Utah," delivered to Provo Central Stake sesquicentennial celebration, 22 June 1980.

"Horton David and Louisa Leavitt Haight," presented at the Haight Family Reunion in Oakley, Idaho, 28 June 1980.

"Joseph Earl Arrington," address prepared for the reception in recognition of the establishment of the Joseph Earl and Genevieve Thornton Arrington Collection of Nineteenth-Century Americana at the Harold B. Lee Library, Brigham Young University, Provo, Utah, 10 July 1980.

"The Meaning of July 24 in Pioneer Utah History," presented at Salt Lake Rotary Club, 22 July 1980.

"Mormon Contributions to the Development of Arizona," presented at a sesquicentennial celebration sponsored by the LDS Institute of Religion at Tucson, Arizona, 16 April 1980.

"Mormon Contributions to Western Agriculture," duplicated by the Ronald Jensen Historical Farm. Presented at Ronald Jensen Historical Farm, Utah State University, Logan, Utah, 17 April 1980. With Scott Kenney.

"The Spirit of Mormonism: The Restoration after 150 Years," presented at a sesquicentennial stake fireside in Los Angeles, California, 12 April 1980.

"On Writing LDS History," presented to the Mormon Pacific History Association Conference, Laie, Hawaii, 1 August 1980.

1981

Books:

A History of Salt Lake Rotary Club No. 24 (Salt Lake City: Rotary Club, 1981), 58 pp.

Rescue of the 1856 Handcart Companies (Provo, Utah: Brigham Young University Press, 1981), 59 pp. With Rebecca F. Cornwall.

Saints Without Halos: The Human Side of Mormon History (Salt Lake City: Signature Books, 1981), 158 pp. With Davis Bitton.

Articles in Professional Publications:

"Church of Jesus Christ of Latter-day Saints." In *Encyclopedia Britannica*, 1981 Year Book, s.v. Religion.

"Foreword" to *Builders of the Kingdom*, by Merlo J. Pusey (Provo, Utah: Brigham Young University Press, 1981), ix–xi.

" 'In Honorable Remembrance': Thomas L. Kane's Services to the Mormons." *BYU Studies* 21 (Fall 1981): 389–402.

"Introduction" to *Atlas of Utah*, by Wayne L. Wahlquist, ed. (Ogden and Provo, Utah: Weber State College and Brigham Young University, 1981), 1–2.

"LDS Settlement of Eastern Utah: A Story of Faith, Courage, and Tolerance." In *Carbon County: Eastern Utah's Industrialized Island*, Philip F. Notarianni, ed. (Salt Lake City: Utah State Historical Society, 1981), 109–29. Address delivered at the Utah State Historical Society Lecture Series, Price, Utah, 23 April 1980.

"The Writing of Latter-day Saint History: Problems, Accomplishments and Admonitions," *Dialogue* 14 (Autumn 1981): 119–29.

Articles in Non-Professional Publications:

"Black Pioneer Was Union Fort Settler," *The Pioneer* 28 (September–October 1981): 8–9.

"The Prayer for a Miracle," *Turning Points* (Salt Lake City: Bookcraft, 1981), 53–55.

Addresses and Duplicated Papers:

" 'I Have the Grit in Me': Brigham Young, From His Private and Public Papers," presented at the Western History Association annual convention, San Antonio, Texas, 16 October 1981.

"Utah's Pioneers Were Prospectors Too," presented at the Utah Mining Association annual convention, Park City, Utah, 11 September 1981.

1982

Articles in Professional Publications:

"Church of Jesus Christ of Latter-day Saints." In *Encyclopedia Britannica*, 1982 Year Book s.v. Religion.

"Making a Living: The Economic Life of Chesterfield." In *Chesterfield: Mormon Outpost in Idaho*, Lavina Fielding Anderson, ed. (Provo, Utah: Brigham Young University Press for the Chesterfield Foundation, 1982), 21–32. With Richard L. Jensen.

"N. Eldon Tanner, Man of Integrity," *Dialogue* 15 (Winter 1982): 8–10.

"New Deal Programs and Southwestern Agriculture." In *Southwestern Agriculture: Pre-Columbian to Modern*, Henry C. Dethloff and Irwin M. May, eds. (College Station: Texas A & M University Press, 1982), 275–92.

"Of Latter-day Saint Men, Women, and Books," *Sunstone Review* 1 (May 1982): 26–28.

"Recalling a Twin Falls Childhood," *IY* 25 (Winter 1982): 31–40. Originally delivered in Twin Falls, Idaho, 25 March 1981, as part of the program "Idaho Small Town Experience," sponsored by the Idaho State Historical Society and Association for the Humanities in Idaho.

Article in Non-Professional Publication:

"LDS Girls in the Pioneer West," *New Era* 12 (July 1982): 16–22.

Addresses and Duplicated Papers:

"The Economic Role of Pioneer Mormon Women," presented at lecture series sponsored by Economics Department, Utah State University, Logan, Utah, 30 June 1982.

"Grass Roots Entrepreneurship in the Frontier West: The Allens of Cache Valley and the Coreys and Wattises of Weber Valley," presented at Charles Redd Lecture Series, Brigham Young University, Provo, Utah, 23 September 1982.

"International Mormonism: Historical Development and Present Challenges," presented at History Week, Brigham Young University, Provo, Utah, 23 March 1982. 27 pp.

"Memories and Traditions," presented to the Old Main Society at Utah State University, 1982. Duplicated.

"Patterns of Economic Organization in the Early West," presented at lecture series sponsored by Economics Department, Utah State University, Logan, Utah, 28 June 1982.

"The Pioneer Mormon Cooperative Village," presented at lecture series sponsored by Economics Department, Utah State University, Logan, Utah, 29 June 1982.

"The Testament of Martin Harris," presented at Aaronic Priesthood Commemoration, The Martin Harris Grave Site, Clarkston Cemetery, Clarkston, Utah, May 1982, duplicated.

"Utah and the Economic Program of the Roosevelt New Deal," presented at lecture series sponsored by Economics Department, Utah State University, Logan, Utah, 2 July 1982.

"Vignettes from the Lives of The Great Economists," presented at lecture series sponsored by Economics Department, Utah State University, Logan, Utah, 2 July 1982.

Reviews:

Nevada Land, Water and Politics in the Nineteenth Century, by John M. Townley. In *AH* 56 (April 1982): 470–71.

Reclaiming the American West: An Historiographical Guide, by Lawrence B. Lee. In *AH* 56 (April 1982): 479–80.

Colorado in the Great Depression, by James F. Wickens. In *PHR* 51 (May 1982): 233–34.

Utah: A Guide to the State, 2nd ed. revised and enlarged, by Ward J. Roylance. In *BYU Studies* 22 (Fall 1982): 502-4.

1983

Articles in Professional Publications:

"Church of Jesus Christ of Latter-day Saints." In *Encyclopedia Brittanica*, 1983 Year Book, s.v. Religion.

"Perpetuation of a Myth: Mormon Danites in Five Western Novels, 1840–90," *BYU Studies* 23 (Spring 1982): 147–65. With Rebecca F. Cornwall.

"Personal Reflections on Mormon History," *Sunstone* 8 (July–August 1983): 41–45. Paper presented at the Mormon History Association annual meeting, Omaha, Nebraska, 6 May 1983.

"The Promise of Eagle Rock: Idaho Falls, Idaho, 1863–1890." *Rendezvous, Idaho State University Journal of Arts and Science* 18 (Spring 1983): 2–17. Prepared for delivery as part of the program "Idaho Small Town Experience," sponsored by the Idaho State Historical Society and Association for the Humanities in Idaho, 22 April 1981.

"The Quest for Interpretation in Local Studies." In *Working Together: A Regional Approach to Community Traditions and History in Idaho*. Published by the Idaho Humanities Council and Idaho State Historical Society, 1983, pp. 8–10.

"Reflections on the Founding and Purpose of the Mormon History Association, 1965–1983," *Journal of Mormon History* 10 (1983): 91–103.

"The Sagebrush Resurrection: New Deal Expenditures in the Western States, 1933–1939," *PHR* 52 (February 1983): 1–16. Presidential address to the American Historical Association, Pacific Coast Branch, San Francisco, California, 16 August 1982.

"Utah, the New Deal, and the Depression of the 1930s," *Weber State College Monograph Series* (Ogden, Utah, 1983). Originally presented as the Dello G. Dayton Memorial Lecture, Weber State College, Ogden, Utah, 25 March 1982.

Addresses and Duplicated Papers:

"Achievements of the 'Second Generation' of Mormon Women," presented at the Eighth Annual Women's Conference, Brigham Young University, 18 February 1983.
"The Looseness of Zion: The Lighter Side of Mormon History," presented to the Phi Alpha Theta Luncheon of the Western History Association, Salt Lake City, Utah, 13 October 1983.

Review:

Rocky Mountain Carpetbaggers: Idaho's Territorial Governors, 1863–1890, by Ronald H. Limnbaugh. In *JAH* 69 (March 1983): 981–82.

1984

Books:

Tracy-Collins Bank & Trust Company: A Record of Responsibility, 1884–1984 (Salt Lake City: Eden Hill, 1984), 252 pp.
Sunbonnet Sisters: True Stories of Mormon Women and Frontier Life (Salt Lake City: Bookcraft, 1984), 161 pp. With Susan Arrington Madsen.

Pamphlets:

Tracy-Collins Bank & Trust Company: A Record of Responsibility, 1884–1984 (Salt Lake City: Eden Hill, 1984), 30 pp.

Articles in Professional Publications:

"Foreword" to *Christmas: A Joyful Heritage*, by Susan Arrington Madsen (Salt Lake City: Deseret Book Company, 1984), ix–xiii.
"Joseph F. Smith: From Impulsive Young Man to Patriarchal Prophet," *The John Whitmer Historical Association Journal* 4 (1984): 30–40. Originally duplicated by Historical Department of The Church of Jesus Christ of Latter-day Saints, 1973. 25 pp. Address prepared for the Joseph Smith Family Reunion, 19 August 1973.
"The Lehi Beet Sugar Factory," *Beehive History*, 10 (1984): 16–21.
"Rural Life Among Nineteenth-Century Mormons: The Woman's Experience," *Agricultural History* 58 (July 1984): 239–46. Paper presented to the Rural Life Conference, Florida A&M University, Tallahassee, Florida, 23 September 1983.

"Tribute to Merrill D. (Sam) Beal," in *Sixty Years of Educational Endeavors in Idaho: Memoirs of Merrill D. Beal* (Pocatello: Idaho State University Press, 1984), i–ix.

Addresses and Duplicated Papers:

"A Brief History of the Salt Lake Valley," delivered to the National Conference of Organ Builders in Salt Lake City, 8 October 1984. 16 pp.
"Traditions," prepared for the graduation banquet at Brigham Young University, 19 April 1984. 9 pp.
"Women in Pioneer Utah," delivered in Las Vegas, Nevada, and in Delta, Salt Lake City, Cedar City, Logan, and other Utah communities. 18 pp.

1985

Book:

Brigham Young: American Moses (New York: Alfred A. Knopf, 1985), 544 pp. Winner of the first David Woolley Evans and Beatrice Cannon Evans Biography Award for a distinguished biography of a significant personality who lived in Mormon Country during the past 150 years.

Articles in Professional Publications:

"Church of Jesus Christ of Latter-day Saints." In *Encyclopedia Britannica*, 1985 Year Book s.v. Religion.
"Foreword" to *The Life and Thought of Orson Pratt*, by Breck England (Salt Lake City: University of Utah Press, 1985), ix–xi.
"Grass Roots Entrepreneurship in the Frontier West: The Allens of Cache Valley and the Coreys and Wattises of Weber Valley," in Jessie L. Embry and Howard A. Christie, eds., *Community Development in the American West: Past and Present Nineteenth and Twentieth Century Frontiers* (Provo, Utah: Charles Redd Center for Western Studies, 1985), 183–200.
"Spencer W. Kimball, Apostle of Love," *Dialogue* 18 (Winter 1985): 10–13.
"Why I Am a Believer," *Sunstone* 10 (January 1985): 36–38. Presented at the annual Sunstone Symposium, Hotel Utah, Salt Lake City, Utah, 26 August 1983.

Article in Non-Professional Publication:

"Brigham Young: American Moses," *Utah Holiday* 14 (April 1985): 48–56.

Review:

Forging New Rights in Western Waters, by Robert G. Dunbar. In *AH* 59 (April 1985): 353–55.

Address:

"History of Livestock in the Great Basin," address to the Society for Range Management, Salt Lake City, 11 February 1985.

1986

Books:

The Hotel, Salt Lake's Classy Lady: The Hotel Utah, 1911–1986 (Salt Lake City: Publisher's Press, 1986). 101 pp. With Heidi S. Swinton.

Editor and author of three chapters in *The Presidents of the Church* (Salt Lake City: Deseret Book, 1986), vii–viii, 3–72, 343–71.

Articles in Professional Publications:

"Foreword," in Edward Leo Lyman, *Political Deliverance: The Mormon Quest for Utah Statehood* (Urbana and Chicago: University of Illinois Press, 1986), ix–x.

"Utah's Ambiguous Reception: The Relocated Japanese Americans," in Roger Daniels, Sandra C. Taylor, and Harry H. L. Kitano, eds., *Japanese-Americans: From Relocation to Redress* (Salt Lake City: University of Utah Press, 1986), 92–97.

"Utah's Great Drought of 1934," *UHQ* 54 (Summer 1986): 245–64.

"Why I Am a Believer," in Philip L. Barlow, ed., *A Thoughtful Faith: Essays on Belief by Mormon Scholars* (Centerville, Utah: Canon Press, 1986), 225–33.

Addresses and Duplicated Papers:

"Historical Overview of Irrigation in the Snake River Valley, Idaho," presented to the Irrigation in Idaho Conference, Boise, Idaho, 26 March 1986, 16 pp.

"A Mormon Apostle Visits the Umatillas and Nez Perce, 1885," presented to the Conference on Missionary Influences on Northwest History, Whitman College, Walla Walla, Washington, 25 July 1986, 12 pp.

"The Mormon Utopia," presented to the American Utopias Lectures at Northern Nevada Community College, Elko, 22 October 1986.

"Mormon Women in Nineteenth Century Britain," presented to students in Religion Courses, Nottingham University, Nottingham, England, 4 March 1986.

"The Scholarly Approach to Church History," presented to the Honor Students of Brigham Young University, 13 February 1986, 14 pp.

Index